The Public Relations Handbook

4th edition

Alison Theaker

Routledge
Taylor & Francis Group

LONDON AND NEW YORK

Fourth edition published 2012
by Routledge
2 Park Square, Milton Park, Abingdon, Oxon OX14 4RN

Simultaneously published in the USA and Canada
by Routledge
711 Third Avenue, New York, NY 10017

Routledge is an imprint of the Taylor & Francis Group, an informa business

First published 2001 by Routledge

Second edition published 2004

Third edition published 2008

British Library Cataloguing in Publication Data
A catalogue record for this book is available from the British Library

Library of Congress Cataloging in Publication Data
The public relations handbook/edited by Alison Theaker. – 4th ed.
    p. cm. – (Media practice)
    Rev. ed. of: The public relations handbook/Alison Theaker.
    3rd ed. 2008.
    Includes bibliographical references and index.
    1. Corporations – Public relations.   I. Theaker, Alison.
    II. Theaker, Alison. Public relations handbook.
    HD59.T474 2012
    659.2 – dc22   2011008644

ISBN: 978–0–415–59813–2 (hbk)
ISBN: 978–0–415–59814–9 (pbk)
ISBN: 978–0–203–80482–7 (ebk)

Typeset in Helvetica and Avant Garde
by Florence Production Ltd, Stoodleigh, Devon

MIX
Paper from
responsible sources
FSC
www.fsc.org   FSC® C004839

Printed and bound in Great Britain by the MPG Books Group

The Public Relations Handbook

The Public Relations Handbook is a comprehensive and detailed introduction to the theories and practices of the public relations industry. It traces the history and development of public relations, explores ethical issues that affect the industry, examines its relationship with politics, lobbying organisations and journalism, assesses its professionalism and regulation and advises on training and entry into the profession.

The Public Relations Handbook combines theoretical and organisational frameworks for studying public relations with examples of how the industry works in practice. It draws on a range of promotional strategies and campaigns from businesses, public and non-profit organisations including the AA, Airbus, BT, Northamptonshire County Council, Cuprinol and Action for Children.

The Public Relations Handbook, 4th Edition includes:

- case studies, examples and illustrations from a range of campaigns from small and multinational corporations, local government and charities
- specialist chapters on financial public relations, internal communications and marketing public relations
- strategic overviews of corporate identity, globalisation and evaluation
- a thorough examination of ethics and professionalism
- more than 50 illustrations from recent PR campaigns
- a completely revised chapter on corporate social responsibility
- a new chapter on risk, issues and crisis management.

Alison Theaker has over 25 years' experience in public relations and management as a practitioner and academic. She was the first Head of Education and Training at the then Institute of Public Relations, as well as Principal Lecturer and Course Leader in Public Relations at Leeds Business School, UK, and Scholar in Residence in the School of Marketing Communication at Emerson College, Boston, US. She is an elected Fellow of the Chartered Institute of Public Relations and co-authored *Effective Media Relations*. She has delivered research papers at conferences in the UK, USA and Australia on team working in public relations, improving students' writing skills and the future of PR as a profession. She is now a PR coach for small businesses, running her own consultancy, The Spark, in Devon, www.thesparkuk.com.

This textbook is supported by a companion website at www.routledge.com/cw/theaker where a range of additional international case studies can be found, along with useful links.

Media Practice

Edited by James Curran, Goldsmiths College, University of London

The *Media Practice* handbooks are comprehensive resource books for students of media and journalism, and for anyone planning a career as a media professional. Each handbook combines a clear introduction to understanding how the media work with practical information about the structure, processes and skills involved in working in today's media industries, providing not only a guide on 'how to do it' but also a critical reflection on contemporary media practice.

The Advertising Handbook
3rd edition
Helen Powell, Jonathan Hardy,
Sarah Hawkin and Iain MacRury

The Alternative Media Handbook
Kate Coyer, Tony Dowmunt and
Alan Fountain

The Cyberspace Handbook
Jason Whittaker

The Documentary Handbook
Peter Lee-Wright

The Graphic Communication Handbook
Simon Downs

The Fashion Handbook
Tim Jackson and David Shaw

The Magazines Handbook
2nd edition
Jenny McKay

The Music Industry Handbook
Paul Rutter

The New Media Handbook
Andrew Dewdney and Peter Ride

The Newspapers Handbook
4th edition
Richard Keeble

The Photography Handbook
2nd edition
Terence Wright

The Public Relations Handbook
4th edition
Alison Theaker

The Radio Handbook
3rd edition
Carole Fleming

The Television Handbook
4th edition
Jeremy Orlebar

Contents

Figures

Tables

Contributors

Peter Brill is Managing Director of communication specialists Net.Mentor. His post-grad Diploma in Radio Journalism from City University led to a career in financial and sports broadcasting before turning to PR. After working in-house at Toyota (GB) and at specialist agency Avenue Communications, Peter moved to RAC Motoring Services where he became Head of Public Relations. He established Net.Mentor in 2002. Peter lectures for the CIPR's Advanced Certificate and CIM's Public Relations courses. In parallel with his corporate career he has also been active in the Third Sector, particularly as a Trustee for Sense (Deafblind and Rubella Association), which included strategic links with the communication team, and as Chairman of Salaam Shalom, the UK's first Muslim/Jewish radio station that launched in February 2007.

Johanna Fawkes Ph.D. was Principal Lecturer at Leeds Metropolitan University (LMU) until 2004, since when she has been an independent writer and researcher. She led the BA in Public Relations at LMU and similar courses at the University of Central Lancashire and the London College of Printing, after 15 years in public sector PR. She has written award-winning papers for a variety of journals, national and international conferences and has contributed chapters to leading PR textbooks. Johanna is a member of the Institute of Communication Ethics (ICE) Advisory Board, the *Journal of Public Relations Inquiry* editorial board, and was Chief Examiner for the CIPR Diploma, 2005–2007. She completed her doctorate in Jung, ethics and PR in 2011.

Liam FitzPatrick is Head of Practice at Bell Pottinger Change and Internal Communication in London. His career includes time in-house running IC teams in the UK and internationally as well as extended periods as a consultant working around the world. He also teaches with the CIPR in London and has created training programmes for a number of clients. He has written on the subject of competencies for communicators. He is a Fellow of the CIPR.

Dr Anne Gregory Ph.D. is Professor Public Relations and Director of the Centre for Public Relations Studies at LMU, one of the UK's leading think-tanks on public relations. Originally a broadcast journalist with the BBC, Anne spent 10 years in public relations practice, operating at senior levels in both consultancy and in-house. She was President of the UK Chartered Institute of Public Relations (CIPR) in 2004, leading it to Chartered status, and is now Chair of the Global Alliance of Public Relations and Communication Management. Anne initiated and edits the CIPR series of 17 books, is Editor-in-Chief of the Journal of Communication Management and publishes regularly in books, academic and popular journals. She is a frequent speaker at international conferences. Anne is still very active in practice, with Centre clients from the Department of Health and Cabinet Office to Tesco and Nokia. She was awarded the Sir Stephen Tallents Medal for outstanding service to public relations in 2009.

Owen Hargie is Professor of Communication, University of Ulster, and is Associate Professor at the University of Chester, England, and at Robert Gordon University, Scotland. He is a Chartered Member, Registered Practitioner, and Associate Fellow, of the British Psychological Society, and is an elected member of the Royal Norwegian Society of Sciences and Letters. He is currently Vice-Chair of the 'Interpersonal Communication and Social Interaction' Section of the European Communication Research and Education Association. His special areas of interest are in the fields of organisational, interpersonal and inter-cultural communication.

Susan Hutchinson (BA) Hons has worked in consumer PR for over ten years and is a divisional director at Grayling, one of the UK's leading consumer PR agencies. She holds the CIPR-accredited postgraduate Diploma in Public and Media Relations from Cardiff University's School of Journalism.

Cinzia Marrocco has worked in charity communications for more than 12 years, having started her career as a secondary school teacher. Following time spent at Scope and St John Ambulance in Australia, from 2003 she worked in the UK delivering strategic communications advice for service providers within the NHS before moving on to Sense (Deafblind and Rubella Association). Her work in the communications field has seen her focus on strategy, change management and brand development and she has delivered many seminars for not-for-profit professionals via the Media Trust training programme. Cinzia returned to Australia at the end of 2009 and is currently working for Quit Victoria, a charity helping individuals to give up smoking, as head of digital communications development.

Dr Mairead McCoy is Lecturer in Public Relations and Public Affairs in the School of Communication at the University of Ulster. She is currently Course Director of the PGDip/MSc in Political Lobbying and Public Affairs and the PGDip/MSc in Communication, Advertising and Public Relations. Mairead is also a member of Ulster's Institute for Research in Social Sciences and has published in the fields of public relations and marketing. She is a member of the European Communication Research and Education Association and the Northern Ireland Government Affairs Group.

Mark Phillimore, MBA, MCIPR, is a Senior Lecturer at the University of Greenwich Business School in London. He is Programme Leader for the MA Public Relations and also lectures on the BA Public Relations at the University. He is a Visiting Lecturer at the ESCEM School of Business and Management in France at the University of Poitiers/Tours. He runs training programmes for the Chartered Institute of Public Relations in social media. Prior to lecturing, he had his own PR consultancy specialising in the technology sector, particularly working with US and Japanese companies entering the European marketplace.

Phil Ramsey Ph.D. (University of Ulster, 2011) is a research associate in the School of Communication at the University of Ulster in Northern Ireland where he also teaches on undergraduate and postgraduate public relations programmes. He is a visiting lecturer in the School of Media, Film and Journalism at the University of Ulster, and has taught on the European Union Peace III funded *Conflicts of Interest* course. He completed a Ph.D. on the political communication policies of New Labour, and has published on public service broadcasting, deliberative democracy and ideology.

Loretta Smith, BA (Hons), Dip CIPR, MCIPR has worked in public relations for over ten years. She currently works in Communication for Severn Trent Water and has also carried out Communication roles for a number of other leading business-to-business and consumer companies in-house, including Airbus as well as agency-side for Grayling. She holds the Chartered Institute of Public Relations Diploma in Public Relations and an honours degree in Marketing from the University of the West of England.

Ian Somerville Ph.D., (Queen's University of Belfast, 1994) is a lecturer in the School of Communication at the University of Ulster in Northern Ireland, where he is Course Director for the BSc Public Relations. He has previously published in the areas of public relations ethics, political public relations and the impact on and use of new media technologies in the public relations industry. Current research interests include public relations strategies in human rights lobbying and public relations in conflict and post-conflict societies.

Simon Wakeman is Head of Communications and Marketing at Medway Council in Kent as well as a freelance consultant and trainer. With more than eleven years communications and marketing experience, he has provided consultancy and training to a wide range of central and local government agencies both in the UK and internationally. His private sector experience included retail product management, marketing online financial products and services, digital and interactive TV services, as well as consulting at a senior level to global brands such as Vodafone and BP. Simon writes a leading UK public sector communications blog at www.simonwakeman.com and holds professional qualifications from the CIPR and CIM.

Peter Walker, FCAM, FIPR, FNIPR is Senior Consultant – PIELLE Consulting. He is a Chartered Public a Fellow of the Nigerian Institute of Public Relations. He is one of the UK's leading international public relations practitioners, an expert in corporate responsibility and governance and a leading authority on the international promotion of economic development. A freeman of the City of London he is a member of the Guild of Public Relations Practitioners and a trustee of its Charity Fund. Peter lectures and writes extensively on public relations and communication management nationally and internationally. He is an adviser to and a member of the World Council for Corporate Governance and an international jurist for the Golden Peacock Awards for Corporate Governance and Corporate Social Responsibility.

Emma Wood MA is Senior Lecturer in corporate communication at Queen Margaret University, Edinburgh. She publishes on corporate identity and corporate communication and is a reviewer for, and former editor of *The Journal of Communication Management*. She is currently involved in researching the use of dialogue in public relations and communications practice. She has a background in communication in both the financial and business sectors and continues to advise clients, ranging from large public sector organisations to smaller consultancies, on a range of communication issues. She is course leader of the CIPR's post-graduate diploma in Scotland and a Fellow of the CIPR.

Heather Yaxley, FCIPR is a hybrid academic-educator-consultant-practitioner. Following a 15-year career working in public relations for consultancies and in-house with major automotive brands, she established Applause Consultancy in 2000 and founded the online professional development initiative, Green Banana in 2006. Heather is general secretary of the Motor Industry Public Affairs Association and lectures at Bournemouth University and as course director for the CIPR advanced certificate and diploma qualifications. She is currently studying a Ph.D. on career strategies in public relations. Heather is active online (@greenbanana), discussing public relations developments at www.greenbanana. wordpress.com and co.managing the international blog: www.prconversations. com.

Philip Young is a Senior Lecturer in Public Relations and Journalism at the University of Sunderland, specialising in media ethics. He is also a lead researcher for the Euprera EuroBlog project. Philip blogs at Mediations http://publicsphere. typepad.com/mediations. He is the co-author of the second edition of *Online Public Relations*.

Preface

When first writing this book, my main aim was to provide a textbook that drew on the UK experience of public relations, having been frustrated during many years of teaching the subject that the majority of textbooks originated from and used case studies from the United States environment. Since the first edition was published, several other excellent textbooks have swelled the ranks of European-based sources. I also experienced teaching in the United States for some years and returned to teach and practice in the UK.

I wanted to bring together the theoretical and organisational framework of public relations with examples of how it worked in practice. This is not a 'how to' book. There are already plenty of books written by experienced PR practitioners that set out the nuts and bolts of writing press releases, producing internal publications and managing campaigns. This edition benefits from a wide spread of new contributors, both academics and practitioners and thus deepens the links between theory and practice.

The first part of this book describes the context of public relations. Johanna Fawkes helps set out the history and development of PR and its role in society. Ian Somerville and Phil Ramsey discuss the relationship between PR and politics that has led to the charge of spin doctoring being laid against the profession. Anne Gregory describes the management role of PR and its relationship with other functions. Finally, I have revised the chapter on ethics, regulation and the development of PR as a profession.

The second part looks at strategic PR. Emma Wood and Ian Somerville discuss corporate communication, image and identity. Heather Yaxley defines risk, issues and crisis management, together with the implications of the rise of pressure groups and their use of public relations techniques. Ian Somerville and Emma Wood review corporate social responsibility. Mairead McCoy takes a fresh look at evaluation and Peter Walker examines global culture and international public relations.

The third part looks at stakeholder PR – addressing specific areas of the economy. Philip Young provides a fresh take on media relations and changes in the media. Liam FitzPatrick provides an insight into internal communications and the qualities of practitioners. Mark Phillimore gives an updated introduction to financial PR. Simon Wakeman reviews developments in the public sector and Susan Hutchinson gives practitioner insight into consumer and marketing communications. Loretta Smith expands on the business-to-business sector and Peter Brill and Cinzia Marrocco update their chapter on not-for-profit public relations. Heather Yaxley examines developments in technology and how they affect the practice of public relations.

Finally, some crystal ball gazing in Part IV examines future challenges for the profession and the issue of trust.

Topical case studies are used throughout the book to illustrate current practice and several have been replaced or updated.

I trust that the book still fulfils its original objectives as well as providing an informative and accessible account of public relations in the UK today.

Alison Theaker

Part I

The context of public relations

CHAPTER 1

What is public relations?

Johanna Fawkes

CHAPTER AIMS

This chapter introduces several definitions of public relations in an attempt to clarify the parameters of the discipline. There is an overview of the UK public relations sector, core tasks and skills are discussed, and distinctions are made between public relations and the fields of marketing and advertising. Finally, an overview of the main approaches to the study of public relations is offered to give context to the subject.

INTRODUCTION

In an end of year review of 2010, an *Observer* journalist (Wachman, 2010) compared the public relations handling of two major incidents by leading British companies, BP and Rolls Royce. The former compounded the environmental disaster in the Gulf of Mexico, in which 11 workers died, with inept comments from the CEO, Tony Hayward; the latter mismanaged its communications following an engine blowout (with no casualties). The journalist comments:

> In themselves these events have little in common. They were different in nature, with the fall-out from the Trent engine failure altogether less severe than the BP conflagration. But the thread that links the two is the hash that both firms made of their public relations afterwards.
>
> Their response undermined confidence in management and, in BP's case, to such a degree that it led to the departure of Chief Executive Tony Hayward.

> In fact BP's reaction amounts to a textbook example of how not to do things and will be studied by students of PR for years to come.

The article highlights misleading statements, inappropriate silences, personal gaffes and failure to engage with key audiences, which contributed to the loss of confidence in these organisations. It also illustrates the consequences that can follow poor public relations: to the organisation, its leaders, shareholders and the various publics, including employees and local residents. While crisis PR is dealt with elsewhere in this book, these examples of 'how not to' offer useful insight into the part that public relations plays in organisations and in society. The foundations of public relations include understanding your organisation and understanding the needs of its many publics, which some call stakeholders. In the case of BP, its publics included the population dependent on fishing and tourism in the Gulf of Mexico, the law makers to whom such groups would turn and, as the concern at pollution escalated, the office of the US President, as well as all the regulators, other companies involved in the Deepwater Horizon oil drilling and those involved in the clean-up. A *Guardian* article at the time (Wray, 2010) lists how relations with each of these groups was made worse by poor communications, including the BP Chairman's remark that 'we care about the small people'.

In the Rolls-Royce case, the major customer was the Ministry of Defence and shareholders were confused by an initial statement that was followed by a long silence as to what had gone wrong and what the costs of putting it right might be. Wachman (2010) concludes:

> But what Rolls and BP really should have learned by now is that the road to redemption lies neither in burying your head in the sand or playing down bad news. The key is to put your head above the parapet and engage via straight, honest talking, even if it means saying 'sorry, everyone, we screwed up'.

It is also interesting to note that it is now common to read about public relations itself, not just the activities of the organisation – a development of recent years as public relations, particularly in the political world, has become the focus of attention. Despite this interest there is still a great deal of confusion with what it is and what it does. For example, the term 'public relations people' was used to describe Ibiza clubbers distributing drugs (Tremlett and Topping, 2010). So the same phrase can be used to describe the implication of global communications and drug dealers!

This chapter aims to cover the issues of definition and distinction of PR from related activities, but a word of warning – these will not solve the dilemma of trying to 'explain' public relations in a phrase. The fact remains that it is a complex and hybrid subject; it draws on theories and practices from many different fields, such as management, media, communication and psychology. These links will be explored more fully in this book. Readers are more likely to have an understanding of the subject and an ability to evolve their own definitions when they have reached the end of the book, rather than the end of this chapter.

DEFINITIONS

Public relations is an emerging profession – various histories of the US and European development of the field place its origins in the late nineteenth century, with rapid expansion through the twentieth century. L'Etang (2004) traces the rise of British PR from its roots in local government and there are now global insights into the development of the field (Sriramesh and Verčič, 2009), as well as the long-standing US-centred histories of public relations (Cutlip, 1994; Ewen, 1996).

In 1976, Rex Harlow scoured 472 definitions of public relations to come up with the following paragraph:

> Public relations is a distinctive management function which helps establish and maintain mutual lines of communication, understanding, acceptance and cooperation between an organisation and its publics; involves the management of problems or issues; helps management to keep informed on and responsive to public opinion; defines and emphasises the responsibility of management to serve the public interest; helps management keep abreast of and effectively utilise change, serving as an early warning system to help anticipate trends; and uses research and ethical communication techniques as its principal tools.
> (Harlow, quoted in Wilcox *et al.*, 2003: 7)

Although this is useful – it contains many key concepts – and saves us ploughing through hundreds of definitions, it describes what PR does rather than what it is. Since then, there have been many more attempts to capture the essence of public relations. It is interesting that one attempt (from the 1978 World Assembly of Public Relations Associations in Mexico) suggested that public relations is an 'art and social science' (Wilcox *et al.*, 2003: 6). The words 'art' and 'social science' are helpful in explaining the continuing tension between understanding PR as a measurable, science-based application of communication tools, and the affection of many practitioners for the looser, more creative, aspects of the work. In the US the social science elements dominate the understanding of PR, as is reflected in their education and texts about the subject. In the UK, there has been a tension between those who see public relations as a management function and those who view it primarily in relation to the media. This is backed up by research (Fawkes and Tench, 2004) into public relations education in the UK, which shows public relations degrees are taught in schools of either media or business, with very different content and emphasis.

The definition framed by the Institute of Public Relations (IPR) in 1987 is still useful: 'Public Relations is the planned and sustained effort to establish and maintain goodwill and understanding between an organisation and its publics.' There are several key words worth noting here: 'planned' and 'sustained' suggest these relationships are not automatic or effortless. Indeed, they have to be 'established' and 'maintained'. Public relations work exists in time – it is not a series of unrelated events. Also, note that the aim is not popularity or approval, but goodwill and understanding. Many think that PR is just about promoting an organisation, whereas most PR work involves ensuring publics have an accurate view of the organisation, even if they don't like what it does. HM Revenue and Customs doesn't expect to be loved for its activities, but it might hope to be respected, or at least understood. More recently, the Chartered Institute of Public Relations (CIPR) extended its definition to: 'Public Relations practice is the discipline concerned with the reputation of organisations (or products, services or individuals) with the aim of earning understanding and support.' This is sometimes simplified further to: 'Public relations is about reputation – the result of what you do, what you say and what others say about you.' This is simple and doesn't attempt to catalogue all the tasks involved in managing reputation. It may even help students and practitioners explain what on earth it is they do, though there is still the danger, as L'Etang and Pieczka (2006b: 375) put it, that attempts to define public relations are largely 'constructed in an attempt to be all things to all people simultaneously'. It also places the emphasis on appearance, which reinforces the somewhat superficial image of PR. L'Etang (2009: 13) outlines the discipline as follows:

> Public relations is the occupation responsible for the management of organisational relationships and reputation. It encompasses issues management, public affairs, corporate communications, stakeholder relations, risk communication and corporate social responsibility. Public relations operates on behalf of many different types of organisation both at the governmental and corporate level, to small business and voluntary sectors. Public relations arises at points of societal change and resistance.

Most definitions (Kitchen, 1997; Wilcox *et al.*, 2003, for example) emphasise that public relations is a management function, developing and executing strategic issues involving two-way relationships and communication. This tends to reinforce the image of public relations as corporate communications, leaving out the PR undertaken by not-for-profit organisations, trade union and other voluntary campaigns. The most recent attempt to describe public relations was produced in the Stockholm protocol (2010), developed by leading PR practitioners and academics, which offers an overview of the work of public relations and communications professionals, stating that they:

- Participate in defining organisational values, principles, strategies, policies and processes.
- Apply social networking, research skills and tools to interpret stakeholders' and society's expectations as a basis for decisions.
- Deliver timely analysis and recommendations for an effective *governance of stakeholder relationships* by enhancing transparency, trustworthy behaviour, authentic and verifiable representation, thus sustaining the organisation's *'licence to operate'*.

- Create an internal listening culture, an open system that allows the organisation to anticipate, adapt and respond.

(WPRF, 2010)

Again, it is worth remembering that organisations come in all shapes and sizes not just corporations.

Before moving away from definitions, it is worth pointing out that many involve that strange word 'publics', which will be discussed more fully elsewhere. It is important to stress that public relations is not about dealing with 'the public', as people often think. In PR we say there is no such thing as the public: there are instead many different groups of people – not just consumers, but suppliers, employees, trustees, members, local and national trade and political bodies and local residents, among many others. One of the key concepts of PR is the idea that these groups – or publics – have different information needs and exert different demands on organisations. Understanding these differences is a vital skill of PR.

Many of the definitions covered above are rather idealistic, with their claims to promote social understanding and mutual goodwill. However, the definitions that most textbooks leave out are those from the critics of public relations (Stauber and Rampton, 2004; PRWatch.org; Spinwatch.com, for example) who assert that it is synonymous with propaganda, citing a constant stream of abuses of public trust by corporate communicators, such as the creation of 'front organisations'. They say huge resources, unavailable to dissenters, are being used to promote corporate and cultural values, as well as goods and political parties. Attacks from critics are not the only problem public relations faces when it comes to sorting out what it is: Hutton (2001: 212–214) believes that public relations has lost the battle for supremacy with marketing (see below for more on marketing and public relations) and is terminally threatened by its failure 'to define itself and to develop sophisticated and progressive theory'. He also castigates the failure to develop its central tenet or core concept, which he sees as managing strategic relationships. Even practitioners seem confused about what public relations is: some are abandoning the term and rebranding themselves as 'perception managers' or 'corporate communications'.

THE PUBLIC RELATIONS INDUSTRY

Another approach to understanding public relations is to describe what people *do*. First, let's look at the industry as a whole. Research on PR in the UK estimates that there are about 48,000 people working in the sector and that PR has a turnover of about £6.5 billion, making it a significant player in the national economy (CEBR, 2005). Public relations workers are either employed by organisations as part of their in-house PR departments or by consultancies, which are retained by a number of organisations and/or individuals to undertake public relations work. According to industry statistics (CIPR, 2009a) 22 per cent of practitioners have a place on the board. Some people also work on their own as freelance PR practitioners. Research suggests that 82 per cent of UK PR workers are employed directly by companies, local and national government organisations and not-for-profit groups (CEBR, 2005). However, the trend is for a growth in consultancies, ranging from full-service agencies offering research, advertising and marketing advice as well as public relations counselling, to specialist agencies that might focus on a particular sector, such as health or music, or on a particular aspect of the public, such as young people or women, or a particular aspect of public relations, such as crisis management or celebrity PR.

Organisationally, international public relations professional issues are coordinated by supra-national bodies, such as the Global Alliance of Public Relations and Communications Management (GA) and the World Public Relations Forum. It should be noted that none of these national or international bodies has control of the work of public relations practitioners who are not obliged to join any such organisation to practice. The UK professional body – the IPR – was founded in 1948 and attained Chartered status in 2005. Its current membership is 9,500 (CIPR, 2010a) out of an estimated public relations workforce of 48,000 (CIPR/CEBR, 2005), though Sriramesh and Verčič (2009) note that such figures should be treated with caution, given the multiplicity of job titles within the broad field of PR.

The CIPR publishes an annual benchmarking report, based on in-depth surveys of its members. The 2009 report shows the majority (65 per cent) of the 1,940 respondents were female, but that 30 per cent of male respondents held boardroom positions, compared to 18 per cent of their female counterparts. Edwards (2010) reports that although 12 per cent of the adult working population in the UK is from black and minority ethnic groups (BAME), only 1 per cent of public relations practitioners is from these groups.

PUBLIC RELATIONS TASKS AND SKILLS

The table below provides a rough guide to the main activities in public relations – most of which are covered in detail elsewhere in this book. These are organised either by the kind of audiences they engage with or the content of the activity. It is important to note that these categories overlap. For example, a company intranet newsletter involves writing, new technology *and* internal communications.

McElreath (1996) suggests that there are two roles commonly assumed by public relations practitioners: technician or problem-solver. This would divide the publications manager supervising the printing of the annual report from the strategic adviser drafting a policy document on the future of the organisation. However, many of the kinds of activity outlined above involve both problem-solving and technical skills.

A well-written media release should reflect understanding of current media practices and channels, and a public affairs adviser also needs a range of technical skills, including writing. As is so often the case in the field of public relations, it is not easy to draw hard lines or lay down absolute rules.

Research among senior European practitioners suggests that their main work includes:

- Building immaterial assets (reputation, brands, organisational culture) – 72 per cent
- Facilitating business processes (influencing customer preferences, generating public attention, motivating employees) – 64 per cent
- Adjusting organisational strategies (identifying opportunities, integrating public concerns) – 49 per cent
- Securing room for manoeuvre (managing relationships, managing crises) – 48 per cent.

(Zerfass *et al.*, 2010)

It is helpful to understand what public relations is by looking at the range of skills different bodies suggest as necessary for entrants to the field. Research (CIPR and the Department of Trade and Industry (DTI), 2003; Fawkes and Tench, 2004; Turk, 2006) shows which skills and topics employers and academics think are the most important for PR graduates.

As can be seen from Tables 1.1–1.5, there is overwhelming support for writing skills/literacy as the key skill for public relations practitioners. It is worth noting that UK employers also rate teamwork and problem-solving very highly. There is also wide agreement that practical experience is a main requirement for entry into the public relations field, and many courses do offer a work placement – which is by far the best way to find out what public relations is.

DISTINCTIONS

Sometimes, of course, it's easier to explain what you *don't* do. The following sections look at areas often confused with PR. As with definitions, the lines are not always clear. To repeat, PR draws on expertise and experience from many fields, it overlaps with other disciplines, it tends to integrate rather than exclude – this is its strength as a practice, but a weakness when it comes to descriptions and definitions.

Marketing

This is the field most commonly confused with PR – not unreasonably since market-ing refers to PR in its texts and practice as part of the marketing mix. To marketing

TABLE 1.1 A rough guide to the main activities in public relations

Public relations activity	Explanation	Examples
Internal communications	Communicating with employees	In-house newsletter, suggestion boxes
Corporate PR	Communicating on behalf of whole organisation, not goods or services	Annual reports, conferences, ethical statements, visual identity, images
Media relations	Communicating with journalists; specialists; and editors from local, national, international and trade media, including newspapers, magazines, radio, TV and web-based communication	Press releases, photocalls, video news releases, off-the-record briefings, press events
Business-to-business	Communicating with other organisations, e.g. suppliers, retailers	Exhibitions, trade events, newsletters
Public affairs	Communicating with opinion formers (e.g. local/national politicians), monitoring political environment	Presentations, briefings, private meetings, public speeches
Community relations/ corporate social responsibility (CSR)	Communicating with local community, elected representatives, headteachers, etc.	Exhibitions, presentations, letters, meetings, sports activities and other sponsorship
Investor relations	Communicating with financial organisations/individuals	Newsletters, briefings, events
Strategic communication	ID and analysis of situation, problem and solutions to further organisational goals	Researching, planning and executing a campaign to improve ethical reputation of organisation
Issues management	Monitoring political, social, economic and technological environment	Considering effect of US economy and presidential campaign on UK organisation
Crisis management	Communicating clear messages in fast-changing situation or emergency	Dealing with media after major rail crash on behalf of police, hospital or local authority
Copywriting	Writing for different audiences to high standards of literacy	Press releases, newsletters, web pages, annual reports
Publications management	Overseeing print/media processes, often using new technology	Leaflets, internal magazines, websites
Events management, exhibitions	Organisation of complex events, exhibitions	Annual conference, press launch, trade shows

TABLE 1.2 Summary of DTI/CIPR recommended key skills and competences

Necessary knowledge includes	Necessary skills include
Understanding of business	Written and verbal communication
Corporate strategy	Creativity
Finance and corporate governance	Media relations
Data analysis	Crisis management
Audience research	Issues management
Management of resources and people	Interpersonal skills
	Credibility and integrity
	Flexibility

Source: DTI/CIPR (2003)

TABLE 1.3 Recommended curriculum

Necessary knowledge includes	Necessary skills include
Communication and persuasion concepts and strategies	Research methods and analysis
Communication and public relations theories	Management of information
Relationships and relationship-building communication	Mastery of language in written and oral
Societal trends	Problem-solving and negotiation
Ethical issues	Management of communication
Legal requirements and issues	Strategic planning
Marketing and finance	Issues management
Public relations history	
Uses of research and forecasting	
Multicultural and global issues	
The business case for diversity	
Various world social, political, economic and historical frameworks	
Organisational change and development	
Management concepts and theories	

Source: Turk (2006)

TABLE 1.4 Ranking of discipline topics by employers

Subject	%
1 Writing skills	86
2 Media relations	81
3 Public relations practice	80
4 One-year work placements	64
5 Media practice	51
6 Live projects for external clients	40
6 Journalism	40
6 Media analysis	40
7 Internal communications	34
8 Business principles	31
9 Public relations theory	30

Source: Tench and Fawkes (2005)

practitioners and academics, public relations is one of the four Ps – product, place, price and promotion – that make up a successful marketing campaign. This is not incorrect: public relations can play an essential role in creating successful products – if the other elements are right, of course. The use of public relations to promote goods and services is sometimes called marketing public relations (MPR). There is some dispute about how useful this term is, but it could reduce the confusion caused by using the same term – public relations – to describe promoting products and planning strategic communications.

So how can MPR support sales? It can help create awareness of the product – especially new technological developments, where consumers need to understand what a gizmo is before they can distinguish between brands of gizmo. Once, campaigns had to explain what a fridge did; more recently the 'market' needed educating about the virtues of broadband and nanotechnology. In competitive fields, such as fast-moving consumer goods (FMCGs), publicity can be crucial to success. Wilcox identifies a number of public relations activities that support marketing efforts by creating new leads through gaining editorial coverage in trade and consumer media and producing sales brochures (Wilcox *et al.*, 2003: 16). While the marketing team may create special offers and sales promotions, the publicity people will be seeking media coverage and arranging launch events. Together, they can create worldwide successes, from the latest Hollywood blockbuster to Viagra. Recent developments in marketing, such as relationship marketing and cause-related marketing, are similar to elements of public relations, and are blurring the distinctions. So what's the difference?

The Institute of Marketing defines marketing as: 'The management process responsible for identifying, anticipating and satisfying consumer requirements profitably.' The two central words here are 'consumer' and 'profit'. Understanding the consumer and producing products or services that will satisfy consumer needs to the profit of the supplier is the traditional arena of marketing. There is a clear exchange – money for goods or services. It is easily measured. Marketing campaigns are often preceded and followed by research to measure the degree to which an attitude or behaviour has changed after the marketing activity. Have more people heard of the product now? Have they bought (or used) it, or are they more likely to?

However, public relations campaigns are often harder to quantify. Many organisations – the armed services, charities, local and central government, for example – may not have goods or services to sell. But they do all have messages to communicate and – importantly – to receive. They need to maintain relationships with all those who may work for them, give time or money, raise complaints, or vote for or against them. These relationships are too complex to be covered by marketing, which is why commercial companies, who *do* have things to sell, also have public relations departments.

Kitchen (1997: 28) explains: 'Public relations and marketing are two major management functions within an organisation, but how they are organised depends upon managerial perceptions, organisational culture, and historical precedent.' Organisations dealing in FMCGs are more likely than not to have a large marketing department containing a PR function. Those who depend on good intelligence about the political environment as well as consumer tastes, especially not-for-profit organisations, will have a larger PR or public affairs function.

In public relations texts (and this is no exception), marketing is described as primarily concerned with sales and sales-related functions. In marketing texts, public relations is rarely considered to be more than publicity. The argument concerning which is the wider discipline can be found in textbooks, university staff rooms, student debates and companies themselves. As quoted above, some scholars, such as Hutton (1999, 2001), believe that marketing has taken over many functions that used to be delivered by PR people. He showed that, in the US at least, many traditional PR functions have gone to human resource departments, finance or public affairs. However, recent evidence suggests a move in the opposite direction, particularly in regard to building relations via social media (Bush, 2010).

Around the turn of the century, the concept of integrated marketing communications (IMC), which suggested that companies could better meet their objectives by combining the various communication elements, gained prominence. This was defined as 'building a synchronised multi-channel communication strategy that reaches every market segment with a single unified message' (Schultz *et al.*, 1992, cited in Kitchen, 1997: 231). In theory, this is certainly common sense. All the elements: public relations, advertising, marketing, direct mail and sales promotion, work best when they are pulling in the same direction, rather than contradicting each other with inconsistent messages.

In practice, integrated communications can mean that one element, often marketing or advertising, achieves a dominant share of resources and relegates the other areas to support roles. Paul Alvarez, former chair of Ketchum Communications, has been quoted as saying that 'to have credibility, [public relations practitioners] must acknowledge the roles played by other communications disciplines . . . By the same token, other disciplines must realise the full potential of public relations' (Wilcox *et al.*, 2003: 19).

Advertising

The distinction between advertising and PR is more easily made: advertising involves paying a medium (TV, radio, newspaper or magazine, for example) for airtime or column inches in which to put across a promotional message. The content of an ad is always controlled by the advertiser, unlike the content of editorial pages or programmes, which are controlled by journalists. Public relations practitioners try to persuade journalists to cover their products and services on the grounds of newsworthiness. An ad doesn't have to satisfy any news value – it just has to be legal and paid for.

The Institute of Practitioners in Advertising (IPA) defines advertising as follows: 'Advertising presents the most persuasive possible selling message to the right prospects for the product or service at the lowest possible cost.' Here, the phrase 'selling message' distinguishes the two disciplines – PR aims not to increase sales, but to increase understanding. Sometimes, of course, understanding a product or service improves sales, but PR does not claim a direct causal link. However, there are grey areas: with corporate advertising an organisation purchases space in a paper, magazine or broadcast programme to put across a general message about itself, not its products. This message might extol its efforts to be green or socially responsible, or it might put the management view in an industrial dispute or takeover. The content of the message is likely to be PR-driven and related to the corporate strategic aims of the organisation rather than product support.

Another grey area is the advertorial, where the space is bought, just like an ad, but is filled with text and images very similar to the surrounding editorial. This is increasingly common in magazines and, although the word 'advertorial' is usually clear at the top of the page, it's in small print and casual readers may well believe they are reading another article about, say, skincare products. As a result, they may believe the text reflects the impartial view of the magazine rather than the more interested view of an advertiser. Harrison (1995: 5) comments:

The strength of advertorials over advertisements is that their style and format give greater credibility to the products they are advertising, by explaining them in apparently objective terms through a third party, the journalist. But what does that do to the credibility of the journalist or the publication in which the advertorial appears? If there is no intention to mislead the reader into confusing the advertising message with a news or feature report, why not just use an advertisement?

SOCIAL MEDIA DEVELOPMENTS

As new technologies offer new channels to reach publics, the convergence between the various communication fields increases. Public relations, marketing and advertising companies are all involved in creating a 'buzz' around a new product or service, often using a mix of traditional media coverage (PR), poster and magazine adverts (advertising) and orchestrated word-of-mouth (WOM) campaigns (either PR or marketing). The enormous impact of social media has transformed communication in general and particularly in public relations. Many campaigns, such as Nike's Facebook ads, now aim entirely at WOM circulation of images, video clips and messages to friends and contacts via web pages, mobile phones and Twitter. It is getting harder and harder to tell which of these are placed by ordinary users and which are carefully planned by PR, ad or marketing agencies. There is also a growth of counter-campaigns using websites, such as the success of Mumsnet in persuading the BBC to change a storyline in *Eastenders*, and nearly 200,000 followers signed up for BPGlobalPR to attack BP over the Gulf of Mexico spill.

APPROACHES TO PR

These days, there are many ways to find out more about public relations and its role in society, including textbooks and websites. However, to make sense of the information they contain, it is helpful to understand their point of view. For example, information found on the UK CIPR website, www.cipr.co.uk, tends to be positive and upbeat about public relations, as it has a duty to represent and promote its members and it believes PR plays a positive role in society. On the other hand, the information on www.Spinwatch.com contains examples where public relations has abused public trust by withholding essential information, disguising the source of information and other underhand practices. This is because it is run by a campaigning group who believe PR distorts public communication.

Textbooks on public relations tend to be written by scholars who base their ideas on a theory or set of theories that help explain how they see the world and PR's part in it. The main theoretical approaches to public relations are set out below (Fawkes, 2010).

TABLE 1.5 Approaches to public relations theory

School/approach	Key proposals/framework	Leading PR scholars
Systems theory	Information is a quantity that is transferred between organisations and various publics, with different degrees of consequent change. PR practitioners manage these exchanges. Studying the systems through which information is transferred enables one to adjust and adapt.	Grunig, Cutlip, Dozier, Wilcox
Rhetoric	Communication involves speech and symbols that can be analysed to understand meanings – shared or otherwise. PR people use signs and symbols to persuade and reflect client values.	Heath, Toth
Relationship theory	Public relations practitioners conduct complex internal and external relationships with key players. Personal relationship theory can be used to explain professional/organisational relationships	Ledingham and Bruning, Jahoonzi
Critical	Exposing the assumptions and value judgements, behind 'neutral' or 'objective' theories helps understand who benefits from not examining these issues. Many of the above PR theories are seen as uncritical of PR.	L'Etang, Pieczka Weaver
Political economy	Information is used by interest groups to protect their own position in society: the mechanisms of control – legal, corporate, economic, political and social – can be studied to see whose interests are best served by the communication. PR is a resource for the powerful more often than not.	Moloney, D. Miller, Chomsky

Excellence

The Excellence project (Grunig *et al.*, 1992, 2007), seeks to measure the dimensions of best practice both in its country of origin (US) and worldwide. Here the practitioner is mostly imagined as a boundary spanner, linking external publics to organisational strategic communications. The boundary spanner role is central to systems theory-based communication and is clear that PR is a management function. It sees the excellent communicator as the key player with access to internal stakeholders via the dominant coalition (such as the boardroom) and important external stakeholders. White and Dozier explain how public relations practitioners interact with the organisations environment to 'gather, select, and relay information from the environment to decision makers in the dominant coalition' (1992: 93). This role achieves its highest level in symmetric communication when the full range of negotiating and diplomatic skills is deployed to secure positive outcomes for all parties: 'In the two-way symmetric model . . . practitioners serve as mediators between organisations and their publics. Their goal is mutual understanding between practitioners and their publics' (Grunig and Hunt, 1984: 22). The highest ideal is symmetrical communication in which both parties are equal (see also Chapter 2 for more on this).

Advocacy

This model recognises that public relations often plays a more asymmetrical or persuasive role than is encompassed by the boundary spanner. Fitzpatrick and Bronstein (2006) see communication as taking place in a 'marketplace' in which all organisations are entitled to have a voice:

> Marketplace theory is predicated, first on the existence of an objective 'truth' that will emerge from a cacophony of voices promoting various interests; second on a marketplace in which all citizens have the right – and perhaps the means – to be both heard and informed; and third, on the rational ability of people to discern 'truth'.
>
> (Fitzpatrick, 2006: 4)

It is strongly US-based, and is the model that is most often cited by practitioners. A more thorough approach to advocacy is based on rhetorical theory (Heath, 2001a; Toth and Heath, 1992), which addresses the role of persuasion in communication, dating back to Aristotle and strongly linked to concepts of democracy. The communicator uses words and symbols to influence the perceptions of others, with varying outcomes. The roles of speaker, audience, the choice of message and the dynamics and characteristics of each provides the focus of study. Rhetoric is rarely taught in the UK (Tench and Fawkes, 2005).

Relationship management

This model is based on relationship theory and centres on the role of public relations professionals in negotiating a complex set of relationships inside and outside client/employer organisations (Ledingham and Bruning, 2000). Positive relationships include trust, satisfaction, commitment, exchange relationship and communal relationship (Hon and Grunig, 1999). Unlike some of the organisation-centred perspective of systems theory approaches to public relations, it takes the standpoint of the publics (Leitch and Neilson, 2001).

Critical theory

Critical approaches, including postmodernism, political economy and propaganda studies, are sceptical of the PR role. L'Etang summarises this grouping as 'an interdisciplinary approach which seeks to define assumptions which are taken-for-granted with a view to challenging their source and legitimacy' (2005: 521). Critical writers scrutinise the power dynamics of organisations and their publics and often reveal persistent involvement of PR practitioners in propaganda and deception, past and present. While the previously covered models share an optimistic view of how public relations can or does contribute to society, this view is not universal. This group can also be expanded to include public relations' greatest critics, Stauber and Rampton (2004) in the US and Miller and Dinan (2008) in the UK, who offer well researched and detailed descriptions of deceptions perpetrated, often by established public relations firms. They particularly highlight the distortions these cause to the democratic process, such as the creation by PR firms of 'artificial' grassroots campaigns, which they term 'astroturfing', or the planting of questions in press conferences by PR staff masquerading as journalists, as well as the systematic campaigns of distortion or suppression allegedly undertaken in the campaign to win the 'climate change' debate, for example, especially with US audiences.

The example of the BP crisis at the beginning of the chapter can be seen from these different perspectives: Excellence theory would look at the systems of communication between the board or dominant coalition and the different publics, assessing the kinds of communication that occurred before, during and after the crisis. It would critique the imbalance of information between the oil company and other groups; advocacy would look at BP's share of the total communication, arguing that BP had to fight its corner, not worry so much about the feelings of other groups, though in the marketplace approach it would seem that BP failed to make its point of view heard because it upset so many groups; a rhetorical analysis would look at the symbols and hidden meanings in the company's main statements and actions (including the decision of the CEO to go yachting at the height of the crisis); relationship management would stress the need to build links with people and politicians who were frightened and unclear about the nature and implications of the oil spill; and the critics pointed out similar problems BP had in the past with safety problems, and suggested this was because it was more interested in profit than its relationships with others.

An article in the *Economist* (December, 2010) echoes the confusion identified above (albeit with its own added sexism):

> . . . after a century of spinning, PR Man remains uncertain of his proper role. Is he a master manipulator? Is he the devil's advocate (as long as Satan pays his fees)? Or is he a benign bridge-builder between the corporate world and the public?

CONCLUSION

This chapter has shown that is it very hard to define public relations, despite many efforts. This presents a problem for the field as a whole as its main ideas are easily adopted by marketing, human resources or other elements in an organisation. Nevertheless, public relations is a growing field, making a considerable contribution to the economy. The key skills required by employers in the field are writing, practical experience and problem-solving skills. Team working is also highly rated. Finally, the chapter looked at the different approaches to the study of public relations, including actively hostile approaches, and the various versions of the role of the practitioner that emerge from these theories.

QUESTIONS FOR DISCUSSION

1 Why do you think public relations is so difficult to define? Which of the existing definitions seems most useful to you?

2 The launch of a Hollywood summer movie might involve: billboard posters; promotional T-shirts; the organisation of a première in the West End of London; guest appearances by stars on TV chat shows; articles about the use of special effects in film or general media; and trailers from the movie on websites and mobile phones. Which of these are public relations? What are the others?

3 Do you think it matters if you can't tell whether a webcam link to a new band has been made in a bedsit and uploaded by the artist(s) or made to look like that by the PR department of a multinational music corporation?

4 Why do you think some people accuse PR of being the same as propaganda? What arguments would you present against this point of view?

5 Can employees be equally committed to their employer's interests and to those of wider society?

6 Is there any kind of company you wouldn't work for/have as a client? Why?

7 Why do you think writing is ranked so highly as a key PR skill?

8 Look at some of the adverts on the PR vacancy pages of the *Guardian* or *PR Week*. How many different job titles can you find? When you look at the details, are they all so different from each other? What do they have in common?

9 You are looking for a PR agency to handle the promotion of a new fragrance for older women. Would you prefer a specialist agency that focuses on this age range or one which has more experience of promoting perfumes across all ages?

10 Do you think it will be harder to tell the difference between PR, marketing and advertising in social media – and does it matter?

FURTHER READING

Ewen, S. (1996) *PR! A social history of spin*, Basic Books.
Heath, R.L. (ed.) (2001) *The handbook of public relations*, Sage.
L'Etang, J. and Pieczka, M. (eds) (2006) *Public relations, critical debates and contemporary practice*, Lawrence Erlbaum.
Moloney, K. (2006) *Rethinking PR: the spin and the substance*, Routledge.
Tench, R. and Yeomans, L. (eds) (2009) *Exploring public relations* (2nd edition), Pearson Education.

CHAPTER 2

Public relations and communications

Johanna Fawkes

CHAPTER AIMS

This chapter looks at different ways of describing the communication process and examines the role of the media in communicating to and between organisations and individuals in society. Topics covered include a definition of communication and its core concepts, a history of communication models and the effects of the mass media. It concludes with a discussion of Grunig and Hunt's four models of public relations communication (1984).

WHAT IS COMMUNICATION?

It is impossible not to communicate – you don't need words, grammar or syntax. Humans communicate before and after they can use language by using sounds and gestures. Babies yell at different frequencies depending on whether they are hungry, frustrated or have a full nappy. Usually their carer can tell the difference. Later, on holiday, people point and smile and nod at strangers, and usually find the beach, bank or souvenir shop.

All you need to communicate is someone else. 'It takes two to speak,' said Thoreau, 'one to speak and another to hear.' In fact, sometimes communication is involuntary. David Bernstein (1984: 1) states, 'Companies communicate whether they want to or not.'

Communication seems so simple until we begin to examine it. Then all sorts of terms and concepts creep into the conversation. Even the definitions add to the

confusion: Windahl *et al.* (1992) point out that there are two main traditions in defining communication – the one-way transmission model and the two-way exchange concept. They quote Theodorsen and Theodorsen, who define communication as 'the transmission of information, ideas, attitudes, or emotion from one person or group to another (or others) primarily through symbols'. The Shannon and Weavor model of communication illustrates this approach. In contrast, Rogers and Kincaid define communication as 'a process in which the participants create and share information with one another in order to reach a mutual understanding' (Windahl *et al.* 1992: 6). Before looking at more models it's worth clarifying a few terms.

Levels of communication

Berger (1995) identifies four levels of communication: intrapersonal (thoughts); interpersonal (conversations); small group communication (like a lecture); and mass communication. He points out that 'talking to oneself' uses the neurological/chemical apparatus of the brain as the channel of communication; talking to another or others uses the airwaves to carry the verbal message, as well as non-verbal communication such as body language, facial expression and so on. Mass media communication uses print, broadcast or phone wires to communicate with a wide range of geographically scattered people.

Core concepts of communication

Burgoon *et al.* (1994) suggest that *intent* is a key concept – where both source and receiver know that communication is occurring. This excludes all the accidents of overhearing or instances where the television is on, but the room is empty.

Meaning is also crucial: without a shared understanding of the meaning of words and symbols, communication is at best limited, at worst impossible. Imagine driving in a country where a red traffic light meant 'go'. The previous discussion on semiotics and Chapter 7, which covers corporate identity, helps explain these issues.

Another issue is *noise*, which is interference between elements in a communication, and can mean technical interference (such as static on the line), semantic interference (where the meaning is unclear) and psychological interference (where the receiver is unable to understand the message because of his or her own state of mind or personality). Shannon and Weaver's model looks at noise.

Feedback is also an important concept. It is what makes the difference between one-way communication, where the sender has no knowledge – or possibly interest – in the receiver's response, and two-way communication, where the receiver can comment or even alter events by responding to a message. Berlo (1960), writing about feedback, said, 'How can anyone know that a communication has taken place unless there is a response from the receiver?'

Finally we must consider the concept of *mediation* – the means by which the communication is transmitted, whether in person, by language or gesture, or via another medium, such as print or broadcast.

Unmediated communication means any two-way contact that does not pass through a channel or medium. This can be one-to-one (a conversation), one-to-many (a speech), or even many-to-one (a protest). It's worth pointing out that even direct communication between individuals contains a number of variables such as voice, body language, proximity and facial expression.

Mediated communication adds a channel – a means of transmitting the message. This could still be one-to-one, such as a mobile phone conversation. Or it could be one-to-many, such as a website announcement. The kind of channel used and its technical efficiency will affect the message (see the previous section on 'noise'); for example, talking on your mobile as you enter a railway tunnel will reduce the efficacy of the message. The development of user-generated websites such as YouTube illustrates how groups can talk to groups via the medium of the World Wide Web. This development in recent years changes the communication landscape profoundly.

Fiske (1990) distinguishes between presentational and representational media. The presentational media are those which are not mediated, such as voice, body language and facial expressions. They require the presence of both the communicator and the receiver to create *acts* of communication. Representational media may include these elements but the communicator does not need to be actually present. This would include television interviews, for example, but could also include paintings, photographs, books, even gardens and buildings – anything, in fact, that makes a statement or 'text' but does not require its creator to be present for a 'reading' to be taken. Fiske calls these *works* of communication. He also examines the 'mechanical' media of television, radio and telephone, and points out the extra technical requirements of these media. Other theorists would describe technical issues as relating to channels not media, but they are often used to mean the same thing.

The media most relevant to public relations are the *mass media* – newspapers and magazines, radio and television and, above all, the internet. These media allow communicators to reach at low cost (compared to contacting them individually) large numbers of people who have already chosen to purchase or consume that paper or magazine or programme. The audience may be vast, like the readership of a national newspaper, or quite small, such as a magazine's subscribers.

To reach these audiences via the mass media involves having your message selected for inclusion by journalists according to formal or informal ideas of what they think the reader or viewer wants, sometimes called news values. The journalist takes on a 'gatekeeper' role, deciding what does and does not get forwarded to the medium's users. Of course, advertisers can reach the same audiences without going through this 'gate', but they lose credibility or third-party endorsement in the process. The growth of web-based communication may bypass this role, by building links between groups and individuals who no longer require journalistic involvement. This is sometimes called 'citizen journalism' and can mean more people's voices are available on any subject, though journalistic standards and selection may no longer apply – Wikipedia is a tremendous resource but often unreliable.

Most public relations communication is mediated, though it is worth remembering that public relations also uses direct media, such as exhibitions, leaflets or corporate videos, where the content is wholly controlled by the sender. Interestingly, the internet allows both kinds of communication. The communication models discussed below help explain these developments.

A BRIEF HISTORY OF COMMUNICATION MODELS

Aristotle (384–322 BC) is often cited as the first authority on communication. His works on rhetoric – the art of influencing others through the spoken word – developed with the growth of democracy in Ancient Greece and are still highly influential. Many political speeches depend on the techniques he advocated, such as the use of repetition in Tony Blair's 'education, education, education' speech. Aristotle believed communication consisted of three elements:

- *ethos* – the nature or qualities of the communicator
- *logos* – the nature, structure and content of the message
- *pathos* – the nature, feelings and thoughts of the receiver or audience.

More recently, in 1948, political scientist Harold Laswell created a formula to describe the communication process:

- who says
- what
- to whom
- with what
- effect?

This has been very influential and reflects the interest at that time in the power of propaganda. But it assumes that communication will always have an effect and suggests that communication is always persuasive. In this model, the communicator or sender decides what and how to communicate and the receiver just waits to be affected – an approach that is now considered very limited (McQuail and Windahl 1993).

Claude Shannon, a mathematician, created a representation of Laswell's formula as a linear, mathematical equation in 1949. He and his partner Warren Weaver worked for Bell Telephones and their interest was driven by the technical requirements of a medium. They introduced the crucial concept of interference in communication, which they called 'noise'. Interference might occur in the handset of the speaker or receiver, or in the lines connecting them. As a result the message could be distorted and misunderstood. The same principle could be translated to different media; for example, radio static, poor TV reception, small print, blurred photographs. Noise was later expanded to include daydreaming, physical discomfort or other kinds of distraction. It was an important reminder that communication sent is not always – if ever – the same as communication received.

A simple communication model will include a source or sender who selects information (encodes) to create a message that will be transmitted by a channel to a receiver who selects a meaning from the message (decodes) and responds with action or no action (feedback). Harrison's adaptation of the Shannon and Weaver model (Figure 2.1) demonstrates this clearly.

This model has some useful elements for public relations, particularly regarding the concepts of noise and the role of feedback. Fiske (1990: 8) describes noise as 'anything that is added to the signal between transmission and reception that is not intended by the source'. Shannon and Weaver were most concerned with engineering noise, such as physical interference on the phone line, which might affect the message. The modern equivalent of physical noise might be the interruption of a mobile phone conversation while the train goes through a tunnel. Shannon and Weaver added the concept of semantic noise, to cover the wider range of possible interference between a sender and receiver of a message, such as the receiver's physical discomfort, or distracting thoughts. The point is that the person you are speaking to may not receive the message you intended to transmit. So, how can you tell? This is where feedback comes in.

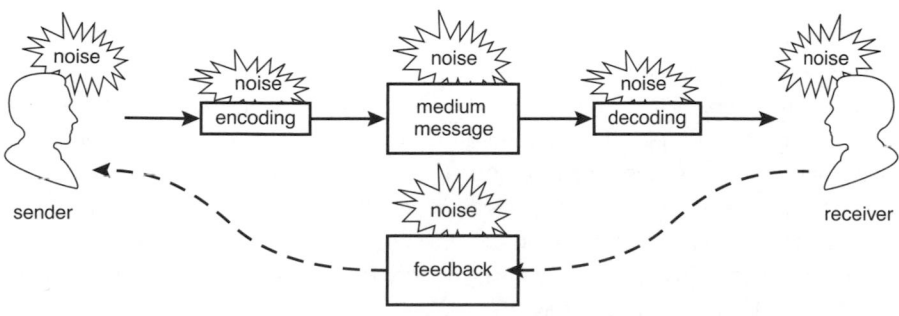

FIGURE 2.1 Harrison's adaptation of Shannon and Weaver's model
Source: Harrison (1995: 30), Figure 3.1. Used by permission of Thompson Learning

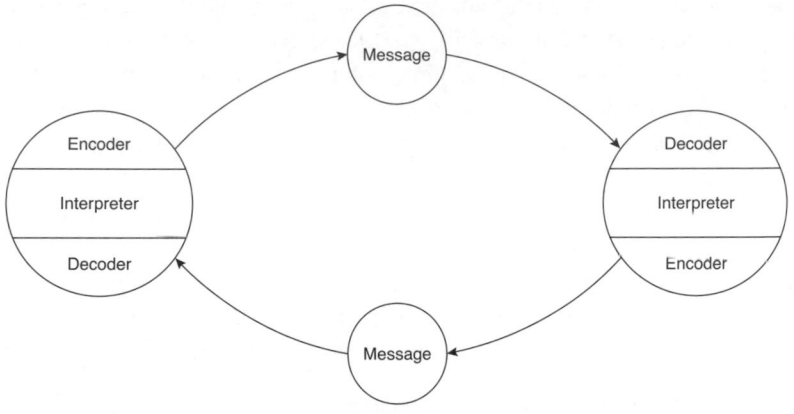

FIGURE 2.2 The Osgood–Schramm model of communication
Source: McQuail and Windahl (1993: 19), Figure 2.2.3. Used by permission of Longman

When two people are in conversation, the speaker is free to adjust his or her tone, speed, language, emphasis and so on, according to questions, nods, smiles and other responses from the listener. Indeed, if something is not understood, it can quickly be made clear. The source and receiver are in a constant feedback and adjustment loop. This feedback element is crucial to effective public relations – we need to know if the message was received, how it was understood and what actions or changes in attitude or behaviour have followed receipt of the message. Feedback is what tells the practitioner that his or her sense of humour or wit has backfired or, more simply, that the language is too complex for a particular audience.

However, this still presents two problems. First, it is linear: feedback is not the same thing as equal participation in the communication; and second, it is hard to place the mass media comfortably in this model. The Osgood–Schramm model (Figure 2.2) suggests a more equal model of communication while the Westley–McLean model describes the role of the mass media in communication.

Osgood and Schramm were central to the development of the second approach suggested by Rogers and Kincaid (in Windahl *et al.* 1992), which was discussed earlier in the chapter when we looked at contrasting concepts of communication. In 1954, they created a circular model that showed that the receiver, as well as the sender, is engaged in a continuous and active act of communication. Each party has to interpret the message and shape a response before sending it out or back. Schramm added, 'In fact it is misleading to think of the communication process as starting somewhere and ending somewhere. It is really endless. We are really switchboard centres handling and rerouting the great endless current of information' (quoted in McQuail and Windahl 1993: 20).

This more equal communication relationship was continued in the work of McLeod and Chaffee, whose co-orientation models (1973) influenced much of Grunig's thinking on two-way communication (see below).

The second problem with the linear models, which also applies to Osgood and Schramm's, is that they do not include a mass media role. Feedback in mass media communications is quite different from personal or group communications. There may be letters to the editor, of course, but often the effect of a communication is very hard to measure. By far the most useful model from this period is the Westley–McLean model of 1957 (Figure 2.3) because it is the first to address the role of the mass media in communication.

Westley and McLean introduce the role of the gatekeeper or channel (C) into the communication flow between (A), which is similar to a source, and (B), which is similar to a receiver. However, they elaborate these roles so that (A) becomes the advocate, the 'purposive role', and (B), the individual or group public, is deemed to have a 'behavioural role'. This model also shows events in the environment (X) and the response of all the players to those events. It is the first to describe the role of the public relations professional so clearly. (A) has to gather relevant information from the internal and external environment and create an appropriate message (X') to pass through the channel (C) or gatekeeper who may alter it (X") before it can reach the public (individual or group) over whose behaviour (B) influence is sought. The model reminds the PR practitioner that the journalist or gatekeeper has access to more information (X3c) than their press releases. The model also describes the complexity of feedback in mass media communication, with feedback

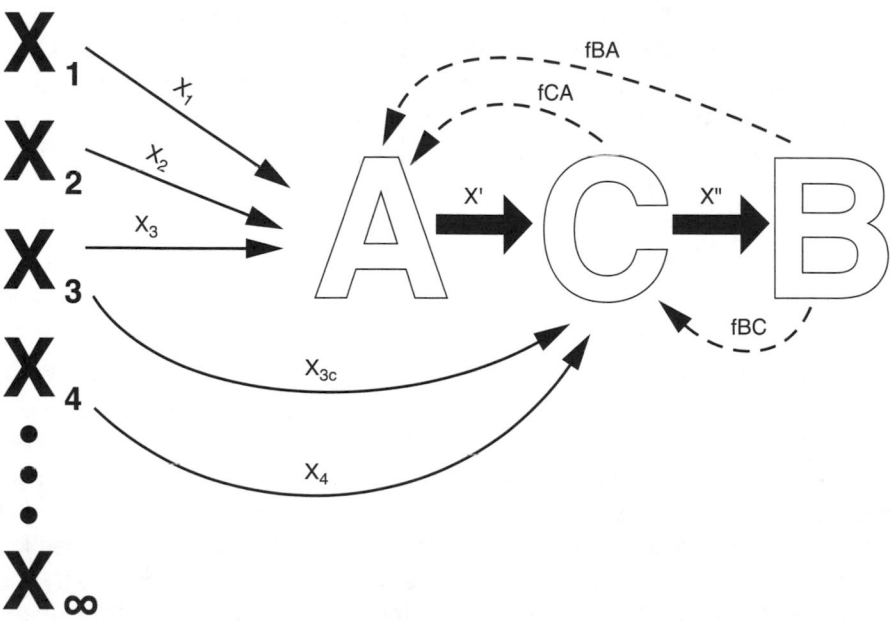

FIGURE 2.3 The Westley–McLean model of communication
Source: Windahl *et al.* (1992: 121), Figure 11.1. Used by permission of Sage

loops running between the PR practitioner and the journalist, the PR practitioner and the public and the public and the journalist – though the feedback via mass media is delayed.

It is worth noting that social media reduce the gatekeeper role of the journalist, as organisations can post whatever materials they choose on their own websites and create direct links with their key audiences. Likewise, the behaviour group (B) is no longer dependent on the mass media for information and can access the events in the environment directly. (B) can also contact other members of the audience and exchange communication without contact with (A) or (C). Increasingly, through blogs and user-generated websites, the audience is shaping and creating its own media content without any involvement from journalists or professional communicators; though some commentators, such as Andrew Keen, author of *The Cult of the Amateur, How Today's Internet is Killing our Culture and Assaulting our Economy* (Smith 2007) are concerned that the content lacks authority and accuracy. The Westley–McLean model has proved a valuable starting point for examining the process of communication, but the emphasis is still on how the sender constructs the message. There are other theorists who see the process and the actions of the sender as quite irrelevant. They emphasise the role of the audience or receiver in constructing meaning.

COMMUNICATION AS MEANING

Semiotics is a vast field of study, pioneered by academics such as C.S. Peirce (1931–1935) and F. de Saussure (1915), originating in the study of language and using theories of signs and symbols that have been adopted and adapted by other communication academics, such as reception theorists. Semiotics cannot be fully explored here, but it is worth pointing out a few elements from this approach that are relevant to students of public relations. The first is that such theorists are not interested in sources, or where messages come from – only in how meaning is created in the mind of the receiver. It argues that audiences 'decode' images and words according to their own personal, cultural or social terms of reference to obtain their own meaning of a message.

All communication is constructed of signs and made of words and gestures. While gestures for food or sleep might be universal, the words are not. Semiotics breaks signs into the thing itself (for example what you eat), the sign for it (the letters F-O-O-D, which are, of course, inedible and that change from language to language) and the meaning you associate with that sign (food means different things to the starving and the bulimic reader). It investigates the gaps between what is intended – or encoded – by the source, and what is understood – or decoded – by the receiver. Unlike some of the earlier models in this chapter, semiotics does not make a distinction between the encoder and decoder of the sign. The issue is not whether the person using or interpreting the sign is a speaker, listener, writer or reader. 'Decoding is as active and creative as encoding', according to Fiske (1990: 42).

Fiske describes semiotics as consisting of: (a) the sign itself; (b) the codes or systems into which signs are organised; and (c) the culture in which these codes and signs operate. As suggested above, Saussure proposed that a sign consists of the physical reality of a thing (the signifier) and the mental concept the decoder holds of the thing (the signified). He also suggested the signified is distinguished by what it is not as much as what it is, e.g. a boy is a Not-man and a Not-girl. The arrangements of meanings gathered in this way can be called codes or systems and reflect the values and culture of the decoder. A brief reflection on the changing meaning of 'teenager' through the twentieth century illustrates that the meaning refers to much more than the age of a person. Moreover, the Western version of a teenager cannot be assumed to be universal – many cultures do not have the same attitudes, positive or negative, towards young people. Roland Barthes' *Mythologies* (1972) is an extremely readable exploration of these issues, often using advertisements to start a discussion of the meaning of images.

In semiotics, meanings can be described as:

1   *Denotative* – what the word means in the dictionary sense, for example, 'chair: a piece of furniture for sitting on'.

2   *Connotative* – the images or associations created in the mind of the receiver; for example, 'school' can evoke the happiest days of your life, or an eternity of terror and boredom.

3   *Ambiguous* – where the same word means different things in a given language; for example, 'bear' can be a noun describing a woolly beast or a verb meaning to carry. Puns and poems depend on ambiguity for their effect.

4   *Polysemic* – where readers/viewers can derive different meanings from the same set of information – pictures or text. This builds on the different connotations people bring to a message, but reflects the wider social context of a message, not just the subjective response. For example, an image of a woman in a swimming costume may represent different meanings to people of different cultures or different political and ideological views.

Semiotics is useful for public relations practitioners because it makes us think about how people use the information – text, image, sound, colour – to construct their own versions of our message. It also emphasises the role of culture in conferring meaning – and reminds the communicator not to assume that others share their values and attitudes. Watts (2004) has investigated the potential of semiotics to enhance PR practice, particularly as visual language is increasingly replacing written communication. Public relations practitioners need to be aware of the varying reactions people can have to the same word or image. Failure to do so can lead to misunderstanding or even offence.

The study of signs and codes has also influenced the study of the media and its effects. There are two schools of theory that reflect this work – media content analysis and reception theory. The first involves a painstaking analysis of the use of language and images in media output over a period of time, originally by hand, increasingly by computer. Searching for particular words in newspapers or broadcasts can help reveal how the media can use language to construct a version of reality. For example, Miller *et al.* (1998) looked at national UK TV news and press reporting of AIDS between November 1988 and April 1990 to understand how HIV/AIDS was being discussed at that time. However, to understand how the discussion was being received or valued by the media audiences, they needed to investigate the reception of the messages: 'it is impossible to determine how people will understand or interpret a text simply by analysing the *content*; it is necessary to examine the *responses* of actual audiences' (Miller *et al.* 1998: 10).

Discourse analysis is linked to these approaches, in that it looks beneath the text and image to discover what is really being communicated, and also grows out of semiotics. It also looks at the complex social rules that are followed when two or more people are in conversation. It suggests that all human communication, whether in person or via the media, can be seen as narrative (van Dijk 1983: 85, cited in McQuail 2000: 346), part of the story we tell about ourselves and about the world. The different 'stories' about HIV/AIDS in the past two decades and in different countries, cultures, gender and sexual orientation groups will be reflected in the media coverage and personal discussion. Again, the subjective experience of reality is emphasised.

Discourse analysis also supports media content analysis, by stressing that media output is the result of social, historical and institutional structures, which produce formal discourses, or ways of discussing issues. Particular news reports can also be studied – it is interesting to note that journalists talk about a good 'story'. The theory certainly suggests that news is structured to follow a clear narrative order, with beginning, middle and end and, preferably, heroes and villains.

USES AND GRATIFICATIONS APPROACH

The importance of audiences is also central to Blumler and Katz's Uses and Gratifications approach. This suggests that people are active seekers of information who choose to read or watch particular magazines or programmes because they expect that medium to satisfy a particular need. McQuail *et al.* (1972) identify these needs as falling into four main categories:

1 *Diversion* – escape from routine or personal problems.
2 *Personal relationships* – such as companionship.
3 *Personal identity* – which might include a fanzine or other entertainment aimed at their age group.
4 *Surveillance* – which means finding out about the world.

Further motivations were suggested by McGuire, who added that needs could be 'cognitive' (searching for knowledge) or 'affective' (looking for emotional rewards); that audiences could be 'active' or 'passive' consumers of media; that they might be driven by 'internal' or 'external' goals; and that they may be seeking 'growth' or 'stability' (McQuail 2000: 388).

The public relations practitioner needs to understand the complex and different ways in which people use each medium – and to remember that people haven't bought a magazine or turned on the TV just to hear the message the PR practitioner wants to put across. Instead, the practitioner can use this approach to think about the state of mind of the media users and try to match the medium and the message to meet their needs.

MASS MEDIA EFFECTS

One of the longest running disputes in communication and media theory is the question of how much the media influence their audiences and how persuasive communication can be. Some academics study the psychology of individuals to understand different responses to messages such as advertisements or health campaigns. Other academics study the connections between violence on television and violence in society. There are those who argue that the media have a powerful role to play in shaping public opinion, and others who say it is actually very hard to persuade others, especially via the mass media. This section cannot cover all of these debates but looks at some of the issues most relevant to the student of public relations.

Early theories of media effects evolved between the two world wars and were heavily influenced by the Nazi use of new media, such as cinema, as propaganda. The Frankfurt School of academics who fled Nazi Germany in the early 1930s carried overwhelming fears that mass media would generate mass effects and that whoever controlled the media would control their society. Their view is sometimes described as the 'hypodermic model', suggesting that audiences are passive and react in a uniform manner to a media message. But US social scientists (especially the Yale School) after the Second World War – also concerned about the power of propaganda – conducted extensive research into voter behaviour, which suggested that people are actually more likely to be influenced by their friends and neighbours or other 'opinion-formers' than the papers they read. This was called the 'two-step flow' theory and was developed by Katz and Lazerfield (1955) (Figure 2.4).

This idea dominated discussion of the media and communication effects and stimulated more research into the psychology of individuals and how people respond to messages. Questions of attitude formation and change, beliefs, values and opinions were investigated as part of the research into persuasive communication. However, in the 1970s some academics (including the Birmingham School) returned

Early mass communication model

Two-step flow model

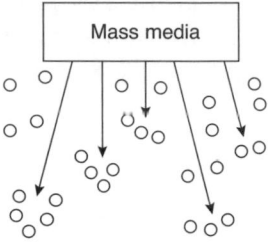
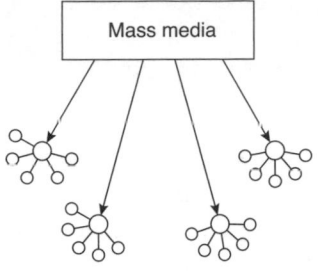

○ = Isolated individuals
constituting a mass

○ = Opinion leader

○ = Individuals in social
contact with an opinion
leader

FIGURE 2.4 The one-step and two-step flow models

Source: McQuail and Windahl (1993: 62), Figure 3.2.1. Used by permission of Longman

to the ideas of the Frankfurt School and re-examined them. They looked at the effect of the media on society and on class and found that the media tended to support the interests of capitalism (and the media's owners, of course). Researchers found negative media images of working people, women, ethnic minorities and others with less power in society. At this time ideas such as 'agenda-setting' were developed, where journalists select what is important to publish according to their implicit or explicit views of society. Unlike the Frankfurt School or the Yale School, this group looked at effects on society as a whole, rather than on individuals. Their more subtle description of effects has gained continuing currency, while questions of effect on individuals – such as those exposed to violence – is still unclear.

The influence of semiotics gave rise to the reception theory of media effects, where meaning is 'constructed' in the reader or viewer (see above). Stuart Hall (1980), a leading member of the Birmingham School, proposed that the media create 'preferred readings' that suggest how reality should be seen. In 2003, many media commentators expressed alarm at the partisan language and images with which US TV reported the Iraq War. There was no doubt about how the audience was meant to respond (see also 'spiral of silence', below). Other theorists rejected the idea that the media promotes a particular point of view, but suggested that there might be a more neutral 'agenda-setting' effect, whereby media reporting does not influence what people think, but what they think *about*. It is certainly true that different issues dominate media debates over the longer term, so that coverage of topics such as education or health will fluctuate considerably over a decade. But the question still remains – if the media select the topics readers talk about, who sets *their* agenda?

Others have looked at the way the media, especially television, 'construct reality' through their use of images. Readers of the *Daily Mail* and the *Guardian*, for example, would have very different ideas about the effects and indeed the extent of asylum seekers in the UK. The way the journalist, the media organisation and the reader 'frame' such stories may affect the way these issues are discussed by individuals, the media and politicians. Where one reading or frame comes to dominate the way the media handles a story, readers/viewers with dissenting opinions may find no reflection of their views in the mass media. According to public opinion theorist Noelle-Neumann (1991, cited in McQuail 2000: 461), because society tends to isolate those with different or 'deviant' views, and because most people fear social isolation, when a person fears their views are not shared by others they are less likely to express their opinions. This has been called the 'spiral of silence' effect: dominant views gain strength; minority views fall silent. Some US residents who did not support the 2003 war turned to the *BBC World TV* for their sources of information. This illustrates the power the media may accrue where the audience has little information about a subject and is highly dependent on the media for information.

Audiences are not the only groups with problems accessing alternative information. The increased deadlines and reduced resources of media organisations, which often produce material round the clock or in many more editions, can in turn make journalists highly dependent on public relations departments. PR people provide a ready supply of material to fill the ever-increasing hours of airtime and acres of newsprint, whether the subject is the latest war or newest celebrity, and journalists do not always challenge these sources. The management of news by public relations is often called 'spin' but is not confined to the political arena. Access to A-list celebrities is probably more controlled than that of senior government ministers. Many movie stars only agree to interviews if the list of questions is agreed in advance and no awkward issues are raised.

It is worth noting McQuail's (2000: 348) reversal of the traditional news sequence. He says the journalistic view is that (1) events are matched against (2) news criteria which, if satisfied, underpin (3) a news report which generates (4) news interest. He suggests instead that (1) news interest influences (2) news criteria, which lead to (3) events, which are covered in (4) news reports. This perhaps provides a more accurate description of celebrity-driven media and shows how public relations may be involved in creating the (3) events that are covered.

The various theories suggest that the media do have a profound influence but it is not a simple case of cause and effect. Often the most attractive theories are not supported by research evidence (McQuail 2000). However, many public relations practitioners still behave as if the stimulus–response/message–effect links are unchallenged (Windahl *et al.* 1992). These communicators have not moved on from the linear model and tend to be engaged in publicity or other one-way communications. It is, after all, hard to explain that your campaign may not work because the theories about the effects of communication are unclear. Better to suggest that as long as people receive the message, they're bound to fall in with it. However, as health campaigners have found over the decades, the reality is very different.

Professional communicators need to be aware of the potential for good and harm contained in their messages – an example is the debate about whether coverage of celebrities aiming for size zero and the use of very thin fashion models affects the rate of eating disorders in young girls. Clearly, those who argue for control of images are not saying that one fashion spread can make a healthy girl ill, but they are saying that through general representations of 'desirable' women, girls and young women receive an impression of an 'ideal' body weight that is actually distorted.

James Grunig and Todd Hunt (1984) suggested four categories of communication relationship with publics, placed in a historical context (see Table 2.1). These have been the most influential models affecting the study of public relations and are worth looking at closely, but with a word of warning. They are often presented as a history of PR as if the field developed from press agency to symmetry. Critics have challenged this view as idealistic and inaccurate, not least because different kinds of communication are undertaken in the same workplace, as more recent writing (Grunig 2001) makes clear.

PRESS AGENCY/PUBLICITY MODEL

This is probably the kind of activity that most people associate with public relations. A press agent or publicist aims to secure coverage for a client, and truth is not an absolute requirement. Grunig and Hunt point out that 'practitioners in these organisations concern themselves most with getting attention in the media for their clients' (1984: 25). Understanding is not necessary for this kind of PR, which is likely to measure success in column inches or airtime. Celebrity PR is the modern version of the stunts circus owner P.T. Barnum used to organise and someone such as Max Clifford is an obvious successor. This is one-way communication, which emphasises the benefit to the sender rather than the receiver, though of course there is general interest in the latest news about soap and football stars.

PUBLIC INFORMATION MODEL

This kind of communication provides information to people where accuracy is essential. This model does not seek to persuade the audience or change attitudes. Its role is similar to that of an in-house journalist (Grunig and Hunt 1984), releasing relevant information to those who need it. The communication is still one way, from sender to receiver, but is more relevant to the receiver than the first example. Ivy Leadbetter Lee was one of the first public relations practitioners in the US who persuaded businesses to be less secretive about their work and release more accurate information. The history of PR in the UK (L'Etang 2004) shows it grew through providing this kind of communication for local government and state organisations.

TWO-WAY ASYMMETRIC PR

This model introduces the idea of feedback or two-way communication. However, it is asymmetric or imbalanced because the intended change is in the audience's attitudes or behaviour rather than in the organisation's practices. It is also described as persuasive communication and can be demonstrated in health campaigns, for example. Persuasive communication relies on an understanding of the attitudes and behaviour of the targeted publics, so planning and research are important to this kind of public relations. Edward L. Bernays, who came to prominence in the US Committee for First World War propaganda, was a pioneer of this model – he was also Sigmund Freud's nephew and used psychological insights to increase the persuasive content of messages. Bernays was the first PR academic and his influence continued throughout his long life (he died in 1995, aged 103). In Britain, Sir Stephen Tallents helped create the Empire Marketing Board in 1924 to promote

TABLE 2.1 Characteristics of four models of public relations

Characteristic	Model			
	Press agentry/ publicity	Public information	Two-way asymmetric	Two-way symmetric
Purpose	Propaganda	Dissemination of Information	Scientific persuasion	Mutual understanding
Nature of communication	One-way: complete truth not essential	One-way; truth important	Two-way; imbalanced effects	Two-way; balanced effects
Communication model	Source → Rec.	Source → Rec.	Source → Rec. ← Feedback	Group → Group ←
Nature of research	Little; 'counting house'	Little; readability, readership	Formative; evaluative of attitudes	Formative; evaluative of understanding
Leading historical figures	P.T. Barnum	Ivy Lee	Edward L. Bernays	Bernays, educators, professional leaders
Where practised today	Sports, theatre, product promotion	Government, non-profit associations, business	Competitive business; agencies	Regulated business; agencies
Estimated percentage of organisations practising today	15	50	20	15

Source: Grunig and Hunt (1984: 22). Reproduced by permission of Harcourt

trade in Empire products, spending more than £1 million on campaigns involving posters, films and exhibitions before going on to help found the Institute of Public Relations in 1948 (L'Etang 2004). Since their time, propaganda has become seen as undesirable and persuasion as suspicious (see Chapter 1), which partially accounts for the general distrust of public relations. There is a major debate about the tensions between propaganda, persuasion and public relations (Moloney 2000 and 2006a; Weaver *et al.* 2006; Fawkes 2006a and 2006b), with some denying any link and others accusing PR of being nothing but propaganda.

TWO-WAY SYMMETRIC PR

This model is sometimes described as the 'ideal' of public relations. It describes a level of equality of communication not often found in real life, where each party is willing to alter their behaviour to accommodate the needs of the other. While the other models are characterised by monologue-type communication, the symmetric model involves ideas of dialogue. It could lead an organisation's management to exchange views with other groups, possibly leading to both management and publics being influenced and adjusting their attitudes and behaviours. Communication in this model is fully reciprocal and power relationships are balanced. The terms 'sender' and 'receiver' are not applicable in such a communication process, where the goal is mutual understanding (Windahl *et al.* 1992). This is communication as – ideally – practised by the boundary spanner outlined in the previous chapter. Critics (Pieczka 2006; Moloney 2000 and 2006a, for example) argue that it is so rarely practised as to be unhelpful. Grunig (2001) has since updated his model to emphasise the mixed motives that may be involved in any PR communication.

CONCLUSION

The chapter has looked at the main elements of communication, in particular the role of sender, receiver and medium, as well as the issues that affect communication, such as noise. Public or audience-centred theories, such as the Uses and Gratifications theory, offer an alternative to the models that focus on the role of senders. Grunig and Hunt's four models describe some of the aspects of public relations communication, though the reality of PR practice often differs from the ideals described.

Many 'how to' PR books suggest communication is easy; in reality it is complicated and involves not only the personalities of the sender and the receiver, the particular requirements of each medium and the public nature of the messages, but also the power to influence, directly or indirectly, society as a whole. The study of communication can improve the practitioner's awareness of the public and their needs and interests. But it can also make it easier to persuade others. Public relations can be a powerful agent – handle it with care.

QUESTIONS FOR DISCUSSION

1 How helpful are communications models in understanding the media? Which one best explains the role of public relations in mass communications?

2 What kind of noise might affect the following communications?
   – web page
   – magazine read at home
   – newsletter read at work/college.

3 Are the media a powerful influence on society or just another source of information? Is the influence direct or indirect?

4 How does the growth in social media sites affect these communication models? In particular, look at their impact on the gatekeeper role in the Westley–McLean model and the idea of feedback in linear models.

5 What is the key difference in the role of the audience between the Shannon and Weaver model and the Uses and Gratifications approach?

6 How might the study of semiotics improve PR practice? Look at the logos of three leading organisations and see if you can detect the meaning they intend to convey.

7 What is the main difference between one-way and two-way communication? Can you find examples of both?

8 Do you think persuasion is always wrong? How much of PR work is normally persuasive communication?

9 Why do you think Grunig updated the four models between 1984 and 2001? What are the key differences?

10 Using the Uses and Gratifications approach, consider what you look for in a:
   – local newspaper
   – student newsletter
   – fanzine
   – favourite TV soap
   – PR textbook.

FURTHER READING

Heath, R. (2001) *The handbook of public relations*, Sage.
McQuail, D. (2000) *McQuail's mass communication theory*, Sage.

CHAPTER 3

Public relations and politics

Ian Somerville and Phil Ramsey

CHAPTER AIMS

Any discussion of the role of public relations (PR) within the political sphere naturally falls into two areas: the use of PR practices by government and the use of PR and public affairs by non-governmental actors in the political process. The first part of this chapter will discuss the role of political PR in liberal democratic societies with a particular focus on governmental bodies within the United Kingdom. It will address the scope and scale of government communication built up under the recent New Labour administration that governed the UK from 1997 to 2010. This section will also address the Lobby system of briefing journalists, discuss the role of soundbites and pseudo-events, and some of the tactics employed by spin doctors, before discussing a case study focusing on how New Labour communicated its policies on welfare reform. The importance of good presentation is hardly a radical new idea in politics but the increasing reliance on 'buying in' PR expertise in this vital area has been controversial, to say the least. This section will conclude by addressing a Habermasian public sphere ideal, and how it relates to public relations and political communication.

The second half of the chapter examines the specialist area of public affairs and lobbying work. It discusses the importance of intelligence gathering and monitoring the policy making processes as well as exploring how organisations can seek to influence governmental actors, policy development and ultimately legislation through various public affairs strategies. There will also be an examination of how the public policy process may vary under different national political systems, as well as in supra-national contexts like the EU or UN. The second half of the chapter is divided into two sections. The first section briefly discusses definitional issues, theoretical perspectives and the influence of political structures and institutions on public affairs and lobbying work. The second section discusses key issues pertaining to practice beginning with environmental analysis and continuing with a description of the three key public affairs strategies – direct lobbying, grassroots campaigning, and coalition building – before concluding with a brief discussion on evaluating public affairs practice.

GOVERNMENT PUBLIC RELATIONS

When Gordon Brown replaced Tony Blair as Prime Minister of the UK on 27 June 2007, he promised a 'different type of politics', that would be marked by 'open and honest dialogue' (*Guardian*, 2007). New Labour had been shaped in its early days by spin, and was built upon making the presentation of policy as important, and sometimes more important than policy itself. Indeed, New Labour's period in government (1997–2010) had been characterised for many by an unparalleled rise in public relations in all socio-economic spheres and particularly in political culture. In government New Labour built a communications structure of unprecedented scope and scale, with large amounts of human and financial resources expended on presenting politicians and policies in a good light.

Spin and indeed the whole PR industry has sustained fierce criticism for playing a role that has been to the detriment of journalism and the democratic process. Journalist Bryan Appleyard complained 'Hacks still naively pursue something they like to call the truth. Their problem is that it no longer exists. For truth has been destroyed by public relations executives, or "scum" as we like to call them' (*Sunday Times*, 2003). This kind of comment is typical of the journalistic distrust of PR that frequently sees it pilloried in the media for its role in contaminating and corrupting the political process in Britain. Spin doctoring, negative campaigning, and the pernicious influence of lobbyists are all highlighted by some commentators as examples of how PR has degraded the political process. There are frequent calls to return to a type of political activity where these somewhat dubious persuasive tactics had no place. This presumption, frequently asserted by the media and politicians, implying a tainting effect of PR on British political culture, should be questioned. Indeed, it could be argued, the media, politicians and PR specialists are increasingly bound together in a relationship that the media and politicians find more beneficial than they care to admit. This does not mean, however, that this is necessarily always a healthy situation for democratic politics but it is the current reality, which this section will describe and assess.

The public relations state?

From its inception, New Labour was a political project built upon a reliance on information management, as it carefully tried to construct an image of a party that had moved on from its internal ideological battles of the 1980s. Indeed, Michie has argued that 'the success of New Labour, indeed its very creation, is the product of spin-doctoring, practised with relentlessness and virtuosity' (quoted in McNair, 2000: 8). It is thus no surprise that when it was elected in 1997, New Labour set about reforming the communication structures within government, enhancing what Maloney (2006) has called 'the most resourced, comprehensive and continuous PR operation in the UK' (ibid.: 121). Under New Labour, the numbers of communications staff employed in Whitehall departments rose from 795 in 1998 to 1,376 in 2008 (*HL Paper 7*, 2009: 34). Specifically, the number of press officers in Whitehall departments rose from 216 in 1998 to 373 in 2008 (ibid.: 35). During its time in office, New Labour also extensively utilised Special Advisers, who are publicly-funded political advisers to ministers. Their number fluctuated from 38 in 1997, to a high point of 84 in 2003, before falling back to 73 in 2007 (ibid.: 25). In 2007, 24 of these special advisers were employed within Number 10 (ibid.: 54). The cost of government communications is also noteworthy. The cost of running the Foreign and Commonwealth Office (FCO) press office was £11.5 million in 2009. Moreover, the Department of Health (DoH) had a total communications budget of £52.2 million in 2007/2008: 'This was made up of an administrative budget of £7.1 million covering the cost of the 122 staff and their day-to-day operations, and £45.1 million of programme costs' (ibid.: 55).

Many commentators note how careful management of information turns it into a very valuable resource. Cockerell *et al.* (1984: 9) suggest that what the government 'chooses to tell us through its PR machine is one thing; the information in use by participants in the country's real government is another'. Negrine (1996: 10) notes the 'increasing use of carefully crafted communication strategies by governments to ensure that . . . the information they seek to impart to their citizens has an appropriate "spin" on it'. Obviously this increased use of PR specialists by the Government may merely reflect a more general 'promotional culture' in Britain (Miller, 1998). However some observers have expressed disquiet at the increasing use of information management techniques by the Government. Deacon and Golding (1994: 7) have noted with concern the rise of the 'public relations state' and Schlesinger (1990: 82) notes that there are important questions:

> [A]bout the nature of information management in a society by a variety of groups in conditions of unequal power and therefore unequal access to systems of information production and distribution and these questions are particularly acute in regard to government because 'the apparatuses of the state . . . enjoy privileged access to the media'.

There are various ways in which governments manage information in order to privilege their own views on an issue. Leaks of important information or documents (Negrine, 1996) are one way in which the Government or powerful interest groups within the state may attempt to control the media agenda, but perhaps the key weapon in the Government's information management armoury is the Lobby system.

The Lobby

The Lobby is the exclusive group of journalists that is briefed twice daily by the Prime Minister's spokesperson (PMS) during sittings of Parliament, so called because journalists historically assembled in the Member's Lobby of the House of Commons. In 2008 it had 176 members, mostly representing the main national news outlets (*HL Paper 7*, 2009: 21), and has been described as 'the Prime Minister's most useful tool for the political management of the news' (Cockerell *et al.*, 1984: 33). All of the national newspapers and television and radio broadcasters are represented in the Lobby, with some media organisations such as the BBC sending numerous journalists. This system is a very important resource that British governments use – and some would argue abuse – for keeping control of information flows to the media and hence to the general public. It remains the best way for political journalists to get the up-to-date position of the government on a developing news story, as it carries the authority of the Prime Minister. On this, Cockerell *et al.* (1984: 33) note that 'what the Press Secretary says at these briefings is what the Prime Minister wants the press, radio and television to report'. Franklin (2004: 44) also suggests that when a government Press Secretary gives a briefing there is a strong likelihood that it will appear as a news item, 'replete with the political spin he places on it'.

The Lobby system, despite claims to the contrary by those who have utilised it (Ingham cited in McNair, 1994) is a unique system within Western democracies. This does not mean that other governments do not attempt to manage information but it is normal practice to appoint a party political spokesperson (such as a Minister of Information) who openly represents the government position and is attributable. This is not the case in Britain. The Prime Minister's Press Secretary is actually a member of the Civil Service and thus officially neutral. Following the *Mountfield Review* in late 1997, New Labour enabled the PMS to be identified regarding statements in the Lobby briefing by their job title, but not by name. Prior to this Lobby briefings were off-the-record and non-attributable; they remain exclusive, however, with the 'only access the public and non-lobby journalists have to the proceedings [coming] in the form of a brief summary posted on the Number Ten website' (Ramsey, 2010: 88). There have been numerous calls for the Lobby to be televised (from government reviews and academic commentators) in an effort to make it more transparent, but they were continually resisted by the New Labour Government. Some compromises have been made, with more on-camera briefing by ministers and monthly televised Downing Street press conferences taking place, following changes implemented by Alastair Campbell in late 2002 after the initial recommendations of the *Phillis Review*. Whether such changes have actually resulted in a dramatic change in the way information is communicated to the media by government representatives is highly debatable, with some commentators suggesting that the systematic practice of favoured journalists being given more revealing off-the-record briefings continuing as usual (Assinder, 2002).

Media management

McNair (2003: 136) notes that in the context of political communication, 'media management comprises activities designed to maintain a positive media relationship, acknowledging the needs which each has of the other, while exploiting the institutional characteristics of both sets of actors for maximum advantage'. At the same time, the relationship between politicians and the media can obviously involve a struggle between two different sets of interests and agendas. Moloney (2006a: 126) offers two conceptualisations of the government–media relationship: one in market terms as an 'exchange relationship' and the other in military terms as a 'contest relationship'. He notes:

> The exchange relationship characterises government and media as traders; the contest relationship as opponents. The exchange relationship implies two equally satisfied parties while the contest one implies winners and losers. The role of the media as watchdogs is consistent with the contest model. Public relations people invariably favour the exchange relationship but are prepared and skilled for the contest one.

From the perspective of the contest model, the journalist attempts to seek out and present the 'facts' while the politician will want to ensure that a news story reflects the 'message' that they wish to convey. There is nothing particularly new in the attempt by the political elites to try and control media representations, as is revealed in various accounts of the development and growth of political PR from the early years of the twentieth century onwards (Pearson, 1992; McNair, 2003; L'Etang, 2004). However, the present discussion will largely focus on the role of political PR over the past three decades in the UK, and in particular New Labour's period in office, a period that witnessed an important and rapid transformation in the role and status of PR within political culture. This expansion of PR activity has unsurprisingly been accompanied by an increasing reliance upon media management strategies. Some commentators (Fairclough, 2000; McNair, 2003; Franklin, 2004) have pointed to the increasing use of the 'soundbite' and the 'pseudo-event' (Boorstin, 1962), of 'image management' and 'spin', as key strategies used by politicians to control media representations of them and their policies.

Soundbites and pseudo-events

As the use of spin and information management by government has increased, the impact upon journalism has been perceptible. Cockerell et al. (1984: 11) note that, in regard to the political process in the UK, 'Very few journalists have had the incentive to dig deeper, to mine the bedrock of power rather than merely scour its topsoil.' It is the broadcast journalists' job to pick out the key details or important points of any political event or speech. If the speech contains memorable phrases (soundbites) that summarise the main points, then there is a good chance that these portions of the speech will be selected and broadcast on the few minutes allotted on the broadcast news bulletins. Tony Blair's phrase 'tough on crime, tough on the causes of crime', from a speech made when he was Shadow Home Secretary, has entered the national consciousness. It is indeed a memorable phrase, but it is important to remember that being 'tough' and talking about being 'tough' was a carefully constructed aspect of the Blair style. Fairclough (2000: 8) argues that 'Blair's "toughness" has been self-consciously built into his communicative style as a matter of policy and strategy.' Occasionally, Blair let the façade of the soundbite communication culture slip, when after the signing of the Good Friday Agreement in Northern Ireland he famously uttered, 'A day like today is not a day for soundbites, really. But I feel the hand of history upon our shoulders' (BBC News, 2007). The Conservative–Liberal Democrat Coalition Government, elected in May 2010, has paid similar attention to the soundbite: David Cameron and his ministers have constantly repeated that with respect of the financial crises and public spending cuts, 'we are all in this together'. Ministers in the Coalition have often repeated the mantra that they are 'fixing the financial mess that Labour left us'.

Spin and image management

Defining political spin is very difficult, and some commentators note that there is a danger that the term is now used to describe so many activities that it is in danger of becoming meaningless. Andrews (2006) points to the fact that today practically all of a government's promotional activities seem to be referred to as 'spin'. Gaber (2000a: 61) argues that 'As long as politicians have been politicking, spinners have been spinning.' There are some definitions that make sense of a phenomenon that is ancient, and yet in its current form, quite recent. Street (2001:1) locates spin within media relations and states that it involves 'getting the right image, making the right connections, and ensuring that both appear on the next day's front page'. McNair (2004: 328) argues that spin is a 'convenient and media friendly shorthand for a particular kind of political public relations, with the negative connotation of spinning a yarn'. Spin is probably best understood as a process that became intensi-fied, and better funded and resourced under Bill Clinton's New Democrats and Tony Blair's New Labour in the 1990s. As suggested above, spin became more professionalised, and increasingly carried out by professional and dedicated inform-ation and communication managers. Describing the role of spin in the New Labour project, Ludlam and Smith (2001: 24) argue that it can be understood as a 'new strategic thinking – against which all programmatic or organisational initiatives were judged – and this dominated the struggle for electability'.

Gaber (2000b: 508) argues that in trying to understand spin, we can break it down into two categories: the 'above the line' and the 'below the line' tactics that a spin doctor may employ. The 'above the line' category includes those activities that would be considered routine, and that 'would have caused an "old fashioned" press officer no great difficulty' (ibid.). These activities may be carried out by civil servants working in communication, without breaking any regulations or straying into the 'politicization' of the civil service. They relate to the everyday business of government

GOVERNMENT COMMUNICATION

Several authors (Jones, 1999; Fairclough, 2000) have discussed the media management surrounding the Government's welfare 'reforms' as a key example that illustrates 'New Labour's management of news and "media spin"' (Fairclough, 2000: 129). Early in their tenure, in 1998, Labour opted to launch a 'welfare roadshow' in a bid to attempt to control the news agenda with Prime Minister Tony Blair going 'on the road' to put his case for welfare reform to the people of Britain. Blair's first speech was in Dudley, and the day before this speech his Chief Press Secretary Alastair Campbell gave private briefings to the media in which he emphasised, with a battery of facts and figures, the costs to the nation of benefit fraud. The next day – the official launch of the welfare roadshow – two national newspapers, *The Times* and the *Mirror*, carried articles 'written' by Tony Blair that were virtually indistinguishable from the briefing Campbell had given the day before. That evening, in Dudley, Blair's speech again reinforced the message, with virtually the same language, that he was determined to do something about benefit fraud. Fairclough (ibid.: 130) notes that, 'The risk of unpredictable and uncontrollable media uptake of the speech is minimised by trailing the speech in a way which presents it in the way the Government wants it to be seen – which puts a particular "spin" on it.' This was of course only the beginning of the welfare reform process, which proceeded through a 'consultation' (Green Paper) stage and eventually to Welfare Reform Bill published on 11 February 2011. Fairclough (ibid.: 129) argues that the whole process, from initial campaign, through the consultative stage, to the presentation of the Bill to Parliament, was 'largely managed through managerial and promotional means rather than democratically through dialogue'. 'Part of the art of "spin" is calculating what additional emphases and foregrounding newspapers . . . will predictably add, which may be an effective way for the Government to convey implicitly messages it may not wish to convey explicitly' (ibid.: 131). In the case of the welfare reform legislation, issues surrounding benefit fraud were only a small part of the Bill, which was largely redistributive, but there was a constant stream of messages about how Tony Blair would 'get tough' on benefit fraud. This allowed politically conservative newspapers such as the *Daily Mail* to use headlines like 'Welfare: The Crackdown'. Fairclough (ibid.: 131) suggests that the *Daily Mail* report 'effects certain transformations which significantly and (from a press officer's perspective) predictably convey a "tougher" message than Blair's', but the key point is that this 'message' will reassure the *Daily Mail's* largely Tory readership.

C@SE STUDY

communication, and as such are often banal, receiving little coverage in the press. These activities might include releasing press releases, holding press conferences, and using ministerial speeches and answers to Parliamentary questions in the House of Commons to communicate information. Gaber (ibid.: 509) also identifies 'Reacting to government/party announcements . . . publicizing speeches, interviews and articles . . . reacting to interviews or speeches . . . reacting to breaking news events' as activities that can all be grouped into this category. The 'below the line' category includes those activities employed by spin doctors that are not conventional, and at times, ethically questionable. Gaber (ibid.: 508) identifies that these activities are 'usually covert and as much about strategy and tactics as about the imparting of information'. 'Below the line' activities include 'staying on message (ensuring a consistent line is taken) . . . setting and driving the news agenda (ensuring that government receives coverage on its terms) . . . kite flying (testing out reaction to a policy before a formal announcement)' and 'firebreaking' (ibid.: 510–512). In the case of 'firebreaking', this involves distracting journalists from a particular story, by planting another of greater significance. Gaber (2000a: 65) notes that an example of this happened in 1997, when the *News of the World* revealed the Foreign Secretary, Robin Cook, was engaged in an extra-marital affair. Promptly, the New Labour spin machine constructed a smoke screen, by releasing two stories, relating to MI6 investigation of Chris Patten, and the possible reprieve of the Royal Yacht Britannia that was due for scrapping at the time. All these tactics represent real events that occurred during New Labour's time in office: the Government Communication case study focuses specifically on how New Labour communicated on the subject of welfare reform.

POLITICAL COMMUNICATION, PUBLIC RELATIONS AND THE PUBLIC SPHERE

The case study discussed above, along with Gaber's analysis of the tactics of spin, raises important questions about the role of PR within the context of political communication in liberal democracies. The increased focus on spin and information management, and the manner in which government presents its policies, have all had an impact on how the public perceive the political process. Fairbanks *et al.* (2007: 23) have noted the decline in public trust in government and suggest that this decline 'is an outgrowth of poor communication between government and its publics, where publics feel that they are not well informed about government actions'. They note that:

> A healthy democracy requires an informed public and demands that governments provide information to the public about policies, decisions and actions. Public relations principles and theories such as transparency, models of public relations and stakeholder management provide guidance on how to most effectively communicate this information to the public.
>
> (ibid.: 24)

It is clearly the case that governments and mainstream political parties have the right to present their policies persuasively to the electorate. However, governments are elected to serve the people and this means they must approach information dissemination in a more open and transparent way than any other institution. They have a responsibility to be accessible and accountable to those who have elected them and in this sense some would argue they have a responsibility to help develop a fully functioning 'public sphere' (Habermas, 1989).

The public sphere ideal

Dahlgren (2001: 33) notes that in its original formulation 'the public sphere as described by Habermas consists of the institutional space where political will formation takes place, via the unfettered flow of relevant information and ideas'. In Habermas' analysis, the public sphere emerged within the bourgeois classes of late eighteenth-century Western Europe, and was aided by the development of mass literacy. The Enlightenment ideals of rational thinking, argument and discussion were, albeit imperfectly, manifested in the clubs, coffee houses, newspapers and pamphlet writing that characterised this era. In his historical analysis Habermas traced the decay of the public sphere as the nineteenth century developed, with the logic of the marketplace coming to dominate the media, resulting in an increasing trivialisation of political debate. Habermas calls this process the 'refeudalization' of the public sphere (Habermas, 1989). Whether or not anything today could qualify as a functioning public sphere has been widely debated (Dahlgren, 2001; Sparks, 2001) but many commentators would argue that at the very least the concept retains a usefulness as a normative vision. Bennett and Entman (2001: 2) suggest that in the ideal public sphere 'all citizens have equal access to communication that is both independent of government constraint, and through its deliberative, consensus-building capacity, constrains the agendas and decisions of government in turn'. They note that this ideal has never been achieved, and probably never will. Nevertheless, the concept 'serves theorists well as an ideal type – that is, as a construct against which different real-world approximations can be evaluated' (ibid.: 3). In respect to the political public sphere Richards (2004: 173) notes that in Habermas' formulation 'the public in the liberal democracies should be a participatory public, the collective of citizens engaged, ideally, in informed and rational discussion, and in dialogue with their leaders'. If this is to occur, citizens must be able to depend on information from government communication that is accessible, transparent and participatory. Based on the evidence presented thus far, a great deal of government communication in the UK and in other democratic societies is still a long way from this ideal.

PUBLIC AFFAIRS

Defining public affairs and lobbying

Harris and Moss (2001: 110) have noted that 'the term "public affairs" remains one that is surrounded by ambiguity and misunderstanding'. Arguably this is much more of an issue in the UK than it is, for example, in the US and this is primarily to do with how public relations and public affairs are conceived of in the two national contexts. The two activities clearly overlap in several key ways although the nature of their relationship tends to be viewed somewhat differently in US literature compared to UK perspectives. A typical US public relations textbook describes public affairs as merely one aspect of public relations work: 'PR counselling firms use the public affairs label for their lobbying and governmental relations services designed to help clients understand and address regulatory and legislative processes' (Broom, 2009: 35). McGrath (2005) argues that it is this conception of public affairs, as a public relations strategic specialism, that is articulated by the majority of practitioners in the US. In the UK the relationship between public affairs and public relations is viewed rather differently; in fact commentators from the UK frequently resist or downplay the idea that there is any necessary connection at all between the two activities. Moloney notes:

> Many professional lobbyists reject their inclusion in PR, joining the flight from it as a work title and preferring euphemisms such as government relations, political communications and public affairs specialists. For these separatists, PR is public campaigning via the media, as opposed to private and confidential approaches to persuade powerful persons face to face.
>
> (2000: 113)

While some may see merit in articulating a conceptual difference between the two activities, public affairs – whether in the UK, the US, or elsewhere – almost always involves much more than just face-to-face 'insider' dealings with those who hold power in public policy arenas. Arguably, a considerable amount of public affairs activity is indistinguishable from public relations activity and indeed one of the arguments of this chapter is that shared conceptual understandings and theoretical explanations of both public affairs and public relations can enrich our understanding and analysis of practitioner work.

McGrath (2005) offers a succinct and useful discussion of definitional issues and points out that many accounts, particularly those written by practitioners, which attempt to define the activity lack clarity at best and, at worst, are rather confusing and contradictory. McGrath cites Milbraith's, straightforward and still relevant, 50-year-old definition to describe the essential features of lobbying. Milbraith notes 'lobbying is the stimulation and transmission of a communication, by someone other than a citizen acting on his own behalf, directed to a governmental decision-maker with the hope of influencing his decision' (Milbraith, 1963: 8). Clearly defining lobbying is a simpler task than defining public affairs. Lobbying, almost irrespective of where it is practiced, is essentially an advocacy activity directed at government/legislators and carried out by actors within or on behalf of a group or organisation. However, public affairs should not be narrowly conceived and limited to advocacy efforts to influence government policy through direct contact with political actors by organisational members or representatives. Harris and Moss (2001: 110) point out:

Those adopting a broader perspective see public affairs as managing a broader range of relationships with organizational stakeholders, particularly those which may have public policy implications, in which they may employ a range of marketing communications and public relations tools.

It is this broader definition that we adopt because public affairs work almost always involves monitoring and intelligence gathering in the public policy sphere and engagement with the wider public sphere through media relations activities. It may also involve building relationships and coordinating activities with other actors engaged in pursuing the same interest or promoting the same cause. Depending on the organisation it may also involve coordinating grassroots activities by members of one's own group and those sympathetic to its agenda.

Pressure groups and interest groups

Who engages in public affairs and lobbying activity? Essentially it is those actors who have an interest in the development of public policy but are not directly engaged in legislating or governing. These actors tend to be described as 'interest groups' in much of the US literature and 'pressure groups' in the literature on the UK/EU context. Typical definitions of what constitutes a pressure group make it clear that the 'pressure' that groups exert is in respect to attempts to influence political agendas and more specifically the development and implementation of public policy and legislation. Grant (2000: 14), writing on the UK/EU context, states that: 'A pressure group is an organization which seeks as one of its functions to influence the formulation and implementation of public policy, public policy representing a set of authoritative decisions taken by the executive, the legislature, and the judiciary, and by local government and the European Union.' Coxall (2001: 5) in his analysis of pressure group politics makes an important distinction between a 'cause' group that 'is formed to promote a particular cause based on a set of shared attitudes, values or beliefs: examples are Greenpeace, the Child Poverty Action Group and Amnesty International', and a 'sectional' group that 'represents the self-interest of a particular economic or social group in society: examples are the Confederation of British Industry (CBI), the Trades Union Congress (TUC), and the British Medical Association (BMA)'. Thomas (2004: 4) in the key US work in the area echoes closely the above definition of a pressure group, when he notes that the interest group is 'an association of individuals or organizations or a public or private institution that, on the basis of one or more shared concerns, attempts to influence public policy in its favour'.

Public affairs theory

Getz (2001: 308) notes that: 'the dominant theoretical approach to political influence is interest group theory. Interest group theory suggests that the democratic public policy process is an attempt to reach a compromise between the competing goals of a multitude of interest groups.' Essentially, as Thomas (2004: 17) notes in a key work on interest group theory, this is an approach underpinned by a pluralist conception. Thomas agrees with Getz that while it is the case that different theoretical approaches make a definitive body of knowledge hard to construct, most theoretical approaches utilise some form of 'pluralism'. Pluralism can be defined as

> the idea that modern societies contain all sorts of competing groups, interests, ideologies and ideas, and in this context democratic politics is seen as a struggle by interests and ideas to predominate, often by inspiring the formation of political parties or pressure groups.
>
> (Budge *et al.*, 1998: 323)

Pluralism does in many ways provide a useful theory for understanding the role of public affairs in liberal democratic societies but there are some important critiques of the pluralist perspective. Hill (2005: 28) notes that:

> [O]pposition to the pluralist perspective can take two forms. One is to argue that this is not a satisfactory model for democracy (it is too indirect or it is impossible to realise the 'general will' through such diversity). . . .The other is to argue that pluralism provides a misleadingly optimistic picture of the way power is organised in those societies described as pluralist.

The pluralist perspective is challenged by a range of theories that identify ways in which power is 'concentrated in the hands of small groups, often described as elites' (Hill, 2005: 50). Hill notes that in much of the literature these perspectives have traditionally been described as 'structural' critiques. The key argument of such critique is that 'there is a range of institutions – the family, the church, the economy, the state – that are linked together in a structure that has a powerfully determining impact on what gets on the [political] agenda' (ibid.: 47). However, Hill suggests that when one examines much of this critique:

> [I]t is open to question whether the phenomena being explored should be described as 'structural'. What is being described is divisions within societies, which are maintained and reinforced in various ways . . . [through] . . . ideas about society and its culture – discourses if you like – that sustain patterns of power.
>
> (ibid.: 48–49)

Arguably, Hill dismisses 'structural' issues rather too hastily. Nevertheless, his reference to 'discourses' is interesting and important because although there have been some notable attempts (e.g. Fisher, 2003) to apply a discourse perspective to public policy formation this has largely remained an underdeveloped theoretical lens through which to view the practice of public affairs (Somerville, 2011). This is unfortunate because the discourse perspective has opened up important new insights into PR practice and it can do the same for public affairs.

Motion and Weaver (2005: 52) argue that: 'In public relations, discourse is deployed as a political resource to influence public opinion and achieve political, economic and sociocultural transformation.' A 'discourse' is the vehicle by which public relations practitioners and public affairs practitioners attempt to 'establish, maintain, or transform hegemonic power [because] . . . public relations discourse strategies are deployed to circulate ideas, establish advantageous relationships, and privilege certain truths and interests' (Motion and Weaver, 2005: 52–53). Viewed in this way, public affairs practitioners as well as public relations practitioners should be 'theorised as working to (strategically) privilege particular discourses over others, in an attempt to construct what they hope will be accepted as in the public interest and legitimated as policy' (Weaver et al., 2006: 18).

Some recent academic accounts of public affairs do adopt something similar to a discourse analysis approach to the activity. For example, McGrath's (2007: 269) advocacy of the tactic of 'framing' – which he suggests involves assessing how 'lobbyists use language consciously to frame policy issues in such a way as to position their organization and its policy preferences to greatest effect' – echoes the discourse perspective. McGrath notes Entman's (1993) definition that the process of framing is in essence

> to select some aspects of a perceived reality and make them more salient in a communicating text, in such a way as to promote a particular problem definition, causal interpretation, moral evaluation and/or treatment recommendations for the item described.
>
> (Entman, 1993, cited in McGrath, 2007: 271)

The parallel here with the notion of promoting a hegemonic discourse is clear. Similarly, Heugen's (2002) analysis of the use of storytelling in public affairs, which obviously involves the construction of a narrative discourse, is an important contribution although the link between this approach and discourse theory is seldom alluded to. Heugens assesses storytelling as an important corporate and activist tool for gaining the support of various external constituencies in the ongoing semiotic wars over biotechnology. By storytelling he clearly means the construction of grand narratives (or discourses) about biotechnology by the key opponents in the battle over GM technologies. He notes that the corporate interests on one side produce a narrative about scientific progress, human advancement and curing starvation. Their opponents, the environmentalists, construct a narrative focused on potential health risks, exploitation of third world farmers and corporate greed. Heugens (2002: 68) concludes that 'every corporate story that was ever written and performed to gain the support of consumers and legislators for the commercialisation of modern biotechnology was quickly reciprocated by an antagonist story that defied and contested the claims of these earlier variants'.

Structures and institutions

Motion and Weaver (2005: 50) suggest 'that discourses deployed for public relations purposes can only be fully understood in relation to the political, economic, and social contexts in which they operate'. The same is certainly true of public affairs and the context always needs to be taken into account to fully understand why some public affairs efforts are successful and others fail, or to use the language of discourse theory, why some discourses achieve hegemony and others do not. Thomas (2004: 67) makes the point that the

> types of groups and interests that exist, and the way they attempt to influence public policy are determined by historical, geographical, cultural, social, economic, political, governmental structural and other factors' and he adds that in turn 'interest group activities help shape and define the nature of a political system.

The significance of political structures, institutions and culture is perhaps thrown into sharpest relief when comparisons between political systems are made. McGrath's (2005: 185) work on lobbying practices in Washington, London and Brussels demonstrates this through a detailed analysis of the role that political culture, institutional frameworks, regulatory environments and executive/legislative relationships all play in determining the differing access points to the policy-making process, which need to be engaged to attempt to influence policy decisions in the three political systems. So the UK, with its strong party system, is different to the US with its weak political party control over legislators and in turn both are different from the EU, where McGrath notes the key 'policy-making institutions are supra-national, and composed of members or appointees from a range of political parties'. Thomas (2004: 1) also draws attention to US constitutional arrangements when he points out that 'largely because of its separation of powers system, its weak political parties, and low level of ideological politics, the United States is an aberrant political system in regard to interest group activity'. He suggests that wider socio-political changes may have the effect of leaving the US less peculiar in this regard. In particular, 'The decline of ideology across the Western world, and particularly Western Europe, is making the factor of parties less significant and more akin to the situation in the United States by increasing the strategy and tactic options for many groups' (ibid.: 76). While it is clear that the Westminster Parliamentary system in the UK means that political parties exert tight control over the legislative process, the decline in party membership and voting figures at election time has led some commentators to argue that there has been a shift of power in the policy arena toward interest groups. For example, Jordan (2004 in Thomas, 2004: 302) notes: 'Given the scale of interest group numbers and memberships, the "decline of parties" and their replacement by group participation, interest groups are now taken seriously in Britain.' It is also important, Thomas (2004: 72) suggests, to bear in mind that 'cultural differences have also led some countries to regulate interest group activity extensively, as in the United States, while in others it is much less stringently regulated, as in Britain and Germany'. For a useful account of regulatory environments in the US, UK and EU the reader is directed to McGrath's study (2005: 167–180).

The various factors discussed above: how one defines public affairs, how its relationship with PR is envisaged and understood, recent theoretical and conceptual understandings of public affairs, and how structural, institutional and cultural factors all impact on practice have been subject to much scholarly debate. In the final section of this chapter some of the key strategies adopted by groups seeking to influence the public policy arena in contemporary democratic societies will be discussed.

Environmental analysis and strategic decision making

Broom (2009: 34) makes the key point that 'lobbyists spend substantially more time collecting information from government than they do communicating to it, since sound lobbying strategies, tactics, and positions are highly dependent on a strong base of information'. In regard to the analytical methods and techniques used by public affairs practitioners, Fleisher (2002: 168) acknowledges that the 'majority of techniques have been borrowed from related fields like administration, management, marketing, political science, public policy and public relations'. The use of typical business and management analytical tools such as the SWOT (Strengths, Weaknesses, Opportunities, Threats) analysis in public affairs has been noted by Shaw (2005). Fleisher (2002) suggests that much of what does occur is not based on a coherent or rigorous methodology, which he argues is a weakness that needs to be addressed more seriously by current practitioners. The identification, monitoring and analysis of legislators, officials, political opponents and other relevant stakeholders is very important in public affairs work, but analysing the political and socio-economic environment is only useful if it enables decision making in respect to the most appropriate strategy and tactics to use in any operating environment.

Although writing in the context of corporate public affairs, Getz (2001: 307) raises important questions that are relevant for most organisations seeking to influence public policy. She points out:

> A clearly important question has to do with the strategies and tactics that might be employed once the decision to participate has been made. Should a firm develop an ongoing relationship with public officials or should it enter and exit the political arena as issues change? Should political decision makers be approached directly or indirectly? Should the approach be intended to inform, to persuade, or both? Which tactics are effective in which situations, and how does one know?

Despite a whole raft of public affairs techniques being identified in the literature, they boil down to a choice between several key strategies or combinations of strategies (Thomas, 2004; McGrath, 2005; Showalter and Fleisher, 2005). These strategies are: direct face-to-face lobbying; indirect lobbying using grassroots pressure; and the formation of coalitions or alliances with like-minded groups to exert broad-based pressure.

Decisions with respect to which strategy to adopt may be influenced by socio-economic and ideological constraints. A key choice facing some activist groups is whether to engage in direct lobbying at all to try to influence policy or whether to eschew this in favour of protest and pressure from the outside. Some of the more ideologically driven environmentalist and animal rights groups have major concerns about compromising their core values by engaging with governments (and other organisations) which perpetuate systems that they are fundamentally opposed to. Groups may decide to deliberately reject some of the avenues or strategies open to them and choose to remain outside parts of the public policy arena. Grant (2000: 16) offers a useful definition of insider and outsider groups: 'An *insider* group is regarded as legitimate by government and consulted on a regular basis. . . An *outsider* group does not wish to become involved in a consultative relationship with public policy-makers or is unable to gain recognition.' Typically outsider groups will adopt non-direct lobbying strategies to exert political pressure, such as grassroots lobbying and direct action.

Direct lobbying

Most groups recognise the importance of putting their case directly to political parties and those holding political office. Fleisher's (2003: 373) advice to public affairs managers is: 'Be prepared to learn as much as you can about the official before meeting them; do not be concerned if the lawmaker is unavailable and a staff assistant is in their place.' Knowledge and expertise of how to engage in and implement traditional face-to-face lobbying still determines the success or failure of many public affairs efforts, particularly in the UK. McGrath (2007: 269) suggests lobbyists using 'language consciously to frame policy issues in such a way as to position their organization and its policy preferences to greatest effect' is of key importance in any direct lobbying activity.

The view that direct lobbying is essentially persuasive communication, tailoring the message and framing it in an appropriate and appealing way, is echoed by many commentators. Mack (1997, cited in McGrath, 2007: 271) suggests that: 'Issues should be framed to show how the public benefits from your side of the argument. Don't go public with a narrow, self-serving issue.' Arguably political discourse in liberal democratic societies is underpinned by utilitarian ideals so it is clear that the 'story' presented must demonstrate how the policy that the organisation supports is in some way benefitting the common good. This is where an understanding of the role and power of discourse becomes significant for the public affairs specialist. Being able to demonstrate that a position on an issue is part of a generally accepted discourse viewed as core to liberal democratic society, such as human rights, women's rights, freedom or equality, will always be advantageous. A clear, coherent narrative works best, as McGrath (2007: 271) notes, 'public policy issues (the focus of lobbying efforts) tend to be complex, involving an array of both factors and alternatives; framing is an attempt by lobbyists to set the boundaries of debate on a given issue.'

To actually present the case, access for the lobbyist to government actors or political figures is a key requirement. Several recent studies have revealed the growing importance of party conferences as an important forum for meeting and engaging in face-to-face lobbying efforts with major political actors (Thomas, 2004; Harris and Harris, 2005). In a UK study Harris and Harris (2005: 224) drew attention to the growth of lobbying activities at political party conferences through the 1990s. They note:

> Tho party conference environment acts as a communications conduit for the sharing and swapping of information as well as an opinion exchange and policy positioning forum . . . It is perhaps the ultimate network opportunity for those interested in government, political processes, and the formation of policy.

Grassroots campaigning

Organisations may be excluded or may choose to exclude themselves from direct 'insider' contact or they might decide other strategies are required. Indirect lobbying using grassroots pressures is likely to be a useful strategy choice. Fleisher (2003: 371) suggests that: 'Very few issues, particularly those captured in the public's attention by the media, escape the onslaught of organised grassroots techniques coming from all sides of the matter.'

Titley (2003) and McGrath (2005) note the increasing importance of 'outsider' tactics, especially grassroots campaigns, which are increasingly supplementing and to some extent perhaps even supplanting 'insider' contact in respect to British and European public affairs. It is clearly a route that is increasingly seen as a useful and legitimate strategy by all interest groups. To some degree then the adoption of what were traditionally thought of as US practices are appearing in the UK/EU context. It is probably fair to say that at the present time – for the reasons to do with political culture noted above – in the US many interest groups use grassroots lobbying much more effectively as a political weapon during key legislative debates. Morris (1999: 132), reflecting on the National Rifle Association's (NRA) tactics, notes:

> [T]he NRA has become incredibly skilled at using its members as a political tool, unlike many special-interest groups, the NRA doesn't even aspire to popularity. When it seeks to influence an election, it doesn't advertise on television or radio. Instead, the NRA sends mailings to its members to urge them to vote for their favoured candidates in elections. The NRA emphasizes its capacity to turn out a disciplined bloc of voters for or against any candidate to strike terror into the hearts of wavering congressmen and senators when gun control legislation come up for a vote.

Web activism can be used to underpin and complement the strategies of grassroots mobilisation and campaigning and thereby transform existing power imbalances that lobbying by powerful groups produces (Kakabadse et al., 2003). There is an accepted wisdom that the internet helps resource-poor groups compete with resource-rich groups in the policy arena. In fact, there is evidence to suggest that the internet may actually be reinforcing the status quo. Rethemeyer's (2007: 199) research indicates:

The Internet appears to foster and intensify closed, corporatized policy networks. The solution may not be IT, as the Internet optimists suggest. Rather, it may be to embrace and reform politics-by-organization. The Internet and other forms of IT have a role – though a small one – in this process.

The power and influence of the grassroots has not gone unnoticed and some organisations in recent years have engaged in the practice of manufacturing such campaigns to try to influence policy makers. Although the creation of 'front' groups is not a new practice, the expansion of the internet has led to a significant amount of debate on groups created to deceive or mislead policy makers about public opinion (Showalter and Fleisher, 2005). Known as 'astroturfing' such front organisations are designed to give the appearance of widespread citizen support, when in reality they often are created to promote narrow interests.

Coalition building

Building a public affairs strategy around grassroots campaigning is sometimes accompanied by the strategy of coalition and alliance building with other interest groups. Fleisher (2003: 373) has noted: 'Through well-conceived coalitions with other allied interests, various groups have been able to achieve important public policy successes.' Showalter and Fleisher (2005: 119) suggest:

> The best coalitions have the involvement and commitment of all stakeholders, clear leadership, group agreement on the vision and mission for the coalition, and assessment of member needs and member resources ... Once these initial building blocks are established, the effective coalition creates short- and long-term objectives, develops an action plan and implements it.

Coalitions that share a similar ideological position, economic interest or that belong to the same socio-economic sector probably have the greatest chance of long-term success.

While alliances between ideologically compatible interest groups are more common, it is possible for organisations that at first sight do not seem an obvious fit to work together for mutual benefit. McGrath (2005: 131) notes the example of the alliance a large Japanese manufacturer of audio equipment and tapes forged with the Royal National Institute for the Blind (RNIB), and educational organisations, to campaign against an increased levy on audio tapes. McGrath cites the views of a senior London lobbyist who helped develop the coalition on behalf of the manufacturer. The lobbyist stated:

> Getting the Royal National Institute for the Blind on board was decisive, and yet it was not difficult because this was a genuinely important issue for them: the government was proposing to do something which would substantially increase costs for their members. The RNIB said 'Yes, we absolutely were planning to campaign against this anyway, but we lack resources.' So we told

them, 'That's fine. We have resources and you have a powerful argument. Let's put those together.' We decided that what the government was proposing was not a 'levy', it was a 'tax', and we launched a campaign against this tax. Essentially it was funded by manufacturers, but most of the action was provided by other parts of the coalition, in particular the blind. That is why in the end the campaign succeeded, because the blind are a very powerful pressure group and they are not afraid to use their emotional pulling power.

There are several interesting elements here. The actors in this coalition not only changed the 'frame' of the debate – a 'levy' was rearticulated as a 'tax' – but even more significantly the discourse of equality/discrimination was brought to the fore and exploited effectively by the partners in the coalition. Coalitions and alliances are frequently fraught with difficulties but groups can work together, even those with radically different worldviews if they can agree on what each can bring to the alliance and what the strengths of each partner are (Showalter and Fleisher, 2005).

Evaluation

There have been various attempts to derive evaluation and measurement criteria for public affairs work but according to Fleisher (2005: 158): 'Unfortunately, the state of performance assessment in public affairs does not actually look all that much better than it did over a decade ago.' One key trend in the literature that Fleisher identifies is the tendency toward quantification in recent years although providing numeric data seems to be being confused with measurement and evaluation in much of this work. He notes:

> [T]his has led to their [public affairs specialists] counting most public affairs activities – in terms of things like the number of meetings with key stakeholders, the number of letters sent to key public policy committee personnel, the number of issues being actively monitored, wins and losses, the number of bills being tracked, the number of persons involved in the grassroots programs, etc.
>
> (Fleisher, 2005: 153)

He points out this is misleading 'Counting is not equivalent to and is only the starting point of measurement' (ibid.: 153). Fleisher (2002, 2003, 2005) has examined the difficulties in measuring or demonstrating the value of public affairs activity from a functionalist, quantitative perspective. Writing specifically on grassroots campaigns he notes:

> [P]ublic affairs does not have a body of procedures established that allows appropriate accounting of the net effect on the investments and uses of public affairs resources as other functions have been accustomed to. In general, public affairs practice and performance have always been more of an art than a science, more qualitative than quantitative, and more conjectural than empirical.
>
> (Fleisher, 2005: 145)

Fleisher, who has published more than anyone else on this topic over the past decade, is largely correct to assert that the effective evaluation of specific strategies and tactics is a problematic area for the public affairs practitioner. Ultimately the key assessment that matters is if there has been an effect on the public policy process and legislation that impacts positively on the organisation or the cause that it promotes. Thus a straightforward way of evaluating any public affairs activity is to examine the legislation adopted in response to the public affairs efforts surrounding an issue. Policy shifts or policy battles may occur over a very long period of time and this should be taken into account when contemplating evaluation and measurement issues. 'Success' in the policy sphere may not mean the achievement, at least in the short term, of legislative change at all. Instead it may be measured in the gradual transformation of what McGrath (2007) refers to as the 'language frame' or the narrative or discourse used to describe the issue. Changing the discourse will in many cases result in a change in policy change, and legislative change will in many cases follow. Public affairs managers and practitioners in all sectors would do well to follow the advice of key commentators in the area (Mack, 1997; McGrath, 2007) and become much more sensitive to the language and narratives used to describe issues.

CONCLUSION

The key issue in respect to the role of PR in government communication practices is whether or not it can actually assist in developing a more accessible, transparent and participatory public sphere. Hiebert (2005: 3) argues that due to economic and political pressures the mass media can no longer be relied upon to fulfil this role. He suggests 'the only possible solution is PR, not in terms of spin or propaganda but in terms of developing real public relationships in the public sphere'. Fairbanks *et al.* (2007: 26) make the point that all organisations, including governments, must be proactive in reaching out to their publics: 'In addition to the open sharing of information, transparency requires organisations to understand and be responsive to the publics they serve.' Some have warned of the dangers of fake government 'dialogic' relationships, engaged in merely in order to legitimise the discourse that it wishes to promote. Motion (2005: 511) argues: 'Participative public relations, in which stakeholders are discursively engaged with pre-determined solutions and conflict suppressed or ignored, may, in fact, simply be a means of masking power relations rather than genuine engagement.' Such strategies encourage cynicism and distrust of government and disillusionment with democratic institutions. PR practitioners working for government may struggle with conflicts of interest. They will have the interests of their organisation and perhaps their immediate political boss as a key influence on their conduct but, like the elected politicians they serve, they have a duty to put the public interest first.

Government policy and legislation impacts on citizens, organisations and institutions throughout society making influencing policy and legislation which benefits one's 'interest' highly desirable and this is the primary task of public affairs. In many democratic societies mainstream political parties are declining in membership numbers while the appetite for joining pressure groups, single interest and voluntary groups is on the rise. Perhaps this reflects a decline in traditional societal institutions or more consumerist approach to politics (Grant, 2000). Whatever the reason the financial and human capital invested in public affairs activity is growing in all sectors; business, public institutions, activist and voluntary/charitable. A range of strategies are employed by the diverse interests and causes that make up the public policy sphere. From face-to-face lobbying to direct action, from grassroots campaigning to coalitions between the most unlikely bedfellows, groups fight to make their voice heard and influence government policy and legislation. Victory in public affairs battles are not necessarily always won by those who have the most resources or have the big battalions. It took the anti-slavery movement over 40 years of campaigning to change British legislation on slavery in what was at that time the greatest superpower in the world. The Committee for the Abolition of the Slave Trade was formed in 1787 but didn't succeed in outlawing slavery throughout the British Empire until the passing of the Slavery Abolition Act in 1833. The campaigners for this legislative change shifted the debate away from an economic discourse (a battleground on which they were bound to lose) to a human rights discourse. They demonstrated that in societies where public opinion matters, and can be expressed in democratic forums, those who can convince their fellow citizens that their story is true, or ethical, or rational, can in the end change the laws by which we all must abide.

QUESTIONS FOR DISCUSSION

1   What are the key media management strategies used by governments in democratic societies?

2   'All political parties and all governments spin. And there is nothing wrong with it' (Finkelstein, 2003). Do you agree with Finkelstein's assessment?

3   Do you agree with Fairclough (2000) that democratic dialogue is being replaced with a 'managerial and promotional' approach to the political process in the UK?

4   How useful is the concept of the 'public sphere' in the context of government communication and PR?

5   Examine a media campaign surrounding a current policy initiative by the British Government. In what ways have politicians and their media advisers attempted to 'manage' the British media to achieve the maximum favourable coverage of their policy?

6 Does lobbying of political elites subvert the democratic process?

7 Why should public affairs practitioners pay attention to 'language frames', 'narratives' or 'discourses' in the policy sphere?

8 Should lobbyists in the UK be more tightly controlled? Would you favour statutory regulation similar to that which exists in the US for the UK lobbying industry?

9 In response to the fuel price campaign in 2000 Tony Blair said 'No government, indeed no country can retain credibility in its democratic process or its economic policy-making were it to give in to such protests. Real damage is being done to real people.' Is pressure group grass roots campaigning a legitimate public affairs activity?

10 Examine a current public affairs campaign in relation to a key policy issue. Which strategies are utilised by those advocating the policy, or policy change and how do they frame the language or discourse in public policy debates?

FURTHER READING

Andrews, L. (2006) 'Spin: from tactic to tabloid', *Journal of Public Affairs*, 6 (1), pp. 31–45.

Fairbanks, J., Plowman, K.D., and Rawlins, B.L. (2007) 'Transparency in government communication', *Journal of Public Affairs*, 7 (1), pp. 23–37.

Gaber, I. (2000b) 'Government by spin: an analysis of the process', *Media, Culture & Society*, 22 (4), pp. 507–518.

Getz, K.A. (2001) 'Public affairs and political strategy: theoretical foundations', *Journal of Public Affairs*, 1 (4) & 2 (1), pp. 305–329.

McGrath, C. (ed.) *Interest groups and lobbying in the United States and comparative perspectives*, The Edwin Mellen Press.

McNair, B. (2004) 'PR must die: spin, anti-spin and political public relations in the UK, 1997–2004', *Journalism Studies*, 5 (3), pp. 325–338.

Motion, J. (2005) 'Participative public relations: power to the people or legitimacy for government discourse?', *Public Relations Review* 31 (3), pp. 505–512.

Moloney, K. (2006) *Rethinking PR? The spin and the substance* (2nd edition), Routledge

Thomas, C.S. (2004) *Research guide to US and international interest groups*, Praeger.

Weaver, C.K., Motion, J., and Roper, J. (2006) 'From propaganda to discourse (and back again): truth, power, the public interest, and public relations' in J. L'Etang and M. Pieczka, (eds) *Public relations: critical debates and contemporary practice*, Lawrence Erlbaum Associates.

CHAPTER 4

Public relations and management

Anne Gregory

CHAPTER AIMS

This chapter aims to do four things:

- describe public relations as a strategic management activity taking the business strategy and systems perspectives as a basis for discussion
- explain the roles of public relations practitioners
- indicate the influences that determine the structure and priorities of public relations within organisations
- describe the working linkages between public relations and other professional areas of organisations.

IMPACT OF CHANGE

The world of public relations has changed radically in the last few years. The challenges faced by society, such as globalisation and global warming, are posing serious questions of organisations. Added to that are the seismic changes that new, communications-based technologies are bringing to the way organisations connect with their stakeholders and the nature of their interactions.

It is not the remit of this chapter to explore the details and ramifications of all these deep and wide changes that are happening, but the impact on the practice and management of public relations overall is profound. A report by the Arthur W. Page

Society (2007) called *The Authentic Enterprise*, examining some of these issues concludes that organisations have reached a point of 'strategic inflection', which requires a new way of operating. Communication is at the heart and the key is authenticity. It goes on to enumerate four new practices and skills for which the more senior public relations practitioner must assume a leadership role:

- defining and instilling company values
- building and managing multi-stakeholder relationships
- enabling the enterprise with 'new media' skills and tools
- building and managing trust in all dimensions.

Unfortunately The European Communication Monitor 2010 (Zerfass *et al.*, 2010) suggests that the majority of European public relations professionals do not align their work to or influence decision-making in their organisations and therefore there remains a question over the capability of practitioners to fulfil the role that senior managers would like them to (Murray and White, 2005). Nonetheless, organisations will have to become adept at responding to societal issues; they will have to engage with a range of stakeholders who, to date, have not been on their radar and who will hold them to account and they will need to engage in new ways. They will have to demonstrate that they are living their espoused values and the mandate, or 'licence to operate' given them by a complex web of multi-stakeholders will be fragile and in need of reinforcement constantly. It follows from this that the opportunities for public relations practitioners to take a place alongside senior management decision-makers in their organisations has never been greater.

BUSINESS STRATEGY AND PUBLIC RELATIONS

As a first step in realising this opportunity, understanding the way organisations work as a whole and the contribution that public relations can make within them is vital. The work of business strategists has been interpreted and applied to private sector organisations by South African public relations scholar Dr Benita Steyn (Steyn, 2007). She points out that there are different strategic levels within organisations and it is important to understand these in order to define the role that public relations can play. Given that more practitioners work in the public and not-for-profit sectors than the private sector, a more generic, but in many ways similar model promoted by the CIPR (Gregory and White, 2008) identifies four levels at which public relations can contribute. Being clear about the levels of strategic contribution helps practitioners to talk about their role in a way that is meaningful throughout the organisation. The four levels are listed below.

Societal level

At the societal level, organisations seek to obtain legitimacy for themselves by trying to gain and maintain overall support from society as a whole. An organisation's place, standing and reputation in society determines whether its licence to operate is granted by public opinion and hence by society. At this level, the organisation's fundamental values, mission and ways of operating are tested and are either found true and worthy of support, or wanting. For example, an organisation whose mission is just to maximise profits without any regard to its operational practices, which may include using child labour, unsafe working practices and a total disregard of the environment, will be deemed to be unacceptable in Western society and will probably find its license to operate withdrawn unless it changes those practices.

Public relations plays a role in assisting the organisation to clarify its values and mission by helping to frame and test these internally and externally. The public relations function also monitors the way society perceives the organisation's performance against its declared values and mission to determine whether they are seen to be acting in an acceptable manner. It does this by acting as the organisational antennae, undertaking the 'boundary-spanning' role (discussed in the next section of this chapter) and constantly monitoring the external environment and public opinion, to bring essential intelligence about potential issues or opportunities into the organisation so that it can act accordingly. It also promotes the organisation by the clear communication of its values and purpose, and by providing evidence that demonstrates consistent performance against them.

Management level

This level is one step down from seeking broad societal acceptance. Here senior managers in organisations seek to operationalise the values and mission by making managerial decisions at corporate level. Often this is about marshalling organisational resources and the temptation is to allow financial considerations to dominate. The public relations function can make a critical contribution at this level by helping managers in making enlightened business decisions that have proper regard for the legitimate interests and concerns of stakeholders. It is vital that the opinions and interests of all stakeholders are properly understood and balanced as decisions are made and the public relations function can ensure that those stakeholder views are represented and fully considered.

It is also the task of the public relations professional to provide intelligence on how the organisation's potential decisions are likely to be perceived by stakeholders and, of course, to involve stakeholders in, and inform them of, management level decisions as appropriate. Thus, for example, it may be that it would make financial sense for a company to build a new facility in a particular neighbourhood, but the local community and protest groups may become so opposed and active that it would be impossible for the company to ever realise the location's potential. The public relations function, being engaged with those communities would be able to bring this intelligence into the company and advise on appropriate courses of action, which might include abandoning the plans altogether or working with the community to ameliorate some of their greatest concerns.

Programme level

At the programme level, it is the role of public relations to liaise with the other areas of the organisation to determine how the function as a whole can contribute to the organisation's mission and objectives. For public relations this will mean planning specific programmes and campaigns that support these objectives, often offering specialist public relations advice and services to other functional areas of the organisation. They will also coach and mentor colleagues throughout the organisation to be 'communicatively competent', or at least communicatively aware, so that they can either undertake certain public relations tasks themselves to an adequate standard, or be alert to when they need to enlist the help of the specialists.

At this level, therefore, a great deal of time is spent on putting together public relations plans in a structured way, and of different types depending on the needs of the stakeholder groups involved. Hence, for example, social marketing programmes may be needed to encourage behavioural change in some groups, such as adopting healthy lifestyles; marketing campaigns will be aimed at potential customers, to help product sales; internal communication programmes help to keep employees up to speed with changes in the organisation and to enlist their ideas and support; and lobbying may be targeted at individual MPs to change voting intentions.

Each plan will be different depending on its purpose, who is involved, their communication channel-use habits, the timing of the campaign, the resources available and so on. However, the disciplines behind the planning process are the same and conform to recognised business planning norms.

Individual level

Clearly, the capability of individual practitioners will determine their performance at each of the three levels outlined above. The more skilled and competent they are and the more able they are to perform the demanding societal and management level roles, the more highly they are likely to be regarded and placed in their organisation.

The point of going through the strategic levels at which public relations can make a contribution is to:

- clarify the types of input that public relations can make to the organisation as a whole, including its input to organisational decision-making
- show that public relations has to be seen within a broader context and ensure all activities are aligned to societal and management objectives
- demonstrate that public relations contributes more to an organisation than just tactical campaigns
- enable the practitioner to articulate and move between the various levels that they must operate at within the organisation.

SYSTEMS THEORY AND PUBLIC RELATIONS

A slightly different perspective on the management contribution of public relations to organisations is taken by a number of public relations scholars largely from America, for example, Cutlip *et al.* (2006); Grunig and Hunt (1984) who refer to systems theory to explain the structure and operation of organisations and their interaction with the environment. In essence, systems theory describes an organisation as a set of parts (or subsystems) that interact within a boundary and which together respond and adjust to the organisation's environment that is outside that boundary.

Systems theory provides a useful theoretical underpinning for thinking about the role of public relations because it stipulates that an organisation's well-being (or otherwise) is dependent on establishing and maintaining relationships both within itself and with its environment. It has to adjust and adapt as both it and its environment change. Thus, while systems theory articulates the contribution of public relations somewhat differently from the language and models employed by the strategic management approach, it can be seen that it is in fact very similar in its practical outworking. Indeed, much of business strategy has its origins in systems thinking (Johnson, Scholes and Whittington, 2007).

Systems theory views organisations as part of a wider social system that consists of individuals or groups of individuals (publics), such as employees, pensioners, suppliers, distributors, online communities and so on, who are all involved with it. The role of public relations is to develop and maintain relationships with these groups in order that the organisation is better able to meet its goals.

From a systems view, public relations professionals' major role is as a 'boundary-spanner'. They straddle the boundaries of an organisation liaising both between its internal subsystems and between it and the external environment that contains its various external stakeholders. They are not the only people within organisations who are boundary-spanners, but they do fulfil this critical function as a formal part of their role.

Public relations professionals also support other internal subsystems by helping them communicate within the organisation itself and by helping them in communicating with external audiences. They provide a counselling role, advising what and how to communicate and they can also provide an implementation role by undertaking the communication on behalf of the subsystems. For example, it will help the human resources department with internal communication programmes or the marketing department with product promotion campaigns. The organisational boundary-spanner, especially those involved in communication has a difficult and complex task interpreting and trying to find a way of reconciling often competing agendas from a range of internal and external stakeholders.

PUBLIC RELATIONS IN STRATEGY MAKING

The main role of the leader of an organisation and its senior managers (or board) is to provide vision and direction. Effective organisations have a sense of purpose. They know where they are going and they know in general how they are going to get there. The vision may be set by a strong individual with a particular driving vision, for example Bill Gates, founder of Microsoft, who wanted to put a PC on everyone's desk; or Richard Branson who brings a fun-orientated and mould-breaking approach to serious businesses such as transport or financial services. Alternatively, the vision may be more broad-based and generic. For example, universities exist to provide higher education; their purpose is broadly the same – to undertake teaching, research and consultancy. However, even within this quite homogeneous sector there are differences; some universities are primarily research driven, some want to focus on serving a regional community, some specialise in certain subjects.

Whatever the type of organisation, successful ones have a strategy that determines long-term direction and the scope of the operation. It is not appropriate in this chapter to examine the different schools of strategy formulation, but suffice to say that strategy-making involves a great deal of information gathering, analysis and decision-making. This decision-making and strategy selection is undertaken by the 'dominant coalition', that group within an organisation that has the power to make and enforce decisions about the direction of the organisation, its objectives and its operations. This is the task of managers at the management level of strategy described earlier in the chapter. Strategy formulation is rarely purely rational and linear. It is essentially an iterative process where managers discuss and debate, make steps forward and then revise their thinking. They explore options and gradually narrow down to certain choices – and often there is a level of 'instinct' about their eventual decisions, although this instinct is informed by years of experience and tacit knowledge. To make these decisions, managers need information and usually from a variety of sources and perspectives so that those decisions can be reviewed and tested robustly. As boundary-spanners, public relations professionals are ideally placed to gather and interpret intelligence from both the internal and the external environment. As described earlier, the contribution that public relations can make to the strategy-making process is twofold. First, helping to collect and interpret information from the internal and external environment so that strategic decisions can be informed. This will include gathering data from a range of sources, but will also involve them talking to stakeholders about their views and opinions, possibly exposing them to interim thinking to see what their reactions are. Second, once decisions have been made this needs to be communicated to important stakeholders with the purpose of gaining their support.

It is worth exploring the way the public relations function gathers intelligence in more detail. Practitioners must be attuned to what is called the 'macro' environment, that is in the elements in the environment largely outside their control. They must also be knowledgeable about the 'task' environment, that is those elements in the environment that they can have some influence over. This means knowing about the attitudes and behaviours of the various stakeholders of the organisation who populate this broader environment and with whom they interact, and being in regular dialogue with those stakeholders. How do public relations professionals undertake this intelligence gathering work?

Environmental scanning

'Environmental scanning' is the term used for gaining information about the macro environment. PR professionals use the same techniques as those available to all strategic planners. They will undertake analysis of the environment using techniques such as PEST. This analytical tool provides a framework that allows analysis of the environment by categorising it under various headings; a short example is given in Figure 4.1 (the capitalised first letter of each section spells out the acronym above).

Some strategists now regard PEST as no longer adequately capturing the complexity of the environment in which modern organisations operate. They recommend an expansion of the framework to encompass *E*nvironment, that is, the physical or green environment, *I*nformation and the *L*egal or regulatory aspects. The acronym EPISTLE describes this expanded categorisation. The physical environment is judged to be one of the major concerns of the twenty-first century. Global warming, pressures to move from car-based transport, sustainability, waste disposal and so

Political	**Economic**
Trade legislation (including overseas trade agreements)	Interest rates
	Inflation
Change of government	Business cycles
Employment legislation	Employment levels
Emergence of new power blocks	
Social	**Technological**
Lifestyles	Internet
Consumer preferences	Rate of change
Social attitudes	Obsolescence
Disposable income	Investment in technology

FIGURE 4.1 An example of PEST analysis
Source: Used by permission

on are all key issues. Indeed, although a concept rather than a group of people, many strategists now regard the environment as a stakeholder – it would be a brave or stupid management team who ignored the claims of the environment on their organisation these days.

Access to and the ability to manage and use information is critical to organisations because information is power. There are many sources of information for organisations including industry research publications, trade bodies and their own market research. For the environmental scanner, the internet is a vital information source. By plugging into sites such as those maintained by the major social research organisations like Ipsos MORI, the political think-tanks, NGOs and activist groups, as well as the many websites, blogs and social networks that relate to their industry and company, professional communicators can keep abreast of the main issues in the wider environment. It goes almost without saying that these issues will also be of concern to employees who will also want to know how the organisation is addressing them.

Organisations operate within an increasingly complex legal environment. In addition to growing amounts of national legislation, there are transnational regulations, such as EU directives, and international agreements, such as those made by the World Trade Organisation. There are also quasi-legal arrangements made by members of fora such as the G20, or World Economic Forum, which often have a moral dimension, such as the agreements to reduce carbon emissions or to alleviate third world indebtedness, all of which may impact on organisations.

Some analysts also recommend that culture should have special consideration. As organisations become increasingly global they need to be aware of national, religious and social differences between and within the countries in which they operate. Organisational cultures differ too and values between suppliers, distributors and organisations or even different parts of the same organisation can be quite distinct. Companies within the same sector can have radically different cultures: Easyjet's approach to airline travel is not that of Singapore Airlines.

The point of this kind of analysis is to identify the key issues that will impact on the organisation. There are no standard responses; the issues will be different depending on the country, sector and organisation. It is also vital to identify the inter-relationships between the key issues. Economic trends may force political decisions and technology often affects lifestyles and social interactions. For example, the banking crisis of 2007–2009 forced difficult political decisions to privatise them in some instances and the internet has transformed working, purchasing and leisure patterns.

Environmental scanning establishes the long-term drivers of change and their impact. These need localising to identify the effect that they will have on the organisation itself. Environmental analyses should not only be done in the here and now, but should also include forward projections so that organisations can plan a variety of futures that they may have to accommodate, try to change or adapt to.

As can be imagined this kind of information is critical to management making decisions. By being a source of this kind of intelligence public relations can position itself firmly as a management capability of equal importance as financial, operational or HR capability.

Knowledge of stakeholders and publics

The second element of intelligence gathering by public relations professionals is a deep understanding of the task environment populated by the organisation's stakeholders or publics. The distinction between the terms stakeholders and publics as used in this chapter needs explaining since the terms are often used interchangeably. If the classic interpretation of stakeholder is used – 'any individual or group who an affect or is affected by the actions, decisions, policies, practices or goals of the organisation' (Freeman, 1984: 25) it can be seen that an organisation may have tens or even millions of stakeholders. However, not all stakeholders are active or even interested in some of the organisations in which they could be seen to have a stake. For example, those living in the developed world rarely even consider who supplies their domestic water despite its importance for everyday life. When an individual or a group does become active and interested, then they may be regarded as a public. Critically, publics collect around issues that concern them and are, by definition, involved in them. Potentially any stakeholder can become a public when they move to being active around an issue. There are other ways to think about publics that are referred to in the further reading. Public relations practitioners are in a privileged and strategic position in that they interact with organisational publics frequently: their job is to facilitate the relationship between the organisation and its publics, often in conjunction with colleagues from elsewhere in the organisation. They are also involved in scanning and categorising the wider stakeholder environment, always alert to the fact that stakeholders may become a public very rapidly. Chapter 6 covers stakeholder theory in some detail, but here it is important to stress that the public relations professional will be alert to the relative power, influence, needs and expectations of publics and stakeholder groups and the shifting dynamics both within and between them.

The public relations professional will also be aware of the attitude towards or behaviour of the various stakeholders and publics in relation to the wider issues identified in the environment and the impact that this might have on the organisation itself. For example, the public relations professional working for a food retailer will be alert to the fact that the genetic modification of food is a major issue for many consumers. They will also be aware of the prevailing attitudes of the scientific community, suppliers, customers, shareholders and employees. They will be conscious that opinion is divided and that they will need to be alert to shifts in public opinion and buying preferences, and any implications this might have for their organisation.

The importance of stakeholder groups to organisations cannot be overestimated. Freeman (1984) first articulated this in a systematic way, arguing that organisations were defined by their relationships with stakeholders and that stakeholders include not just those groups that management believe to have a stake in the organisation, but those who decide for themselves that they will take a stake in the organisation. This latter group, because they are especially active, will be a public who must be taken seriously. The actions of activist groups have made this a painful reality for some organisations. Indeed, in some instances, these activist groups have caused organisations to rethink their business strategy, as was the case for Monsanto following activist protests over its development of genetically modified crops. Monsanto was forced to set back its production of such crops by several years as a result.

Given that organisations are dependent on stakeholders for their existence it is obvious that the strategic management of those relationships is a critical function in its own right: reputation and ultimately the existence of organisations are determined by the opinion of these stakeholders.

A typical organisation interacts with an enormous number of publics. Esman (1972) usefully categorises these into four types of organisational linkages, as illustrated by Grunig and Hunt (Figure 4.2). This categorisation is still helpful and has stood the test of time.

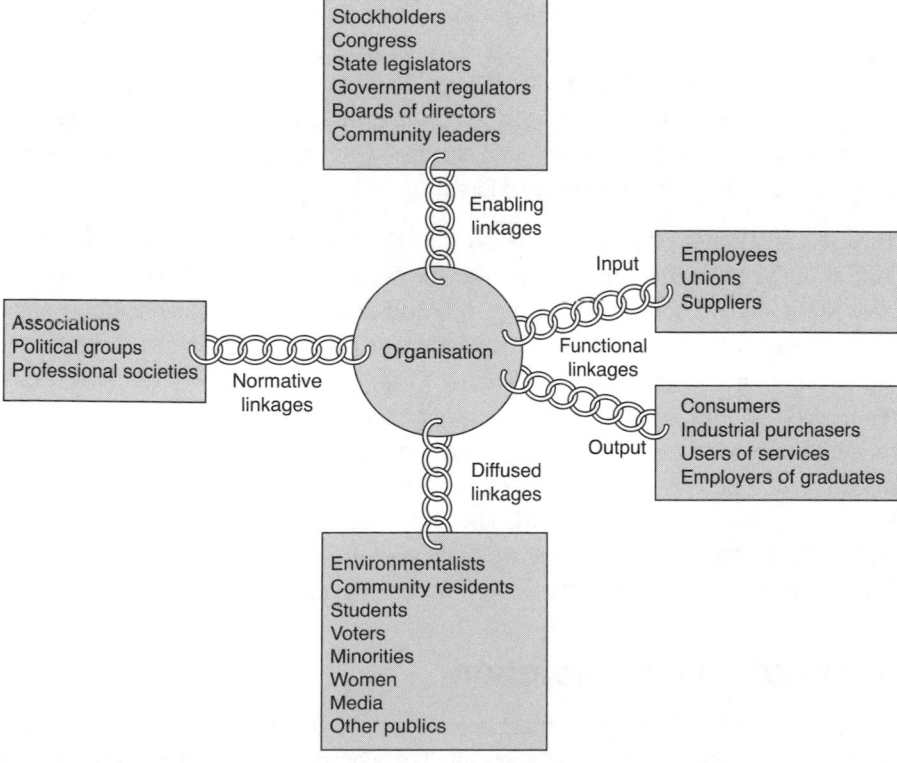

FIGURE 4.2 Organisational linkages

Source: Grunig and Hunt (1984: 141). Used by permission of Harcourt

Enabling linkages are those with organisations and groups that have the authority and resources to permit the organisation to exist. Functional linkages provide input into the organisation and consume its outputs. Normative linkages are those with peer organisations, and diffused linkages are with those who have no formalised relationship with the organisation, but have an interest in it.

This categorisation not only demonstrates the number of different publics that the professional communicator interacts with, but the range of interest of those publics.

The reality of management is that there is not only a need to identify stakeholders, but there has to be a way to prioritise them since it is not only impossible to give each an equal amount of time and attention, but is also not necessary. The importance of different groups varies depending on circumstances, but determining the priority of different groups is a highly skilled science. Gregory (2007) has shown how different techniques can be used to categorise stakeholders and how different communication strategies can be employed to engage publics depending on their level of priority and activity.

Engaging with stakeholders may be a defensive action, but it can also be regarded as a positive strategic activity that organisations can and should develop. By integrating the economic resources, political support and specialist knowledge that publics can offer, both organisations and stakeholders can gain mutual benefit. The role of managers is to facilitate a coalition that draws partners together (Steyn, 2007). This collaborative working is especially important in the new media age where stakeholders can organise quickly and effectively if they feel their concerns are not being responded to or adequately addressed.

Thus, it can be seen that public relations is a sophisticated management activity that at its highest articulation is the careful negotiation of relationships with and between dynamic, constantly forming, evolving and dissolving stakeholder groups and publics, many of whom see themselves as having a legitimate stake in the organisation either directly or indirectly. Organisations can no longer impose themselves on their environment; they have to constantly prove their legitimacy and renew their license to operate at a time when literally the people of the world can hold them to public account for their actions. The navigation and negotiation of these complex interrelationships calls for skills of the highest order. Regular research and audits of the environment and the opinion of their publics in particular, is a vital job for the public relations professional and an organisationally strategic activity.

Information interpretation

White and Mazur (1995) suggest that because they have such extensive contacts with sources and information, public relations staff may be in a position to provide a central collation and interpretation function. Managing and interpreting information requires both research and analytical capabilities and are an indication of the expanded skills set required of senior practitioners beyond their usual communication abilities.

Where the environment is turbulent and creates uncertainty, those individuals who are capable of interpreting what is happening are invaluable for decision-making. Public relations practitioners are used to dealing with complex situations and to making sense of inter-linked issues involving a variety of publics so are ideally placed to be the organisational 'seer'.

Public relations practitioners are also ideally placed to be able to access sources of information early and can interpret that information to identify emerging issues and those that may have a profound effect on an organisation. For example, media content, social network and Twitter analysis can identify matters of emerging importance and help clarify the direction in which public opinion is moving on a particular issue. Public affairs departments are often plugged into government thinking on prospective legislation or have access to think-tanks who specialise in futures. Importantly their boundary-spanning role and connection with the outside world helps public relations professionals maintain an independent perspective. This independence is valuable to other managers who are often too tied into the 'organisational view' to act objectively or to understand the ramifications of their decisions and the impact they will have on stakeholders.

Risk management

Knowledge of the environment and of stakeholders is vitally important in another respect too. Organisations find themselves increasingly at risk from a number of directions. In the wider context, we live in an increasingly interconnected, dependent, pluralistic world (Gregory, 2004), where no one and no organisation can isolate itself from any of the 'big issues' that are emerging. For example, the increase in international terrorism by cause-related activists has led organisations to appraise all kinds of issues that affect their business, for example, how much should executives travel? Are their products or services culturally sensitive? Are their buildings secure? With whom do they make strategic alliances? The big-picture political and economic issues such as these can and should be tracked and monitored by public relations professionals as part of their environmental scanning duties. Indeed, issues tracking and management are part of the strategic communicator's basic toolkit.

Furthermore, as far as stakeholders are concerned, it is possible for small groups to challenge and hold to account large organisations, as the protests against McDonald's over the impact of securing new grazing for beef cattle in environmentally sensitive areas has demonstrated. By knowing stakeholders well and understanding what motivates them, what their thinking is and how they are likely to act, the public relations professional can bring an early and invaluable perspective to management thinking and advise on the appropriate way to manage these relationships. Thus, helping to manage risk is a vital role for communicators. Issues management and agenda-setting are not only possible but necessary in an environment where publics themselves define and then seek to satisfy their information needs.

It is for this issues and risk management skill and judgement that many of the most senior communicators either sit at board tables in their own right or are direct advisers to CEOs and chairs of large organisations. It is a vital strategic information role and highly valued in boardrooms throughout the world (Gregory and Edwards, 2004; Murray and White, 2005). For an in-depth examination of risk, issues and crisis management see Chapter 8.

THE ROLES OF PUBLIC RELATIONS PRACTITIONERS

Within this discussion of public relations as a management function, it is appropriate to look at the specific roles of public relations practitioners in order to differentiate their roles as manager from those requiring just technical proficiency. Work spear-headed by Glen Broom and David Dozier (summarised by Moss et al. 2005) has identified two dominant public relations roles and their view still dominates thinking.

The communication technician is often a highly skilled individual who carries out communication programmes and activities such as writing news releases, editing house-magazines and developing websites. They probably do not undertake research, except to decide which communication mechanism suits their prescribed purpose best; implementation is their focus. They will not be involved in organisational decision-making. The technician is typically associated with the programme level of strategy as outlined earlier in the chapter.

The communication manager on the other hand is in the dominant coalition, counsels management, makes policy decisions, and plans, manages, evaluates and facilitates communication programmes. The communication manager is more likely to be associated with the societal and management level of strategy mentioned earlier with all its attendant potential issues and risks.

Other researchers such as Toth et al. (1998) and Moss et al. (2000) have identified another highly specialised 'senior adviser' role, someone not actually on the board of companies, but directly responsible to CEOs and who advises on public relations matters at the highest level.

More recently Moss et al. (2005) reported the findings of empirical work undertaken in the UK and US that identified a more precise role for the senior public relations manager operating at board or near-board level. They isolated five elements to the communication manager role; four relate to managerial responsibility: monitor and evaluator; key policy and strategy adviser; trouble shooter/problem-solver; and issues management expert. There was also a technical aspect labelled communication technician. Senior communication managers not only manage departments, but are personally involved in implementing what might be regarded as high risk or complex communication work, for example, media relations on corporate earnings.

These studies extend earlier work that identified the key role of the senior practitioner as being environmental scanning, issues identification and evaluative research (Dozier and Broom, 1995).

Gregory (2008) in her empirical work identifying the competencies, or behaviours of board level communicators in both the public and private sectors in the UK, noted that skills and knowledge are not in and of themselves enough to secure seniority. Enacting the senior manager role is required and the visible demonstration of board level competencies is essential.

The role practitioners play in organisations is ultimately determined by senior management, but this is critically informed by how practitioners enact them. If they act principally as technicians, focused on implementation, then this is how they are likely to be regarded. If, however, they display an ability to make a more strategic contribution and become an essential asset and resource at a higher level in the organisation, then they are likely to find themselves being recognised at that level. Besides an ability to negotiate to an extent their own contribution within organisations, there are a number of other factors, however, that will influence the role of the public relations practitioner.

INFLUENCES ON PUBLIC RELATIONS' POSITIONING WITHIN ORGANISATIONS

Public relations practice varies from organisation to organisation and so does its position. There is no single blueprint for either the location, structure or the range of activities that should be undertaken, and priorities will differ in every organisation. There are a number of influences that will establish priorities for public relations in an organisation and determine the way it is practised and whether or not it fulfils a management role. Some of the most significant are given here.

Sector

Working in a well-established, relatively stable sector will be more conducive to planned and sustained long-term public relations programmes with public relations teams often having very senior representation in the organisation. The pharmaceutical and automobile sectors are typical examples. New, fast-growing and turbulent sectors such as the IT environment will require fast-moving, reactive as well as proactive programmes where the speed of development and the in-built capability to change direction quickly will be more of a prerequisite. In some such organisations, for example Google, there is also a very clear understanding of the importance of public relations and communication generally. It is not true that only established organisations have substantial and highly placed public relations functions, although working in different sectors requires different emphases.

A manufacturer or retailer of FMCGs could well require a heavier marketing communication focus whereas working for a trade or professional body may mean that membership communication or lobbying are the primary public relations activities. In both cases there is a solid argument for all these activities being strategic and integral to management thinking.

Public relations for the public or not-for-profit sector, where public accountability is critical, generates one way of working, whereas working in the private sector, where shareholder accountability and profits are key, generates a different set of priorities. Traditionally in the public sector public relations has not played a part in decision-making at the most senior level, but that too is changing as the public services find they are having to become more 'customer' focused and are ever more accountable for the way they spend public money.

Size

Small organisations tend to have small multi-skilled public relations departments, indeed public relations may be subsumed into another department, typically marketing, or be just a part of a single individual's job. It may even be outsourced to a freelance practitioner or consultancy. The range of activities may well be restricted and undertaken by a public relations generalist. This generalist typically has a heavy implementation role, with their ability to contribute at a strategic level being limited because of this. Alternatively, their input may have significant importance because the relationship-building role could be regarded as central to the operation of the whole organisation.

Large organisations often will have larger public relations departments. Within those departments the public relations remit may well be broken down into task or functional areas with individual specialists taking on specific roles (see Chapter 1). The size of the organisation and its range of public relations activities could well mean that the most senior practitioner is required to enact the manager role outlined earlier rather than being focused on implementation.

Publics and stakeholders

The range of public relations activities undertaken and the seniority of the senior post-holder can clearly be influenced significantly by the types of publics and stakeholders involved. A number of factors need to be considered:

- *Range*, that is, the breadth of publics involved. Some organisations, for example, niche manufacturers of space components, may have a limited range of publics, but these may have immense importance and require very senior public relations counsel and handling by perhaps a relatively small, but highly-placed team. Others, for example the DoH, have an extended range of publics and will need a variety of practitioners at a number of levels to deal with stakeholders varying from 'the general public' to the most senior government ministers.

- *Numbers and location.* Some organisations have publics that form fairly discrete and more readily manageable blocks; for example, car dealers have groups of customers, suppliers and employees. Others, for example, public relations consultants, will have potentially a large range of publics attached to each project and client they are handling. Some organisations have publics in a wide geographical area or covering several socio-economic and demographic bandings. Others focus on concentrated areas and groups. Clearly, a public relations function will have to be structured in a way that appropriately addresses these issues and seniority normally increases with complexity.

- *Influence and power.* There are publics that, although small in number, can have a disproportionate level of influence and power, for example, large institutional shareholders or pressure groups, especially if they enlist public support. Practitioners who work with these difficult to handle groups, or who are employed in industries that attract controversy, such as the drinks or arms industries, are usually working with the board or top management and tend themselves to be placed at senior manager or board level.

Development stage

Public relations activities are usually prescribed by the stage of development that the organisation has reached:

- *Start-up.* Organisations start small. The owners know suppliers, customers and employees. The public relations effort will often be one-to-one even where web-based communication is used and the emphasis is often on growth, thus marketing communication will be a priority. Nonetheless, because of the importance of personal relationships and the need to build trust based on those relationships, public relations could be at the heart of senior management and indeed be the responsibility of a founding director.

- *Growth.* More employees, customers and suppliers mean that one-to-one communication becomes difficult. At this stage a generalist public relations professional may be engaged to raise awareness of the company, its products and/or services. Internally, a formal and structured communication programme may begin. Activities such as government and financial public relations are likely to be low priority, if done at all. It is ironic, but at this stage often the public relations function become dis-established at senior levels. It becomes the responsibility of a professional who was not a founding director and who is not appointed at that level. The founders of organisations become more pre-occupied with growing and sustaining the business and their personal commitment to public relations slips down their priority list – it is a task to be done by other professionals on their behalf. It tends to become more tactical – in support of other functions rather than as a core management function in its own right. Of course this is not always the story, but there are many instances where it is.

• *Maturity*. Now the organisation is likely to be well established. The range of public relations activities will be expanding and could include financial public relations if a floatation is being considered. Employee communication is likely to be well developed, community relations will be a part of the agenda as the organisation takes on CSR programmes and developing and maintaining a cohesive corporate brand will be a priority. The in-house department of several staff, usually with specialisms, could well be complemented by engaging public relations consultancies to work in such areas as government affairs and investor relations. This is a critical point for public relations. Either the function is recognised as strategic with activity such as financial and employee relations exemplifying a more profound recognition of the importance of communication, or it remains as a 'tool' to be deployed in a support capacity and as largely a 'messenger' function used to attempt to convince others of the rightness of management decisions.

• *Decline*. Open organisations usually avoid decline by adjusting their activities or moving into new areas. However, organisations do move into periods of temporary or permanent decline, for example through takeover, legislative change or bad management. Here public relations has a key role to play in identifying issues in the environment in order to avert crises. Ultimately, there is nothing public relations can do if a business is non-viable. However, it is possible to cease trading or to look for a strategic alliance or takeover with dignity and with reputation intact, and public relations has a key role to play. Furthermore, if an organisation has been unsuccessful in defending itself against a hostile takeover bid, the public relations teams in the acquired and acquiring company have a critical management role in re-building the confidence and commitment of the acquired company's stakeholders and in building a new and successful corporate culture and identity.

PUBLIC RELATIONS AND LINKS TO OTHER FUNCTIONS

To complete this chapter on the role of public relations in the management of organisations it is important to look briefly at links to other functions. There are three areas where there are clear links and overlaps and occasional conflicts.

Public relations and marketing departments

It is the relationship between public relations and marketing that usually takes up most space and generates most heat. There have been extended and at times unprofitable debates about whether public relations is a part of marketing or marketing is a part of public relations: just three themes are identified for discussion here.

Terminology

To public relations people, public relations means managing the total communication of an organisation with ALL its publics and stakeholders. To most marketers public relations means publicity, that is, obtaining (usually) free media coverage in support of products and services, but increasingly, managing the social networking spaces (Rogers, 2007c). To distinguish between public relations in its broad strategic sense and public relations as a part of the marketing communications mix, the latter has been called marketing public relations (MPR).

Again, public relations professionals have tended to restrict the meaning of marketing to the notion of a profit-based exchange between an organisation and its customers. This is now an outmoded concept. Marketing has broadened its parameters to include relationships with internal customers (employees) and the broader external stakeholder community. As organisations become more open, more porous and greater integration of communication is required, the justification for distinct functions is less and less clear. Furthermore, employees are usually required to be multi-skilled and flexible. Even so, different professional outlooks do contribute diverse perspectives that are of value to organisations.

The fact is that in modern organisations the communicative functions need to be aligned and to work together to be effective. A visitor to a website is not at all concerned if it is the marketing or the public relations department who has designed it and put together its content, as long as information needs are satisfied. What is obvious is that internally there needs to be a clear understanding of the roles of each discipline and where the responsibilities lie along with a clear and consistent narrative that permeates all communication.

Encroachment

Public relations professionals fear 'encroachment' or the taking over of the discipline by non-specialists, especially marketers, but also management consultants. However, there is rejoicing when a public relations professional is made a chief executive or director of corporate communications (with marketing as a subservient partner). What is good for public relations is that as many people as possible from as many disciplines as possible are aware of the contribution that public relations can make in both strategic and tactical ways.

Status

For some public relations professionals it is important that public relations is seen to be a dominant and ascendant communication discipline. It is a sign that public relations has come of age that its unique contribution in stakeholder relations is recognised.

Some go further and say that the social media age requires the sophistication and knowledge of public relations professionals to handle the very complex world of internet communication, and the power plays between cyber groups and their interaction with the organisation. It is true that the dialogue skills that public relations staff acquire with a range of stakeholder groups will be invaluable, but organisations also need to sell or obtain support for their products and services to survive. A good general reputation, often maintained through sustained public relations activity, will attract customers and users of services. Good service and products enhance reputation. Organisations need both marketing and public relations.

Public relations and human resources departments

There are potential areas for co-operation and conflict between these domains:

- *Structural re-organisation.* The human resources department has a clear role vis-à-vis contracts and liabilities in situations where there are mergers, lay-offs, acquisitions and re-organisation. The communication aspects of these matters, including how to communicate with employees and external stakeholders, would normally involve public relations expertise.

- *Internal communication.* Control of employee communication and the division between what is rightly communicated by human resources and public relations are areas of potential debate.

- *Community relations.* This might involve communication with employees who are located within the local community and also with potential employees, and again requires careful assignment of responsibilities.

Again, as with marketing, it is important that each area recognises the expertise and contribution that they and their fellow professionals can make. It is also vital that, as with all good public relations, a frequent, honest dialogue is maintained with willingness on both sides to give ground in order for the organisation's best interests to be served.

Public relations and legal departments

When organisations are under threat or handling crises there is often a tendency or even a necessity to turn to legal counsel. Legal concerns normally revolve around liability and risk and the natural instinct in the past has been to close down communication with the legendary 'no comment'. Lawyers are concerned that what is said may rebound on the organisation and often point out that there is no requirement to say anything.

However, there is an increasing recognition that corporate responsibility requires a more helpful response and that public interest should be served by providing information. 'No comment' implies something to hide, and will be seen as obstructive or insensitive by many stakeholders.

Public relations professionals are aware that expressions and demonstrable actions of sensitivity, concern and responsibility enhance reputation. They see the value of openness and want to maintain dialogue. They are also acutely aware of the need to respond quickly to given situations – again the legal process usually takes time.

The recent trend has been for public relations professionals and legal advisers to work together in difficult situations. Product recalls and libel cases usually include both a public relations and a legal dimension and it is not uncommon for legal representatives and public relations professionals to speak on the same issue for an organisation. Again, the touchstone is a clear understanding of roles and a recognition of the contribution of each specialist, cemented by regular and open dialogue.

CONCLUSIONS

This chapter has argued that there is a requirement for public relations input at all levels in organisations. They can help surface and clarify organisational values and purpose, understanding what it takes for an organisation to maintain its 'license to operate'. As expert boundary-spanners, public relations professionals can play a key role in the dominant coalition by gathering and interpreting information from the external and internal environments and presenting this as strategic intelligence. On the basis of this, organisations can adapt and change or initiate a dialogue so that the continued support of their key stakeholding publics can be assured. Furthermore, public relations plays a key role in identifying issues and protecting the organisation from undue risks. It also promotes the organisation to its stakeholders with the expressed intent of gaining their support.

It has also been demonstrated that public relations practitioners' roles vary according to the remit they are given in organisations. If restricted to the tactician role, they will never provide the full benefits that an organisation can derive from public relations, that is, informed decision-making, good relationships with stakeholders and a solid basis on which to build a good and lasting reputation.

It is recognised that there are several influences on the role that public relations' plays in organisations, including their size, the nature of their stakeholders and the stage of organisational growth.

Finally, the link between public relations and other disciplines has been commented on. The plea is for mutual understanding, recognition, respect and co-operation with fellow professionals for the benefit of the organisation. In short there is a call for genuine public relations within the management context.

QUESTIONS FOR DISCUSSION

1 How helpful are the strategic management or systems approaches in explaining public relations as a strategic activity? What are their strengths and weaknesses? Are there other more appropriate approaches?

2 What information resources might you use to enable you to undertake a comprehensive EPISTLE analysis for your organisation?

3 What research techniques might you use to find out what your target publics think of your organisation?

4 Sometimes public relations practitioners are also called risk managers. What contribution do you think practitioners can make to risk management?

5 What training do you think practitioners need to be equipped to analyse information accurately?

6 What personal skills do you think a boundary-spanner requires?

7 What are the business environment and sectoral influences that would affect easyJet airlines and Routledge, the book publisher?

8 What factors might turn a stakeholder into a public? Give three examples.

9 Why do you think public relations is undervalued in some organisations?

10 What do you think is the most powerful contribution public relations can bring to an organisation?

FURTHER READING

Cornelissen, J. (2011) *Corporate communications* (3rd edition) (Chapters 2, 6, 8 and 16), Sage.

Cutlip, S.M., Center, A.H. and Broom, G.M. (2006) *Effective public relations* (9th edition), (Chapters 3 and 7), Prentice Hall.

Dozier, D.E., Grunig, L.A. and Grunig, J.E. (1995) *Managers guide to excellence in public relations and communication management*, Lawrence Erlbaum Associates.

Edwards, L. (2009) 'Public relations theories – an overview' in R. Tench and L. Yeomans (eds) *Exploring public relations*, (2nd edition), FT Prentice Hall.

Gregory, A. (2009) 'The management and organisation of public relations' in R. Tench and L. Yeomans (eds), *Exploring public relations* (2nd edition), FT Prentice Hall.

Gregory, A. (2010) *Planning and managing public relations campaigns: a strategic approach*, Kogan Page.

CHAPTER 5

Ethics, professionalism and regulation

Alison Theaker

CHAPTER AIMS

In this chapter we will begin with an examination of the main ethical doctrines – utilitarianism, deontology and rights theories and how they relate to public relations. This will lead to a discussion of how the industry is addressing the question of professionalism. Prerequisites of a profession are examined, and a number of them are addressed: entry qualifications, research and the body of knowledge; training and professional development; and codes of practice.

MORAL RULES

Societies have developed various kinds of social rules, such as legal rules, or even the rules of etiquette, which act as a framework or guide to behaviour. Moral rules and legal requirements have a very close relationship, but they are not necessarily synonymous. The 'race laws' in the US, or the 'apartheid laws' in South Africa, were eventually perceived to be so immoral that the only moral course was to disobey them. Clearly, in all societies, a majority of people accept that they *should* adhere to certain fundamental moral rules. Breaking these rules will meet with sanctions of various kinds, from disapproval and ostracism to, in certain cases, legal penalties. Moral rules help to structure social relations and many of the decisions that individuals and businesses make must take account of them.

ETHICAL THEORIES

Ethical theories, which argue that it is possible to know right from wrong, can be divided into two groups. There are those, such as utilitarianism, which assess moral right and wrong in terms of the consequences of actions – the *consequentionalist* perspective – and those, such as Kantianism and 'rights' theories, which do not – the *non-consequentionalist* perspective. From the consequentionalist perspective, the results of actions are assessed to make a moral judgement about those actions. From the non-consequentialist perspective, there is no immediate appeal to beneficial or harmful consequences to determine whether actions were morally right or wrong.

UTILITARIANISM

Utilitarianism is the notion that an action is right only to the extent that it causes more good than ill to be produced. The classic formulation of this position is that of the English philosophers Jeremy Bentham (1748–1832) and John Stuart Mill (1806–1873). Bentham and Mill identified utility with happiness. From a utilitarian perspective, actions are right to the extent that they maximise happiness or minimise unhappiness. Bentham was not particularly concerned with the happiness or unhappiness of individuals, the 'common good' was what was important. His *greatest happiness principle* proposes an action can be classified as good when it provides 'the greatest happiness for the greatest possible number'. Individuals assessing whether an organisation's actions could be justified from a utilitarian viewpoint must take into account their effect on society.

The common objection to utilitarianism is that it requires the promotion or maximisation of 'goods', such as economic growth, in order to achieve *utility* and permits the sacrificing of individuals and minorities 'for the greater good'.

This ethic may allow the telling of lies to protect the reputation of the corporation and consequently the jobs of employees. So, for example, if a company was saved from bankruptcy because its image and reputation were enhanced by lies told by company representatives to journalists this may well be seen as a permissible act. From a utilitarian point of view, the welfare of those human beings whose jobs had been saved is weighed against the breaking of trust with other human beings. However, whose happiness should be taken into account when judging whether an action is morally right?

DEONTOLOGY: AN ETHIC OF DUTY

Non-consequentionalist ethics argue that it is *motivation*, rather than *consequences* that is the determining factor in deciding whether actions are ethical or not. This perspective is generally referred to as *deontological*, from the Greek word for duty (*deon*), and is a doctrine that is primarily associated with the German philosopher Immanuel Kant (1724–1804). Kant argues that some actions are morally obligatory regardless of their consequences. According to Kant, an act is carried out from a sense of duty when it is performed in accordance with what he calls the 'categorical imperative'. Kant explains this as follows:

> I ought never to act except in such a way that I can also will [desire] that my maxim should become a universal law . . . Act in such a way that you always treat humanity . . . never simply as a means but always at the same time as an end.
>
> (1964: 70–96)

Thus, an action is only moral if you can make your reason for acting into a rule that everyone can follow (Dienhart 2000: 117–118).

Considering the case of lying to protect the reputation of the company in order to secure jobs, a deontological perspective would suggest first that you shouldn't be prepared to act in this way unless you are willing to live in a world where everyone can lie if they think it is justified. Second, lying for your own purposes is also immoral as it treats another human being as a means to getting what you want.

The chief problem is when there is a clash of categorical imperatives. One has a duty never to lie but what if by lying one is fulfilling one's duty to preserve the life of another human being? A frequently cited example is what do you do when the Gestapo ask you the whereabouts of the Jews you have hidden in your basement (Singer 1979). Kant actually insisted that if a murderer was to ask you the whereabouts of his or her intended victim you had a duty to tell him or her and not break the precept regarding lying.

UNIVERSAL RIGHTS

Deontology has much in common with theories that proclaim that there are 'rights' to which every human being is entitled. To infringe a person's human rights is to fail to treat them as a being with intrinsic value. This viewpoint adopts the position that individuals and minorities cannot be sacrificed to the common good as this would infringe their human rights.

The foundational assumption of 'rights' theories is that over and above mere human law there is an objective moral order, the 'natural law', which confers rights on all individuals. The generally agreed list was life, liberty, and sometimes, property. These were proclaimed as 'natural rights' bestowed on people by the natural law. They were rights that the sovereign or government could neither grant nor take away; people possessed them by virtue of being human. Governments could rule but they were bound 'contractually' to honour these basic rights.

John Locke (1632–1714) developed this into a social contract between people to set up and empower a government. This influential concept has been enshrined in various 'declarations', from the United States' 'Declaration of Independence' (1776) and the French 'Declaration of the Rights of Man' (1789) to Article 1 of the 'Universal Declaration of Human Rights' which states: 'All human beings are born free and equal in dignity and rights.'

Again, problems arise when two different 'rights' clash. In the case of lying to protect the reputation of the company and therefore jobs, how does one weigh the 'right' to work against the 'right' of people to be told the truth?

All of the classic ethical theories have inherent problems and it is fair to conclude that none of them seem satisfactory unless they are qualified by each other. Chryssides and Kaler (1993: 103) note:

> [T]he the aim of serving the common good has to be tempered by the admission of rights and responsibilities. Likewise rights and duties cannot generally be examined separately and neither can they be pursued regardless of any consideration of collective welfare.

CULTURAL RELATIVISM

Some perspectives on business ethics reject the idea that there are 'objective' standards of right and wrong. Pearson (1989) offers an argument that places public relations at the centre of efforts to construct a business ethic. According to this view, all 'truths' emerge out of a process of negotiation and debate. There are no objective standards of right and wrong, only subjective views, shaped by the social and cultural environment, on what constitutes right and wrong. This view contains the suggestion that public relations, as it plays 'the central role in corporate communication' also 'plays the major role in managing the moral dimension of corporate conduct' (1989: 111). This is similar to Grunig and Hunt's (1984) two-way symmetrical model.

However, there are several issues here that need to be resolved. First, the issue of 'power' seems to be largely ignored. It might be possible to think of a situation where all relevant groups are represented regarding an issue but it is difficult to imagine a situation where all the participants will be accorded equal status. The process of dialogue has to stop somewhere and a resolution to which everyone agrees might not be possible. A decision might have to be made that is only in the interests of the majority.

VARIETIES OF MORAL ETHOS

Snell (1993) builds on Kohlberg's models of individual moral development and relates it to organisations. He suggests that punishment avoidance is the lowest stage, where obeying those in authority is a guide to how to behave. Next, people may try and maximise their own personal advantage. Stage three shows an awareness of what others might approve of, and 'One gets things done by reading the unwritten rules' (1993: 89). Next, we might be aware of what those in our profession or organisation might approve of and decisions are subject to rules and regulations, laws or professional codes of conduct. Stage five is 'principled', where the organisation acts in a utilitarian way to produce the greatest happiness. At this stage, the organisation may take account of ecology and justice. Finally, the 'philosophical' stage sees the organisation valuing individual reflection and acting as a member of the world community.

Reidenbach and Robin (1991) also devised a way of analysing corporate behaviour. The amoral organisation has a culture that regards ethical violations as a cost of doing business, and that anything goes as long as one is not caught. A legalistic organisation regards the law as the arbiter of behaviour. They suggest that Nestlé and Philip Morris fit into this bracket. A responsive organisation may see that 'ethics pays' and start to encourage a more 'responsible citizen' attitude. However, at this stage, profit is still the main driver. An emerging ethical organisation wants to do the right thing, and a truly ethical organisation has a 'balanced concern for ethical and economic outcomes' (1991: 282).

Gregory (2009) discusses several duties that a public relations practitioner should pay attention to. A duty to one's own value system should come first and then the duty to the client. While practitioners represent organisations, there is no obligation to provide a service if this goes against one's own moral code. A duty to the public involves bringing all facts into the public domain to allow them to make up their own minds, and a duty to the profession calls for adherence to a common standard of behaviour or code of conduct. Finally, she raises the question of a duty to society's interests.

Gregory also points out that it may not be possible to serve all these interests at the same time. In 2006 she suggested using Potter's Box to weigh up conflicting values. This process of ethical reasoning first sets out to analyse the situation and then identify the different values that are important. She used the example of being asked to lie for an employer, and suggested that honesty, integrity and loyalty should be considered. Then the relevant ethical principles should be defined, which may include codes of conduct, the CIPR code, one's own ethics and any other regulatory issues. Finally, one should prioritise the various stakeholders affected and choose which ones are most important (Gregory 2006: 10–11). While this does not suggest a 'right' answer, as she points out, 'Ethics in public relations is important, complex and challenging' (Gregory 2009: 288).

PROFESSIONALISM

The *Concise Oxford Dictionary* definition of profession is 'a vocation or calling, especially one that involves some branch of advanced learning or science'. Some practitioners, who see themselves as creative rather than scientific, have resisted the general feeling that public relations is maturing into a profession. The growth of degrees at both undergraduate and Masters levels and the development of vocational qualifications have been greeted with suspicion rather than as evidence of professionalism.

Originally, the professions were law and medicine, and were practised by the sons of wealthy landowners after they had been to Oxford or Cambridge universities. Private income was necessary as the professions offered little pay. Later, specialised knowledge became the basis for entry. Elton (1993: 137) suggests the following prerequisites for a profession:

- an underlying discipline or cognitive base
- a body of practitioners
- a disciplinary organisation
- induction, training and licensing of members
- communication channels between members
- rewards and sanctions for members
- self-reflection, leading to improvement
- professionalism and regulation
- corporate evaluation and feedback
- a code of ethics and accountability to the profession
- corporate accountability to society
- quality assurance of the profession
- the ability to ensure high standards of remuneration.

The establishment of professional bodies worldwide has led to the introduction of codes of conduct and calls for regulation of certain parts of the industry, such as lobbyists. The IPR in the UK is over 70 years old, having been established in 1948 by a group of practitioners, with aims such as 'to provide a professional structure for the practice of public relations' and 'to enhance the ability and status of our members as professional practitioners'. Grunig and Hunt (1984: 4) put forward the view that PR was a young profession and only really started to approach that status in the 1980s:

> The profession has its roots in press agentry and propaganda, activities that society generally holds in low esteem. Most of its practitioners have little training in the social sciences. Few have been trained in public relations . . . We must admit that many people today who call themselves public relations practitioners still do not measure up to professional standards.

They continue:

> True professionals possess a body of knowledge and have mastered communication techniques that are not known by the average citizen. They also have a set of values and a code of ethics that discourage the use of their knowledge and technical skills for antisocial purposes.

L'Elang and Pieczka (2006a) review the historical development of calls for the professionalisation of public relations. They suggest that this was seen as a way to improve social respectability. They feel that the idea of public relations as the conscience of the organisation sounds moral and alluring, but that 'The role of public relations is necessarily partisan on behalf of client or employer, which makes it difficult to claim that the function necessarily operate in the public interest' (2006a: 421). Bowen (2007) disagrees. He suggests that public relations 'is ideally informed to counsel top management about ethical issues . . . (they) . . . facilitate trust which enhances the building and maintenance of relationships . . .the ultimate purpose of the PR function'.

One of the first protocols agreed by the Global Alliance of Public Relations Associations, founded in 2000, was a declaration of principles that stated that a profession's characteristics included:

- mastery of a particular intellectual skill through education and training
- acceptance of duties to a broader society than merely one's clients or employers
- objectivity
- high standards of conduct and performance.

The declaration also pledged the Alliance members to conduct themselves with 'integrity, truth, accuracy, fairness and responsibility to our clients, our client publics and to an informed society'. The Alliance currently comprises 45 member organisations. Its Global Protocol on Ethics in Public Relations is discussed later in this chapter.

In June 2000, the City of London Guild of Public Relations Practitioners was formed with the aims of promoting and maintaining 'excellence in the practice of our profession' and to 'support education and training of practitioners'. While a Guild could be thought of as a retrograde step, harking back to old fashioned cliques, the Guild felt that 'since the practice of public relations is an essential activity of all companies . . . within the City, it seemed entirely appropriate that PR professionals should . . . (create) their own Livery company'.

In January 2003, the IPR was awarded DTI funding to conduct a best practice overview of the UK PR industry. The objectives of the study were both to spotlight best practice and to show how public relations contributed to the national economy and the competitiveness of British industry internationally. The Chair of the IPR-DTI Steering Group, Michael Murphy, stated:

> Maintaining and improving the UK's competitive position demands an ethical, dynamic and strategic public relations industry that works to promote transparent corporate governance and a full understanding of the management of the relationships on which the 'bottom line' success of every business depends.
>
> (IPR 2003: 1)

In early 2005, the IPR was awarded its Royal Charter and became the Chartered Institute of Public Relations. (The Institute will henceforward be referred to as the CIPR throughout this chapter.) Director General Colin Farrington (2005) declared that this was 'an official recognition of the important and influential role that public relations plays in business and society'. He stated that such external third-party approval and endorsement was in the public interest as it indicated a significant degree of government regulation of the Institute. President Chris Genasi (2005) felt that Chartered status showed an 'emphasis on quality control and standards. It shows rigorous standards exist and are enforced and that we are serious about PR's future as a respected profession'. He announced a major social impact study intended to demonstrate both 'how PR makes a difference to the bottom line' and that 'our impact is benign and valuable, helping people to make informed choices'.

However, Cornelissen (2008: 168) suggests that an occupation will be seen as a profession only when it is socially valued as such. As we will see, public relations still has some way to go to achieve this condition.

There are many who regard the drive of public relations towards the status of a profession with extreme cynicism. Corporate Watch (www.corporatewatch.org.uk/?lid=412) suggests in its latest report on the industry '[this] . . . demonstrates a clear link between the rise of public relations and the increasing alienation of the public from mainstream politics [and] . . . how modern PR, in fact, subverts the fundamentals of democracy'.

Hill and Knowlton's representation of Citizens for a Free Kuwait, which drew the US into the Gulf War in 1991, has been well documented (Newsom *et al.* 2000: 59–60). A witness to the congressional hearing was found to have been the daughter of the Kuwaiti ambassador rather than a disinterested party, as claimed, and stories of Iraqi soldiers taking babies from incubators and leaving them to die were thus considered highly suspect.

PR Watch (www.prwatch.org/prissues/1998Q2) is also scathing about the intentions of practitioners to improve standards:

> Watching the public relations industry discuss ethics is a little like watching tourists from a foreign country attempting to speak a language they barely understand. They seem enthusiastic and sincere, and many of the right words come out of their mouths, but they just don't quite manage to make sense.

Cynicism about professional standards is not confined to the public relations industry. Cortese (2002) relates that while more companies are starting to develop 'sustainability reporting' on their environmental, health and safety and social performance, this lacks credibility and is viewed as 'greenwash'. Rising expectations of stakeholders and how corporations and governments are responding recur in several chapters of this book. McCusker (2006) suggests that the behaviour of a minority of practitioners is proving disastrous for public relations' professional reputation. He quotes a study by Texas State University that showed that negative connotations and commentary dominated media reports discussing public relations.

ENTRY QUALIFICATIONS

One element of a claim to a professional status is an emphasis on well-qualified practitioners. Years of training are necessary to become a doctor, lawyer or accountant, followed by more years of on-the-job training.

Public relations education is more developed in the US, where university-level courses date from 1920, with early courses in publicity being offered at the University of Illinois and Indiana University. The first PR course was offered in the journalism department of the New York University School of Commerce, Accounts and Finance, taught by Edward Bernays. Courses tended to be part of journalism qualifications, with students able to specialise in PR through taking options. The 1981 Commission on Public Relations Education recommended that the content of undergraduate and postgraduate courses should include mass communications, PR theories, media relations techniques, research methodology, case studies, work placements and PR management (Cutlip *et al.* 2006: 150). A further commission in 1987 added ethics, law and evaluation to the list (IPRA 1990). This was updated by the work of the Public Relations Education Commission set up by the Public Relations Society of America (PRSA) in 1999, which looked at the knowledge and skills that should be included in undergraduate and postgraduate courses. Business context, finance, communication theory and a supervised work placement in practice were felt important at degree stage, with the emphasis shifting to management science and research design at postgraduate level (Commission of PR Education 1999). Bowen (2007) refers to the Commission's 2006 report, which added that a consideration of ethics should pervade all content of public relations education. However, Bowen's own research for the International Association of Business Communicators (IABC) found that the majority of practitioners had received little academic study or training in ethics, and that 70 per cent felt ill prepared to counsel management on ethical decisions. Coleman and Wilkins (2009) reviewed a small sample of public relations practitioners using the Defining Issues Test (DIT). This is a measure of individual moral development based on Kohlberg's framework that had been administered to practitioners in several professions. They found that public relations practitioners ranked seventh highest among professionals, and above adults in general.

FIGURE 5.1 IPRA wheel of education

Source: Used by permission of the International Public Relations Association

The International Public Relations Association (IPRA) published guidelines for PR education in 1990. It stated that, 'public relations courses should be taught by individuals with a sound experience and understanding of both the academic and professional aspects of the field ... We also strongly recommend [teachers] to continue to develop their professional experience while they hold teaching appointments' (IPRA 1990).

Achieving Chartered status necessitates having a majority of practitioners with a relevant vocational qualification, as well as an emphasis on continuous professional development. A number of years ago, the CIPR tightened its entry requirements. From 1992, if they had fewer than 10 years' experience in public relations, all full members had to have a relevant vocational qualification or (since 2000) give a commitment to participating in the CIPR's continuous professional development scheme.

The CIPR approved six courses in 1989, including vocational, undergraduate, postgraduate and Masters programmes in the UK. The criteria for approval have been revised and updated, and cover the content of the course, the qualifications and experience of the teaching staff, links with industry, the inclusion of some form of practical work experience and the employment record of those who complete the course. Since then, the number of approved courses has risen to 35 BA programmes, and 20 Masters provided at 30 institutions. (A list of approved courses is available on www.cipr.co.uk.) On completion of one of these, there is still a requirement for three years' experience in PR before full membership is awarded. In addition, in 1998, the CIPR also introduced its own qualifications, the Advanced Certificate and Diploma, which provide a part-time route to qualification for those who are already working in the profession and who are unable to return to full-time education. On completion of the Diploma, a practitioner may progress directly to full membership. These courses are available at several approved venues (again, details are on the CIPR website). Applications to take the Diploma have shown an upward trend, so it seems that practitioners do wish to become qualified in their discipline. The Public Relations Consultants Association (PRCA) have also introduced their own qualifications, a Foundation, Advanced Certificate and Diploma. Each course is modular in structure and the emphasis is on practical skills.

There are still many in the industry who do not have a relevant qualification, although with the number of graduate entrants rising, there are few who do not have any qualifications at all. It is still possible to enter the profession without a degree but Wolf (2005) notes a 2001 survey that stated that PR was in the top three career choices for graduates. Some consultancies or in-house departments have a specifically designed graduate training scheme in public relations, but often training tends to be ad hoc. The CIPR's Professional Development Committee works to improve the standard of training provision within the profession. The Institute is recognised as a major supplier of training to the communications profession, and also accredits external employer based training and development. The CIPR also benchmarks the provision of commercial training organisations with its Approved Training Provider Kitemark™.

The IPR–DTI report mentioned above concluded that the CIPR 'should recommend work placements on all its managed and approved public relations undergraduate courses'. In addition, a work placement charter should be developed setting out the requirements and expectations on both sides for all organisations offering such placements.

Despite the changing picture with regard to the education of entrants, Montagu Smith (2006b) quotes Simon Anderson, Head of Corporate Communications at M&G as saying, 'In the long run there is nothing that beats good work experience.' An article in *PR Week* celebrating 'The grads are back', about graduate recruitment in UK consultancies still contained the opinion that, 'they look less favourably on a PR degree, which they still deem to be too theoretical', unlike their regard for English and history degrees – hardly practical courses (H. Gregory 2006). On the other hand, organisations that have relationships with their local degree course often find that they make a huge saving on recruitment advertising and also on training as

PR graduates come equipped with practical skills as well as a foundation of relevant theoretical knowledge. Research for the CIPR in 2000 found that 85 per cent of graduates with approved degrees found employment in PR or related industries. Ralph Tench, then Course Leader at LMU, pointed out that 'a history graduate from Oxford does not arrive in the job with an understanding of what it is about. Our graduates are able to start working straight away' (Montagu Smith 2006b).

L'Etang and Pieczka (2006a) suggest that education has been seen as a tool to achieve status, but that there is a reluctance to identify the abstract knowledge required to practice. Thus they feel that the CIPR has always deferred the decision on compulsory qualifications in favour of allowing an experiential route as well, and that the emphasis has been on skills rather than academic rigour.

CIPR CEO Jane Wilson adds a note of caution about pressing for graduate entry:

> If degrees or postgraduate study are the (only) recognised methods of entry, it will exclude those who do not have these opportunities open to them. This would mean that we will not be a profession which is reflective of the society we represent.

RESEARCH AND THE BODY OF KNOWLEDGE

There has been a rather uneasy link between academic research, PR theory and practice in the UK, with many practitioners resistant to the idea that PR could be taught. Cutlip *et al.* (2006: 152) suggest that 'Few practitioners subscribe to or read the field's research journals.' The US Commission on Public Relations Education reported:

> Most public relations educators – not having attained PhD level – have not been required to do research . . . most are teaching skills courses that have little relationship to basic research. Public relations practitioners . . . have generally been too busy at their jobs to engage in basic research, not connected with specific public relations tasks.
>
> (IPRA 1990: 21)

There are signs that the body of knowledge in PR is growing and that academics and practitioners are more willing to enter into a dialogue, but progress is slow. The professional associations are also taking upon themselves the role of assembling case studies and links to research on their websites. Members of the CIPR, PRCA and PRSA in the US can all search databases of best practice. While the majority of the information is practice-based, the CIPR has a strong academic membership and close ties with UK and overseas centres for learning. CIPR research can be found on the CIPR website. The European Public Relations Education and Research Association (EUPRERA), an association that brings together European academics in the field, supports a variety of academic projects. A Delphi survey was undertaken in 2000 to attempt to draw up a common definition of the practice, although it concluded that 'it is difficult to find any pattern in the naming of the field'. This research led to further definitions of the practice and parameters of public relations, suggesting that there were four characteristics of European public relations:

- *reflective* – analysing standards in society to enable the organisation to adjust its own standards
- *managerial* – developing plans and maintaining relationships with publics
- *operational* – carrying out communication plans
- *educational* – helping the members of the organisation to become effective communicators.

van Ruler and Verčič 2002

Professor Betteke van Ruler believes that these are important steps to demonstrate a European approach to the area: 'We need a European body of knowledge. There is no point in imitating the US way.' She also thinks that,

the general level of academic research on public relations in Europe is too low. I am convinced that more research will lead to an increased professionalism ... We all need to be on the same team, whether we are academics or practitioners.

(Hansen 2003)

Cornelissen (2008: 171) suggests that 'the development of the body of knowledge is the crucial plank in the field's quest for professional status'. Cornelissen recommends increasing the level of academic research into crucial questions in communication management and greater links between academics and practitioners in order to produce reflective practitioners using research-based knowledge.

TRAINING AND PROFESSIONAL DEVELOPMENT

Bines and Watson (1992) suggest three models of professional education. The first is apprenticeship or pre-technocratic, where professional education takes place mainly on the job, with some associated learning through day release at a relevant institution. The emphasis is on practical techniques. The technocratic model is more associated with professions and consists of a systematic knowledge base founded on academic disciplines, the application of that base to practice, and supervised placements in practice. This most closely reflects the systems of CIPR-approved courses mentioned above. The third model, or post-technocratic, emphasises professional competence and bridges the gap between education and employment. There is still a debate on what constitutes competence and there are difficulties in identifying the competences needed.

To address the issue of lifelong learning, in April 2000 the CIPR introduced Developing Excellence, a continuous professional development (CPD) scheme. This scheme, while voluntary, aims to encourage members to continue their development by undergoing vocational training, achieving subsequent academic qualifications, participating in the work of the Institute and contributing expertise to public relations students.

By ensuring that its members are properly qualified and engaged in current training, the CIPR aims to ensure that they will be professional in their business conduct and that clients and employers will be able to use the standard of membership as an indicator that they are employing a competent practitioner.

Four suggested levels of development were devised:

- *Level 1* – PR executive
- *Level 2* – account manager or PR officer
- *Level 3* – account director or head of department
- *Level 4* – board member, managing director, chief executive.

Particular skills are included at each level, from basic media training at Level 1 to strategic issues management and board skills at Level 4. All CIPR workshops carry an indication of their level, and the overall structure can be used by both individuals and companies when planning their training requirements. Courses of the Approved Training Providers are also linked to level and subject. The framework has been constantly updated, and contains an indication of the skills needed to ensure that PR practitioners can use new technology. All members can now create and manage their own integrated CPD programme via the CIPR website.

Francis Ingham, PRCA Chief Executive, felt that training was a key issue in staff retention:

> Employees now expect to receive significant, quality training as part of their terms of engagement. As the recovery began, and the labour market started to move once more, employers started seriously to re-examine their training offering, to help keep staff.

In 1998, PRCA members were spending only half a per cent of their payroll on training, whereas management consultants recommend about 8 per cent. By 2008, that figure was 0.68, which translated to an average spend of £728 per employee.

The area of training and development was one which was highlighted in the IPR–DTI study. Less than half of consultancies and in-house departments had formal training and development programmes and it was felt that there was a 'need for public relations practitioners to be more capable across a wide range of competency areas' (IPR 2003: 4). There was a need for a 'more rigorous approach to training and skill acquisition, particularly management skills at middle and senior levels' (ibid.: 7). There was a lack of appreciation of the need for planning, research and evaluation (PRE) skills, which it was felt was holding the profession back from being seen as a strategic rather than tactical discipline.

The Guild of PR Practitioners is developing a mentoring programme for senior practitioners, and the PRCA also has a similar scheme. In 2005, Cowlett (2005b) stated that while places on training courses were up by 20 per cent, consultancies took up fewer than a third of places. By 2010, Frances Ingham felt the situation had changed dramatically:

> We launched practical, skills-focussed training in early 2008, responding to a feeling that the existing offering in the market was theoretical rather than practical, and over-priced. The take up was encouraging, and a year later we launched online training, via interactive webcasts. Our most popular webcasts are 'attended' by in excess of 100 people. Agencies are no better or worse than in house teams at investing in training; and PR is no worse than many other industries.

PROFESSIONAL BODIES AND REPRESENTATION

The PRCA is the trade body for consultancies in the UK, and members are companies rather than individuals. It opened membership up to in-house teams in late 2009, and freelancers in 2010. It has strict criteria for membership. While the CIPR has a Code of Conduct, the PRCA has a Professional Charter and Consultancy Management Standard (CMS) that its agency members are obliged to follow. An in-house version is being developed now, at the request of in-house members. We will look at the content of these codes below. One problem with the raising of standards within PR is that these organisations do not represent all of those working in PR in the UK. The CIPR has over 9,500 members, while the PRCA has 235 agency members, and in excess of 50 in-house teams, such as Marks & Spencer, Visa, the Metropolitan Police and Royal Mail. This represents another 8,000 practitioners. The latest figures quoted by the CIPR put the size of the industry at 48,000, with an annual turnover of £6.5 billion, making a significant contribution to the economy (Ingham 2005). While membership has been increasing, the professional bodies together still account for just over a third of practitioners. The requirements for qualifications and professional and ethical behaviours can only apply to association members.

Other influential professional bodies include the PRSA, which with 21,000 members is the largest association of individual practitioners in the world. It was founded in 1948 by the merger of the National Association of Public Relations Counsel and the American Council on Public Relations. In 1966, the PRSA merged with the American Public Relations Association to form a strong national association. The PRSA signed an agreement with the CIPR in April 2000, which stated the intention of both bodies to cooperate in the fields of professional practice, training and education.

The IPRA was founded in 1955 with only 15 members in five countries. Small by national association criteria, the organisation represents around 1,000 members in 100 countries.

The CIPR is a member of the Confédération Européenne de Relations Publiques (CERP), which has 15 member organisations, and of the Global Alliance, mentioned above. The PRCA is also a member of the International Communications Consultants Organisation (ICCO), which has 1,400 member companies in 28 countries.

CODES OF PRACTICE

The CIPR Code of Conduct, which was updated after a major consultation in 2000, covers members' practice of PR: how the practitioner deals with the media, the public, employers, clients and colleagues. The Code emphasises 'honest and proper regard for the public interest, reliable and accurate information'. The member is required to 'maintain the highest standards of professional endeavour, integrity, confidentiality, financial propriety and personal conduct' and to bring neither the Institute nor the profession into disrepute. Professional activities must be conducted with 'honest and responsible regard for the public interest', and any conflicts of interest must be declared to clients as soon as they arise. Members must 'deal honestly and fairly in business' and 'never knowingly mislead clients, employers, colleagues and fellow professionals about the nature of representation'.

Members are expected to 'take all reasonable care to ensure employment best practice', which includes 'giving no cause for complaint of unfair discrimination', and safeguarding confidences. Members must also be aware of legislation and regulation in all countries where they practice. Maintaining professional standards specifically encourages members to undertake the Institute's continuous professional development programme and to encourage employees and colleagues to become members also. The Code sets out a highly detailed process governing complaints relating to professional conduct.

The PRCA's Professional Charter covers similar ground, and indeed many of the clauses are identical. The Charter is written with its member consultancies in mind. Terms can be negotiated on the basis of the complexity of the issue and the difficulties associated with its completion; the specialised skills needed and the time to be spent; the amount of documentation needed; the place and circumstances where the work is to be carried out; and the value of the task to the client. Accuracy, openness about interests and regard to the public interest are also stressed. The PRCA has specific codes that relate to investor relations, healthcare and parliamentary advice, which are in addition to the provisions of the Professional Charter. The specifics of these codes are concerned with the particular environments and sensitivities that exist. There are recommendations for those in investor relations about dealing with price-sensitive information. Healthcare professionals are directed to legislation and other relevant codes, and must ensure balanced and accurate information is given. Public affairs practitioners have an extensive code that relates to their conduct towards MPs and clients. Both the CIPR and the PRCA gave evidence to a series of Parliamentary Committees on Standards in Public Life (see below). This led to the establishment of the UK Public Affairs Council (UKPAC) comprising the PRCA, CIPR and Association of Professional Political Consultants (APPC).

The Global Alliance agreed in April 2003 that all member associations would standardise their codes of ethics by the end of 2005. The 2009 Annual Report stated that 'a majority' of members had filed the necessary certification. All new members are expected to certify their compliance with the code within 12 months of joining. The minimum elements that are to be included are:

- an obligation to protect and enhance the profession
- to be informed about practices which ensure ethical conduct
- to actively pursue professional development
- to define what public relations can and cannot accomplish
- to counsel members on ethical decision-making
- a requirement that members observe the recommendations of the Protocol.

Clauses on advocacy, honesty, integrity, expertise and loyalty are also required. The Alliance made a further bid to talk the language of business with the Stockholm Accords, which set out principles for corporate governance, management and sustainability as well as communications (Global Alliance 2010).

The IPR–DTI study recommended that the CIPR should set up a UK Public Relations Industry Corporate Social Responsibility Report and, together with the PRCA, improve communication of industry ethics and promote their ethical clauses (IPR 2003: 6).

Tobin (2004) points out that despite these ideals, the CIPR is not a judicial body and has no teeth legally. UK business culture prefers voluntary codes of practice to legislation.

REGULATION OF PRACTICE

Both associations have committees to which complaints can be made if a breach of the codes of conduct is discovered. Most of the problems that the PRCA committee has had to investigate have been cases resulting from poor systems of consultancy management, rather than problems of bad behaviour or ethics. To remedy this, the CMS was devised and, by the end of 2000, all PRCA members had to conform to it or be disqualified from membership. In 2003, the CMS was revised and now all new members must complete the process within 12 months of being admitted. There are eight elements in the CMS, and member consultancies must score at least 50 per cent in each section to pass with an overall score of 75 per cent. The first element concerns the business plan, the next financial systems. Other sections cover audited accounts, adherence to the Professional Charter and campaign evaluation. Client satisfaction must be measured and service delivery monitored. A commitment to training and development is also included. Essentially, the CMS combines elements of both the ISO 9000 benchmark and IP standards.

Quality management, management responsibility, resource management and measurement, and analysis and improvement are stressed. In addition, consultancies are reassessed every two years to ensure that they are keeping up with the standards set. The CMS has now been adopted by 15 countries, franchised from PRCA via ICCO to national associations.

Some of the problem has lain with the question of professional competence. 'Too many PR consultancies still fit the stereotype of being excellent, creative outfits, but lacking in business skills. The CMS is designed deliberately to address that issue,' says Francis Ingham. 'Years ago the PRCA and the IPR were old boys' clubs, now that is long gone. A lot of people have put a lot of work into developing professional standards, and we are committed to upholding them.'

The CIPR changed the conditions for invoking an investigation by its Professional Practices Committee (PPC) in 2006 (Lewis 2006). The PPC can now act proactively if a member's poor conduct is apparent, rather than waiting for a complaint. Martin Horrox (2010), a consultant appointed to work with the PPC, stated that the main focus would be to effect agreement through information and conciliation: 'If a complaint reaches the committee, I have already failed in part of my job.' However, penalties still only range from a public reprimand to expulsion from the Institute. Offenders could still practise public relations.

Lukaszewski (2010) pointed out on the PRSA website that codes were 'aspirational, educational, procedural practice guidance', and that legislation was required to force compliance. He raised the question, 'Do we want to be known for the numbers of practitioners we try to kick out each year, or by the thousands of practitioners we help to be more ethical and professional?' Horrox (2010) felt that complaints mostly arose from disappointment, when clients had been promised more than was delivered.

The question of compulsory registration and licensing has long been debated. In 1993, Bernays was a proponent of licensing of practitioners in the US as a way to enhance credibility (Cornelissen 2004). However, a benchmarking exercise carried out by the Global Alliance in 2004 called for standardisation to be resisted (O'Connor and Falconi 2004). Global general principles and local specific applications were recommended rather than rules and constraints affecting practice. Tobin (2004) regarded the drive for Chartered status as effectively self-regulation and that licensing could both extend membership of the professional institutions and improve credibility of practitioners. However, Molleda and Athaydes' (2003) work on licensing in Brazil, Nigeria and Panama found that the licensing process was bureaucratic and that practitioners used other titles to avoid regulation. The law tended to be violated without punishment and there was still a problem of 'quacks' giving the profession a bad name. Even Bernays (1992) had admitted that licensing did not ensure competence.

In the past some have claimed that the problem may often lie with clients or employers. Jane Wilson, CEO of the CIPR felt that individual practitioners needed to take responsibility:

> We must stop referring to the profession and its ethics or ambitions for greater professionalism as if they were abstract notions that are someone else's responsibility. We must each play our part in demonstrating improved standards. Only then will the industry change. If we believe that minimum moral and ethical standards should apply then we must adhere to them. To say that we do something because it's what the client wants belittles the skills we bring and shows that we are not properly communicating our value. Would a Chartered Accountant agree to manipulate figures if a client asked? No, because there would be too much at risk professionally for the individual.

The CIPR consulted the Department of Education and Skills to develop a framework for Chartered Practitioner status, which it introduced in 2008, its sixtieth anniversary year. The process of achieving such status involves three stages, including a detailed application form on which the applicant sets out how they have achieved the criteria of strategic counsel, leadership, learning, innovation and communication. The final stage requires the submission of a 3–4,000 word piece of critical reflection. Jane Wilson, CEO of the CIPR, stated,

> Chartered Practitioner is a senior professional status that recognises and celebrates professional expertise. It is not only a benchmark for those working at a senior level, but a 'gold standard' to which the CIPR believes that all PR practitioners should strive to reach. Chartered Practitioner will be awarded to CIPR members who can demonstrate an outstanding level of professional practice and knowledge, and a commitment to continuous professional development.

To date there are 28 Chartered Practitioners.

CREDIBILITY OF PRACTITIONERS

'Honesty begins at home. It is synonymous with trust and trust is the lubricant that makes our practice function.' Despite this aspiration, John Budd (1994: 5) relates the example of Hill and Knowlton chief, Robert Dilenschneider, who in 1988 warned against:

> twisting the facts 'a little'; unquestionably doing the unquestionable thing; ducking the truth, doing anything you knew 'in your bones' was wrong. Two years later [he] . . . advocates an array of highly questionable stratagems . . . publicly attack the competitor; steal his best people; insert Quislings into his ranks; and pre-empt his access to the media.

We have already noted Hill and Knowlton's involvement in questionable campaigns above. The conduct and regulation of lobbyists has been a key issue in raising questions about the ethical conduct of those engaged in public affairs. Back in 1956, Tim Traverse Healey warned that 'the further development of public relations depends on the confidence of the community in the integrity of our practitioners' (quoted in Budd 1994: 4). In the run-up to the UK general election in 1997 a number of MPs lost their seats as a result of revelations in the media that some firms had allegedly been involved in paying them to raise questions in the House, while Ian Greer Associates, a long-standing firm of lobbyists, was forced out of business. Subsequently, one of Labour's parliamentary aides, Derek Draper, was accused of boasting that he could secure access to ministers for those who wanted to make their case. He was forced to resign. The various cases caused a media frenzy about 'spin doctors' and lobbyists, with calls for more regulation and slurs cast upon public relations practitioners of all kinds, not just those engaged in public affairs.

In October 1994, the then Prime Minister, John Major, set up the Committee on Standards in Public Life under Lord Nolan. Its first report recommended a ban on advocacy by MPs on behalf of companies and organisations with which they had a paid relationship.

The Committee continued under the new Labour government with Lord Neill as chair. Submissions were made to the Neill Committee by the CIPR, the PRCA and the APPC. The three bodies adopted supplementary and virtually identical codes to govern practice in this area. The APPC also made clear that its members were not permitted to have financial arrangements with members of parliament or peers.

The Public Administration Select Committee (PASC) published its report on *Lobbying: Access and influence in Whitehall* in December 2008, recommending that a public register of lobbyists should be created. The first meeting of the UKPAC took place in July 2010, with representatives from the three trade bodies and three independent members. Also in July, Deputy Prime Minister Nick Clegg announced that legislation would be introduced to make the register statutory.

However, in February 2007, in the *PR Week* Ethics Debate, the motion 'PR has a duty to tell the truth' was defeated. The editor, Danny Rogers, paradoxically commented, 'the fact that PR people admit they need to lie occasionally is a sign of growing honesty and confidence in what they do' (Rogers 2007a). Booth (2010) suggested that London was the reputation laundering capital of choice and that public relations firms were earning millions of pounds by promoting foreign regimes with the worst human right records. Lord Bell defended his company's work by saying, 'I am not an international ethics body. We do communications work. If people want to communicate their argument we take the view that they are allowed to do so.' CIPR President Jay O'Connor (2010) pointed out that organisations had the right to present a viewpoint and practitioners could effect change for the good by engaging with them. However, they had to 'be prepared to walk if it can't be done'.

PROFESSIONAL OR NOT?

In conclusion, PR possesses several of the prerequisites to be considered a profession, and the professional bodies show a clear desire to address the issues of entry, training and conduct of practitioners. Cutlip *et al.* (2006: 148) state 'to qualify as a profession, practitioners – both individually and collectively – must act as moral agents in society'.

This message must also be communicated to the relevant stakeholders. The DTI report concluded that there was an opportunity for public relations practitioners to change their role to that of strategic advisers, although there was much work to be done on improving practitioners' competences.

Jane Wilson added, 'Another key aspect of *professionalising* public relations is to educate beyond the profession. It is not enough for us all to be in agreement about what constitutes best practice. The real measure of success will be when the perception of what constitutes good professional public relations is understood and demanded by wider business and social communities. We should actively bring those outside the profession into the debate and get their understanding of what professionalism would look like.'

When presenting at the PRIA conference in 2007, the author suggested that the answer to the questions, 'Can public relations ever be a profession? And does it matter?' should be 'No' and 'No'. However, as then CIPR Director Colin Farrington said, 'There is nothing which detracts from the basic view that people should behave professionally, and I think we all know what that means.' Bowen (2007: 67) added a quote from Plato, 'Good people do not need laws to tell them to act responsibly, while bad people will find a way round the laws.'

QUESTIONS FOR DISCUSSION

1 Should the professional public relations associations in the UK merge to increase their representation of the industry?

2 Do you feel that 10 years' experience is equivalent to the completion of an academic course in public relations? Should the CIPR drop this option to qualify for membership?

3 Has Chartered status for the CIPR improved the image of public relations?

4 Would mandatory licensing improve the reputation of public relations?

5 Is the Global Protocol on Ethics realistic?

6   What are the benefits of membership of a professional association to public relations practitioners? To their clients or employers?

7   Does a voluntary system of CPD address the need for practitioner competency? If not, how might that need be addressed?

8   How does the Chartered Practitioner designation affect the perception of public relations? Do the requirements allow for the demonstration of competency in practice?

9   Discuss Farrington's opinion that we all know what behaving professionally means. What do you think constitutes professional behaviour?

10   How might professional behaviour be promoted within the industry?

NOTES

Unless otherwise stated, quotes are taken from interviews with the author.

Thanks to Ian Somerville for the discussion of ethics at the beginning of this chapter.

FURTHER READING

Cornelissen, J. (2008) *Corporate communications*, Sage.

Gregory, A. (2009) 'Ethics and professionalism in public relations' in R. Tench and L. Yeomans (eds) *Exploring public relations* (2nd edition), FT Prentice Hall.

Harrison, M. R. (2005) *An introduction to business and management ethics*, Palgrave Macmillan.

Tobin, N. (2004) 'Can the professionalisation of the UK public relations industry make it more trustworthy?', *Journal of Communication Management*, 9 (1), pp. 56–64.

Part II

Strategic public relations

CHAPTER 6

Public relations and corporate communication

Emma Wood

CHAPTER AIMS

This chapter uses a case study to raise some of the moral or ethical debates surrounding public relations practice as well as demonstrating the importance of a strategic approach to corporate communication.

Corporate communication has been defined in a number of different ways – in relation to public relations perhaps the most significant is as the process of establishing trust, social capital and legitimacy.[1] Another popular conceptualisation is the functionalist view that corporate communication is about 'harmonising' all communication within an organisation to ensure consistency with corporate missions and objectives – a view that is contested by critical scholars:

> Whilst it may seem appealing to align all messages inside and outside an organization, a deeper examination of this position reveals logical, practical and even ethical problems. With our organizational approach, we want to demonstrate that plurality and diversity of opinions and expressions are necessary for organizations operating in complex environments and having multiple constituencies.
>
> (Christensen, Morsing and Cheney 2008 : ix)

Consequently, it is argued here that corporate communication should be seen less as harmonising all communications and more as establishing *meaningful* (Christensen, Morsing and Cheney 2008) values communicated in a way that encourages the organisation (and organisational members) to *behave* in a way that is consistent (but not homogeneous) with them in order to build *social capital* and establish *legitimacy* thereby encouraging stakeholder support (expressed through local communities being open to corporate plans, employees feeling highly motivated, top performers seeking employment with an organisation, investors wanting to invest and legislators not jumping to introduce punitive legislation *as well as* potential consumers being more open to promotional messages aimed at getting them to purchase goods or use services).

Corporate communication is such a multi-faceted practice that the use of a case study has been selected here as one of the best ways of illustrating the different dimensions – and the importance to the organisation of managing these effectively. For anyone wanting to justify the *strategic* importance of effectively managed corporate communication in *commercial* terms, the case study used demonstrates the impact that poorly managed communication can have on 'the bottom line'. But it goes further than this and shows the importance of ethical, transparent, decision making, of building social capital or trust and relationships with a whole range of stakeholders – and how effective communication with stakeholders other than shareholders/funders is important and can significantly affect an organisation's image, reputation and consequently its ability to conduct its business effectively. The analysis goes further than providing a functional 'how to' guide and points to some of the conceptual frameworks that can be used to guide decision making and practice in this area. It illustrates what can happen if dialogic relationships with key stakeholders are ignored. This case has had a real impact on senior thinking about corporate public relations and is often referred to as the 'Brent Spar' of the financial sector.

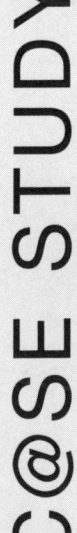

THE BANK OF SCOTLAND

The Bank of Scotland (BoS) is a leading UK clearing bank, headquartered in Edinburgh. Following its merger in 2001 with Halifax plc, it has been known as HBOS (Halifax Bank of Scotland). It has 22 million customers (two out of five UK householders) and is the largest mortgage and savings provider in the UK. The company currently employs around 65,000 people in the UK, and 73,500 worldwide. It issues a range of credit and charge cards (including cards to supporters of affinity groups ranging from charities to universities) and is known for its pioneering electronic and telephone home and office banking service.

In the early part of this century, its community mission statement clearly signified a stakeholder approach to its business:

> Throughout Bank of Scotland's 306-year history, we have been keenly aware of our responsibilities as good corporate citizens. We know that our own business will be stronger if the communities where our existing and future customers live and work are stable and healthy.
>
> (www.bankofscotland.co.uk: September 2003)

Its 'statement of business principles' specified that:

> In three centuries of doing business, we have learned how to win trust in all of our relationships – and how vital it is to retain that trust. The highest standards of business conduct and fair dealing in all our operations is our aim.
>
> (www.bankofscotland.co.uk: September 2003)

It seems highly significant then that following the Robertson debacle (the case explained below), these principles were changed. Instead of referring to trust and fair dealing, the statement of business principles or 'The Way We Do Business (WWDB), our commitment to our stakeholders about the standards and values we aspire to deliver' became:

> Our main contribution to society is the value we can add through our success in business. We seek to be a positive influence on those social and environmental issues which, having listened responsibly to our shareholders, customers, colleagues and suppliers, we think are important, for example upholding human rights.
>
> We will observe the laws and regulations of all countries in which we operate, not just in the letter but also the spirit. We will not countenance bribery, corruption, insider trading or the concealment of conflicts of interest.
>
> (www.hbosplc.com/community/includes/WWDB)

The statement doesn't clarify who the 'we' is in terms of the people who will determine which issues are important and which aren't. Clearly not the colleagues or other stakeholders who will be listened to, but will not be part of the decision-making process. One can assume then that it is a top-down process with decisions made by a 'dominant coalition'.

Perhaps the bank changed its rhetoric in response to accusations of hypocrisy regarding its behaviour in relation to the US TV evangelist, Pat Robertson.

The bank and the TV evangelist

In March 1999, the bank announced its intention to team up with Pat Robertson to set up a direct bank in the US. The new bank would operate only through telephones and computers.

Robertson is well known in the US as a religious broadcaster, entrepreneur and rightwing politician who ran unsuccessfully for the US presidency in 1988. His Christian Broadcasting Network provides programming by cable,

C@SE STUDY

broadcast and satellite to approximately 180 countries with a mission of converting 500 million people to Christianity. As direct banking was less developed in the US than in the UK, the combination of BoS expertise and Robertson's access to a vast network of potential customers seemed to guarantee a highly profitable business venture.

Soon after the announcement, the press published details about Robertson and his extreme right-wing views. Robertson's attacks on homosexuals, feminists, Muslims, Hindus and other religious groups were reported, particularly in the Scottish media. Pressure groups were quick to publicly denounce Robertson, and the bank for being associated with him. Utilising the internet and other media, these groups coordinated attacks on the deal. They set up websites with links to the media and the bank to help the public to learn more about the issue and to register their condemnation. Direct action included calls for bank accounts to be closed and protesters handcuffing themselves to the bank's headquarters.

The bank remained adamant that it would not succumb to public or media pressure. Its PR strategy seemed to alternate between refusing to comment and blaming the media for distorting or exaggerating Robertson's views. Robertson's approach was similar; in addition he attempted to place legal restrictions on press reporting of his opinions. Far from diminishing interest in or coverage of the issue, this resulted in the media becoming more entrenched. Rather than being frightened off by threats of legal action, the media substantiated their attacks with evidence of Robertson's comments, using direct quotes from his TV shows, books and an open letter that claimed: 'The feminist agenda is not about equal rights for women. It is about a socialist anti-family political movement that encourages women to leave their husbands, kill their children, practice witchcraft, destroy capitalism and become lesbians' (*The Scotsman*, 24 April 1999).

The bank was reported to believe that these views should not affect their potentially lucrative joint venture. Peter Burt, BoS Chief Executive, defended the deal by drawing a distinction between the intrinsic moral and ethical values of a commercial decision and the ethics of the individuals involved: 'An individual's personal religious views do not form the basis on which the Bank makes its business and commercial judgement. And nor should it' (*The Scotsman*, 22 April 1999). However, key opinion formers disagreed and major institutions began to publicly register their disapproval of the bank's association with Robertson.

The logical extension of this disapproval would be for these key institutions to disassociate themselves from the bank. Media coverage became dominated by reports of city councils, universities, trade unions, charities and churches threatening to close their accounts. Several high

C@SE STUDY

profile MSPs were happy to be named in condemning the deal and called for the Scottish Parliament's account to be removed from the bank if the deal went ahead (*The Scotsman*, 2 June 1999).

The bank's defence of Robertson ceased in mid-May when he was reported as condemning Scotland as a 'dark land' overrun by homosexuals (*The Scotsman*, 2 June 1999). In early June the bank announced that it was abandoning its joint venture. A joint statement said:

> Dr Pat Robertson and Peter Burt, following a meeting in Boston yesterday, agreed that the changed external circumstances made the proposed joint venture . . . unfeasible. In reaching this agreement Dr Robertson expressed regret that the media comments about him had made it impossible to proceed.
>
> (*The Scotsman*, 7 June 1999)

The announcement was seen as terse by some and interpreted as still blaming media distortion for the failed venture rather than the bank fully condemning Robertson's views. *The Scotsman* deemed it an 'apology that leaves a lot to be desired' (7 June 1999), the *Guardian*, 'a grudging, gritted-teeth apology' (19 June 1999). Tim Hopkins of gay rights campaigners Equality Network represented a number of views with his comments:

> People are still very angry with the Bank and it will have its work cut out getting back their confidence. We would like to see the Bank reaching out to minority groups to rebuild its reputation for equal opportunities, which before the Pat Robertson business was very good.
>
> (*The Scotsman*, 7 June 1999)

It was only after a more full and personal apology was given to shareholders at the annual general meeting that public opinion was reported as mellowing towards the bank. At the AGM, the bank's deputy-governor, Sir John Shaw, said:

> The board of the Bank regrets any concern to customers, proprietors [shareholders] and staff caused by the events of the past few weeks. The Bank failed to predict the strength of public reaction after announcing the deal with Dr Robertson. The last straw came when he described Scotland as an overly 'dark land'. We have a long-standing commitment to ethical values, tolerance, equal opportunities, and nondiscrimination in all our dealings. Determination to uphold these principles as we develop our business world-wide will continue to characterise the Bank of Scotland.
>
> (*The Scotsman*, 11 June 1999)

C@SE STUDY

Analysis

This case study demonstrates several important aspects of corporate public relations practice. Before moving to consider the strategic elements, it's important to reflect on what this tells us about some of the philosophical ideas that could influence practice, particularly in relation to establishing legitimacy and building trust and social capital.

Stakeholder approach

In 2008, HBOS made a pre-tax loss of £10.8 billion and in 2009 had to be taken over by The Lloyds Banking group to save it from collapse (*The Scotsman*, 3 December 2009). This was during the dramatic change in global economics when an era of financial liquidity or 'easy money' was replaced by the 'credit crunch', leading to an erosion of trust in financial institutions and, indeed, for some a questioning of the very foundations of capitalism. A number of commentators blame the financial crisis on banks' philosophy and priorities in pursuing profits. The Robertson case illustrates this type of adherence to profit making that sees the shareholder as the most important public and contradicts a *stakeholder* approach to business, an approach deemed by many to underpin the most effective approach to corporate public relations (although it was eventually forced to adopt a stakeholder approach and ditch the Robertson deal).

The extreme focus on shareholders at the expense of other stakeholders has been construed as short-termist and ultimately damaging. At a 2009 forum *The Global Financial Crisis: What Happened and Lessons for the Future*, Will Hutton, one of the UK's most pre-eminent economics commentators, blamed the banking crisis on the 'intellectual and moral failure' not just of financial institutions – but also of legislators, regulators, business leaders and academics basing their ideas on a 'narrow ideological theory and consumer culture' with a business mantra deemed 'a short termist philosophy and amoral way of doing capitalism'. Hutton reaffirmed his beliefs expressed in *The State We're In* (see below) that stakeholder capitalism is the ideology necessary for a sustainable future and Margaret Curren MSP speculated on the need to return to the 'third way'.

In his best-selling book, *The State We're In*, Will Hutton argues for a democratic political economy that relates to the whole of British society. He criticises business for being short-termist and relentless in pursuit of some of the highest financial returns in the world: 'Companies are the fiefdoms of their Boards and sometimes of just their Chairmen; and companies are run as pure trading operations rather than productive organisations which invest, innovate and develop human capital' (Hutton 1996: 25).

In contrast to this view of companies being dominated only by the idea of improving returns for shareholders, the concept of stakeholding advocates a democratic approach to business that values relationships with a range of *stakeholders*.

The term 'stakeholder' refers to groups or individuals who have an interest or stake in an entity such as an organisation, community or country. In corporate terms, a company's stakeholders typically include:

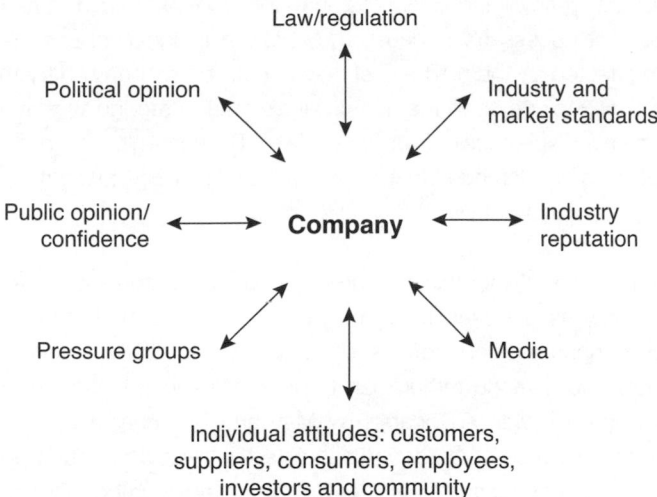

FIGURE 6.1 Various forces in the external environment combine to influence a
company's licence to operate
Source: RSA inquiry (1995). Used by permission of the RSA

certain individuals and groups that have legitimacy in the eyes of management.
That is, they have a legitimate, direct interest in, or claim on, the operations of
the firm. The most obvious of these groups are stockholders, employees and
customers. But, from the point of view of a highly pluralistic society, stakeholders
not only include these groups, but . . . the community, competitors, suppliers,
special interest groups, the media and society.

(Caroll and Buchholtz 2009: 85)

Each of these groups can affect or are affected by the 'actions, decisions, policies,
practices or goals of the organisation' (Freeman 1984: 25).

From an organisational perspective, stakeholderism is linked to notions such as
'death of deference' – whereby people no longer automatically defer to professionals
or large organisations but can feel more powerful in granting a 'licence to operate'
– consequently, to be successful, organisations must maintain public confidence in
the legitimacy of their operations and business conduct.

There is no firm consensus on the meaning of stakeholder theory.[2] It has been
described variously as being based on Keynesian economics (Hutton 1996), communitarianism (rights matched by responsibilities) (Burkitt and Ashton 1996) and the
Kantian notion of duty (as opposed to utilitarianism) (Etzioni 1988 in Burkitt and
Ashton 1996; see also Chapter 9).

Burkitt and Ashton (1996: 10) describe New Labour's stakeholder economy as
hinging on:

the idea that many interest groups may be said to have a 'stake' in certain activities, not necessarily because they have a financial interest, but because they are affected by them. These stakes should be recognised by those whose actions may impinge upon them. Individuals should recognise that their behaviour can have repercussions upon society. They should act in a responsible way that does not damage others . . . Stakeholder firms must act with responsibility to their stakeholders.

In political terms, stakeholder theory is premised on the interrelation of state, society and the economy as opposed to a 'free market' approach (where the market is not primarily concerned with notions of social responsibility and regulates itself through supply and demand rather than through state intervention). In the UK, the free market approach was advocated by Margaret Thatcher and the New Right, whereas stakeholder theory has been associated with New Labour's philosophy of social inclusion, a philosophy labelled 'the third way' by a number of political thinkers including, perhaps most notably, sociologist and adviser to Tony Blair, Antony Giddens who sees the third way as:

a label for upgrading left of centre thinking in the face of the profound changes affecting social and economic life today . . . The 'first way' was traditional social democracy – in the context of [the UK] Old Labour based on an unswerving faith in the state . . . The 'second way' was Thatcherism, or free market fundamentalism . . . founded on the belief in the primacy of markets the need to reduce the scope of the state and minimize taxes, and upon a relative indifference to social justice.

(Giddens 2007: 15)

Both stakeholder capital and the third way are closely connected to the concept of social capital (Franklin 2003).

Social capital

A number of key thinkers have noted an erosion of social capital in contemporary cultures – notably, Putnam (1996, 2000) in the United States. In the UK, Hutton notes 'In the early 90s . . . mainstream culture moved away from public purpose and fairness; the new priorities were individual self fulfilment, personal experience and loyalty to self' (Hutton 2008: 2). And the ideas inherent in the theory of social capital – building trust and connections between individuals and social networks – clearly resonate with David Cameron's rhetoric in relation to 'Broken Britain' and his ambitions for a 'Big Society'. The debate surrounding the Conservative party's utilisation of the concept reflects a wider debate whereby some thinkers such as Bourdieu (1983) see social capital as belonging only to elites, and a way in which they access and sustain power and resources, whereas commentators such as Coleman (1988, 1990, 1994) see it as a way in which all socioeconomic groups can build capacity in their communities.

At an organisational level, social capital can refer to the impact that organisations can have on sustaining cohesive societies (through employment creation, community relations and CSR activities and so on), but also in a more commercially strategic sense, it refers to the *value* accrued by an organisation being deemed a trustworthy, productive actor in society and part of a network: 'the type of connections that an organisation has with competitors, politicians, journalists, bureaucrats, researchers and other relevant groups' (Ihlen 2009). This can be particularly relevant to earning 'a license to operate' through legitimation. In 2011, it is interesting to consider this within the context of what we know now has happened to the banking sector as part of the financial crisis, and in particular in relation to the comments of the chair of the Financial Services Authority (FSA): '[the financial sector] has swollen beyond its socially useful size . . . I think some of it is socially useless activity' (Turner 2009: 1).

The public and media outcry provoked by BOS's joint venture with Robertson certainly demonstrates a transgression of several of the tenets of stakeholderism. Consequently, far from deferring to the bank's decision to go ahead with the deal, a range of stakeholders publicly debated the bank's *licence to operate*, and lack of public confidence in the moral *legitimacy* of the venture eventually resulted in its demise. Communities insisted on their rights being respected, and the bank conceded – preferring to find a new and less controversial partner than Robertson, despite the millions of pounds that could have been quickly realised through the proposed deal. The bank opted for sustainable development.

Stakeholder management

Hutton's argument for an end to short-termism in the financial community could be seen to resonate with a number of public relations scholars and practitioners' calls for public relations practitioners to take a long-term view in managing organisational *relationships* with a range of stakeholders and publics (Scott 2007; Hung 2002, 2007; Jo *et al.* 2004; Ledingham 2003, 2006a, 2006b; Ledingham and Bruning 2000; J. Grunig and Huang 2000; L. Grunig 2002).

They argue that practitioners do not wait until publics are actively campaigning before communicating with them. Effective public relations strategists are involved in organisational decision-making (see Chapter 4). Before decisions are made they would draw a stakeholder map[3] identifying their stakeholders and anticipating the ways in which they may be affected by organisational decisions and how they would react to them. 'After thoroughly researching their stakeholders, public relations managers should rank or assign weights to them to indicate their impact on the organisation or the extent to which the organisation believes it should moderate its consequences on them' (Grunig and Repper 1992: 126).

Grunig and Repper advocate a strategic approach to managing public relations based on research into stakeholder perceptions as illustrated in Figure 6.2. If the BOS used this type of strategic approach it is difficult to understand why it did not either actively manage its stakeholder relationships or 'moderate their consequences'

1   *Stakeholder Stage*: An organisation has a relationship with stakeholders when the behaviour of the organisation or of a stakeholder has a consequence on the other. Public relations should do formative research to scan the environment and the behaviour of the organisations to identify these consequences. Ongoing communication with these stakeholders helps to build a stable, long-term relationship that manages conflict that may occur in the relationship.

2   *Public Stage*: Publics form when stakeholders recognise one or more of the consequences as a problem and organise to do something about it or them. Public relations should do research to segment and identify these publics. At this stage focus groups are particularly helpful. Communication to involve publics in the decision process of the organisation helps to manage conflict before communication campaigns become necessary.

3   *Issue Stage*: Publics organise and create 'issues' out of the problems they perceive. Public relations should anticipate these issues and manage the organisation's response to them. This is known as 'issues management'. The media play a major role in the creation and expansion of issues. In particular, media coverage of issues may produce publics other than activist ones – especially 'hot-issue' publics. At this stage, research should segment publics. Communication programmes should use the mass media as well as interpersonal communications with activists to try to resolve the issue through negotiation.

Public relations should plan communication programmes with different stakeholders or publics at each of the above three stages. In doing so it should follow steps 4–7.

4   Public relations should develop formal objectives such as communication, accuracy, understanding, agreement, and complementary behaviour for its communication programmes.

5   Public relations should plan formal programmes and campaigns to accomplish the objectives.

6   Public relations, especially the technicians, should implement the programmes and campaigns.

7   Public relations should evaluate the effectiveness of programmes in meeting their objectives and reducing the conflict produced by problems and issues that brought about the programmes.

FIGURE 6.2 The strategic management of public relations
Source: Grunig and Repper (1992: 124). Used by permission

on its stakeholders by deciding not to venture into a relationship with Robertson in the first place. It's important to note that the process outlined above advocates organisations adjusting their goals to accommodate stakeholder views. This is the key to public relations people implementing a stakeholder approach, and a lack of this type of symmetrical activity could be seen as the basis for accusations of the bastardisation of term. Some approaches have stripped away the philosophical context to focus on a purely functionalist approach as illustrated in one of the perspectives considered by Caroll and Buchholtz (2009: 92): 'Let us approach stakeholder management with the idea that managers can become successful stewards of their stakeholders' resources by gaining knowledge about stakeholders and using this knowledge to predict and take care of their actions.' Critical scholars debate the basis for this type of managerial approach, which can be identified as an 'almost exclusive analysis of stakeholders from the perspective of the organisation' (Friedman and Miles 2002: 1), an approach that they argue 'hampers' stakeholder theory:

> Generally stakeholder theory has been approached from the point of view of business ethics, corporate governance and/or corporate social performance. This puts the organisation at the centre of the analysis and discourages consideration of stakeholders in their own right as well as discouraging balanced viewing of the organisation/stakeholder relation.
>
> (2002: 2)

Stakeholder engagement

In recognition of the difficulties (both practical and ethically) of managing stakeholders (or even relationships), the concept of stakeholder *management* is being increasingly replaced by the notion of stakeholder *engagement* premised on a dialogical approach (de Bussy 2010; Heath 2007). Effective stakeholder engagement is key to the success of corporate communication conceptualised in this way, but the ability to achieve real engagement is highly contested. A significant body of knowledge points to dialogue theory and dialogic and deliberative approaches (see Anderson *et al*. 2004; Deetz and Simpson 2004; Kapein and van Tulder 2003) as being the best way to achieve engagement, and views are emerging that point to the importance of this approach to public relations (Kent and Taylor 2002; Heath *et al*. 2006; Bruning, *et al*. 2008; Pieczka forthcoming). Following this approach, the more traditional adversarial behaviour witnessed in the case study could be argued to ultimately undermine social capital. Alternatively, a stakeholder engagement approach, based on dialogic principles of facilitating dissensus, could have resulted in more sustainable outcomes.

This discussion demonstrates that stakeholder theory can used by public relations practitioners to inform a pragmatic, strategic approach to practice, but its implications are more far-reaching. Stakeholding is 'intimately connected to societal values and power relations and interactive with them. Culture, polity and society are conceptualised as inextricably connected with the economy, each being highly interactive with each other' (Burkitt and Ashton 1996: 5). The BOS case seems to illustrate that public relations practitioners ignore the values of stakeholding at their peril.

CSR

Stakeholderism is inextricably linked to broader concepts of corporate social responsibility (CSR) and the role of public relations in relation to democracy. CSR is covered in depth in Chapter 9 but the application of some of these ideas is important to highlight here. Amnesty International's Peter Frankental believes certain paradoxes evident in organisations' application of CSR suggest that far from embracing a real duty to society, CSR has become a 'PR invention'. He argues that CSR can only have:

> real substance if it embraces all the stakeholders of a company, if it is reinforced by company law relating to governance, if it is rewarded by financial markets, if its definition relates to the goals of social and ecological sustainability, if its implementation is benchmarked and audited, if it is open to public scrutiny, if the compliance mechanisms are in place and if it is embedded across the organisation horizontally and vertically.
>
> (Frankental 2001: 18)

In other words, these ideas must not only influence the language chosen by PR practitioners to communicate with publics, as a way of spinning an organisation's activities, but must permeate thinking at all levels of strategic decision-making and implementation. The buck does not stop with organisations – government and other regulators must guarantee a regulatory framework that forces organisations to comply with these ideas. Frankental endorses the call for auditing according to a triple bottom line that is 'financial, environmental and social' (Frankental 2001: 19). Annual social reports must be more than gloss or spin. In a properly regulated world 'the terms of reference will be more comprehensive, standard methodologies will be developed and issues of definition, measurement, monitoring and verification will be . . . addressed' (Frankental 2001: 20).

Clearly though, it is significant to note the *criteria* of measurement of corporate social responsibility.

HBOS's key performance indicators for 'contribution to society' very much focus on Frankental's 'financial' and 'environmental' impact but only seem to encompass the 'social' if this is interpreted as wealth creation and providing tax revenue to the government to spend on social infrastructures. They were:

- taxation paid
- dividends paid

- total payroll
- energy use
- water use
- waste
- business travel
- protection of the environment
- prosecutions/reported cases of bribery/corruption
- regulatory fines or reprimands.

(www.hbosplc.com/community/includes/
HBOS_CR_Report_14Aug_2005.pdf)

The case can be seen as evidence to substantiate an argument that CSR or CSR(S) Corporate Social Responsibility and Sustainability, is not about corporate development of policies or activities designed to build a socially responsible image or to help achieve pre-determined strategically important objectives; but is about the process of understanding an organisation's impact on a broad range of stakeholders, relates to social capital and is located in a broader social context (Beckmann *et al.* 2006: 26).

The attitude-behaviour gap

In their research into whether consumers really care about corporate reputation when making purchasing decisions, Page and Fearn criticise research that investigates what participants *say* will influence their buying behaviour rather than examining their *actual* buying behaviour (Page and Fearn 2005). Their large-scale, quantitative research project finds that although consumers profess to care about ethical behaviour, this doesn't mean that they will purchase goods or services according to the vendors' reputation. It also grades the type of corporate social responsibility most valued by consumers:

The elements of corporate reputation that seem to matter most to consumers in practice are perceptions of fairness toward consumers, and perceptions of corporate success and leadership, rather than public responsibility. Consumers want good business practice but when it comes to brand strength and purchasing, more personally relevant factors take precedence.

(Page and Fearn 2005: 306)

These findings are replicated by a qualitative study conducted in 2001: 'If they liked and regularly used a product they would find it hard to boycott. The most important purchasing criteria were price, value, quality and brand familiarity. Customers bought for personal reasons rather than social ones' (Carrigan and Attalla 2001: 564).

This would seem to be borne out by HBOS's corporate success despite its reputation for poor public responsibility in relation to Pat Robertson and Farepak.

This gap between consumers' *attitudes* towards companies and their purchasing *behaviour* (Boulstridge and Carrigan 2000) seems to demonstrate that CSR is not about increasing sales but in line with the corporate PR goals of establishing legitimacy and increasing social capital.

Reputation

Better-regarded companies build their reputations by developing practices that integrate economic and social considerations into their competitive strategies. They not only do things right – they do the right things. In doing so, they act like good citizens. They initiate policies that reflect their core values; that consider the joint welfare of investors, customers and employees; that invoke concern for the development of local communities; and that ensure the quality and environmental soundness of their technologies, products and services.

(Fombrun 1996: 8)

The aims outlined in the BOS's corporate statement reflect an understanding of this approach to reputation-building. However, its actions or *behaviour* (teaming up with Robertson and defending the deal by attempting to distinguish between the ethics of commercial decisions and the personal views of business partners) is not congruent with the core values its statement expresses. Its problems could be judged to have stemmed from its failure to 'integrate economic and social considerations'.

A consideration of the bank's withdrawal from the deal also provides a useful insight into this perspective of reputation building. The bank stood to make tens of millions of pounds' profit as a result of the Robertson deal, which would have resulted in the opening of millions of new accounts by American customers. At the time it withdrew from the venture, only 500 accounts had been closed by British customers (compared with more than 21,500 opened during the same period) (*Guardian*, 16 June 1999). Clearly the potential gains would vastly outweigh the losses. An analysis of the bank's early statements and subsequent apology seems to indicate that it did not abandon the deal because of ethical considerations. The motivation for the decision can be interpreted as stemming from concern that direct action from key stakeholders might escalate, irreparably damaging its British business (and profits). Clearly, the bank recognised its long-term reputation as being more valuable than the short-term profits it could have made as a result of going ahead with the venture.

The case not only illustrates how a reputation is earned (and damaged) but also its value and the relationship between a good reputation and profits. As Fombrun (1996: 81) explains:

Corporate reputations have bottom line effects. A good reputation enhances profitability because it attracts customers to the company's products, investors to its securities, and employees to its jobs. In turn, esteem inflates the price at which a public company's securities trade. The economic value of a corporate reputation can therefore be gauged by the excess market value of its securities.

Crisis management

If a company at the centre of a crisis is seen to be unresponsive, uncaring, inconsistent, confused, inept, reluctant or unable to provide reliable information, the damage inflicted on its reputation will be lasting – and measurable against the financial bottom line.

(Regester and Larkin, in Kitchen 1997: 215)

'Tell it first, tell it fast' is one of the mantras of effective crisis management. However, both the bank and Robertson were often reported as being unresponsive, refusing to comment or blaming media distortion for their predicament. Eventually Robertson changed his PR approach and invited the press to the US to visit his organisation and speak to him directly. However, media views were already entrenched.

The bank was also criticised for failing to apologise quickly enough to its customers for Robertson's offensive comments. As Dugdale Bradley, co-founder of *Tomorrow's Company* in Scotland, said: 'The bank did not come clean about it and apologise, like Perrier did in the 1980s. They have got in a muddle. But if people say "sorry, we made a mistake", people will be more forgiving' (*The Scotsman*, 12 June 1999).

Commentators consider that a strong reputation helps companies survive crises with less financial loss. In the second edition of this book, Wood (2004) stated: 'BOS's reputation was good before the Robertson debacle; it will be interesting to track how it weathers the storm and recovers its former position.' In the third edition, through an analysis of HBOS's management of a new crisis – its withdrawal of overdraft facilities for the Christmas savings company Farepak that many say led to its subsequent collapse, resulting in 150,000 savers from low-income families collectively losing around £35 million (an average of £400 per family) just before Christmas 2006 – the authors concluded that a damaged corporate reputation is not as important as some would believe.

Despite the Robertson affair, BOS was welcomed as a partner by the Halifax building society and was making record profits and the major institutions such as the Scottish Executive and councils still banked with HBOS. This seems to support the view that there is a gap between attitudes expressed and action taken.

Impact on share price

Advocates of a stakeholder approach to business, do not disregard the shareholder as a vitally important stakeholder based on the argument that, by adopting a stakeholder approach an organisation will be well managed and therefore able to deliver greater value to its shareholders. In contrast, 'organisations that continue to act as if shareholders are the only important group will colour the financial community's view of the quality of management and endanger the interests of the very group they seek to satisfy' (RSA Inquiry 1995: 1). The effect of the Robertson venture on the BOS share price seems to bear this out. When the deal was first announced the share price rallied, but when public outcry emerged, it fluctuated – falling significantly following the publicity surrounding Robertson's 'dark land' comments.

Opinion formers

An analysis of the people and organisations that influenced the bank's decision is useful in identifying the range of opinion formers public relations practitioners should communicate with. Council leaders, MSPs, church leaders, individual shareholders, the unions, pressure groups and civil rights leaders' views were all reported in the press.

Communication technology and globilisation

The internet played an important role in the case. Not only did it enable pressure groups to mobilise public pressure, it also facilitated fast and effective access to information about the American preacher. For example, while Robertson complained about being misquoted, *The Scotsman* printed instructions for readers to download real-time video footage of the programme in which Robertson denounced Scotland as a 'dark land' (2 June 1999).

These developments are also significant in the process of globalisation (and antiglobalisation movements) and multiculturalism. Indeed, Kruckenberg and Starck (quoted in Heath 2001a: 52) identify 'communication/transportation technology, multiculturalism and globalisation' as the 'three phenomena that promise incalculable continuing effects on human kind' resulting in 'immense societal changes'. They identify communication as the 'indispensable component' in negotiating this 'increasingly globalised, diversified and multicultural world' (quoted in Heath 2001a: 57). See Chapter 19 for further discussion of these concepts and Holmstrom (2010).

PR AND REASONED PERSUASION

Any discussion of the role of PR in society necessarily impacts on ideas of democracy and the democratic process. A major concern in considering public relations practice rests on notions of manipulation and uneven distribution of power and resources allowing 'rich' organisations to dominate less powerful actors in society.

In a world where public trust in big organisations has been largely eroded by numerous corporate scandals, the BOS case shows how companies can be called to account. In this way it could be seen to support Moloney's call for an 'internal reform' of PR to ensure it has the following characteristics: 'known source, clear intent, reasoned argument, factual accuracy, and positive but limited emotional appeal. It is dialogic, respectful of its audiences, open to challenge, ready to amend and willing to reply.'

Clearly the BOS fell down on several of these; it could be argued that it did not respect its stakeholders' views, was not open to challenge or 'willing to reply' and was, therefore, forced to 'amend' its activities in a way that damaged its reputation.

In relation to the role of PR in the democratic process, Moloney argues that 'PR should encourage outcomes favoured by our society: outcomes such as reasoned, factually accurate, persuasive public debate amongst all individuals, groups and organisations wanting to speak and listen' (Moloney 2000: 150). This argument develops the stalemate in thinking about 'excellent' PR practice as it clearly resonates with both the notion of two-way symmetrical practice and ideas of amoral persuasion.

In an environment dominated by accusations of spin and sleaze and the anti-democratic nature of public relations, it is interesting to consider Moloney's view that PR:

> is a set of techniques amenable for the promotion of values, done by an industry, done by an individual alone or by voluntary groups, and available in paid professional form or in 'personal kit' and 'cottage industry' forms. This shift in UK society to more expression by individuals of different personal values via voluntary, often local, groups is identified here as value pluralism and group pluralism of a civic kind.
>
> (2000: 35)

In other words, if adequate access to public relations could be achieved, the practice has a valuable contribution to make to the democratic process.

The BOS case study seems to illustrate how this process can work in action. The large and powerful resource-rich organisation (BOS) had to bow to the views of seemingly less powerful individuals and groups who promoted their views via public relations (particularly through effective media relations).

In his extremely useful book, Moloney goes further and argues that:

> For democracy, societally beneficial PR is reasoned persuasion. Such PR is the consequence of choosing to persuade by reason (supported by accurate data) rather than by emotion. Reason and emotion are alternative communication modes of being persuasive and of achieving persuasion. PR in a democracy should proceed more by reason and less by emotion. Beneficial PR in a democracy is a means of promoting the public good through a contribution to informed choice.
>
> (2000: 151)

Following Moloney's viewpoint, it could be argued that BOS was pursuing reasoned persuasion by divorcing Robertson's emotionally provocative comments about homosexuality from the reasoned business case that the deal would result in vast profits for the organisation. The BOS data certainly supported this perspective. However, in this case, the emotional response of a diverse spectrum of stakeholders carried the day.

Perhaps further clarification of what Moloney means by 'reason' and 'emotion' would be useful. Humans are emotional beings and are often governed by emotional responses. The concept of emotion could be inextricably linked to values or ideological views of what is just.

ENVIRONMENTAL SCANNING

At the AGM, Sir John Shaw was reported as saying: 'The Bank was well aware that Mr Robertson was a controversial figure in the United States. We did not expect that the controversy he was associated with there would have transferred to here where he has no political constituency or business.'

Critics could argue that in a global economy, geographical boundaries do not operate in the way Sir John had anticipated.

Effective public relations input at board level should have forewarned the bank that Robertson would be a controversial figure, particularly in the current business environment where discussions of ethical practice and social responsibility are prevalent on business and political agendas. The case serves as an effective argument that public relations expertise should be included in the strategic planning process and should be able to influence dominant coalition decision-making (see Chapter 4).

QUESTIONS FOR DISCUSSION

1   How does corporate communication differ from consumer public relations?
2   What constitutes a 'good' reputation?
3   To what extent can HBOS build or erode social capital?
4   What is the role of communication in establishing legitimacy?
5   Why is a stakeholder perspective important? Can it be used cynically?
6   How can PR practice damage or benefit the democratic process?
7   Draw a stakeholder map for HBOS.
8   Should an organisation-centric view of stakeholders be avoided?

9   What criteria should be used to measure a company's 'contribution to society'?

10 Bearing the attitude behaviour gap (Boulstridge and Carrigan 2000) in mind, does 'A good reputation enhance profitability because it attracts customers to the company's products'? (Fombrun 1996: 81)

NOTES

1   The concepts of trust, legitimacy and social capital as explicated in the works of Weber (1922/1968); Habermas (1984, 1987); Bourdieu (1983); and Putnam (1996, 2000) are very usefully debated in relation to public relations practice in Ihlen and Fredrikson (2009). Hazelton and Kennan (2000) and Kennan and Hazelton (2006) also offer interesting insights into the significance of social capital for public relations practice.
    All figures published on the BOS website, May 2007 (www.hbosplc.com/abouthbos/History/HBOS_history.asp).
2   See Clarke (1997), Mitchell, Agle and Wood (1997) and de Bussy (2008) for a useful analysis of different approaches to the concept of stakeholding and stakeholder theory.
3   For a comprehensive guide to stakeholder mapping see Johnson *et al.* (2008) and Caroll and Buchholtz (2009).

FURTHER READING

Christensen, L.T., Morsing, M. and Cheney, G. (2008) *Corporate communications: convention*, challenge, complexity, Sage.

Ihlen, O. and Fredrikson, M. (eds) (2009) *Public relations and social theory:key figures and concepts,* Routledge.

Mitchell, R.K., Agle, B.R. and Wood, D.J. (1997) 'Towards a theory of stakeholder identification and salience: defining the principle of who and what really counts', *Academy of Management Review*, 22 (4), pp. 853–886.

Page, G. and Fearn, H. (2005) 'Corporate reputation: what do consumers really care about?', *Journal of Advertising Research*, 45, pp. 305–313.

Wood, E. (2009) 'Corporate communication' in R. Tench and L. Yeomans (eds) *Exploring Public Relations,* Pearson Education.

CHAPTER 7

Corporate identity

Emma Wood and Ian Somerville

CHAPTER AIMS

A strong corporate identity and positive corporate image are believed to deliver tangible bottom-line benefits for a wide range of organisations. But how easy are they to achieve? This chapter will explore the meaning of corporate identity and image and consider some critical approaches. It will then consider ideas affecting identity and image management and consider how concepts dominating PR thinking (such as stakeholderism) can be incorporated into corporate identity (CI) management – an area often informed by a marketing paradigm. It concludes with a case study exploring an identity change programme to demonstrate the application of many of these ideas.

DEFINING CORPORATE IDENTITY

From a communications management and public relations perspective, corporate identity management can be defined as the strategic development of a distinct and coherent image of an organisation that is consistently communicated to stakeholders through symbolism, planned communications and behaviour.

(Cornelisson and Elving 2003: 116)

The above definition, building on van Riel's (1995) conceptualisation by introducing the ideas of coherence and consistency in communication, encapsulates current thinking in effective CI management.

Nike is tough, aggressive and trendy. The Co-operative is socially responsible and ethical. The term 'corporate identity' refers to the combination of ways in which an organisation's personality is expressed. Red flag or red rose? Rule Britannia or cool Britannia? Identity includes design aspects such as logos, colour, typeface and architecture but also embraces less tangible elements such as behaviour, culture, values, mission, communication style and associations (with personalities, charities, political parties or other organisations via donations or sponsorship). CI management is considered by many to be a vital aspect of motivating stakeholders (including voters, employees, shareholders and consumers) and securing a host of benefits ranging from recruiting top employees and attracting consumers to products, brands or services, to helping companies manage issues and recover from crises.

Identity – mapping the conceptual terrain

As such a fundamental part of what it is to be human, the concept of identity has been explored and expounded for hundreds of years. Space precludes an in-depth analysis of the different ways in which it has been theorised, interpreted and understood, but some of the ideas most relevant to the concept of corporate identity are mapped here to encourage further exploration of specific underpinning frameworks.

Identity in cultural studies

Hall and du Gay have written extensively on identity from a cultural studies perspective. Key to this is the idea that identity is not a naturally occurring aspect of a person or organisation waiting to be uncovered but is a construction, a 'discursive practice' (Hall in Hall and du Gay 1996: 2):

> Precisely because identities are constructed within, not outside discourse, we need to understand them as produced in specific historical and institutional sites within specific discursive formations and practices, by specific enunciative strategies. Moreover, they emerge within the play of specific modalities of power, and thus are more the product of the marking of difference and exclusion, than they are the sign of an identical, naturally-constituted unity – an 'identity' in its traditional meaning (that is an all inclusive sameness, seamless, without internal differentiation.
>
> (Hall in Hall and du Gay 1996: 4)

This approach is clearly of particular importance to any analysis of, and subsequent attempt at construction of, a corporate identity. Curtain and Gaither (2007) adopt a cultural studies perspective to analyse public relations practices and develop a number of ideas including those of Hall and other key thinkers in relation to the construction of identities.

Identity in organisational studies

The term 'organisational identity' could be argued as an attempt to distinguish conceptualisations of identity formulated within an organisational studies domain from those formulated within a marketing centric domain. Unfortunately, just as there is no firm definition of the term corporate identity, there is also lack of consensus in regard to the term 'organisational identity' – however, one of the most enduring conceptualisations is Albert and Whetten's (1985) definition: 'Organisational identity is (a) what is taken by organisational members to be *central* to the organisation; (b) what makes the organisation *distinctive* from other organisations (at least in the eyes of the beholding members) and (c) what is perceived by members to be an *enduring* or continuing feature linking the present organisation with the past (and presumably the future)' (in Whetten and Godfrey 1998: 21) or *Centrality, Distinctiveness* and *Temporal Continuity* (Whetten 2006).

Ravsai, van Rekom and Soenen (in Lerpold *et al.* 2007) provide a useful distinction between organisational and marketing conceptualisations of identity, image and reputation, but do still largely represent conceptualisations of corporate identity from within a marketing domain.

These conceptualisations regard organisational identity as pertaining to the beliefs and aspirations of *internal* stakeholders and corporate identity to be the communication of these to *external* stakeholders. This runs contrary to 'public relations centric thinking', a perspective that views corporate identity as a communicative process, which includes culture, involving both internal *and* external stakeholders and that therefore impacts on the formation of a particular image in the minds of both groups (see Bronn in Heath 2010 and Hatch and Schultz 2000). This view also holds that external stakeholders will be involved with organisational members in affecting aspects of organisational identity as is illustrated in the case study at the end of this chapter.

CORPORATE IDENTITY VS CORPORATE IMAGE

The terms 'corporate identity' and 'corporate image' are sometimes confused with each other.[1] In our definition, *corporate identity* is what the organisation communicates (either intentionally or unintentionally) via various cues, whereas its *image* is how its publics actually view it. An image is a perception and exists only in the mind of the receiver. To formulate an *image*, publics interpret an *identity* in a wider context with broader frames of reference.

For example, Nike's corporate identity is a carefully managed amalgam of associations (with fashionable sports personalities and major sporting events such as the Olympics as well as local and charitable events), clear design and mission. Many people exposed to these aspects of its identity may well formulate an image of Nike as a high-quality and fashionable arbiter of good design. Others, aware of some negative media coverage of Nike's manufacturing policy in third-world countries (interpreting the identity in a broader context), may form an image of Nike as exploitative and thus boycott its products.[2]

Clearly, then, organisations cannot *construct* a corporate image because they cannot control the context in which their communication is received, interpreted or understood. Nevertheless, a clear, well-managed corporate identity can go some way to effecting a strategically important image, and a neglected corporate identity may send out all the wrong messages: 'An organisation may commonly assume that it only communicates when it wants to, but unfortunately for many companies, a failure to control communications results in a confused image' (Ind 1997: 21).

But managing an identity well means embracing all aspects of what van Riel (1995) calls the CI mix – symbolism, communication and behaviour. The Nike case illustrates this well. Despite well-managed *symbolism* and *communication*, perceptions of aspects of its *behaviour* (reported treatment of third-world workers) have affected some publics' image of the company.

REPUTATION

Having delineated the rather contested concepts of organisational identity, corporate identity and corporate image, the introduction of the concept of *reputation* may cause further confusion. It is sometimes difficult to distinguish from image, as reputation is also something that belongs to the receiver, not the sender. However, the consensus is that an image is an immediate, or fleeting, impression whereas reputation is an assessment or judgment developed over time that relates to an organisation's historical and future performance. Consequently it is bound up with concepts such as 'trust' (Bronn in Heath 2010) and, according to van Riel and Fombrun's (2007) analysis: visibility, distinctiveness, authenticity, transparency, consistency and responsiveness (in Bronn 2010: 313). Vella and Melewar (in Melewar 2008: 13) represent a number of published views in their definition of reputation:

> Whereas image reflects the more recent beliefs about the organisation, reputation is the perception of an organisation built over time (Balmer 1998). Reputation results from a reflection upon historical accumulated impacts of previously observed identity cues and transactional experiences (Melewar 2003). In other words, it is evaluative and is image endowed with judgment.
>
> (Simoes and Dibb 2002)

Figure 7.1 maps the relationship between the concepts of organisational identity, corporate identity, corporate image and reputation to help avoid confusion.

So, can corporate identity be effectively managed? And, if so, how?

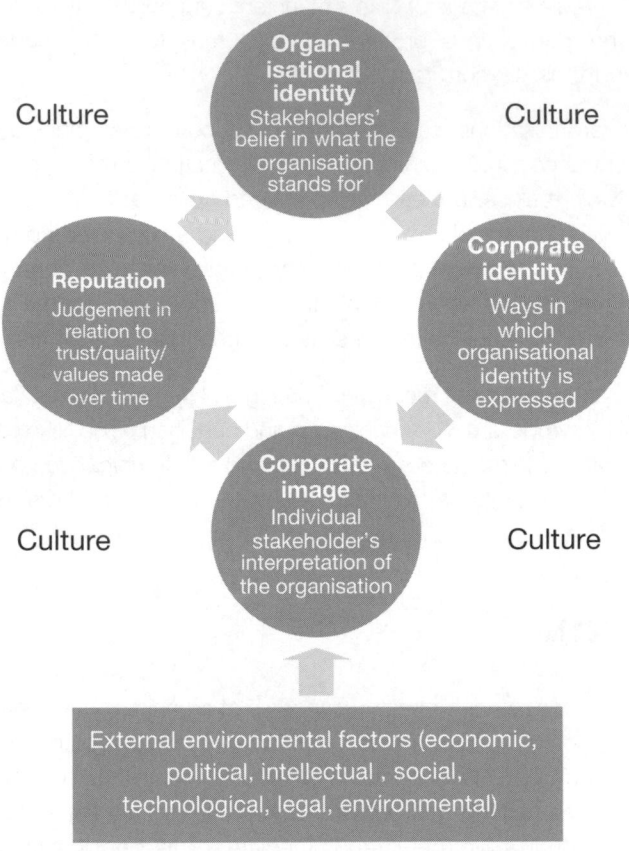

FIGURE: 7.1 Mapping the relationship between relevant concepts

ISSUES RAISED BY CORPORATE IDENTITY MANAGEMENT

Corporate identity management commonly involves:

- conducting research to determine senior management and a range of stakeholders'[3] views on an organisation's actual and desired image
- an audit of all elements of corporate identity to determine if they are congruent with the desired image
- formulating a plan to adjust the corporate identity if necessary.

It all seems simple enough. Clearly though, controlling identity is not simple or straightforward or perhaps even possible. Consequently, before considering the management process, it is important to consider a range of questions and issues.

CORPORATE STRATEGY

One of the key issues of corporate identity management is its role in achieving overall organisational strategic objectives.[4] The aim of a corporate identity plan is to determine and communicate a corporate identity to meet these future strategic objectives. For example, the Labour Party's introduction of a new corporate identity in the 1990s (involving the introduction of a new logo, a red rose, and a new name, New Labour) was linked to its overall strategic plan to modernise the party to make it electable. Interestingly, immediately after Tony Blair's resignation announcement on 10 May 2007, the Labour website dropped the term 'New' from the party's name and reverted to the designation 'Labour'. It also changed the dominant colour on the web pages from red to purple. The end of the Blair era was swiftly indicated in these new visual identity signifiers. It is also worth noting that the Conservative Party has also recently abandoned the blue torch of freedom, its logo from the days of Margaret Thatcher's premiership, and replaced it with a green oak tree. This is meant to symbolise the embracing of environmentalism as a key policy by the party.

However, a number of thinkers in this area, most notably Grunig,[5] would argue that the corporate identity management process should not just be designed to help implement a predetermined strategy. Instead, strategy should be formulated partly in response to stakeholders' needs and views and should adapt their corporate strategies according to stakeholders' opinions identified through research. Indeed, many would argue that the Labour Party's strategic objective to modernise was formulated in response to research conducted into publics' perceptions of the party's image.[6]

SYMBOLISM

Using cultural codes and associated meanings, designers choose particular colours, shapes and typefaces to provoke particular emotional responses or to connote particular meanings. For example, a serif typeface such as Times New Roman used in broadsheets (the 'quality' press) has connotations of tradition, longevity and quality. A sans serif typeface, favoured by the tabloids, is often deemed to invoke modernity.

The controversy triggered by Labour's adoption of the red rose logo to replace the red flag illustrates the power of the symbol. The change in visuals was interpreted as symbolising a major ideological shift from hard left to centrist politics. A semiotic[7] analysis would infer that 'Labour abandoned the symbolism of the red flag (viewed by the leadership as a sign with negative connotations of bureaucratic, Soviet-style socialism) in favour of the red rose, a logo first successfully employed by the French socialists' (McNair 2003: 150).

Olins (1999: 73) suggests that:

> The problems in developing symbols are complex. In addition to avoiding negative connotations, technical, creative, fashion and cost requirements all have to be considered. Creating something which will encapsulate the idea behind the organisation, that won't go out of date, that is flexible and cheap in use and that will evoke strong, positive emotional feelings in all those who come into contact with it, is actually a very difficult thing to do.

Of course, the significance of symbols within an organisation goes beyond aspects of design, such as the logo. It includes the existence (or absence) and distribution of status symbols such as executive washrooms, plush carpets and parking spaces. This aspect will be referred to later as part of a consideration of organisational culture. The study of semiotics, where signs signify particular meanings is also of real significance here.

CONSISTENCY

To ensure that a *visual* identity communicates the messages for which it was painstakingly designed, it must be applied consistently across all media. So 'house style' manuals are developed to control every aspect of application, from Pantone number (representing exact colours) to typeface. But not all organisations want to represent themselves as a homogenised unit. Some are decentralised and a corporate identity should signal this.

This seems relatively straightforward, but can, and should, other aspects of identity, such as communication and behaviour, be homogenised? Markwick and Fill (1997) argue that 'it is important to establish consistent and sustainable internal images among all employees in order that this consistency is projected as a positive cue to other stakeholder groups'. Clearly, organisations should involve a range of stakeholders in determining core philosophies and values and clearly communicate the agreed goals. But different stakeholder groups often have differing needs and expectations of single organisations, so expecting uniformity seems an unrealistic goal. This demonstrates the importance of defining what is meant by the term 'consistency'.

Van Riel (1995) overcomes the problematic notion of imposed uniformity with his concept of 'common starting points' (CSPs). CSPs are central values developed by communications staff from research into an organisation's desired corporate identity and image. Examples of CSPs include reliability, innovation, quality, profit-making and synergy (ibid.). CSPs function as 'wavelengths' or 'parameters' to guide communication activity. The concept of CSPs fosters a notion of an organic process of developing and communicating organisational images rather than a top-down approach that limits staff to static, agreed perceptions. As Leitch and Motion (1999:

195) explain: 'An organisation may present multiple images to its various publics provided that these images are consistent, not with each other, but with the organisation's CSPs. The corporate identity task is to manage the multiplicity rather than to suppress it.' Christensen, Morsing and Cheney (2008) and Christensen, Firat and Torp (2008) provide interesting insights into how approaches that seem to be about facilitating multiplicity or diversity can actually be controlling and offer alternative *process* rules.

The CSP approach has also been progressed in relation to developing a 'sustainable corporate story' (van Riel in Schultz *et al.* 2000).

> A corporate story is a comprehensive narrative about the whole organisation, its origins, its vision, its mission. However, the emotionally formulated core story is much more than just a vision or mission statement. By incorporating elements such as competencies, fundamental beliefs and values, it mirrors something deep within the organisation and provides a simple yet effective framework guiding the organisation in all its actions.
>
> (Holten Larsen in Schultz *et al.* 2000: 197)

Perhaps it is important to note that the source of these carefully constructed stories is an issue: 'To have employees internalise corporate narratives requires a more direct involvement of them in the articulation of the organisation's identity' (Christensen and Cheney in Schultz *et al.* 2000: 256). Christensen and Cheney (ibid.) critique the creation of corporate identities on a number of levels – an important one being that over-enthusiastic CI zealots can get carried away with their mission and only pay lip service to employee involvement. Another dimension of their criticism is the level at which employees want to become involved; they argue that managers can misinterpret the importance of the intricacies of corporate identity to most employees (Christensen, Morsing and Cheney 2008).

ORGANISATIONAL CULTURE

An organisation's behaviour reflects, or is reflected in, its culture, sometimes referred to as 'the way we do things around here'[8] (Hatch 1993, Schein 2004 in Vella and Melewar 2008). Changing organisational cultures to improve performance in our global economy is the subject of an entire industry of 'culture change' gurus. And a plethora of recipes for changing organisational cultures is currently on offer. Known as 'culture change programmes', as Wilson (1992) explains, these often offer 'generalised templates' developed from analysis of a handful of 'successful' processes observed in particular companies (or sometimes productive national cultures such as in the Far East).

These approaches indicate that strong unified cultures can be created through strong leadership. The 'recipes' promise that cultures will become more effective by re-engineering particular aspects such as leadership styles or communication techniques.

Space precludes a lengthy analysis of the concept of organisational culture and attempts to change it, but Wilson (1992) offers an interesting critical appraisal of many ideas and approaches.

Some thinkers view culture as a context for identity rather than being part of it (Hatch and Schultz 1997; Cornelisson and Elving 2003) and others argue that it is part of organisational identity and not corporate identity (Ravasi and Schultz in Lerpold *et al.* 2007) but we share the view that *organisational* culture is part of an organisation's corporate identity that is made sense of or interpreted through the lens of the broader cultural environment that we inhabit. Culture is not something that is easily manipulated to project a particular or desired image, but it is a vital part of researching the current identity of an organisation and in establishing gaps between actual identity and desired identity.

For example, an organisation may be fantastic at communicating carefully crafted messages and values through corporate literature and websites. Content analysis of these plus interviews with senior staff would indicate that the corporate identity was clearly consistent with the desired corporate image, but research into the culture of the organisation could give a fuller picture. This was the case at a shipyard where the author was employed as a consultant and noted that all seemed well until going into the staff restaurant for lunch – there half of the room was carpeted and had high quality tables and chairs and the other half was not. The reason for this was that the nice half was for the administrators who were 'clean' and the other half was for the shipyard workers who were 'dirty'! Everyone washed and removed dirty clothes before going for lunch, but this ritual symbolised a huge problem in the organisation – a real divide between management/administrators and people who worked on the shop floor – an attitude that was manifest through the culture and affected the image of the organisation and its reputation. Clearly then, it is essential to research culture as part of the ways in which organisational identity is signified, or communicated, to both internal and external stakeholders.

Johnson *et al.*'s (2008) cultural web (see Figure 7.2) is a very useful tool for mapping and understanding organisational culture. The cultural web illustrates the complexity of organisational culture and, in practical terms, the areas that should be investigated as part of any attempt to audit culture as part of corporate identity.

Understanding the realities of a corporate culture, revealed through research, will influence the CI management process. Johnson *et al.*'s model refers to an organisa- tion's paradigm which can be explained as its 'taken for granted assumptions' (2008: 197) or the link between structure and culture (Grundy 1993). It could also be argued as being a similar concept to corporate personality.

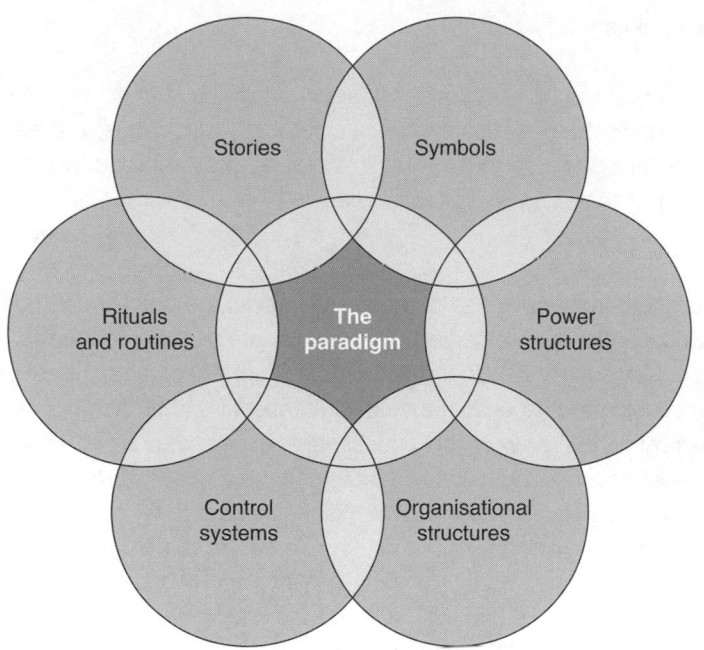

FIGURE 7.2 The cultural web
Source: Johnson *et al.* (2008). Used by permission of Prentice Hall/Pearson

However, this notion becomes problematic if the projected personality does not reflect reality.

REFLECTING REALITY?

> Our preoccupation with, and reliance on, images has important implications for the study and practice of corporate communications. The image without any clear or certain relation to 'reality' is perhaps becoming the dominant form in both external and internal corporate public communications.
>
> (Cheney 1992: 173)

The media revelled in ridiculing the BBC for spending reputed millions to adjust its logo from a slanting to an upright typeface. They gloried in maligning the Labour Party for replacing the red flag with a red rose. The source of the criticism was the perception that highly paid 'spin doctors' were concentrating on style as opposed to substance – trying to gloss over the problems both institutions were experiencing by creating an illusion of sleek professionalism. Whether this perception was fair or not will be debated elsewhere. The point here is that public relations practitioners must carefully consider the motives and ethics of their practice.

As Cheney points out:

> Contemporary public relations is fundamentally concerned with representing major organisations and institutions of our society with values, images, identities, issue positions and so forth. Thus, it is crucial that we probe the structure and meaning of that process of representation.
>
> (Cheney 1992: 170)

In constructing carefully planned corporate identities, the practitioner must not lose sight of whose interests are served. The practitioner truly committed to the notion of a stakeholder society (which in this context emphasises employees' interests in particular) should strive to ensure that identity reflects, rather than conceals, reality. If an organisation's 'reality' is too undesirable to promote, an ethical practitioner would set about counselling management to change the reality rather than designing a corporate identity plan to mask it. We must remember to be careful when seeking 'truth' or 'reality': 'Authenticity is as much a creative construction as an inherent quality of the organization itself. We should always ask: Whose authenticity? Where do we find it? How do we know it?' (Christensen, Morsing and Cheney 2008: 78).

RESEARCHING CORPORATE IDENTITY

> To know the identity of a person is to be able to identify him or her – to distinguish him or her from others and to recognise him or her as a unique individual. Addresses, nationalities, ages and physical features are observable data, which are frequently used to identify an individual. Does this mean that one person really knows the identity of another person after having read his or her passport? Simple observation quickly becomes an insufficient method for understanding identity. Truly to know the identity of people, we must go much further. We must have long discussions with them, we must ask them about their tastes and convictions, and we must learn their histories.
>
> (Moingeon and Ramanantsoa 1997: 1)

To gain a real insight into a personality, it is also important to talk to a whole range of friends, family and acquaintances to assess their views and experiences. In the same way, when attempting to determine an accurate picture of the corporate identity, a range of stakeholders' views must be sought. Stakeholder analysis techniques (discussed in Chapter 6) should be used to identify the relevant stakeholders to be used in the research.

So how can we engineer 'long discussions' to learn more about an organisation's tastes, convictions and histories?

A combination of research methodologies must be adopted, targeted at a range of stakeholders. These could include content analysis of corporate documents, surveys, focus groups, interviews and critical incident analysis.[9]

RESEARCHING THE CORPORATE IDENTITY – A PRACTICAL APPROACH

One of the first steps any public relations practitioner should take when joining an organisation or taking on a new client is to audit its corporate image and identity. The purpose this process (researching the actual and desired image and identifying which aspects of corporate identity should be changed to connote appropriate meaning) is to use this information to formulate a corporate identity plan. Such a plan would often aim to manipulate the variables of corporate identity to ensure they suggest a coherent and desirable image. But is it really possible to manipulate the appropriate variables (symbolism, communication and behaviour) effectively?

Corporate identity is such a complex concept, it is difficult to imagine that it is easily manipulated and controlled. However, consultants sometimes claim just this. Schmidt (1997), for example, promotes an approach to corporate identity management involving five dimensions: 'products and services, communications and design, corporate behaviour, market conditions and strategies and corporate culture.' He claims, 'our successful holistic approach made it possible to analyse, structure and control all relevant dimensions, including culture' (1997: 40).

Others hold conflicting views, Hatch and Schultz (1997) argue:

> Strategies and visions are created and interpreted through culturally-mediated language such as metaphor, stories and humour and demonstrated by material artefacts of culture such as products, buildings and physical arrangements. Corporate identity can, therefore, never be wholly managed.

Although perhaps it cannot be 'wholly managed', important inroads can be made into identifying and communicating a strategically important corporate identity. Provided readers retain a realistic mindset about what can really be effected, a number of useful multistep corporate identity management plans are available in the literature and Lerpold et al. (2007: 235–245) offer a useful appraisal of the most interesting. Van Riel's (1995) model of the process, however, remains among the most useful (see Figure 7.3).

Comprehensive research (of the type investigated above) affects the corporate identity management plan. It should be conducted among a range of stakeholders, include environmental monitoring to identify any emerging issues, trends or policies and enable the following questions to be answered:

1   What is our current image?
2   In order to meet strategic objectives, what do we need our image to be (what is our aspirational image)?
3   What is the difference between 1 and 2?
4   Does our existing corporate identity reflect our aspirational image (2 above)?
5   What changes must be made to our corporate identity to help narrow any gap between 1 and 2?

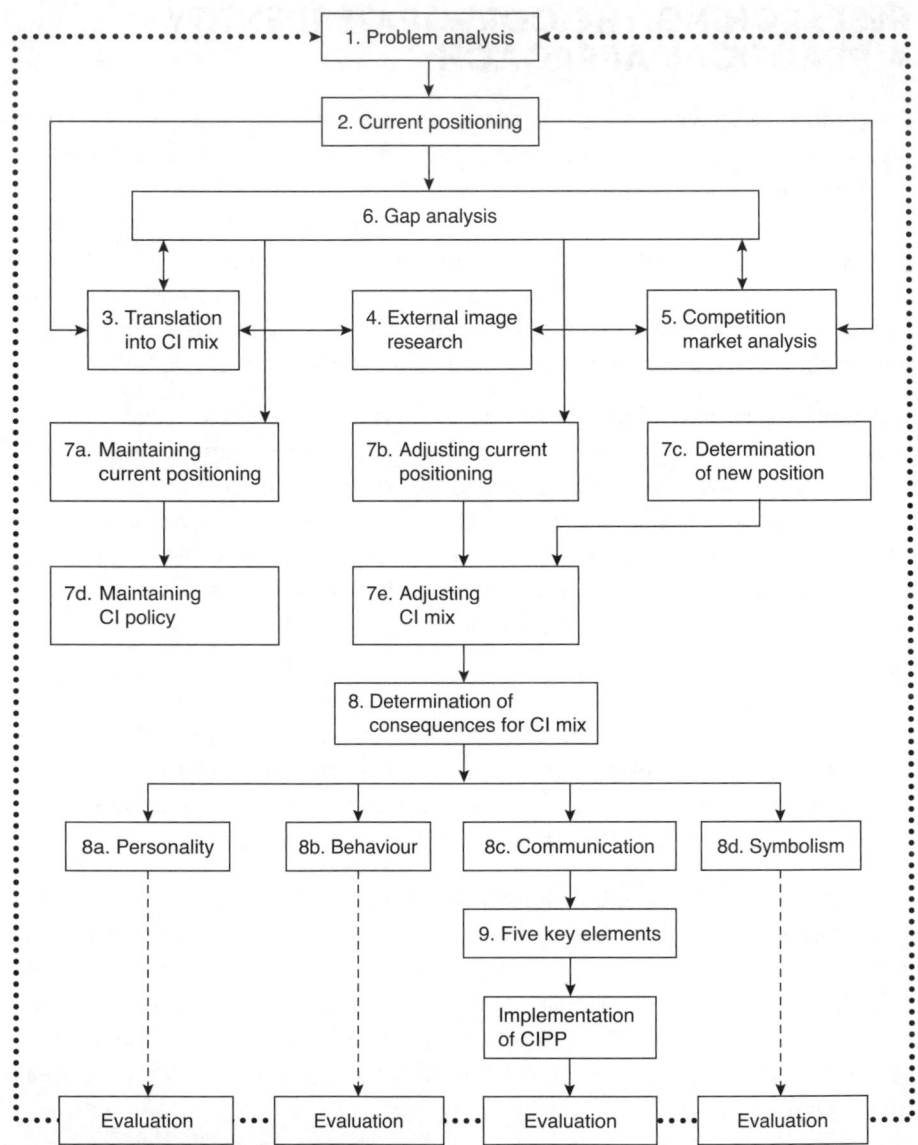

FIGURE 7.3 Adapted version of van Riel's model of corporate identity management
Source: Adapted from van Riel (1995). Used by permission

The objectives of the corporate identity policy programme (van Riel 1995) could be:

- to maintain an organisation's current position (research shows that 1 and 2 are the same)

- to adjust its current position (1 and 2 are slightly dissonant) or
- to determine an entirely new position (1 and 2 are vastly dissonant).

The design of a corporate identity plan involves consideration of a range of 'components', 'dimensions' or 'determinants' (Cornelisson and Elving 2003; Melewar 2003; Melewar and Karaosmanoglu 2006; Vella and Melewar 2008). These are perhaps most usefully represented in Figure 7.4, an adapted version of Melewar and Karaosmanoglu's (2006) revised categorisation of corporate identity dimensions and their sub-items.

Melewar and Karaosmanoglu's very useful model is based on a thorough examination of the literature to identify theoretical dimensions of corporate identity that are then tested against practitioners' experience to identify an 'operational definition'. It is a fairly comprehensive guide to the dimensions that could be considered by practitioners in the formulation of a CI strategy and is useful for academics in helping to establish some common ground in defining what is meant by corporate identity.

It has been adapted here, as we feel that Melewar and Karaosmanoglu's original (2006) model does not give enough weight to the impact of external environmental factors such as political thinking and legislation (areas represented in EPISTLE analysis: environmental, political, information, social, technological, legal and economic) that will affect the strategic design of corporate identities. For example, many mission and value statements involve concepts such as sustainability and social responsibility – would this have been the case if Thatcherism and Reagan-onomics had continued to dominate political thinking in the UK and US? It is often strategically important for organisations to project a 'responsible' identity to negate the need for legislation. And surely organisations' approaches to communication have changed as a result of developments in technology, particularly the internet – a phenomenon known as technological determinism (Somerville *et al.* 2007).

Melewar and Karaosmanoglu do recognise environmental forces as influencing identity but represent this in their model only as the influence of sectoral responses to external elements in the 'industry identity' dimension but do not reflect the source of these influences in detail. Perhaps this is because their research has been developed within a perspective that views public relations as part of the '4Ps of product, price, place and promotion . . . aimed at supporting the sales of an organisation's products' (Melewar and Karaosmanoglu 2006: 850). This has been called a marketing-centred conceptualisation of public relations:

> In what can be termed a marketing-centred approach to corporate communication, which is evident throughout much of the literature, significant stakeholders such as politicians and local communities are routinely absent and public relations is represented as promotion of a product or service.
>
> (Wood in Tench and Yeomans 2009: 544)

We do not share that perspective and prefer a conceptualisation centred on public relations that regards environmental scanning, issues management and lobbying as

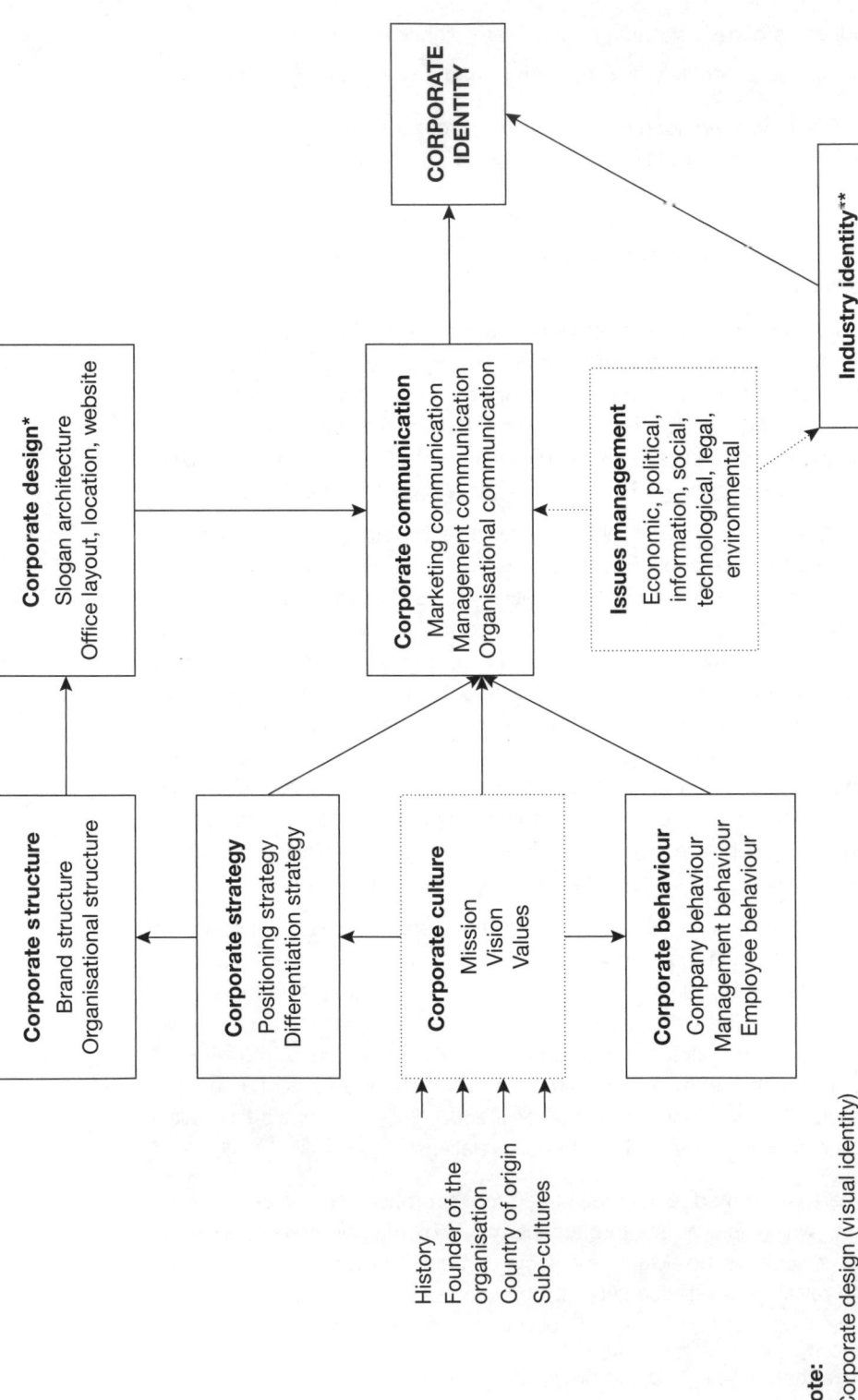

Note:

*Corporate design (visual identity)

**The most salient external factor mentioned by the interviewees

FIGURE 7.4 Adapted version of Melewar and Karaosmanoglu's revised categorisation of corporate identity dimensions and their sub-items (2006)

Source: Adapted from Melewar and Karaosmanoglu (2006). Used by permission

major imperatives in corporate communications practice. Even though practitioners may not always recognise the pervasive influence of political thought or social policy on their decision-making, issues management and environmental forces – including political, social, environmental and economic – should be recognised as influencing and shaping corporate identities (Cornelisson and Elving 2003) and Melewar and Karaosmanoglu's model has been adapted to reflect this.

RESEARCHING ACTUAL AND DESIRED CORPORATE IMAGE

Identifying the desired corporate image

From a public relations perspective, this is one of the controversial aspects of CI management. This is because much of the literature has emerged from a marketing paradigm and often considers an ideal identity as being determined by senior management and communicated to an audience (often of consumers). A public relations perspective may well consider that formulation of a desired identity should *involve* a range of stakeholders in a dialogic (or two-way) process. In other words allow key stakeholders (including employees) an influence. 'Large organisations have become so preoccupied with carefully crafted, elaborate and univocal expressions of their mission and "essence" that they often overlook penetrating questions about stakeholder involvement.'(Christensen and Cheney in Schultz *et al.* 2000: 265)

In addition, public relations planning involves issues management, and therefore consideration of the environment (often encompassed in an EPISTLE analysis)[10] informs public relations aims and objectives. It could be argued, then, that appropriate methodologies should be devised to ensure that identification of a strategically important identity is informed by an organisation's current and projected situation within its broader environment as well as stakeholder expectations. So the first step in the corporate identity planning process is to research the existing image and the desired (strategically important) image:

So when researching what the desired corporate image should be, a range of stakeholders should be consulted (via interviews, focus groups or questionairres) not just senior management. The actual corporate image would be researched using the same methodology.

Auditing existing corporate identity

Having determined what type of *image* needs to be projected, it's time to research its corporate *identity* or the 'cues' that the organisation uses to communicate about itself in an attempt to effect a particular corporate image in the minds of its stakeholders. Van Riel's (1995) CI mix (behaviour, communication and symbolism) provides a useful guide to the aspects of identity to be audited. Figure 7.4 details Melewar and Karaosmanoglu's (2006) dimensions of corporate identity and provides a useful guide to what should be investigated. For example, content or discourse analysis could be used to analyse corporate communication and corporate strategy, perhaps supplemented by interviews. An appropriate methodology should be devised to ensure all dimensions are investigated.

Communication and behavioural audits: behavioural audits, more commonly known as attitude surveys, measure job satisfaction, gather feedback on the effectiveness of internal policies and provide insight into the attitudes and behaviour of staff at all levels. The term 'behaviour' also refers to consequences for external publics, however, and implies aspects such as the manifestation of an organisation's corporate social responsibility. As discussed elsewhere in this book, a comprehensive audit of 'behaviour' would include analysis of an organisation's impact on the environment as well as a full range of stakeholders.

Communication audits survey the 'communication climate'[11] including communication style and structures as well as content.

Clearly communication and behaviour are 'inextricably linked'. Communication must be defined as more than merely communication techniques or styles of delivery. Organisations must not see the introduction of a team briefing system and some presentation training for managers as the panacea for all the problems identified through a communication audit or attitudes survey. As Grunig and Hunt (1984: 248) explain:

> Too often, management wants an easy way to gain the loyalty of employees and get more work out of them. And it's much easier to change the methods of communication than it is to change the organisational structure and role relationships – more realistic ways of affecting performance and satisfaction.

This raises broader issues relating to organisational structure and power. For example, if an organisation professes innovation as a core value, but has a highly bureaucratic structure involving layers of decision-making and centralised power, then innovation will not be fostered. A corporate identity analysis must address corporate 'behaviour' in its broadest sense and embrace all aspects of corporate culture discussed in the previous chapter, as well as structure and power. Johnson *et al.*'s cultural web (Figure 7.2) and Lewin's (1935) force field analysis[12] are useful for mapping a number of dimensions of corporate behaviour. Johnson *et al.* (2008: 200) detail a whole range of appropriate research questions investigating areas such as the type of behaviour encouraged by particular routines; core beliefs reflected by stories; ways in which power is distributed in the organisation; and the status symbols favoured. Forcefield analysis can then be used to map which of these 'enable' or 'constrain' the aspirational image.

The visual or design audit:

> The design audit is led by one of the designers on the corporate identity consultants' team. Its task is to study and document the way in which the different parts of the organisation present themselves in terms of the three

traditional areas of design – factories, showrooms and so on; product, packaging and information material; vehicle liveries, signs, brochures, advertising, instruction manuals and every other form of graphics. What does it all look like? What message is it meant to convey?

(Olins 1999: 162)

A visual audit is not superficial and should reveal more than where a new coat of paint is needed. Baker and Balmer (1997: 378) illustrate the value of the visual audit as a research tool and its contribution to strategy formulation at Strathclyde University, for example, where 'the visual audit revealed important characteristics of the University's identity; i.e. the University was highly decentralised and had fragmented corporate communications'.

However, the design audit is only one aspect of the research into an organisation's corporate identity. 'The design audit is in a sense both complementary to, and an integral part of, the communications audit, and both are inextricably involved with the behavioural audit' (Olins 1999: 162). Again, the visual attributes can be added to the forcefield analysis to help practitioners make judgements about which help or hinder the formulation of an ideal corporate identity.

So what does all this mean in practice? An example of an organisation acting on feedback from extensive research into its corporate identity is given below. The Queen Margaret University case study illustrates many of the points made in the text. It shows the value of research and how organisations can react to research findings, and provides a real insight into a comprehensive corporate identity management programme involving key stakeholders.

C@SE STUDY

QUEEN MARGARET UNIVERSITY'S CORPORATE IDENTITY

Queen Margaret College (QMC) was founded in Edinburgh in 1875, a time when women were excluded from most universities. At the forefront of women's fight for access to higher education, it was originally a cookery school and then became known for health education. At that time, research was just beginning to demonstrate the link between poverty and ill health. The college worked to improve standards of health and living conditions and campaigned for the introduction of district nurses to care for women in their homes. Within a generation, infant mortality in Scotland was reduced by 50 per cent. QMC's contribution is still a source of pride, an important aspect of its culture often emphasised in speeches (which is interesting in relation to Johnson et al's (2008) stories and myths and the idea of corporate storytelling (van Riel et al. in Schultz et al. 2000)).

Now the much-expanded Queen Margaret University (QMU) has some 5,500 students from some 50 countries worldwide studying a wide range of subjects, from dietetics to drama, from radiography to retail business and public relations.

Despite these developments, QMU's history still influences its corporate personality, as its mission statement makes clear:

> Queen Margaret University's mission is to enhance the well-being of individuals and the communities we serve through socially and economically relevant education and research.

> This mission is enhanced by our strong commitment to economic, social and environmental sustainability.

Strategic aims and objectives

In 1999, the Privy Council awarded Queen Margaret College the title *University* College. The full 'university' title could not be conferred because the college had fewer than 4,000 students (full university status was conferred in 2007).

The addition of the word 'university' into Queen Margaret College's title meant that its visual identity had to be updated. Rather than simply inserting the new word into the existing logo, however, the Principal and senior management recognised the necessity of a more fundamental and wide-ranging corporate image audit to help the University College achieve its future strategic aims. As Marketing Manager Gregor McMeechan explained: 'We took an integrated and holistic approach and considered our identity in its fullest sense. Not just thinking about how we look, but about our culture, our values, and how we communicate an accurate image of who we are.'[13]

Corporate identity plan

The aim of the corporate identity programme was to ensure that Queen Margaret University College's (QMUC's) corporate identity consistently communicated its university level status ('universityness') to all of its stakeholders.

The plan was also informed by a number of organisational objectives outlined in the University College's strategic plan. Primarily:

- to extend and develop the profile and reputation of the University College locally, regionally, nationally and internationally

- to continue to review organisational systems and structures to secure improvements in corporate policy formation and implementation,

C@SE STUDY

operational efficiency, flexibility and responsiveness to change and opportunity.

(QMUC Strategic Plan 1999–2000)

The corporate identity plan also underpinned objectives highlighted in the strategic plan relating to high graduate employment rates, international student recruitment and the development of strategic links.

Research

Several qualitative and quantitative research methods were employed to identify a range of stakeholders' views on QMUC's current and desired image:

- content analysis of documents ranging from prospectuses and strategic plans to media coverage and the internet
- surveys and questionnaires
- corporate personality mapping exercise with senior management
- semi-structured interviews
- focus groups
- visual audit.

Purposive sampling was used to ensure sufficient disclosure from a range of key stakeholder groups. These included the following:

Internal publics

- academic staff (course leaders, admissions tutors, lecturers involved in seeking research funding and/or commercial consultancy, heads of research institutes or commercial centres)
- administrative staff from areas such as business development, commercial services, marketing, student services, students' union
- governors and students.

External publics

- prospective undergraduate and postgraduate students
- professional and industrial contacts such as research sponsors and partners, placement hosts, members of advisory panels, commercial consultancy clients and the funding council.

C@SE STUDY

C@SE STUDY

Research questions

The problem with focusing a discussion on corporate identity is that most people associate corporate identity with design, which is often judged according to personal taste with everyone having views on what they like or dislike. The facilitator's major task in the focus groups was to explain the concept of corporate image and the role of corporate identity and keep the discussion focused on QMUC's corporate identity in relation to its strategic objectives. When staff considered a desired image for the University College, for example, conversations were steered towards what needed to be achieved over the next 10 years and how a particular corporate positioning could contribute to success, rather than becoming stuck on favourite colours and preferred typeface.

That said, asking for views on the existing logo and the image it communicated served as a useful icebreaker. Having expounded often dearly held opinions, participants could then be led through the group processes[14] up the conceptual ladder to a stage when valid and interesting views were proffered.

The research mapped participants' views on current and desired corporate image in relation to other universities and against expectations of what a university should be like.

Key findings

A number of attributes were identified. Some were commonly well regarded by participants while different publics held distinctive views about some important aspects. A summary follows.

Attributes valued by all constituents

- The name 'Queen Margaret', with its connotations of credibility, authority and prestige often associated with the old established universities.

- QMUC's Edinburgh location (although an overemphasis on Scottishness should not imply parochialism and obscure QMUC's international status).

- The use of the crest in QMUC's visual identity, with its connotations of longevity, tradition, quality and learning.

Attributes valued by staff and professional contacts

- Quality teaching, research and consultancy and distinctiveness of character. Perceptions of quality include issues such as the high grading obtained in the independent quality assessment exercise, the high level of individual attention given to students and the high graduate employment rate (the highest in Scotland).

- The relatively small size of the University College is an important aspect of staff perceptions of a friendly, caring and supportive nature.

- QMUC's strong research culture and history of academic achievement make staff feel more aligned with 'old' universities than with the 'new' university sector.

- The 'applied' nature of QMUC's academic expertise and strong vocational links with a range of professions.

- Caring and community values linked to concepts such as 'serving society', 'enhancing quality of life' (particularly for health faculties) and 'lifelong learning' were also highlighted.

Problematic areas identified by staff

- Confusion regarding a clear strategy to manage increasingly conflicting demands (such as the need to earn income to offset government cuts, the need to meet research targets, and the need to manage increased competition while still meeting student needs).

- Poor internal communication.

- The perception that QMUC's strategy to purchase a new campus had resulted in a lack of investment in existing facilities and buildings.

Attributes valued by students and prospective students

Specific attributes chosen as being particularly motivational showed students are looking for: quality and up-to-date teaching provision to make the most of their abilities, relevant knowledge and skills, a degree that is well regarded by employers, a high level of individual attention and support, a pleasant environment and an exciting social life.

Conflicting perspectives

Staff deemed concepts of 'serving society' and 'lifelong learning' as important attributes of the corporate personality, whereas students rejected this image. Students were motivated by elements that would benefit them as individuals rather than notions of universities being about enhancing public quality of life. (This is particularly interesting in relation to the discussion of consistency above.)

C@SE STUDY

Recommendations

Having considered the range of views expressed, researchers System Three[15] made the following recommendations:

- The desired identity for QMUC is one that effectively communicates: the key areas of activity, product quality in terms of established and independent endorsement (heritage, Quality Assessment ratings, graduate employment rate), a caring and supportive environment, as well as excitement and dynamism.
- The desired tone of QMUC both on behalf of staff and students is a stamp of established quality and prestige, as well as modern relevance, advancement and innovation.
- The high number of pressures placed on the University College necessitates a clear strategy for prioritising demands on staff and establishing a logical way forward guided by meaningful and non-conflicting objectives.

Implementation of the new corporate identity

Symbolism

From the sea of research findings, the designers distilled the following desired perceptions to inform the new visual identity:

- heritage and established quality
- Queen Margaret title
- innovation
- modern relevance of courses
- quality of teaching
- individuality of the organisation
- Edinburgh location
- friendly, supportive approach.

The single most important message was identified as 'established quality'. So, how could design communicate these attributes? Figure 7.5 (A and B) shows the old and new logos for QMUC. Lauren Rennet, Creative Director of Graphic Partners, explains the design concept:

> The concept of a crest was retained to communicate QMUC's heritage but was simplified and updated to reflect the current and future offer

C@SE STUDY

Queen Margaret University College
EDINBURGH
established 1875

FIGURE 7.5A Queen Margaret University College, old logo
Source: Used by permission

Queen Margaret University College
EDINBURGH

FIGURE 7.5B Queen Margaret University, new logo
Source: Used by permission

FIGURE 7.6 Queen Margaret University new campus
Source: Used by permission

FIGURE 7.7 Queen Margaret University library, new campus
Source: Used by permission

C@SE STUDY

of the University College, not that of its early years when the original crest was drawn.

With this in mind, the symbols within the crest were adjusted to more distinctively represent the University College. The main focus, Queen Margaret's crown, provides a memorable symbol of power, leadership and excellence.

Vibrant royal blue, futuristic silver and timeless typography complete this modern, streamlined crest without losing the valuable sense of established quality.

Staff have unique access to a corporate identity manual available solely online. The new visual identity is consistently used across applications ranging from letterheads and vehicle livery to uniforms and websites.

Figure 7.6 illustrates the application of the new identity at QMUC's Corstophine campus.

The corporate identity mix

Van Riel (1995) highlights the importance of all aspects of the CI mix. Symbolism has clearly been affected by the QMUC corporate identity plan. But what about the other important aspects, behaviour and communication?

Research conducted among QMUC staff indicated a need for improved communication and leadership in prioritising and balancing demands on lecturers. A number of initiatives were launched in response.

An improved career development and appraisal scheme provides a structure for staff to agree individual objectives within a framework that clearly connects with organisational aims and objectives. Staff are involved in determining their own criteria for success.

Dorothy Wright, Director of Human Resources, planned more far-reaching cultural developments:

> The strategic plan specifies flexibility, commercial awareness, quality, innovation and creativity as key attributes of the culture we need to foster in order to achieve our corporate aims and objectives. My job is to look at the way we need to behave in order to deliver in these areas.

Her first task was to run a facilitated session with senior management, using tools such as force field analysis to identify changes that needed to be made. Then, a full attitudes survey was commissioned to determine staff views.

Part of the attitudes survey was designed to audit communication, and resources were made available to implement more effective two-way communication systems.

In 2011, QMU, now a full university, has moved to an entirely new campus. This latest development reveals other aspects of corporate identity management in practice, as architecture is commonly identified as a significant aspect of symbolism – the vision for the new building was 'to create an attractive, distinctive campus that represents the unique characteristics of QM'. Rosalyn Marshall, Vice Principal (Resources and Development), said,

> The corporate identity project carried out in 2000 was an important part of the work preparing this institution for a new phase in its development, which would include the award of full university title and relocation to our innovative new campus. As we have continued to develop the vision for Queen Margaret University at our new campus, this corporate identity work has provided a firm foundation on which to build. The positive attributes and desired perceptions identified back in 2000 hold true today, illustrating the effectiveness of the approach taken to corporate identity management.

C@SE STUDY

QUESTIONS FOR DISCUSSION

1 Can a carefully managed corporate identity affect a strategically important corporate image?

2 What ethical issues should be considered when formulating and managing corporate identity?

3 How can stakeholders be involved?

4 Critique the assumption that corporate identity can be 'wholly managed'.

5 What is the effect of a marketing centred perspective of corporate identity management as opposed to a public relations centred approach?

6 To what extent is issues management part of CI management?

7 Specify how an existing corporate identity can be audited.

8 Critics such as Christensen and Cheney consider CI management to be the domain of a small elite within organisations who become self-absorbed and deluded about the role and importance of identity:

> In a world saturated with symbols, where there is a great demand for every organisation to keep communicating, it is easy to think that each message and every campaign are taken seriously and received in the ways designed. But such meanings are often malleable, unstable and of only ephemeral interest. In fact in many cases, cynicism may be the most prominent outcome.
>
> (Christensen and Cheney in Schultz *et al.* 2000: 267)

How could this view influence approaches to CI management?

9 How would you justify the resources necessary for the introduction of a CI management programme to a sceptical CEO?

10 To what extent is consistency important to managing corporate identity and how can multiplicity and diversity be facilitated?

NOTES

1 Gregory (1999a) provides a useful summary of current thinking:

> The two concepts of identity and image have suffered from a lack of clarity stemming partly from confusion between and conflation of the terms. Broadly speaking, corporate identity was originally seen as the visual symbols an organisation used such as logos, house style and other representations associated with design . . . For some practitioners, that view still persists . . . However, more recently the concept of corporate identity has been broadened to include linkages between corporate strategy and

communication . . . In Margulies' (1977) terms 'identity means the sum of all the ways a company chooses to identify itself to all its publics'.

2   Nike has launched a number of initiatives to overcome this image, which can be explored via its website.
3   The term 'stakeholder' refers to groups of publics (typically employees, suppliers, shareholders, customers and the local community) who have a significant effect on, or are affected by, an organisation. For a more detailed consideration of the concept, see Chapters 4 and 6.
4   For an explanation of corporate strategy and the strategic role of public relations, see Chapter 4.
5   For explanations of Grunig's (1984) symmetric and asymmetric models, see pp. 35–36.
6   For further discussion, refer to Franklin (1994) and McNair (1994).
7   The semiotic approach is outlined in Chapter 2.
8   'The way we do things around here' originated at management consultancy McKinsey & Company.
9   Van Riel (1995) provides a comprehensive summary of approaches.
10 EPISTLE analysis encompasses research into an organisation's macro environment under the headings Economic, Political, Information, Social, Technological, Legal, Environmental.
11 See Hargie and Tourish (2000) for an in-depth guide to communication audits.
12 Grundy (1993) provides a useful guide to using force field analysis.
13 Unless otherwise stated, quotes are taken from interviews with the author.
14 Social scientists often refer to groups moving through several stages (forming, storming, norming) before they 'perform' and contribute more truthful and useful opinions. For further information refer to Vernelle (1994: 28–29).
15 Research was conducted by a number of consultants, including research company System Three and the author.

FURTHER READING

Balmer, J. and Greyser, S. (eds) (2003) *Revealing the corporation: perspectives on identity, image, reputation, corporate branding, and corporate level marketing*, Routledge.

Bronn, P.S. (2010) 'Reputation, *communication and the corporate brand*' in R.L. Heath (ed.), *The SAGE handbook of public relations*, Sage.

Cornelisson, J.P. and Elving, W.J.L. (2003) 'Managing corporate identity: an integrative framework of dimensions and determinants', *Corporate Communications, An International Journal*, 8 (2), pp. 114–120.

Curtin, P.A. and Gaither, T.K. (2007) *International public relations: negotiating culture, identity, and power*, Sage.

Lerpold, L., Ravasi, D., Van Rekom, J. and Soenen, G. (eds) (2007) *Organizational identity in practice*, Routledge.

Melewar T.C. (2003) 'Determinants of the corporate identity construct: a review of the literature', *Journal of Marketing Communications*, 9, pp. 195–220.

Melewar, T.C. (ed.) (2008) *Facets of corporate identity, communication and reputation*, Taylor & Francis.

CHAPTER 8

Risk, issues and crisis management

Heather Yaxley

CHAPTER AIMS

This chapter considers the role of public relations in the fields of risk, issues and crisis management, looking at both organizational and activist perspectives. It presents and assesses traditional 'best practice' recommendations as well as the purpose of corporate apologia. Alternate approaches, reflecting the challenges of an increasingly complex world, are introduced and limitations of the involvement of public relations are recognized. In this way, the topic is extended beyond the usual consideration of planning and communications to address questions about the contribution of public relations to this evolving area.

SETTING THE SCENE

The modern world comprises a risk society (Beck 1992) with numerous dangers that impact on communities, organizations and individuals. From a public relations perspective, some of these have the potential to develop into an issue; defined as 'a contestable point, a difference of opinion regarding fact, value, or policy, the resolution of which has consequences for the organization's strategic plan and future success or failure' (Heath and Palenchar 2009: 93). In a 24:7 global communications environment, the immediacy and interconnectedness of mobile, online and social media are able to amplify what might otherwise be issues of low or no significance. This occurs often before mainstream media, organizations, or professional activists have a chance to plan their involvement and react. As such, consideration of risk, issues and crisis management occur in an increasingly dynamic and complex environment.

Within this environment, there may be diverse opinions and varying expectations of how situations should be addressed – or even if they should be addressed. Such considerations extend to public relations responses. Not only are a host of cases examined and critiqued after the event in memoires, textbooks and journal articles, but news reports and social media increasingly provide judgements and advice on what could, should and is being done by public relations practitioners in real time while an issue or crisis is occurring.

The term 'PR disaster' may be heard (defined as 'anything that could catalyse embarrassing or negative publicity for any given organization', McCusker 2006: 311); implying that practitioners are responsible when issues have not been addressed effectively (in the opinion of the critics). At the same time, attempts to explain an organization's position may be labelled as a 'PR exercise' (defined as 'a situation of communication with no substance within it', Green 2007: 215). The use of public relations by organizations is exposed by Stauber and Rampton (1995: 16) as able to 'only manipulate while it remains invisible'. Hence, increasing discussion about public relations arguably means that practitioners are no longer simply 'invisible persuaders' (Mitchie 1998). Indeed, being visible means the role of public relations in managing risk, issues and crisis can increasingly be recognized and critically examined.

VISIBLE PERSUADERS

Involvement in the management of risk, issues and crisis situations positions public relations as a strategically valued function within organizations (Holtzhausen 2007); particularly when there may be significant consequences as a result of adopting a particular course of action.

Such acceptance of PR counsel reflects arguments for its boundary spanning role, where it takes on responsibility for 'bringing the problems of stakeholder publics into decision making' (through managing relationships with media, politicians or other opinion formers) and 'helping organizations to adapt, or match, themselves to their environments' (Moss *et al.* 2000: 283).

The core dimensions of work executed by PR managers (Moss *et al.* 2005) focus on responsibilities of clear relevance to the topic of this chapter. Managerial functions include acting as: monitor and evaluator, key policy and strategy adviser, troubleshooter/problem solver, and issues management expert; while the communication technician dimension may reflect a role for public relations managers in crafting communications in response to issues or crises, including corporate apologia. Holtzhausen and Voto (2002) also advocate a postmodern view of public relations whereby practitioners act as organizational activists; challenging the dominant Model of Excellence paradigm (Grunig 2001) that positions the function as part of the senior management team for issues and crisis scenarios to be handled effectively (Holtzhausen 2007).

The boundary spanning role may also involve a senior PR practitioner acting as a spokesperson, which could be a highly visible position. During the Kosovo conflict in the 1990s, NATO Director of Information and Press, Jamie Shea, became a household name as the organization's lead spokesperson. Even if, as Fearn-Banks (2007) argues, the head of PR is not normally the spokesperson during a crisis, their role is presumed and may be critiqued publicly by commentators in the media or online. The *Guardian*'s City editor, Richard Wachman commented: 'BP's reaction [to the Gulf of Mexico oil spill] amounts to a textbook example of how not to do things and will be studied by students of PR for years to come' (26 December 2010).

Recognition of the need for professional PR advice in times of trouble is particularly noticeable in relation to celebrities or members of the public who are the focus of media attention. In the UK, Max Clifford is well known not only as a publicist, but for his ability to keep clients out of the news; reflecting a protectionist approach to crisis management. This defensive strategy is also evident in high profile legal firms who position themselves as experts in crisis management; primarily recommending the use of media injunctions or other legal measures to protect their clients who include major corporations, heads of state and high profile individuals. In contrast, public relations consultancies specialising in crisis management tend to maintain a lower profile and rarely speak about their specific clients.

UNDERSTANDING RISK

Within organizations, public relations expertise has the potential to extend beyond protecting clients or managing public interest after a situation has occurred to involve anticipating and managing understanding of risk as a precursor to issues or crisis management. Such risks may emerge from within the organization or from external eventualities. The involvement of public relations may help alleviate threats (for example, to lessen or avoid risk), or to increase understanding of the necessity or context of risk. It may also, as L'Etang (2008: 80) observes, position PR practitioners as 'apologists for inexcusable dangers or accidents'. Alternatively, public relations may help achieve activist or organizational goals by increasing recognition of hazards in order to stimulate responses from the public, government, organizations or individuals.

Risk as a concept is 'multidimensioned and nuanced' (Haimes 2009: 1647) and hence difficult to define. McComas (2010: 462) opts for the National Research Council definition: 'things, forces, or circumstances that pose danger to people or to what they value.' A traditional, organizational approach to understanding risk considers three questions (Garrick and Christi 2008):

1   What can go wrong?
2   How likely is that to happen?
3   What are the consequences if it does happen?

For most organizations, there are innumerable potential risks and the cost of addressing these may seem prohibitive. Although the classic Tylenol crisis case is held up as a best practice case study (Regester and Larkin 2008), the painkiller's manufacturer, Johnson & Johnson, introduced tamper-resistant bottles only after the deaths of several customers in the US in the 1980s. The risk of someone deliberately poisoning over-the-counter medicines had always existed, but until this situation actually happened, its probability may have appeared so low that the costs of introducing new packaging were not justified.

However, when incidents occur, organizations may act proactively to be responsible or be forced to respond by legal, financial or reputational consequences. For example, McDonalds' coffee cups carry a statement: contents are hot; which derives from a legal case involving a customer who received extensive burns as a result of spilling coffee in her lap (Somerville 2007). For McDonalds, considerable legal and financial consequences led to inclusion of the warning statement. From a PR perspective, it is debatable whether reputational risk can be eliminated entirely by warning labels.

In the UK, a health and safety culture has increased recognition of potential risks – and required organizations to look at ways that they, and the public, can be protected, at least legally. PR practitioners are encouraged likewise to protect the organization's reputation in the face of potential risks. However, Sutherland (1992) observed how even experts (such as engineers or management) frequently make decisions that fail to understand how people will react in a situation and this increases the risk of unforeseen consequences. Risk management is not an exact science, particularly when human behaviour is involved.

For example, following debate about the issue of the high risk of young car drivers having road accidents, a successful PR campaign in the UK by road safety campaigners led to the New Drivers Act in 1997. This was felt to be a solution that targeted only unsafe newly qualified drivers who would lose their licence by incurring fewer penalty points than drivers with more than two years' experience. However, the logical, legislative solution failed to anticipate how other road safety initiatives, such as speed cameras, would increase the likelihood of gaining points, and the rise in the number of drivers prepared to drive without a licence (AA Foundation for Road Research 1999). More than a decade on, young drivers are still considered to be at greatest risk of accidents; with the added danger that they may be driving without a licence or insurance (Figure 8.1).

Risk management traditionally involves assessing the likelihood (risk assessment) and possible impact (risk analysis) of foreseen consequences. Some organizations also undertake causal modelling and forecasting of different outcome scenarios to anticipate unforeseen consequences. Theaker (2007) cites Ansell and Wharton (1992) who view risk as unavoidable; although they claim risk assessment and analysis enable informed decisions to be made to select from possible choices of action.

FIGURE 8.1 Newly qualified drivers are considered to be at greatest risk of accidents
Source: Used by permission of the Automobile Association

Schwartz and Gibb (1999) argue this is driven by a focus on the cost of insuring against organizational liability in such circumstances. They believe organizations tend to concentrate on risks where there are predictable financial consequences, whereas reputational risks are often more difficult to evaluate.

The emergence of formal risk management processes within organizations is the result of concerns about corporate governance and other strategic matters relating to how organizations are being managed, as well as recognition of the possible costs of a crisis (financially, legally and to reputation). Data is used to evaluate hazards and ensure financial and other stakeholders understand the possible consequences of problems and how well the organization's management is addressing these. The scientific approach to risk assessment has seen auditors and management consultancy groups take on this analytical and reporting role. If PR is to claim equal status and enact its boundary spanning strategic role, it may be argued that the function needs to take responsibility for undertaking similarly robust calculation of stakeholder relationships, emerging issues and reputational risk. Decision making would then be based on assessing hazards and outlining the benefits of different options drawing on research data and scientific analysis.

This systems-based, management approach supports analytical decision making to assess possible outcomes (Figure 8.2). The likelihood of each outcome, along with its benefits and drawbacks can be mapped. Where possible a financial or other measure, such as impact on stakeholder relationships or reputation, can be determined to aid decision making.

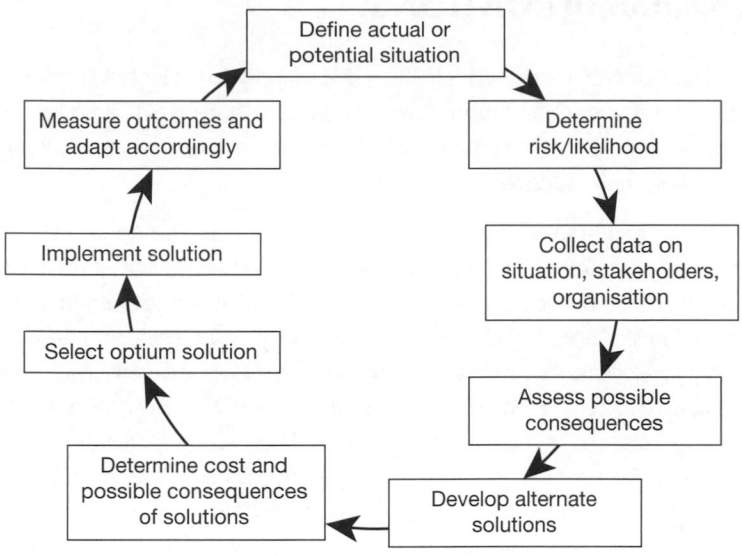

FIGURE 8.2 Circular decision making process

It should be emphasized, however, that this approach involves predicting possible outcomes (consequences) and calculating the likelihood of these occurring. As such, it remains guesswork, even if based on research data and logical deductions.

Also, in undertaking risk management, public relations practitioners need to take account of perceptions and acceptance of risk among stakeholders and publics. L'Etang (2008: 79) notes that risks are 'perceptions manufactured partly through our own sense-making and judgements'. Similarly, McComas (2010: 462) observes 'the challenge for risk management is that while some people seek zero risk in their daily lives, others are willing to accept some level of risk to obtain some type of benefit'. Indeed, there is a certain level of risk inherent in day-to-day life, often as a consequence of the benefits gained from modern society (Beck 1992).

Understanding of risk can also be affected by the media and other communicators (including public relations practitioners) who act to socially amplify risk and attenuate public responses (Kasperson *et al.* 1988). L'Etang (2008) notes the potential for panic to spiral from the type of media coverage that Feldman and Marks (2005: xix) feel often reflects expression of opinion (rather than fact) originating from 'over zealous pressure groups or presentations by special-interest lobbies'. A more positive role for public relations in communicating risk is evident in L'Etang's (2008: 138) statement that 'accurate, trustworthy guidance is a public good'.

RISK COMMUNICATIONS

McComas (2010: 462) notes that 'effective risk management includes risk communication with affected publics'; which she defines as 'a purposeful, iterative exchange of information among individuals, groups and institutions related to the assessment, characterization, and management of risk'.

The circular decision-making process presented in Figure 8.2 applies to the public as much as organizations. That is, when faced with situations that involve perceived risk, members of the public may similarly seek information to help with their decisions. The elaboration likelihood model proposed by Petty and Cacioppo (1986) details a central cognitive route that involves extensive consideration of issues, particularly among those who have high motivation and the ability to think about messages. In such circumstances, simple messaging is unlikely to be sufficient to meet their needs. Indeed, Rucker and Petty (2006: 49) suggest risk communications can be improved by making people aware of the lack of benefits as well as risks associated with behaviours. For example, they propose cigarette packaging 'might not only note the health dangers associated with using the product but also specifically emphasize that the product does not offer any health benefits'.

Similarly, Grunig's situational theory of publics (Grunig and Hunt 1984) considers when and how people will act in relation to an issue of interest to them; advocating that 'lasting behavioral effects can occur when attitudes are formed through elaborated cognitions, highly developed constructions about an issue' (Ehling and Dozier 1992: 175). It proposes that those with a greater level of interest in a situation should be the primary focus as they will engage in proactive consideration of messages.

These cognitive models therefore suggest public relations practitioners need to pay attention to publics who are likely to act, and ensure they are able to access detailed information to address any concerns and prevent criticism of the organization. McComas (2010) notes, however, that risk communications have traditionally been one-sided, becoming persuasive if publics do not respond to information presented. She claims that more recently, the emphasis of risk communications has shifted to seeking to involve publics on the basis of understanding psychological and social factors affecting their decision making. Palenchar (2010: 451) supports 'shared dialogue' over 'information push' in encouraging 'vigilant community stakeholders'.

Risk communications can help influence choices (Palenchar 2010) and reduce uncertainty felt when people are faced with risk. As such, communications help minimize or eliminate cognitive dissonance (mental discomfort) experienced by those who face conflicting information or inconsistent feelings. From a PR perspective, practitioners may be involved in communicating risk from the perspective of helping organizations address emerging issues or potential crises, or they may be involved in highlighting risk, increasing understanding of issues and mobilizing others against organizations.

As risk communications can be used to reduce or to increase public perceptions of the need to take action, this raises questions of ethics. Even if not deliberately lying, communicating risk means information could be selected purposefully to obfuscate or at least to downplay or overplay the situation depending on the aims of the client organization.

In particular, careful consideration is required in communicating scientific facts and statistics that emerge from risk analysis. Technical information may be difficult for non-experts to understand, and those affected by an issue may react instinctively or engage in peripheral processing (when little thought is given to issues, particularly by those with little motivation or who are unable to consider messages in any depth, Petty and Cacioppo 1986). This presents a danger that rational and informed debate is replaced by simplistic communications leading to the type of over-reaction that has accompanied recent health risks (from SARS to swine flu). Consequently, the public may ignore valid warnings becoming risk averse (reflecting the cry wolf phenomenon, Kam 2004) or lose all motivation to respond (reflecting the learned helplessness phenomenon, Badhwar 2009). The public could also feel disempowered by communications involving 'risk experts' (L'Etang 2008: 80) who may present contradictory evidence or disagree over its interpretation.

There is little sense of these considerations in traditional PR recommendations for managing risk communications. For example, on a tactical level, Seitel (1998) cites William Adams' seven steps to plan a risk communication programme:

1   Recognise that risk communication is part of a larger risk management programme based on politics, power and controversial issues.

2   Encourage management to participate in communications and undertake a media training programme.

3   Develop credible outside experts to deal effectively with news media.

4   Become an in-house expert in your own area of risk to improve credibility.

5   Approach news media with solid facts and figures before they approach you. Ensure the veracity of your data.

6   Research perceptions of your organization by the media and other publics to gauge credibility and help determine if your messages will be believable.

7   Understand your target audiences and how the news media can help you communicate effectively.

The advice presents a linear communication process, with research evident only in the final steps, where it is used asymmetrically to improve the messaging process. Grunig and Repper (1992) offer a more relationship approach, albeit focused on the organizational perspective. Their model features four stages:

1   *Stakeholder stage.* Involves understanding of, and building effective relation-ships with stakeholders (defined as those who affect or are affected by

the organization in achieving its objectives, Freeman, 1984). Environmental scanning enables the potential consequences (risks) of stakeholder behaviour on the organization (and vice versa) to be identified (Kim and Ni 2010).

2   *Publics stage*. Relationships with stakeholders are seen as serving to reduce the negative impact of publics (defined as 'connected social actors . . . who seek, select and share information in their problem-solving process'; Kim and Ni 2010: 44). Monitoring stakeholder opinion enables early identification of the emergence of concerns that may lead to the formation of publics who will act against the organization. PR practitioners may also involve publics in the decision-making process at this stage (Kim and Ni 2010).

3   *Issues stage*. PR's boundary-spanning role enables situations to be anticipated and analysed on the basis of the organization's relationships with various stakeholders or latent publics (those affected by an issue but not yet aware of it), in order to develop planned PR and communication solutions. Issues are identified at an early stage at which point their impact can be minimised.

4   *Public relations/communications programmes and plans*. Consequently, strategic responses are determined on the basis of knowledge of those involved in the scenario and the nature of the issues that concern them.

This model's linear approach led Moss and Warnaby (1997) to propose an adaptive framework that showed how public relations strategies should integrate with organizational strategies and the external social, political, economic, technological environment. Grunig (2009) likewise reflects the interdependence between an organization and the external environment with a revised strategic management model where stakeholder relational outcomes and cultivation strategies are presented as central to managing issues, crises, organizational reputation and achieving organizational goals.

Grunig's original situational theory has been developed by Kim and Ni (2010: 44) to include the concept of active communication behaviours by publics, notably with the selection and transmission of information within 'social communicative networks'. They argue for symmetrical (dialogic) communications to develop quality relationships that will increase positive communication actions and decrease negative ones.

Such models echo the evolution of risk communication noted by Palenchar (2010) towards working in partnership with publics to mutually manage risk. However, they do not acknowledge any differential in power that may be at the heart of consideration of risk; it is normally others who face risk as a result of organizational decisions or action. The extent to which risk communications are executed in order to achieve organizational goals, improve public understanding and engagement in developing outcomes, or reflect corporate responsibility in doing the right thing are matters of debate in the latest phase in risk communications according to Palenchar (2010). He claims such concerns are reflected in contemporary best practice approaches that emphasize building trust, transparency, respect for others and ongoing communications that acknowledge the uncertainty of risk situations.

ISSUES MANAGEMENT

Although L'Etang (2004) notes the antecedents of issues management in the intelligence service enacted by British public relations practitioners in the 1930s, the term 'issues management' is credited to Howard Chase in 1976, who had concerns about the influence of activists and non-governmental organizations on public policy, at the expense of corporations (Jaques 2010). During the 1980s, issues management became viewed as an important preventative step in proactive crisis avoidance.

Jaques (2010) notes a lack of agreement in defining issues management, although Tucker and Broom (1993, cited by Regester and Larkin 2008: 44) believe it enables organizations to 'reduce risk, create opportunities and manage image (corporate reputation) as an organizational asset'. As such, an issue is seen not simply as a problem. A problem is a situation or question for which there may be several solutions that are not necessarily controversial or involve opposing sides. For example, the past few winters in the UK have seen increasing incidents of extreme snowfall and local authorities face the problem of planning for such eventualities. There are many possible solutions to the problem, not all of which may be controversial (for example, that they should ensure adequate supplies of road grit). However, considering whether or not local authorities should invest in expensive specialist equipment in anticipation of extreme snowfall is an issue that has caused considerable public, media and political debate.

A proactive approach to issues management is seen as important, with Cutlip *et al.* (2000) defining its essence as early identification and designing strategic responses to mitigate or capitalise on possible consequences. Grunig and Hunt (1984: 296) quote Buchholz (1982) as saying 'The interactive corporation tries to get a reasonably accurate agenda of public issues that it should be concerned with . . . and develops constructive approaches to these issues.'

These statements do not explicitly recognize the opportunity for public relations to engage others and L'Etang (2008: 86) expresses concern that issues monitoring implies a 'surveillance' approach, whereby organizations seek to exert power, often in partnership with other institutions, over those being investigated.

Research may identify several, possibly opposing, points of view surrounding an issue. When faced with a variety of perspectives, it may be possible to identify common themes or groups of people who hold similar views. This enables responses to be developed to meet particular needs or to engage with the most frequently raised aspect of the issue. It should be remembered, however, that the organization should be consistent in its response to avoid communicating potentially conflicting messages. Responses should also be clear about the organization's position and not include statements merely to gain favour that are at odds with its actions.

Identification of issues should also acknowledge that an operational response, rather than a persuasive communications one, may be required from the organization. An issue may be a matter of legitimate concern where public relations practitioners need to act as activists within organizations (Holtzhausen 2000) and insist on internal change.

It is also important to understand that issues do not exist in isolation and may be linked to other issues. For example, the issue of genetically modified food relates to the wider debate on food poverty, which depends on factors such as population numbers, food technology, transportation, political structure, cultural traditions, and so forth. An organization's response may need to be placed in the wider framework of debate, or consider the impact of related issues on stakeholders and publics.

Similarly, any response to a situation can cause different issues to arise. For example, criticism of car companies for their reliance on fossil fuels led to a switch to biofuels such as ethanol, which can be made from crops such as corn, barley, wheat, sugar cane or beet. However, demand for biofuels raises issues such as deforestation and food poverty as a result of their production.

The traditional approach to issues management proposes a rather narrow developmental life cycle with public relations action seeking to prevent public, media and political debate that could lead to restrictions on an organization's practices. As such, issues management is closely linked to public affairs or political lobbying and underlines a role for public relations in maintaining an organization's license to operate (Ihlen and van Ruler 2009).

Jaques (2010: 436) notes that issues management is also 'used by government agencies themselves to promote and implement new policy, and by NGOs [non-governmental organizations], activists, and community groups to facilitate public participation in the process'. Issues management has predominantly been considered from the organizational perspective, and primarily as a defense mechanism against activist opposition (L'Etang 2008). Those who are most critical of public relations, such as Stauber and Rampton (1995), focus on this dominant paradigm to highlight the actions of organizations; while ignoring the use of PR tactics when employed by activists. Indeed, Smith and Ferguson (2010: 405) note that activism has not been embraced as a 'legitimate public relations practice' despite its close linkage to issues management.

Nevertheless, Jaques (2010: 437) feels the idea of disputation is useful in emphasising that to be considered as an issue a matter must involve 'contending opinions' between two or more parties. He states the potential impact of issues should be an important consideration, particularly in focusing attention on matters that are most significant; listing six factors that justify formal issues management:

1   Involvement of external parties
2   No black-and-white answer
3   Likely involvement of public policy or regulation
4   Emotion rather than data likely to prevail
5   Occurring in public, or via news media
6   With greatest risk of failure or becoming a crisis that threatens the entire organization.

Linking into approaches already considered in relation to risk management, issues management literature has tended to propose simple linear models. First, process planning models include stages that can be seen in the circular decision making model (Figure 8.2) and can be summarized broadly as: defining the issue, analysis, considering potential solutions, implementation and evaluation. Second, temporal models are proposed to illustrate how issues develop through sequential stages showing escalation of interest and debate before the issue peaks, is resolved (possibly by legislation) or declines in relevance. Jaques (2010) observes these models generally, arguing that if an organization does not act promptly, it will face fewer choices, greater costs and less chance of achieving a positive outcome.

One problem with such models is that they present a simplified, linear perspective suggesting that organizations can control the development of issues and prevent crises arising. They also remove any wider social context and ignore the involvement of others affected by the issue (positively or negatively). As noted by L'Etang (2008), presenting issues management as research undertaken prior to communications campaigns may limit its ability to contribute to wider corporate strategy development. This suggests public relations practitioners need to do more than focus on com-munications solutions when considering their role in issues management.

Such considerations arise when looking at issues where the limits of organizational influence are evident. One high-profile area relates to ethical sourcing and fair-trade practices within an organization's supply chain. For example, although Nike initially used media relations to defend its position in response to criticisms of labour prac-tices in its global supply chain (Neef 2004), it has subsequently taken a leadership position based on monitoring, industry codes, transparency in its operations and social responsibility (Ferrell *et al.* 2009).

Jaques (2010) highlights the necessity for organizations to take issues management seriously and ensure the intelligence generated during this process can translate into action. As with the examples of McDonalds and Tylenol discussed above, the potential for a crisis situation is often known – but for various reasons, no action is taken to avoid a potential risk from becoming a real crisis. Jaques (2010) also emphasizes the need for post-crisis management, which again requires action to be taken (as in the Nike example) to avoid recurrence and development of the initial issue into other areas.

Many crises can have long-term legacies, particularly when litigation or political inquiries keep an issue alive potentially for many years. As such, an issue or crisis that initially reveals operational or management problems, can become a significant reputational issue and result in a lasting decline in trust. Jacques (2010) therefore recommends issues management needs to continue after an immediate crisis is resolved and become embedded into ongoing strategic management.

Jaques (2010) presents a relational model that offers a holistic viewpoint of issues management and avoids the inference that steps are to be undertaken sequentially. He includes issues and risk management within crisis prevention, which is distinct from crisis preparedness, crisis event management and post-crisis management. Crisis preparedness involves formal systems necessary in case a crisis occurs (such as producing manuals, policies, training and resource allocation). In contrast, issues management seeks to avoid a crisis from occurring alongside actions such as audits, risk assessment, and environmental scanning.

ACTIVE APPROACHES TO ISSUES

An alternative view of issues management from being solely a defensive precursor to crisis management is its use by organizations as 'opportunity management' (Jaques 2002: 142) or voluntarily to raise issues of concern. Indeed, rather than viewing an issue as a matter of disputation (Jaques 2010), organizations could engage with active publics and authorities to agree mutually acceptable solutions.

The Chase-Jones model (1979, cited by Gaunt and Ollenburger 1995) includes two somewhat pro-active strategies reflecting this perspective: adaptive (being open to change) and dynamic (being an advocate of change). Jaques (2002) additionally cites the catalytic strategy proposed by Crable and Vibbert (1986) as offensive (rather than defensive), affirmative action to create potential issues and ensure these are discussed in a way that is favourable to the organization.

These approaches are echoed in models of social responsibility that present responsiveness in seeking to contribute – and gain a reputation – as a leader in ethical or philanthropic matters as superior to meeting legal obligations or reacting to social expectations. In being responsive to society's needs, it could be viewed that issues management enables an organization to seek out opportunities to advance its strategic position – and demonstrate social responsibility.

Smuddle and Courtright (2010: 184) call for responsible public relations practitioners as members of professional bodies to advocate ethical responsiveness to 'serve the public interest' and 'aid informed public debate'. As such, practitioners may reflect a post-modernist perspective by challenging organizational behaviour from within as internal activists (Holtzhausen and Voto 2002) or as the organization's conscience or 'ethical guardian' (although this is seen as problematic in reality; L'Etang 2003).

Citing L.A. Grunig, Holtzhausen (2000) notes public relations practitioners routinely deal with external activists, necessitating skills in building relationships and accepting that others may have more power (for example with the media) than the organizations they represent. As noted in the introduction, the 24:7 global communications environment enables mobile, online and social media to be used to amplify issues, increasing the power of individuals and activist groups. This means it will be increasingly necessary, and difficult, for public relations practitioners to identify, and engage with, those who have the power in influencing the development of any issue.

An active approach to issues management is also evident in the work of organizations that seek to 'elevate a society's value standards' (Smith and Ferguson 2010: 396). Examining the role of public relations within community, NGO or activist groups, enables their work to be considered as part of the field (not opposed to it) and encourages a less traditional organizational-centric or defensive approach to issues management.

There is a long history of charities, NGOs and independent groups of highly active publics using public relations tactics to raise the profile of issues or stimulate crisis situations, in order to get their voice heard and change public opinion (Bourland-Davis *et al.* 2010).

Activists, including investigative media, have been putting pressure on government and organizations for hundreds of years, and in the 1960s and 1970s global activist movements began to form (e.g. Amnesty International, Greenpeace, Worldwide Fund for Nature). These large organizations became expert at engaging and motivating stakeholders through high profile public relations campaigns. Bourland-Davis *et al.* (2010) believe the success of activist organizations highlights weaknesses in traditional PR models, notably through the way in which such bodies heighten perceptions of conflict (often through press agentry activities) rather than seek collaboration. As such, they argue the 'default position of excellent public relations' (p. 419) as part of the dominant coalition within corporate environments should be reconsidered.

Smith and Ferguson (2001) cite Heath's (1997) cyclical model of activism comprising five stages:

1   *strain* – recognise, define and seek legitimacy for issues
2   *mobilisation* – form groups, establish communication systems, mobilise resources
3   *confrontation* – push government or organizations to resolve problems
4   *negotiation* – exchange of messages
5   *resolution* – temporary/permanent solutions.

Many activist organizations being already established may be thought to focus primarily on confrontation – with their goal being to maintain their organization to pursue its purposes rather than to rectify the conditions they seek to address (Smith and Ferguson 2001). This means attracting and motivating members to a particular cause or position could be viewed as directing public relations resources away from drawing attention to an issue, positioning the activists as legitimate advocates and successfully arguing for a particular solution. From this perspective, the role of public relations within activist organizations may be more akin to that in corporate environments, where it is involved at a strategic level with matters of organizational sustainability.

The need for collaboration may also be evident in the need for activist groups to work together (or even merge) to better fight a particular issue. The Make Poverty History campaign in 2005 brought together a broad coalition of hundreds of organizations that could share a common purpose in seeking global political action on the issue of world poverty (Sireau 2008).

At other times, groups splinter as different elements refine their objectives. In this way, there are often moderate and more extreme groups working around any particular issue. For example, in the animal rights movement, groups may be divided into reformists or abolitionists (Guither 1998); the former being more willing to work within the system to address issues of concern.

Arguments already considered for building relationships and achieving mutually acceptable solutions apply to organizations and activists, although both may be suspicious of the other and question their motives for seeking a dialogue.

CRISIS MANAGEMENT

A quick scan of the news, or social media, shows that crises have an ongoing impact on individuals, organizations and communities every day of the year. From the organizational perspective, Coombs (2010: 477) defines a crisis as 'the perception of an unpredictable event that threatens the important expectations of stakeholders and can seriously impact an organization's performance and generate negative outcomes'.

At the international level, you will find major disasters such as terrorist attacks, product recalls and environmental emergencies. Organizations also hit the headlines and online grapevine for customer relations issues and ill-judged public statements – for example, BP CEO Tony Hayward's infamous remark: 'I'd like my life back' at the height of the Gulf of Mexico oil crisis. Crisis situations also affect public sector bodies, charities and even small local businesses.

Crisis communications is one area where the value of public relations should be indisputable. Organizations facing crises (driven by external or internal forces) rely on goodwill, and being able to communicate with key publics, the media and other influencers. Helping to avoid or resolve a crisis can be seen as the pinnacle of the public relations role when it has strategic significance, and engages the attention of senior management. However, as already noted, this is a field where legal firms and media relations specialists challenge the role of public relations. The involvement of public relations is also criticized by those opposed to conventional crisis communication approaches (Dezenhall and Weber 2007).

The way in which an organization responds to a crisis and ensures that it is effectively resolved – in the long term – may affect its reputation for many years. Companies such as Nestlé, Coca-Cola, McDonalds and Nike have all experienced major crises that continue to be associated with their name some years after the original incident has been resolved. Crisis scenarios affecting BP and Toyota dominated global head-lines (online and in mainstream media) in 2010, costing millions of pounds to resolve and affecting perceptions of the competence of their management, and public relations teams. Indeed, in a digital age, any crisis remains visible through archived media coverage, activist sites, blogs and social media postings.

As discussed above, traditional theories propose a scientific management approach (Gilpin and Murphy 2008) whereby public relations practitioners can employ techniques that ensure negative situations do not arise – and if they do, crisis pre-paredness comes into play to mitigate any effect. This presents a rationale approach based on modernist, linear perspectives that imply crisis situations can be predicted and their impact avoided.

Gilpin and Murphy (2008: 4) state that 'a dominant paradigm has emerged' based on a process of intelligence gathering through environmental scanning as a defense against potential crisis situations. This approach can be seen in examples used to validate a mantra of 'golden rules' (Regester and Larkin 2008) or commandments (Seitel 1998). Indeed, adherence to prescribed practices means an organization (such as Johnson & Johnson over Tylenol) is held up as an exemplar (winning industry awards), while those who do not conform (such as Exxon with the Valdez crisis) are slated as the worst (Pauly and Hutchison 2005). In this way, public relations practitioners are encouraged to follow a 'right way' regardless of the actual crisis situation they may face.

Murphy (1991) applies a different approach to considering crisis situations using game theory to examine a number of cases. Looking at the strategy of entering a duel (by remaining silent), benefits of delaying disseminating information (as well as dangers) can be considered; showing openness may not be the best policy. Search and pursuit (hide and seek) can also be a successful strategy, although it raises ethical questions as the organization seeks to avoid discussing the crisis. Escalation is a financially driven game where denial at early stages raises the stakes of a higher ultimate settlement – its only merit is in using delay before opening negotiation and reaching an agreement reflecting a bargaining game. While reflecting that unwritten rules may govern actions in crisis scenarios, Murphy believes game theory also challenges ideas about rationale mindsets and supports the concept of uncertainty in crisis management.

Gilpin and Murphy (2008: 5) argue against 'overly rigid crisis planning procedures' as these position public relations as capable of delivering more than may be possible and so risks practitioners appearing to fail as a result of misplaced expectations. A more flexible approach enables consideration of the actual situation being faced by the particular organization at a specific time and presents public relations not as controlling the crisis, but as capable of working as proficiently as possible.

The traditional systems approach further advocates developing plans for specific types of crisis (Fearn-Banks 2007) based on action lists necessary to prepare and manage the particular eventuality. It implies a simplified predictability of crisis emergence and development rather than the reality of complex situations, involving multiple stakeholders and interests (inside and outside the organization), changing scenarios and dynamic communications networks.

Rather than expecting a crisis to behave in a particular way, and respond with particular solutions, public relations practitioners need to be equipped to assess shifting events and respond with an appropriate range of tools. Gilpin and Murphy (2008: 7) suggest learning from complexity theory by recognizing 'uncertainty and unpredictability' in crisis situations with a focus on 'flexibility and alertness'.

Unpredictability is often apparent in the first indication of a crisis (Seitel 1998), which may be the surprise of a media call (or increasingly an online comment in social media) indicating that an incident has occurred. Initial reports may lead to ongoing discussion, speculation (ill-founded or justified) and both escalation and spread of awareness. The public relations function will be expected to respond – even if verifiable information is not yet available. Without the organization taking action, the linear crisis management models propose loss of control results with others presenting information and views on the situation – often critical. This leads to further scrutiny and potentially a siege mentality (with legal advice to avoid admission or fault) or panic within the organization.

Public relations advice traditionally recommends that prompt, honest, full disclosure is made as soon as possible; with a general rule to: tell it all and tell it fast. This addresses one aspect of crisis communications (Coombs 2010): managing information. Coombs (2010) asserts that crises are perceptual and consequently public relations practitioners also need to manage how situations are understood and interpreted by others. This implies crisis management is a narrative process requiring rhetorical approaches. It is natural for public relations practitioners, as communicators, to focus on this aspect of a crisis.

However, it must be remembered that crises generally occur for a reason – and operational or managerial causes and consequences need to be addressed, not simply replaced by corporate apologia or image management techniques. In such cases, any underlying issue is likely to reoccur and when it does, any initial goodwill that may have supported communications initially is likely to have dissipated, resulting in a more serious situation second time around.

The focus on managing perceptions rather than solving underlying causes reinforces the idea that public relations practitioners alone can control a crisis. Indeed, it relates to the tactics employed by publicists and lawyers where connections, manipulation, threats or legal restraints are all that are required to make an issue or crisis disappear. Online communications have shown that it is not so simple to stop bad news from emerging. Indeed, seeking to prevent disclosure often exacerbates the resulting crisis and puts the organization in a much worse light.

The changing nature of crisis management necessitates a new approach involving continuous learning 'to equip key managers with the capabilities, flexibility and confidence to deal with sudden and unexpected problems/events—or shifts in public perception of any such problems/events' (Robert and Lajtha 2002: 181). Likewise, Gilpin and Murphy (2008) advocate a different type of expertise with a model based on establishing strong relationships and robust knowledge of the organization; as well as developing competencies in intuition, active sense-making, sensitivity to change, and rapid decision-making. They advocate maintaining dialogue within networks of relationships within and outside the organization (including communities of practice to facilitate problem resolution). These ideas require a shift towards improvization and away from rational planning; although Gilpin and Murphy (2008) see this as evolution rather than revolution and extend its use to issues and reputation management (2010).

APOLOGIA

The term 'apologia' was conceived initially by Aristotle as 'the rhetoric of self-defense, image-repair or crisis management' (Campbell and Huxman 2003: 293). As we have seen earlier, there are 'well-defined rhetorical expectations' of crisis responses (p. 287) and violating these is likely to generate additional negative attention. Despite advocating honesty and openness, the primary focus of these 'best practice' rules seems to be on making an apology – which from the organizational perspective is a discourse of defence (Hearit 1994) rather than contrition. This can be seen in the case of Tiger Woods and demands for a public apology for exposure of his marital infidelities, where arguably, this was a private rather than a public relations issue (Sowell 2010).

As discussed in the case of activist groups, alternative discourse or 'rhetoric of subversion' (Campbell and Huxman 2003: 292) can be a successful approach with the use of confrontation, mass rallies, shock tactics and other techniques that would be unacceptable if used by public relations practitioners working on behalf of organizations.

In using apologia as a strategy, public relations practitioners are seeking to influence judgements in terms of presenting facts about the organization's actions (from its point of view), to control the nature of debate (and influence any outcomes that may be sought by those affected by a crisis) and engage in image repair by altering perceptions. Apologia may be used to reinforce the good character of the organization, deny wrong doing, differentiate problematic actions, transcend the current situation, shift blame or attack the accuser, present corrective action or make a confession (Campbell and Huxman 2003).

Such speeches may be carefully crafted by public relations experts, reflecting a one-way method of communications seeking to persuade rather than engage others in resolving a crisis. Lazare (2005: 7) observes an 'apology phenomenon' in the media; reflecting what he asserts are pseudo-apologies, where sorrow is expressed conditionally rather than acknowledging responsibility (Hearit 2001). Interestingly, Campbell and Huxman (2003) conclude that well-publicized speeches of self-defence tend to fail, despite modern society's demands that they be made.

Corbett (1988: xi) states: 'What perversity is there in the human psyche that makes us enjoy the spectacle of human beings desperately trying to answer the charges leveled against them? Maybe secretly, as we read or listen, we say to ourselves, "Ah, there but for the grace of God go I".' However, such apologies may be a form of power-rebalance when the media, and public, are able to exert some form of contrition from organizations or celebrities. Indeed, such apologies may not be taken seriously; with public apologies seen as a form of entertainment where powerful figures are required to embarrass themselves. Their continuing dominance as a 'best practice' crisis response strategy highlights the need for traditional approaches to be reconsidered.

IMPORTANCE TO PUBLIC RELATIONS

Risk, issues and crisis management are important to the self-image of public relations as the function is positioned in a strategic boundary-spanning role within the organization's dominant coalition of senior management. Traditional models reflect rational management approaches presenting public relations as able to monitor, evaluate, address and control areas of risk, even if they develop into issues or crisis situations. They reinforce the status of public relations as a profession based on a body of knowledge and expertise, which may be delivered by PR specialists within the organization or external consultants. However, this territory is contested by publicists and legal firms who advocate primarily protectionist and defensive strategies.

Risk management involves identifying hazards, assessing their likelihood and potential consequences (financial, legal or reputational) in order to prioritize which need to be militated against. Linear models propose that monitoring not only identifies risk, but emerging issues that are of concern to stakeholders and around which publics may emerge to oppose organizations and prevent them achieving their objectives. This organizational-centric focus dominates public relations literature, ignoring the opportunity presented by activist involvement in issues to consider a different perspective and encourage co-operation (although dialogue may be viewed cynically by both parties).

Emerging theories propose a role for public relations based on relationship building and co-orientation in managing risk, addressing issues and resolving crisis situations. This needs to be contingent on the particular organization, specific situation and other varying factors rather than driven by generic rules. PR practitioners are also advised to accept uncertainty and complexity within the modern world where the idea of organizations, or expert PR practitioners, being in total control is replaced by recognition of the need for flexibility and accommodation.

A shift in focus also questions corporate apologia as a defensive or subversive tactic that, although unsuccessful, may have entertainment or power-rebalancing value to the media and public.

Case studies in public relations literature (and award programmes) tend to support a narrow view of crisis management where hero status is bestowed on those who follow accepted practice (and villain status given to those who do not). This creates a mythology of crisis management and limits the depth of analysis and reflection regarding actual practice concerning managing risk, issues and crisis situations.

Simplified cases and linear models mask the fact that a modern risk society exists in a 24:7 dynamic global communications environment, which presents challenges to rationale management of issues and crisis, not least because of the immediacy and interconnectedness of mobile, online and social media. The focus placed on emerging situations, and the involvement of public relations in managing these in real time, further questions the usefulness of traditional linear, modernist models and historic case studies.

Risk should be recognized as unavoidable, with public relations used to increase understanding rather than excuse organizational behaviour. At the same time, greater realism about what public relations can, and cannot achieve is required. This could affect the status public relations has sought as a controller of crisis situations, but avoid the function being seen to fail when its 'best practice' approaches do not deliver miraculous results.

The role for public relations may increasingly be as internal activists, raising and addressing issues within an organization on the basis of a toolkit of appropriate techniques, rather than a limited 'best practice' approach.

QUESTIONS FOR DISCUSSION

1 What are the primary arguments for the jurisdiction of public relations in risk, issues and crisis management?

2 How is risk identified and managed in your organization – and what role does public relations play in this?

3 Consider an area of risk that could impact on your organization – what factors would make it develop into an issue?

4 Why do you think commentators use the term 'PR disaster' and what impact does seeing organizational problems in this way have on the occupation of PR?

5 Are there any differences in how activists and other organizations use mainstream and online media to address risk, issues and crisis situations?

6 Why are the ideas of power imbalance and disputation important in addressing issues or crisis situations?

7 What are the benefits and drawbacks of establishing 'best practice' rules for risk, issues and crisis management?

8 Why do organizations often ignore warning signals that could indicate the potential for a crisis situation?

9 How could PR operate as an internal activist in your organization to challenge management decisions?

10 What challenges does an increasingly complex world present for the involvement of public relations in this area?

FURTHER READING

Dezenhall, E., and Weber, J. (2007) *Damage control: why everything you know about crisis management is wrong*, Portfolio.

Fearn-Banks, K. (2007) *Crisis communications: a casebook approach*, Routledge.

Gilpin, D.R. and Murphy, P.J. (2008) *Crisis management in a complex world*, Oxford University Press.

Heath R.L. (ed.) (2010) *The Sage handbook of public relations* (2nd edition), Sage.

Regester, M., and Larkin, J. (2008) *Risk issues and crisis management in public relations: a casebook of best practice*, Kogan Page.

CHAPTER 9

Public relations and corporate social responsibility

Ian Somerville and Emma Wood

CHAPTER AIMS

Corporate social responsibility (CSR) is a key legitimising practice for business organisations in contemporary society. This chapter focuses on the relationship between this activity and public relations, the main communication management tool of CSR. Explaining and justifying the practice of CSR is usually regarded as a public relations function because this is where the company meets the public outside of the usual roles of producers (or service providers) and customers. The literature explaining and justifying most CSR programmes has utilised the ethical perspectives of utilitarianism and deontology. This leads to significant claims for CSR. Companies may maintain that such activity is the fulfilment of the duties and responsibilities that they have to the wider community, or that they contribute to the common good by benefiting both the company and society. The first part of the chapter outlines some of the main theoretical debates in respect to CSR and discusses the arguments for and against it. The second part of the chapter discusses how ethical concepts and the language used to express them in PR discourse relate to the actual practice of CSR. The chapter ends with an analysis of issues surrounding CSR evaluation, reporting and stakeholder engagement and the role PR might play in these key tasks.

SOCIALLY RESPONSIBLE BUSINESS?

Definitions of CSR differ widely, ranging from the idea of charitable giving to the notion that business can help government achieve everything from social inclusion to environmental protection. Many definitions frame CSR activity as an intervention in society: 'To be socially responsible corporations must co-operate with other groups – such as competitors, nonprofits and government agencies to help solve social problems' (Bowie 1993 quoted in Daugherty 2001: 389). Other definitions, such as that offered by the UK government, extend the responsibility to include the environment, people (employees and customers) and the economy:

> The Government sees CSR as the business contribution to our sustainable development goals. Essentially it is about how business takes account of its economic, social and environmental impacts in the way it operates – maximising the benefits and minimising the downsides. Specifically we see CSR as the voluntary actions that business can take, over and above compliance with minimum legal requirements, to address both its own competitive interests and the interests of wider society.
>
> (www.csr.gov.uk/whatiscsr.html)

While some argue that the concept is defined in so many different ways that it is practically meaningless (Sen and Bhattacharya 2001), at the very least CSR involves the idea of business being proactive in its relationship with a range of social actors and doing more than just trying to avoid transgressing widely accepted ethical rules or obeying the law. The term 'social responsibility' implies that business is motivated by more than just self-interest and is, in fact, an activity that aims to promote the interest of society at large. This can be differentiated from, for example, corporate sponsorship where 'the company's managers will expect a tangible return for their money' (Varey 1997: 118).

The following two sections discuss widely contrasting views of CSR. In some senses they represent the extreme poles of opinion on this issue. In practice the attitude of most business organisations to CSR will occupy a position somewhere between the two. Ethical doctrines play a role in justifying both perspectives. For example, Milton Friedman, who rejected the concept of CSR, attempts to justify his 'free-market approach' to some extent from a utilitarian standpoint. His position appears to be a vague echo of Adam Smith's 'invisible hand' theory of capitalism – that an unregulated free market, while proving disastrous for some, ultimately works to benefit the majority in society. On the other side of the debate, CSR is viewed as a necessary and integral part of the 'stakeholder approach', an approach that is ultimately justified from a Kantian or deonotological ethical perspective.

THE SOCIAL RESPONSIBILITY OF BUSINESS IS TO INCREASE PROFITS

Milton Friedman, the economist and advocate of *laissez-faire* capitalism, argued against the idea that business has a social responsibility in the sense defined in the section above. He claimed that 'there is one and only one social responsibility of business – to use its resources and engage in activities designed to increase its profits' (Friedman 1993: 254). Friedman insists that it is wrong to suggest that corporations can have social responsibilities – for him only individuals can have responsibilities. He claims that the actual responsibilities of the corporation should be narrowly defined and limited to making 'as much money as possible while conforming to the basic rules of the society, both those embodied in law and those embodied in ethical custom' (Friedman 1993: 249). By claiming that businesses have only one social responsibility, to maximise their profits, Friedman is in effect saying they have no social responsibilities in the generally accepted sense of the term. He does not say that moral rules have no place in relation to business practice, in fact while pursuing profits business must conform to what he refers to as 'ethical custom'. As Chryssides and Kaler (1993) point out, he seems to be making a distinction between first and second order ethical rules, the basic moral rules of society (an obligatory first order) and social responsibility precepts (an optional second order). He does not elaborate on what the rules based on ethical custom are, but he does give some indication as to what the second order rules might involve. Friedman castigates businessmen for 'preaching pure and unadulterated socialism' when they speak of 'responsibilities for providing employment, eliminating discrimination, avoiding pollution and whatever else may be the catchwords of the contemporary crop of reformers' (1993: 249).

According to Friedman those who 'preach' the doctrine of social responsibility are making two claims, both of which he disagrees with. These are, first that business must actively seek to do good, that is, not just avoid transgressing 'ethical custom'. Second, this 'good' must not be done for profit, that is, it must not be done with self-interest in mind (if this was the motivation Friedman would have no objection to it). This raises an important question, that is, is actively seeking to do good easily distinguishable from the mere avoidance of doing evil? Friedman seems to believe this to be the case but it is difficult to see how the examples that he points to demonstrate this and indeed overall his position appears to be riddled with flawed arguments. It could be agreed that some of the examples he lists, 'eliminating discrimination' or 'avoiding pollution' are doing 'good', but at the same time they are actions that are intended to eliminate what are widely perceived to be social or environmental evils. Thus ironically what Friedman's own examples actually illustrate is that on many occasions the moral choice is between doing good or, by default, doing evil. Chryssides and Kaler note:

> Friedman's assumption of a neat division between 'ethical custom' and business social responsibility takes too narrow a view of both. The first cannot be confined to simply the passive avoidance of evil or the second to just the active pursuit of good because very often good and evil are simply two sides of the same moral coin. Friedman is therefore wrong to assume that acceptance of 'ethical custom' has no implication for the adoption of socially responsible policies by business. Clearly it has; if only because such is the power of business over people's lives that its failure to do good will very often result in great evils being permitted to flourish.
>
> (1993: 232)

It is not only Friedman's conceptual understanding of CSR that is flawed, there are also problems with the arguments he presents in respect to what he perceives to be the responsibilities of a corporation. One of his key arguments, sometimes referred to as 'the agency argument' (Chryssides and Kaler 1993: 234), is that managers of corporations are merely *agents* of the shareholders in the companies they work for. Friedman states, 'In a free-enterprise, private-property system, a corporate executive is an employee of the owners of the business. He has direct responsibility to his employers. That responsibility is to conduct the business in accordance with their desires' (1993: 249). In other words the owners of the corporation, the share-holders, are the only people to which managers are accountable and the only responsibility managers have is to act in their interests. This means maximising profits so that the shareholder will make as much money as possible from their investment. Friedman presents his premise about a manager's role vis-à-vis the shareholders as a 'statement of legal fact' (Chryssides and Kaler 1993: 234). Clearly Friedman is correct to state that the managers of a corporation have a primary duty to serve the interests of the shareholders. However, his attempt to imply that this is a straightforward issue of legality is completely spurious. In both British and US law the corporation is a separate legal entity and is not identified solely with any particular group – employees, shareholders or directors (Chryssides and Kaler 1993: 229). Managers therefore are not directly the 'agents' of the shareholders in the way that Friedman wishes to imply, although, shareholders are, in roundabout way, the owners of the business. Friedman's assertion that the interests of the corporation ought to be exclusively identified with its shareholders must be seen in the context of his advocacy of the values of free enterprise. These values involve a combination of ethical egoism and, as we noted above, a rudimentary version of classical utilitarianism that makes the assumption that if everyone pursues their own self-interest within a free market, the result is the greatest happiness, or economic well being, for the greatest number of actors within that market. Friedman's argument that only the interests of shareholders are important is, of course, something upon which there is not universal agreement. There is, in fact, an argument that the managers should act, in some senses, as the 'agent' of all groups associated with the corporation and not just the shareholders. Those who support this view reject Friedman's 'stockholder' or 'shareholder' model in favour of what usually referred to as the 'stakeholder' model.

KANTIAN CAPITALISM AND THE STAKEHOLDER APPROACH

The 'stakeholder' model is so named because those who propose it argue that the task of the corporate manager is to balance the interests of the different groups who have a 'stake' in the company. The interest of the shareholders in increasing their profits is only one interest, albeit an important one, among many that the manager must consider. This model requires the corporation to take account of its social responsibilities and to consider all of its stakeholders when developing business strategies. Evan and Freeman (1993) argue from a Kantian perspective for the adoption of the stakeholder model. They employ Kant's categorical imperative: 'Never use people simply as a means to an end; always treat yourself and others as beings with infinite value' (Dienhart's formulation 2000: 117–18) to argue that corporations have a duty never to treat any human beings as if they have only an instrumental value to the business. In fact they go on to argue that all groups affected by a corporation should play a role in determining company policy. Evan and Freeman state this deontological or Kantian ethical doctrine explicitly:

> We can revitalize the concept of managerial capitalism by replacing the notion that managers have a duty to stockholders with the concept that managers bear a fiduciary relationship to stakeholders. Stakeholders are those groups who have a stake in or claim on the firm. Specifically we include suppliers, customers, employees, stockholders and the local community, as well as management in its role as agent for these groups. We argue that the legal, economic, political, and moral challenges to the currently received theory of the firm, as a nexus of contracts among the owners of the factors of production and customers, require us to revise this concept along essentially Kantian lines. That is, each of these stakeholder groups has a right not to be treated as a means to some end, and therefore must participate in determining the future direction of the firm in which they have a stake.
>
> (1993: 255)

They argue that, in the US, changes in the legal system have been progressively circumscribing the idea that the corporation is only run in the interests of the 'stockholders'. They point to a number of legal cases in the US, which show that although stockholders' interests are still paramount, other interests, customers, suppliers, local communities and employees have increasingly secured protection under the law (Evan and Freeman 1993: 255–57). Friedman's viewpoint, they would argue, is slowly being overtaken by changes, in legislation and business thinking, more in line with a stakeholder approach.

In the stakeholder model the role of the corporation co-ordinates stakeholder interests. It is through the corporation that each stakeholder group makes itself better off through voluntary exchanges. They argue that the 'corporation serves at the pleasure of its stakeholders, and none may be used as a means to the ends of another without full rights of participation in that decision' (Evan and Freeman 1993: 262). From the stakeholder perspective corporate social responsibility is not an optional extra it is integral to the responsibilities of the company and the company must pay as much attention to its social duties as it does to maximising its profits.

THE PRACTICE OF CORPORATE SOCIAL RESPONSIBILITY

This part of the chapter will analyse the practice of CSR by examining the language corporations use to explain this increasingly important corporate activity. It will then go on to discuss key recent issues surrounding CSR reporting and evaluation utilising recent academic analysis and practitioner research. First, however, it is important to locate the role of PR within the practice of social responsibility. When business organisations decide to involve themselves in local community initiatives there is usually an attempt to construct a narrative to explain the organisation's actions. This task of explanation is usually allocated to the company's PR department. This is hardly surprising since public relations specialists frequently play a key role in setting up CSR programmes in the first place. It is also clear that the evaluation and reporting of CSR policies and practices is increasingly a function of PR departments or consultancies.

PUBLIC RELATIONS AND CORPORATE SOCIAL RESPONSIBILITY

L'Etang notes that CSR

> is often managed by public relations practitioners for public relations ends, and therefore corporate social responsibility is seen as part of the public relations portfolio and as a technique to establish relations with particular groups (for example, in the local community) and to enhance reputation with key stakeholders.
>
> (2006a: 414)

There is, however, another key reason why PR specialists have tended to be associated with CSR, namely, the claim that PR can be a mechanism within liberal, pluralist society to enable the realisation of 'laudible social goals' (Gandy 1992: 133). For J.A. Pimlot, the historian of PR in the US, the activity is intimately connected with what he views as democratic ideals. He writes: 'They [the public relations specialists] are experts in popularizing information . . . the better the job of popularization, the more smoothly will society function' (quoted in Pearson 1992: 257). Heath, echoing J.S. Mill, argues that 'professional communicators have a major voice in the marketplace of ideas' but that ultimately these voices 'compete to achieve cooperation – the collective and coordinated actions of people in society' (1992: 20). Cutlip et al. go further and argue that PR practitioners 'must operate as moral agents in society' and they must be prepared to place 'public service and social responsibility over personal gains and special private interests' (1995: 134).

It is clear that there is a significant strand within PR theorising which claims that the practice can have a positive contribution within society, although this usually comes with the proviso that practice needs to be transformed (Grunig 1989). There is bound to be a tension between this conception of PR serving the interests of society and the requirement that it serves the interests of the corporation. L'Etang notes that the 'area of corporate social responsibility thus highlights a dilemma which arises generally in the role of public relations: the tension between organisational goals and declared responsibility for "the public interest"' (2006a: 416). This tension between responsibility to the needs of the company and responsibility to the needs of society is sometimes revealed by the language used in corporate documents that attempt to explain the practice of CSR.

THE LANGUAGE OF CORPORATE SOCIAL RESPONSIBILITY

Companies frequently justify their CSR programmes with the utilitarian argument that 'everyone benefits' in the sense that the company's reputation is enhanced and a local community materially benefited. Neil Shaw, a former chairman of Tate & Lyle plc. explains the mutual benefits of community programmes:

> Our community activities, both in the UK and abroad, focus particularly on initiatives in the localities of our plants and the provision of direct assistance for individuals seeking further educational attainment. In addition, we also encourage secondment of employees to particular projects in the belief that, not only can this make a worthwhile contribution to community activities, but in doing so, the experience will enable volunteers to develop their own management potential.
>
> (quoted in Newman 1995: 99)

Some commentators (L'Etang: 2006a) note that while CSR programmes are indeed justified on utilitarian grounds there is in many instances little attempt to actually measure and evaluate the effects of such programmes. L'Etang points out that if such evaluation is lacking then companies 'will not be in a position to claim that they have contributed to the general "happiness". In short, CSR justified on utilitarian grounds needs to demonstrate cost-benefit analysis from the perspectives of donor, recipient and society in general' (2006a: 415). Evaluating and reporting the effects of CSR practice is an exceptionally important issue and one we will return to in the next section because there is perhaps here an opportunity for public relations to fulfil the public service aspirations referred to above.

Many companies frequently allude, in deontological language, to their responsibilities or duties to the community, or society as a whole. Lord Raynor, when he was Chairman of Marks & Spencer stated: 'There rests on all companies, particularly large organisations like ours, a responsibility to assist through donations and help, the charities and agencies which exist in the community' (quoted in L'Etang 1996: 91). L'Etang (2006a) makes the point that such aspirational claims are seldom matched by the practice of corporations. She argues that a deontological approach to CSR would focus on the motivation behind the programme, because seeking benefit from carrying out your responsibilities would not be ethical. From this perspective a CSR programme needs to demonstrate that it is motivated by duty, and not self-interest (enlightened or any other kind). If a company were attempting to improve its image or reputation via community involvement then it would be treating beneficiaries as a means and not as ends in themselves and thus breaking Kant's categorical imperative. L'Etang (2006a) points out that if corporations took on board Kantian principles then their CSR programmes might be managed rather differently. If the beneficiaries of CSR are to be treated as ends in themselves then they should be accorded equal status in defining and developing their relationship with the corporation and indeed in designing the CSR programmes they are meant to be benefitting from. If the language of the classic ethical theories is adopted to explain and justify CSR but companies do not fulfil the full implications of these ethical doctrines then they can leave themselves open to the charge of cynicism.

When reading corporate literature on CSR it becomes clear that companies sometimes do not restrict themselves to justifying the activity solely from a utilitarian, or a Kantian perspective. Robert Clarke, Chairman of United Biscuits, states: 'Our commitment to community involvement stems from our strong sense of social responsibility combined with the realization of the commercial benefits that it brings . . . a generous and far-reaching sense of community responsibility – are essential to effective long-term business performance' (quoted in Newman 1995: 99). L'Etang notes that in 'many cases corporate literature is confusing because it appears to appeal to both utilitarian and Kantian principles yet apparently delivers on neither' (L'Etang 1996: 93). This point, while indisputable, can perhaps be explained to some extent by the fact, noted above, that the classic ethical doctrines need to be qualified by each other in order to arrive at an ethic that balances rights and obligations with the 'greater good'. It could certainly be argued that, given that moral philosophers have found it difficult to come to a wholly satisfactory resolution when debating the relative merits of the classic ethical doctrines, it would be asking a lot to expect business managers or public relations practitioners to avoid some confusion when dealing with complex ethical debates. Nevertheless, whether or not a company appeals to a combination of ethical doctrines to justify its CSR policies and practices it should be expected to make a meaningful and committed attempt to fulfil the requirements of those ethical doctrines. Thus a deontological approach, motivated by the principle that regards others as intrinsically and not just instrumentally valuable will entail a commitment to genuinely 'engage' with stakeholders to find out how a CSR initiative can really fulfil their needs. This is quite different from merely 'managing' them and ultimately exploiting the process for the reputational benefits of the corporation. A utilitarian approach, which is meant to ensure benefit to all sides, should be prepared to measure and demonstrate that benefit clearly and transparently. The final two sections of this chapter explore these two key issues of engagement with responsiveness to stakeholders and the measurement and evaluation of CSR practices in more detail.

EVALUATING AND REPORTING CSR POLICY AND PRACTICE

L'Etang (2006a) has noted that it has long been argued that PR practitioners need to develop more comprehensive research and evaluation skills, and we would suggest that this is particularly important in respect to CSR initiatives in communities. Recent commercial communications research and academic analysis has also emphasised this point. For instance, Richard Coope, Head of CSR practice at CTN, commenting on the 2004 CSR Online Survey by CTN Communications notes:

> The UK's top companies are still not taking CSR seriously, making little effort to improve their online communication of CSR to investors and other key stakeholders . . . Despite a lot of noise about the growing importance of CSR to reputation and brand, most companies still seem content to produce long-winded CSR reports. These are more often designed to meet the requirements of the regulators and specialist CSR agencies than to connect with the general public. Only the most committed net visitor will be prepared to plough through a 90 page long pdf.
>
> (www.csr-survey.org)

Owen (2005: 1) also highlights this point, commenting that recent years

> have witnessed a significant increase in the number of major companies in Europe, the US and Australia proclaiming their social responsibility credentials, and backing up their claims by producing substantial paper, or web-based, environmental, and more recently, social and sustainability reports.

Accompanying this expansion in the reporting of CSR activity, companies have also claimed that they now carry out much more research into stakeholder views and requirements. Scottish Power's statement in their 2003 CSR report is fairly typical. They state that they: 'commissioned research to establish stakeholders' views on the relevant issues to cover in this report. We also incorporated multi-stakeholder feedback from previous Scottish Power Environmental Sustainability and Community reports' (Owen 2005: 7). This all seem very laudable but Scottish Power's own assurance process highlights that while the company's activity in regard to stakeholder research is to be commended, the actual use to which this research is being put is less clear. A recent trend in company CSR reporting is to have one of the specialist CSR bodies verify the report in much the same way as an accountancy company verifies the financial annual report. Interestingly, *csrnetwork's* Verification Statement for Scottish Power's CSR Report concludes:

> Commendably, formal dialogue is undertaken with selected stakeholder groups to understand the information they require. Future reports would benefit from an explanation of how this, and the constant dialogue that happens during the running of the business, informs the issues, actions and performance data included in the report.
>
> (Owen 2005: 10)

Carrying out research and reporting it has happened is all very well but a company must spell out clearly and in detail how they are evaluating stakeholder feedback and what impact the results of this research actually has on corporate decision making. There is an opportunity here for PR but they need to do more to develop the research, evaluation and reporting skills that will enable them to monitor the attitudes and expectations of stakeholders more successfully. The same skills will also enable them to demonstrate how the company's CSR policies and practice have actually benefited stakeholders as well as the corporation in a much more transparent way. A recent initiative by Business in the Community (BITC) sets out 'principles of measurement' that would make an excellent starting point for public relations practitioners wishing to develop more robust methodologies for both assessing stakeholder needs and measuring CSR impacts (see 'More than making money' at www.bitc.org.uk).

It is vitally important that public relations practitioners engage more competently in research and evaluation in this area because it is becoming clear that in the absence of wholly transparent corporate communication stakeholders will increasingly access alternative sources of information to find out about, and make up their own minds about, a company's behaviour. A recent (2007) major CSR survey carried out by Fleishman Hillard International Communications and the National Consumers League in the US has shown that among consumers, 'online sources' and 'word-of-mouth' vastly outweigh traditional media sources as preferred ways to learn about a company's CSR record. Reponses indicated that consumers increasingly rely on the internet to find out about CSR-related information but not in ways that will provide much comfort for corporations. Only 7 per cent of respondents said they would rely on the company website whereas 49 per cent said they would use internet search engines or the websites of discussion groups. Additionally 77 per cent of consumers feel that WOM recommendations from peers are more powerful than recommendations from traditional media outlets. The authors of the report note that: 'These findings, taken together, may indicate that traditional media sources may be lacking in credibility because the information they disseminate is viewed as incomplete, censored, edited, and therefore tarnished in some way' (www.csrresults.com).

In today's information society the corporate website, which seems to be the natural mechanism to use to report CSR policies and practices, is in danger of being bypassed by consumers and other stakeholders. Coupland (2003) notes,

> With interest from potential customers and employees to current shareholders, the remit of attracting, entertaining or satisfying the website reader is a complex one . . . This has relevance as companies are increasingly competing in discursive space where winning the 'argument' is important.
>
> (www.accountability.21net/aa1000/default.asp)

If, as seems to be the case, consumers and other stakeholders are not engaged by current CSR reporting processes then this is an issue that must be taken seriously by PR practitioners. A recent study of corporate websites by Capriotti and Moreno (2007: 89) notes that in respect to CSR 'the websites assume a mainly unidirectional/ expositive function, focusing on the presentation of the information content. A high predominance of expositive resources (graphic and audiovisual) rather than interactive resources is observed'. In other words information is displayed for the reader but there is little attempt to use the interactive capabilities of the internet to engage with stakeholders and potential stakeholders.

ENGAGEMENT AND RESPONSIVENESS IN CSR POLICES AND PRACTICE

Simply publishing increasingly elaborate and lengthy CSR reports is not enough to convince stakeholders that their views are being taken into account and, more importantly, being acted upon at the corporate governance level. This means that the public relations role in CSR should not just be about presenting information but about engaging with stakeholders and most importantly demonstrating responsiveness to stakeholder views. In its Rating Report 2006 of global corporations, *AccountAbility*, the global think-tank on organisational and corporate accountability, two of the key measurement factors they list in their analysis are 'stakeholder engagement' and 'governance'. They define these factors as follows:

> **Stakeholder engagement** – Does the company engage in dialogue with people who have an interest in, may be affected by, or may affect its business?

> **Governance** – Do senior executives and the advisory board properly consider stakeholder issues when setting strategy and formulating corporate policy?
> (www.accountabilityrating.com)

In respect to the issue of stakeholder engagement the study by Capriotti and Moreno (2007: 89) would seem to indicate that the engagement process is lacking or at best in its infancy. In respect to the websites they studied they note that:

> [N]o evaluation tools (such as interactive opinion polls, opinion forms, etc.) are provided, nor are there interactive feedback tools (such as chat rooms, forums, blogs, etc.) that would allow visitors to interact with the companies or with other people about CSR topics in real time . . . They are in a very initial phase of interaction or dialogue with their publics, considering that the resources used to present the information are mainly expositive, and the feedback resources available are minimal. The use of corporate websites for CSR issues is partial and limited, focusing primarily on the dissemination of information, rather than favouring dialogue and interaction with different publics.

Owen (2005: 10–11) suggests that the crucial question from a stakeholder accountability perspective has to be whether the engagement and dialogue processes they are invited to participate in do meaningfully influence specific aspects of corporate decision making, and in particular can lead to situations where their interests prevail over those of shareholders in matters of distributional conflict.

He notes that a particularly noteworthy level of responsiveness to stakeholder concerns appears in the Co-operative Bank's 2002 Partnership Report. This approach is rare and more typically, suggests Owen (2005: 9), commentary in CSR reports regarding responsiveness to stakeholder feedback is couched in more general and vague terms making it impossible to gauge 'how, if at all, stakeholder feedback influences corporate strategic decision making'.

CSR reports may devote significant space to describing the stakeholder dialogue processes that have taken place but according to Owen (2005: 26), 'For stakeholder accountability to be established and associated reporting exercises to be meaningful in empowerment terms, a far more pluralistic form of corporate governance must be instituted.' A key demonstration of goodwill from the deontological perspective is that the company/stakeholder relationship in respect to CSR policies and activities is based on the mutual recognition of rights and responsibilities on both sides. Many corporations report the inclusion of external members on their advisory panels that help shape CSR policies and practices. While such measures are a step in the right direction toward more accountable and transparent corporate governance structures, Owen (2005: 14) notes:

> [I]t is debatable as to how much such initiatives achieve in terms of empower-ing stakeholders and thereby democratising the whole CSR process. The crucial point here is that the external participants (as far as may be ascertained) are appointed by corporate management, rather than being elected by those they purport to represent. Quite bluntly, these individuals represent no-one but themselves and are therefore directly accountable to no-one but themselves. Significantly forums at which stakeholder groups (predominantly employee and local community groups) are directly represented are confined to consultative committee type structures, completely separated from the key strategic decision making arena.

How a company responds to its stakeholders is key. AccountAbility AA1000 (2003: 18) issued an Assurance Standard for CSR relationships and they highlight the key principle of responsiveness, which requires that 'the Assurance provider evaluate whether the reporting organisation has responded to stakeholder concerns, policies and relevant standards and adequately communicated these responses in its report'. This is an important opportunity for PR representatives who can facilitate a process that will offer stakeholders a meaningful voice in the corporate decision-making arena and demonstrate concretely the deontological concepts of duty and responsi-bility that underpin many statements in CSR documentation. Arguably they must do this to avoid the charge that their role, and that of CSR initiatives in general, is nothing more than the cynical instrumental exploitation of stakeholders for the benefit of corporate reputation.

CSR, THE CREDIT CRUNCH AND STAKEHOLDER COMMUNICATION IN THE IRISH BANKING SECTOR

The Irish banking sector is in some senses an extreme example, and in other ways entirely typical, of the catastrophe that overtook financial institutions around the world at the end of 2008 and early 2009. The fracturing of the global financial system has had a disastrous impact on all Irish financial institutions. Irish banks listed on the London Stock Exchange saw their share prices plunge 90 per cent in the 12 months up to December 2008 (Bloomberg.com 21 January 2009). Facing a financial sector meltdown at the end of 2008 the Irish government took the unprecedented step of guaranteeing all bank deposits and debts in Irish banks for two years (a loan guarantee worth over 550 billion euros, a sum that exceeds the German government's guarantee to German banks and that amounts to almost three times Ireland's annual GDP of 160 billion euro). It also announced a multi-billion euro bailout for three of the biggest banks, Bank of Ireland, Allied Irish Bank and the Anglo Irish Bank taking a 25 per cent stake in each and it has since nationalised several banks in the sector. In March 2009 the Irish government announced a plan to buy up the toxic debts of most of the Irish registered banks, both domestic and foreign owned, at a potential cost of 80 billion euros. One price that the domestic banks have had to pay for this government help was to sign up to a range of Irish Banking Federation requirements, one of which is that they will produce joint bi-annual transparent CSR reports and present them to the office of the Irish Finance Minister. This was quite a culture change for Irish banks, some of which, in what was a relatively unregulated system, had never provided any kind of dedicated CSR report in the past.

This case study compares the CSR activity and reporting of two banks operating in Ireland. One is the Dutch owned Rabobank, which entered the Irish market by purchasing the Irish bank ACC in 2002, the other is the Bank of Ireland, the last remaining bank listed on the Irish Stock Exchange. One thing that the Dutch bank brought with it to the Irish financial sector was a focus on CSR issues and a concern to engage with a range of stakeholders on all aspects of its business practice. This was the way it operated in the Netherlands and it claimed to import this culture to all its overseas operations including its Irish subsidiary. Given that the Irish taxpayer is now a partial owner of the Bank of Ireland one may also expect to see a high level of transparency in respect to its CSR activities and a commitment to dialogue with its stakeholders. Following the approach of Capriotti and Moreno (2007: 89) this case study will investigate best practice in CSR disclosure and stakeholder engagement by analysing the presence of key

C@SE STUDY

C@SE STUDY

CSR indicators on the websites of the respective banks. It will also assess the nature of the stakeholder communication, with a particular focus on how 'expositive' or 'interactive' the communication approach is. A predominance of expositive communication would mean the bank relied on merely displaying information about its CSR activities, which, as we know from the Fleishman Hillard (2007) study cited above, does not meet with the approval of stakeholders. A high level of 'interactive' communication capability is viewed as potentially resolving this communication barrier between stakeholders and corporations (Capriotti and Moreno 2007). Key to the development of interactive communication, on this view, are online technologies and social media that can facilitate in dialogue (blogs, forums), create opportunities for feedback (dedicated email contact addresses, online opinion forms) and 'converse' with stakeholders through the new Web 2.0 media (Facebook, Twitter). Organisations may exaggerate claims that they engage in interaction with stakeholders, therefore the information presented in the websites will be examined to assess the real level of stakeholder engagement and just how much the views of relevant stakeholders actually influence CSR policy and practice.

Like previous studies (O'Donovan et al. 2001; Capriotti and Moreno 2007), this case study has relied upon a combination of internationally recognised CSR indices to construct a table of best practice measurement. The CSR indicators identified are based on the requirements for disclosure in CSR reporting from the following sources: World Business Council for Sustainable Development (2000), United Nations Global Compact (2002), Global Reporting Initiative (2006) and BITC. BITC operates in both the UK and the Republic of Ireland, and the categories adopted are from their 2007 Responsibility Index. The CSR issues are listed below (Figure 9.1), along with a brief definition and an indication of the reference source.

It is not enough for the organisation to merely claim it is committed to a particular CSR principle, e.g. environmental impact. The minimum requirements are that it must present a clear explanation of what it means by this indictor and how it applies it in practice.

As can be seen from Figure 9.2, the presence of CSR issues on corporate websites in Rabobank and Bank of Ireland (accessed on 2 and 3 February 2011) reveal an apparently fairly similar picture. Most key CSR issues are present on the website of the Bank of Ireland and all are present on the Rabobank website. There is no explanation of how the Bank of Ireland in its business activities discharges its responsibilities toward human rights or the economic impact of its activities. Interestingly, despite the bank being listed as a member of BITC in both Northern Ireland and the Republic of Ireland there is no indication of how it applies the BITC Responsibility Index in

CSR Issue	Definition	Source
Corporate governance	Explanation of the organisation's decision/policy making structure and how it ensures transparency in respect to accountability and disclosure.	WBCSD (2000) GRI (2006) BITC (2007)
Employee rights	Explanation of the organisation's systems of contract, evaluation, promotion and dismissal.	WBCSD (2000) UNGC (2002) GRI (2006) BITC (2007)
Human rights	Explanation of the organisation's approach to human rights (discrimination, child labour etc.)	WBCSD (2000) UNGC (2002) GRI (2006) BITC (2007)
Economic impacts	Explanation of the organisation's economic impact at the local, regional, national and supranational levels.	WBCSD (2000) GRI (2006) BITC (2007)
Social impacts	Explanation of the organisation's activities in relation to social issues.	WBCSD (2000) GRI (2006) BITC (2007)
Environmental impacts	Explanation of the organisation's involvement in/action on environmental issues.	WBCSD (2000) UNGC (2002) GRI (2006) BITC (2007)
Stakeholder relationships	Explanation of the organisation's actions in relation to its stakeholders/publics (shareholders, customers, and suppliers).	WBCSD (2000) GRI (2006) BITC (2007)
Corporate ethics	Explanation of the organisation's ethical framework in relation to its business activities and its stakeholders/publics.	WBCSD (2000) UNGC (2002) GRI (2006) BITC (2007)
External criteria on CSR	Explanation of the organisation's incorporation of national and international criteria on CSR.	WBCSD (2000) GRI (2006) BITC (2007)

FIGURE 9.1 CSR issues, definitions and indicator sources
Key: World Business Council for Sustainable Development (2000), United Nations Global Compact (2002), Global Reporting Initiative (2006), Business in the Community (2007)

CSR Issue	Rabobank/ ACC	Bank of Ireland
Corporate governance	✔	✔
Employee rights	✔	✔
Human rights	✔	
Economic impacts	✔	
Social impacts	✔	✔
Environmental impacts	✔	✔
Stakeholder relationships	✔	✔
Corporate ethics	✔	✔
External criteria on CSR	✔	

FIGURE 9.2 Presence of CSR issues on the corporate websites (including online CSR reports/corporate annual reports) of Rabobank and Bank of Ireland

C@SE STUDY

practice. Some of the documentation of the Bank of Ireland's CSR activity actually appears in the joint Irish Banking Federation CSR Report submitted bi-annually with the other Irish owned banks in the Irish financial sector. This is to comply with the requirements imposed by the Irish government after the financial bailout of these institutions. This joint report (last published 22 September 2010) is included as a pdf file on the Bank of Ireland website, as it is on websites of the six other Irish banks covered under the Credit Institutions (Financial Support) Scheme.

In contrast, how Rabobank engages with each of the CSR issues is explained and discussed in depth with a wealth of pertinent information and case study examples of the bank's activities. The information is not just presented as written text, there is frequent use of audio-visual material such as podcasts, webcast and web films. There is also a detailed explanation of stakeholder dialogue and 20 different stakeholder groups, which the bank regularly consults on policy and practice issues, are listed. Rabobank explains in detail how it measures its practice against a range of CSR indicators including the United Nations Global Compact and the Global Reporting Initiative and it publishes the reports of several independent CSR rating agencies including the Corporate Sustainability Assessment of SAM (Sustainable Asset Management Group) and Oekom. The bank is not selective in its reporting. It highlights that it received an A+ rating from the Global Reporting Initiative but publishes in full Oekom's

CSR Issue	Expositive		Evaluative				
	Textual	Audio-visual	E-mail	Opinion forms	Blogs	Face-book	Twitter
Corporate governance	□ ▲		□ ▲	□		□	□
Employee rights	□ ▲		□ ▲	□		□	□
Human rights	□		□ ▲	□		□	□
Economic impacts	□	□	□ ▲	□	□	□	□
Social impacts	□ ▲	□	□ ▲	□	□	□	□
Environmental impacts	□ ▲	□	□ ▲	□	□	□	□
Stakeholder relationships	□ ▲	□	□ ▲	□	□	□	□
Corporate ethics	□ ▲	□	□ ▲	□		□	□
External indicators	□		□ ▲	□		□	□

Key: Rabobank □ Bank of Ireland ▲

FIGURE 9.3 Expositive and interactive resources

Corporate Rating report that awards it a C+, a rating that suffered because of its relatively poor score in 'eco-efficiency'. The fact that both banks appear to tick most or all of the boxes in regard to the presence of CSR issues in their corporate reporting should not obscure the fact that on closer analysis the Bank of Ireland falls along way behind Rabobank when it comes to transparency and detailed explanation in respect to its actual CSR policy and practice.

A key difference between the banks is immediately apparent in Figure 9.3 when one assesses how the two banks deploy the interactive capabilities

C@SE STUDY

of new media technologies to open up the potential for dialogue and engagement with stakeholders. The only interactive resource on the Bank of Ireland website is the email facility, which is a general email address so it theoretically can be used to contact the management on any of the CSR issues. Rabobank has several dedicated email addresses in the different CSR areas to allow the user to engage with a specific expert on an issue and there are also contact forms on each CSR web page where issues can be raised or a complaint made about Rabobank's CSR policies and activities or that of any of its clients. In either case the bank promises to provide a written answer within 30 days. Rabobank have an easily accessible fully interactive blog (available via RSS feed), which various staff members from across the organisation participate in and comments are invited from all stakeholders. Many of the topics focus on issues such as investment or pensions but debates about the environment and social and ethical issues, such as investing in countries with poor human rights records, are also present. Rabobank's website provides links to its social media such as Facebook and Twitter, which are up to date and widely used by a wide range of stakeholders.

Western governments sought to communicate to citizens during the recent massive bailouts of the financial sector that the banking industry underpins capitalism in a fundamental way. If this is the case, this invites consideration of the relationship between financial institutions and society. Western governments presumed an obligation or responsibility to the banks and this was the justification for propping them up with enormous amounts of taxpayer's money. Does this obligation work both ways? Do banks now have an additional responsibility to society? Some banks such as Rabobank, now the only AAA rated bank in Ireland, take the view that CSR is an integral part of what underpins their business activities while others, such as the Bank of Ireland, despite being partially owned by the ordinary citizens of Ireland offer very little detailed explanation of how CSR is integrated with their business activities. The corporate websites, increasingly the public face of all organisations, illustrate this difference.

CONCLUSION

With regard to the role of public relations in CSR, there would appear to be two clear choices. Public relations practitioners can use CSR as just another element in the 'the creation, or "engineering" of consent' in order to foster 'a favourable and positive climate of opinion toward the . . . institution' (Steinberg 1975: 15 quoted in Gandy 1992: 133). Or they can try to realise the idea that public relations can also serve the public interest (Cutlip *et al.* 2006). This will involve making genuine attempts to discover the requirements of community stakeholders through real engagement and partnership. To achieve this, the stakeholder model, built as it is upon deontological foundational assumptions, is a prerequisite. This model argues that a corporation should take account of the interests of all the groups that have a stake in it. It would mean that all stakeholder groups, including the potential beneficiaries of such programmes, should be able to engage in debates about CSR policy and contribute to the decision-making process. This would demonstrate that companies are treating the beneficiaries of corporate social responsibility with 'good will' and as ends in themselves. When they first formulated it, in the early 1980s, Evan and Freeman admitted that a stakeholder approach may seem 'utopian' (1993: 265), but it would appear that more recently the tide has turned to an extent and the stakeholder concept has infiltrated business and political thinking to a remarkable degree.

While the stakeholder concept has achieved widespread acceptance, much more needs to be done to put it into practice and public relations – utilising the full potential of new information and communication technologies – can and should play a key role in this task. As the key organisational group responsible for liaising with stakeholders, public relations practitioners are best placed to help design and shape a participatory process to meet the needs of stakeholders. They are also in a position to capture stakeholder views through qualitative and quantitative measurement. All this will involve developing more robust research methodologies for gathering stakeholder perspectives, a commitment to report and evaluate these viewpoints completely and transparently, and a willingness to engage with and respond to stakeholder needs and concerns.

QUESTIONS FOR DISCUSSION

1 Assess Milton Friedman's claim that 'there is one and only one social responsibility of business – to use its resources and engage in activities designed to increase its profits' (1993: 254).

2 Assess the practicalities of achieving Evan and Freeman's view that stakeholder groups have 'a right not to be treated as a means to some end, and therefore must participate in determining the future direction of the firm in which they have a stake' (1993: 255).

3 In what ways may CSR highlight a dilemma (L'Etang 2006a) at the heart of PR practice?

The remaining questions require you to research your own case study example of CSR practice. Chose a company and analyse the documentation – its website is a good place to start – that outlines and explains its CSR programme.

4   Does the company tend to adopt the language of 'utilitarianism' or the language of 'deontology' when explaining and justifying its CSR initiatives?

5   What independent reporting indices does the organisation use in its CSR reporting? Does its report, for example, reflect recognised indicators from the United Nations Global Compact (2002), the Global Reporting Initiative (2006) or the UK/Ireland BITC guidelines?

6   Assess the overall standard of reporting and evaluation of the company's CSR activities. Is this clear, detailed and transparent?

7   Does the CSR report include research on stakeholder feedback? If so how is this reported? Which stakeholders are cited?

8   How does the company use its website to measure stakeholder views on CSR issues? Does the website include evaluation tools such as online opinion forms?

9   Does the website incorporate interactive feedback tools (e.g. chat rooms, forums, blogs, etc.)? Is there evidence that Web 2.0 capabilities are being utilised to their full potential?

10   How are stakeholders included in corporate governance in respect to CSR? Does the organisation explain how their views ultimately feed into decision making surrounding policy and practice?

FURTHER READING

Capriotti, P. and Moreno, A. (2007) 'Corporate citizenship and public relations: the importance and interactivity of social responsibility issues on corporate websites', *Public Relations Review* 33 (1), pp. 84–91.

Daugherty, E.L. (2001) 'Public relations and social responsibility', in R.L. Heath (ed.) *Handbook of Public Relations*, Sage.

Day, K.D., Dong, Q. and Robins, C. (2001) 'Public relations ethics: an overview and discussion of issues for the 21st century', in R.L. Heath (ed.) *Handbook of public relations*, Sage.

Dienhart, J.W. (2000) *Business, institutions, ethics*, Oxford University Press.

Evan, W.M. and Freeman, R.E. (1993) 'A stakeholder theory of the modern corporation: Kantian capitalism' in G.D. Chryssides and J.H. Kaler (eds) *An introduction to business ethics*, Chapman and Hall.

Freidman, M., (1993) 'The social responsibility of business is to increase its profits' in G.D. Chryssides and J.H. Kaler (eds) *An introduction to business ethics*, Chapman and Hall.

L'Etang, J. (2006) 'Corporate responsibility and public relations ethics' in J. L'Etang and M. Pieczka (eds) *Public relations: critical debates and contemporary practice*, Lawrence Erlbaum Associates.

Moloney, K. (2006) *Rethinking public relations* (2nd edition), Routledge.

Owen, D. (2005) *Corporate social reporting and stakeholder accountability: the missing link* at www.nottingham.ac.uk/business/ICCSR/research/paperseries.html.

CHAPTER 10

Measurement and evaluation

Mairead McCoy and Owen Hargie

CHAPTER AIMS

The chapter provides an overview of the main theoretical and practical issues involved in evaluating public relations. It begins by introducing the area of evaluation and discussing the importance of objectives. Models of PR evaluation are then reviewed and the key research findings regarding the practice of PR evaluation and the main barriers to implementation are summarised. Some of the initiatives undertaken by the PR industry are then outlined before two particular areas of debate – media evaluation and online evaluation – are highlighted. Finally, the chapter concludes by presenting a case study of evaluation in practice.

EVALUATION IN CONTEXT

Evaluation has been described as a 'transdiscipline' (Scriven, 1996: 402) that can be applied in many areas where efficiency, effectiveness and impact are important concerns (Rossi and Freeman, 1989). Developing from efforts to assess education and public health programmes prior to World War One, the field has extended and diversified rapidly. Some years ago, Weiss (1972) defined evaluation as measuring the effects of a programme against its goals. However, while still recognising the element of comparing results with objectives, other definitions broadened the concept of evaluation to emphasise the importance of evaluation before and during the pro- gramme, and stressed that evaluation is not solely a retrospective analysis conducted after the programme is over. For example, Berk and Rossi (1990: 8) suggested that, 'evaluation research includes the design of . . . programs, the ongoing monitoring of how well programs are functioning, the assessment of program impact and the analysis of the program benefits relative to their costs'. Thus, evaluation can be both formative and summative, and can involve assessment of needs, programme theory, implementation, impact and efficiency (Rossi *et al.*, 2004). Key inherent issues include the formation of goals and objectives, identification of measurement indicators, the specification of the programme and cost benefit analysis (McCoy and Hargie, 2001).

In terms of public relations, Lindenmann (2005: 8) pointed out that,

> measurement and evaluation in the public relations field is not a brand new issue or topic that has suddenly emerged just in the past few years. It is an issue and topic that has been widely discussed, actually carried out, and grown and evolved over a 60-year period of time.

Furthermore, Hon (1997) stipulated that PR can be evaluated at the individual, programme, organisational or societal level, although programme effectiveness is the most common focus of evaluation activity. It is argued that the ability to evaluate programme effectiveness is a key skill in strategic communication planning (Smith, 2009). Indeed, evaluation routinely appears in many models of strategic PR management (e.g. Marston, 1963; Kelly, 2001; Cutlip *et al.*, 2006; Hendrix, 2006). Although often depicted as the final stage in the process, as outlined above, evaluation contributes to all phases of PR programmes.

According to Anderson *et al.* (2009: 6) proving the value of public relations is one of the profession's most 'vexing challenges'. In a business and social environment that is increasingly competitive, PR practitioners need to understand how to manage research and evaluation practices that contribute to success and accountability, and allow them to demonstrate in a measurable way how PR programmes are of benefit to their organisation (Austin and Pinkleton, 2006). In addition, evaluation is seen as a fundamental component of professional practice (Stufflebeam and Shinkfield, 1985), so that L'Etang (2008) contended that evaluation has the potential to increase the credibility of the PR industry and help it to gain professional status. Moreover, the topic of PR evaluation consistently emerges as one of the top research priorities for practitioners, academics and researchers (Watson, 2008).

As pointed out above, objectives play an important role in evaluation. We will now examine this relationship in more detail.

SETTING OBJECTIVES

The most prevalent approach to evaluation is Tyler's (1942) objective-based model, which proposes that goals and objectives must be defined and specified as a prerequisite to evaluation. Therefore, at the outset, practitioners should be able to stipulate exactly what they want to achieve with their public relations programme.

According to Watson and Noble (2007), setting appropriate objectives is the bedrock of effective evaluation. However, writing PR objectives has been described as one of the most difficult tasks that practitioners face (Broom and Dozier, 1990; Kerr, 1999). A common source of confusion regarding objectives is the tendency for practitioners to describe their tactics or activities (e.g. 'to distribute 20 press releases') rather than their intended consequences (Cutlip *et al.*, 2006). Objectives can be cognitive, affective or conative (Gregory, 2000b) or set at output, outcome, outgrowth or outflow levels (see evaluation models later in this chapter for more information). While most will be familiar with the advice to define objectives that are 'SMARRTT' – **s**pecific; **m**easurable; **a**chievable; **r**ealistic; **r**elevant; **t**argeted; and **t**imed (Watson and Noble, 2007) – many authors have outlined key guidelines for formulating measurable objectives (e.g. Gregory, 2000b; Rossi *et al.*, 2004; Austin and Pinkleton, 2006; Anderson *et al.*, 2009). Their main recommendations can be distilled as illustrated in Figure 10.1.

Calculating a realistic magnitude of expected change can be especially problematic and is usually determined via a combination of research and practitioner judgement. It also requires some baseline measurements to provide a comparison for later figures in order to identify any progress made. This is one valuable function of formative evaluation.

Likewise, the seemingly commonsense suggestion that objectives should be 'achievable' also causes difficulty in practice. Familiarity with theories of mass communication effects and persuasion can help practitioners to understand what communication can achieve in order to set realistic objectives and to avoid misguided and exaggerated expectations of the effects that a PR campaign may have

• Begin with 'to' followed by a 'strong' active verb
• Specify a single end-product or result/outcome
• Be precise and specific
• State the size of change or level to be maintained in quantifiable terms
• Specify the expected time for achievement
• Link to organisational objectives
• Set objectives that relate to PR
• Ensure targets are achievable

FIGURE 10.1 Key recommendations for writing measurable objectives
Source: Adapted from Gregory (2000b) and Rossi *et al.* (2004)

(McCoy and Hargie, 2003; Macnamara, 2006). It is important to bear this in mind, not only when setting objectives, but also when interpreting evaluation results. In addition, some effects may develop over time and only become apparent in the longer term. Therefore it is essential that evaluation activity is appropriately scheduled.

In essence, objectives identify the criteria by which the success of PR programmes can be evaluated (Fill, 2005). However, in practice, links between specific campaign objectives and corresponding evaluation methods are small. For example, research has found that action objectives expressed in terms of achieving action among target publics were rarely measured by behaviour change techniques (Pieczka, 2000). Similarly, Gregory's (2001) analysis of PR award entries indicated a clear discrepancy between objectives and evaluation where 73 per cent of objectives focused on impact but only 40 per cent of evaluations were impact oriented. To illustrate with a case study, Veil et al. (2009) described a situation where local emergency planners were tasked with increasing community members' compliance with the US Department of Homeland Security's recommendations that all residents have household emergency plans and kits. The evaluation of this exercise appears relatively straightforward, i.e. the number of households who have developed emergency plans and stock emergency kit. However, the campaign evaluation focused on the transmission of messages via the media, and did not attempt any research to discover if it had achieved increased awareness or behaviour change among its targets.

In recognition of the problems associated with objective setting, some authors have proposed an alternative evaluation approach. For example, Scriven (1996), questioning the efficacy of criteria-based evaluation and relegating goals/objectives to minimal importance, introduced the concept of 'goal-free' evaluation. In his view, evaluations exist to make value judgements on whether the programme was of use to its stakeholders. This is a concept that may be applicable in the PR context.

EVALUATION MODELS AND METHODS

Several models of PR evaluation have been developed. This chapter focuses on four key models: Cutlip et al.'s (2006) Preparation, Implementation and Impact (PII) Model; Macnamara's (2002b, 1992) Pyramid Model of PR Research; Lindenmann's (1998) Effectiveness Yardstick; and Watson's (1997) Short Term and Continuing Models.

Preparation, Implementation and Impact Model

Cutlip et al.'s (2006) 'PII' Model, originally conceived in the late 1970s, depicts the possibility of evaluating PR at three different levels of preparation, implementation and impact. Evaluation undertaken at the preparation level assesses strategic planning in terms of the adequacy of background information gathered to design the programme, as well as the appropriateness and quality of message content and presentation. At the implementation level, evaluation examines the adequacy of the tactics and efforts applied to the PR programme. During this phase the number of PR materials produced and distributed is documented, opportunities for exposure are determined from the number of messages placed in the media and the number of people who received and attended to programme messages are also measured. The final level of the PII Model involves assessment of programme impact where the extent to which programme goals and objectives have been achieved is investigated. Accordingly, changes in targets' knowledge, opinion, attitude and behaviour become the focus of evaluation efforts. Additionally, the determination of PR's contribution to social and cultural change is proposed as the ultimate summative evaluation.

Cutlip *et al.* (2006) argued that each step within the model increases understanding and accumulates knowledge so that an evaluation is not complete without addressing criteria at each level. However, they cautioned against substituting measures from different levels, for example, using measures of column inches (implementation level) to infer changes in target publics knowledge, attitude or behaviour (impact level). While the PII Model does not propose evaluation methodologies, nevertheless its focus on separating the various levels at which PR can be evaluated is valuable and it serves as a useful checklist for evaluation planners (Watson and Noble, 2007). However, arguably its main contribution lies in clarifying the parameters surrounding each evaluation level.

Pyramid Model of PR Research

Building on the PII Model, Australian author Jim Macnamara developed a 'Macro Model' of PR evaluation (Macnamara, 1992), which was later revised and re-titled the 'Pyramid Model of PR Research' (Macnamara, 2002b). As illustrated in Figure 10.2, this model conceptualises PR programmes in the form of a pyramid that rise from a broad base of inputs, narrowing through outputs and outcomes until reaching a peak where objectives are achieved.

The Pyramid Model differs from the other models discussed in this chapter in the fact that alongside each stage it proposes a menu of appropriate evaluation methodologies. While the list is not exhaustive, it nevertheless serves as a practical illustration of the wide range of informal and formal research and evaluation methods and tools available to practitioners. In particular, it highlights a number of 'no cost' or low cost avenues including secondary data (both internal and external). This is an important point for PR practitioners to note as cost is frequently advanced as the reason for not undertaking evaluation. The inclusion of indicative methodologies in the model also underscores the point that different methods are required at different stages and measure different things. In other words, it is important for PR practitioners to understand what research methodologies to use and when.

Although the Pyramid Model has been criticised for its seemingly summative approach and lack of a dynamic feedback element (Watson and Noble, 2007),

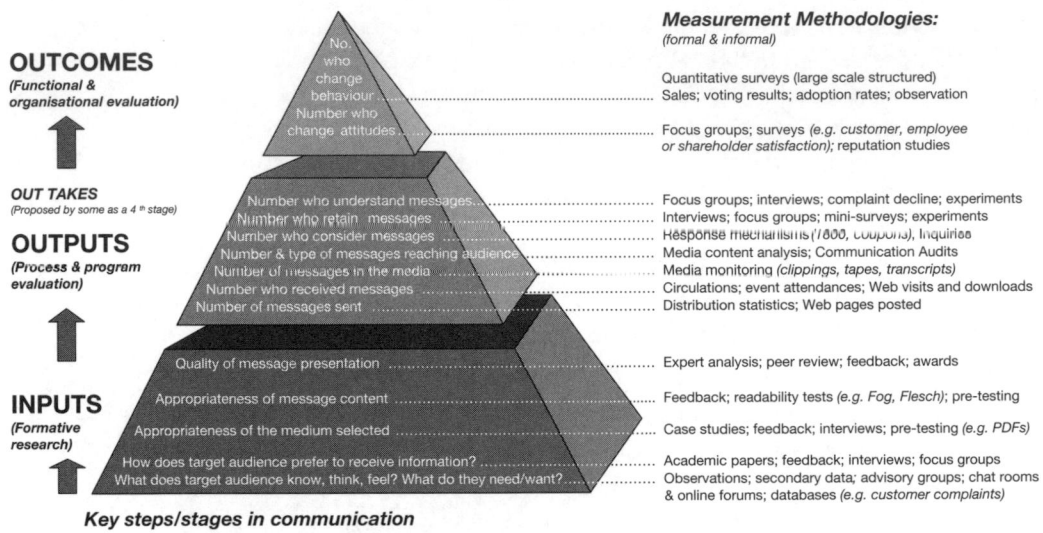

FIGURE 10.2 Pyramid model of PR research (Macnamara, 1992; 2002b)
Source: © Jim Macnamara 1992 and 2002b. Used by permission of Jim Macnamara

Macnamara (2005) argued that while not overtly acknowledged, nonetheless the model implicitly proposes that research findings from each stage are continually incorporated into planning. Thus, if initial pre-testing at the input stage finds that a chosen medium is inappropriate, no practitioner would continue to the output stage and use that medium to distribute information.

Effectiveness Yardstick Model

In keeping with the theme of depicting the multi-stepped nature of PR evaluation, American practitioner and researcher Walter Lindenmann (1998) developed the Effectiveness Yardstick Model that established three levels for measuring PR. However, unlike the previous two models discussed, Lindenmann did not explicitly include the assessment of PR planning in his vision. Rather he proposed that effective PR measurement and evaluation was a two-step process that involved, first setting specific and defined PR goals and objectives and second, determining levels of measurement. At the basic level, PR outputs are measured. These centre on media relations efforts involving media placements, impressions and reach. At level 2, deemed the intermediate stage, the model introduces an additional stage that focuses on assessing PR outgrowths, that is whether target audiences received, attended to, understood and retained the PR messages. It is argued that these elements represent cognitive processes that should be distinguished from behavioural results. Finally, PR outcomes are evaluated at the advanced Level 3 phase, which includes measures of opinion, attitude and behaviour change.

The Effectiveness Yardstick Model is noteworthy because it was one of the forerunners in asserting a hierarchy of levels in which the relative importance of each type of evaluation was established so that, 'as important as it might be to measure PR outputs, it is far more important to measure PR outgrowths' (Lindenmann, 1998: 69) and furthermore, 'the ultimate test of effectiveness – the highest outcome measure possible – is whether the behaviour of the target audience has changed, at least to some degree, as a result of the PR programme or activity' (ibid.: 70).

Like the PII Model, the Effectiveness Yardstick does not include possible evaluation methods. However, Lindenmann (1993: 9) has outlined a number of data collection techniques corresponding to each level of the model where he emphasised that, 'an array of different tools and techniques is needed to properly assess PR impact.' Nevertheless, it has been argued that models that do not provide methodological guidance remain purely theoretical frameworks that offer little practical assistance for practitioners (Macnamara, 2006).

In comparing the PII, Pyramid and Effectiveness Yardstick models, it is evident that each uses varied terminology to describe essentially similar stages. Moreover, these models have been criticised because they appear too complex, static and lacking in dynamic feedback (Watson, 1997; Watson and Noble, 2007). However, this conclusion has been refuted by Macnamara (2006: 21) who argued that while the models depict a chronological illustration of the order of activity, 'in reality, input, output and outcome research is part of a dynamic and continuous process and these models should be read that way.'

Short Term and Continuing Models

In response to the perceived need for accessible and dynamic models, Watson (1997) developed the Short Term and Continuing Models of PR evaluation. After empirically investigating evaluation practice via four case studies, he concluded that PR actions operated according to two broad structures of short-term media relations campaigns and longer-term programmes that utilised a variety of strategies and tactics to create effects among target groups. Thus, 'two different evaluation models are needed to judge two very different scenarios' (Watson and Noble, 2007: 95). Watson's Short Term Model follows a single track, linear process wherein awareness objectives are implemented through media relations and evaluated by way of media or target response analysis. To meet the needs of longer-term PR programmes, Watson designed a Continuing Model with an iterative loop to depict a dynamic and continuous evaluation process. The model initially begins with a research stage from which objectives are set. Following this phase, strategies are selected and tactics chosen. Multiple formal and informal analyses are then applied and the information is fed back to each programme element. Thus, throughout a programme, the objectives, strategies and tactics are continually adjusted.

Watson claimed that his models are simple, accessible and do not require rigid adherence to evaluation methodologies. In addition, the models recognise the fact that information can be used to adjust programmes so that summative evaluation data can actually be used in a formative manner. Furthermore, with seeming reticence to recommend appropriate evaluation techniques, Watson and Noble (2007: 101) maintained that,

> these models are not detailed prescriptions for undertaking evaluation of public relations programmes. This is a complex problem that does not lend itself to simple, straightforward solutions; nor is a long list of potential evaluation techniques useful for similar reasons.

In summary, the reviewed models offer four principal insights into the evaluation of PR. In broad terms they:

- depict PR as a multi-step process (input, output, outgrowth, outcome)
- clarify that different methods are appropriate at different stages
- underscore the importance of avoiding level substitution
- offer debate about the usefulness of prescribing evaluation methodologies.

Having said this, however, the practical application of these models is in doubt. It has been claimed that most practitioners have not adopted these approaches due to a lack of knowledge, too narrow and academic a dissemination base or practical and universal appeal problems (Watson and Noble, 2007).

In addition, others have proposed that in recognition of the paradigm shift towards relationship management (Ledingham and Bruning, 2000), there is also a need for a specific level of evaluation that focuses on how measurable relationships with stakeholders could be linked to business outcomes. This has been dubbed 'outflows' (Thellusson, 2003). Zerfass (2010) also defined this as the value created by communication processes in terms of the impact on strategic/financial targets (value adding) and tangible/intangible resources (capital-building). The empirical measurement of relationship indicators in PR is a developing area of research. In an early study of organisation-public relationships, Hon and Grunig (1999) proposed six indicators of a successful public relationship as: control mutuality; trust; satisfaction; commitment; exchange relationship; and, communal relationship. In addition, Huang (2001) has developed and validated a cross-cultural OPRA (organisation-public relationship assessment) instrument. Other researchers have focused on quantifying the link between relationship indicators and organisational outcomes. For instance, Bruning (2002) found a quantitative link between relationship attitudes and outcome behaviours while later research also discovered that mutual benefit was a specific and measurable outcome that provided competitive advantage (Bruning et al., 2006).

PR EVALUATION IN PRACTICE

Nature and extent of evaluation practice

A number of empirical research studies have investigated the nature and extent of PR evaluation practice in countries around the world, including the United States, Canada, Australia, Europe and the United Kingdom. Results show remarkable consistency across these geographically diverse regions. The main findings can be synthesised as follows.

Practitioners generally seem to support the idea of PR evaluation, recognising its professional benefits (Chapman, 1982) as well as its importance to the credibility of PR (PRCA, 2009). However, there is also a feeling that PR is difficult to measure in precise terms (Walker, 1997) with one fifth of respondents to a *PR Week* survey maintaining that PR could not be measured (Fairchild, 1999). Indeed, it has been found that practitioners recognise that research is talked about more than it is actually conducted (Lindenmann, 1990; Walker, 1997).

The majority of practitioners appear to rely on techniques involving the measurement of media coverage as well as experience and informal judgement. For instance, a recent European study found that 82.3 per cent of respondents monitored clips and media response (Zerfass *et al.*, 2010). However, there is evidence to suggest that despite the ubiquitous nature of media evaluation, practitioners are not fully satisfied with the approach and use these types of measurement more extensively than they value them (Pinkleton *et al.*, 1999). For example, Baskin *et al.*'s (2010) research revealed that although 89 per cent of respondents regularly utilised 'clip reports/press cuttings books,' only 65 per cent regarded them as an effective evaluation method. Similarly, 93 per cent identified 'pre- and post-surveys' as an effective means of measuring impact, yet, only 50 per cent made frequent use of the technique. Nonetheless, the overall evidence suggests that most PR evaluation takes place at the output level with low levels of input, outcome and outflow measurement (Gregory, 2001; Xavier *et al.*, 2006; Zerfass *et al.*, 2010). Analysing award-winning PR case studies in the PRIA Awards during the period 1997–2001 to examine whether the use of evaluation techniques had changed over time, Xavier *et al.* (2005) discovered no significant differences in the frequency of use of output methods and, while the popularity of outcome evaluation fluctuated significantly between certain periods, no general trend towards increased use was detected.

Typically, a variety of evaluation techniques are used representing a 'continuum from virtually no evaluation to formal and ongoing efforts' (Hon, 1998: 123) with averages of 3–6 methods per campaign being reported (Pieczka, 2000; Xavier *et al.*, 2005). However, Pieczka (2000) attributed this to 'fluke' or luck rather than a deliberate intent to employ systematic triangulation.

In his research among American practitioners, Dozier (1984) identified three styles of PR evaluation: scientific impact evaluation; seat-of-pants evaluation; and, scientific dissemination evaluation. Reflecting a formal scientific approach, the scientific impact evaluation style involved the measurement of public reaction to the organisation and PR programmes both before and after implementation. In contrast, the seat-of-pants style consisted of informal and subjective techniques that focused on preparation, dissemination and impact stages. The final evaluation style of scientific dissemination revolved around the scientific measurement of message distribution. Dozier found evidence that practitioners adopted styles simultaneously with scientific evaluation supplementing rather than replacing more informal approaches.

There are also suggestions that evaluation activity varies across the four specific programme content areas of: problem definition; planning and preparation; implementation/dissemination; and, impact assessment. Piekos and Einsiedel (1990) found that overall, intuitive techniques such as discussions with top management/ colleagues, informal meetings with media personnel and reactions of contacts, significant publics and top management, were used significantly more often than scientific methods with the exception of the implementation/dissemination phase. During this particular phase, scientific procedures to monitor the distribution, placement, potential exposure and audience attention were most common.

In terms of financial support, expenditure on evaluation is low with generally less than 5 per cent of the PR budget allocated for evaluation (Lindenmann, 1990; Watson, 1995; PRCA, 2009). However, on a more positive note, 60 per cent of respondents to a PRCA survey claimed that they had experienced no reduction in the proportion of budget spent on evaluation despite the economic downturn (PRCA, 2009). In fact, there is evidence to suggest that the recession at the end of the decade may boost evaluation activity with 40 per cent of European practitioners claiming to have experienced a higher demand for evaluation of PR (Zerfass *et al*., 2009). As the Executive Director of AMEC pointed out, 'in a recession, evaluation is already playing a more important part in PR campaigns as clients demand proof that the programme is working' (PRCA, 2009: 1).

Despite this picture of evaluation as a somewhat haphazard activity, it is worth noting that there are many excellent best practice examples of PR campaigns that have been evaluated effectively. A number of them are referenced within this chapter and also include, for example, Spencer and Jahansoozi (2008) who described how research and evaluation was used throughout London's bid to host the 2012 Olympic Games. Nonetheless, on the whole, the previously reviewed studies, which span over three decades, demonstrate little in the way of substantial improvement with regard to the widespread execution of systematic and formal evaluation approaches. It is therefore important to examine the barriers that stand in the way of developing and using evaluation in PR.

Barriers to evaluation practice

A number of reasons have been put forward to explain the limited progress in implementing PR evaluation in practice. Universally, the most common barriers have centred on limited resources. Time and again, the twin themes of insufficient budget and lack of time have emerged from surveys of practitioners as the principal constraints to conducting PR evaluation (Hauss, 1993; Kerr, 1999; Walker, 1997; Xavier *et al.*, 2005; Xavier *et al.*, 2006; Baskin *et al.*, 2010). In addition, there has been widespread acknowledgement that PR practitioners lack knowledge of, and training in, evaluation methods and processes (Walker, 1997; Xavier *et al.*, 2005; Baskin *et al.*, 2010). This is particularly concerning given that research suggests that most PR research and evaluation is conducted by PR-trained personnel rather than by research specialists (Lindenmann, 1990; Watson, 1995; Walker, 1997). Moreover, many practitioners have claimed that clients lack understanding of PR and evaluation (Walker, 1997) so that the emphasis on media-oriented evaluation stems from pressure from clients who want a tangible, easily understood, standardised evaluation approach (Xavier *et al.*, 2005).

The role of senior management in influencing evaluation activity has also been raised. For instance, in Kerr's (1999) study, practitioners admitted that they were not proactive enough regarding evaluation because management did not request it. On the other hand, a more structured, scientific approach to evaluation often ensues when senior management support or demand evaluation (Piekos and Einsiedel, 1990; Hauss, 1993). This issue seems to stem from perceptions about PR itself, with CEOs claiming that they instinctively knew when PR was effective (Campbell, 1993). In White and Murray's (2004) study of UK CEOs there was also an acknowledgement that while the effects of PR occurred over time, few managers were willing to wait for longer-term results. Their main concerns seemed to revolve around the calibre of PR personnel. As White and Murray (2004: 18) concluded: 'value is recognised in the quality of the advisors at work in the practice. The CEOs interviewed who have as advisors practitioners that they know, respect and trust, and in whose abilities they have confidence, are quite prepared to rely on their judgement that they are receiving valued support from public relations.'

Nonetheless, Macnamara (2007: 3) proposed that lack of budget, time and demand were 'excuses' rather than valid reasons for not evaluating PR. He argued that other, underlying reasons came into play, namely that practitioners do not see evaluation as relevant because they mainly operate in a technical role that is primarily output oriented. Indeed, it is suggested that PR practitioners' own attitudes towards research and evaluation may also exert an important influence on their evaluation activity. For example, a significant positive relationship between the belief that research and evaluation was important and actual use of formal research and evaluation approaches has been found (Judd, 1990). However, most data on practitioner attitudes suggests a more negative viewpoint. Feelings that evaluation could be perceived as 'checking up' on staff, that criticism would be taken personally rather than professionally, apprehension about the implications of negative evaluation results and a preference for informal evaluations have been recorded (Kerr, 1999).

The tools of evaluation are another concern for practitioners (Xavier *et al.*, 2005). Kerr (1999) found that practitioners were hesitant about employing available measures because of perceived problems and called for the development of a quick and easily administered measurement instrument. However, many commentators disagree with this desire to reinvent the wheel (Cline, 1984), instead maintaining that the industry already has access to existing research tools and techniques that are ready and waiting to be used (Phillips, 2001b; McCoy and Hargie, 2003; CIPR, 2005; Lindenmann, 2005).

Industry response

Against this backdrop, PR professional associations and related organisations around the world have developed a range of initiatives to support and encourage the development of PR evaluation, with varying degrees of success. Over the years, they have held numerous seminars, workshops and conferences and issued a number of white papers and guidelines for various aspects of evaluation, many of which are referred to throughout this chapter. Focusing on the UK, *PR Week* launched their 'PRoof' campaign in 1998 recommending that 10 per cent of budget should be allocated to evaluation. However, research findings suggest that this did not yield fruitful results. The same year, the CIPR (then the IPR) published a 'Public Relations Research and Evaluation Toolkit', which is now in its third edition. In 2002, two UK-based organisations, the IPR and PRCA created 'PRE-fix', a joint PRE forum that aimed to establish a standard form of media evaluation. Unfortunately, this venture failed to reach agreement on a meaningful standard and was dissolved. In conjunction with various partners, the CIPR also commissioned a number of reports examining the UK PR industry (e.g. DTI/IPR, 2003; CEBR, 2005).

However, perhaps the most significant event in recent times occurred at the second European Summit on Measurement in Barcelona held in June 2010. Here, leaders of five international professional measurement and evaluation bodies (AMEC, Global Alliance, IPR Measurement Commission, PRSA and ICCO) and 200 delegates from the world's top measurement companies and PR agencies gathered together to agree the first ever global standard for PR measurement. Named the 'Barcelona Declaration of Measurement Principles', the agreement comprises seven key principles as shown in Figure 10.3.

Early reaction to the 'Barcelona Principles' has been mixed. AMEC Executive Director Barry Leggetter, described them as an important framework for future development (Magee, 2010). Likewise, Jay O'Connor, CIPR President, supported the principles, saying they provided a clear position on measurement fundamentals, although she also acknowledged that they could create challenges for practitioners if their clients wanted measures that did not reflect the principles (Magee and O'Reilly, 2010). However, the Declaration has been criticised by some practitioners who feel it is too pedestrian and does not go far enough (Magee, 2010). Nonetheless, Richard Houghton, President of ICCO and former chairman of PRCA defended the Declaration, saying that, 'These principles will be the building blocks that enable us to tailor evaluation techniques to each individual market – enabling us to reflect

	The Seven Barcelona Principles
1	Importance of goal setting and measurement
2	Measuring the effect on outcomes is preferred to measuring outputs
3	The effect on business results can and should be measured where possible
4	Media measurement requires quantity and quality
5	AVEs are not the value of public relations
6	Social media can and should be measured
7	Transparency and replicability are paramount to sound measurement

FIGURE 10.3 The Barcelona Declaration of Measurement Principles
Source: Magee and O'Reilly, 2010

the undeniable fact that PR markets around the world are at different stages of maturity' (Magee and O'Reilly, 2010: para. 19).

Following the measurement summit, two taskforces were set up to further examine Principles 5 and 6. In addition, AMEC and PRSA with support from PRCA and CIPR, organised a Measurement Metrics conference in London in November 2010. At this event, the CIPR committed to a number of actions including: updating its CIPR Measurement and Evaluation Toolkit; setting clear guidelines for its awards entrants and judges regarding acceptable measurement practice; continuing to focus on measurement in its education and professional development programmes; placing greater emphasis on effective measurement in its own communications campaigns and ensuring it forms a key strand of the CIPR's agenda for 2011; and, working with the wider business and public sector communities to improve the value of Public Relations (Wheatcroft, 2010). Similarly, the PRCA announced that it would include a compulsory evaluation section on its awards entry form, and create a specialist evaluation module within its CMS accreditation process (PRCA, 2010).

At the beginning of the new decade, it appears that there is significant momentum in the industry towards encouraging and supporting the widespread use of PR evaluation. It remains to be seen whether this can translate into practice and overcome the many barriers to evaluation.

We now highlight two specific areas that often generate particular debate. These are media evaluation, followed by an overview of online evaluation.

THE MEDIA EVALUATION DEBATE

As highlighted in the previous section, PR is commonly evaluated at the output level using content analysis of media coverage. This can range from basic to sophisticated, be quantitative or qualitative and may be performed manually or via computer software systems. The simplest form of content analysis is the counting of press clippings and/or radio/TV segments that mention an organisation or its products and services or those of its competitors. Articles that contain other key words or issues that an organisation identifies as relevant can also be gathered. In addition, the press/broadcast coverage can then be measured in terms of column inches/centimetres or seconds/minutes of airtime. Circulation or readership analysis may also be carried out using Opportunities To See (OTS). These indicate audience reach and are calculated from circulation or ratings figures of the medium in which the item appeared. Advertising Value Equivalency (AVE) is also a common, though controversial, measure of PR. This is assessed by multiplying the column inches/ centimetres or seconds/minutes of air time gained by the corresponding media advertising rates. In essence, AVE aims to determine what the print/broadcast coverage generated by a PR campaign would have cost if equivalent advertising space had been purchased. In particular, AVE has been the subject of considerable debate within the industry and is therefore worthy of further discussion.

Over the past two decades, AVE has been widely condemned as an evaluation metric (Jeffrey et al., 2010). Jeffries-Fox (2003) argued that the method suffers from a number of conceptual and practical problems. First, the relationship between news stories and advertising is too complex to simply assume that a news story of a particular size has the same impact to an advertisement of equal size in that publication. Second, AVE cannot reflect the value of keeping stories out of the media. Third, while both can have an effect on consumers' awareness, perceptions, attitudes and behaviour, public relations and advertising are different disciplines. For instance, any given advertisement will repeatedly appear in the media in exactly the same way, but public relations news stories about an issue or an event can be highly variable with regards to placement and presentation (Macnamara, 2006). Thus AVE has been described as comparing a boat and a car – they are both means of transport but operate in different environments and although passengers can end up at the same destination, they get there in different ways (Fairchild, 1999).

In terms of practical difficulties with AVE, Jeffries-Fox pointed out that it is impossible to determine AVE for media outlets that do not permit advertising (e.g. BBC). Second, calculating AVE for the total amount of coverage gained does not take into account the possibility that some or all of the publicity could have been negative or indeed neutral. Finally, each piece of media coverage may not focus exclusively on one issue or organisation and can include favourable references to competitors. From a wider perspective, Macnamara (2006) argued that AVE is deficient because it cannot measure the range of PR activities that do not have media publicity as their goal (e.g. events, community relations, etc.).

Criticism of AVE is further compounded by the fact that in some cases, 'multipliers' are applied to basic AVE calculations on the assumption that news coverage is more credible than advertising, and therefore more persuasive. This is referred to as 'PR value'. Multipliers can vary widely, ranging from two to thirteen. However, there is little empirical evidence for such weightings (Michaelson and Stacks, 2007) and they are generally applied in an arbitrary manner. In fact, some practitioners decrease the AVE figure because of PR's lack of control over message, audience and publication schedule (Austin and Pinkleton, 2006). Lindenmann (2003: 10) asserted that, 'most reputable researchers view such arbitrary "weighting" schemes aimed at enhancing the alleged value of editorial coverage as unethical, dishonest, and not at all supported by the research literature.'

In addition, many professional bodies and associations have been long-term critics of AVE. This was most recently reflected in the Barcelona Principles outlined earlier. The Institute for Public Relations recently published a position paper rejecting the 'term, concept and practice of Advertising Value Equivalency' (Rawlins, 2010: 1). It stated:

> There is no evidence to suggest that advertising and editorial space hold equivalent value . . . The two are not equivalent concepts and should not be treated as such. Additionally, AVE is not a proxy for measuring the return-on-investment of public relations. AVE subjugates the value of the messages delivered through public relations simply to the cost of the space and/or time occupied by advertising, not the impact or effectiveness of public relations in its broadest definition . . . The Commission recognizes that the use of AVE is a common practice because calculating AVE is inexpensive and accessible but this does not justify the practice as appropriate.

Other professional associations are focusing on industry award schemes as a way to wean practitioners away from AVE. For instance, the method will no longer be deemed an acceptable form of measurement and evaluation within CIPR Excellence awards (Wheatcroft, 2010). There is already some evidence of movement towards this in the industry, as in late 2009 the Central Office of Information removed AVE from their set of compulsory metrics (Magee, 2010).

However, despite its many critics, AVE remains a popular evaluation method among practitioners. As AMEC Executive Director Barry Leggetter acknowledged,

> it doesn't matter who you speak to, people use AVE because it is an easy thing to figure out. The metric is flawed, but it provides a number. That's what a CMO or CEO demands, a number to show the PR programme is working.
>
> (Magee, 2010: para. 7)

Simon Warr, Board Director of Communications and Public Affairs at Jaguar Land Rover agreed, 'in the absence of anything that is more relevant, we do use AVE

. . . internally, they have a degree of recognition and are something people can easily understand' (Magee, 2010: para. 28). AVE amounts can also be impressive as Claire O'Sullivan, Director of media measurement company Metrica pointed out, 'often AVE figures returned are much higher than any PR budget and they make PR people look good' (Wallace, 2009: para. 4). Demand from clients/managers for AVE is often cited as a reason for their continued popularity. As Emma Cohen, MD of Skywrite put it, 'like it or not, if clients want to use AVE, you use it' (Wallace, 2009: para. 8).

Nonetheless, because of the recognised flaws in the system, efforts are underway to develop alternatives to AVE. For example, the Central Office of Information has introduced a new measure of 'cost per impact'. This divides the amount spent on PR by 'impact', which is calculated by multiplying reach by opportunity to see. This metric is already is use by other marketing disciplines and thus places PR on a par with its peers (Magee, 2010). Unwilling to completely discount the value of analysing the cost of media space and time, Jeffrey *et al.* (2010: 8) proposed a Weighted Media Cost (WMC) metric. This differs from AVE in that it does not equate editorial to advertising in value and impact terms and is defined as, 'the practice of utilizing the cost of media to the broadcast time or print/internet space occupied by a client as an objective market proxy number for comparative analysis against historical performance, against objectives, or against competitors.' It also attempts to overcome some of the limitations of AVE by,

> including the subtraction of all negative coverage; assigning costs to only the space or time occupied by an organization; using audited, negotiated media costs to the extent possible; and refraining from claims that WMC scores are outcomes of public relations campaigns.
>
> (Jeffrey *et al.*, 2010: 21)

It is too early to tell what impact the Barcelona Principles and other recent initiatives will have on the use of AVE. Although client demand for AVE may remain strong, Macnamara (2006: 37) urged PR professionals to resist such pressures arguing that they have a duty to advise, counsel and educate their clients and thus,

> Public relations practitioners who are aware of the invalidity and irrelevance of AVEs – and few could be unaware of at least serious questions about AVEs after years of debate – but still provide these to clients and employers, could be held to be knowingly and intentionally providing misleading information. Such behaviour, under most codes and guidelines, is patently unethical.

Rather than relying on somewhat blunt measures of the volume of coverage gained or financial metrics such as AVE, it also recommended that practitioners carry out assessments of the *quality* of their publicity. According to Macnamara (2006: 42) in-depth media content analysis takes into account: media type; prominence; positioning; size of articles or length of a radio/TV segments; share of voice of quoted sources; and, the position/credibility of key sources. In addition, 'tone' is also a key variable in media content analysis in terms of whether coverage is negative, positive or neutral (Watson and Noble, 2007). Moreover, Michaelson and Griffin (2005) recommended that the accuracy of overall coverage as well as specific messages should be taken into account by determining the presence of: correct information; incorrect information; misleading information; and, omitted information.

Media evaluation can be a source of valuable intelligence not only in terms of an organisation's own coverage, but also competitors, as well as societal issues and trends. Watson and Noble (2007) outlined how it can provide information on areas such as:

- whether key corporate messages are being reported in the media
- which journalists/publications are providing favourable coverage
- the sources of the press coverage achieved
- comparing an organisation's coverage to its competitors
- identifying trends in media coverage
- detecting emerging issues that may affect an organisation.

According to Austin and Pinkleton (2006), media content analysis is a five-step process involving: establishing objectives; selecting sample of texts; determining units of analysis; identifying categories of analysis; and, coding content. Technological developments offer the potential for automatic analysis of text (Fekl, 2010) although some are sceptical of the ability of software to fully appreciate and interpret meanings from text (Macnamara, 2006). Nevertheless, several software programs for media content analysis are available, some of which can be used by practitioners, while others require specialist research firms to undertake more sophisticated analyses.

However, one of the main limitations of media evaluation is that it cannot measure actual impact or results among target publics. One of the dangers inherent in the popularity of media evaluation is that practitioners may infer such results. Cutlip et al. (2006) cautioned against this type of 'level substitution' in their PII model. Nevertheless, Neuendorf (2002) claimed that media content analysis, if conducted rigorously and scientifically, could be useful for 'facilitating' inference and helping to predict likely effects on publics. Similarly, arguing that because news media summarise ongoing social debates, analysis of the news media is an efficient way to indirectly measure public attitudes, Bengston and Fan (1999) described how they used computer content analysis of online news media text to evaluate the achievement of strategic planning goals of the US Department of Agriculture Forest Service.

The final section of this chapter now focuses on a developing area of research and practice – that of online evaluation. It is not possible to provide a comprehensive discussion of this topic within one chapter, however, an overview of the main issues is presented.

ONLINE EVALUATION

The 2010 European Communication Monitor (ECM) (Zerfass et al., 2010) revealed that media relations on the web, social media and online communication have been some of the largest growth areas of PR across Europe in the last three years. As with all aspects of PR, there is a need to monitor, measure and evaluate these types of communication (Phillips and Young, 2009). However, the ECM found that most respondents had not yet got to grips with monitoring and evaluation. For instance, only 28 per cent had implemented tools for monitoring social media, 26 per cent intended to plan these during the coming year and 46 per cent had no plans in place. Similarly, only 18 per cent had established key performance indicators for measuring social media, 27 per cent planned to do so in the next year and 55 per cent had not yet planned this activity. It is small wonder that online monitoring and evaluation has been described as a 'black hole' in evaluation (Watson and Noble, 2007: 208).

Despite this, a number of guidelines have been developed that offer advice for monitoring and evaluating online PR. As an overarching framework, Paine (2002) identified six essential 'tools' to:

1   find out what the cyber media is writing about you and what your constituencies are seeing about you (and your competition)

2   ascertain the size of the impact you are having

3   discover what your constituencies are saying about you

4   determine what your constituencies think about you

5   reveal what action, if any, your constituencies are taking

6   decide whether it's all worth it.

Lindenmann (2003) suggested that cyberspace analysis of PR outputs should comprise an examination of a) website traffic patterns and b) online discussions. Duncan (2010) outlined how web analytics tools can be used to identify where website visitors are coming from and how they interact with an organisation's website. These can track the number of unique visitors; number of visits; number of page views; time on site; bounce rate; number of goals reached; and, conversion rates. More advanced statistical techniques that draw upon demographic and message content of referring sources can also provide further insights into the messages that are most effective at driving traffic and how messages and specific outcomes could be matched to optimal effect. Some of the advanced analyses require the expertise of specialist firms, but basic types of analysis can be accessed by practitioners from readily available free sources such as Google Analytics.

A number of other approaches to evaluating websites have also been developed. For instance, Hallahan (2001) advocated that usability research should be conducted in order to understand how users navigate an organisation's website. Similarly, Ingenoff and Koelling (2009) carried out a content analysis of websites using a framework created by Taylor *et al*. (2001) where they examined the five principles of: ease of use; usefulness of information; conservation of visitors; generation of return visits; and, dialogic loop.

In terms of examining online discussions, Lindenmann (2003) advised that the criteria applied in analysing offline editorial could also be used with internet postings. Paine (2007) detailed a number of specific measurement techniques for analysing blogs at output, outtake and outcome levels. She also pointed out that as well as quantitative metrics, it was also important to examine the quality of the content. Blogs can also be analysed from the perspective of their ability to build and maintain relationships online. Using Hon and Grunig's (1999) PR Relationship Outcome Scale, Kelleher and Miller (2006) found that blogs were perceived as conveying a 'conversational human voice' and as such, correlated positively with the key relationship outcomes of trust, satisfaction, control mutuality and commitment. However, the CIPR's (2010a: 29) toolkit proposed that the measurement of social media should focus on, 'identifying what conversations the organisation should participate in (or initiate) and understanding how all of these interactions and mentions (the "outputs") impact the organisation. In other words, what impact (outcomes) do these outputs have on the organisation's goals?'

The social media taskforce established after the Barcelona summit reported their conclusions in late 2010. They outlined a metrics grid that cross-referenced three phases of PR (PR activity, intermediary effect and target audience effect) with five stages of communication (awareness, knowledge, interest, preference and action) and identified measurement techniques for each intersection (Marklein, 2010). Their guidelines included the advice that social media outcomes and goals should be defined in advance and that while quantitative data is easy to measure, an increasing emphasis is needed on quality and context. In this regard, the underlying principles mirror those that apply in offline PR.

CONCLUSION

Gregory and White (2008: 307) likened the evaluation debate to,

> a car, stuck in mud or snow, trying to move forward. The engine revs, the wheels spin, exhaust fumes and friction smoke clouds the scene, but – in the end – the car remains stuck. So, too, the evaluation debate: a great deal of discussion but no forward movement.

As outlined in this chapter, evaluation of PR has a strong theoretical underpinning, there is a plethora of frameworks offering advice as to how PR can be measured and evaluated and a vast array of methods and tools exist for doing so. Despite this, the uptake of systematic and formal evaluation among practitioners has remained disappointingly low. It is important to garner a greater understanding of why the implementation of evaluation appears to be so problematic in practice and to devise strategies to overcome these barriers. Only then can evaluation regain some traction and continue on its forward journey.

The following case study provides a practical example of PR evaluation in action. The campaign won Gold in the 'Measurement and Evaluation' category of the 2009 CIPR Northern Ireland PRide Awards.

C@SE STUDY

BT YOUNG SCIENTIST AND TECHNOLOGY EXHIBITION

Introduction to campaign

BT is the sponsor/organiser of the annual BT Young Scientist and Technology Exhibition (BTYSTE), an all Ireland competition and one of the largest science fairs in the world (see Figure 10.4). The aim of BTYSTE is to encourage students with interests in science, technology, engineering and mathematics (STEM subjects) to pursue their passion into third level education and careers in order to benefit the future economy of Northern Ireland (NI) and the Republic of Ireland (RoI). With entries from NI much lower than those from RoI, Aiken PR (APR) was tasked with developing and implementing a campaign to increase awareness and drive entries over a six week period.

Objectives

- Increase NI entries by 15 per cent.
- Achieve entries from all six counties in NI.
- Reinforce BT's association with the long standing exhibition.

FIGURE 10.4
BTYSTE
exhibition
main hall
Source: Provided
by APR

In order to meet the objectives in a short period of time, APR had to be sure it was getting the correct message to the correct people. A campaign was designed to change perceptions and position BTYSTE as achievable and something that students and teachers in NI would aspire to be part of.

Strategy

- Use existing research from previous entries to identify opportunities.
- Conduct research among key stakeholders.

Implementation

Research

- Research was conducted among 100 second level students and teachers. This identified two stumbling blocks to participation in NI: (1) it was perceived as a competition for students based in the ROI; (2) it was seen as elitist and of a level that was unachievable for average students.
- APR compiled a document detailing the wide range of qualifying entries from previous years. This showed that the subject matter was broad and ideas varied from extremely simple to the complex. However, all the entries were innovative and revolutionary.
- Media engagement alone was not enough and budget was tight. APR identified that motivated teachers played a key role in encouraging entries to the competition. We investigated channels of communication for this key audience and identified outlets that previously had not been targeted with the BTYSTE message.
- A key objective was to ensure that entries were submitted from each county in NI. However, County Fermanagh had not submitted an entry in a number of years. We gathered data on schools in this area and identified teachers to target.

Planning

- An internal workshop was conducted with BT to share knowledge and establish NI specific key messages as our research indicated that using the same messages across the island was unproductive.
- A 'messages document' was created and circulated for use in all BTYSTE communications in NI.
- A media and stakeholder tracker was generated.
- A critical path detailing an ideal balance of media and stakeholder activity was developed.

C@SE STUDY

Engagement

- Key media were briefed on BTYSTE and issued with a follow up email detailing information on the competition.

- A story bank was created for the various media channels. For example, BTYSTE was pitched to the business media from the angle of the long-term skills shortage in STEM subjects and the threat this would pose to the future of the NI economy.

- APR reacted to topical stories in the media. For instance, The CERN Experiment took place on 10 September and APR identified a previous YSTE entrant who had since worked at CERN and leveraged this in media.

- Interviews were set up with students who had previously taken part as well as with BT personnel. The interviews were aired on UTV Life, BBC Radio Ulster, Citybeat, U105, Downtown Radio and all stations across the Northern Media Group.

- Press releases were issued announcing the deadline for entries.

- BT secured NI government support for the first time. This information was conveyed in a press release issued ten days before the deadline for entries as a reminder to schools.

Stakeholder engagement

Building on its research, APR specifically targeted stakeholders through a number of channels:

- Relationships were developed with teachers unions including NASUWT, which has 11,000 members in NI. BTYSTE information was carried in newsletters and bulletins encouraging teachers to participate.

- An appeal was made to the Council for Catholic Maintained Schools (CCMS) to communicate with its schools regarding BTYSTE. A letter was circulated from its deputy chief executive to principals and heads of science encouraging them to submit entries to BTYSTE.

- Teachers in the Fermanagh area were contacted and encouraged to enter the competition. This provided the opportunity to dispel any myths and to offer mentoring as required.

- Links were made with Council for the Curriculum, Examinations and Assessment (CCEA) and information was given to headmasters to encourage participation.

- Contacts were established in Education and Library Boards and information distributed accordingly.

C@SE STUDY

C@SE STUDY

- A link to www.btyoungscientist.com was provided on the teachers' mini site of wholeschool.tv. The mini site is used by over 13,000 teachers in NI for curriculum mapping.

Evaluation and measurement

- All print, broadcast and on-line coverage was positive.
- One TV interview, eight radio interviews, 14 pieces of print editorial and four pieces of online editorial were secured in a six-week period.
- NASUWT carried the information in its newsletter.
- CCMS issued a call to action.
- Wholeschool.tv carried link on curriculum mapping mini site.
- Entries from NI increased by 25 per cent.
- Entries from all counties were achieved including three from schools in Fermanagh.
- All communications referred to the exhibition as the BT Young Scientist and Technology Exhibition.

With thanks to BT and Aiken PR

QUESTIONS FOR DISCUSSION

1 Is evaluation essential in helping PR to gain credibility as a profession?

2 Could 'goal-free' evaluation be applied in the PR context?

3 How can senior management/clients be persuaded to invest in evaluation?

4 Will AVE ever be replaced as an evaluation method?

5 How could PR be evaluated at the societal level?

6 Are professional judgement and experience acceptable forms of evaluation?

7 What is the main reason for low levels of impact evaluation in PR?

8 What can be done to encourage more evaluation among practitioners?

9 Do the Barcelona Principles represent a significant step forward for PR evaluation?

10 Does online evaluation differ from evaluating offline PR?

FURTHER READING

Chartered Institute of Public Relations (2010) *Research, planning & measurement toolkit* (3rd edition). October 2010. Available from: www.cipr.co.uk/content/policy-resources/for-practitioners/research-planning-and-measurement/toolkit, accessed 18 November 2010.

Gregory, A. (2001) 'Public relations and evaluation: does the reality match the rhetoric?' *Journal of Marketing Communications*, 7 (3), pp. 171–189.

Lindenmann, W.K. (2003) *Guidelines for measuring the effectiveness of PR programs and activities*. Available from: www.instituteforpr.org/files/uploads/2002_MeasuringPrograms_1.pdf, accessed 25 November 2010.

Macnamara, J. (2005) *Jim Macnamara's public relations handbook*, Archipelago Press.

Watson, T. and Noble, P. (2007) *Evaluating public relations* (2nd edition), Kogan Page.

CHAPTER 11

Public relations and globalisation

Peter Walker

CHAPTER AIMS

Globalisation has moved on someway since a little known Scottish town planner, Patrick Geddes advanced the idea in 1915. The implications for public relations have changed since Marshall McCluan developed the concept of the Global Village in 'Understanding the Media' in 1964 to describe the impact of technology and later of telecommunications and the World Wide Web on society and communication. Some of the main writers and observers on the commercial, social, political and cultural impact of globalisation are reviewed with current thinking on how public relations is practiced in a diverse and globalised world.

DEFINING INTERNATIONAL AND GLOBAL PR

Public relations practice and programmes will always reflect the needs and strategic imperatives of the organisation they serve. Szondi (2006) sees the international-isation of the profession reflecting the standard definition of globalisation as 'taking advantage of global operational differences, similarities and opportunities to meet global objectives'. This is true for public relations in the multinational enterprise and to a lesser extent to the use of web based and digital technologies by practitioners worldwide.

In contrast, internationalisation – investing and operating in another country and shaping the enterprise or organisation to meet national needs – is reflected in

Wilcox's (2003: 283) definition of international public relations as the planned and organised effort of a company, institution or government to establish mutually beneficial relations with the publics of other nations. Wakefield (2003: 180) adds that international public relations (IPR) is a multinational programme that coordinates activities between a company's headquarters and various countries, with potential consequences or results in more than one country. Szondi (2006) suggests that IPR can be preparative (cultivating the environment), situational (dealing with a single issue or situation) or promotional (supporting global marketing).

No consideration of global and IPR in the twenty-first century is complete without reference to 'public diplomacy'. The phrase was coined in 1965 by Edmund Gullion, Dean of the Fletcher School of Law and Diplomacy at Tufts University and a distinguished retired foreign service officer, when he established the Edward R. Murrow Center of Public Diplomacy.

Speaking to the Diplomatic Academy in London in 2008, Sir Malcom Rifkind defined public diplomacy as public relations for diplomats, reflecting the intellectual and operational investment made by the US State Department under Condeleesa Rice (2005–2009). Her Under Secretary of State (2005–2007) Karen Hughes, a former Global Vice-Chair at Burson Marsteller, led the Bush administration efforts to improve the image of the US abroad, involving US business in the process of making public diplomacy strong and central to US foreign policy. Criticism of the Bush administration has overshadowed the profound change public diplomacy made to public relations practice in diplomacy for nation states and for global public relations strategies and plans for many, mainly US, multinational enterprises.

THE GLOBAL PUBLIC RELATIONS COMMUNITY

No consideration of the global public relations community today can ignore the reshaping of the world economy, the rebalancing of global political power and the reality of professional public relations practice in the emerging economies from Argentina to Zimbabwe and the BRICs (Brazil, Russia, India, China).

The global public relations community has been stronger, more professional and more organised than any of the IPR research has ever recognised or identified. Jolly Kaul, the 90-year-old former head of public relations for Indian Oxygen (part of the BOC International Group), published his *Public Relations in India* in 1976. It makes interesting reading 40 years later. Anyone thinking that CSR is a new US or European concept should ponder on Kaul's report of the proposals from the TATA Group founder, J.R.D. Tata. He suggested that some voluntary machinery for independent management and social audits should be set up and business should voluntarily submit to them to tackle 'suspicion and hostility towards private industry in our country' (Kaul 1976).

From Australia to Zimbabwe public relations practice and the public relations communities are well organised, professional, and in many countries have their position recognised and registered with national government.

Australia's national Institute (PRIA) is part of its government's immigration assessment and approvals process and is consulted over immigrants claiming to be public relations professionals. In Nigeria and Ghana public relations and the role of the national Institutes have a defined place in the post-colonial constitution of both countries. The Nigerian Institute of Public Relations (NIPR) was given the status of a Chartered body in 1990. With rights of direct access to a sponsoring cabinet minister and the constitutional authority to object to the appointment of a non-professional to senior government public relations posts comes the responsibility to apply a considerable rigour to professional training, development and examination processes. Until the political upheavals of recent years the Zimbabwean Institute of Public Relations (ZIPR) had an enviable professional education programme based at the University of Harare. An examination of the training and development certification programme run for many years by the Public Relations Institute of South Africa (PRISA) reveals a national government recognised programme that would be the envy of most practitioner and academic bodies.

The founding priority of the Global Alliance in 1998 was to establish a proper framework for exchange and information gathering between individual associations facing similar problems. Other priorities were to benchmark certification and professional development processes across national boundaries and to compare regulations affecting the development of the profession. The underpinning objective was to move to the mutual recognition of national membership criteria as a means of driving up standards of practice and of facilitating international mobility of public relations practitioners in a fast globalising world (Farrington 2003).

The world of international and global public relations has changed. Not because practitioners are increasingly involved in international accounts, but because of the re-balancing of the world economy. It is a change made more dramatic because of the 2008 US, UK and European led global financial crisis; the comparatively high economic growth rates of the economies of Africa, Asia, Russia and South America at a time when the so-called developed world was in recession; the youth demographics of those emerging economies; the growth of digital and social media; and the incredible growth and penetration of mobile phones.

The strengths and importance of well-regulated domestic stock exchanges, the growth of well-regulated banking and finance sectors not just in the BRICs and latterly South Africa, but also in the Goldman Sachs 'next eleven' – those economies that they forecast will be among the world's top 20 economies by 2020 – have stimulated national and regional public relations practice.

Membership of the ICCO has grown to include 1,000 consultancies in 29 countries, representing 25,000 staff. Moss and De Santo (2002: 3) counted 150 national and regional PR associations with a total of 137,000 members. In China alone, there were 100,000 practitioners, with another 450,000 students of the discipline. 'One of the key challenges for practitioners and students of PR . . . will be to become more conversant with how PR is understood and practised around the world' in order to develop communication programmes that span national boundaries (ibid.: 6). Falconi (2003) estimated that there were 3 million individuals in the global PR community, 400,000 of whom were in Europe.

PUBLIC RELATIONS PRACTICE FROM A FIRST WORLD PERSPECTIVE

In 1997 IPRA published a survey of eight countries (comprising the UK, the US, South Africa, Brazil, Japan, Singapore, Switzerland and Australia), which looked at the effects of globalisation on corporate communications. The most important task for PR in the future was thought to be the maintenance and improvement of corporate social evaluation. In order to communicate globally, companies would have to use PR professionals native to the different areas of operation. The fact that media were now reaching across national borders also had to be taken into account. The main problems for the future included the challenge of dealing with product liability issues across national borders, managing confidential information in the internet age and maintaining a global standard (IPRA 1997).

The question of a European consensus as to what the PR industry represents was identified as a problem in moving forward. Reviewing a plethora of definitions, a common theme was found to be that PR 'helps organisations to establish and maintain good relationships with all kinds of publics which are important for reaching the organisation's goals'. However, the practice of PR was felt to be diverging from this, in that many practitioners were operating in circumstances where they were not allowed to consider strategic activities. Other practitioners were working in integrated marketing communications.

Setting up a European standard for PR that allowed for different regional and national cultures, as well as recognising the different stages of development of practice, was proposed (van der Laan 2000). As part of the attempt to find an agreed definition of PR, the Confédération Européene des Relations Publiques (CERP) commissioned research in April 1999 among organisations and experts across Europe to ascertain the components of PR practice. The CERP definition of PR practice is: 'Public relations is the conscious organisation of communication. PR is a management function. The task of PR is to achieve mutual understanding and to establish a beneficial relationship, between the organisation and its publics and environment, through two-way communication' (www.cerp.org). However, visitors to the website are still instructed to view individual members' websites for further definitions.

The European Communication Monitor annually reviews trends in public relations (see also Chapter 20). Initiated by the European Association of Communication Directors this is an accurate and well-researched insight into the depth and breadth of public relations practice.

Its 2009 edition provides valuable insights into the evolution of strategic communication in Europe: 'Based on a sample of more than 1,850 professionals from 34 European countries, this research is one of the most comprehensive transnational studies ever conducted in the field of public relations worldwide.'

It is remarkably honest when it says that:

> as there is no knowledge about the population of communication departments and agencies in Europe, the findings presented here cannot claim representativeness. It is also necessary to note that economies, communication landscapes and PR professions are in rather different stages of development throughout Europe.

In looking at public relations and management decisions the study reports that:

> All over Europe PR professionals are trusted advisors with 73 per cent reporting that their recommendations are taken seriously by senior management. . . . In general, statistical analysis shows that influence depends on the geographical location of the organisation as well as on practitioners' experience and position, but not on their age and professional or academic education.
>
> (Zerfass *et al.* 2009)

While Heath (2001b) stated that the future of public relations could not escape global influence, practitioners felt that they lacked the knowledge and skills for effective practice in global situations. He recommended that they need not leave their domestic skills behind, for there were several similarities in practising public relations between different countries. Areas for study included behavioural and communication theories, the mass media, interpersonal communications, research methods, markets and public policy arenas. These cultural differences could make or break successful campaigns.

Wakefield (2001) reports the contradiction between the fact that while there are now 40,000 multinational entities, financial markets are converging and new technologies are facilitating communication, there has also been a rise in more entrenched stereotypes. He found that most PR people in the US feel unprepared to practise internationally and that global positions were often filled by employees with little experience outside their own countries. Thinking and acting at both local and global levels is necessary rather than simply extending domestic practices. IPR is similar to domestic work in that it is strategic, dealing with media relations and promotions. PR practitioners will still communicate with targeted publics, deal with issues and crises, and develop community relations.

DEFINING INTERNATIONAL AND GLOBAL PR

Szondi (2006) makes the distinction between global PR, which he defines as the internationalisation of the profession, and IPR, which is the 'planning and implementation of programmes involving two or more countries'.

In 2005, the Ford Vice President of Communications declared at the ICCO summit: 'There is no such thing as local, globalisation is a reality' (Crush 2005). An interesting comment from a company that does not have a single global product and addresses each regional market with products designed specifically for those markets. Manufacturing has globalised with engines from Wales to electronics from China and motor manufacture is an assembly process of a globalised production process as manufacturing cost dictates operational priorities.

When the CEO of Weber Shandwick was equally forthright saying that: 'All PR is local,' he was also being disingenuous as the former head of communication at BP in 2010 will attest. At the same conference delegates debated whether the best response would be to adopt a single brand identity, as few consumers see brands as having a country-specific origin, or whether increased connectivity did not necessarily bring more harmonisation. The fact that in several countries it is normal to charge for editorial meant that practice could not be standardised (ibid.).

Speaking at the Cambridge Marketing College lecture in 2005, Judge put forward the thesis that the improvement of trade between nations could lift 128 million people out of poverty. While charity donations to the developing nations total around US$20 billion and government aid US$80 billion, exports from those countries amount to US$2.4 trillion. By reducing tariffs on raw materials and basic manufactures and reducing subsidies to Western farmers, a substantial difference could be made to the level of world poverty. He felt that marketing communications was the key to bring this about (Judge 2005).

What Judge didn't deal with was the World Bank's (2006) assessment that some 30 per cent of all aid and development projects (worth $60 billion) did not achieve their objectives because of a failure in communication or community engagement. At the World Bank 2006 World Congress on Development Communication, the term 'public relations' was avoided despite the fact that so many of the examples of success could have come straight from a community relations chapter of a standard public relations text. He did not address the potential for the development of value added and branded products and services from emerging economies. The role public relations could and will play in the process of developing brands for export in such countries has yet to be explored.

THE GAME CHANGERS FOR GLOBAL PUBLIC RELATIONS PRACTICE

Consider this calendar:

2001   **Wikipedia** the collaborative reference was launched. It now handles 78 million enquiries a month.

2004   **Google** launches its first public offering – it now handles 1 billion search requests each day.

2004   **Facebook** incorporated – its current population makes it the third most populous country on earth.

2006   **Twitter** founded – now 190 million users post 80,000 search questions per day.

Social media have become the profit drivers for all the global advertising and marketing services groups. For the cost of a full page advert in *The Sun* an organisation can employ an executive to manage their global digital presence and messaging (see also Chapter 19).

In 2008, 'there was a choice between the risk of the total collapse of the global financial system or injecting government and tax payers funds into the financial systems and an array of companies threatening the economies of those countries themselves' (FCIC 2011). The G8 was forced to become the G-20, recognising the reality of both the economic shift in power towards what were still being called the 'emerging economies' and acknowledging that in the main their banks and financial regulators had protected their economies from the excesses that created the financial and economic crisis for the US and Europe in particular.

International diversity and the development of diasporas

It is not just international business that raises questions of diversity. Wilson and Eng (2003) point out that the population of the UK is changing rapidly and dramatically. While 29 per cent of the population in London is referred to as minority/ethnic, it is the emerging majority of tomorrow. Diversity must be recognised in all public relations programmes and organisations must create product lines that truly speak to the needs of each market. They advise a holistic approach, integrating PR, marketing, advertising, and community relations, to build trust and understanding.

Homogenous cultures are rare. Jandt (2004) states that 95 per cent of the world's countries are ethnically heterogenous. Post-communist Russia contains 148 million people from 100 nationalities, living across 11 time zones. The expectation in countries such as Australia and the US, with high levels of immigration, was that children of immigrants would simply assimilate. In the 1980 census, only 6 per cent identified themselves as American, however. Learning the language of the host country is normally a three-generation process. The old 'melting pot' idea held that people acculturated to American society by assimilating into the dominant culture and losing their old one. Now, people acculturate by integrating – learning the dominant culture and language but not losing their original one.

Billingsley (2002) refers to the diverse market in the US. In the 2000 census, there woro 36 million blacks, 35 million Hispanics, 12 million Asian-Americans, and 4 million American Indians. The cultural background of targeted publics can change which media channels practitioners should use. Simmons Market Research Bureau in 2001 surveyed Hispanics and found that they paid more attention to products advertised in Spanish. On the internet, the highest usage is among Asian-Americans, as 60.4 per cent use this medium, compared to 39.8 per cent of blacks and 31.6 per cent of Hispanics. She refers to a successful health campaign to target the black community that used churches and engaged pastors to launch the African-American Diabetes programme.

Wilson and Eng also point out that while the Hispanic community is 40 per cent of the population in the US, there are many different Hispanic cultures. These publics are not insignificant in terms of economic power, either. Hispanics, Asians and blacks in the US constitute a US$1.3 trillion market (Wilson and Eng 2003). Clarke (2000) defined the differences between the religious, royalist culture of the Thais; the assertive, workaholic culture of Hong Kong; the international sophistication of Singapore; and the heavily restricted media in Japan, and warned against regarding all Asian cultures as the same.

DEFINITIONS OF CULTURE

Sriramesh and Verčič (2003: 8) found no universally accepted definition of culture. They quote Tylor (1871), who defined it as 'that complex whole which includes knowledge, belief, art, morals, custom, any other capabilities and habits acquired by man as a member of society'. In 1952, Kroeber and Kluckhohn (cited in Sriramesh and Verčič) described a 'set of attributes and products of human societies . . . transmissible by mechanisms other than biological heredity'.

Hofstede is the third most cited author in international business studies published between 1989 and 1993 (Schneider and Barsoux 2003: 90). He defined culture as 'collective programming of the mind which distinguishes the members of one category of people from another' (Lewis 1999: 23) and Lewis reflects that 'comparisons of national culture often begin by highlighting differences in social behaviour' (ibid.: 8). MacManus (2000) states that culture is one of the four central influences on modernity and that the interrelationship between culture and communications is in the form of PR.

Anthropologist Edward Hall's *Silent Language*, set out in the *Harvard Business Review* in 1960. Hall suggested four categories of cultural variables that may drive surface behaviour:

- Relationships – if the focus is on relationships, deals arise from already developed relationships. If it is on the deal, relationships develop after it has been agreed.

- Communication – whether indirect, high context with non-verbal cues or direct and low context. In the US, communication should be to the point, whereas in China people like very detailed data.

- Time – monochronic or polychronic? Anglo-Saxon schedules are fixed, people do one thing at a time. Latin schedules are fluid, interruptions are common, interpersonal relationships take precedence.

- Space – moving too close in some cultures produces discomfort, and in others, backing away may convey disdain.

(Sebenius 2002)

Hofstede (Schneider and Barsoux 2003: 87–91) built on Hall's Silent Language. Based on an employee opinion survey of 116,000 IBM employees in the 1960s, across 40 different countries, he identified four value dimensions. Power distance is the extent to which unequal distribution of power is accepted. Uncertainty avoidance refers to society's discomfort with uncertainty and preference for stability. Individualism/collectivism looks at the individual or group focus and masculine/feminine reveals the bias towards masculine assertiveness and competitiveness as against feminine nurturing, quality of life and relationships.

On studying Asian cultures, a fifth dimension appeared, referred to as long-term orientation, reverence for persistence, thrift and patience. While there have been critiques of Hofstede's findings, several studies confirmed similar differences. A table of rankings was produced for each country, showing that the US ranked most highly in individualism and in the top third for masculinity, but low on uncertainty avoidance and power distance. Japan was the most masculine culture, and also seventh in uncertainty avoidance. Arab countries were halfway down the rankings in terms of individualism, ranked seventh in terms of power distance, and were surprisingly less masculine orientated than the US or Japan. Greece was ranked highest in uncertainty avoidance and Malaysia in power distance. Comparing societies with a high long-term orientation, building of relationships and market position were emphasised rather than the short-term bottom line. High power distance is reflected in more levels of hierarchy and centralised decision-making. High uncertainty avoidance results in more rules and procedures and risk avoidance. High collectivist organisations prefer group decision-making. High masculinity rates task accomplishment higher than social relationships. The rankings were then translated into country clusters: Anglo, Nordic, Latin and Asian.

While actions can be copied, understanding thought processes and concepts is more difficult, as people will have different notions of the same concept, such as duty or honesty. For example, in Britain and the US, a contract is a document that should be adhered to once signed. In Japan, it is a starting document that can be modified as needed. In South America, it is regarded as an ideal that is unlikely to be achieved but that is signed to avoid argument.

Hofstede's value dimensions can be redrawn to divide cultural norms into outer and inner layers (Marx 2001: 43–46). Symbols are the most obvious signs of cultural differentiation, including dress, small talk and table manners. Next, it is useful to examine which personalities are seen as heroes and how that illustrates which qualities are revered. Rituals mark the boundary between inner and outer, with a ceremony that marks particular occasions that have meaning. Lastly, values are the standards or principles considered valuable or important, expressing what people believe, and are often complex and subconscious.

Marx (2001: 47–57) sets out three dimensions of problem-solving. While problems that are encountered may be the same in different cultures, how people deal with them will be different. Orientation refers to the emphasis on task or relationships, which also includes whether individual action is regarded more highly than collective. In an individualistic culture, performance-related pay is a meaningful motivator but not in a collectivist culture.

In the latter, it is important to see tasks as interrelated so that people can see that they are part of a group. The second dimension, the task approach, reveals whether the culture is tolerant of ambiguity or not. At one end of the spectrum is the German regard for structure, at the other the Brazilian emphasis on objectives rather than planning, so that the schedule is unimportant as long as the task is done. This also includes the approach to time. It is suggested that the English monochronic approach was learned as a result of the Industrial Revolution, as workers in factories were needed to be present at a particular time, but that it seems logical and natural now. The third dimension is communication and presentation style, including the display of emotion. In the US, regret and self-effacing behaviour are not acceptable; communication is preferred to be positive rather than neutral. In Asian cultures, showing guilt or shame is regarded as loss of face. Informal, democratic attitudes can be contrasted with formal, predicted roles based on seniority, age, class and gender. Marx suggests that there is no right or wrong, but that in order to be effective, people must adapt their methods of doing business according to the cultural context. Hampden-Turner and Trompenaars (2000: 11) proposed six dimensions of cultural diversity.

- Universalism versus particularism. Rules, codes, laws and generalisations versus exceptions, special circumstances, unique relations.
- Individualism (personal freedom, competitiveness) as against communitarianism (social responsibility, cooperation, harmonious relations).
- Specificity (analytic and objective), or diffusion (holistic and relational).
- Achieved status (what you have done), or ascribed status (who you are and your personal connections).

- Inner direction where convictions are located internally, or outer direction where examples and influences are located externally.
- Sequential time, where time is a race along a set course, or synchronous time where several things may happen at once.

Stevens suggested the following cultural profiles in 1991 (Schneider and Barsoux 2003: 92–93):

- *Anglo/Nordic*. Village market. Decentralised, entrepreneurial, flexible, delegation, informal personal communication. Output control.
- *Asian*. Tribe or family. Centralised, paternalistic, strong social roles, personal relationships. Social control.
- *Germanic*. Well-oiled machine. Decentralised decision-making. Narrow span of control, compartmentalised, throughput control. Efficiency.
- *Latin*. Traditional bureaucracy. Centralised decision-making, less delegation, pyramid of people, elitist, input control.

Selmer, in 1998, added a Viking form of management, with decentralised decision-making, emphasis on consensus and avoiding conflict, informal channels of communication and long-range objectives. These cultural preferences affect how information circulates and is shared. In French companies, the flow of information between groups is limited, as information is a source of power and not easily given away. In Sweden, communication patterns are much more open and informal, whereas information sharing is not widely practised in Russia, especially with outsiders in case of misinterpretation. In Japanese companies, intensive and extensive discussion is encouraged at all levels (Schneider and Barsoux 2003: 92–93).

DIFFERENT CONVENTIONS

Dealing with clients and publics in different countries and cultures requires sensitivity to different conventions. Silence in conversation in the US, Peru or Kuwait is awkward, whereas in Asia it can be a response and a part of social interaction. Lewis (1999) draws attention to listening societies such as Japan, Korea and Finland, where people think about their reply to remarks in silence. He examines the different ways of gathering information, from the data-oriented Northern European emphasis on solid information to the dialogue-oriented Latin societies that put this information in a personal context, to the more complicated listening society of Japan, where information will also be gathered from a web of relationships, memberships of clubs and schools.

The Japanese regard the underdog as inefficient, so banks don't like to lend to struggling small businesses. Lewis recommends moving away from chauvinism and a belief that one's own culture is the best to developing intercultural sensitivity.

Schneider and Barsoux (2003: 85) also question 'the logic of universal "best prac-tices"'. They suggest that theories about organisational structure are products of societal concerns at the time, such as Weber's bureaucracy, the French administra-tive model of Fayol and the American scientific management of Taylor. Different approaches reflect different cultural assumptions about human nature and the importance of task and relationships. This leads to questioning the transferability of management ideas and structures, such as the US and European trends towards participative management and empowerment, which have been frustrated in Russia where employees expect strong, paternalistic management.

In most agrarian economies or societies cohesion and sensitivity to society is important. 'The nail that sticks up will be hammered' is a Japanese saying but it carries a warning for the public relations practitioner that holds true for most emerging economy countries.

The issues of acceptance in society and a high regard for protocols are conventions the public relations practitioner ignores at their peril.

ORGANISATION STRUCTURES

Hampden-Turner and Trompenaars (2000: 50–52) differentiate between global, multinational and international companies, and suggest a new form of transcultural corporation. They suggest that the normal form of global corporation is centralised, which expects offices in the 'Rest of the World' to be integrated with its own way of doing things, and these overseas offices are managed by nationals of the global corporation's country, normally American, such as in AT&T (now Comcast). Econ-omies of scale are gained from producing essentially the same product in all markets. Multinationals are decentralised, locally responsive and overseas offices are managed by indigenous people, and may produce different products in different markets according to local needs, such as Unilever. International companies' prime export is knowledge, mainly American or Japanese, with local variations on centrally supplied know-how, using elements of both the previous two forms. Transcultural organisations are offered as a new model, taking advantage of diverse ideas across the world with common themes to be more competitive. Thus each function would be situated where the expertise exists, for instance research and development may be in India or Japan. The communication network is vital so that learning and know-ledge can be transmitted throughout the organisation. Multiple perspectives are accepted as legitimate, along with a commitment by individual units to a shared vision. They suggest that Phillips, GE, P&G and Matsushita are moving in this direction.

Melewar and McCann (2004) suggest that communication for corporate brands should operate on both micro and macro levels. Company values should be delivered in a consistent message to all stakeholders, while at the local level the brand needs an interactive relationship with each stakeholder by meeting their needs and wants. It is easier to uniformly convey corporate values than communicate product differences. They note two approaches to communicating globally: a waterfall approach launches in developed countries first, with communications trickling down to the less developed; while the sprinkler targets all world markets at same time. The key to building an effective corporate brand is doing simple things well: listening and involving customers and employees, developing relationships and integrating consistent internal and external communications.

Coulson Thomas (2004) puts forward a variety of recommendations for successful international operation. He suggests adopting different approaches and adapting behaviour. He regards being open to alternative views, welcoming cultural diversity, and developing cross-cultural awareness to avoid standard solution as good practice.

Szondi (2006) lists the main players on the global stage as multinational organisations (MNOs), governments, intergovernmental organisations such as the EU and UN, international NGOs such as Oxfam and Greenpeace, global PR consultancies such as Burson Marstellar and Edelman, and the virtual communities on the internet.

The media have also become multinational corporations, with news gathered and distributed by a few transnational companies like CNN and the BBC.

HOW GLOBAL ARE WE?

Schneider and Barsoux (2003: 271) question whether organisations are truly international. They quote Farnham, who said, in 1994: 'We are living in a world which is about as integrated as the world of the nineteenth century . . . Fewer than 10 per cent of the businesses that inquire about going global actually try it'. Moss and De Santo (2002: 3) admit that the majority of enterprises have fewer than ten employees and operate on a small, local scale, yet they suggest that even these companies may take advantage of opportunities to trade internationally. Szondi (2006) notes that many global companies use English-language slogans even in non-English-speaking countries without translation. Lufthansa even used an English slogan – There's no better way to fly – in Germany.

Joffe (2003) states that we know more about each other through travel, television and technology. The global citizen is mobile, well travelled, cross-culturally aware and speaks several languages, but this is a small elite group. However, the more we want to be the same the more we emphasise our differences, and it is increasingly important not to talk to masses but to individuals. She quotes the work of Holden, who suggested that culture in the workplace is an important socialisation process and that organisational culture represents a deeper level of basic assumptions and beliefs shared by all employees. In this approach, the life of the project or work group is more important than the background or cultures of the work team. Joffe advises: 'Assume difference until similarity is proven.'

Whatever the extent of international interaction in most people's everyday lives, public relations practitioners are having to cope with organisations that are themselves composed of culturally different individuals, communicating with increasingly diverse publics. Public relations can adapt communications to suit the needs of this diverse population; global brands may be marketed differently in different parts of the world.

PUBLIC RELATIONS AND GLOBALISATION

Morley (2002: 35) suggests that 'there is not likely to be a phrase you will hear in your career in public relations as often as "think global, act local"'. He claims that British public relations practitioners were at the forefront of internationalist awareness, especially those who worked in the European headquarters of major American companies, educating their foreign 'parents' in the customs, sociology, politics and media of the local market. The rise of the multinational corporation was seen as commercial colonisation and a threat to local communities in Europe. The benefits of 'acting local' were that global companies became members of the community rather than being seen as foreign invaders. Morley proposes an emphasis on thinking local, to 'reach a level of understanding of the mindset of each group of people with whom you must communicate . . . [to] make your dialogue much more successful' (2002a: 39). This is much more than translating, customising and localising news releases. He uses the example of the Japanese ignorance of volunteerism and private donations, as social responsibility in Japan manifests itself in ways such as lifetime provision of employment. This led to the refusal of offers of help after the 1994 Kyoto earthquake, as they had no system for accepting contributions to the costs of medical care, which made them appear arrogant and insensitive. Alternatively, Western companies in China must pay attention to the concept of feng shui when building or refurbishing new premises. Sometimes, public relations' boundary-spanning role must take on the task of explaining these differences to clients.

Clarke (2000) recommended local solutions with local understanding as a best practice model, although never at the expense of a global perspective. Core strategy should always come from the lead office, with local offices adapting it to local conditions. For example, it is rude to send an email release to a Japanese journalist unless there is a close working relationship. 'Information technology enables us to manage and damage reputations at the touch of a button,' she said. 'Public relations is intended to resolve conflicts and misunderstandings.' Lerbinger (2001) adds: 'The essence of PR is cultural context.' Communications exist in the context of intentions and interpretations of participants, so that effective communication can only happen when a relationship is established. He quotes Bank's six primary dimensions of diversity: age; ethnicity; gender; physical abilities; race; and sexual orientation. Secondary dimensions are education; occupation; income; marital status; and military and work experience.

Wakefield (Rosborough and Wakefield 2000: 3) found that 'larger European multinationals have more sophisticated global PR programmes than those based in the US'. In terms of structure, he confirmed that the majority have a central PR strategy and relegate tactical delivery to local units.

Most had full-time PR officers in fewer than 50 per cent of international units. Conflict between central and local units could be a barrier to global success. Therefore, solid internal communication was increasingly important. He reiterated that: 'The most effective approach balances central and local needs.'

'Domestic work will not sustain the British PR industry,' says Gallagher (2007). The rise of India and China will cause shifts in the global power equations that British PR can capitalise on. He suggests developing multifaceted, multinational coordination from a global hub. Even domestic budgets may be spent on services abroad. PR Business (2006) reported a global union of PR agencies. PR Network (PRN) was an international alliance of 16 consultancies, from Europe, the US, Australia, India and Asia Pacific.

Szondi (2006) lists various specialisms in the IPR field. It may deal with tourism, and branding a country itself; culture, emphasising heritage and arts; diplomacy and military policy that may involve propaganda and supporting anti-democratic regimes. Diplomacy involves communicating with elite foreign publics to establish a positive image of a nation, but sometimes IPR creates a positive image that does not reflect reality.

THEORETICAL APPROACHES

Taylor (2001) reviews a number of ways in which research has examined IPR practice. Some studies extend Grunig's (1984) four models, even suggesting a fifth model of personal influencer. Sriramesh (2003) found that practitioners in Slovenia had similar ideals of excellent PR but did not practise it as often as in Grunig's studies. Chen and Culbertson (2009) suggest that PR is influenced by cultural variations. Taylor also examines differences in education and ethics, quoting Hatfield's 1994 study, which found that PR majors did not exist in UK universities – rather a shock to the many academics teaching in the UK at this time! Taylor concludes that US theoretical frameworks and practices may not hold up in other cultures and that assumptions need to be critically examined. Szondi (2006) suggests that Grunig's excellence model is a useful benchmark.

FRAMEWORKS FOR GLOBAL PRACTICE

Several writers have assembled books of case studies to examine both the diversity and the commonality of public relations practice. Moss and De Santo (2002) and Sriramesh and Verčič (2009) offer comprehensive collections. Both admit that there have been few international comparative studies, and that most try to test the applicability of a US model of practice in other countries rather than examining indigenous characteristics.

Sriramesh and Verčič relate the development of public relations to three elements in the infrastructure of a particular country. These are the political system, the level of economic development and the level of activism. Public relations thrives on public opinion, and so is most developed in democratic systems. The Freedom House survey of political change in the twentieth century found that there was a general shift towards pluralism (www.freedomhouse.org; Sriramesh and Verčič 2003: 4–5). Definitions of public relations assume a democratic structure that is not always the norm. Greater economic freedom in market economies favours the development of strategic public relations. As the discipline is yet to be widely considered, on a global scale, as an essential, core managerial function, where resources are scarce they are devoted to more urgent needs. Thus, public relations thrives in developed countries, where suppliers have to compete for public attention, approval and support. The level of economic development also affects the communication infrastructure and impacts on the wealth and literacy of the population. Activism is another element that influences the development of public relations. It is unlikely to be high if the bulk of the populace are more concerned about where their next meal is coming from, and so is present in more developed countries. It provides an opportunity in that practitioners can represent both sides of an activist movement. Increasing pressure from activist groups can force organisations to be socially responsible and require public relations practitioners to communicate changes in policy as well as provide feedback on trends in public opinion to management.

The nature of the media is also crucial in the development of public relations within society. As media relations is an integral and pivotal element of public relations, there is a need for a 'solid working relationship based on mutual respect for each other's work' (Wilcox and Nolte, quoted in Sriramesh and Verčič 2003: 11). The media has a powerful influence on the international images of nations and organisations, as we have seen from several of the case studies presented in the text. In developing countries, the media may reach only a small, homogenous group because of illiteracy and poverty. People may not be able to read or afford television, even assuming that the infrastructure allows them access to electricity. Thus practitioners may have to adapt to using traditional and indigenous media. Access to the media will determine whether various segments of the population can approach the media to disseminate messages. In Japan, press clubs are gatekeepers between the media and other publics. In Eastern European countries, it is normal practice to pay for editorial coverage.

Sriramesh and White's 1992 study related Hoftede's categories to Grunig's model of excellent PR and suggested that the latter was more likely in countries with low power distance, low individualism, low masculinity and low uncertainty avoidance – ironically, neither the US nor the UK conformed to this description (MacManus 2000).

Szondi (2006) charts a number of possible relationships between MNOs and PR practitioners in consultancies in the home country and host country, suggesting that programme objectives may be standardised but that messages should be adapted in different countries. Systematic research is needed to ensure that messages are not dominated by the MNO's organisational or societal culture.

All PR exists to preserve corporate reputation, and the PR manager should act as a cultural integrator, controlling global PR programmes and resolving any conflicts (Wakefield 2001). PR should maintain a broad base across the organisation, ensuring a balance between global imperatives and local strategies. Wakefield recommends using local practitioners and recognising that there is 'no one best prescription'. Szondi (2006) adds that local agencies can add more credibility to messages as they will be tailored towards the needs of the publics of the host country. He also suggests that PR can help the MNO adapt to the culture of host country.

EXAMPLES OF PRACTICE

Sometimes adapting practice means changing the emphasis on both brand and approach. In 1995, Dow Corning published a variety of materials for its products in different markets. One product was promoted with four different brochures in nine different languages. Local needs were overemphasised. The public relations function was strengthened, and a new set of visual identity standards developed. The intention was to speak with one voice, albeit in different languages.

The director of corporate communications reported directly to the CEO, and the worldwide communications team instigated regular global meetings, both face-to-face and by teleconferencing. Weekly global teleconferences of communications staff had rotating start times to deal with different time zones. Not all operational managers were based at headquarters; for example, the Online magazine has one editor in Brussels with a network to gather stories. The meetings are used for information sharing and planning strategy and implementation, and those who are responsible for each communication project are identified. 'It wasn't a revolution,' says Amy Rosborough, 'It took commitment and patience' (Wakefield and Rosborough 2000).

Despite the rise in democratic societies and the shift towards market economies, Moss and De Santo (2002) found little evidence as yet of the widespread adoption of Grunig's two-way symmetrical system of public relations.

The most sustained rapid economic growth in the past 50 years has occurred in China. PR revenues had increased to US$740 million in 2005. PR is beginning to have an important role in introducing foreign brands to China as well as helping Chinese brands raise their visibility on the global stage. The scale of the Chinese media – 8,000 magazines and journals, 2,000 newspapers, 1,250 radio and 2,100 TV channels – shows the opportunities for media relations alone. The vast majority, 70 per cent of PR revenue, originates from Beijing, Shanghai, Guangzhou and Chengdu. However, the government exercises strict control over media content (Gray 2006a).

Africa is a vast and untapped market of 800 million people across 53 states. These countries vary enormously in wealth, although the average share of GDP is US$684, compared to US$780 in China and US$440 in India. In 2006 Gyroscope developed an Africa Communications Index (ACI), examining range and reach of media, the existence of a professional PR body and the ease of access to trained staff. An update is badly needed but the rankings of South Africa, Nigeria and Egypt at the head of the index probably reflects the state of development of public relations practice in the 24 countries included in their largely desk based research study.

There are two PR associations in the Ukraine. The Ukrainian Association of PR is affiliated to ICCO and the CIPR, and is delivering the CIPR Advanced Certificate and Diploma in an effort to demonstrate that a good reputation is essential for the country to attract much-needed foreign investment. However, the larger PR Liga, supported by local Burson Marstellar, Ogilvy & Mather and Edelman affiliates, conforms to the status quo. Advertising law states that any mention of a company is advertising and should be paid for, which has led to black PR where commission is earned on stories placed. This has resulted in thinly disguised commercial propaganda, so that newspapers have lost readership and TV audiences are low (Nunn 2006).

Liu and Reddy (2006) discuss the main characteristics of communications in China and India, two of the world's fastest-growing markets. While in China the media is monitored by the government, India prides itself on being the world's biggest democracy and media criticism is rife. Print, broadcast and online media have widespread coverage in China, but poor infrastructure has restricted the growth of the internet in India. Television remains the main vehicle for media relations. Neither Chinese nor Indian consumers can be 'squeezed into convenient demographic boxes', and require multiple PR initiatives taking account of different languages and dialects. More important are the national behavioural drivers that underpin public relations practice in these, the two most populous economies in the world.

In India, the basis of any effective public relations campaign is public benefit. If an organisation does not serve the needs of the public, the public will not support it. Contrast that with the view of TC Ajit the former head of Public Relations for South and South East Asia for Ogilvy & Mather that public relations has been caught up in what he describes as institutionalised media corruption. If payment to journalists for favourable consideration of press releases or the unquestioning acceptance of investor relations messages and announcements was an ethical dilemma for public relations practitioners the media have made it easy. There is a published tariff for the publication of press releases or announcements in even the most illustrious of India's media.

Payment for publication in China is an accepted practice. China, unlike India, is not a democracy. For most practitioners, communication is based on managerial requirements rather than audience needs.

SHELL INTERNATIONAL – 'LISTENING AND RESPONDING'

The following case study demonstrates a multinational corporation's approach to tackling negative views of its policies.

Shell is a global group of energy and petrochemicals companies that operates in more than 140 countries and territories. The aim of the Shell Group is to meet the energy needs of society, in ways that are economically, socially and environmentally viable, now and in the future. This aim is underpinned by the core values of honesty, integrity and respect for people that sit at the heart of Shell, defining the organisation and how it works. Shell's strategy and priorities for the future are regaining upstream strength and delivering downstream profits; improving performance across all its activities; and a focus on creating what it calls an 'Enterprise First' culture.

A strategic approach

Like most major companies, Shell has had to respond to the changes in stakeholders' expectations of multinationals that have become evident over the last 10 years. Increasingly, the extent of the social and environmental responsibilities of any business is being questioned.

In 1998, Shell began a global stakeholder engagement programme to stimulate two-way engagement around sensitive, topical subjects such as social investment, environmental responsibility and human rights. The shell.com website was used as a crucial tool for education, engagement and dialogue. All communications used the www.shell.com address to drive people to the website where they could join a discussion forum about the issues or email Shell Centre directly – Tell Shell. A team of issues experts handled queries. Numerous stakeholder forums were held,

C@SE STUDY

whereby small groups of Shell's management and special publics got together for a day to share ideas and debate issues. 'Listening and Responding' literature explained Shell's approach in detail and was used to keep in regular contact with key special public audiences. To encourage dialogue and debate, a joint annual writing prize with *The Economist* was launched in 2000. The prize was aimed at opinion-formers, inviting them to submit essays about topical subjects such as 'The world in 2050' or 'How much freedom should we trade for our security?'

However, in recent years, Shell has found itself in an increasingly noisy environment, with other global energy companies looking to stake out a position on issues such as sustainable development, climate change and renewable energy. The campaign required a refresh to generate cut-through with the 'hard-to-reach' special public audience, which research suggested is more effectively influenced by results, direct contact and business partnerships than by advertising, and to demonstrate that Shell is a company that is meeting the world's energy challenge.

Working in partnership with the media

A new phase of the 'Corporate Identity' programme was launched in 2005. Central to the new programme is a series of partnerships with high-profile media partners including *Time*, *Fortune*, *CNN*, *CNBC*, *BBC World*, *Newsweek*, *EuroNews*, *European Voice*, the *Financial Times* and *The Economist*.

The partnerships take a 'through-the-line' approach, enabling Shell to engage stakeholders through what they watch on TV, read in print media and view on the internet. They were developed to engage stakeholders in a dialogue about issues of importance to multinational companies and those working in the energy business, such as security of supply, climate change, globalisation, innovation and trust.

Through the partnerships, Shell has created opportunities in which stakeholders can discuss issues of common interest – both with Shell and with each other. These discussions take place virtually, through online interaction, and physically at face-to-face events.

Facilitating the discussion provides a legitimate springboard for Shell to offer its own perspective on the issues being debated. Shell's senior management, including members of the Executive Committee, Heads of Business and local Country Chairs, have been pivotal in giving status and authority to these partnerships.

C@SE STUDY

C@SE STUDY

Principal Voices is a partnership with *Time*, *Fortune* and *CNN*. Global figureheads – principal voices – address some of the major issues facing the world today via vignettes broadcast on CNN, print pieces published in *Time* and *Fortune* magazines and at events held around the world, where stakeholders are invited to hear them speak and put their questions from the floor. Principal Voices have included Jeffrey Sachs, Amartya Sen and Muhammad Yunus.

Questions for the Future, in partnership with CNBC, enables Shell to discuss major issues of relevance to its business in filmed sessions taking place in key markets around the world. Topics have included extreme energy engineering and security of energy supply.

World Challenge, with *BBC World* and *Newsweek*, is an annual search for individuals or groups who have shown enterprise and innovation at a grass roots level. The call for nominations is made via *BBC World* and advertorials in *Newsweek*, driving traffic to a dedicated website. A panel of judges, including representatives of *BBC World*, *Shell*, *Newsweek* and authoritative external organisations, shortlist 12 projects from all of those nominated, which will then be the subject of a 15-minute *BBC World* TV programme. The overall winner, voted by viewers and readers, receives US$20,000 from Shell, and two runners-up receive US$10,000 each. The winners are announced at a filmed awards presentation in The Hague.

Comment, in partnership with European Voice and EuroNews, provides access to the important Brussels and Strasbourg opinion-forming audience and an opportunity to express views on hot EU news topics via a dedicated Comment microsite.

Working with the *Financial Times*, Shell is holding a series of intimate dinners with stakeholders around the world to discuss energy-related issues. A similar piece of activity is underway with *The Economist.*

It is important that the outcomes of the media partnerships are reported back to the businesses so they are aware of how stakeholders feel about key issues. After each event, Shell representatives complete a questionnaire and feedback form. These questionnaires, along with summaries of the event discussion, are then sent on to relevant parts of the business for them to review and act on any specific comments about Shell's performance.

To help facilitate an even greater dialogue, a new website was created. The www.shell.com/dialogues site brings stakeholders into direct contact with Shell senior managers via webchats and online forums.

Think global, think local

The programme has been tailored to have even greater resonance with local stakeholders in some of the key markets in which Shell operates around the world, including China, India, The Netherlands, Russia, Mexico and the Middle East region.

In each market, the strategic direction remains the same, but local teams partner with local media to arrange stakeholder engagement sessions and events.

Measurement and evaluation

Anecdotal research suggests that the programme has resulted in the creation of more meaningful relationships with stakeholders around the world. However, as in previous years, the CI programme has used independent market research to help evaluate the activity and to provide guidance for future development. The research inputs used to measure the effectiveness of the above-the-line activity and media partnerships included the Shell Reputation Tracker (SRT), an annual assessment of reputation conducted in 14 countries among Shell's special publics, and quantitative research that was conducted among the media owners' readers and viewers in six different countries.

According to the 2006 SRT, the level of recall of at least one element of the CI programme varies by market, but on average across the 14 markets stands at 69 per cent. Recall is the highest in Oman and China, mainly driven by TV and print advertising, which is heavily concentrated in media consumed by special publics in these areas. In most markets, this is higher than in previous years, mainly driven by increased levels of advertising recall.

Research among readers and viewers of the target media in selected markets shows an encouraging response to the partnership activities, with six in ten who saw or read about the partnerships programmes saying they found them interesting.

In 2005 and 2006, half of the viewers and readers said that Shell's involvement in these activities made them more favourable towards the company for the following reasons:

- Shell showing social responsibility
- Shell researching and developing renewable energy
- effective PR and communications
- Shell correcting its negative image.

C@SE STUDY

C@SE STUDY

In addition, there is a positive correlation between exposure to the activity and improved views of Shell in specific areas. This is particularly noticeable in perceptions of Shell's honesty and integrity and its attempts to minimise environmental impact. People who recall the partnership activity have a better view of Shell in these areas than people do in general.

The future

The programme is constantly evolving and Shell uses both direct feedback from stakeholders at the events and information from the Brand Tracker to inform and update activity each year. Feedback from stakeholders is also shared within the business to inform business planning and approaches. This constant evolution is essential to keep the partnerships fresh, to make sure that the special publics find these dialogues interesting and relevant and to make sure that Shell maintains its leadership in this area.

With thanks to Fishburn Hedges and Shell

C@SE STUDY

PAKISTAN'S PINK RIBBON CAMPAIGN

Background

For the past 15 years the Pink Ribbon has become symbol of support for breast cancer awareness worldwide or at least throughout the developed world. It has become an emblem of hope for breast cancer sufferers and for those working to fight this curable disease that still claims the lives of too many women in particular. The Pink Ribbon Campaign was brought to Pakistan in 2004 by the Pakistan Women's Empowerment Group (WEG). It was their response to the chilling fact that Pakistan has the highest rate of breast cancer of any Asian population in the world. It is the commonest cancer observed in females, representing more than one third of female cancers and about one fourth of all malignancies. Approximately 35 per cent of Pakistani women are likely to suffer from breast cancer at some point in their lives. Every fifth woman in Pakistan develops breast cancer after the age of 40. About 77 per cent of invasive breast cancers occur in women over 50 years of age but the average age at diagnosis is 64. Advanced breast cancer accounts for 43.7 per cent of cases, accounting for 40,000 deaths per year in Pakistan.[1]

Cultural, religious and economic factors limit availability of public health education information on breast cancer and access to advice, early discovery and treatment. In a first for Pakistan, and any Islamic country, the Women's Empowerment Group addressed these issues head on, launching and establishing a nationwide Breast Cancer Awareness Campaign. The story of that campaign is an object lesson in the role of public relations and communication management in overcoming cultural barriers to social development.

Planning and objectives

WEG had been established in 1999 by a group of young professionals from marketing, public relations, the law and medicine. With initial seed funding from USAID they had established a reputation for their programmes to take women's healthcare into rural communities, establish basic business education programmes for women and took the bold step to break the age-old taboo of conservatism in respect of breast cancer. They took up the challenge to create awareness of breast cancer and in so doing, ran an enormous risk to the group's own standing and reputation, possibly even of violence against volunteers and staff by venturing into previously forbidden territory.

Working with PIELLEVision the professional public relations firm headed by Omer Aftab, one of those behind the creation of WEG, the Group established Pink Ribbon Pakistan – the National Breast Cancer Awareness Campaign. This was set the goal of becoming a self-funded, self-sustaining, nationwide volunteer-driven organisation charged with making breast cancer a premier public health concern in Pakistan and the task or mission to become the Centre of Excellence for Breast Cancer Care Information.

Public relations and communication management objectives for the Breast Cancer Awareness Campaign were set as:

1   Make breast cancer an acceptable topic in the public domain in Pakistan.
2   Secure 'leadership' support at the highest level.
3   Promote understanding and the practice of self-diagnosis among women.
4   Evoke empathy in the right quarters to support the cause.
5   Motivate people to contribute funds for campaign execution.
6   Build a long-term, sustainable platform for future Pink Ribbon campaigns and similar women's health and well being programmes.

C@SE STUDY

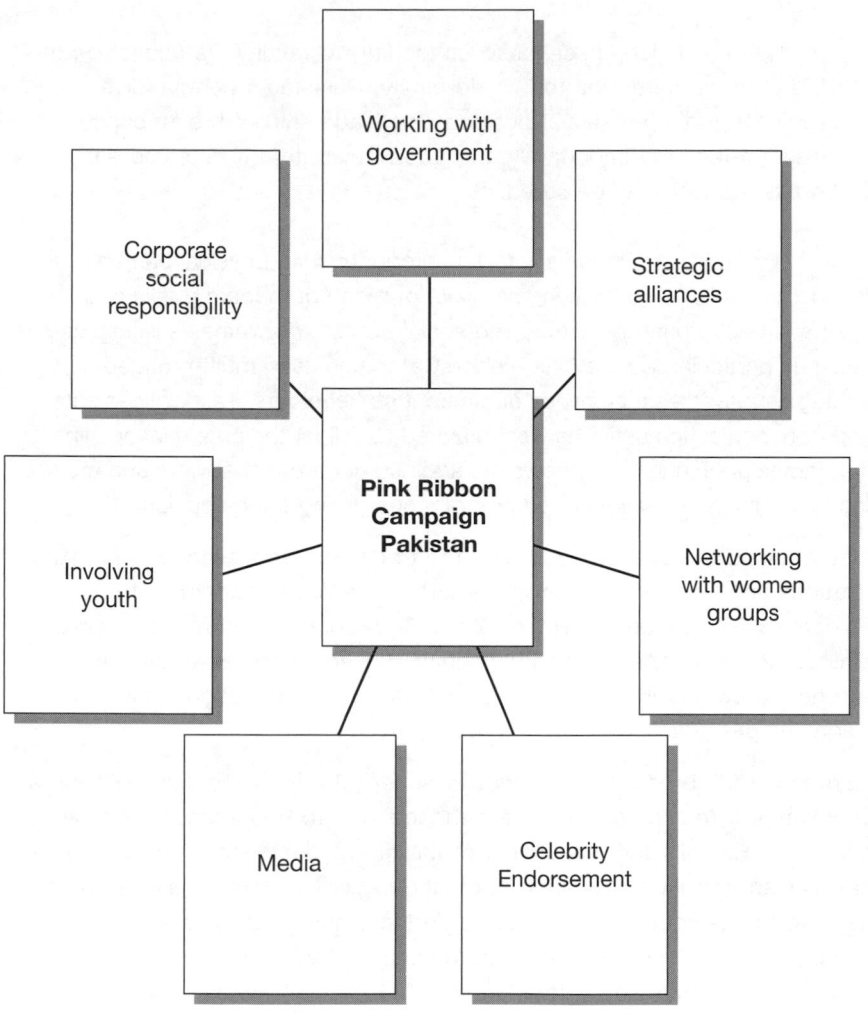

FIGURE 11.1 Stakeholder areas for the Pakistan Pink Ribbon campaign

7   Stimulate campaign and issue awareness in the Pakistani Diaspora and
     the wider world of Islam.

Strategy and tactics

A clear overriding strategy was established and articulated clearly
throughout the organisation and among all those associated with it:

create widespread awareness about breast cancer and all the key
aspects for Pakistan.

Its high incidence, its seriousness leading to fatality, its impact on the life of the sufferer and the whole family, Pakistan's comparative regional and international position and leadership of breast cancer death rates, and importantly, the good news, that if detected early, breast cancer may be cured.

Essential strategies, but no easy task in a country with physical barriers, among a very large population, many out of reach of modern media and against a background of cultural and social barriers on women's issues and health in particular. So the Pink Ribbon Campaign used multi-pronged strategies to address the needs of different stakeholders. Tactically, events and communication activities were planned to reflect the core relationships of the campaign. Figure 11.1 shows the stakeholder areas that were and are the focus for discrete but integrated programmes during the campaign.

Media relations and press publicity, the traditional anchor for any public relations led campaign posed the greatest challenge. According to Pakistan's Press Freedom Report 2001–2002 'under the present code of ethics, the difference between obscenity and education is a blur, for example a programme on breast cancer is not an educational one but a vulgar programme'.

Getting media, broadcast and print to accept the Press Freedom Report's criticism and recommendations for change was to become a secondary challenge. Establishing recognition of the high prevalence of breast cancer in Pakistan and the importance of creating awareness of the issue and the need for mass communication among editors and journalists alike was the campaign's greatest trial. It is some measure of the value of the Pink Ribbon Campaign's strategic approach that it made media realise the gravity of the issue and breast cancer became an integral part of the health programmes they editorialise and broadcast.

National media coverage and interviews with leaders of the campaign gave a boost to the campaign by bringing to the limelight different events organised at the national and provincial levels. Similarly, various newspapers and magazines printed special articles on the situation of breast cancer in Pakistan and the services Pink Ribbon Pakistan is extending to curb this deadly monster. Along with these special transmissions and publications, the media also gave due coverage to various Pink Ribbon activities carried out throughout the country on an ongoing basis.

In 2006 the Press Information Department (PID) aired Public Service adverts for the first time ever on breast cancer, from all State run TV channels. These adverts were aired in support of the campaign and the wife of the Prime Minister of Pakistan delivered the message.

International media from the BBC to *Voice of America, Yahoo News, Daily Mail, The Times, Khaleej Times, Oman Times,* and *Hindustan Times* also gave momentous exposure to the campaign by giving significant coverage to different events, such as the visit of Jagjit Singh as cultural ambassador for the Indian Government through his peace concert for the campaign, and the support from former Miss World Ashwariya Rai.

For the BBC Fiona Bruce made a documentary on the visit of Cherie Blair to Pakistan as Patron of Breast Cancer Awareness UK. This 30-minute documentary showed the warm welcome and celebrations organised in honour of the wife of the UK Prime Minister and depicted the plight of a young girl named Minahil residing in a Punjab village and the impact on the family after the death of her mother from breast cancer. It was aired on all BBC channels throughout the world for over a month.

Print, electronic and broadcast media were not the only communication tools used. WEG Pink Ribbon Publications, viral marketing and merchandising – Pink Ribbon pins, badges, wrist bands, nursery rhyme books and CDs – all played their part. Advertising, strategically and tactically generated publicity were most effective for creating awareness, though the role and effectiveness of different advertising media varied as the campaign moved from one state to another.

Electronic and outdoor media and newspaper articles were the most effective in sustaining awareness and establishing comprehension about the issue among the target audience. Newspaper advertisements, brochures and mounted posters were devised and developed to match religious strictures. Posters and leaflets were produced that went beyond cultural norms for display in the waiting rooms of different clinics. They all gave detailed information increasing knowledge about the issues and were most appropriate for disseminating detailed information and creating better understanding and comprehension. Seminars and conferences were used to effectively complement these efforts.

Celebrity endorsement was extended beyond the national and internationally recognised. It created a new group of celebrities who had actually benefited from having the disease diagnosed and treated in its initial stages, using them as everyday heroes to re-enforce the message 'that life after cancer is not only possible but is worth living'.

Results, reviewing progress

WEG has achieved its goal of a self-funded, self-sustaining, nationwide volunteer-driven organisation. Breast cancer is now a premier public health concern in Pakistan.

C@SE STUDY

Every year since October 2004 WEG has:

- distributed explanatory brochures in easy to understand language to millions of women across the country through various means – utility bills, bank statements, handouts in girls' colleges

- managed a communication campaign through the media including press releases, articles and interviews in the print media and investigative news stories and interviews in the electronic media

- prompted and promoted live discussion programs on FM radio and national television

- staged seminars and workshops in various cities and focused presentations to targeted audiences like college girls or members of women's organisations

- advanced the campaign objectives through quantifiable incremental progress with every one of its stakeholder groups.

It has also established a bi-lingual interactive website that enables women to seek and exchange information, ideas and views with each other and Volunteer Support Groups nationwide.

A subject that was taboo and very sensitive for an Islamic country such as Pakistan is now part of the national agenda for women. There is continuing active public support from the Prime Minister's wife to the commitment of national and international business in Pakistan.

Women, including in the rural communities, have involved themselves in creating awareness, providing public education materials and promoting women's action to reduce the incidence of breast cancer. International Aid Agencies – GTZ (Germany), USAID, UNDP and UNESCO have funded WEG campaigns run with PIELLEVision on women's health and issues.

The Pakistan Pink Ribbon Campaign Group joined with Breast Cancer Care in the UK to reach out to the British Pakistani and British South Asian communities.

In Pink Ribbon month, October 2008, one of Pakistan's leading newspapers – *DAWN* – dedicated one of its weekly magazines to breast cancer awareness.

The work for the campaign for 2011 is well advanced.

With thanks to the Women's Empowerment Group of Pakistan and PIELLEVision London and Lahore

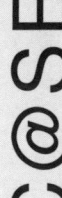

C@SE STUDY

ACKNOWLEDGEMENTS

With thanks to Alison Theaker for the material on cultural theory, public relations and globalisation and frameworks for global practice, which appeared in the third edition of this text.

QUESTIONS FOR DISCUSSION

1 Do social media make the reality of globalisation of public relations practice more likely?

2 To what extent has the acquisition of business and brands in Europe and America by businesses from emerging economies been made easier by public relations? How has public relations supported dialogue with different publics?

3 What instances of different cultural sensitivities to time have you experienced? How were they resolved?

4 Is country of origin more important than place of work? Do you agree with Holden's view that organisational culture is more influential than societal culture?

5 How do you see 'Western public relations practice' adapting to achieve an organisation's objectives in countries with an aural tradition and high penetration of mobile phones but limited access to the net?

6 Think of a successful PR message disseminated in the UK by a global company. How might this be received in China? In India?

7 What research would you need to carry out to implement a successful campaign across the US, the UK and Australia? What similarities and differences would you expect to find?

8 How would you improve the image of the US in Arab countries? Could this be done by communications alone?

9 How would you respond to the norm of paying for editorial coverage in India, China, Russia or the Ukraine?

10 To what extent do you think that the Karen Hughes model for public diplomacy with a country's multinational businesses taking responsibility for promoting the country's image abroad is integral to global public relations?

NOTE

1   *Journal of Pakistan Medical Association* Vol. 53 No. 8.

FURTHER READING

Chen, N. and Cuthbertson, H. (2009) 'Public relations in mainland China: an adult with growing pains', in K. Sriramesh and D. Verčič (2009) *The global public relations handbook: theory, research, and practice*, Routledge.

Jandt, F.E. (2004) *An introduction to intercultural communication* (4th edition), Sage.

Seth, P. (2008) *Chindia rising*, Tata McGraw Hill.

Szondi, G. (2009) 'International context of public relations', in R. Tench and L. Yeomans (eds) *Exploring public relations,* FT Prentice Hall.

Part III

Stakeholder public relations

CHAPTER 12

Media relations in the social media age

Philip Young

CHAPTER AIMS

This chapter aims to investigate one of the most visible manifestations of public relations activity. It looks at some of the cultural conventions of journalism and their implications for organisational communication, setting this against the background of a changing media landscape, including the rise of digital communications and social networking.

THE STATUS OF MEDIA RELATIONS

In the 1961 novel *A Crooked Sixpence* by Fleet Street legend Murray Sayle, two investigative reporters challenge a shady character to describe his work. 'Well, it used to be called publicity,' he says. 'We've only recently reached the status of a profession, if you know what I mean. The proper term is public relations.' The interview over, one sceptical hack asks the other, 'What the hell is public relations, anyway?' While it is fiction, and the book was written 50 years ago, the reply still holds good for many critics: 'It means getting stories into papers without paying for them.'

Most modern public relations practitioners will wince at this formulation, but, as Hitchins (2008: 205 in Theaker 2007) wrote, 'It would not be overstating the case to say that for many organisations public relations *is* media relations.'

That said, an understandable desire by 'the profession' to highlight the broader contribution public relations can make to the management of organisations often leads it to accord media relations a lower status and significance than perhaps it merits. But even a cursory study of the realities of PR practice might suggest such thinking is open to challenge; certainly some would see media relations as sitting on a faultline between theory and practice, between those committed to the 'professional project' (including many academics) and the people who actually do the job. Morris and Goldsworthy (2008: 105) put it strongly:

> The PR industry's reluctance to admit to the centrality of media relations . . . flies in the face of the understanding of PR in wider society. To most outsiders PR is forever, and overwhelmingly, associated with journalism and the media, with press releases and press conferences.

Public relations practitioners seek to influence the mass media, partly because of its reach but also because of its credibility with the target audiences they wish to engage. Even with the rise of the internet, newspapers, magazines, television and radio are still widely seen as the most effective channel for reaching large numbers of people with product information or corporate messages in a short space of time. It is partly to do with technology – *reach* (Phillips and Young, 2009) – and partly because media content managers (journalists and editors) are presented as being of 'independent of view and opinion', thereby offering an 'impartial' validation of organisational messaging. This *third party endorsement* framing is closely aligned with notions of reputation management, wherein reputation can be equated with what the press say about an organisation. For some, media exposure *is* reputation, so if practitioners can influence the media to present a positive image, the job is done. Interestingly for a discipline that places great emphasis on trust and legitimacy, the endorsement is sought from Fourth Estate media institutions, which many studies suggest are rapidly losing public credibility.

The changing status of media relations tells us a lot about PR. Media relations is visible, not least because it directly concerns journalists, and thus becomes the part of the practice that is most often written about and commented upon. Indeed, despite its best efforts, the public image of public relations remains one that is defined by journalists whose relationship with practitioners puts them in a position that does not invite objectivity.

Furthermore, the tangible outputs of media relations arise from (junior) 'technician' functions, which can be seen as devaluing the status of those wishing to join the dominant (boardroom) coalition; certainly, media relations is primarily tactical work rather than the strategic management function that is lauded as the 'holy grail' (L'Etang, 2008: 29) of PR.

CHANGING MEDIA LANDSCAPE

One of the attractions of effective media relations is a claimed ability to target specific audiences, defined by a range of socio-demographic measures. Media planners believe themselves able to deliver publics, by geography, by income, by age, perhaps by gender, and often, with some certainty, by specialist interest; to reach pig breeders, target *Pig Breeders Weekly*. Likewise, to publicise an event, the local or regional newspaper is the way to do it. The narrative of the last 30 years has been one of media fragmentation and, most notably for newspapers, one of decline. With very few exceptions newspaper circulations are shrinking, and the pain is being felt particularly acutely by the regional dailies, which traditionally offered a trusted and credible vehicle for targeted messaging. It is possible to argue that this mirrors a decline in sense of community, perhaps allied with an increase in mobility, but a significant reason must be the dramatically increased competition for time and resources.

The steady erosion of print media circulations predates the explosion in internet usage but technological advances of the last 15 years have undoubtedly presented enormous challenges. Online requires less start-up investment, carries lighter production costs, and has fostered an environment in which many people no longer recognise the need to pay for content. As readerships shrink, fewer eyes see stories, so the return on investment of media relations becomes less attractive. At a deeper level, people are beginning to consume media in different ways. Whereas a casual reader might flick through a newspaper, glancing at every page, and having at least an opportunity to investigate most of the content, the on-screen browser travels a different path. There are only a certain number of content opportunities on a single web page, and it is can be difficult to persuade readers to explore deeply. Hyperlinks encourage skimming, and thereby work against sustained 'investigation' while also presenting endless temptations for the visitor to leapfrog to a rival content provider.

Although declining circulations are a significant threat to the business models of traditional publications they present some short-term advantages for the PR practitioner. Declining revenues lead to shrinking staffs and much greater reliance on news releases and other PR-driven content. For the competent practitioner it has never been easier to get material into a newspaper, but the rewards may be proportionately less valuable. Disgruntled journalist Nick Davies (2008: 75) paints a grim picture of the modern newsroom: 'The churnalists working on the assembly line in the news factory construct national news stories from raw material which arrives along two primary conveyor belts ... the [national news agency] Press Association and public relations.'

It is undeniable that young people consume media in dramatically different ways than their counterparts of only a decade or so earlier. University lecturers are well-used to asking undergraduates where they get their news from, and discovering that perhaps one in 10 reads a newspaper (other than, perhaps, free titles such as *The Metro*, which they picked up on the way to college).

This is a profound shift that requires the media relations practitioner to radically rethink the notion of news. There is a tendency to consider news to be the retelling of important events that are captured by 'newspapers of record' for the immediate public good and for the benefit of future historians. As McNair (1998: 15) points

out: 'In capitalist societies journalism is a commodity which must be sold to sophisticated and demanding consumers in an increasingly competitive marketplace.'

Perhaps it is more useful to characterise news as something the consumer wasn't
previously aware of that might influence their opinions, attitudes and behaviours,
and, ideally to such an extent that they will pass it on to others. Information may
be legitimated by a news portal, but the value of the portal will be determined by
peers, and the value of the 'story' is measured by 'likes' and 'shares'.

Digital media and internet connectivity have led to a changed information dynamic.
Shirky (2010: 37) observes: 'Publishing used to be something we had to ask
permission to do: the people whose permission we had to ask were publishers.
Not any more.'

THE PR PRACTITIONER AS NEWS CREATOR

To practice media relations effectively a practitioner must learn to think like a journalist. This means developing news sense, and adopting the conventions of news
narrative. In the simplest of terms, this involves appreciating that while 'Dog Bites
Man' is of concern to the man (and perhaps those close to him, or to the dog),
'Man Bites Dog' is of wider interest. Moreover, the newshound knows instinctively
that if the dog were to be one of the Queen's corgis and the man were to be
Barack Obama or Simon Cowell, it is a very big story indeed.

It is no coincidence that many of the early recruits to the PR discipline that emerged
after the Second World War were journalists. As Grunig and Hunt (1984) have
famously observed, one of the earliest models of public relations activity was that
of press agentry; a calling that required skills of news manufacture, and Morris and
Goldsworthy (2008) refer to as PR's 'skeleton in the cupboard'. The objective of
the press agent was to create publicity via media exposure, a decidedly one-way
information flow that now ranks low in what might be termed the Whig history of
public relations, which emphasises the discipline's inexorable progression towards
ever greater liberty and enlightenment.

Certainly media relations can be seen as forming a dissonant continuum with journalism. The shared objectives may include identifying attractive pieces of information
and packaging them for a target audience, but journalism has developed a distinctive
set of cultural norms that seek to place distance between its activities and those
of 'publicists'. This constructed divide, not always as glaringly obvious in practice
as newsroom crusaders might wish to believe, provides a fertile breeding ground
for distrust and approbation. The faultlines in this often fractious relationship most
regularly splinter along the tensions between partial truths and 'objective facts'.

Whether or not the channel employed is the news media, there is a further overlap
in that one of the properties of newsworthiness is that it catches attention in a

manner that encourages people to pass on the information. PR has to identify and tell a story, and sometimes this resonates with accepted news values. A shared characteristic is topicality or 'freshness', but the major difference is partiality. Journalism privileges objectivity whereas PR places emphasis on persuasion, often derived from the careful presentation of selected truths. In reality, both sides can show an astonishing lack of self-awareness.

THE TECHNIQUES OF MEDIA RELATIONS

The ability to identify what is newsworthy is vital to the effective practice of media relations. The practitioner needs such understanding both to generate attractive material and also to anticipate journalistic inquiry. They will know how to find a news hook for a news release, and also develop the skills to be an effective internal reporter – what is happening inside an organisation that can be packaged as a news story that not only attracts attention but also carries positive messages that reinforce objectives set out in a communications plan.

It is one of the reasons for the early prominence of former journalists in PR practice. Wearying of long and irregular hours, and attracted by better pay and conditions, it was not unusual for reporters to turn to 'the Dark Side'. L'Etang (2004: 204) quotes Richard West's *PR: The Fifth Estate:* 'Journalists know in their heart of hearts that they too may become PROs when they fail at their profession; they tend to see in PROs the embodiment of their own future failure.'

The framing of 'poacher turned gamekeeper' reveals many of the assumptions that underpinned the complex relationship between the two disciplines. Certainly, experience of news values (how to spot a story, or anticipate likely questions) as well as an appreciation of news culture has benefitted many a career in media relations. To an extent news is defined by editors, and in response to perceived values of the target readership – an economic decision. In an overused 1965 study Galtung and Ruge (1973) identified 12 elements employed in gauging newsworthiness. Some students are tempted to see this study as a checklist when in fact it was an empirical study, no longer contemporary and of countries that might be considered obscure, although media teams should appreciate Harcup and O'Neill's (2001) reworking that highlights 10 values, one or more of which must characterise an event in order for it to be selected as 'news'. Richardson, in Franklin *et al.* (2005: 174), summarises these qualities as reference to the power elite, to celebrity, entertainment, surprise, good news, bad news, magnitude, follow-up stories and the newspaper's ideological agenda.

What all this is boils down to is that news is about people. Pick up any newspaper and the front page picture is most likely to be of a person, rather than a place or an object. Selling a story often involves identifying and amplifying a 'human interest' angle.

This differs between publications. Look at this morning's printed newspapers, and the front pages may feature several entirely different stories, or perhaps the same story from several different angles. The 'objective' press will approach the event being reported from a range of political and socio-demographic perspectives, from the overly serious to the apparently inane. In the last few days, it is inevitable that an event of international historical significance will have occurred but a 'down market' tabloid will have splashed on a perceived fissure in a celebrity relationship. Such distinctions can be seen to delineate what used to be characterised as the difference between tabloid and broadsheet press, but now the outside observer can gain a further perspective by looking on news websites and comparing the stories featured most prominently with those most read and most shared.

In many organisations the media relations function has traditionally been located in a 'press office'. Although the term is used less often today, it reflects a framing in which part of the communications function can control the flow of information between an organisation and the media. This may be in the form of outputs, the identification of information that can be packaged in a way that may be processed and distributed by news organisations, and also influence the seepage of sensitive or prejudicial information from the organisation. It is common for organisations to insist that employees may only speak to journalists with the permission of the press office. This 'gatekeeping' process may involve the press officer assessing the desirability or otherwise of presenting the employee as a public face, identifying topics suitable for dissemination and advising on positive phraseology. Many argue that any pretence that an organisation can in practice command and control messages is fast disappearing as online channels encourage *porosity* (Phillips and Young, 2009).

As well as issuing information through news releases the press office may also stage press conferences, set up interviews, draft statements, and create photo opportunities. Knowing what makes something newsworthy leads naturally to developing an ability to create story opportunities. This may be as simple as organising photography with appropriate props.

Other tried and trusted techniques involve milestone events, including anniversaries of a launch or the achievement of a sales or visitor target; hence 'Attraction X has welcomed its 10,000th visitor,' or that in January 2011 Gail Davis, from Orpington, Kent, who downloaded the 10 billionth app from iTunes (Apple, 2011) becomes a news story. In many presentations, but not the original Apple news release, the narrative is enhanced by quotes from Gail: 'I had no idea, when Apple called me. I thought it was a prank call and I declined to take it' (BBC, 2011a). This was swiftly followed by stories such as 'A Gloucestershire software company has been congratulated by Apple for designing the 10 billionth app to be downloaded from its online store. Neon Play, which is based in Cirencester, developed the free Paper Glider game' (BBC, 2011b).

Story creation can also involve commissioning research, of varying degrees of scientific value, which illustrates the need for a certain product or organisation.

Statistics sell stories, as do lists – the Top Ten this, or Britain's sexiest/ most boring/ dirtiest/cleanest city are staples of many Monday newspapers put together on slow news Sundays.

This same news sense that identifies news hooks provides an invaluable radar for picking up on things that a journalist will want to know about a company. Second guessing what a reporter will ask and providing an informative, accurate answer that serves the organisational interest is a vital skill.

Many organisations invest in media training, preparing senior staff for interviews. This can range from coaching on body language and dress, to including pre-prepared sound bites and mastering techniques for not answering questions. One of the hardest concepts to impart is to stop interviewees saying too much; savvy reporters quickly learn the value of silence, of leaving spaces that the interviewee is tempted to fill, usually by saying more than they intended to say.

THE IMPACT ON PRACTICE

Online has a different rhythm to the conventional news cycle. Media relations used to be orchestrated to the predictable and regular tempo of content production deadlines, and the ability to deliver messages at the optimum time was a sophisticated and effective tactical weapon. Magazines take a lot of planning and a practitioner wanting to 'hit' a Christmas or Valentine's Day issue needs to think well ahead. Weekly newspapers were effectively closed for most new stories a day or more before distribution. Timing was everything. Online changes that. News still has rhythms, but the edges are blurred. Daily papers are still 'put to bed' at set times, and the physical edition appears roughly once every 24 hours but most news organisations are now comfortable with breaking stories online. Operationally, the arrival of real time news has a significant impact on media relations practice. For even quite small organisations, it is important that practitioners can respond around the clock, and that they are on top of the news agenda. The challenge is two-fold: both to ensure procedures and protocols are in place for the media team to acquire and verify accurate information at high speed but also for those involved to build disciplines that give them the confidence *not* to react prematurely to apparently damaging situations.

For some time, public relations practitioners were able to convince themselves they had a degree of control, sending out news releases with embargoes – stamped, addressed and by post – and more recently, by carefully timed fax. Now, of course, email is the channel of choice, offering global reach, instant transmission and negligible distribution costs.

It is increasingly unhelpful to think in terms of newspaper, magazine, radio programmes, or TV broadcasts. Most newspaper websites carry sound and video, radio stations offer listen again and downloadable podcasts, TV programmes have red button interaction, and all can be complemented by often extensive websites.

In today's media relations, the challenge is to provide the information in a whole range of formats, and anticipate need. Some characterise an appropriate delivery mechanism as a 'social media release' (SMR) and there have been various attempts to create effective templates for the new content. One interesting characteristic of some SMR templates is an attempt to eschew the artifice of PR packaging and present the constituent parts as apparently 'raw' information that will be assembled for purpose by the online outlet. This might include links to background information sources, or to content hosted on image or video sharing sites such as Flickr, Vimeo or YouTube.

This evolution was fuelled by Tom Foremski's (2006) incendiary blog post, titled 'Die! Press release! Die! Die! Die!', in which he observed: 'Press releases are nearly useless . . . This madness has to end. It is wasted time and effort by hundreds of thousands of professionals.' His solution was to 'deconstruct the press release into special sections and tag the information so that . . . a publisher . . . can pre-assemble some of the news story and make the information useful.'

Today, the most well-known and most used vehicle for news distribution remains the news release. It is still at the heart of the media relations toolkit and must accommodate journalistic conventions, which can both blur disciplinary boundaries and highlight cultural differences of objectivity, style, even consistency and rigour. As Moloney observes (2006a: 5): 'Writing a press release is an imitation of a journalistic form in order to serve an interest.'

In terms of narrative structure, the news release and the news story are broadly similar. They need a headline that catches the reader's interest, and a first paragraph that gives enough information to tell the story. News stories traditionally answer six questions: What? Where? When? Who? Why? and How? So should a news release. This information is presented in a news inverted pyramid, with the most important information at the top, sketching in less relevant detail as it progresses. They very seldom have a linear narrative.

In theory at least, the news release is directed at a journalist who will rewrite as necessary to meet the house style of their publication, and to an appropriate length, as well as synthesising other content from other, often contradictory sources. It is this selection process that legitimises the PR message, and adds the authenticity of endorsement.

The news release writer is unlikely to stress negative information about a client, but a wise practitioner will nonetheless include less positive information if it is important to wider understanding. This can be tricky in that without careful management most clients will be unwilling to use valuable resources to underline negatives.

Ideally, a news release should spark the interest of a reporter to explore a topic more deeply but in reality, as newsroom staffs contract, they will have less time for independent investigation; it is far from unknown for whole releases to appear as news content, with the only journalistic intervention being the use of cut and paste keys. One way of encouraging such beneficial behaviour is to follow advice given by Edward Bernays, that in the best press release each sentence should have no more than 16 words and one idea (Tye, 1998: 102). Another is for the release writer to mirror closely newspaper practice (*house style*) thereby inviting a minimum of changes. A simple example would be dates; one might speak of May the 25th but the convention shared by UK newspapers is May 25; each time a journalist is invited to 'correct' information to conform with style offers an opportunity for error to creep in.

News stories are brought alive by quotes. For the reporter, this adds authenticity and the human touch. Quotes attributed to those with a client organisation are often crafted by the PR practitioner, though 'signed off' by the person into whose mouth they are to be placed. Broadly, the body of a news release should stick to presenting facts, avoiding excitable adjectives. Opinion can then be presented in a quote by a named individual.

One of the skills the practitioner must develop is to create quotes that sound as if they could have been spoken by a human being. Crafting a memorable 'soundbite' is a valuable skill, but gluing together jargon into jarring corporate speak only serves to highlight the differences in intent between the two texts. In theory at least, journalism stresses simplicity and concise delivery. It disdains 'puffery' and hyperbole, but many outlets thrive on sensationalism, delivered in a 'tabloidese' that is not – and could not – be spoken by a 'real' person.

Those who issue news releases need to consider the journalistic convention of balance, a laudable aim that informs the view that there are 'two sides to every story'. If an organisation makes a claim about its prowess in a particular field it is reasonable, even desirable, for such claims to be tested. The problem for the public relations – and for the wider public understanding of complex issues – arises when this testing gives equal weight to two sides of an argument, even when the weight of conventional belief or scientific opinion leans overwhelmingly in support of one view. This convention works well for those promoting the cause of an underdog but can be exhausting for those of sound standing whose statements are nonetheless coloured by apparently unjustified contrary opinion.

Depending on the organisation for which the media relations practitioner is working, there is comfort or challenge in Davies's assertion that mainstream journalists tend to produce a consensus account of the world that repeatedly reflects the interests of the rich and powerful (2008: 13). He adds: 'Our stories overwhelmingly tend to cluster around the same narrow set of political and moral assumptions about how the world should be run' (ibid.: 15). Later, he puts the process in rather more pragmatic context: 'Balance means never having to say you're sorry' (ibid.: 126).

Practitioners can learn a great deal from thinking through the contradictions inherent in news production that are eloquently highlighted by Andrew Marr (2004: 62):

> Journalists are taught inconsistent things. We are taught to 'play it straight' or 'tell both sides' or 'refrain from comment' – all good enough mottos. But we

are also taught to 'make it human' and 'engage the reader'. And that really means playing it bent – taking a viewpoint and telling one side more vividly than the other; in other words, commenting.

The tensions in 'playing it bent' are but some of the many reasons why media stories can contain inaccuracies and untruths, or an apparently unacceptable bias. Consequently a good part of media relations is about the refutation of wrong stories – from defamation to apologies and corrections. Journalism academic Adrian Monck says: 'If we know it is a rag that is published for the profit of the proprietor and as a distraction for the nation's population of plumbers and shopkeepers, tearing our hair out over every lie and sensation is an unproductive waste of time' (Monck and Hanley 2008: 20).

Those practitioners who have faced an MD or CEO waving a newspaper that seems to have slighted their product or organisation may take a similar view . . . but know also that, with a fair wind, in a few weeks time they will be waving the same newspaper, under the same boss's nose, showing off wonderful coverage that more than justifies their salary.

Finally, it is worth considering two other perspectives on news. There has been a tendency for newspaper magazines and online equivalents to move away from hard news – crime, courts and councils, to softer features and lifestyle based topics. This reflects social change and is also a good example of following the money. Clearly this helps the PR practitioner working in such fields.

It is worth remembering that a vast range of publications work to a different business model. Media relations can involve softer outlets from regional magazines, to business magazines who work hard to reflect the perceived goals of business, and put a premium on upbeat, positive stories. Some would argue that they lack credibility, but that does not diminish their value to PR.

To sum up, it is hard for the aware practitioner to argue with Davies's (2008) *Flat Earth* contention that, 'All local and regional media outlets in Britain – print and broadcast – have been swamped by a tide of churnalism.'

He adds 'This is the heart of modern journalism, the rapid repackaging of largely unchecked second-hand material, much of it designed to service the political or commercial interests of those who provide it' (2008: 59–60).

MEDIA AS RELATIONSHIP MANAGEMENT

Although managing relationships with the media are but one facet of the broader public relations remit, it is undeniable that there are many circumstances in which media coverage can make or break an organisation. The continuing adherence in some quarters to AVE reflects the importance some organisations place on securing coverage that can then be expressed in terms that appeal to accountants. It would be stupid to discount the sales boost that can be achieved by positive media coverage, ideally positive celebrity or opinion former endorsement expressed through a media channel. It would be equally stupid to deny the potentially disastrous impact of negative coverage. Despite some impressive challenges, the fall of the jewellery chain Ratner after its chief executive Gerald Ratner was reported as referring to his company's merchandise as 'crap' retains prominence as a chilling illustration of the fragility of reputation.

There are convincing arguments to be made that suggest reputation does no more than reflect the underlying culture of an organisation, and that skilful PR can only deflect adverse opinion to a limited degree, but this should not diminish the value placed upon establishing a good working relationship with influential journalists who have the power to shape the media image of an organisation.

Apart from personal chemistry, such repartee requires an understanding of the rules of engagement, and of the basic needs of the journalist. Although some can successfully characterise the interaction as a symbiotic relationship, arguing that the journalist needs the PR practitioner as much as they need the journalist, it is as well to remember that some animals never do make safe family pets. Such understanding needs to encompass key terms as 'background' or 'off the record', through to an appreciation of the commercial pressures of newsroom life. Journalists who may never reveal their sources can feel an equally strong obligation to deliver a story regardless of who it might hurt. The arch-publicist Max Clifford may boast of his skills in keeping stories out of the news but it is not a business service he can guarantee. Not many practitioners have the equity to make the 'if you don't run X I will give you Y in return' deals that are open to Clifford, but even he must recognise the limits of such wheeling and dealing.

Few practitioners will have the power to advise, as Alastair Campbell did in a Government Information Service memo to all Heads of Information (Franklin, in Cottle): 'Decide your headlines, sell your story and if you disagree with what is written, argue your case.'

THE ETHICS OF MEDIA RELATIONS

One of the charges that serious journalism levels against PR is that it trivialises, distorts, even blocks access to information that belongs in the public domain. To an extent, public relations must plead guilty as charged.

It is quite natural that a function that positions itself as the interface between an organisation and the media channels that connect that organisation to the wider world will invite such accusations.

In a full-blooded assault on alleged stonewalling by a police press office campaigner, Heather Brooke (2010a) argues 'PR exists for control purposes, to *hinder*, rather than to inform'. Brooke, author of *The Silent State* (2010b), says:

Public officials also often complain about the irresponsibility of the press. Yet here we see a responsible reporter who writes stories based on facts and in the public interest being frozen out of a press conference precisely because of the strength of his journalism, by a police force already accused of misleading the public with false information.

The journalist seeking to develop a story is guided by the commercial imperative to deliver a saleable story, and what broadly boils down to a professional distillation of two maxims with which most people broadly agree: 'There is no smoke without fire' and 'Those with nothing to hide have nothing to fear.' Here social media is doing a great deal to forefront transparency, as the *Wikileaks* episode that unfolded from late 2010 illustrates, but it is worth remembering that the damage was multiplied by involvement of traditional media outlets, such as *The Guardian* in the UK.

Brooke is talking cover up and suppression. Appleyard (2003) took a broader line of attack when he wrote:

> The virus of aggressive PR has compromised the claim that must underpin all the activities of the media – the claim that the story they are telling is true or is an honest attempt at the truth. To my dismay, much of my profession can no longer make that claim.

Appleyard may be arguing for greater journalistic integrity, but the underlying reading is that public relations at best distorts the truth, at worst goes much further, and that it is journalism's duty to challenge this state of affairs. As Moloney observes 'There is a PR-isation of the media happening in the UK (producing) a dependency of journalists on PR, leading to a disablement of their critical faculties' (2006a: 151).

Certainly one of the most visible elements of the news creation industry is the pseudo-event, which is often played out in the arena of celebrity. Just as inviting a well-known person to cut the ribbon at a supermarket opening can generate column inches, newspapers and magazines know that celebrity stories sell newspapers and magazines. This complicity in artifice famously flowered in *The Sun*'s March 1986 splash, '*Freddie Starr Ate My Hamster*' where the fact that the story was almost bereft of truth mattered little to either the newspaper or the fading celebrity and set new standards for complicity between publicity seekers and the Fourth Estate.

Such incidents are as much an embarrassment to those who see effective communications being grounded in trust and legitimacy as they are for journalists who prize accuracy and integrity as the cornerstones of their profession.

Truth is the slipperiest of concepts, and means something different in the minds of almost everyone who seeks to define it. That said, it is perhaps harder than ever to pin down when claimed by Clifford (2005), who has been reported as saying 'Lies are an important part of PR – I have always admitted that.'

However much the profession may distance itself from Clifford, he remains the single person most readily identified with public relations, not only in the eyes of the general public but also for a significant number of journalists. If that wasn't bad enough, the next in line must be that epitome of poacher turned gamekeeper, Alastair Campbell, the former *Daily Mirror* man who became the living incarnation of spin. Clifford offers this criticism of Campbell: '(His) position went to his head, or he didn't understand the fundamentals of PR because instead he upset a lot of people and only fed stories to his friends, which anyone can do and doesn't require any skill' (2005: 160).

THE FUTURE

One of the challenges for practising media relations is to decide what constitutes a 'journalist'. This query informs part of more fundamental questions about what media channels offer. The two advantages of traditional, conventional or mainstream media are reach and credibility. Online potentially allows direct access to stakeholders, and in certain circumstances allows conversation and interaction that truly builds relationships. The challenge is to attract audiences, which can be more difficult. Good social media builds relationships with those stakeholders who know of an organisation's existence and have some understanding of what it offers, but are less good at bringing it to the attention of those who aren't looking.

The challenge now is to identify online portals that provide a marketplace for information. One way is to treat Google as a news or media aggregator, but again this needs prior awareness, for people to have at least begun to look for relevant or related information. An effective route that takes many of its cues from 'traditional' media relations is to identify the influencers or 'mavens', whose online presence forms the hubs of social media conversation. Some of these 'content generators' will act rather like journalists – but it is for PR practitioners to recognise that many may never have learnt the etiquettes and protocols that accrue from exposure to mainstream news culture. The independence and freedom of spirit embodied by many bloggers presents advantages for PR. The cynical might suggest that some are easier to impress, but they can invite fury and retribution.

CONCLUSION

The importance of media relations lies in its ability to leverage a high degree of exposure for organisational messages by complementing the needs of a range of commercial media outlets. Public relations achieves its ends by exploiting the media as channels to audiences, stakeholders and publics, and goes on to gain value and credibility by the endorsement implicit in the refraction of its messages. While not challenging the view that media relations is but part of a much broader discipline, it is also clear that the skills, techniques and protocols inherent in effective media relations will have an important role to play in PR practice for the foreseeable future.

The challenge for media relations practitioners is to identify and engage with the changing topography of interest hubs that focus audience consumption of media content. Put another way, PR will continue to work out what it wants to say, who it wants to say it to, and then find the best way of reaching them. It appears that this may include putting much greater emphasis on direct engagements that have little need for intermediaries, but attracting and retaining interest will still require many of the selection and presentation skills that are developed by journalism.

If this evolution was not challenging enough already, the effective media relations practitioner will have to work simultaneously to educate clients who cling to the reassuring if illusory support of press cuttings and AVEs. There are good grounds for fearing that it may be some time before accountants go beyond seeing PR success as getting the boss's face in the newspaper.

WHICH? MAGAZINE

Organisations such as Which? (formerly the Consumers Association) have a high media profile and receive hundreds of calls from journalists each year seeking information and opinion on consumer issues. But when they wish to pursue new and previously unpublicised policies a more proactive stance is needed.

For 50 years, Which? has been championing the cause of consumers by testing goods and services and publishing the results in *Which?* and a range of other magazines and books covering holidays, gardening, money, computers and other consumer issues. It also challenges business and government and campaigns for a fairer deal on behalf of consumers.

The organisation puts media relations at the heart of its campaigns. Many staff are media-trained to talk on behalf of the organisation and make themselves available to talk to the media if required. The quality of down-the-line interviews is ensured by the presence of an ISDN link at their offices in central London. Embargoed news releases on the most interesting articles in *Which?* magazine are distributed by mail and email several days before the publication of the magazine and more specialist articles are sent to targeted journalists. Key consumer journalists are invited to meet the editor each year and by using a password they are able to access Which? news releases and reports online.

'If we get almost blanket print coverage for an issue of the magazine it is not uncommon,' says Nicola Frame, the Which? press manager.

Between fifteen to twenty broadcast interviews are usually conducted on publication day, but we often release three or more stories from

C@SE STUDY

Strictly embargoed until 10:00 hrs, Thursday 8 February 2007
Martin Chapman 020 7770 7373, martin.chapman@which.co.uk

PRESS RELEASE

Which? kicks off over football shirt rip-off

Consumer champion Which? has warned JJB Sports it intends to sue on behalf of people who have been unlawfully overcharged for football shirts.

The sportswear retailer was one of seven companies fined by the Office of Fair Trading in 2003 for running a cartel that unlawfully fixed the price of England and Manchester United football shirts in 2000 and 2001.

Using its new legal powers under the Enterprise Act 2002, Which? is the only organisation in the UK so far given powers to launch a representative action of this kind.

Although JJB Sports has paid a £6.7m fine to the government, Which? now plans to bring an action for damages to pay back the people who were overcharged.

The not-for-profit organisation is appealing to people who bought certain shirts during 2000 and 2001 - even if they no longer have a receipt - to log onto **which.co.uk/football-shirts** and register their claim.

If Which? succeeds in winning a pay-out to consumers at the Competition Appeals Tribunal, it will be able to deal the payment back out to those who were ripped off.

Malcolm Coles, Online Editor, Which?, says:

"We hope it will soon be payback time for JJB Sports. They ripped off their customers, so we think it's only fair they should have to pay them back.

"A case like this has never been launched before, so we need as much evidence as we can get. If you bought an England or

Manchester United football shirt in 2000 or 2001, register your claim at which.co.uk/football-shirts.

"We can't promise a big payout, but we'll do all we can to get justice for consumers."

JJB Sports has two weeks to respond. After this time, Which? will consider filing the action at the Competition Appeals Tribunal.

which?

FIGURE 12.1A Press release announcing the *Which?* court case against JJB for overpricing replica football shirts
Source: *Which?* Used by permission

For immediate release 9.30am, Tuesday 13 March 2007
Adam Williams 020 770 7563, adam.williams@which.co.uk

Which? issues legal proceedings against JJB Sports

Consumer champion Which? has issued proceedings against JJB Sports to sue the high street retailer for damages on behalf of consumers.

Which? is taking the company to court to claim back money for people who were unlawfully overcharged for football shirts in 2000 and 2001 by a cartel made up of JJB Sports and six other companies.

The companies were fined a total of over £16m in 2003 by the Office of Fair Trading for fixing the price of England and Manchester United football shirts in 2000 and 2001.

Using its new legal powers under the Enterprise Act 2002, Which? is the only organisation in the UK so far given powers to launch a consumer representative action of this kind.

Lawyers acting for Which? have issued proceedings in the Competition Appeal Tribunal (CAT) against JJB Sports. Malcolm Coles, Online Editor, Which?, says:

"JJB Sports and their fellow cartel members tried to ensure the market was all sewn up, so it would have been difficult to find these shirts for sale at a fair price.

"Although JJB has already paid a fine, the money went to the government. We're suing now to try to get money back for the people who paid more than they should have - and whose money only went to line this greedy cartel's pockets.

"This case is as much about justice and fairness as anything else. We want to teach companies that rip off their customers a lesson - Which? has new legal powers and we will come after you."

Which? wants people who bought certain shirts during 2000 and 2001 to come forward and register a claim on **which.co.uk/football-shirts** - even if they no longer have a receipt.

which
?

FIGURE 12.1B Press release announcing the *Which?* court case against JJB for overpricing replica football shirts

Source: *Which?* Used by permission

FIGURE 12.2 Press coverage of *Which?* case
Source: *Daily Star* (9 February 2007). Used by permission of Express Syndication

C@SE STUDY

each issue of *Which?* and they can continue to attract coverage throughout the month. Key messages for media work are agreed with the researchers and editor of the magazine.

In terms of new media, Which? also targets online news sites and uses podcasts to provide information on the latest consumer news and updates on campaigns.

News conference: the case of the rip-off football shirts

Unless you are announcing a major news story and can be sure of a good attendance by journalists, Nicola's advice is not to hold news conferences:

There are many other ways to convey information to the media and journalists are extremely busy, so you need to think carefully about whether a press conference is really necessary or if there's a more appropriate method of distributing the information.

C@SE STUDY

Which? was thus faced with a dilemma when, at the beginning of 2007, it sought publicity for its intention to sue JJB Sports for damages for selling 'rip-off' football shirts to thousands of England and Manchester United fans. This was a big story ideally launched at a news conference, but because of legal proceedings the name of the company involved could not be revealed to the press before the conference began. How could journalists be persuaded to attend?

> We invited consumer, legal and sports journalists. [says Nicola Frame] They pressed very hard to know what the story was about and we said we were launching unprecedented legal proceedings against an unnamed company. Given our reputation in the media for providing good news stories we were able to attract around twenty-five journalists and a BBC film crew to the news conference, by which time we were able to reveal JJB Sports as the company we were intending to launch legal proceedings against on behalf of football fans.

For most people working in public relations, especially those in consultancies, generating the level of coverage obtained each month by Which? in the national media is never going to be possible unless they represent large companies in which the media has ongoing interest. But by being more modest in their ambitions and targeting relevant sections of the specialist, trade and consumer press – and there are close to 10,000 different magazines in the UK, including large-circulation customer magazines published by most large retailers – media relations practitioners can obtain valuable publicity for their products and services.

The National Readership Survey (2005) shows that while only 36 per cent of adults read a national newspaper, 77 per cent read a consumer magazine. And the Periodical Publishers Association says that 87 per cent of 'decision-makers' use business and professional publications regularly for work purposes (May *et al.* 2007).

With thanks to John Hitchins and Which?

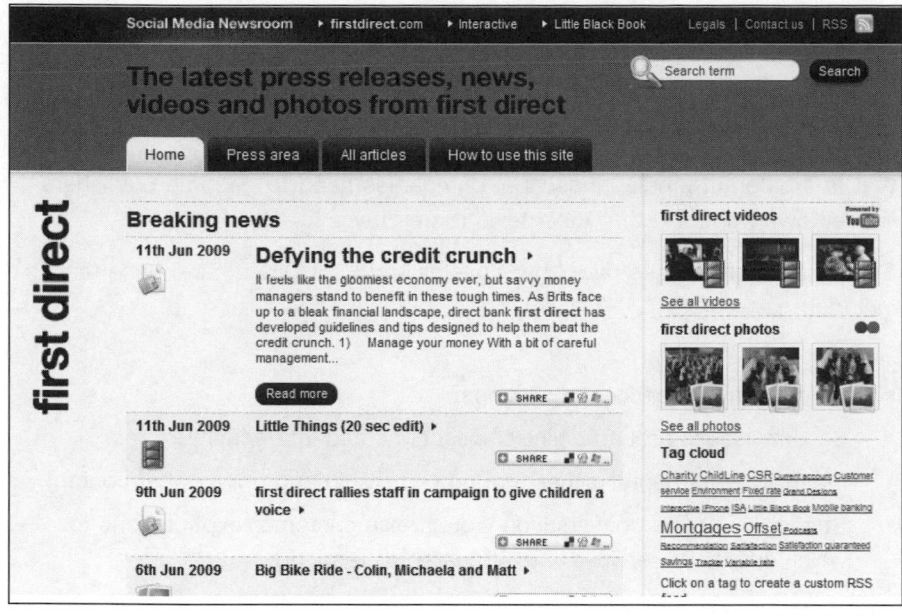

FIGURE 12.3 First Direct's online newsroom

C@SE STUDY

FIRST DIRECT

One of the challenges facing those practising media relations in an increasingly online world is to provide relevant and accessible information in a manner suitable to a range of platforms and channels. Here is a description of how Wolfstar set up a social media newsroom as an integral part a wider communications programme for First Direct bank.

First Direct, a division of HSBC, was the UK's first telephone bank and believes it has continued to lead the way in banking innovation and was keen to engage with social media. It appointed Wolfstar (http://wolfstarconsultancy.com) to provide strategic public relations social media consultancy. The social media newsroom went on to receive over 2,400 hits a week and First Direct made the news as the first bank to use Twitter.

The brief

First Direct wanted to continue promoting its brand image as the first 'black and white bank', being transparent and open towards its customers.

Wolfstar's strategy was to create a news room www.newsroom.firstdirect. com that was designed to be fast, flexible and media rich. The platform allows the bank to reach its customers directly and improves service to journalistic audiences. Its design was based on the fundamental principle that in a different media landscape, companies need to become publishers in their own right and that their news rooms need to reflect this.

Some of the challenges faced by Wolfstar and First Direct's in-house team included:

- Strict financial services regulations.
- Security issues around online transactions and interactivity.
- Internal departmental issues around ownership and approval of content.
- Starting an online conversation would raise customer expectations to which customer services wasn't geared to respond.

Strategy

Wolfstar recommended that First Direct start its social media presence with a social media newsroom to replace its existing static online press room. This approach meant that First Direct was primarily restricting its social media engagement to journalists, who were governed by a different set of regulations to those covering consumers.

Advantages of creating a social media newsroom included:

- Ability to publish 'soft' news – a key strength of First Direct is its excellent working environment for team members, which improves the service to customers when they answer the phone and its excellent CSR policies covering philanthropy, environment, community relations etc. These stories aren't strong enough to make national news stories, but are still of interest to journalists and key stakeholders.
- Ability to publish multimedia content such as YouTube videos and photographs on Flickr providing visitors with a much richer user experience and ability to find and use content on their own online news sites.
- Ability to publish content quickly without the need for involvement of the IT support team.

Wolfstar also helped First Direct to improve the quality of the multimedia content available via the social media newsroom by adding the following features:

C@SE STUDY

- Making the newsroom easily accessible with just one click from the home page (or any page) of the website.
- Providing a broad range of photographs, images and videos.
- Users can filter and search content or find it via tags covering subject areas such as mortgages, CSR etc.
- Using tags, users can also subscribe to custom RSS feeds.
- A 'How to use this site' page explains how to subscribe via RSS, download photos and video, for journalists and bloggers not too familiar with social media.

The third element of the new SMNR was Wolfstar helping First Direct's in-house team become more 'social' in the way it interacts with journalists:

- Using Twitter to initiate and respond to conversations with journalists.
- Creating new and more multimedia content including video and photographs.

Outcomes

- The previous online press room received five visits a week – the new SMNR receives approximately 2,400 visits a week.
- First Direct was first bank in the UK to use Twitter and create a SMNR.
- Banking4tomorrow.com: 'First Direct – they have their social media listening post working very well. *Impressive!*'
- Total blog: 'First Direct are pretty much leading the vanguard action in changing this and can lay claim to the title of the UK's only Social Bank.'

Conclusion

Although some of the advantages accrued to First Direct from being first with new ideas, the basic principles underpinning Wolfstar's approach would now apply to most businesses that try to engage with the media. It is also worth noting the constraints that come with working in a highly regulated industry, and, of course, the possibility of attracting negative criticism. Few sectors were as unpopular with the press and media as banking at the time of this launch.

C@SE STUDY

QUESTIONS FOR DISCUSSION

1 Should PR students study practical journalism?

2 Should PR students still learn to produce a traditional 'news release'?

3 Has the arrival of digital media meant PR needs to rethink the term 'journalist'?

4 Do former journalists make good PR practitioners?

5 Is the growth in 'Churnalism' claimed by Nick Davies good or bad for PR?

6 Why don't young people read newspapers? Does it matter?

7 Who cares if Freddie Starr didn't really eat a hamster? Why should PR be concerned if facts get in the way of a good story?

8 How valuable is third party endorsement when readers don't trust the endorser?

9 Why do the vast majority of all news releases end up in the recycle bin?

10 Should a news release be balanced, fair and accurate?

FURTHER READING

Bland, M., Theaker, A., Wragg, D. (2005) *Effective Media Relations* (3rd edition), Kogan Page.

Davies, N. (2008) *Flat Earth news,* Chatto & Windus.

Gillmor, D. (2010) *Mediactive,* Lulu.com

Harcup, T. (2003) *Journalism: principles and practice*, Sage

Hobsbawm, J. (2010) *Where the truth lies: trust and morality in the business of PR, journalism and communications* (2nd edition), Atlantic Books.

Morris, T. and Goldsworthy, S. (2008) *PR: a persuasive industry?*, Palgrave Macmillan.

Zappala, J.M. and Carden, A.R. (2010) *Public relations writing worktext* (3rd edition), Routledge.

CHAPTER 13

Internal communications

Liam FitzPatrick

CHAPTER AIMS

This chapter looks at how organisations and their employees communicate with each other. Good internal communications matters not just because it effects external reputation, but because it helps organisations perform better, build employee commitment, and is a pre-requisite for change.

A variety of current management thinking will be reviewed, effective media will be explored and considerations that come into play when planning internal communication will be discussed. Finally, the organisation of internal communications and the skills needed by practitioners in this field will be examined.

INTERNAL COMMUNICATIONS IN CONTEXT

Internal communication (IC) is a specialism within the broad discipline of public relations that is gaining increasing interest among practitioners having once been seen as a minor area of importance. Professionals often saw IC as a box only to be ticked as they accumulated experience on the way up their career. Commonly managing messages for workers was a role that was given to a colleague at the end of their career; a secondment for a blameless and loyal but ineffectual manager.

In the last 20 years things have changed. Shifts in industrial relations and attitudes towards workplace relations (Sparrow and Cooper 2003: 32) have led employers to think about how they communicate with their employees. Alongside the reinvention of 'Personnel' as 'Human Resources', questions have been asked about how we should talk to staff, and about the relationship between effective communication and organisational effectiveness.

Recently, senior managers have become more aware of their responsibilities as communicators. In the 1980s, discussion about employee communications was framed in terms of union relationships (Bland 1980: 37). The days are gone when the CEO's only connection with front line staff was limited to the occasional factory visit and the Christmas message. Today, leaders expect to be talking with employees on a continual basis and are willing to pay high salaries for skilled communication specialists (MacLeod and Clarke 2009).

As IC has become more important as a specialism, greater thought has been given to good practice, evaluation and the skills of those who practice it. It has spawned its own network of specialist suppliers, consultants, publishers and recruiters.

DEFINING THE PRACTICE

Any discussion of employee or internal communication can quickly become confused for a number of reasons.

Everyone communicates at work. People talk to their friends and colleagues about work, share opinions towards the boss or the departments on the next floor and about what was on the TV last night (Downs and Allyson 2004). Hargie and Tourish (2005: 5) cite Mintzberg who observed that a manager does not break off from working to communicate – communication is the essence of a manager's work. In the modern world, this is probably true of a great many jobs, regardless of status or hierarchy.

It is therefore always useful to distinguish between 'organisational communication' (Conrad and Poole 1985: 28) – the day-to-day intercourse that takes place in the workplace between colleagues as part of their regular work, and the processes by which an organisation discusses context, news, plans and performance with its people.

Systems thinkers (Conrad and Poole 1985: 30) offer some explanation as to why this is a challenge for IC people. Essentially, organisations are defined by the relationships that they generate. If there were no communication in a workplace one might argue that organisations would cease to exist, let alone operate efficiently (Wim 2006: 132). Practitioners can find themselves drawn into the challenges of helping individuals manage their relationships with colleagues if they are not sufficiently clear about the boundary of their role.

It is also worth remembering that a wide range of terms are used to describe the concepts underpinning internal communication (Welch and Jackson 2007: 177). The term 'engagement' seems to be used to mean interested, committed or merely present, depending on who is using it and includes a wide range of concepts (Alfes *et al.* 2010: 5).

Finally, anyone working in IC will be familiar with the belief that all problems are communication problems. Often it is easier to pretend that a workplace issue is simply a matter of misunderstanding. Managers can happily ascribe dissatisfaction with pay, a poor safety record, resistance to change or a broken IT system to 'communication failure' (Downs and Allyson 2004: 2). Clearly, most workplace challenges have a communication component somewhere but successful IC professionals tend to be adept at spotting what they can fix and what is the proper responsibility of other functions or professions.

IC here is defined as a planned management process designed to create common understanding and commitment towards defined goals (Yeomans 2006: 334).

This assumes that internal communication is a mutual process – not a one-directional broadcast of management information. While it is possible, in other PR specialisms, to attempt to practice communications that Grunig would describe as press agentry or asymmetrical, there is little point in anything but two-way internal communication.

This definition also assumes that there is an objective for communication – it's not about making internal noise for the sake of it.

In North America, employee communication seems to be the preferred term for what we refer to in this chapter as IC.

WHY BOTHER WITH INTERNAL COMMUNICATION?

PR practitioners often concentrate on the role of good IC in helping improve the external reputation of an organisation. Anyone who has watched the news and seen workers interviewed at the factory gates following a difficult announcement will know the importance of getting the right message to staff. There is wealth of writing on the subject of why organisations should bother with IC for reasons that go beyond creating internal ambassadors.

Some caution is needed in quoting exact claims about the likely return on investment to be had from spending on IC – it is very hard in research studies to isolate the factors that drive growth or profitability. However, it is obvious that organisations that communicate well and have staff focused on the same results tend to perform well to some extent or another.

It is also clear that IC is not a universal prescription for automatic success. Organisations have to be properly run, led, resourced and have the right products or services to satisfy their stakeholders. If an organisation has serious weaknesses in these and many other areas, no amount of inspired IC is going to save it.

Broadly, there are five main reasons for good communication internally:

- meeting legal obligations to communicate
- building the community
- helping get the job done
- promoting advocacy
- supporting change.

In most jurisdictions around the world there are specific obligations placed upon employers to communicate with their employees. At the most basic there are normally requirements to educate employees about safety rules, and labour law commonly entitles staff to be informed about things such as their terms of employment, rights of redress during disputes and disciplinary procedures.

European law also guarantees workers' rights to be consulted over issues such as safety, the transfer of jobs, site closures and job losses. In some countries, national law gives employees a very involved role in business planning during difficult times and in others workers are represented as voting members on the supervisory boards of businesses.

Most internal communication is concerned with helping to...

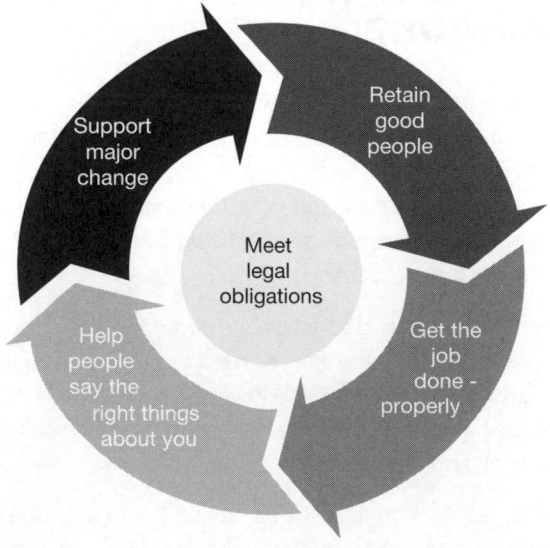

FIGURE 13.1 Reasons for internal communications

In addition, European Union directives have enshrined continuing rights for employees to be informed and consulted about strategy and plans (EU Framework Directive 2002/14/EC).

In practice, it is the legal obligation to consult employees in hard times that is probably the greatest concern to the IC manager. The IC function is always the last stop in the process before a message is published and so the IC manager should know enough about local employment law to be able to spot when an embarrassing or costly mistake is about to be made.

This might, for example in the UK, include knowing the minimum period for consultation before redundancies can be made or workers' rights to privacy. Additional regulations apply in specific sectors or situations such as when a company is listed on a stock exchange; normally significant announcements have to be made to stock markets before anyone else, including employees (see also Chapter 14).

BUILDING THE COMMUNITY

A consistent theme in writing about human resources is the cost of employee turnover (the number of staff joining and leaving an organisation) and the value of employee commitment. Simply put, the costs of finding good team members, training them and avoiding service or production gaps are considerable (MacLeod and Clarke 2009: 16). Organisations normally aim for a level of stability in their workforce and try to avoid unplanned resignations. Holding onto experienced and skilled people comes up time and time again in surveys of what concerns senior managers (PriceWaterhouseCoopers 2010) and HR people.

While high unemployment, good salaries and good working conditions are supposed to go a long way towards discouraging staff from leaving, the most powerful reasons for staying are more emotional – and emotional factors rely heavily on good communications (Russo 2010: 147).

Hertzberg, in the 1960s, suggested that relationships with supervisors or peers are significant motivation factors for employees. Good salaries or added benefits only matter when they do not live up to expectations. People will be encouraged to work harder by their membership of a work group (Robertson in Wright 2009: 150).

The concept of the psychological contract is often used to explain what makes employees stay and work harder. Most people, in return for working hard, expect their employer to deliver unstated obligations such as training, opportunities for promotion or even small perks such as a few extra hours off at the end of a very busy week. Crucially, the relationship relies on mutual trust – if people don't believe that their boss is going to be grateful when they have made an extra effort, they are probably less likely to do anything out of the ordinary (Goudge 2006: 28).

While much of the psychological contract is shaped by personal relationships between an employee and his or her supervisor, communication has a clear role to play in creating a climate of trust and ensuring that people have reasonable expectations of how they will be treated by the organisation.

Gallup (Hartner *et al.* 2002: 271) have developed an employee satisfaction survey that asks just 12 questions to test levels of motivation in any given workplace. Of the 12 indicators, at least five are directly related to communication behaviours:

- knowing what is expected of me at work
- receiving recognition or praise regularly
- having your opinions taken seriously
- understanding the overall mission well enough to see your own job as important
- having regular opportunities to discuss progress.

Work by the Institute of Employment Studies (Robinson *et al.* 2004) has also highlighted the importance that communication plays in creating an engaged or committed workforce. In particular, their research stresses the need for employees to feel that they are listened to at work, and have the chance to speak up on issues that they think are important. These are things that the IC team should facilitate.

This theme was also developed in a UK study entitled *Engaging for Success* (MacLeod and Clarke 2009), which indentified that staff who feel a high level of commitment to their employer work harder and are more productive. In short, communication has a vital role in making employees feel good at the organisations where they work.

IC managers support this role in a number of ways. They provide context around what the organisation is trying to achieve, they ensure that individual and collective achievements are celebrated in news stories in internal publications or through awards ceremonies and they provide opportunities for colleagues to come together socially or during activities such as charity or CSR campaigns.

HELPING TO GET THE JOB DONE

While it is the role of local managers and supervisors to ensure that day-to-day work is done properly, the IC function contributes to driving performance.

Consultants Towers Watson (Yates 2006) claim that companies that have robust internal communications can be shown to be more profitable and enjoy more sustained growth than their less-communicative peers. Similar claims are made by bodies such as the Great Companies Consulting Organisation (Leary-Joyce 2004: 5).

More specifically, Quirke (2003: 5–15) talks about good IC as a mechanism for:

- creating a point of competitive difference
- developing new products and markets
- finding cost savings and improving processes
- offering a way to build support for business strategy
- promoting innovation
- fostering continuous improvement
- promoting knowledge sharing
- prompting networking.

Commonly IC teams find themselves involved in explaining strategy and priorities as well as performance. Often they publish information internally about market conditions, changes to operating procedures or to promote campaigns around quality, safety or customer service. In the last decade, for example, more and more businesses regularly publish annual reports to employees covering everything from profitability, environmental performance or social policy.

Most importantly, an organisation is unlikely to be successful unless everyone understands what it is trying to achieve and is excited about those goals. IC is also often involved in equipping line managers and supervisors to explain the local implications of organisation-wide messages. Studies (Yates 2006) mentioned earlier strongly argue that business success is linked very closely to the ability of local leaders to create a clear connection between day-to-day work and corporate objectives.

ADVOCACY

A very common theme among public relations practitioners is the value of turning employees into 'ambassadors' – people who are active in their community, speaking up for their organisation.

The internet and social media make this role more and more significant. Disaffected employees have more and more places to voice their opinions and committed employees are often quick to challenge negative comments posted online.

The strength of employee advocacy does not just come from the sheer number of staff who are available to act as spokespeople. There is evidence that an employee is considered a more credible source about an organisation than either advertising or the words of official representatives.

A 2003 study by MORI looking at the drivers of corporate reputation found that 'knowing someone who works there' is a very powerful driver of an organisation's reputation. People are likely to place considerably greater weight on the opinions of a direct personal contact than they are on what they read in the press about an organisation or even their own experience (Dawkins 2003: 186).

The IC team's role in this area tends to be about making sure people understand corporate policy and positions on key issues. This can be as simple as publishing internally the substance of media statements through to more involved education programmes on specific issues. For example, drinks companies invest considerable energy in helping staff understand messages about responsible alcohol consumption and many firms with active CSR programmes work hard to give employees a chance to take part themselves within a community activity or a detailed awareness of what the organisation is trying to do.

Naturally, the growth of social media creates a dilemma for an organisation that hopes to control its message tightly. On one hand the influence of many employee voices is considerable, on the other hand there is no guarantee that employees will remain consistently 'on message'. Organisations that have punished employees for voicing legitimate or mild criticism are seen as bullying (Guardian 2005). Some organisations such as IBM actively encourage their employees to participate in online industry debates – within clearly laid-out guidelines (IBM).

SUPPORTING CHANGE

Change is a consistent theme in most organisations and the need for employee support seems to be axiomatic except in the most drastic of situations. Employees are commonly thought to respond to announcements about change with some cynicism (Stanley *et al.* 2005: 429–459) or fear (Wim 2005: 133).

Quirke (2003: 124) points out that change initiatives often fail simply because no one really cares, the bigger picture isn't properly understood, people resent a loss of stability or because no one has actually explained either 'what's in it for me' or the basics of what employees are expected to do differently. All of these are clearly challenges for the communications team.

Practitioners should make the distinction between change and transformation. Managers might change processes or physical aspects of a workplace but unless employees are ready to undergo some form of personal transformation in their thinking or behaviours then it is unlikely that the change is going to work as planned. It is argued that change programmes normally fail because leaders fail to communicate effectively throughout their process (Kotter 1996: 3–17).

Herrero suggests that as social media has developed, traditional attempts to control change by senior leaders are potentially futile. Change is a viral or organic process, driven through personal networks (quoted in Ruck 2010: 31).

Whatever model of change is being discussed, there are clear roles for the IC team. At its most basic, changes to physical processes, products or organisations need announcing in ways that employees can understand. Where shifts in behaviour are needed, the communications team need to ensure that context and direction are consistently understood and that managers are able to guide their teams through it. Finally, it is the role of the IC team to gather intelligence about employee understanding, attitude and preparedness for change to initiate the process.

IT ALL STARTS WITH THE AUDIENCE

As with any branch of communication, planning in IC begins with an understanding of the public or audience with whom the organisation wishes to connect. Without a clear picture of the character, composition, motivation and attitudes of the people being addressed, it is unlikely that any useful understanding will emerge from the conversation.

The challenge for internal communicators is that they serve the corporate interest and work with senior leaders who may see the world very differently from employees who may earn considerably less than the bosses, understand little of the processes and pressures of managing external stakeholders and who have probably seen several CEOs come and go. As with other professional specialisms within communications, the IC manager has to work to provide a bridge between the concerns of leaders and employees to make sure that they understand each other.

In order to do this, the IC manager should understand that few workforces are homogenous – most are made up of a diverse mix of people, professions, mindsets and cultures. For example, if one looked at the people who worked in a hospital it is clear that doctors might have different information needs to those of kitchen staff; office-based administrators will see the world differently from nurses working on an intensive care unit. Attempts to communicate with everyone in exactly the same way can only be partially successful. When dealing with a multinational organisation one needs to take into consideration a number of different issues including language, culture and different legal frameworks.

IC teams will naturally have a clear idea of how many employees they are dealing with, where they are based and what they do. Figure 13.2 contains an example of a page from an audience report detailing the breakdown of a workforce produced by an IC manager. Some managers will plot out additional demographic information such as average age, typical length of service and pay grades as an aide to understanding how best to talk to a section of the workforce.

It is useful to know any significant recent history that might colour employee attitudes. For example, a redundancy programme five years ago may well be remembered and influence reactions to a mildly worded message about cost savings. A merger several decades back can decide how employees respond to

Every good internal communication manager knows their audiences. This is an example of a page from a simple log for a manufacturing company's distribution centre. It may not exactly match what appears on the HR database, but it provides enough to tell the IC manager how to reach some key people.

Locations	
Name of site	Hemel Hempstead
Role of site	Warehousing, distribution and sales
Numbers employed	Warehouse: 50 Drivers: 48 Sales admin: 10 Field Sales: 5
Senior manager contact	Site Logistics Manager – Terry Smarts Regional Sales Director – Helena Saxon
Key contacts	Malcolm Royal – Warehouse chargehand/ social club Emma Carter – Field Sales Manager
Local media	*The Goods* (Logistics Newsletter 2 pa) print (editor Nigel Farr) *Terry Talk* – Terry Smarts' biannual staff meeting *Hemel Update* web page – update Malcolm Royal
Recent history	Logistics division merged 2003 with Cardiff operation CEO Roadshow April 2005
Emergency	– Email List 14 – Frances Wiles will print and post on notice boards/add to driver inventory sheets – Call Michael Devonshire (Site HR) to liaise with union
Contacts	Ext 12345

FIGURE 13.2 The demographics log book

announcements about trivial things such as Christmas bonuses or attempts to change working practices.

Within any given population of people there is likely to be a wide spectrum of attitudes. Quirke (2003: 12) talks about dividing employees according to their understanding of change and willingness to help into:

- unguided missiles (they want to help but are unclear where the change is headed)

- hot shots (they understand the direction of change and are keen to be involved)

- slow burners (they don't understand the need for change but don't want to help anyway)

- refuseniks (they understand the change but simply don't want to be involved).

A communications manager needs to understand if these mindsets are represented in their audience groups and in what proportion.

Another important point when considering specific messages is the fact that not everyone will be impacted in the same way. When talking about a change, some people will just need to know about it, some will need a more detailed understanding while others will often need to be consulted in some detail. This thinking has been developed further by practitioners experimenting with social media and viral messaging. Gladwell (2000: 60) identifies the importance of knowing who in an organisation are 'mavens' – ordinary people known for being the font of all knowledge and 'connectors' – people who have abnormally large personal networks who are the epicentre of the informal grapevine.

Some writers suggest that the tools of social media allow IC people to pick out the most influential people in an organisation and target them directly (Ruck 2010: 33). This approach likens communications to a virus – a message spreads without needing to use orthodox management chains of command. Because people are more trusting of their peers than they are of remote senior leaders, these virally-spread messages are more impactful.

Whatever approach taken to dissecting an audience it is important to remember that the audience itself has a firm view over what it wants to know. Before an employee is ready to listen to corporate messages, they need to have personal questions answered. Arnott suggests that there is a hierarchy of questions that need addressing in the following order (Hargie and Tourish 2004: 9):

- What is my job?
- How am I doing?
- Does anyone care?
- How are we doing?
- How do we fit into the whole?
- How can I help?

The lesson for an internal communicator is that they must have a clear understanding of both the formal structures of their organisation and of the informal networks that exist externally.

Neither is by any means simple to understand, which may explain why IC managers can struggle to collect more than the most basic demographic data. A 2006 report stated that less than 5 per cent of practitioners use attitudes as a formal basis for segmenting their workforces, relying instead on more simple audience breakdowns based on divisional or functional structures (Melcrum 2006a: 21).

RESEARCH APPROACHES

Like all management activities, IC needs data in order to be effective (Walker in Wright 2009: 7). Although there is a high degree of creativity and personal judgement involved in communications, professionals should not depend on guess work about what people are thinking at the beginning of a communication task involved in changing attitudes. Senior leaders also commonly expect their advisers to use data to add weight to their arguments; where the discussion of possible tactics depends on personal opinion, the IC manager can struggle to establish their authority or credibility among other managers who are likely to have their own prejudices about how to talk to staff.

Broadly speaking, internal communicators use four main approaches for tracking employees understanding and attitudes:

- informal networking
- process feedback
- qualitative research
- quantitative research.

These techniques will be core elements in a communication audit, which is a prerequisite for the planning and development of any IC function.

Informal approaches

Informal networking approaches tend to be relatively simple and consist of little more than escaping from the office to have lunch in the canteen or taking any opportunity to meet colleagues and talk about current issues. However, it is worth approaching informal networking in a systematic way.

For example, some communications teams regularly decide on themes or issues that they plan to explore over a defined period. This might be about asking contacts around the organisation what they thought of a recent CEO's podcast or what experiences people are having with a new working procedure. The team might then discuss the informal feedback.

Clearly, such approaches are unscientific and there are obvious risks of reading too much into the feedback, which will often be incomplete, partial or subject to interpretation bias by the communications team – after all, it's easier to hear positive feedback about a beloved newsletter or intranet than acknowledge that no one likes them!

The importance of informal networking is that it can throw up early warning of significant issues and suggest where messages are failing to be understood. It can also provide insights very quickly – in much less time than it takes to launch a survey or a series of focus groups. Essentially, senior managers expect their IC team to be informed about the employee sentiment and to be able to provide answers to the question 'what are the staff saying?'

While IC teams do not have the monopoly of insight when it comes to employee attitudes, other managers will have their own prejudices or agenda when it comes to hearing what staff in their areas of responsibility are discussing.

Process feedback

Process feedback is the commentary and intelligence that finds its way directly to the IC team – perhaps as letters to the staff magazine, comments on intranet stories or contributions to online fora. The level of interest in a particular announcement on the intranet is demonstrated through the number of employees looking at the relevant online page. Equally informative would be the numbers attending 'town hall' meetings (all staff meetings held in a single room) or participating in social events.

Although process feedback is often highly selective and occasionally little more than the concerns of an unrepresentative individual, it can be useful to indicate the strength of feeling that exists around an issue. Some IC teams adopt a systematic approach to collating this sort of intelligence, perhaps at a monthly team meeting.

Qualitative approaches

IC managers find it useful to develop a more formal qualitative approach to gathering intelligence and feedback. The most popular approaches tend to be in the form of focus group mechanism or interviews.

The strength of a qualitative approach is that it allows the IC manager to probe deeper into certain issues. Sometimes people may be reticent about their views on a sensitive issue or the researcher might want to clarify how improvements can be made. A skilful questioner can extract a wealth of information that provides deeper insights than can be taken from the results table of a survey (Noble in Ruck 2010: 83–92).

Interviews can be done face to face or over the telephone and can vary from a loose conversation to a highly structured conversation using a pre-planned topic guide (Dickson in Hargie and Tourish 2004: 96). Some teams routinely conduct a monthly call schedule where each colleague calls a small number of employees and asks them a handful of questions about communications issues. The answers are collated and discussed and feedback for senior leaders prepared.

The interview is a useful tool for understanding communications preferences and forms a valuable part of an audit. Respondents can be asked about the channels that they use and the type of information that they expect from those channels.

Focus groups use the interaction between a number of people to generate rich insights, establish the likely range of opinion about an issue or test likely solutions to a problem. If handled sensitively they are useful at teasing out points of view that perhaps do not emerge naturally because people might be nervous of voicing them.

IC managers continually run the risk of seeing the world through the eyes of senior leaders. Over familiarity with the head office mindset can reduce the IC manager's effectiveness at translating messages into a language understood by regular employees. Spending time discussing issues with teams of colleagues in a programme of focus groups is a powerful way to stay focused on the audience and not the transmitter.

The numbers of people involved in a focus group and the format of the session can vary considerably depending on the issues to be discussed. External facilitation is sometimes used, especially when a particular skill is needed or when there is a chance that people will not speak up because they do not want to offend the editor of the staff magazine who is sitting in the room or the subject matter is very sensitive.

Quantitative approaches

Quantitative approaches provide data through methods such as surveys. Most organisations conduct some form of employee opinion survey on a regular basis. The frequency can vary depending on the size of the organisation, the cost of the exercise and the interest of senior leaders in the results

Typically, an all staff survey will cover a wide range of issues, of which communications is only one. Employees will be asked about subjects as diverse as attitudes to pay, relationships with line managers, the quality of training and general satisfaction levels. Often these surveys are the province of the HR department and IC managers can struggle to extract meaningful insight about communications from the results beyond being told simple percentages. This is partly because of a genuine desire on the part of survey managers to limit access to the base data in order to protect the anonymity of respondents.

Where additional analysis is possible, key driver analysis will help explain issues like the relationship between employee satisfaction and communication or the relative importance of different channels and an employee's belief that they are well informed

(Sinickas 2009). Segmentation analysis provides insights into the issues that drive employee engagement. The usefulness of detailed statistical analysis will depend on the quality and volume of the questions asked. If the survey is very short or answers only come as a 'yes' or 'no' it is hard to extract much useful additional insight.

This does not suggest that short surveys are not useful. Many communicators use short online surveys regularly to track communications understanding or awareness. Modern tools such as Survey Monkey or Zoomerang make the collection of such data easy, although some skill is required in preparing questions and thought is needed about sampling and recruiting respondents.

The main value in gathering even the most basic data is that it tells the communications team whether campaigns are working and it also reinforces the status of the IC manager as the person who really understand the internal publics. Good quality data is also essential for measuring the effectiveness of channels and their changes over time.

AUDITING

From time to time, internal communicators will want to conduct a full audit of their operations. A number of tools exist to help a communicator plan their review. A particularly good example is the HELiX Model (HELiX 2008) that has been developed in the UK specifically for the higher education sector, but which, with some minor adaptation would be a suitable foundation for studies in other areas.

It provides a checklist of areas to explore eight main themes, which are summarised as:

- Organisation Goals, Ambitions and Character
  - Is there a clear set of goals that are reflected in local plans and which staff can explain externally?
- Leadership
  - Are senior leaders committed to communication?
- Strategy, accountability and evaluation
  - Is there a properly resourced and evaluated communications strategy that has clear roles for departmental heads?
- News and message dissemination
  - Are there robust channels?
- Information sharing
  - Are there tools in place so people can access and share the information that they need to do their jobs?

- Space and collegiality
  - Does the organisation have facilities and processes that bring everyone together?
- Crisis, safety and security
  - Are there procedures for handling emergency communications?
- The employee journey
  - Is the staff experience consistent with the messages we want to sent them?

Other audit models might place additional emphasis on issues such as the cost of operations relative to staff numbers or industry norms (where they can be defined), the quality and frequency of employee feedback and the ability of the IC team to reach all employees regardless of location, culture, role or language.

PLANNING – WHERE DO WE WANT TO GO?

Earlier IC was defined. As with any management activity, planning needs to begin with a final destination in mind. Objectives can be grouped into three categories:

- What do we want them to *know*?
- What do we want them to *think* or *feel*?
- What do we want them to *do*?

How these might look in practice is illustrated in Figure 13.3.

Knowledge

Clearly most communication contains some sort of information. Without essential information it is unlikely that a message will work.

Typical knowledge components might be quite simple things, such as:

- knowing where to find the new Health and Safety rules
- knowing that the CEO thinks our costs are too high
- knowing when the Christmas party is happening
- knowing how my job is changing.

Think or feel

There is no guarantee that two employees will interpret information in the same way. The views of the CEO and their senior managers at head office may be the exact opposite of those held by junior staff. Just because the boss thinks that costs are too high it doesn't mean front line staff will agree when they are trying to deliver great customer service. Just because someone knows the date of the Christmas party, it doesn't mean that they think it is worth attending.

Defining the desired interpretation of a piece of information by staff starts the process of thinking who to deliver the message to in the most convincing way. Context, explanation and opportunities to discuss the message can then be provided.

Do

Few organisations communicate with their staff just for the fun of it. Normally the organisation has a specific outcome in mind. They want employees to behave safely, to work harder, to sell particular products, deliver customer service or change the way they work.

Drawing out a specific behaviour is very useful for three main reasons. First, many people rely on a practical example of how they are expected to behave before they can understand the message that they are receiving. People are continually bombarded by massive volumes of information at work and the corporate message will be quickly ignored or forgotten unless the practicalities can be explained.

Second, a clear statement of what people should do as a result of the communication immediately tests whether the information provided or the process to be used will be sufficient. For example, if an organisation wants staff, for the very first time, to start using a very complicated and novel IT system, sending a memo or not bothering to listen to employee concerns may not be sufficient. Outlining the final behaviour required makes it easier to see what communications are going to be needed.

Finally, it challenges managers to acknowledge whether employees will actually be able to do what is asked of them. Not all problems are communication problems and if the organisation has not provided enough resources or not trained staff to do the job, this step of the objective planning process stops everyone fooling themselves that good communications alone will make change happen.

There are times when there is no specific positive action that employees are expected to take. Some communications might be asking people to act safely or know that there is a new procedure for something that might interest them at a future date. This step of the planning process is useful to ensure that the communicator is not adding to the volume of unnecessary communications that fly around most workplaces. If there is no real or substantive reason why an employee should care, then the communicator should ask whether they need to be targeted with the communication at all.

As with all other forms of communication objective-setting it is worth testing each element of the communication objectives to see if they are SMART, i.e.:

- *Specific*. Are we clear exactly what outcome we want? (we want people to be aware of the new IT security policy and see how it impacts them).

- *Measurable*. How will we know when we have got there? (75 per cent of staff to have visited the IT Security website and taken the online learning module).

- *Agreed*. Have the relevant stakeholders signed off? (All divisional managers and regional II directors will have been consulted on the plan)

- *Realistic*. Does it make sense? (75 per cent of all staff is achievable – 100 per cent take-up will never happen).

- *Timed*. When will all this happen by? (by the end of September next year . . .).

HEAD +	HEART +	HAND
What do we want people to KNOW?	**What do we want people to FEEL or THINK?**	**What do we want you to DO?**
• We make more profit when we sell multiple products to existing customers • Trust Gold is a new personal insurance plan aimed at high income customers aged over 50 • Branches introducing the product to suitable customers can earn an extra 3% team bonus in Quarter 1	• Trust Gold is very good value for our customers • It has been developed to meet the specific needs of this group of customers • None of our competitors offer anything like it – it puts us ahead of the game • Branch staff are not being asked to sell this product – they only need to persuade customers to talk to our financial advisors • The incentive for making introductions are attractive and achievable	• Make sure you have read the on-line tutorials on the product, its features and ideal customer • Make sure you understand the introduction process • Discuss in your team the incentives • Talk to customers about insurance

FIGURE 13.3 Example of how objectives can be broken into different components covering knowledge, attitude and behaviour

CHANNELS

For many years the media was the main focus of IC. Organisations often had staff magazines or in-house film units long before they employed people called internal communications managers. IC is a management activity with the aim of driving specific behaviours and managers should begin planning by thinking about the desired outcome. Only when they have defined the end result are they in a position to think about which channels or media to use.

Quirke (2003) makes the important point that different channels have different uses and that the IC manager should begin with the outcome that he or she wants before deciding on the best route for delivering the message. Simply put, if people are to feel involved or consulted in a decision, sending a memo or putting a poster on the wall probably won't have the desired impact. If people only need to be aware of a change in canteen opening hours perhaps a series of all staff briefings might be excessive.

Every communicator needs a repertoire of techniques or channels that allow them to:

- *push* out messages
- enable employees to *pull* information
- *campaign*
- collect *feedback*
- build the *community.*

Push

Frequently communicators will need to broadcast messages and want channels that let them reach every employee in the organisation. Channels that 'push' messages out to employees might include the staff magazine, a memo passed through managers, an email to everyone, a notice posted on a wall or a New Year's present left on every desk.

Such channels are surprisingly difficult to set up and manage. Distribution can be a challenge even for organisations based on a single site or it can be hard to create consolidated mailing lists from HR or IT colleagues in complex organisations. Letters to home addresses can be a problem in some cultures while they are quite acceptable in others. Some channels are controlled by other people, e.g. HR may decide when messages in pay packets are used or the facilities team may have installed locked notice boards that they guard jealously. IC managers will need to use a number of different channels when they want to reach all staff quickly.

Of course no one should be under any illusion that communication has been achieved because some form of broadcasting or distribution has taken place. All staff emails get deleted, videos on the intranet get switched off after 30 seconds, managers may not pass on emails or notice boards get ignored. Crucially, people may disregard a message if it does not seem relevant at the moment it is received.

Pull

Often information is not received at the moment it is needed. Employees don't need to be aware of the details of a new policy on annual leave at the moment they are unveiled – they will probably only be interested when they come to plan their summer holidays.

Organisations need repositories where staff can access messages at the point when they are ready to absorb them, when they are most useful or when they want to understand an issue in more depth. Intranets should be ideal examples of 'pull' channels. Before their arrival in the 1990s organisations tended to rely on either librarians, staff handbooks or more informal processes.

In reality, most organisations still benefit from individuals who tend to be super-informed – 'mavens' (Gladwell 2000: 62) – who seem to accumulate information and expertise much more than their peers. People will often rely on them as easy points of reference. Work on viral communications confirms that, along with people who have bigger than average personal networks, they are a common and potent feature inside organisations. The potential importance of harnessing these informal super-communicators explains the considerable interest in using social media inside workplaces.

Analysis of intranets (McGovern 2011) suggests that managing 'pull' channels can be problematic – not least in ensuring that information is easily accessible and up to date. Furthermore, IC teams often put a great deal of effort into generating 'push' news pages for their intranets but employees might use it exclusively as a 'pull' channel, to look up telephone numbers, the canteen menu and job vacancies.

Uses and Gratification theory is particularly useful when considering pull channels (Dainton and Zelley 2005: 212). People choose to look at different media depending on their own immediate motivations, whether entertainment, information, to confirm personal identity or to develop personal relationships and have social interaction. This would suggest that the most attractive intranets would offer employees entertainment, perhaps through interesting stories or features on co-workers. People are unlikely to make a point of viewing the news and features if the system is used just as an electronic notice board.

Employees will want ready access to reliable information about a range of subjects. Frequently staff complain about the search features on their systems at work, suggesting that the seeking of information is the main use that they have for the system.

Some organisations have special areas on their intranet catering for particular interests. For example, engineers may want to be able to discuss technical problems with colleagues or sales people might want to contribute materials that have helped them win contracts. Commonly social clubs will have places where they can announce events and a short review of the conversations taking place in many internal chat rooms will normally uncover a number of individuals who use it to express their personality.

Feedback and reaction

Feedback and dialogue are essential elements of any IC repertoire. When communicating, organisations need to know if the message has landed, give space for employees to check that they have understood and, crucially, express their opinion about it. As mentioned earlier, studies of employee engagement have stressed that workplaces that make staff feel that they are contributing are more likely to enjoy higher levels of personal commitment and better performance than their peers. Feedback is an essential tool when trying to give staff a sense of involvement and commitment.

Broadly speaking, face-to-face channels are particularly useful for managing reaction and gathering feedback. People like to test their understanding with real people. Local managers and supervisors are well placed to translate the thoughts of head office into practical terms and handle questions. Team members often feel safer expressing views to someone who knows them, reinforcing the role of the line manager.

It is often helpful to expose senior leaders to the views of regular staff. Common techniques include CEO breakfasts, small scale meetings or 'back to the floor' exercises when a leader spends a day or longer working alongside front-line colleagues to get an understanding of the current issues that concern them.

Online discussion boards and emails to the CEO are also used, although they require careful management. Not every senior leader welcomes feedback and often questions the need to respond to reasonable questions. Sometimes questions from employees can sound aggressive, irrelevant, picky or negative, but once they have been invited, they deserve an answer; in fact suppressing or ignoring them may send unhelpful messages about the honesty of leaders. When setting up fora, careful thought is therefore needed about the willingness of leaders to genuinely address staff concerns.

Community

As mentioned earlier, giving people a sense of membership and community in their organisation is an important objective for IC. People who feel connected to other people at work are more likely to be committed and perform better. Therefore, providing opportunities to meet other colleagues – either in person or online – and to feel that their work is useful, are important. Thus many IC teams are heavily involved in running employee recognition schemes, promoting CSR and volunteering programmes or mounting 'meet the customer' campaigns. The IC team needs the capability to manage events and facilitate interaction in the workplace.

Campaigning

The problem facing all communicators is that people can become habituated to messages, especially when they come through the same media. In order to influence behaviours, communicators need to offer channels that hold their attention, create a sense of urgency, allow them to seek clarification and to celebrate success. In short, a communicator needs to be able to innovate continually and to develop methods that complement the basic push, pull, feedback and community-building channels.

The communication media you choose will depend on what you want to achieve from your communication and the audience you need to reach. The right channels for raising awareness would probably be the wrong ones for gaining ownership and commitment. Similarly, the needs of a manager working in head office will be very different from an engineer working in the field. Assuming you're already thinking about both these things, Figure 13.4 reviews some of the main channels used by internal communicators (with thanks to Sue Dewhurst).

THE ROLE OF LINE MANAGERS

Time and again writers talk about the importance of line managers as a channel of internal communication. In the 1980s Larkin and Larkin (1994: 1) identified the pivotal position that immediate supervisors play in creating meeting and making sure that employees understand how corporate messages affect them.

The IC manager needs to be very clear about the purposes for using supervisors as a channel. Some organisations have created processes that involve a message 'cascading' through successive levels of management with each level adding or tailoring the message as they see fit. The challenge comes in preventing dilution or distortion while ensuring that local managers can interpret the message in ways that are relevant to their teams.

The Larkins reject the mindset of the military style briefing where managers are used as animated notice-boards to read out scripted messages that no one believes. Processes that rely on managers reciting a notice tend to have little credibility and quite possibly break down from head office.

Sinickas (2009) stresses that line managers are not always the most preferred channel for employees – staff want to hear from the expert on an issue. If it's not their manager, they want to be briefed by the leader who understands the issue at stake.

Where line managers are most effective is when an organisations needs:

- a high level of personal understanding that relies on discussion
- to tailor the message to specific teams
- to make sure context is appreciated
- to hear feedback
- to build emotional commitment which comes through debate.

Line management communication is less useful for:

- transmitting simple information
- explaining issues of which the manager has limited understanding
- when the organisation can not be candid
- debating practices over which the team has little control.

Practitioners will readily talk about the challenges of creating a consistent quality of line manager briefing. Clampitt (2005: 265) explains that not all managers are offers the following categories:

- *spray and pray* – oversupply information and hope some of it makes sense.
- *tell and sell* – assume that staff are a passive audience ready and willing to receive the leader's wisdom.
- *underscore and explore* – limit the message and give staff a chance to explore the meaning.
- *identify and reply* – anticipate what staff will be concerned about and focus on them.
- *withhold and uphold* – treat information as power and assume that staff are too daft to see what is really going on.

Getting a robust line manager system seems to rely on getting five elements in balance as illustrated in Figure 13.5.

It is not always clear to supervisors that they are expected to communicate. Sometimes managers are uncertain whether they are meant to pass on specific information. IC managers address these issues by working with HR to ensure that communication appears as a core competency and that when communications are sent to supervisors there is no ambiguity about what is to be shared.

If a line manager doesn't know anything more than the information that has been already announced, they are unlikely to want to discuss the subject with their teams. As they have an important role in explaining context and background and finding ways to make it meaningful locally it is worth investing time to give them additional

The communication media you choose will depend on what you want to achieve from your communication and the audience you need to reach. The right channels for raising awareness would probably be the wrong ones for gaining ownership and commitment. Similarly, the needs of a manager working in head office will be very different from an engineer working in the field. Assuming you're already thinking about both these things, here's a simple summary of the key channels to choose from (with thanks to Sue Dewhurst).

Channel	At its best	Potential downsides	Think about
Team meetings	• Draws out local implications • Opportunity for discussion, feedback, questioning and ideas – making sure that people understand • Good line managers can facilitate lively and interactive sessions • Can help build understanding and involvement	• Success depends on skill of leader • It takes time to do right • Beware of content overload. Other channels are more effective for information delivery • Managers don't automatically understand – build-in time to brief them	• Making sure managers know what is expected of them • Training line managers • How are you going to capture their feedback?
E-mail	• Can reach mass audiences fast • Cost effective and simple to use • Consistent and controlled message • Reaches the recipient directly • Good for information/awareness/ instruction – or just proving you've sent it	• Not everyone may have access • Impersonal and open to misinterpretation • Can result quickly in information overload – sending it does not mean it's been received, read or understood • Doesn't prioritise messages • Can't generate dialogue/discussion	• Controlling access to mass distribution lists • Using the subject box to get across your key message • Keeping it short and simple • Using headings and bullet points for key messages and to break up the text
Intranet	• Fast and consistent • Possibilities are endless – can be entertaining and visually snappy • Good for information store, reference and awareness raising • Information shares and bulletin boards good for involvement and discussion • Webstats show who is reading	• Not everyone may have access • Relies on people seeking out information • People may not have time to read it • Difficult to maintain consistent quality of contents • Needs proper management if it is not to become unwieldy, hard to navigate and full of outdated information	• Including 'killer content' to draw people in (expenses forms, classified ads, processes people need to do their jobs) • Finding ways to involve people across the organisation in developing content

Channel	At its best	Potential downsides	Think about
Video	• Creative and entertaining – brings dry facts to life • Can show real people talking about real stories • Makes people and places accessible for a mass audience • Consistent, controlled message	• Not interactive on its own • Can be seen as glossy corporate propaganda • Talking heads alone are rarely engaging – especially if viewed in a web browser • Can be difficult for mobile workforce	• Using as part of a briefing session to stimulate debate • Using 'real people' to talk about their experiences, not just senior executives
Print magazine	• Reach the entire organisation with a consistent message • Even time-pressured staff can read in coffee breaks/on trains etc. • Can address/ reflect staff feedback and respond • Can show how everything fits together and reinforce company brand	• Can be seen as biased and not credible • Information dates quickly • Challenging to make it relevant to all audiences • No automatic opportunity for discussion/checking understanding	• What will hook people to open it? E.g. a competition • Using a staff editorial board to test content and make sure articles address the real issues • Co-ordinate with other channels – e.g. follow up articles with a team discussion
Audio tapes/ podcasts	• Good for remote workforces • Easy to distribute • Effective for information and instruction	• Relies on people choosing to play it • Still has to be interesting	• Producing content that compares with regular broadcast radio in terms of interest and colour
Notice boards	• Visible and may catch people's eye when too time pressured to read anything else • Good for instructions and information	• May not be read/people become quickly habituated • Lose their impact if over-used by every project in the company	• Putting a 'display until' date on posters • Posting in surprising places such as in the lift, or in cloakrooms

FIGURE 13.4 What media?

Channel	At its best	Potential downsides	Think about
Text messaging	• Good for reaching remote workers • Good for crisis communication • Can be used to direct people to further sources of information • Can update senior managers on important news whilst on leave	• Will annoy people very quickly if overused • Is seen as impersonal so should not be avoided for sensitive or emotive issues	• Making sure you have mobile contact details for all your senior team in case of crisis
Events/road shows	• Opportunity for key people to reach mass audiences face to face • Flexible and responsive • Can include Q&A sessions, break-out groups and involve people • Can build team spirit and motivate • Can be used to address controversial issues by the best communicators	• Can be one-way 'tell' sessions • Weaning leaders off endless PowerPoint shows can be hard • Agenda set by HQ may not be what the audience wants • May seem expensive • Takes time to prepare and do properly	• Involving staff in setting the agenda and format • Involving staff in event itself, as hosts or facilitators • Finding entertaining ways to deliver the message – games, activities, video
Open forum	• Gives opportunity to raise and discuss the real issues • Genuine open dialogue • Helps leaders to understand how things really are	• Dismissive or aggressive response to questions can close down dialogue • Line managers can feel disempowered if their decisions are over-ruled or contradicted	• Issuing a summary of discussion for everyone to see • Asking for questions in advance to prompt the real debate
Site visits by senior leaders	• Shows leaders are listening and want to see what the real issues are • Keeps leaders in touch with the real issues • Promotes dialogue and understanding	• Leaders won't experience the real issues if treated as 'royal visits' • May do more harm than good if leaders show by what they say that they are out of touch – preparation is vital • Time-consuming for senior leaders to visit multiple sites	• Use small groups or work shadowing so that the manager and the staff get a real feel for each other • Giving leaders a good brief on site issues before they visit • Tracking issues raised and reporting back on actions

Channel	At its best	Potential downsides	Think about
Voice mail	• Helpful for remote workers • Opportunity to hear about issues from senior leaders	• People will hang up if the message is too long	• Using a text message to alert remote workers to an urgent voice mail announcement
Web-casting and similar	• Opportunity for senior leaders to reach mass audiences with consistent message in real time • Can involve Q&A sessions	• Distraction is easy – content has to be compelling • May be difficult for all staff to be available at the same time (e.g. call centres)	• Involving several different speakers and interspersing with recorded content • Watching a small screen is tiring – keep it interesting
Teleconferencing	• Live and two way, good for debate and discussion • Connects people across distances in a cost-effective way • Some companies will provide managed conference call facilities, particularly helpful for large groups	• Managed calls can be costly • People can be reluctant to ask questions • Some managers are tempted to skip preparation	• Inviting questions in advance and using a MC to make things flow
The rumour mill	• Great for understanding what are the hot topics and concerns	• Not the way you really want people to be getting their information • Limited control and very easily distorted	• Making sure you have a few informal routes of tapping into what rumours are circulating
Gimmicks and incentives incentives	• Captures people's attention • May entice them to become involved or look at key information • Can add a light-hearted and humorous dimension	• May be seen as an unnecessary waste of money – environment needs to be right • Doesn't guarantee even awareness	• Doing something different – don't just buy something from an catalogue

FIGURE 13.4 What media?—*continued*

Five questions
great line manager communication boils down to a few basics

do they know it's their job?	who's talking to them?	are they trained?	have they got the right tools?	is anyone listening?
have they been told to do it? – in general – on specific topics • competencies • senior pronouncements • specific briefing packs.... 'We need you to discuss this...'	**they can't add value if it is dumped on them without briefing** • annual/biannual briefings on context and strategy • monthly update calls/webex with senior leaders .... • ... with real opportunities to ask questions and check own understanding	**does it make sense?** • reflection with peers 'people like me' • is it about skills or adopting a process? • position as part of a wider project – e.g. HSSE, ethics etc. • little and often • on-line follow-up?	**do they get materials that actually work with their teams?** • not just a re-cut of the board PowerPoint • based on what they need • doesn't have to be PowerPoint – learning maps and games work well • how are other managers using it? • what have they asked for?	**who cares if they don't do it or gather feedback?** • are they measured in staff survey? • is their feedback publicly noted? • does anything happen as a result of their feedback? • do they get a straight answer themselves?

FIGURE 13.5 Five questions

Source: Bell Pottinger, reproduced with permission

briefing. A senior leader who spends time with line managers are always appreciated and are a powerful model of the communicative behaviour that supervisors need to display themselves.

As Clampitt (2005: 6) points out, communication skills don't come naturally to everyone and so it is worth considering some form of training. This can either be part of general management training or focused on a specific issue such as managing cost savings, introducing an environment policy or improving customer service. Some organisations supply managers with simple manuals that explain how to manage team meetings or to think through their personal communications.

Managers are often grateful if they are supplied with materials that they can use in meetings with their teams. These are unlikely to be copies of the presentations used for City analysts and may not necessarily be PowerPoint slides at all. Large drawings called rich pictures or transformation maps equip managers to discuss complex issues with their teams (Scarlett in Wright 2009: 349).

Finally, supervisors need to feel that someone is interested in the feedback that they are collecting. If, month after month their comments and reports are met with silence, line managers will soon stop bothering sending it and may well give up holding meetings to gather it in the first place.

EVALUATION

Measuring the effectiveness of IC is an enduring conversation among practitioners and comes up frequently as a topic on discussion boards and at conferences. Quirke (2003: 249) talks about the value of evaluation to assure the efficiency of processes, measure changing attitudes, gather feedback and to understand the impact that communications are making.

Communicators often rely on a similar structure to that developed by Kirkpatrick (1998: 21) to understand the effectiveness of training programmes. This model says that there are four levels on which a training programme can be judged:

- Reaction (did participants rate the experience well?)
- Learning (did participants change their attitudes?)
- Behaviours (did participants do things differently?)
- Results (did the organisation get the intended benefit from the training programme?)

In IC terms evaluations tends to look at:

- *User perceptions*. Do you feel well communicated with? Do you like the intranet? Are you reading the newsletter?

IC managers may want to judge the effectiveness of a specific channel or the impact of individual events. They will review data such as user statistics for an intranet, comment sheets from an all staff meeting or the results of a staff survey. This data can be the simplest to capture, but it will always need considerable interpretation. Furthermore, it may have little significance for a senior manager without years of experience working in communications. How would a non-specialist interpret the news that 10 per cent of employees read a particular story on the intranet?

• *Learning*. What did the audience take away from the communications?

The main way of assessing effectiveness here is through either a staff survey or less formal means. Surveys can ask people how well they understand certain messages or whether they agree with particular statements as a way of gauging understanding.

Less formal approaches may include listening to candid remarks from colleagues, reviewing the quality of comments posted on intranet fora or asking line managers what feedback they are receiving.

• *Behaviours*. Are people doing things differently? Have they stopped doing things?

One of the main aims of IC is to change specific behaviours in the workplace. So evaluation might focus for a safety campaign on a reduction in the number of incidents or a marketing campaign might be linked to sales figures. The strength of this approach is that it moves the conversation about IC away from a discussion of channels or writing style and focuses it on what managers are seeking to achieve.

The difficulty of evaluating communications according to specific behaviours is that IC is often not the only reason why people adopt certain behaviours. A campaign around safety at work might reach everyone in a way that resonates with them and motivates them to act more safely, but pressure from local managers or customers, poor tools or a badly-lit workplace might still encourage unsafe practices. Not every problem has a communications solution.

• *Results*. Is our business performing better as a result of good IC?

Linking IC to the overall performance of a business is a consistent theme on discussion fora (Sinickas 2009) where the potential link between bigger budgets and business results is explored.

Achieving a robust model of the links between IC and business performance was one of the outcomes of work done by US retailer Seers (Rucci *et al.* 1998) that highlighted, through a statistical analysis of customer profitability and employee attitudes to service, a causal link between the two. Some quite complex models

(Yates 2006: 71) have been developed to explain the connection between good IC and business outcomes. The challenge of evaluation communications in this way is the volume of data required and the assumption that the organisation has clear objectives in the first place.

SKILLS AND ORGANISATION

What then are the skills of an IC manager? For some time there has been considerable debate about whether the IC manager should be a public relations or a human resources professional – indeed IC teams are regularly based in a range of functions including IT, marketing and operations. This is because IC is the concern of a wide range of functions in the organisation and because IC managers need a range of skills that are associated with a broad range of professions.

An understanding of segmentation might be most commonly found in marketers, the ability to facilitate group discussions might be developed in a HR team while skills around messaging may be the natural province of public relations professionals.

WHAT DO IC MANAGERS DO?

Helsby and Croton (2009: 1) observed that recent years have seen expectations raised of IC professionals. They comment that the days are gone when an IC manager was mainly seen as a magazine editor and suggest that such managers are generally accountable for some standard activities, which they listed as:

- developing and communicating the corporate story internally – making sure that communications about brands, plans, operations etc make sense in a coherent single narrative
- innovating and making use of a range of communications channels, which are increasingly online and make greater use of social media
- running CEO and other leadership communication programmes – including coaching senior figures on personal style and content together with event management
- working to improve management communication throughout the organisation
- ensuring that campaigns and communications programmes are focused on real business outcomes
- communicating news and business updates
- supporting formal 'employee engagement' or 'employer brand' initiatives
- planning and executing crisis communications strategies
- conducting basic measurement of the impact of communication on employee satisfaction and similar metrics.

While Helsby and Croton highlight the interest taken in good IC by CEOs and other senior managers they also stress the importance of good tactical delivery as well as a strategic mindset (Kernaghan in Tench and Yeomans 2001: 338).

This echoes Quirke's observation (2003: 205) that IC professionals fulfil a number of roles in an organisation:

- *distributors* – circulating messages without an input into the content – perhaps posting notices on an intranet
- *craftsmen* – preparing copy or media without particular regard to the underlying message or the strategic relevance of the work
- *technical advisers* – helping managers decide what routes to use to deliver messages that have already been decided
- *planners* – working with managers to shape messages and think through tactics and timings
- *facilitators/consultants* – helping a leader understand why and what they need to communicate and how it will influence business success.

As IC practitioners (Melcrum 2006b: 18) frequently work in small teams, even a senior communicator will need to be skilled as both adviser and implementer. In larger teams there has increasingly been a division of labour between craft or delivery specialists and business partners who work as advisers to senior managers (Pilkington in Ruck 2010: 143). These business partners will operate to help leaders understand their communication needs and then develop specific requirements for the craft or delivery specialists who might concentrate on, for example, generating copy for newsletters, organising conferences or developing web applications.

WHAT SKILLS DO THEY NEED?

In a 2006 study, 860 practitioners were asked about the skills that they needed in their jobs (Dewhurst and FitzPatrick 2007b). This drew on Quirke (2003: 205) in that communications roles tend to be defined by two issues: how strategic it is and how focused are IC managers on providing advice rather than delivering specific tools and channels. Senior people need to understand the connection between communications and the overall success of their organisation, as well having well-developed consulting skills. More junior people are defined by their skills at delivering specific channels to a high standard.

Dewhurst and FitzPatrick suggested 12 core competencies for internal communicators around the world. A competency is a mix of knowledge, skill and experience needed to do a job. These are set out in Figure 13.6.

One of the competencies – Specialist – reflects the reality that often IC teams play host to an eclectic range of professionals, many of whom might sit happily in other

Competency	Definition
Building effective relationships	Developing and maintaining relationships that inspire trust and respect. Building a network and being able to influence others to make things happen.
Business focus	Having a clear understanding of the business issues and using communication to help solve organisational problems and achieve organisational objectives.
Consulting and coaching	Recommending appropriate solutions to customers; helping others to make informed decisions; building people's communications competence.
Cross functional awareness	Understanding the different contributions from other disciplines and working with colleagues from across the organisation to achieve better results.
Craft (writing and design)	Using and developing the right mix of practical communication abilities (e.g. writing and design management) to hold the confidence of peers and colleagues.
Developing other communicators	Helping other communicators build their communications competence and develop their careers.
Innovation and creativity	Looking for new ways of working, exploring best practice and delivering original and imaginative approaches to communication problems.
Listening	Conducting research and managing mechanisms for gathering feedback and employee reaction.
Making it happen	Turning plans into successfully implemented actions.
Planning	Planning communication programmes and operations, evaluating results.
Specialist	Having specific subject matter expertise in a specialist area.
Vision and standards	Defining or applying a consistent approach to communication and maintaining professional and ethical standards.

FIGURE 13.6 Dewhurst and FitzPatrick's communication competencies

Source: Reproduced with permission

functions. Some IC teams have event organisers who might as well work in a marketing department or web designers who could equally belong in the IT organisation.

Twelve competencies are probably far more than any individual can hope to master. Dewhurst and FitzPatrick concluded that the mix and level of proficiency needed for any single practitioner depended on the challenges facing the organisations for which they worked. Somewhere with a large workforce with high staff turnover might want an IC manager with strong listening skills; an organisation facing a financial crisis and large scale job losses might want someone who works closely with lawyers and HR.

A clear message from the study's respondents is the importance of soft skills – the ability to get on with other people, to listen and gather intelligence and to develop or coach colleagues are as prominent as craft skills such as writing.

GETTING THE PRIORITIES RIGHT – MCDONALD'S UK

With 85,000 people working in 1,200 restaurants, McDonald's UK has a very clear idea about where internal communications makes a difference to its business; it's about developing a workforce that is 'confident, committed and competent'.

The company's head of internal communications, Linda McGee, explains; 'Our mission is about harnessing the energy of people who come into work everyday so that they are able to deliver the experience we want for our customers.'

At a basic level the restaurant chain works hard to explain operational matters to its people. This covers everything from service standards to forthcoming promotions.

'Our operational communication is intended to support specific business priorities that feature in our annual plan,' says McGee. Her team reviews the company's annual 'Plan to Win' (its internal statement of goals and targets) and identifies specific activities that IC needs to do to help achieve the plan.

For example, IC manages the company's intranet to ensure that important changes to restaurant procedures are explained in a clear and concise way that people can understand and action if required.

'It's also important that we do things with a sense of fun,' adds Linda. 'When we launch a promotion we want colleagues to understand what it's

C@SE STUDY

all about so we run competitions and stories across our internal communications channels to give people a taste of the vibe we're trying to create.'

This means that IC works hard to communicate management ideas in a way that is easy to understand for all areas and levels of the business. Although staff surveys have shown that people universally know about the company objectives and targets, communications are careful not to assume that people fully grasp how those targets impact on them on a day-to-day basis. 'Our job is about continually finding ways of keeping the message meaningful and engaging to the people who see customers day in and day out.'

Another priority is celebrating the opportunities that the company offers its staff. In addition to its renowned learning and career development programmes, McDonalds is heavily committed to supporting staff in community activities. In recent years internal communications has not only profiled individuals who have made significant achievements through the company's education programmes, but has also provided communication toolkits to restaurants to make it easier for teams to get involved in voluntary or social activities.

Clearly, creating internal awareness of training and advancement opportunities helps build employee commitment. In addition IC works on campaigns such as the McDonald's Cup – an internal national five-a-side football competition – to bring people closer together.

However, keeping messages fresh is a continuous challenge, made more difficult by the ever changing nature of the business. Because customers' tastes shift, menus have to keep pace; restaurants are now open for longer hours and McDonald's works with increasing numbers of franchisees. IC has to provide business support in an environment that is dynamic and which makes demands that are constantly evolving.

As a result, the IC team continually wonders whether its channels are right for the job in hand. In the last few years its print magazine has been replaced by online tools and they are exploring the use of social media to ensure that they are having a conversation with staff.

According to McGee,

> We know very well that one way or 'tell' communications are not always going to fully engage our people. And as our brand is about trust we have to think all the time about how to build the relationship internally and involve our people in discussing the context behind decisions or changes.

C@SE STUDY

USING DATA TO SHAPE COMMUNICATIONS – MAERSK LINE

When planning significant change at the world's largest shipping company, Maersk Line, the communications team use a very simple set of metrics to assess their performance.

The team began by wrestling with the question: 'How many people are getting and understanding our messages?' Significant transformations in how the business was managed meant that the company's 25,000 employees around the world needed to understand what was happening and how change might affect their jobs. As the process was happening over many months and was driven from the headquarters in Copenhagen, having a clear picture of what was working and where more emphasis was needed was essential to the communication team.

Head of Communication Klavs Valskov explains,

> We were mindful that the change message takes time to filter through an organisation like ours and that people in the head office who are involved in planning change can be way ahead of everyone else in their understanding and enthusiasm for new ways of working.

The team decided to introduce a simple monthly online survey that asked a random sample of employees 20 questions. Staff were asked if they were aware of key messages, whether they understood or agreed with the messages and whether they felt able to implement the changes being asked of them.

Over the months the survey showed the rate at which people were moving from basic awareness, through understanding into indications of behavioural change. And it highlighted which messages were penetrating better than others.

The key to the effectiveness of the survey was its simplicity. The limited number of questions made analysis quick. Crucially, each month, the CEO was given a very simple set of figures and commentary limited to a few lines.

Gathering data in this way enabled the communications team to identify when issues needed more explanation or decide which channels needed attention. Early on, the team identified the need to support local managers with more tools and information.

'The other significant benefit,' explains Valskov,

> was that we were able to bring evidence to our discussions with the executive team. Although our process is not exhaustively rigorous, it is

C@SE STUDY

speedy and provides us with a general indication of what works and what doesn't. That's often enough for day-to-day communication management and it removes the risk of running things on guesswork or speculation.

The team has gone on to develop the reporting of the study to draw connections with specific communication activity. The executive feedback also reviews intranet traffic and external media coverage.

Says Valskov, 'The report has been very well received in the organisation and added to our credibility as a true value-adding team.'

QUESTIONS FOR DISCUSSION

1 Thinking of an organisation you know, why do they undertake internal communication? Can you see the connection between IC and organisation success?

2 Thinking about an organisation you know, how would you segment the internal publics? How might different employee groups react differently to a current issue?

3 How would you go about gathering intelligence in an organisation? What data might be currently available about employee attitudes and what information might you want to collect?

4 Thinking about an internal campaign in an organisation, perhaps about safety, customer service or diversity, what objectives might you set for your communications?

5 What channels exist for communications in a workplace with which you are familiar – what types of communication do they work well for?

6 How well prepared are line managers in your organisation to communicate? Using the five questions assess how you might help line managers become more effective as communicators.

7 Thinking of a communication campaign you have seen at work, how might you go about evaluating its effectiveness?

8 Thinking about Quirke's descriptions of the generic roles of IC practitioners, what type of people do you think are needed in an workplace that you are familiar with?

9 What obstacles can you imagine might get in the way of a line manager or supervisor being an effective communication – and how might you overcome those obstacles?

10 Looking at Dewhurst and FitzPatrick's model of competencies – which do you think are strengths that you have and which could be personal development areas for you?

FURTHER READING

Clampitt, P. (2005) *Communicating for managerial effectiveness*, Sage.

Dewhurst, S. and FitzPatrick, L. (2007) *How to develop outstanding internal communicators*, Melcrum.

Hargie, O. and Tourish D. (eds) (2004) *Handbook of communication audits for organisations*, Routledge.

Quirke, B. (2003) *Making the connections*, Gower.

Ruck. K. (ed.)(2010) *Exploring internal communication*, Pearson.

Russo, D.F. (2010) *17 rules successful companies use to attract and keep top talent: why engaged employees are your greatest sustainable advantage*, Pearson Education.

Wright, M. (ed.) (2009) *The Gower handbook of internal communication*, Gower.

CHAPTER 14

Financial communications

Mark Phillimore

CHAPTER AIMS

This chapter provides an understanding of financial communications and its role in helping organisations communicate with financial markets. An historical perspective of the growth of the profession and the important role played by financial communication consultancies is covered. How financial communications may be influenced by the wider discussion about the management and practice of financial markets after the financial crash is considered.

INTRODUCTION

Financial PR or financial communications has become one of the most profitable and highly paid sectors of the PR industry. For PR practitioners working within medium or large businesses, the role of financial communications will be an important communications priority within the overall corporate communications agenda.

In a recent survey, eight out of the ten top PR consultancies in the UK's top 150 (*PR Week*, 2010) have a strong involvement with financial communications. PR consultancies with a particularly strong focus on financial communications such as Brunswick, Financial Dynamics (FD) and Finsbury, with strong global networks of offices have particularly high fee income per employee, with Finsbury achieving £285,000 fee generation per employee in 2009. This high level of fee income further drives the salaries and bonuses of this sector of the communications profession (which are generally higher than other areas of PR practice).

Financial Times commentator and entrepreneur, Luke Johnston, who has also owned financial PR consultancies wrote 'A consumer PR agency should generate 20 per cent net profit margins on revenue; a financial PR agency more like 30 per cent' (2010).

So what is financial PR or financial communications and why is it generally such a profitable area of PR practice? A number of commentators (Dolphin, 2003; Davis, 2006) have highlighted it is not a well understood area of public relations practice and has not had the same level of exposure in books and academic papers as other areas of the profession. This is starting to change, and the recent financial crash in 2007–2009 has led to more focus on the workings and role of financial communications within financial markets.

Financial communications has traditionally split into two main areas of activity: communicating and relationship building with financial media that was seen as a financial PR function; and investor relations that encompassed an organisation's communications and relationship building with professional investors in debt and equity markets. This separation of activity was reinforced by the development in the US of the function and professionalisation of investor relations from the 1950s onwards, separate from the PR function and with a strong focus on the shareholder.

Modern financial communications practice by the major consultancies such as Brunswick, Finsbury, Citigate, Abernathy McGregor Group, Maitland and many more is to integrate all financial communications – whether media or investor relations – in one operation. This development, particularly by US companies with a strong separate investor relations tradition, is relatively recent and significant. There is an even more recent development by these leading consultancies to provide government relations and regulatory support alongside financial communications, highlighting that the role and power of financial markets also has a growing political and social dimension.

Within companies, the investor relations team may report both into the finance director of a major company or to the director of corporate communications, but whichever way there will be a strong matrix reporting structure reflecting its importance across the organisation. The changing lines of communications reflect the origins of investor relations. The corporate communications function was slower to professionalise than disciplines such as finance and accountancy but public relations' influence in organisations at a senior level has grown over the last 15 years. Peter Hall, former Director of Investor Relations at BP talked about the changing lines of reporting during his career at BP. 'Within BP, over the past ten years, investor relations has reported to the CFO, the Group Treasurer, briefly the CEO and, as now, the Director of Corporate Communications' (Hall, 2010).

Increasingly, the financial communications function both in-house and within the major financial communications consultancies would seem to be adopting a corporate communications model of services such as outlined by leading corporate communications authors such as Cornelissen (2009: 31). Financial communications is part of a range of corporate communication services for major global companies alongside government relations, reputation management and crisis communications among other services.

This chapter will seek to reflect these changes in providing an understanding of the role of communications in financial markets. While the communications aspects of investor relations will be covered, there will be no attempt to describe in anything more than an outline the very detailed technical aspects of the investor relations function. Readers are encouraged to consult relevant literature and key websites for further research are provided. The chapter will not focus on the extensive area of financial services communications that is involved with communicating products and services to the consumer market.

HISTORICAL CONTEXT

To understand financial communications it is necessary to have a brief overview of its historical context. The growth of newspapers in the latter part of the nineteenth century saw growing coverage of financial and business news, particularly of share prices as financial markets particularly in the US and Europe reflected growing industrialisation and expansion of world trade. It was during this period that newspapers such as the *Financial Times* (1888) and *Wall Street Journal* (1884) were founded (Kynaston, 1994: 397). As historians of PR have pointed out, the growth in media covering business and financial stories was a catalyst in the growth of public relations from the 1900s onwards.

The big change in media coverage of business came with the 1950s and the great expansion particularly in the US of the post-war economy and growth in shareholding by US citizens. This led media to increasingly take an interest in looking after the interests of ordinary shareholders particularly as they accounted for a growing affluent readership for their newspapers and magazines. It was in this time, that the first in-house investor relations department was set up by Ralph Cordiner, Chairman of General Electric (NIRI, 2010). According to NIRI's it was the failure of public relations departments and consultancies to handle the function of investor relations professionally that led to this separate development and uneasy relationship between the two functions.

In the US, these first steps by GE led to the growing development of the role of investor relations function and in time in the 1960s, to its professionalisation separate from public relations practice, which was also echoed in the formation of the Investor Relations Society in 1980 in the UK. This development can also be seen in the context of the growing professionalisation of financial functions generally such as investment analysts (NIRI, 2010).

In the UK and Europe, small investors were not an important constituency, except briefly under Margaret Thatcher in the early 1980s, but institutional investors were the main holders of equity. This led to financial communications and investor relations in the UK being focused on institutions and an approach based on City opinion formers (Davis, 2006).

The growth in financial markets in the 1980s and 1990s led to further development of financial media with CNN's creation of a 24-hour television news service focusing on financial and business stories. Even more significant was the formation of the proprietary financial information network, Bloomberg, in the 1980s. Bloomberg's success led to the creation in the 1990s of Bloomberg TV, the first 24-hour TV channel dedicated to financial and business information followed by CNBC. The growth of the internet was to have increasing influence on financial media from the mid-1990s.

The cultural and professional differences between financial PR and investor relations are becoming less relevant as the major financial communication consultancies offer a range of integrated communication services to global brands spanning global markets. This can be seen on the FD website (2010), describing its role as the 'world's leading investor relations and financial communications consultancy'. It goes on to highlight its ability in terms that show its ability to articulate vision and narrative, familiar concepts to PR practitioners:

> we help our clients achieve their aims by helping them clearly articulate their strengths and goals, whatever they do and whatever their size. In an environment where markets and audiences are increasingly blurred, we advise management teams and boards of directors how to tell the story behind their strategic decisions and business imperatives.

THE WORKING ENVIRONMENT

In simple terms, financial markets are an exchange or market bringing together people and institutions who have money (investors) and people who need money (companies). In developed markets these two are brought together in regulated exchanges such as the London Stock Exchange or New York Stock Exchange and increasingly in a variety of online exchanges. In these large, very liquid markets, listed companies can raise large amounts of capital both through the issuance of equity or shares and also raise debt in the form of corporate bonds.

Companies become listed for a number of reasons: to raise capital so they can fund further growth; to enable original investors (such as venture capitalists) to realise their investment; to raise the company's profile; to provide employees with incentives. The aim of all capital markets is to act as a catalyst for growth and a company will be expected to raise capital more than once to ensure continued growth. To encourage investment, a company therefore needs to be attractive to potential investors and maintain the support of existing investors, which is where financial communications comes in.

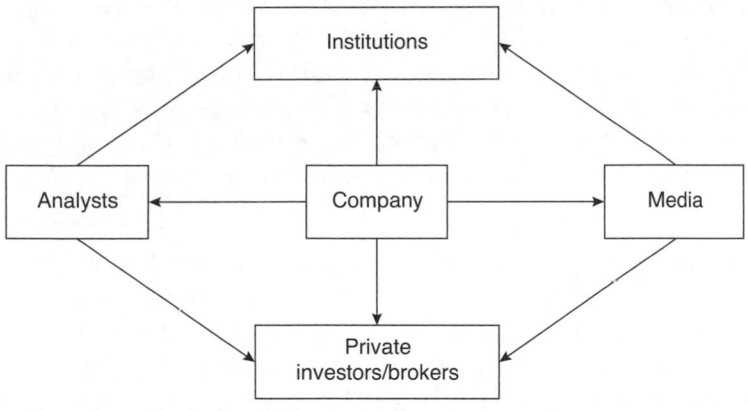

FIGURE 14.1 Flow of information
Source: Used by permission

FINANCIAL AUDIENCES

Financial markets are extremely complex and inter connected and have developed a wide range of intermediaries who play a key role in the whole process of capital markets. Each of these can be important stakeholders for companies communicating financial information and seeking to build medium- to long-term relationships. Listed below are some of the main audiences for financial communications.

Institutional investors (existing shareholders, potential shareholders or past shareholders)

The main investors in quoted companies are large institutions such as pension funds, insurance companies and investment banks. When individuals put money into pension funds or insurance policies, it goes into bigger pots of money known as 'funds' that are subsequently invested in listed companies. Large institutions are influential investors, as they may hold a significant stake in an individual company, anything between 1 and 20 per cent. A company's relationship with its institutional investors is actively managed by its investment relations team (in-house and external as well as by broker or investment bank). Institutions will be greatly influenced by 'third party' or independent comments in the media and from analysts, and by the company's regulatory communications.

New capital sources (hedge funds, private equity, venture capital)

Financial markets have innovated and developed significant new sources of capital and investment over the last 20 years that have become important influences on quoted businesses particularly during times of difficulty such as restructuring or in mergers and acquisitions. Some of these new sources of capital such as hedge funds have become highly controversial, particularly as many have short-term trading strategies, making an investment relationship strategy for an organisation difficult. Kraft's takeover of the famous British chocolate business, Cadbury, had a share register at the end with 20 per cent of shares held by hedge funds (Wiggins and Guthrie, 2010).

The power and influence of these sources of capital, even though controversial, have become key audiences for financial communications teams and are now a regular feature of the investor relations scene. The short-term nature of some of this capital has made the monitoring by the investor relations team of an organisation's share register a key area of activity to spot share building.

Analysts

Analysts are key opinion formers, identifying trends and anomalies and generating ideas for investment. There are two types of analyst: buy side and sell side. A buy-side analyst works solely to provide information to fund managers working either for these large funds or independently. Sell-side analysts work for the brokers or investment banks who look after listed companies. Both types provide independent analysis about the workings and prospects of a company and the market in which it operates. They usually specialise in a particular sector and will make recommendations about whether shares in a particular company should be bought, sold, held or avoided, making them an important audience for listed companies and their financial communications. It is the unique responsibility of financial communications to encourage and manage the relationship between a company and the analysts who follow it. A financial communications person is most likely to be the first point of contact between a company and an analyst and will be the gateway for subsequent information gathering.

Analysts have an important relationship with the press. Journalists can add weight to an article by quoting an analyst. An analyst will also watch key press such as the *Financial Times*, *Wall Street Journal* and key national media, as well as key trade media for new ideas or independent information on companies and sectors. The growth of social media, particularly specialist blogs has also provided new sources of information and ideas for analysts.

The media

With the growth of financial markets, particularly into new global markets such as BRICs (Brazil, Russia, India, China), the leading financial media such as the *Financial Times* and *Wall Street Journal* have transformed themselves in the range and scope of their coverage. Where once the *Financial Times* was the house newspaper for the City of London and the *Wall Street Journal* on Wall Street, these have become powerful news organisations in the range and coverage of international news. They have also become increasingly confident and independent of financial markets about setting news agendas with the *Financial Times* running a famous series in 2009, on the 'Future of Capitalism'. Both have invested heavily in online coverage with innovative use of social media including video and bulletin boards. Both are key outlets for financial communications teams both in reporting key financial information and developments but also in helping set agendas.

A key outlet for financial information is Bloomberg via its terminal and Bloomberg TV. While the terminal will report key financial information, often before other media outlets, Bloomberg TV would be seen as an important outlet for interviews with chief executives at the announcement of important financial results such full year results. CNBC would also be seen as an important outlet for executive interviews along with Fox News in the US.

As financial markets have become increasingly influential, coverage in leading national media in most major markets has also increased. Robert Peston from the BBC became the leading financial commentator, able to move markets and influence political opinion during the financial crisis of 2007–2009. Coverage in the City pages of the national newspapers would be a key target for the financial communications team.

TRADE AND TECHNICAL MEDIA

While trade and technical media are not generally the target of financial communications, there are some media that are particularly influential in certain sectors and read by analysts and the market generally. These would be part of the media audience targeted by financial communications. Also, within a corporate communications team, such key industry media would be targeted with awareness that stories and features may have the ability to influence the organisation's reputation with financial markets among its target audiences.

Wire services

Wire services provide the starting point for the announcement of key financial information across financial markets that comply with European and US regulations on disclosure of price sensitive information. The London Stock Exchange RNS service has become a popular service (London Stock Exchange, 2010) feeding into other news wire services and specialist information networks such as Bloomberg. In the US, Business Wire is a leading provider.

Private investor services

While Bloomberg and Reuters serve the information needs of professional markets in particular, there are a range of online sites serving the information needs of private investors. Many are subscription-only sites and have become a key source of information and trading for retail investors. Examples include Citywire, Hemscott and Money AM.

Private client brokers

Less important than they used to be, they are still a feature of some global markets such as the US. As well as the growing power of institutional investment, the growth of trading online has led to their role being disintermediated further with private clients able to now dealing directly online. Stockbrokers act for private individuals who have money to invest, buying and selling shares on their behalf. They can offer advice to clients, if asked, about which companies to invest in. A stockbroker's opinion about a company will be influenced by what information is available, either through what is written in the press or if he/she has access to analysts' research. Financial communications manages this relationship, through the provision of information and by arranging meetings between the stockbrokers and the company at appropriate times, such as financial reporting.

The retail investor

Over the last 10 years, the small retail investor has become more sophisticated and more powerful. Website providers such as Hemscott and Citywire allow the retail investor access to levels of information similar to the larger institutional professional investors. Discussion in chat rooms have existed for many years where investors could share ideas and information, but now added to this there are also a growing number of financial blogs.

REGULATORY ENVIRONMENT

The financial crisis of 2007–2009 has resulted in moves towards more regulated markets – not just at a national level but also with growing international measures, particularly in EU markets. The ideology that financial markets were efficient and rational and could regulate themselves were badly undermined (Kaletsky, 2010; Turner, 2009), resulting in further regulation which is still in the process of being developed.

In fact, regulation has become a growing feature of the financial communications process over the last 10 years. Legislation in the US following the Enron collapse led to the Sarbanes-Oxley Act (2002) and was followed in Europe by the EU Transparency Directive 2004. The Transparency Directive, which was created as part of the harmonisation of the European Capital Markets, has implications for financial reporting and for shareholder disclosure. It was brought into the UK Companies Act 2006, and impacts on the regulatory environment for quoted companies.

Both measures placed greater requirements on disclosure of information, particularly the need to inform all shareholders at the same time. This has resulted in much greater use of the company website for web casting of quarterly and annual results with ordinary investors able to watch and listen in as chief executives are questioned by leading City analysts from the major investment banks.

The trend in all regulation is to ensure growing transparency and fair disclosure of information to protect investors in listed companies and to ensure the fair treatment of all. The rules that specifically concern financial PR regard the dissemination of information, in particular price-sensitive information. There is no strict definition of what price-sensitive information is, other than any information that the market does not know about, which if known would cause the share price of a company to move. Large deals, such as mergers, acquisitions or takeovers, must be disclosed to the market through one approved regulatory wire services such as the London Stock Exchange RNS.

Stock Market rules prior to the Financial Services and Markets Act 2000 were the responsibility of the London Stock Exchange. Since the Act, statutory powers have been given to the Financial Services Authority (FSA). The FSA is an independent non-governmental body that regulates all financial markets. For the rules governing the Stock Market, the FSA is referred to as the UK Listing Authority (UKLA). The UKLA Sourcebook is the definitive publication for the Listing Rules and the UKLA guidance manual. The FSA will become part of the Bank of England under proposed new legislation.

FINANCIAL COMMUNICATIONS

Aims of financial communications

The main purpose of financial PR is to ensure the share price of a company adequately reflects its value and to help the liquidity of its shares. It does this by using communications to manage the relationship between the listed company and its financial audience, creating and maintaining awareness and understanding of the company.

Financial PR exists for companies listed on the stock market and for major private companies or institutions that need to communicate with professional financial audiences. A company needs to have 'liquidity' in its shares, i.e. sufficient shares traded to create a market. Investors can be discouraged from investing in stocks that are 'illiquid' as it may be difficult for them to sell at a later stage. Companies with little liquidity are more likely to have a lower share rating and volatile share-price movements, making buying and selling of their shares extremely difficult.

Communicating what exactly?

The City judges a company by its financial performance and its growth potential. Financial communications can help to communicate this through raising awareness of a company's activities and business strategy and profiling its management. The communication also involves managing financial market expectations of a company. Investors will use the available information about a company to try and predict how it will perform in the future. If financial markets, using information given by a company, predict a 20 per cent growth in profits and that company fails to meet the prediction, the result is disappointment. Disappointment may lead to investors selling their shares and may discourage other investors from buying, which would bring the share price down. Analysts rely on companies to provide clear information that allows them to make realistic predictions about a company's future performance. New regulations have encouraged businesses to be much more careful and cautious about future forecasts.

When to communicate

All listed companies have what is known as the financial calendar, consisting of preliminary results, publication of the annual report, half-yearly results and an annual general meeting (AGM). In the US quarterly reporting is also standard. These are the times the listed company is legally obliged to disclose its financial performance. These announcements also provide an opportunity to build strong relationships with financial audiences.

Financial reporting

When a company reports full-year figures, the statement is referred to as its preliminary results; it is a shortened version of the annual report. The hard copy of the annual report is produced subsequently, but must reach shareholders not more than four months following the company's year end. A company is also required to report its half-yearly figures in the same way and a smaller hard copy report is produced for shareholders that must also reach them within four months of the half-year end. From January 2007, companies have also had to make interim management statements that give a description of any material events or transactions which have taken place during the reporting period. These announcements are made to the market via one of the approved regulatory wire services.

Commonly at the preliminary results and the half-yearly results, meetings are held with major investors, usually institutions, and also with analysts and the media. These meetings are typically webcast ensuring that all information is available to all investors – large and small at the same time.

The presentation of results is key to creating understanding. Little notice will be taken of a badly written, uninformative chairman's statement or presentation. The chairman's statement must contain everything the company wishes to convey to its financial audiences, as all information for subsequent press releases and presentations must come from this. One of the main roles of financial PR is to assist in the writing of the chairman's statement and presentation, ensuring that the key messages are communicated effectively. Ahead of the announcement, Q&As should be prepared to ensure the consistency of information given.

A few days following the results, feedback is obtained from analysts who follow the company and who attended the analysts' briefing. This provides valuable information on how a company is being perceived and can help inform the communications strategy.

The annual report

All listed companies are legally required to produce an annual report for their shareholders within 4 months of their financial year end and 21 days before the AGM. The UKLA Sourcebook contains a list of items that must be included, which refer in the main to the disclosure of the financial accounts and significant corporate or business activity for the year just ended. The annual report also provides the company with an important communication tool. Shareholders, the media and analysts will refer to it throughout the year. It is a marketing tool and can be used to introduce the business not only to potential investors, but also to potential customers.

The AGM

The AGM is a legally required meeting, held after the financial year end for shareholders. This is the only formal opportunity for smaller investors to meet the company's management face-to-face and to ask them direct questions. The AGM's purpose is to seek approval for the resolutions set out in the annual report, to re-elect the company's directors and auditors and for the annual report to be formally accepted.

The event varies from company to company. Small companies can have as few as two or three investors attend, while large companies could have hundreds. The AGM is an opportunity to communicate and deepen understanding, but not all companies capitalise on the advantages of meeting their main audiences face-to-face.

Any price-sensitive information given out at the AGM must either be announced prior to the AGM or be simultaneously announced to the market.

The location varies and is dependent upon the location of the company's head office and the number of shareholders expected to attend. A company that produces an interesting or clever product could hold its meeting close to the factory and give shareholders the opportunity to visit the site, to bring about a better understanding of its activities.

COMMUNICATING OUTSIDE THE FINANCIAL CALENDAR

Activities outside of the calendar might include analysts' site visits to see the operations of the company. This can help create a greater understanding about a company and allows analysts to get a better feel for how the company works and also provide an opportunity to meet the management below board level. There may also be meetings with private client brokers if a company has a large number of private investors on its register, or, if it would like to have more. A company always has to exercise extreme care when hosting visits and meetings not to disclose any information other than what is already in the public domain.

COMMUNICATING DURING TRANSACTIONS

Flotations

An Initial Public Offering (IPO) or flotation is when a private company goes public and becomes listed. The process involves finding investors to buy the shares when they are first traded on a named day. In this situation, financial PR and IR work very closely together. The private company will appoint a nominated broker and a corporate financier who are responsible for the technicalities of the float and also for marketing the company to large institutional investors. It is the role of financial PR practitioners to support the IR role by raising awareness and creating understanding in the City about the company. This is achieved through gaining appropriate media exposure and through private client broker and analyst briefings. Typically a major financial PR consultancy will be retained and will play a key role in this process.

Mergers and acquisitions

Globalisation and the search for increasing profits continue to be the key drivers behind mergers and acquisitions. Financial markets expect that most listed companies will at some point complete a merger or acquisition as part of a growth strategy. Financial PR helps manage the City's expectations about the nature and timing of a likely deal. A company may do this by making reference to its acquisition strategy at the time of its results. However, confidentiality and UKLA rules on shareholder information restrict what can be said outside of a formal announcement.

Many large mergers or acquisitions may require money to be raised on the market through the issue of new shares and may also need the permission of shareholders. The company's broker and other advisers will prepare a legal offer document for shareholders setting out all details of the deal. This will be sent directly to shareholders who are asked to vote either by proxy or by attending an extraordinary general meeting (EGM). In most cases, shareholders must have the 'offer document' no fewer than 21 days before the EGM so they have adequate time to analyse and assess the deal.

The role of financial PR in these transactions is twofold: to encourage shareholders to vote in favour of the proposed deal, and to encourage new and existing investors to buy the new shares issued through raised awareness of the deal. Ahead of the document being posted, an announcement (a summary of the legal offer document) is prepared for issue via one of the approved regulatory wire services. On this, the City will base its first opinions. Press and analyst briefings will be arranged on the day of the announcement. Briefing meetings help to create a deeper understanding of a deal, ensuring accurate comment in the financial press and a positive reaction from analysts.

Hostile take overs

When a listed company tries to take over another one without the agreement of that company's board, it is a hostile bid. One of the most famous hostile bids was when Granada took over Forte in 1997. The aim of the financial PR and investor relations in this situation was to persuade Forte's shareholders that they would be better off if the company was bought by Granada. Forte's board were not prepared to sell the company to Granada and so Granada had to communicate directly, and indirectly though the media, with shareholders to persuade them to vote against the board of Forte, allowing the sale to take place.

The PR programme ahead of Granada's announcement ran for two years, with financial PR and investor relations working hand in hand. Granada, long before it approached Forte, ensured it had good communications with its own shareholders and with third-party audiences, such as press and analysts, and made clear that its strategy for growth was to be by acquisition. Forte, on the other hand, had a record of poor communication with its investors. Granada successfully took over Forte and the deal demonstrated the importance of good communication. Sadly, the takeover was not a success and resulted in significant destruction in value for Granada shareholders who continued to hold its shares.

Each hostile bid is unique and complicated. Financial PR and investor relations programmes are tailored accordingly, but as a general guide, if working to fight off a hostile takeover the company's shareholders must vote to reject the other company's offer, so the focus of financial PR would be to persuade shareholders to this effect. When working to take over another company via hostile means, financial PR needs to persuade the target company's shareholders with the argument and rationale to convince them they would be better off voting to agree the takeover. The activities of all parties involved are closely governed by the Takeover Code.

ONGOING COMMUNICATION

The investor relations section of the company website

The immediacy and depth of investor relations information that is available to all Investors has been transformed in recent years by the Investor Relations part of company websites. These are now extensive productions with detailed presentations on all activities of the organisation. A key feature of these sites is that they include a wide range of webcasts and presentations. They also have a range of features allowing investors to be kept up to date with new announcements via RSS feeds and email alerts. The Investor Relations Society and NIRI run competitions each year for the best investor relations site on a company website, allowing best practice to be observed.

Evaluation

The main measure of financial communications is share price, particularly in relationship to its peer group. If similar companies in a sector such as IT are on a particular price/earning band, then the share price of the company would be expected to perform to a similar level or better. In the recent financial crisis when share prices for nearly all companies slumped by 20–30 per cent, this approach to evaluation would allow a sensible evaluation of work undertaken.

Investor relations has developed a wide range of metrics to evaluate performance based on a strong understanding of the share ownership structure. If a company was making a major long-term move into the Asian market, it might also seek to develop investors from the region to have a better balance of international investment in its shares and debt products.

FUTURE ISSUES

The following are a number of issues, some inter-connected, facing financial communications in the years ahead. Many relate to the implications of the financial crisis of 2007–2009 and the potential impact on financial communications practice in the years ahead.

Sustainability not profitability?

Professor Michael Porter (Porter and Kramer, 2010), famous for his works on competitive strategy and industrial clusters called for business to re-connect with society and seek 'shared value' not short-term profits. His opening lines leave no room for doubt: 'The capitalist system is under siege. In recent years business increasingly has been viewed as a major cause of social, environmental, and economic problems. Companies are widely perceived to be prospering at the expense of the broader community.' Along similar lines, the concept of 'stewardship' was prominent in the Walker report on corporate governance following the bank crisis (UK Treasury, 2009). In the Stockholm Accords, a global mission statement and agenda for the PR industry, launched in 2010, organisational sustainability and stakeholder governance are two key agendas for PR practitioners.

All these agendas are arguing that an organisation has a wider remit than just shareholders. It could be argued that these are all a development of ideas based round the concept of stakeholders rather than shareholders that have become increasingly current over the last 20 years. However, financial communications and investor relations have fundamentally been about putting the shareholder or capital markets agenda at the top of its priorities. What are the implications for its practice as wider sustainability agendas become more widely adopted – if they are adopted?

Controlling agendas

A number of commentators including senior politicians and media as well as recent research by LSE academic Dr Damian Tambini (2008) highlighted the unhelpful role of financial PR in the 2007–2009 financial crisis. There was criticism of the attempt to control information and access to senior management by the media. This was not a growing trend but according to earlier research by Davis (2006: 9) was a fact of life for City financial journalists from the 1980s.

Davis (2007) later examines the role of 'elite power' groups such as the City of London and its ability to set political and media agendas. His premise is that financial communications and financial communication consultancies such as Brunswick, FD, Finsbury, Maitland and Citigate have played a key role in promoting and defending the 'elite power' held by financial markets. He notes (ibid.: 61), 'When conducting interviews it became apparent that a substantial proportion of corporate communication time is indeed taken up with blocking journalists and stifling negative coverage.'

Clearly the level of control over information concerned the regulatory authorities and the International Monetary Fund commissioned research on the role of lobbying by sub-prime mortgage companies in the US (Igan *et al.*, 2009). The opening remarks state: 'anecdotal evidence suggests that political influences of the financial industry contributed to the 2007 mortgage crisis, which in the fall of 2008, generalised in the worst bout of financial instability since the Great Depression.'

The attempted control of communications by organisations using an asymmetrical or one-way messaging approach described by Grunig and Hunt (1984) is seen by old-fashioned approach to PR and is not feasible with the growth of social media. It is worth considering why the use of one-way communications seems particularly strong in financial communications. Certainly the power and influence of financial markets and the major financial communications consultancies must be a factor.

Investor relations has a professional code that has always encouraged a symmetrical approach to communications, which contrasts with financial media relations. Recent research in the US suggests a symmetrical model of communications is adopted by the investor relations function within an organisation (Kelly *et al.*, 2010).

Western financial markets have suffered considerable loss of prestige and influence as a result of the crash and it will be interesting to see how financial communications responds and develops in a more sceptical and questioning environment, with greater political influence and use of social media.

The impact of social media in financial markets

The financial crisis of 2007–2009 also coincided with the growth of social media such as Twitter, Facebook, YouTube, blogs on news sites and forum-type features on main news sites. It was the first financial crash where the voices of many could be heard and sampled leading to a great outpouring of comment – informed and otherwise – on financial markets for the first time.

Several examples are worth highlighting. Robert Peston, Business Editor of the BBC writes a very popular blog with many readers commenting on and reading the debate taking place on his website. A fairly standard blog entry, 'Faith in Banks' (2009) resulted in over 400 comments being made.

The *Financial Times* developed a site called *FT Alphaville* with continual reports from journalists on global markets during the trading day and commentary from market participants and informed viewers. During times of crisis around financial markets, this site witnessed extensive dialogue.

The development of social media raises many challenges for PR practitioners. Other sectors such as retail, IT, travel and fashion have risen to the challenge and use the new forms of media to build relationships with stakeholders. Financial communications, restricted by regulation and by culture may have more difficulty in its development.

Methodology of investor relations undermined?

A number of commentators, including Lord Turner, Head of the FSA (2009) and more recently Kaletsky (2010: 176), have questioned the role of market efficiency and the concept of the rational market. Both financial PR and investor relations can be seen as a product of the 'efficient market hypothesis' that has been the dominant methodology behind the growth of financial markets and financial products over the last 30 years. This hypothesis says that markets are inherently competitive, efficient and rational, and the price of an asset or share price fully reflects the information available. In this context, the role of financial communications can be seen as assisting market professionals by providing information, admittedly from the company's perspective, to enhance market efficiency.

Economists such as Keynes and Hayek, in contrast, took the view that financial markets were inherently unstable and were prey to 'mood swings, herd instinct, self-reinforcing momentum trading, and other positive feedbacks in financial markets' (Kaletsky, 2010: 176). Taleb (2007) critiqued the use of normal probability distribution in financial markets and the way it became an important foundation for many mathematical models underpinning the 'efficient market hypothesis'.

The impact of this questioning and loss of confidence in traditional approaches to markets and market making may be short lived as markets settle down. However, the primacy and influence of ideas from financial markets has been questioned and disturbed for the first time in a generation and the implications will not likely be settled or apparent except over the medium term.

KRAFT TAKEOVER OF CADBURY

C@SE STUDY

The takeover in January 2010 of the iconic British chocolate brand and manufacturer, Cadbury, by the US global food processing company, Kraft provides an interesting case study of the range of communication issues that can be triggered by a large takeover battle.

Cadbury is a famous name in British industrial history and consumer culture. Formed by a Quaker family in Birmingham in the 1820s, the Cadbury family were pioneers in corporate governance in Victorian times creating an industrial, leisure and domestic environment in Bournville, Birmingham, which was famous for its care of employees. Although, as the *Financial Times* reported, the company had moved away from these roots particularly after it floated in 1960 and more recently adopted a strongly shareholder agenda as the family ceased to be involved from 2000 onwards with global expansion and increased manufacture outside the UK (Guthrie and Kuchler, 2010). Kraft's origins were more recent (1920s) and mergers and acquisition were part of its organisational strategy from its earliest days taking it from dairy products including the famous Kraft cheese into the world's 'second largest food company with annual revenues of $48bn' (Kraft, 2011).

In September 2009, Kraft made an opening indicative offer of £10.2 billion based on a 745p a share takeover offer that included both a cash and share composition. The offer was seen as the opening gambit by Kraft in a longer takeover approach. Irene Rosenfield, the CEO of Kraft was quoted in the *Financial Times* (Wiggins, 2009) referring to Cadbury as 'a portfolio of beloved iconic brands with a very strong heritage.' Highlighting that

Cadbury management was, like Kraft, driven by a shareholder approach, the *Financial Times* said that management hoped that the Kraft bid would lead to other bids for the company. This immediately alerted Kraft and its advisers that the board and management were not going to broaden the defence into the political arena drawing on Cadbury's significance in British industrial history, but were purely going to be driven by getting the best price possible for the company.

UK takeover rules require bidding companies to formalise the process of making a bid from an initial indicative and discussion process. This is called the 'put-up or shut-up regime', and does not allow a firm to destabilise the market in a quoted company for long before it must make a formal offer, otherwise it is banned from making an offer for a period of six months. Kraft made a formal, unsolicited bid only four hours before the deadline on 9 November 2009. The offer was 300p per share plus 0.259 Kraft shares per Cadbury share equal to 717p per share. The *Financial Times* reported that Kraft had raised $9 billion in loan finance from nine banks to help fund the takeover. The offer was seen as applying further pressure on Cadbury to get round the table and agree a figure.

Commenting on the publication of the Offer documentation in December 2009, Rosenfeld, said,

> We remain confident that the unique combination of Kraft Foods and Cadbury would create a significant growth opportunity for both businesses. That's why we believe this Offer is in the best interest of both companies' shareholders. Our Offer is fully financed, represents a substantial premium to Cadbury's unaffected share price and provides both immediate value certainty and meaningful longer-term upside potential.
>
> (Kraft, 2009)

In December, Kraft raised its offer to 360p in cash. In December, and then again in early January 2010, the Cadbury's defence team responded to the Kraft bid calling it derisory. Todd Stitzer, CEO of Cadbury said, 'We are delivering now and don't need to be subsumed into a lumbering corporate monolith' (Jones, 2009).

Within a week, the papers were reporting that the takeover was nearing conclusion and that Cadbury and Kraft were round the table discussing the terms of the takeover. On 19 January both sides agreed terms based on 500p per share in cash plus 0.1874 Kraft shares valuing Cadbury at £11.6 billion. The Cadbury's Chairman, Roger Carr, announced that he had achieved a good price for shareholders, highlighting that the shareholder focus was key for Cadbury's board.

C@SE STUDY

C@SE STUDY

A year later, he fought back at the criticisms about selling not just a British company but a famous British brand. He said, 'It wasn't a family business and it wasn't very British. The brands were loved all over the world, but the company was pretty much unloved by investors, particularly those in the United Kingdom.' He pointed out that just 28 per cent of shares were British before the takeover began, with 49 per cent owned by US investors (Bow, 2010).

His comments can be seen in the context of the heated communication issues that developed after the takeover. Kraft had promised to keep open a factory near Bristol that was due to close under Cadbury. Following the takeover it changed its decision. This led to major criticism in the media and questions in Parliament. It also led to a censure by the UK Takeover Panel in May 2010, the first censure of a company in three years. Rosenfeld refused to speak in front of a Parliamentary committee but sent her deputy. In the same month, the *Financial Times* reported that the new combined company was losing a number of key staff as a result of the takeover. In January 2011, 12 months after the takeover, in a major retrospective piece, the *Financial Times* questioned the success of the takeover. 'More than one former employee points to the "Orwellian" feel of Cadbury under Kraft' (Lucas, 2011), highlighting the problem of large mergers and acquisitions bringing two strong corporate cultures under one roof.

The Kraft takeover of Cadbury has generated more negative publicity than any other recent acquisition. Both companies and management with strong shareholder agendas seem particularly ill-tuned to understand the wider stakeholder agendas that are increasingly part of large takeovers and Kraft as a brand is widely perceived to have suffered reputational damage as a consequence, even if only in the short term.

ACKNOWLEDGEMENTS

The author would like to thank Keeley Clarke for her major contributions to the text.

QUESTIONS FOR DISCUSSION

1 Identify some financial blogs and discuss how they could influence investment in a company.

2 Analyse what impact communicating detailed financial data has on the communications narrative.

3 Analyse the Investor Relations page of a major publicly quoted company and examine the sources of information available to an investor.

4   Do you think financial communications employs asymmetrical or symmetrical communications in mergers and acquisitions?

5   Analyse the Kraft takeover of Cadbury in a shareholder and stakeholder perspective and its influence on communications strategy. Are stakeholder perspectives becoming more important in communications around takeover bids?

6   Discuss the importance of traditional print media and compare with that of online and social media.

7   What information about a company most influences investment decisions?

8   Compare a company's financial results announcement with the press coverage it receives the following day in the print and online media.

9   Evaluate communications problems in a hostile takeover.

10 Join a fantasy share-trading scheme such as www.bullbearings.com. How do you choose the companies you invest in?

FURTHER READING

Financial Dynamics (2010) *Capital markets and investor relations*, www.fd.com/en/homepage/practice-areas/capital-markets-and-investor-relations.aspx.

Davis, A. (2006) 'Role of mass media in investor relations', *Journal of Communication Management,* 10 (1).

A SELECTION OF RELEVANT WEBSITES

AMO: www.amo-global.com
Brunswick: www.brunswickgroup.com/index.aspx
EU Single Market: http://ec.europa.eu/internal_market/finances/index_en.htm
FSA – Financial Services Authority (UK): www.fsa.gov.uk
EU Transparency Directive: www.fsa.gov.uk/pages/About/What/International/td/index.shtml
—— : www.pwc.com/gx/en/ifrs-reporting/pdf/transparency.pdf
Finsbury: www.finsbury.com
Investor Relations Society: www.ir-soc.org.uk
Maitland: www.maitland.co.uk
NIRI – National Investor Relations Institute (US): www.niri.org
London Stock Exchange: www.londonstockexchange.com/home/homepage.htm
London Stock Exchange – A practical guide to investor relations: www.londonstockexchange.com/home/ir-apracticalguide.pdf

CHAPTER 15

Public sector public relations

Simon Wakeman

CHAPTER AIMS

This chapter gives an overview of the origin and state of public relations in the public sector. The characteristics of national and local government and health sector PR are examined and the future challenges of the sector are discussed.

CONTEXT AND ORIGINS OF PUBLIC SECTOR PR

Before considering the nature of public sector PR, it is worth identifying the organisational make-up of the sector. The Office for National Statistics (ONS) defines the public sector as comprising of central government, local government and public corporations. It comprises organisations that deliver one or more services to stakeholders and which are not primarily operated in a commercial manner.

The operations of central government include the work of bodies such as the National Health Service. It is usual for public sector services to be funded through a form of taxation or levy, although this is not always the case. Many local authorities operate leisure facilities or cultural services (such as theatres) that exist in direct competition with similar services in the private sector. According to ONS figures about 6 million people worked in the public sector in 2010 (ONS, 2010).

The public sector is a dynamic entity that constantly evolves in response to the political climate and the environment in which it operates. At the core of the sector are the directly-elected democratic bodies and the organisations that exist in response to their policy decisions. Nationally these are government departments, ministries and their executive agencies. Regionally these are devolved administrations in Scotland, Wales and Northern Ireland. More locally these are councils that exist at a range of spatial levels to serve communities. In many places there are often two or three tiers of local government, comprising county councils, district councils and parish councils.

Tho UK's largest employer is the National Health Service, which employs around 1.3 million people. While in practice the service comprises a range of differently constituted local or regional organisations, the past decade has seen as significant growth in the role of public relations in the National Health Service. The advancement of the engagement agenda has moved hand-in-hand with the growth of health service public relations. Legislation, which came into force in 2003, placed a duty on certain NHS organisations to involve and consult people about changes to services. The Local Government and Public Involvement in Health Act 2007 subsequently clarified and strengthened these duties. Delivering these duties has significantly increased the role of public relations within NHS organisations. However, in April 2011 the government began a consultation on rescinding much statutory guidance for the public sector. These proposals included removing the duty to consult local residents on significant policy and service changes.

The public sector includes the police, fire and ambulance emergency services and often a complex arrangement of partnerships designed to co-ordinate the work of different public sector bodies in delivering coherent public services to a geographic area or other audience.

The public sector also includes bodies known as quangos – an acronym for quasi-autonomous non-government organisations. Such bodies are set up by the government to deliver specific policy aims or services at arm's length from political control. Such bodies have grown significantly in number over the past 20 years although the Coalition Government is now reducing the number of quangos in existence. The public relations functions of quangos vary in size and scope with the larger organisations maintaining significant public relations operations to help them communicate with recipients of their services to and other stakeholders.

THEORETICAL CONSIDERATIONS

Since the early twentieth century, public relations has played an increasingly important role in the public sector. L'Etang (2004: 20) identifies the origins of the profession as arising from 'developments in local government, both in terms of the growth of public relations work and in terms of the professionalisation of civil servants'.

Nationally the Crombie Committee was set up in 1947 to establish terms of reference and to advise on the creation of a professional group of civil servants to provide the necessary links between government and the media. The Crombie Report set out the role of the information officer. There were four objectives:

- to create and maintain an informed opinion about the subjects with which each department deals
- to use all methods of publicity where suitable to help the department achieve its purpose
- to assist and advise in all matters bearing on relations between the department and its public
- to advise the department on the public's reaction to the policies or actions of the department.

The information officer envisaged by Crombie was not regarded as anything other than a press officer and there was no hint of the enormous range of responsibilities that now make up public sector PR.

Harvey (1995: 73) identifies six objectives for public relations in contemporary local government within the sector. These include a responsibility for 'corporate character and identity', as well as an extremely broad remit to keep customers informed about the activities of the organisation. He also identifies a specific role for responding to criticism of the organisation, identifying the balance of organisational communications, particularly in media relations, being responsive to a media agenda that is critical to the organisation. Harvey's observations are also relevant to the broader public sector, particularly those parts of the sector that are politically-led.

Harvey identifies an important internal role for communications. As the professional communicators within an organisation, comprising a myriad of professional, skilled and semi-skilled workers, it falls to the communicators to educate colleagues about the value of communicating with customer groups and the importance of being responsive to customer needs and opinions.

The first five roles identified by Harvey are relatively tactical in nature. They are primarily focused on supporting the organisation's activities with a communications response. His final objective articulates the strategic value of communications, which is becoming increasingly important and recognised among professional observers (Karian and Box, 2007).

These objectives reflect the breadth of challenges that exist in public sector communications. For them to be fulfilled successfully, modern day public relations practitioners working in the public sector typically use two broad types of proactive public relations campaigns: public information campaigns and public communications campaigns (Yeomans, 2006).

The distinction between these two types is that 'information' campaigns involve one-way (sender to receiver) communications, while 'communications' campaigns involve two-way communications (sender to receiver to sender). It could be argued that the growth of social media and citizen-led journalism is blurring the distinction envisaged by Yeomans.

Information campaigns, by virtue of their one-way nature, fit into Grunig and Hunt's (1984) public information model of public relations. This characterisation is reinforced by the requirement for accuracy in public sector communications, which is consistent with the importance of truth in the public information model.

Dozier *et al.* (2001) argue that public communications campaigns can be considered as examples of two-way asymmetric communication, where the sender's intention is to influence knowledge, opinions and actions of the target audiences. The increasing responsibilities of the public sector to engage with publics and stakeholders are likely to support increased two-way asymmetric communication and in some cases development of new two-way symmetric communications.

PRACTICAL ASPECTS

One of the distinguishing characteristics of public sector PR compared to other areas is the complex nature of the stakeholder landscape in which it operates. The political dimension does not exist in private sector public relations yet it is core to the business of public sector PR, whether directly in the case of central and local government or indirectly in the case of the broader sector.

Professionals working in public sector PR have to be constantly aware of the political context of the organisation's operations and decision making. The way a policy or service is perceived among the voting electorate is an important environmental factor that communicators must consider, yet that perception often arises from politically-led beliefs or emotions as well as more rational drivers such as quality of service or outcomes delivered.

The universal nature of many services provided – for example roads – leads to overlapping stakeholder groups. While all road users can be considered stakeholders for the Highways Agency (an executive agency of the Department for Transport) or a local authority's highways services, those users will also be members of other stakeholder groups.

In many areas the combined public sector dominates the employment market. For example, the public sector is proportionately larger in the North East than in other areas – here the sector employs 287,000 people, representing just over one quarter (25.7 per cent) of employment in the North East, 4.5 percentage points larger than the UK proportion (21.2 per cent) (Hunt, 2010). In such areas one stakeholder group – service users – overlaps heavily with another – employees. This leads to a complex environment in which public relations must deliver targeted and relevant messages effectively as part of its work. The size of the public sector in such areas can also have an impact on public relations in the private sector as there will be more public sector contracts available for public relations services in these areas.

In the local public sector conflicting communication goals can easily arise, especially if local public sector organisations such councils and the police are not working effectively together. Without well-planned partnership working a local police force may be striving to promote its work and contribution to a local community through publicising its work dealing with crime and anti-social behaviour, while a local council may be trying to improve the reputation of a local area. While the two goals need not be mutually exclusive, they can easily leading to conflicting messages for stakeholders and ineffective public relations.

CENTRAL GOVERNMENT

Central government is made up of ministerial departments, non-ministerial departments and a number of executive agencies. Most departments and agencies have their own teams responsible for public relations. These departments are staffed by civil servants who are politically neutral and implement the policies of the elected government. Ministers are also able to appoint a number of special advisers who do not need to be politically neutral. Their responsibilities can include advising on public relations issues.

The most established centre for public relations within central government is the Central Office for Information (COI). Originally set up in 1946 from the production division of the Ministry of Information, including its regional organisation and film unit, COI was set up to provide services for all government departments at home and overseas (COI, 2011). It reports to the minister for the Cabinet Office, who determines policy and the financial framework, approves business plans and sets performance targets.

In 1990, COI Communications was established as an Executive Agency and has developed into the government's specialist agency for buying publicity and marketing services on behalf of government departments and agencies. By using its aggregated buying power, COI Communications can get the best price for the publicity materials needed by these clients. COI staff also advise client departments on selecting creative options and improving and evaluating campaign effectiveness.

In April 2002, the COI further expanded its role. The chief executive became the government's chief adviser on marketing, communications and information campaigns, reporting directly to the Director of Communications and Strategy at 10 Downing Street. In addition, the Regional News Network and Distribution Service transferred to the Government Information and Communication Service in the Cabinet Office and the COI was tasked with conducting more departmental research into understanding hard-to-reach audiences, such as the socially excluded. The COI inclusivity unit investigates how to reach BAME groups, small- to medium-sized enterprises (SMEs) and other hard-to-reach groups such as youth and older people. The COI also manages mass media campaigns on behalf of the government and in 2009/10 spent £193 million on advertising (COI, 2010b). Mass media advertising has the advantage of reaching a wide audience, but needs to be supplemented by other methods to explain issues.

The COI was also responsible for developing the government's expertise in social marketing. This discipline has grown in prominence as a branch of marketing that is focused on delivering public good from marketing rather than the commercial benefits that sit behind much conventional marketing theory.

One of the key facets of social marketing theory is the application of social psychological theory and behavioural economics to delivering change in people's behaviours – understanding the thought processes people go through that lead to changes in behaviour for personal or public good.

The principles of social marketing are consistent with underpinning notions of public relations. Bernays (1928: 32) identified a role of public relations as 'engineering public consent and organising the habits of the masses in order to create social order'. While his terminology may not sit comfortably with current language, his meaning is entirely compatible with the concept of social marketing.

An example of a campaign that emerged from social marketing thinking is the nationwide Change4Life initiative. It aims to prevent people from becoming overweight by encouraging them to eat better and move more. It uses a variety of approaches including marketing and public relations to achieve this.

However, since the 2010 general election and the subsequent creation of the Coalition Government, expenditure on public relations and marketing has been reduced. A freeze was placed on all non-essential marketing and public relations expenditure by all government departments. This has led to the COI reducing its staffing levels and the services it provides (COI, 2010a). This trend is also common across the central government public sector where the number of people employed in public relations has been decreasing in response to the need to reduce public sector expenditure generally.

LOCAL GOVERNMENT

Local government in the UK is a complex structure of authorities responsible for different types of services. In many large cities all local government services are provided by borough councils (London) or metropolitan councils (other large cities outside London). Outside these areas there are unitary authorities that provide all local government services to a given area, while in other areas there are a further two tiers of councils that work together to provide services. These are county councils and district councils.

The Local Government Acts of 1986 and 1988 form the basis of the legal constraints placed on public relations for local authorities. These and the subsequent legislation mentioned below were introduced by the Thatcher government, which sought to limit the powers of local government. The 1986 Act prohibits local authorities from issuing political publicity. A separate account of expenditure on publicity must be kept, and publicity is defined as 'any communication, in whatever form, addressed to the public at large or to a section of the public'. The 1988 Act set out the factors to be taken into account in deciding whether any publicity material is considered to affect public support for a political party. In December 1987, the Local Authorities (Publicity Account) (Exemption) Order was passed, setting out what items could be excluded from the account. The original definition of publicity was so broad it could have been taken to cover any correspondence or message, so making the account meaningless.

In 1988, the Code of Recommended Practice on Local Authority Publicity was published, covering content, style, subject matter, costs, dissemination, advertising, recruitment, publicity about individual members of an authority, timing and assisting others in providing publicity. The code urges a responsible approach, and that content must be relevant to the functions of the local authority. Cost-effectiveness is emphasised. The need for local authorities to publicise and explain their policies and decisions is recognised, but a warning is given about the use of public funds to persuade the public to hold a particular view on a question of policy. 'Objective, balanced, informative and accurate' are the key words. The careful targeting of information is recommended, but at the same time information should be made available to all those who want or need it.

One of the challenges of implementing the code has been the lack of guidance relating to the internet. The provisions of the code were stipulated before the widespread adoption of the internet as a communications channel and local government public relations officers have had to interpret the code's applicability to internet communications themselves.

In October 2010 the Department for Communities and Local Government launched a consultation about major revisions to the 1988 publicity code (DCLG, 2010). Following the consulation the new code came into force in April 2011. The revised code sets out seven principles that local government public relations must comply with. These set out that public relations should be lawful, cost-effective, objective, even-handed, appropriate, have regard to equality and diversity and be issued with care during periods of heightened sensitivity.

There are no restrictions on publicising comments made by council officers, but publicity about individual members of the authority is currently limited to those who represent the council as a whole, such as the mayor or the leader of the council or a particular committee. The proposed new publicity permits council PR to promote the work of any elected member, regardless of whether they hold a position of authority within the council.

Publicity that deals with controversial issues cannot be issued between the notice of an election and polling day – this time is known colloquially as the purdah period. During this period the activities of local government PR practitioners are curtailed and an enhanced awareness of the potential political sensitivies of PR is required. However the purdah period does not prevent PR that supports the day-to-day operation of a council, such as communications in an emergency situation or about the operation of a specific council service.

The Local Government Officers (Political Restrictions) Regulations 1990 set out a salary level above which staff become politically restricted. Officers would have to resign from their jobs before announcing an intention to stand for election as an MP, MEP or local councillor. There is no other sector of public relations that finds itself with such a range of rules within which it must operate. Any local resident can challenge local authorities and their public relations officers in the courts or through the district auditor (Fedorcio *et al.*, 1991).

One of the most controversial issues concerning local government public relations recently has been local government publications – typically newspaper or magazine-format printed communications produced by councils. These publications are typically delivered to residents' homes or available to pick up for free from locations such as libraries, leisure centres and garages. Publishing such a magazine has been one of the recommendations of the LGA Reputation campaign since 2005 (LGA, 2005).

In 2009 LGCommunications published research looking at local authority publications (LGCommunications, 2009). It showed that 94 per cent of councils produce either a council magazine or newspaper (66 per cent produce a magazine, 28 per cent a newspaper). Almost two thirds of publications carried advertising for council-run services or for private sector companies.

The research also looked at nationally available research into resident satisfaction with their councils and identified trends for councils publishing their own newspapers or magazines. It showed that the longer a council has had a publication the better informed and satisfied their residents are. The results also suggested that shorter, less frequent publications have more impact for most councils. The optimum frequency of publication appeared to be no more than one publication every quarter.

The Newspaper Society, a trade body for local media, has campaigned for restrictions on local government publications since early 2008 (Newspaper Society, 2008). It claims that local government newspapers and magazines represent unfair competition to local commercial media through competing for advertising expenditure against commercial rivals. The society has also raised concerns about the lack of transparency of expenditure and performance of local government newspapers and magazines. It has consistently called for restrictions on such publications to protect local commercial media.

Following early representations on the issue, the government's Digital Britain report, published in summer 2009, noted 'the adverse impact on local newspapers of the increasing role of local authorities in taking paid advertising to support local authority information sheets' (BIS, 2009). The Audit Commission was subsequently asked to investigate local government publications and published its findings in January 2010 in a letter from Chief Executive Steve Bundred (Bundred, 2010).

While noting that its remit to examine the issues raised more broadly by critics of council publications, the commission produced seven conclusions from its research:

- Over 90 per cent of councils produce a regular publication, but almost of all these are published once a month or less often.

- 47 per cent of council publications contain private sector advertising of some sort.

- Only 5 per cent of council publications contain statutory notices and 6 per cent contain recruitment advertising – reflecting the frequency of most publications being impractical for the timely publication of such notices and adverts.

- Around one third of one per cent of council spending (£257 million) in 2008/9 was recorded as being on communication with the public, although the commission recognised the limitations of this methodology as much expenditure is not coded accurately or consistently between different councils.

- Claims about value achieved by communication spending are not well supported by evidence.

- Councils should review their editorial policy to ensure that it is politically neutral and publicly defensible. The political neutrality should be inherent in council publications to ensure they comply with the publicity code, but the editorial policies of council publications are more flexible and dependent on local circumstances.

- The current framework for accountability provides adequate safeguards against misuse of public money for political ends – reflecting the strength and effectiveness of the existing provisions of the publicity code in preventing politicians from unduly influencing the content of council publications for political means.

In the consultation on the local government publicity code, it was proposed that councils would be limited to producing a newspaper or magazine a maximum of four times each year. According to the Audit Commission's research this would mean around a quarter of councils would need to reduce how often they publish their magazines. They claim this would reduce their ability to communicate effectively with the residents they provide services for and would increase the cost of their communications as they would be forced to use more expensive ways of reaching residents.

The Local Government Association (LGA), which represents the interests of councils, has argued that council publications provide information about councils, their services and the democratic process (LGA, 2009). This information used to be provided by local newspapers, but as circulations decline and newspapers no longer send journalists to council meeting to report on proceedings regularly, the amount of coverage of council issues has reduced. Councils argue that their own publications are replacing this coverage, although their critics suggest that such coverage is not objective and does not replace the role of the media in scrutinising the democratic process.

THE REPUTATION CHALLENGE

The consistent challenge for local government public relations has been managing council reputations and increasing satisfaction rates in line with the increasing performance of services. In 2005 the LGA undertook research that showed perceptions remained where they were 10 years ago (LGA/MORI, 2005). Most respondents thought that councils were low profile, remote and bureaucratic. Only 1 per cent would talk favourably about their councils unprompted, while 22 per cent would be critical if asked; another 8 per cent would be critical without being asked. Only 5 per cent thought they knew a great deal about what their councils did.

While there was no substitute for excellent service delivery, the research also found that good communication had a greater effect on a council's reputation than issues such as council taxes. Twelve core actions in the two areas of environmental issues and communications were found to have the most effect on reputation. These were:

Environment

- Adopt a highly visible, strongly branded, cleaning operation.
- Ensure there are no gaps in council cleaning and maintenance.
- Set up one phone number for the public to report environmental problems.
- Deal with grot spots.
- Remove abandoned vehicles within 24 hours.
- Win a Green Flag for at least one park.
- Educate the public to improve the environment.

Communications

- Manage media relations.
- Provide an A–Z guide to council services.
- Publish a regular magazine to inform residents.
- Ensure the council brand is clearly linked to services.
- Communicate with staff so they become advocates.

This research was based on statistical analysis of local government performance and reputation measures and represented a significant advance in the use of empirical analysis to demonstrate the value of effective public relations in local government.

In 2010 the local government communicators' group LGCommunications published an updated version of the LGA's 2005 research. *The New Reputation Guide* uses data from the 2008/09 national Place Survey – a mandatory piece of research undertaken by all councils – to analyse the reputations of councils and how they had been affected by public relations activities (LGCommunications, 2010).

The guide recognised once again that while improvements continued to be made in service performance, satisfaction with public sector organisations was at stubbornly low levels. In response to this the authors outline five 'rules of reputation' that public relations in local government should focus on to achieve measurable improvements in council reputations:

- *Proving that the council provides value for money* – as this is the strongest factor that influences satisfaction with council services.

- *Always inform and engage residents and staff* – this recognises that many members of the public do not understand the full range of services that are provided by councils and also the importance of an engaged and informed workforce in reputation management.

- *Build trust and confidence in what councils do* – this is particularly important against the backdrop of declining trust in public bodies and politicians more generally. The guide advises councils to demonstrate links between residents' wishes and council actions to help increase trust in councils.

- *Improve key services and show you are doing so* – this recognises the importance to a council's reputation of a small number of services that councils deliver – such as waste collection, street cleaning and parks. By improving these services in particular and communicating this, councils can significantly improve their overall reputation.

- *Focus on changing lives for the better* – this recognises the role of councils as community leaders, particularly in a time of significant change in public services. Councils should take a lead role in establishing effective working relationships between public and voluntary sector organisations in their areas to deliver improvements for their residents.

The scope of these recommendations recognises that the remit of public relations within local government has expanded significantly from the traditional practice of media relations that has dominated local government public relations until recent years. This shift demands a new mix of skills and experience from the public relations practitioner working within this sector.

PR IN THE NHS

Kuteev-Moreira and Eglin (2004) provide a thorough account of the considerations that corporate communicators in the health sector need to take into account. They refer to Ansoff and McDonnell's two communication strategies: consensus building and building implementation. Both necessitate consulting stakeholders and informing them about the progress of change. They suggest that corporate communications is central for successful implementation of change in European healthcare systems. The diversity of internal audiences, from senior managers, clinical team members, physicians, and service staff to volunteers, is matched by that of external stakeholders. The latter may include patients and primary service users; organisations representing patients and service users; non-care customers who rent space, such as florists; contractors; health authorities; regulators who evaluate the service; partners such as primary care organisations and diagnostic services; suppliers; and competitors. Reputation plays a fundamental role in assisting or damaging staff recruitment.

The media is a central stakeholder here also, interested and aware of critical events. The main stories covered are problems: management failures, clinical errors, professional corporate conflicts, staff shortages and hospital-originated pollution such as incinerator combustion. Corporate communication is carried out in an environment of constant scrutiny, where service provision is balanced with resource scarcity.

Kirdira (2008) considered the role of public relations in creating brand reputations for health services. He argues that hospitals use public relations activities to achieve competitive differentiation, to engage with stakeholders and to create a strong hospital brand and culture. He also notes the importance of public relations in achieving recommendations for new patients from those that have already been treated by the hospital. This role for public relations has increased as successive policies have increased the role of patient choice in the NHS – in an environment where the patient is able to choose where they are treated, the reputation of the healthcare provider and the effectiveness of its public relations will be very important in the financial viability of the hospital or service provider.

The size and complexity of the NHS and the institutions that make it up presents a challenge for public relations. Tony Ellis, Head of Communications at Southport & Ormskirk Hospital NHS Trust describes how a national issue can affect public relations at a local level:

> People's own rating of the local NHS services they have used is generally very high. The perception of the NHS as a national organisation, while still good, is not as high. That means communications needs to emphasise the local experience – particularly if a national issue causes local concerns. For example, infection control has always been a high priority at Southport and Ormskirk – we never had an MRSA problem in the way some trusts did. However, patients

still came here concerned about the issue even though our infection rates were low compared to others.

(Finnegan, 2010)

Like many areas of the public sector, the NHS is expected to undergo radical transformation in the next four years. The 2010 health white paper, *Liberating the NHS*, removes a number of NHS institutions involved in the planning and commissioning of health care and proposes new consortia of general practitioners working together to commission services (DoH, 2010). This will place a requirement on NHS public relations to engage a wider range of general practitioners as well as effectively communicate any changes to services to the public.

FUTURE CHALLENGES

While the past 15 years have been a period of growth for public relations in the public sector, the profession is entering a more challenging period. The need to reduce the public sector budget deficit means that all parts of the sector are being forced to scrutinise their activities and scale back or cease many things they do. Politicians in all tiers of government have committed to protecting frontline services as much as possible from the impact of spending cuts. The public is unlikely to consider public relations a frontline service compared to, for example, nurses, police or rubbish collections. This means that the public relations profession must improve its ability to empirically identify what it contributes towards delivery of a particular public service.

Public relations within the sector cannot expect to be unaffected by reductions in spending. The challenge of the public sector budget deficit is too great for that. However, without being able to demonstrate the value of public relations in outcomes that contribute directly to the delivery of public service, the profession may be vulnerable to more extreme cuts than otherwise would have happened.

While effective and meaningful evaluation of public relations is more important than ever, the public sector budget challenge means that innovative models for delivery of public relations are being implemented. For example, Westminster City Council undertakes public relations on a consultancy basis for other councils and directly manages the public relations functions of a number of other councils on a long-term basis. Other councils, for example Peterborough City Council, have merged their in-house public relations teams with those of other public sector bodies in their local area such as the NHS. This trend is likely to accelerate as it offers councils the opportunity to exploit economies of scale, share expertise and reduce their own spending on public relations.

Within the Civil Service public relations structures are under review. The role of the COI is changing and in-house teams within government departments are striving to become more efficient and identify new ways of working to meet the budget challenge. Wherever public relations practitioners work within the sector, they need to show creativity and innovation in their approach to public relations to ensure the profession continues to thrive within the streamlined public sector.

The Coalition Government is also committed to increasing transparency in the way the public sector makes decisions and spends money. The Minister for the Cabinet Office Francis Maude said,

> It is our ambition to make the UK the most transparent and accountable government in the world. I want the public to hold us to account for what we do and by publishing this data today, taxpayers will be able to see exactly how we spend their money.
>
> (Maude, 2010)

Much data has already been published online so that anyone can see where central and local government spends money and on what. However, critics of this approach have argued that without context and explanation this information can be misleading and easily or maliciously misinterpreted. It is important that public relations practitioners in the public sector understand this significant shift and what it means for managing organisational reputation.

However, the nature of change is not purely internal to the sector. The rapid adoption of social media presents some unique challenges for public relations in the sector. Direct communication between public sector organisations and those they service is more important than ever before because of the network effect of citizens connected via social media. While remaining important, the traditional focus on media relations is less important than before for reputation management.

The growth of social media also challenges those working in public relations to clearly identify their role in managing social media use within the organisation. Social media does not fit comfortably within the remit of a single team or department within a public sector organisation, yet it is becoming an important driver of reputation and source of information for citizens. Because of this, public relations practitioners within the sector must gain the skills and knowledge to be able to advise about the use of social media and develop policies that allow the public sector to use and engage with citizens using social media while safeguarding corporate reputation and meeting the standards expected of the sector.

NORTHAMPTONSHIRE COUNTY COUNCIL – YOU CHOOSE CAMPAIGN

Like all councils, Northamptonshire County Council expected to have to make changes to services as a result in the reductions in public sector spending. However, the council's own research showed a large majority of its residents had little sense of impending cuts and believed that if they continued to pay council tax then services would not suffer.

The council recognised that it needed to actively gauge the priorities of its customers to help inform the decision-making process about budget cuts and to prepare residents for significant changes in how services are delivered in Northamptonshire. It also wanted to enhance its reputation through positioning the council as a 'trusted advocate' that listens to its customers.

Objectives

*   To raise awareness of the likely £100 million budget reduction that the council expected by 2012 and record the opinion of at least 1,000 residents with a particular focus on those who usually choose to not engage with the council.
*   To rate which services provided by the county council are most important to residents, and should be prioritised when managing budget reductions.

Strategy and tactics

The campaign began in December 2009 with market research activity to help inform the direction and targeting for the overall campaign. The project team undertook interviews with key community stakeholders and ran three focus groups with residents. These activities gave the team a good insight into the general themes about which engagement activities would be most effective.

The team also recognised the importance of involving council staff in the campaign as well as senior officers and politicians. Four half-day interactive events were run for community and voluntary groups, council staff and young people. Sessions were held with Northamptonshire County Council cabinet members and directors to agree the objectives for the campaign and outcomes it sought to achieve. This was an important way of securing buy-in to such a high-profile campaign on a politically sensitive subject.

One-to-one briefings with key journalists were also arranged to help local media understand the campaign objectives and secure future opportunities for media coverage.

To help select the most appropriate ways of engaging different audiences within the Northamptonshire community, the team used a value-based segmentation model. This used empirical evidence to predict the effectiveness of different engagement methods with different demographic segments. The methods employed and targeted in this way ranged from a simple one-word answer to a long and detailed one-to-one conversation.

C@SE STUDY

This model was an important way of ensuring that the tactics selected would be most likely to deliver the desired objectives for the campaign.

The campaign was launched at a media event where the 'Northamptonshire Superhero' was unveiled. This provided a media story that helped the team gain coverage for the campaign website and face-to-face roadshows that followed.

A dedicated website was created for the campaign. This site was designed to enable visitors to participate in conversations about council services. Residents could respond to questions posted, add their own suggestions as well as commenting on and endorsing other people's suggestions. Detailed background information was provided and a campaign blog was set up. The site was linked to popular social media websites to extend its reach.

Nine regional face-to-face roadshows were held in high footfall locations such as shopping centres. At these events residents could speak directly with cabinet members and directors. The roadshows launched with a fruit and veg market stall manned by the Leader 'selling' public services in a tangible way – for example, the cost of running the library service was around £1 per person per year – this was represented by a bunch of bananas that costs around the same amount. This use of analogies was important in breaking down large sums of money into more easily understood amounts that they could relate to.

A video diary room was set up at each roadshow to provide an alternative way for residents to submit their feedback. This recognised that some of the target audience were more comfortable providing verbal feedback than written responses. A large graffiti wall was used for people to write their feedback on. Mobile advertising vans were used in the local area on the day of the roadshows to raise awareness and the team targeted their pro-active media relations work at local publications in the areas where roadshows were being held.

Comment cards were made available through the council's information points and offices as well as being handed out at the roadshow events and printed in the council's publication that was delivered to every residential property in the county.

The team also ran presentations at a number of community groups such as churches and local organisations to raise awareness of the campaign among harder to reach audiences. Community toolkits were developed to help local groups hold their own debates about the campaign topics and then feed back the results to the council.

Throughout the campaign the team worked to secure coverage in local and national media. Week-long features were placed in local publications and

C@SE STUDY

programmes, focusing on a different council service each day. The team also secured national media coverage by linking the campaign messages with themes from the national news agenda such as a nationwide BBC survey of council budget cuts.

Local artist Daxa Parmar was commissioned to create a montage forming a superhero with local landmarks, using 500 photos of local faces. This was intended to represent the combined power of residents working together. This photo collection formed the basis of all campaign artwork. By doing this the team added a personal dimension to the campaign materials and increased engagement as participants liked to identify photos of people they knew.

Evaluation

The campaign gained significant media coverage. The council's analysis showed that residents had 95,000,000 opportunities to see and hear this campaign. This equates to 125 opportunities per county resident. Coverage was secured in a range of local and national media including *BBC Panorama*, *BBC News 24*, *Daily Star*, *Metro*, *ITV Anglia Tonight* and *BBC Radio 5 Live*.

The campaign website had 5,939 visits with an average time on the site of six minutes. This length of time reflected a strong level of engagement with the site content. The offline campaign activities demonstrated significant reach and engagement with 20 community toolkits completed and returned, more than 1,000 comment cards received and more than 150 comments on the graffiti wall.

The council's reputation was also improved by the campaign. Satisfaction levels increased across all communications related categories in the council's quarterly survey. In particular, more people felt they could get involved in local decision making (+13.2 per cent) and residents felt better informed about local public services (+7.1 per cent).

The campaign was recognised by other councils as good practice and the team ran an event in July 2010 to share their experiences. This was endorsed by trade publication *Local Government Chronicle*. The team has also made the campaign tactics and creative available for sale to other councils that wish to run similar campaigns in their area. This demonstrates the potential for more cost-effective PR in local government through sharing and reusing successful campaigns across different areas.

The team behind the You Choose campaign won the Communications Team of the Year at the CIPR Local Public Services Group 2010 awards. The You Choose campaign was also highly commended in the Campaign of the Year category at the same awards.

With thanks to Northamptonshire County Council

C@SE STUDY

Most important services

Below are our most important services, judged by times mentioned through customer engagements.

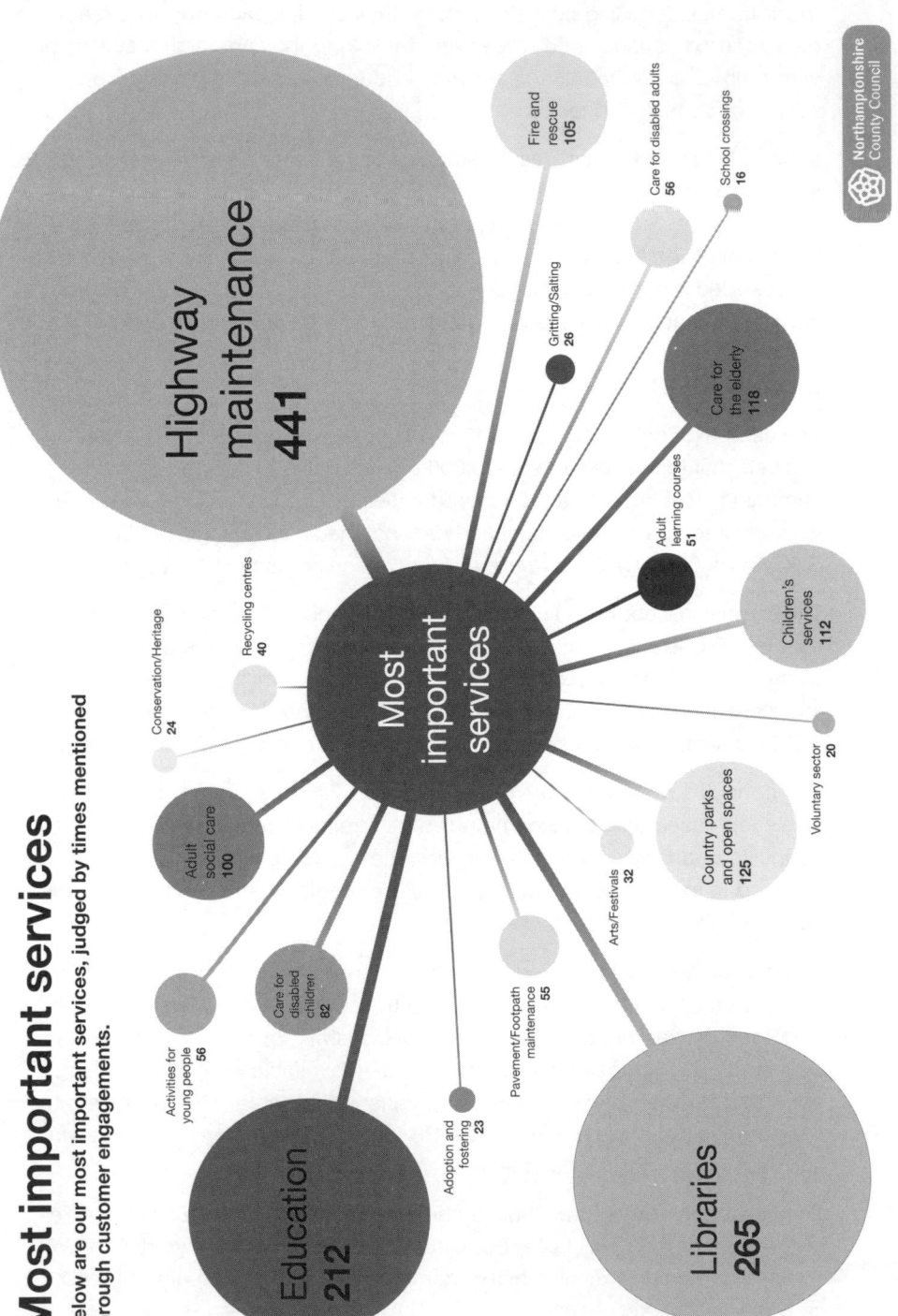

FIGURE 15.1 Northampton County Council You Choose – Diagram summarising campaign feedback

FIGURE 15.2 Residents speaking to council representative at Brackley roadshow, March 2010

ACTIVE STOCKPORT

Obesity currently costs the economy around £16 billion. This includes costs to the NHS, days off sick and incapacity benefit. In Stockport this rising cost is estimated at £76 million. Stockport Council became concerned that they were sitting on a demographic time bomb as the current generation could be the first to die younger than its parents. The council was also concerned about the impact that obesity would have on the local economy and the need for additional public sector spending on health and social care.

A recent Citizen's Panel Survey of 1,000 people showed more than 20 per cent of residents said that lack of time and constraints were a factor in them exercising and eating healthily.

Objectives

- To promote council-owned facilities such as parks and leisure centres as helping people lead healthier lives in Stockport.
- To raise awareness of health benefits of being more active.
- To reduce the perceived barrier of lack of time by promoting that just five sessions of 30 minutes of exercise per week is needed to keep adults healthy, with an hour a day recommended for children.

Strategy and tactics

The council set up a range of different communications methods, ranging from traditional forms of media to social media to target a range of target audiences:

- Young people in Stockport (52,900 young people aged 0–15).
- Adults in Stockport, including parents (228,100 people aged 16+).
- People in a number of specific disadvantaged groups in Stockport. (approximately 16,000 people).
- 6,000 employees of Stockport Council (77 per cent of whom live in Stockport).

The project targeted adults using traditional media relations techniques. Interviews were organised with TV channels Channel M and BBC Northwest Today, as well as on local radio stations BBC Radio Manchester, Imagine FM and Pure FM. Data on radio audiences showed that 43 per cent of Imagine FM listeners are aged between 25 and 44, while Pure FM targets listeners in the 25 to 55 age group.

C@SE STUDY

Local newspapers were targeted and close working relationships were built with reporters. This resulted in strong articles in local publications. These articles often included key messages, creative photographs and a call to action. The campaign's key messages were identified as:

- There are hundreds of ways to get active in Stockport.
- Get involved by walking to work and cycling to school.
- It's easy to fit in 5 x 30 minutes of exercise per week.

The Active Stockport Facebook page was set up to help the campaign reach younger audiences. This launched in January 2010 and included a number of free and low-cost ways people in Stockport could get active. Data showed that more than half of the page's fans were aged 13–17. The page is used extensively to promote events and engage residents in two-way communication.

The council's newspaper, which is delivered to every household in Stockport, was also used to reach adults, with a focus on the disadvantaged groups for whom other techniques were less effective.

Throughout the campaign the council partnered with local sports celebrities. These included Paul Gerrard from Stockport County, cycling Olympic medallist Jamie Staff and Olympic swimming medallists for swimming, Kerri Anne Payne and Cassie Patten. The use of relevant celebrities helped secure coverage for the campaign and add weight to the campaign's messages through endorsement.

The campaign also launched children's bike and scoot week and linked with national campaigns such as Walk to Work Week and Walk to School Month to highlight low cost and easy ways to get active. A range of integrated communication techniques was used. These included bus advertising panels, flyers and merchandise including jute bags. These were sent to schools, disadvantaged groups within Stockport and handed out to adults at events.

Recognising the value of communicating to young people through schools, the campaign launched a Key Stage 1 and 2 Resource Pack to promote sustainable ways to travel to school. To measure the success of these activities, two competitions were run, a slogan competition for Key Stage 1 and a design a cycling jersey for Key Stage 2. A 'cyber bike' was also taken to events at colleges to promote cycling.

To engage with the council's internal target audience, a Senior Council Officer cycled to work for a week and wrote a diary. Two employees documented their experiences taking different modes of transport to work

C@SE STUDY

each day for a week, highlighting the health benefits and difference in stress levels. Both diaries were included in the council's internal newsletter, which is sent out to 2,500 council employees and included on the council intranet. Information was included in elected members' briefings, intranet pages and staff newsletters.

Evaluation

The campaign's objectives were surpassed, generating significant interest externally and internally. Media coverage was positive and there were more than 2,500 visitors to the website during the campaign.

Specifically the campaign exceeded its objectives in engaging residents, employees and local businesses with walking and cycling. Highlights included:

- Children walking to school rose by 10 per cent since 2008.
- Half of primary schools took part in bike and scoot week and 3,000 children cycled or scooted to school.
- More than 60 schools in Stockport signed up to Walk to School month.
- More than 20 schools used Active Stockport workbooks during lessons and over 300 children entered the competition.
- Questionnaire results showed that 25 per cent of respondents confirmed they took part in Walk to Work Week and 70 per cent were aware of Active Stockport.
- Awareness of the recommendation to take part in at least five sessions of 30 minutes of physical activity per week rose from 78 per cent in 2008 to 96 per cent in 2009.
- Those claiming they made changes in their life to allow for at least five sessions of 30 minutes of physical activity per week increased by 11 per cent.
- Half of the colleges within Stockport took part in Bike Week.
- Eight major local employers requested Walk to Work Week bags and Active Stockport literature, including Stockport PCT and PZ Cussons.
- Coverage including 23 positive media articles including regular stories in the *Stockport Times* and broadcast coverage on *North West Tonight*.
- 60 per cent of press coverage contained at least two key messages.

The Active Stockport campaign won the Campaign of the Year award at the CIPR Local Public Services Group 2010 awards.

With thanks to Stockport Metropolitan Borough Council

C@SE STUDY

QUESTIONS FOR DISCUSSION

1 What are the challenges of working in public relations in the public sector?

2 What are the differences between the types of public relations used in local government compared to police services?

3 Should councils be allowed to publish their own magazines or newspapers? Do they represent unfair competition to local commercial media or are they fulfilling an unmet need for information about what councils do?

4 What skills are important for a public relations practitioner in local government today compared to those that would have been important ten years ago?

5 Read your local newspaper and note the stories about your local council. What could be done to improve the number of positive stories about the council in the local media?

6 How is social media affecting the model of public relations undertaken by the public sector?

7 What does the government's drive for public sector transparency mean for the practice of public relations within the sector? Will it make public relations simpler or more difficult?

8 In the age of financial austerity in the public sector should local councils have public relations departments at all?

9 What does the drive to increase patient choice in the provision of healthcare mean for public relations in the health sector?

10 One of the reasons corporate reputation is important in the private sector is to differentiate a company from its competition. Why is corporate reputation important in the public sector when often there is no competition among providers?

FURTHER READING

Hastings, G. (2007) *Social marketing: why should the devil have all the best tunes?*, Butterworth-Heinemann.

Kotler, P. and Lee, N.R. (2006) 'Marketing in the public sector: a roadmap for improved performance', Prentice Hall.

CHAPTER 16

Consumer public relations

Susan Hutchinson

CHAPTER AIMS

The primary goal of consumer public relations is to help build relationships between an organisation and existing or potential consumers. The emergence of new technologies, new media and new influencers presents significant implications for all marketing disciplines. The purpose of this chapter is to investigate the evolving role of consumer PR and the interplay between consumer marketing activities, such as advertising, within the twenty-first century.

WHAT IS CONSUMER PR?

Consumer PR forges meaningful connections with consumers to help stimulate the sale of goods or services. Willis (2009: 410) states that its role is 'often more subtle and sophisticated than more direct forms of communication'. He goes on to describe consumer PR as a facilitator for attitudinal and behavioural change, which in turn can enhance the sales environment and help to drive purchase. Each critical intervention point within the consumer decision journey provides opportunities to interact with the consumer, build relationships and converse meaningfully with them. The power of PR to capitalise on opportunities these is arguably greater than ever.

PR AND THE MARKETING MIX

As C. Murphy (2005) points out, PR has traditionally been regarded as inferior in the marketing mix – popularly known as the 4Ps: product, price, place and promotion (Kotler, 2003). Price can indicate good or bad value for money; in some cases, a high price signals quality or prestige. Place means the channel of distribution and the kind of outlet where the product can be obtained – a product will be viewed differently if it is sold on a market stall rather than a high street department store. Promotion refers to the media and messages used to influence buyer decisions. It is here that PR contributes the most, ideally working in tandem with other marketing activities such as advertising, sales promotion and direct mail to achieve maximum impact.

The unprecedented expansion of consumer choice and media channels has had a profound effect. In 2009 (Court *et al.*), McKinsey published research on the buyer decisions of 20,000 consumers across five industries and three continents. The research showed that 'the proliferation of media and products requires marketers to find new ways to get their brands included in the initial-consideration set that consumers develop as they begin their decision journey'. They also found that 'because of the shift away from one-way communication – from marketers to consumers – toward a two-way conversation, marketers need a more systematic way to satisfy customer demands and manage word-of-mouth'.

This is increasingly echoed by today's marketing leaders. As Irwin Lee (2010) Vice President UK and Ireland, Procter & Gamble, states:

> We need to look at how we innovate for the consumer, how we connect today and tomorrow. We live in a multi-tasking, multi-sensorial, multimedia world so the question for the future of consumer connections isn't how we shift from traditional to new media, but how do we maximise multi touch points.

According to Willis (2009: 412), when it comes to adapting to this new consumer environment, PR's capacity to influence, persuade and explain gives it a distinct advantage over other marketing disciplines. This shift is reflected in PR's increasingly influential role within the marketing process, with spend often diverted from advertising, direct mail and other activities. In 2009, UK PR agency income increased 0.75 per cent (*PR Week*, 2010), despite the challenging economic environment. Davis (2004) suggests that PR is a more cost-effective alternative to advertising. Advertising alone is not persuasive enough. Smith (2008: 13) highlights the emerging recognition of the impact of PR and the effect on other marketing communication activities, quoting a marketing executive: 'If you advertise in a time when you're getting bad PR, it doesn't work. Conversely, if you advertise in a time of really good PR, there's a leveraging effect – it actually has more impact than it would, all things being equal.'

Moloney (2006) agrees that PR and marketing together are better able to handle promotions across a variety of channels such as media relations, events, sponsorship, exhibitions, road-shows and web-based materials.

INTEGRATED MARKETING COMMUNICATIONS (IMC)

The concept of IMC has become a key element of the marketing and brand communications of many organisations. The approach first emerged in the 1980s, and as Gurău (2008: 170) reflects, 'a series of articles written between 1991 and 1996 have outlined the specific dimensions of the IMC concept, presenting it as a logical answer to the problems by many businesses and non-profit organisations.' Since then, the concept of IMC has attracted much debate, with many, and often contradictory, definitions.

The development of an integrated approach across the four 4Ps in a campaign is, according to Schultz (1996) meant to address the fact that integration happens at the consumer level – consumers aggregate all communications messages from a company (whether advertising, PR, direct mail, sponsorship, or sales promotion) in making a decision to interact with the brand. Consequently, this necessitates the strategic synchronisation of all communication activities at a corporate level into a 'single persona and voice' (Hallahan in Smith, 2008: 4).

Kitchen and de Pelsmacker (2004: 18) argue that the emergence and growth of IMC is rooted in the following factors:

1 Movement of marketing budget below the line away from mass media advertising
2 Media explosion and accompanying fragmentation
3 Market demassification and splintering
4 Greater segmentation and emergence of niche and unitary markets
5 A revolution in information technology that is still sweeping the world
6 More development, easier access to and usage of huge consumer databases that effectively underpin marketing communications of all types
7 The importance of retaining customer loyalty via relationship marketing
8 The importance of building and increasing a brand's image based on equity
9 Generally, the brand was recognised as the primary driver of corporate success
10 Development and diffusion of digital technology
11 Spread of multinationalism and globalism, supported by economic and political means.

Pickton and Broderick in Gurău (2008: 171) maintain that marketing activities that were traditionally separated into either 'above the line' or 'below the line' should now be integrated under the IMC concept. Marketing communications are 'strategic-ally driven by the most relevant function' (Duncan, 1993: 18) and companies must 'lead with the marketing communication function that most effectively addresses your number one problem and use a marketing communications mix that utilises the strengths of various communications functions that relate to your brand's particular situation'.

The focus of this definition is on tactical implementation as opposed to building relationships with a range of stakeholders beyond the target consumer. Other definitions widen the scope of IMC to include communications with a much broader range of audiences and emphasise the importance of strategic coordination, where effective planning, targeting and positioning underpin consistency of message and complementary use of media. A good example is the definition offered by Schultz and Kitchen (2000: 65): 'IMC is the strategic business process used to plan, develop, execute and evaluate co-ordinated measurable, persuasive brand communication programs over time with consumers, customers, prospects and other targeted, relevant external and internal audiences.'

As quoted by Gurău (2008: 171), Duncan (1992: 8) provides a more 'conceptual perception' of IMC: 'A cross-functional process for creating and nourishing profitable relationships with customers and other stakeholders by strategically controlling or influencing all messages sent to these groups and encouraging data-driven, purposeful dialogue with them.'

This definition also highlights the ongoing consumer–brand relationship dialogue. Today's marketers are continually looking at new and creative ways of delivering brand messages to their target consumers.

As Keith Weed (2010) CMO of Unilever, suggests:

> We're in a revolutionary time and the speed of change is amazing. We're trying to find new ways . . . to find a sustainable model to create content. One way is to turn to the people that Unilever is talking to and ask them to talk to us about the brands.

As a result many brands have adopted more channel neutral strategies instead of relying on big budget TV campaigns. Hughes (2009: 515) explains that channel or media neutrality

> advocates a shift away from what might be called 'traditional' forms of media, such as TV for branded goods . . . towards other media, including direct mail, sponsorship and PR. It also promotes a more even allocation of resources across media channels rather than the dominance of one major medium.

THE DEVELOPMENT OF MARKETING PUBLIC RELATIONS

Smith (2008: 2) refers to a report from the Council of Public Relations Firms, which revealed that the disciplines of corporate communication are converging, and states:

'Past norms rendering public relations departments separate from marketing departments are no longer appropriate.' According to Weed (2010), 'we are seeing more companies moving towards combining marketing and communications and it's a trend I think you will see grow.'

Kitchen and Papasolomou (2010) prefer to use the term MPR to talk about the area where marketing and public relations merge. They refer to Kotler's description of MPR as 'a healthy offspring' of the two disciplines. They also cite Duncan's findings that MPR was thought to be particularly effective in some areas that may have originally been served by advertising, and also in brand building. They recommend Shrimp's definition of MPR as public relations that 'involves an organisation's interactions with consumers . . . regarding marketing matters'. In addition, objectives for this area of public relations are related to Harris' suggestions of introducing new products, cultivating new markets, influencing opinion-leaders and positioning companies as leaders and experts in order to extend the reach of advertising and gain exposure for products that cannot be advertised to consumers (quoted in Kitchen, 1997: 258–267). Davis (2004) quotes Kotler's 1991 definition of MPR as 'a variety of programmes designed to improve, maintain or protect a company or product image'.

Kitchen and Papasolomou (2010) also use Kotler's thoughts on the different tasks that could be undertaken by marketing, MPR and public relations. The first deals with market and customer assessment and segmentation as well as product advertising. MPR is concerned with corporate advertising, media strategy and surveys into employee attitudes and customer satisfaction. Public relations then takes responsibility for news, community relations, lobbying and social investments (Kitchen, 1997: 255).

Willis (2009) suggests that 'many marketing professionals now view PR as an effective way to win over hearts and minds of consumers', and so stimulate sales of products and services. PR techniques are seen as particularly useful in changing attitudes and behaviours of consumers. Media relations can produce third-party endorsement by journalists, which is more credible than advertising. Davis (2004) adds that PR can contribute to four marketing objectives: awareness, credibility, stimulation of the sales force and holding down promotional costs. Kitchen concluded that 'in the real world, [PR and marketing] need one another', and that MPR helped build relationships between consumers and brands (Jardine, 2006).

BRANDING

As Willis (2009: 417) explains: 'it is necessary to understand the role and power of effective branding more fully to appreciate the benefits that PR can generate within the context of a successfully executed consumer strategy.'

Willis goes on to cite Adam Morgan's 1999 definition of a brand as an entity that satisfies the following four conditions: (1) something that has a buyer and a seller; (2) something that has a differentiating name, symbol or trademark; (3) something that has positive or negative associations in consumers' minds for reasons other than its literal product characteristics; and (4) something that is created, rather than naturally occurring.

Successful brands appeal to emotional drivers and add resonance to a product or service. 'Nobody in the world ever bought anything on price alone,' argued L.D. Young (2006) in the Annual Cambridge Marketing Lecture. Brands enable corporations to add price premiums, such as Heinz baked beans, which (at that time) retailed for 44p against a supermarket's own label at 15p. Young quotes a blind test of Heinz ketchup against an own-label brand, where 71 per cent of consumers preferred the own label. However, when they saw the label, 68 per cent preferred the Heinz ketchup.

Traditionally, the value of a company has been measured in terms of its material assets, e.g. real estate, plants and equipment. However, in recent years it has been argued that 'brand equity' is the prime source of a company's value. As Helm and Jones (2010: 545) point out: 'Although other key resources may have finite lives – material assets and research and development will be amortised, key people may leave and proprietary technologies become commodities – a successful brand is a long-term strategic asset.' Tuominen (2007) summarises Aaker's (2004) hypothesis as follows: 'it is now increasingly recognised that a firm's real value lies outside the business itself – in the minds of current and potential buyers.'

In a lecture delivered to the British Brands Group in 2001, Jeremy Bullmore, Non-executive Director of communications and marketing services group WPP, declared:

> Products are made and owned by companies. Brands, on the other hand, are made and owned by people . . . by the public . . . by consumers. A brand image belongs not to a brand – but to those who have knowledge of that brand. The image of a brand is a subjective thing. No two people, however similar, hold precisely the same view of the same brand.

BrandFinance PLC produces an annual report on the world's 500 most valuable brands, placing a monetary value on the brand equity of an organisation or product. As a result, Morley (2009) argues:

> Public relations professionals should begin to see their role as that of corporate brand managers, rather than simply as communicators. Enhancing brand value by securing an excellent reputation should be our holy grail. It is when that reputation is reflected in a dollar value – the equity of the brand – that the importance of our work will achieve the recognition it deserves . . .

CONSUMERISM AND CONSUMER BEHAVIOUR

Tuominen (2007: 182) states that 'consumers are not passive recipients of marketing activities, and branding is not done to consumers; rather, branding is something that customers do some things *with*'. Godin (2004) uses the analogy of the 'brand cocktail party', where 'the marketer doesn't get to run the conversation . . . You get to set the table and invite the first batch of guests, but after that the conversation is going to happen with or without you'.

There can be no doubt the relationship between the brand 'owner' and the consumer has fundamentally changed. In recent years there has been a profound shift in power from the organisation to the individual, driven by the impact of technology and social media, as well as increasing consumer scepticism of mass market messages. Quigley (2009) refers to the emergence of an 'era of democratic consumerism' where the 'empowered consumer provides the opportunity to improve and innovate . . . they are also there as a mouthpiece for your business . . . an advocate spreading the good word. On the flip side, they are there to criticise you when you get things wrong'

Helm and Jones (2010: 546) highlight the 'ever empowered consumer' as one of the major challenges to brand equity:

> consumers are . . . better informed, educated, sceptical, more self-directed and increasingly seeking value in the form of self-realisation from the brands that they feel are right for them . . . if dissatisfied with a brand experience, they can often switch and go elsewhere easily and at little or no cost . . . These 'postmodern' consumers of the experiential, digital, price-transparent economy are difficult to reach, let alone engage with, and capturing long-term value from them is getting harder.

The public voice of the 'empowered consumer' was seen during the launch of Gap's new logo (*Marketing Week*, 2010). The retailer revealed a new logo across its website in the US, but it was immediately derided on online forums. Gap then attempted to initiate a 'crowdsourcing' project by asking its Facebook fans to share their preferred designs. This drew further criticism and Gap scrapped the new logo and crowdsourcing project and announced it was retaining its original, 20 year-old 'blue box' logo. Gap North America president Marka Hansen said: 'We've learned a lot in this process. We recognise that we missed the opportunity to engage with the online community'

New communications platforms, including social media tools such as blogs, forums, podcasts, online video and social networks, are giving voice to the opinions of millions of consumers. Pavlik (1996) maps the consequences of technology on public relations and the impact of the internet, which 'enables anyone to own a digital press'. The traditional role of media as gatekeepers is in a state of unprecedented flux as mainstream media becomes increasingly influenced by these online conversations.

In addition, distrust and disillusionment with mass market messages has resulted in a growing tendency for consumers to turn to the person-to-person channel of WOM – both off- and online. According to the inaugural TalkTrack Great Britain study, the average consumer talks about ten different brands a day (Barnett, 2010).

Among the most frequently mentioned brand categories are food and dining (mentioned by 64 per cent of people each day), media and entertainment (63 per cent), and beverages (57 per cent).

The challenge for marketers is to leverage these same dynamic tools to speak directly to their consumers. How brands react to, manage, engage and ultimately capitalise on this phenomenon will fundamentally dictate their future success or failure. Weed (2010) says: 'I want to be able to leverage this fantastic revolution to create real engagement with the people who are buying our products, and allow them to help build our brands.'

Cooper (2011: 12) interviewed 30 marketers from brands about their plans for the future and found that many were changing how they spend their marketing budget, in response to reaching increasingly fragmented audience: 'They are engaging with new technologies and adopting fresh channels such as mobile platforms and tablet devices to communicate with consumers. Cooper quotes Ashley Stockwell, Virgin Media's departing executive director of brand and marketing:

> It's not just about driving people into stores or onto the phones, it's driving them wherever they want to go. Part of the challenge is getting the balance right between all of the sales and marketing channels that you have because consumers are probably more in control than they've ever been, in terms of how and where they get their information and how and where they purchase.

More and more brands are enabling their audiences to experience the brand, create a compelling story around the brand and helping them form a community to share their brand experience. In this environment, 'PR's potential to harness third-party editorial endorsement – both online and offline – assumes an even greater importance than before, as does its ability to target and connect with individuals in a way that advertising cannot match' (Willis, 2009: 423).

THE EVOLUTION OF CONSUMER PR

The traditional tools and techniques of consumer PR include media relations, events and sponsorship. However, creating an integrated, interactive, experience-rich campaign and establishing a two-way dialogue with consumers is becoming increasingly important. The likes of buzz marketing, brand ambassador programmes and high impact stunts are just some of the activities deployed to generate talkability or 'stand out' for products and services, and critically secure engagement and participation in the brand.

A good example of this is T-Mobile's 'Dance' campaign. The mobile phone operator launched a new three-minute TV advert featuring 350 dancers breaking into a mass dance routine at Liverpool Street station. The filming of the advertisement was done in 'guerrilla-style', with hidden TV cameras placed around the station to capture the spontaneous reactions of London commuters. A YouTube channel was also created where people could learn the dance, add their faces to it and watch the many tribute dances from both the public and celebrities. Press and TV coverage featuring viral videos of the flashmob dance ensured the T-Mobile advert had much greater impact and longevity than that of a traditional ad. Costa (2011: 28) quotes T-Mobile advertising and channel manager Kelly Engstrom: 'telling your director that you are putting a lot of budget into a stunt is a scary thing.'

For Daniel Cohen (2009), Director at PR agency Grayling, it was worth it. Naming T-Mobile as the brand that, in 2009, best caught the public mood in its communication, he said: 'it has delivered a series of experiences across all channels and disciplines that have increased brand affinity while catapulting affinity scores. You can't help but smile'

The case studies below have been selected to illustrate different approaches to consumer PR. The first concerns work undertaken by PR consultancy, Grayling, and the in-house PR department at Diageo. The other focuses on how the same PR consultancy helped to generate mass exposure for leading DIY company AkzoNobel.

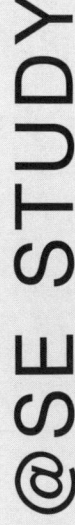

THE TALISKER BOUNTY BOAT EXPEDITION, GRAYLING AND DIAGEO

Background

Diageo is the world's leading premium drinks business, with an outstanding collection of beverage alcohol brands across spirits, wines and beer categories. One of these brands is Talisker – situated on the Western shore of Skye is the Talisker distillery, possibly the most remote distillery in the world.

With bays, sea arches, caves, cliffs, waterfalls and tidal islands, the shoreline of Skye has been shaped by the sea over thousands of years. This sea gives the Isle its unique character and is embodied in Talisker, the only single malt Scotch whisky made on the shores of the Isle of Skye.

Talisker's relationship with the sea was already encapsulated by a formal fundraising partnership with the RNLI, which enabled the brand to target the grassroots sailing community. However, in order to reach new audiences the brand needed a campaign that would lift Talisker out of its traditional media space and into the public limelight.

Objectives

* Bring to life Talisker's relationship with the sea and reinforce its provenance.
* Broaden appeal and reach to new audiences by lifting the brand out of its traditional media space (food and drink pages).

Strategy

- Create a wholly ownable and unique nautical property to amplify the brand platform 'Made by the Sea'.

- Integrate all communications channels to create multiple brand-to-consumer conversations.

- Work with sailor 'ambassadors' to keep the brand at the heart of the piece.

- Create a seamless communications framework to ensure distance is not a barrier to delivering PR success in the UK.

Creative

This led Diageo and Grayling to the Talisker Bounty Boat. The proposition was immense – take four adventurers, one boat and sponsor a 4,000 mile voyage from Tonga to West Timor, to re-create Captain William Bligh's epic journey following the 'Mutiny on the Bounty' 221 years ago. The expedition would be the first ever authentic recreation of one of the greatest open boat voyages ever undertaken.

In addition, the aim of the voyage was to raise as much money as possible for the Sheffield Institute Foundation (SIF) for Motor Neurone Disease (MND), which is building the world's first research Institute into Motor Neurone Disease, Parkinson's and Alzheimer's.

The PR journey took Diageo and Grayling from announcing the trip and running a last-minute promotion to find a new crew member, to creating and managing media partnerships, using the latest technology to connect the sailors with their target audiences and celebrating their success.

Execution

On 28 April 2010, one of the greatest Australian adventurers of all time, Don McIntyre, embarked on an incredible nautical journey to re-create one of the most extraordinary stories of survival and determination.

With on-board conditions authentic in every way, the only exception was the addition of twenty-first-century technology to tell the story throughout the journey. A micro-site (www.taliskerbountyboat.com) was created to host a blog that was updated daily by crew members before, during and after the expedition. The digital content was used to populate the Talisker Bounty Boat Facebook page and engage media on a weekly basis with regular news alerts. A satellite phone was also used to facilitate down-the-line interviews with key broadcast media throughout the expedition and maintain 24-hour contact with the PR team.

C@SE STUDY

Prior to departure an exclusive editorial partnership was negotiated with the *Daily Telegraph* giving exclusive access to certain content from the expedition. The partnership proved vital as 10 days prior to departure UK crew member Mike Perham was forced to withdraw for health reasons. The search was on for another crew member with an appeal launched in the *Daily Telegraph* for a brave volunteer to step up to the challenge. With two days to spare, 18-year-old Chris Wilde was selected and embarked on a journey of a lifetime with no sailing experience.

The crew successfully landed on 15 June 2010 and was received like royalty in West Timor. The completion marked a milestone in history as the first crew to successfully re-enact Captain William Bligh's journey – an angle that was dialled up for the world's media. With Diageo on the ground at landing, interviews were co-ordinated with the world's media as camera crews fed VNRs (Video News Release) and photography to the networks within hours of landing.

Later Chris Wilde and the expedition captain Don McIntyre flew back to the UK for media interviews that included *BBC Breakfast*, which was syndicated across *BBC World Service* and many other broadcast outlets. The crew was also invited to dinner with the Duke of Devonshire (patron of SIF) with footage filmed and made available to the media.

Results

Creating a seamless communications framework to ensure distance was not a barrier was vital to delivering success in the UK. The resulting coverage delivered over 300 pieces of coverage, 800 million opportunities to see (OTS) and has been showcased throughout Diageo as a best in class example of PR exploitation.

Highlights include:

* Significant broadcast feature coverage: *BBC Breakfast*, *GMTV*, *London Tonight*, *BBC Radio 2*, *BBC Radio 4* and *BBC World Service*.
* Over 30 pieces of national print coverage in UK national print: *The Times* (x3), *Daily Telegraph*, *The Independent* (full page), *Metro* (1/2 page), *The Guardian* (x2).
* High-profile online hits including a link to the URLs: Mirror.co.uk, dailymail.co.uk, CNN.com, bbc.com, timesonline.com, guardianunlimited. com, dailytelegraph.co.uk, yahoo.com.
* 3,000 fans on the Talisker Bounty Boat Facebook fan page.
* 100 per cent of coverage included at least one key message and 100 per cent of all coverage was favourable.

With thanks to Diageo and Grayling

C@SE STUDY

FIGURE 16.1 Talisker Bounty boat landing

FIGURE 16.2 Talisker Bounty boat crew

CUPRINOL SHED WEEK 2010

Background

With over 75 years of experience and knowledge, Cuprinol is the number one brand in garden woodcare. Cuprinol operates in an increasingly competitive market and one of the main challenges for 2010 was to differentiate itself from its competitors in order to retain market share in the garden woodcare category.

Objectives

- Maximise brand awareness and bring Cuprinol to front of mind among target consumers during its key sales period.
- Extend media coverage beyond homes and gardens pages into mainstream news.

Strategy

- Create a campaign that adds the 'feel good factor' to garden woodcare, making it more appealing and injecting fun into the category.
- Shift focus from product to brand and from task to the aesthetic.
- Demonstrate Cuprinol's relevance and passion by owning an engaging property that helps make woodcare memorable and resonates with target audience (strong male bias).

Creative

The strategy led Grayling to National Shed Week, a quirky, online celebration of garden sheds and an annual competition to find the 'Shed of the Year'. Wholly conceived and run by one man in his shed, Shed Week started in 2007 and since then has built up a following of true shed fanatics (80 per cent of them male), otherwise known as 'sheddies'. Each year 'sheddies' upload photographs of their sheds to be in with the chance of winning the highly coveted 'Shed of the Year' accolade.

Shed Week was identified as the ideal vehicle for Cuprinol to own and amplify, thereby transcending the 'functional' nature of woodcare. For 2010 Shed Week became 'Cuprinol Shed Week 2010'.

Execution

The campaign ran from March until the winning shed was announced at the beginning of July 2010, which coincided with the key sales period for

C@SE STUDY

Cuprinol. The first stage of the campaign was the website takeover, which included incorporating a Cuprinol presence into the existing Shed Week website, www.readersheds.co.uk, without taking away from the website's homemade appeal.

A new 'We love sheds' logo was introduced and relevant content – providing 'sheddies' with top tips on how to get their sheds looking great (using Cuprinol products) prior to entering the competition – was also added. A panel of celebrity judges, including Sarah Beeney, were recruited to judge the overall shed winner and add celebrity appeal to the competition.

The second phase of the campaign worked to spark initial media interest for Shed Week, using case studies of previous Shed Week winners and strong images of their sheds to capture the media attention and encourage more entries.

As part of the pre-Shed Week activity, consumer research was undertaken to uncover the mystery of 'what men get up to in their sheds'. The findings were then utilised as news hooks for national and regional newspapers as well as online and radio, utilising Andrew Wilcox, the founder of Shed Week, as campaign spokesperson.

A series of quirky news stories, led by key phases in the competition, were pitched into national and regional newspapers, online and broadcast media, as well as consumer and specialist titles. These included case studies and images of the 2010 shortlisted sheds, and ultimately the winning shed and its owner. Providing the media with fresh collateral and keeping them informed at each stage of the competition helped to sustain interest and build momentum. Andrew Wilcox also 'Tweeted' constant updates to build up a strong Twitter following in the run-up to the announcement of the winning shed.

To coincide with Shed Week, Cuprinol also ran a high impact 'Guess Who's in the Shed' promotion on Absolute Radio. In addition, to get high-profile radio DJs/presenters talking on air about Cuprinol Shed Week, bespoke shed-themed biscuits were delivered to key targets along with information on the winning shed.

Results

Results exceeded key performance indicators (KPIs) agreed at the start of the campaign, generating over 70 pieces of coverage and 180 million opportunities to see (OTS).

- Significant broadcast feature coverage including ITV *This Morning* and 10 regional BBC radio stations.

C@SE STUDY

C@SE STUDY

- Twelve pieces of coverage appeared in UK national print including *The Sun*, *The Times*, *The Independent*, *The Daily Star* and *The Mirror*.

- High-profile online hits included thesun.co.uk and gmtv.co.uk as well as specialist interest sites including lets-do-diy.com.

- The number of Cuprinol Shed Week Twitter followers reached 1,670.

- readersheds.co.uk received 21,304 visits during the period 11 June–11 July, with 80 per cent of visitors new to the site.

- The total number of entries to the Cuprinol competition on Absolute radio was 7,433.

- The campaign successfully shifted the focus from product to brand, taking Cuprinol out of the homes and gardening specialist press and into the national news agenda, and most importantly the male consciousness.

With thanks to Grayling and Cuprinol

FIGURE 16.3 Winning Cuprinol shed entry

FIGURE 16.4 Cuprinol Shed Week logo

QUESTIONS FOR DISCUSSION

1 How do public relations and marketing overlap in the area of consumer public relations?

2 Should all campaigns be carried out from an integrated marketing communications viewpoint? What challenges does this present?

3 How has the balance of power changed between brands and their consumers?

4 What are the consequences of new technologies and social media channels on consumer PR?

5 What is your reaction to the T-Mobile 'Dance' campaign? Are you aware of any other similar engagement activities?

6 Investigate the range of tools and techniques deployed by Talisker whisky in its PR programme. How did these bring the brand personality to life?

7 Think of three common brands. How is their brand personality conveyed through their communications?

8 When might it be advantageous NOT to use an existing brand name when launching a new product?

9 Which corporate brands are the most respected in your opinion? What qualities make them respected?

10 What part has 'place' in consumer PR? Which companies have used this to their advantage?

FURTHER READING

Davis, A. (2004) *Mastering public relations* (Chapter 8), Palgrave, pp. 115–128.
Hughes, G. (2009) 'Integrated marketing communications', in R. Tench and
    L. Yeomans (eds) *Exploring public relations*, Prentice Hall, pp. 498–516.
Moloney, K. (2006) *Rethinking public relations* (Chapter 10), Routledge,
    pp. 134–149.
Willis, P. (2009) 'Public relations and the consumer', in R. Tench and
    L. Yeomans (eds) *Exploring public relations*, Prentice Hall, pp. 409–424.

CHAPTER 17

Business-to-business public relations

Loretta Smith

CHAPTER AIMS

This chapter deals with the particular characteristics of public relations for organisations whose publics are other businesses, rather than target sections of the 'general' public. Several case studies illustrate success stories and demonstrate the variety of techniques that can be used.

CHARACTERISTICS OF B2B PR

Cornelissen (2004: 184) defines business-to-business public relations (B2B PR) as 'relating to the sale of a product for any use other than personal consumption'. He gives examples such as a government body, a manufacturer or reseller. Many products and services are sold to other businesses rather than to consumers.

Kelly (2009) sets out the characteristics of B2B PR as:

- a small number of buying publics
- a specific application for the product or service
- defined terms of technical specifications
- purchasing decisions often negotiated individually and subject to finite contract periods.

STRATEGY

B2B PR strategy is similar to that of consumer PR. Tom Bowden-Green, Associate Director at Grayling and a B2B PR specialist,[1] advises that communication plans should be created in a similar way to consumer PR, with objectives, key messages, implementation and evaluation outlined at the outset. He adds that in terms of approach, as with consumer PR, Grunig's (1984) two-way symmetric model of communication is an ideal but not often fully achievable in reality. However, businesses should aim to generate a two-way exchange with other businesses as much as possible, creating engagement, meaning and facilitating feedback.

B2B PR TECHNIQUES

Although the strategy may be similar, B2B PR differs from consumer PR in terms of the tactics deployed. Whichever techniques are used, Bowden-Green warns that practitioners must not forget that B2B audiences are ultimately still people. Therefore, they are likely to be interested in the people behind businesses and less switched on by 'corporate speak'. PR campaigns should try to involve people as 'brand ambassadors', rather than just presenting a corporate entity. Effective internal communication is essential to transforming employees into 'brand ambassadors' as they deal with suppliers and customers. They need to be well informed so that what they say complements and adds value to the PR messaging.

Historically, media relations has been central to B2B PR. Bowden-Green warns that although coverage in the nationals is good for creating a 'big splash' and generating wider awareness, the proportion of readers belonging to the intended target audience for a campaign may be small. Coverage in trade publications should not be undervalued as there are many niche publications covering the B2B sector. They do not have the circulation figures of national newspapers but they often reach a high percentage of a specific target audience. This means that it can be simpler to effectively target a particular segment than it is with consumer PR. Another benefit he notes is that the target audience is an interested one – they often open up a trade publication with their 'business hat' on, something they may or may not do when they open up one of the nationals.

Kelly (2009) states: 'Trade press journalists have a thorough understanding of their subject area.' He advises practitioners to 'assume expertise' when dealing with them, suggesting story ideas and news angles. He lists a raft of media relations techniques that can be used in B2B PR, including briefings, photocalls, feature articles and case studies, press conferences and facility visits. Advertorials are also popular in the B2B sector (this is where paid-for advertising space is filled with copy to make it look like editorial). Bowden-Green adds that to raise awareness of a new business, repeated coverage needs to be gained over a short period in specific publications to help the audience remember the brand name and what it does.

To gain coverage, it is important to have a good story to tell. This may be a product or service launch, a new business development or expansion plan, for example. News can be generated. For example, carrying out a representative survey and publishing the results or a white paper that would benefit a publication's readership. A reputable 'industry celebrity' can be used to endorse or enhance the story and help to build trust. Bowden-Green advocates a particularly effective method, which is to put senior people in the business forward as 'thought leaders' to the media. Getting them to comment on topical news items gives a different slant to the story to make the opinion stand out.

While media relations may be the core of B2B, other techniques are also used extensively. For particular clients, a series of presentations to key decision-makers may be used. Exhibitions are useful for demonstrating products, although they are becoming increasingly expensive. Newsletters may also be sent to clients and potential clients, informing them of company developments. B2B is an area that is seeing increasing use of new technology in communications. Facility visits also help to demonstrate the product to potential buyers and journalists, but should have a proper structure and be worthwhile for the journalist.

Other methods that can be used effectively include staging events and seminars on relevant topics to the buying public. Sponsorship and corporate hospitality events can encourage prospective buyers to engage with the product and attendance at carefully targeted exhibitions can put the product in front of the relevant public and enable them to experience the benefits hands-on.

Digital media can add an additional dimension to campaigns. It can be used to run demonstrations, webinars, virtual events and competitions, for example. Many companies also have press centres online that provide further information for journalists.

The rise in social media usage has opened up new opportunities for B2B PR. Social media provide platforms for engaging directly with the audience. They can be used to generate 'water-cooler banter' whereby business people talk about what they have heard. The views of trade publications with limited circulation also can be heard across the world in a short period of time if they are discussed in social media channels.

Bowden-Green says that social media can be used to create a buzz around a campaign, even in the B2B world. Where possible, employees should be allowed to reach outside of the boundaries of the business using social media. They are likely to talk about the company to family or friends and in other forums. However, comments on Twitter (for example) are more visible, enabling businesses to track discussion and take feedback onboard. It's vital to ensure employees are given the information they need to speak about the company accurately. He indentifies LinkedIn as a useful B2B PR tool, arguing that it is good for networking and for promoting discussion around particular topics. There are many discussion groups covering a host of different industries and they can easily be found using the search facility. It is another forum for thought leaders to share their viewpoints within their industry.

Blogs can also be effective here. Awareness of blogs can be raised through LinkedIn and Twitter. It is a good idea to tweet a link each time the blog is updated. It is also important to be clear on the search terms used within the blog to enable accidental discovery of it. For example, when targeting an engineering audience through blogging, sharing links plus the tag or word 'engineering' may improve the chance that the target audience picks up the blog when searching for something about engineering on the internet. A large audience may not read a blog, but those that do are likely to be highly interested in the topic. The feedback posted by them can also be useful.

EFFECTIVE TARGETING, TAILORING AND REPACKAGING

As with consumer campaigns, effective targeting is essential. The publics targeted are likely to be much smaller. In some instances, each separate individual approached within that public can be targeted separately. PR creates the atmosphere in which items can be sold. The reasons for the buying decisions are also professional, rather than personal. Buyers are looking for equipment to help them do their jobs, or to ease the process for others.

Bowden-Green says that B2B markets are often segmented by profession, which can simplify the task of reaching a specific 'public' (in comparison to trying to reach a mass consumer market). The range of trade titles means that publics can be precisely targeted. Some specialist publications work across an industry, and others reach people in particular job functions in several industries. Research pays off when it comes to targeting. There are many tools that can be used to assist with effective targeting. Several databases identify media outlets, detailing their audiences and reach (such as circulation figures). They can be used for seeking out trade publications relevant to the target audience. There are also demographic tools that give details of the profiles and behavioural patterns of people in different geographic or demographic groups. This could be useful when targeting specific business audiences, such as those in a particular region.

It is important to ensure message consistency, while tailoring that message to the particular concerns of the public. However, businesses that other businesses may want to communicate with are not homogeneous, either. They may be suppliers of raw materials, and so have to understand the company's systems, needs and market opportunities. They may distribute a company's products – few manufacturers sell direct to the consumer, but operate through retailers and agents.

PR must reach all members of the company who contribute to a buying decision, sometimes referred to as a decision making unit (DMU). Fill and Fill (2004: 115) warn against simply targeting organisational buyers, stating that they are not 'the only representatives of an organisation to be involved with the purchase decision process'. The whole DMU must be considered. There are those that initiate and manage the buying process, the end users, those that influence the decision as well as those that make the decision.

Sometimes products have to be repackaged to show customers the unique features of a particular supplier. Selling energy to businesses is fairly difficult, as buyers tend to concentrate purely on price. Eastern Electricity found that it was too expensive to pursue domestic consumers, and that business clients were more profitable. On talking to the sales team, they found that most businesses wanted to feel that Eastern understood their particular needs. While Eastern is not the cheapest in the market, savings can be made by some manufacturers. Those who can manufacture their product at any time and stockpile until needed can take advantage of cheap tariffs overnight. One such business was cement, so a package was put together for cement manufacturers, showing how they could run their machinery and make substantial savings. Eastern also found that by analysing electricity demand, other information about a business could be deduced. A holiday camp owner could tell which nights were the most popular because of changes in demand.

GETTING THE LANGUAGE RIGHT

Information should be presented clearly avoiding using abbreviations and terminology without explaining what they mean. This applies to both written content and in media interviews.

It is also important to bear in mind that not all members of the target audience are experts in the field. If this is known to be the case, careful attention needs to be given to information to make sure that it is understandable to everyone targeted. For example, the audience for a complex engineering product may not only be engineers but may be other members of the DMU within businesses such as the finance and procurement teams who need to be persuaded of the benefits.

Bowden-Green advises using inclusive language as much as possible, presenting a human voice (and face or name where appropriate). Speaking in the third person can be alienating. This is of course dependent on the objectives of the activity and sometimes a more formal tone or technical information is required.

Victoria Tomlinson, Managing Director of Harrogate-based Northern Lights,[2] believes that few companies really understand about getting their products across to buyers through the media:

> I spent a day with a regional newspaper's business desk and could not believe the large numbers of press releases that failed to make any point. They were

written in heavy technical jargon, had no story and did not highlight the 'so what' aspect to readers. An example was the launch of a new valve with a long description about its technical features but absolutely no mention as to why it was better than a competitor's or how it would change a manufacturer's product. The most complicated process can be written in plain English and understood by a non-technical person.

WORKING WITH OTHER COMMUNICATIONS DISCIPLINES

Kelly (2009) feels that PR practitioners in this area need to be aware of other disciplines. He says: 'PR practitioners working in B2B often display an in-depth understanding of advertising, direct mail and sales promotion and of how PR can act as a unifying mechanism.' Advertising can place the specific message in front of the target public, without being interpreted by journalists. It is good for building brand awareness and can be complemented by PR. Direct marketing aims to put promotional material in front of prospective buyers rather than expecting them to gain information from a retailer or salesperson. Sales promotion can also be effective. If the promotions are of significance, PR may be able to help gain attention for these in the media.

MEASURING SUCCESS

Tomlinson is a champion for measuring success of PR activities against business goals and says that it is a sad fact that many PR practitioners feel their work cannot be evaluated or that it can be evaluated solely on the basis of media coverage. She advocates setting clear business objectives for each PR campaign, such as numbers of enquiries, increased sales, improved recruitment, better share price or reduced staff turnover:

> It is hard relating PR to these sorts of results but it is worth doing. Just the process of setting measurable goals is a good discipline. It concentrates the mind on what you want to happen as a result of the PR, ensures you have evaluation processes in place, and makes sure that success or failure can be measured. This gives a good base to improve on for the future.

All proactive PR campaigns need to make sure that they measure and track return on investment. It is important to ensure that any activities have a positive impact on a business's marketing and bottom line.

Advertising Value Equivalency (AVE) measures the value of media coverage in terms of how much it would cost to advertise in that outlet in terms of column inches for print and time slots for broadcast. It is quantitative, cheap and easy to calculate, so many businesses take this approach to evaluation. However, this method is too simplistic and lacks meaning. There are more effective methods that can be used.

Bowden-Green recommends that the first step is to measure output, for example the number of press releases issued and key messaged covered. Next the outtakes should be measured, such as circulation figures and space in trade publications. Finally the outcomes need to be evaluated, for example hits on the website, number of mentions of a business's name on social media sites, number of visitors to a stand at a trade exhibition and the number of sales leads generated. The output, outtakes and outcomes should be measured in terms of how well the activity met or exceeded the objectives that were set in the beginning as recommended by Tomlinson.

CASE STUDIES

Case studies from Airbus, Lloyds TSB Autolease and the University of the West of England have been used to demonstrate how B2B PR can be approached effectively.

THE AIRBUS CONCEPT PLANE – A PLATFORM FOR AN INNOVATION LEADER

Background

Airbus is one of the world's leading aircraft manufacturers and it consistently captures approximately half or more of all orders for airliners with more than 100 seats. It is infamous across the world for its flagship double-decker A380 aircraft. Its latest development programme, the A350 Extra Wide Body (XWB) also captures a lot of trade and business media attention. Airbus also has a military division that is best known for the A400M versatile airlifter.

Airbus is continually working to anticipate the global needs of a better and more sustainable world. Its 2010 Global Market Forecast (an outlook for the 20-year period to 2029) anticipated a 4.8 per cent annual increase in overall world passenger traffic and a demand for 26,000 new commercial aircraft and cargo aircraft (valued at US$3.2 trillion) in this timeframe (Airbus, 2010b). The challenge for the aviation industry will be to balance the global demand for growth in aviation with a better environment.

To work towards tackling this well-publicised challenge, Airbus engineers, all experts in the fields of aircraft design came up with their 'dream' Concept Plane, an icon that represented Airbus' long-term vision of

C@SE STUDY

FIGURE 17.1 The Airbus Concept plane
Used by permission

C@SE STUDY

aviation (2030+). It was designed in the spirit of the 'concept cars' regularly produced by automotive manufacturers but was a first for the aerospace industry. The Airbus Concept Plane was created to stretch engineers and push thinking beyond the usual boundaries. It featured many significant technological advances. While all are feasible, an aircraft is unlikely to ever come together in this manner. However, it is more than a flight of pure fantasy. It was instead designed to help refine the technologies of the future. The Airbus Concept Plane illustrated what transport could look like in 2050 – even 2030 if advances in existing technologies continue apace and is a representation of the main technological fields that are being explored to face future needs: a significant cut in fuel burn and emissions, less noise and greater comfort.

Strategy and objectives

The aim of the campaign to promote the Concept Plane was to enhance Airbus' image as an innovation leader in conjunction with communicating about breakthrough innovations in service today and coming up next on the A350 XWB and A400M.

The campaign targeted several publics (including employees, governments, industry, investors and passengers). The B2B industry element of the campaign targeted airlines, partners and suppliers. The objectives were to:

- support Airbus' position as a global innovation leader
- encourage partners and suppliers to keep investing in research and technology
- give airlines confidence in the future of Airbus.

The key B2B messages, which complemented communication with other publics, were that Airbus:

- is the number one innovator
- is an aircraft architect and integrator with a long-term vision for aviation
- is investing in tomorrow, today (through €2 billion invested in research and design) by anticipating market and passengers' needs
- is continuing to deliver and drive eco-efficiency through step-changing technology.

Other messages were aimed at specific audiences:

- keep innovating and investing with Airbus to develop new ideas for a sustainable aviation sector (aimed at partners and suppliers)
- keep counting on Airbus to deliver the most advanced, eco-efficient aircraft (aimed at airlines).

Implementation

- Airbus unveiled the Concept Plane at Farnborough Airshow in the UK during Futures Day (for which the company was one of the lead sponsors) on 23 July 2010. Farnborough is an iconic global event and arguably one of the most prominent Airshows in the world. During the 2010 trade week, US$47 billion worth of orders were announced (Farnborough International Airshow, 2010), demonstrating the importance of effective B2B PR at the event. Futures Day was designed to inspire youngsters aged between 7 and 21 to go into careers in the aerospace and defence and security sectors. As it was run on one of the Airshow's trade days, it was an ideal opportunity for B2B PR activity surrounding the Concept Plane.

C@SE STUDY

- Print, broadcast and digital media were invited to the unveiling, including trade media. A news hook was created by launching a new research report that painted a picture of the world in 2050, authored by leading futurologist, Robin Mannings. The report covered potential, quirky aircraft developments that could be talking points for an industrial audience, such as walls that become see-through at the touch of a button to afford a 360-degree view and holographic projections of virtual decors, allowing travellers to transform their private cabin into an office, bedroom or even a Zen garden. It also covered the potential of sustainable developments such as using fuel cells, solar panels and even passengers' own body heat.

- Digital images were created of the Concept Plane for use by the media. A tangible model of the aircraft was also created to include in broadcast interviews. 'Morph men' in Airbus-branded suits carried out acrobatic stunts near the entrance to the Airbus stand. This was a fun way of reflecting the concept of interiors designed to 'morph' to each passenger in the future. It also created an interesting way to get the Airbus branding into the media.

- Media relations activity was underpinned by the findings of an online survey carried out with 2,243 respondents aged over 18 years in the UK, just before the event. The findings showed that passengers would become more environmentally aware while also recognising the many benefits of air travel in the future.

- Twelve media interviews were carried out, most with Charles Champion, Executive Vice-President, Engineering at Airbus who is seen as a thought leader in the industry. Charles also presented a video covering the Concept Plane called, *A glimpse of air transport's future*, available on Airbus' website, which had an industry audience.

- Dr Gareth Williams, another thought leader, who leads business development and partnership for the Airbus research and technology programme, was also put forward to join a panel for the lively Flying Matters Debate at the event entitled: *Is the future mobile?*, at which the Concept Plane was discussed. Flying Matters 'seeks to contribute to a balanced and informed debate on aviation's contribution to climate change' (Flying Matters, 2010) and is formed by a wide coalition interested in supporting the sustainable growth in aviation, which includes members of the wider business community in addition to the aviation industry. This was an excellent opportunity to influence Airbus' target audience.

C@SE STUDY

Results and evaluation

- Over 130 pieces of international coverage were gained across print, broadcast and digital media. Airbus' share of voice was 88 per cent compared to 12 per cent for its main competitor. 70 per cent of coverage featured an Airbus spokesperson and 70 per cent also featured a photo. The UK media was particularly attentive (which was anticipated as the Airshow was held in the UK).

- The A350 XWB and A400M, whose technology was promoted through the Concept Plane campaign also received almost 50 items of media coverage each (Echo, 2010), although some coverage of the latter would largely have been influenced by the fact that the A400M made its first UK public appearance at the show.

- Coverage about Airbus on Future's Day was the second highest in terms of volume, favourability and rating compared to other days of the Airshow and communication surrounding the Concept Plane contributed to the perceptions of Airbus' leadership (Echo, 2010).

- There were 55,000 hits to the Airbus website each day of the Airshow, including Futures Day, compared to the 1,500 hits on a regular day.

- There were 120,000 trade visitors overall.

- The Concept Plane was a talking point among airlines, partners and suppliers following the unveiling. Tim Clark, President of Emirates Airline, one of Airbus' biggest customers said: 'I'm a great believer in the future of aerospace and the airline industry; it will never go away as long as Airbus continues to design and build quality aeroplanes and to innovate' (Airbus, 2010).

- Airbus achieved 255 orders and commitments worth a catalogue price of US$28 billion at the Airshow. Although this cannot be attributed specifically to the Concept Plane campaign, it would have gone some way to cementing confidence in the future of Airbus in the minds of its customers.

With thanks to Katherine Bennett, Vice-President, Head of Political Affairs

(Katherine was Director of Communication and Government Affairs for the UK at the time of the campaign)

C@SE STUDY

LLOYDS TSB AUTOLEASE – A THOUGHT LEADER IN FLEET MANAGEMENT

Background and objectives

Lloyds TSB Autolease (LTSBA) is one of the largest fleet management and funding organisations in the UK, owning one in 200 vehicles on the road.

In the highly competitive and contracting fleet market, it is essential to stay ahead of competitors by being an innovator in fleet management services and products. LTSBA used Grayling to strategise and implement an ongoing campaign that would position it as a thought leader, with the aim of gaining market share from competitors and opening up unexplored business opportunities. The team constantly refreshed its approach to come up with proactive ideas for achieving differentiation.

Strategy, planning and research

The fleet market has become much more competitive over the last five years, with large investors backing a number of competitors, allowing them to build scale through acquisition. LTSBA, however, had not made any acquisitions in the three previous years, so the campaign strategy was to maintain market presence with ongoing proactive press office activity and at the same time raising the bar in the fleet industry by creating peaks of activity around innovative initiatives. Every story issued, including contract wins or appointment releases, was always linked back to the key concepts of innovation and thought leadership.

Although LTSBA's marketing function was strong, no above the line spend was authorised at the time. With no advertising, media relations became critical to promoting the organisation and defending its leadership position in the industry.

Grayling worked closely with key personnel at LTSBA to gain a thorough understanding of the business and its areas of expertise. The team focused on innovators within the business who could provide thought leadership on important industry issues such as environmental impact and duty of care, having regular briefings with them to keep on top of key topics.

Strong links were built with top fleet titles by offering exclusive briefings with key personnel and contributing regularly to set features with meaningful, unique content as well as suggesting proactive feature ideas to set the agenda.

C@SE STUDY

Grayling also helped broaden LTSBA's media focus from the fleet press to targeting wider media, which would be read by decision makers.

Action and implementation

Key messaging was developed to be at the core of all communications. LTSBA needed to position staff as consultants who could add value to customers' businesses by offering advice as well as value for money.

LTSBA had some fantastic assets in their senior executive team, who had insights and opinions about current and future issues to help shape the fleet industry and fill the pages of the media that they wanted to reach.

A quarterly Executive PR Forum was set up to stimulate round table discussion to unearth hidden gems and spark thoughts in order to access and mine opinions and knowledge.

The success of this sort of approach was easy to demonstrate. For example, a member of the board was discovered to have strong opinions about the reliability of the vehicle recall system used by manufacturers in the UK. Research was carried out into this topic and found that at the time, each year around 160,000 cars that should have been recalled were never taken in for corrective action, potentially jeopardising lives.

This issue was taken into the public domain in a way that would prompt government and industry action, as well as positioning LTSBA as thought leaders. An open letter to Dr Stephen Ladyman, Minister for Transport, was drafted and issued with the subject 'Vehicle Recall – A Legal and Moral Responsibility'. LTSBA's expertise was turned into a news story.

National news and consumer media were targeted, enabling LTSBA to reach a much wider audience and make a huge impact. The open letter was not only the biggest single news story generated for LTSBA but other organisations backed the campaign and the Minister for Transport at the time announced a review of the manufacturer recall system.

Another example is how the company was positioned appropriately in relation to environmental issues that were topical and relevant to both LTSBA and its customers. Media stories were developed and comment opportunities secured on the subject, giving customers solutions for helping the environment, such as ways to be fuel efficient.

Evaluation and results

- The number of pieces of coverage was increased year-on-year from 62 in 2004 to almost 300 in the first nine months of 2008.

C@SE STUDY

C@SE STUDY

- Audience reach was increased year-on-year from under 2 million in 2004 to more than 6 million in the first nine months of 2008.

- Monitoring share of voice against its top five competitors indicated that the company was consistently out-performing rivals in volume and quality of coverage.

- The open letter drafted to the Minister for Transport created a huge amount of coverage for LTSBA and generated backing from other organisations, which led to the Minister for Transport at the time reviewing the manufacturer recall system.

In a contracting and highly competitive market, LTSBA was taken out of its comfort zone and its media relations programme was challenged. Without the support of any above the line spend, campaigns were created that demonstrated LTSBA's expertise in the industry and moved it up the value chain in media coverage. The firm now regularly features as providing expert comment on legislation and topical issues, increasing its share of voice, giving LTSBA the leading voice in the fleet industry

With thanks to Paul Barnard, Associate Director at Grayling

C@SE STUDY

UNIVERSITY OF THE WEST OF ENGLAND – KNOWLEDGE TRANSFER PARTNERSHIP INSPIRED BY THE BLOODHOUND SSC PROJECT

The University of the West of England (UWE) is based in Bristol and is one of the UK's fastest growing research institutions. It was founded in 1970 as Bristol Polytechnic. It gained University status and adopted its current name in 1992 as a result of the Further and Higher Education Act.

The University's ethos is built around fostering genuine partnerships with all its stakeholders. 'U+WE' is used in its branding to underpin this. Its vision is 'to be the UK's best Knowledge and Learning Partnership University' and its mission is 'to make a positive difference to our students, business and society'.

UWE is a not-for-profit organisation with a key ambition to engage with the business community by forming partnerships. The University is close to many businesses supplying advanced technology industries. Through collaboration with these businesses, the University aims to encourage more students to study science, technology, engineering and maths (STEM) subjects to address the shortage of engineers and help improve

FIGURE 17.2 BLOODHOUND banner
Used by permission

competitiveness of advanced technology in the UK. UWE works with businesses in this sector to provide opportunities for undergraduates to improve their practical skills and understanding of the industry before entering the workplace.

Background

On 17 March 2010, UWE held its annual lecture during Science and Engineering Week. The event focused on the University's involvement with the development of BLOODHOUND SSC, a car designed to take the land speed record to over 1000mph/Mach 1.4. UWE is the lead sponsor of the project, which is led by Richard Noble. The development activity is taking place on the University's grounds. It is an exciting project that can be used as a hook to get local business interested in being partners.

Strategy

The objectives of the event were to:

* increase visibility of UWE to businesses in the advanced technology industry;
* promote Knowledge Transfer Partnerships, which give academics great opportunities to apply research to real world business projects;
* gain more industry contacts;
* inspire future engineers at the University and to encourage youngsters at local schools and colleges to go into engineering.

The key message was that 'great things can be achieved through partnership'.

The event format meant that a two-way approach could be facilitated. Delegates had the chance to ask questions, experience the mock-ups first-hand and network with other business people in the advanced technology industry as well as those at the University.

Implementation

- The event itself was used to build relationships with business stakeholders and deliver key messages.

- The campaign was people-focused throughout. A scale mock-up of the car, and the cockpit designed by UWE Product Design students was showcased.

- Media relations activity targeted regional TV and radio stations, national and regional press as well as technology-related websites.

- A dedicated BLOODHOUND SSC area was set up on UWE's website where businesses (and other stakeholders) could go to find out more.

Results and evaluation

- A full house of 280 people in senior positions in the region, including many for advanced technology companies, joined the event. New relationships with local businesses were built to foster future partnerships and existing relationships were strengthened.

- Coverage was gained on regional TV and radio stations, national and regional press and on a product design website. It was also featured on the BBC's *Politics Show*. The people-focused approach to the photographs offered to the media meant they were of interest and therefore used.

- On the day of Science and Engineering Week there were 138,000 hits on the UWE BLOODHOUND SSC Page. The page still appears in the Top 10 most hit pages of the UWE website.

- At the time of the event, the University did not use social media. However, it has since started using Twitter, Facebook and a YouTube channel to keep up the momentum of its involvement with BLOODHOUND SSC and keep businesses informed. Content is carefully targeted for use on social media, with stories that will be of interest to businesses. There are now over 900 followers on Twitter and 2,000 fans on Facebook.

With thanks to Keith Hicks, Director of Marketing and Communications at UWE

C@SE STUDY

QUESTIONS FOR DISCUSSION

1   What is the main difference in the audience for B2B and consumer PR?
2   How are B2B and consumer public relations similar and in what ways do they differ? (You may want to refer to Chapter 16, which covers consumer PR.)
3   Why is targeting considered to be easier in B2B PR?
4   How could the media relations techniques discussed in Chapter 12 be applied to B2B PR?
5   Earlier in the chapter, it was said that when dealing with trade journalists, it is important to assume expertise. If you worked for a PR agency and were selling a story about a firm's groundbreaking renovation project to an architectural trade publication, how would you prepare?
6   Look at the lead headline story in a national newspaper. Consider how a thought leader could give a new perspective or angle on the story to generate media attention.
7   If you were responsible for the PR for an aircraft manufacturer, how would you go about organising a campaign targeted at trade journalists that involved a facility visit? How could you ensure there were enough exclusive stories or angles during the visit to maximise the breadth of coverage?
8   Identify the potential characteristics of members of the DMU responsible for purchasing a piece of high-technology machinery for a large organisation. How would you raise awareness of the product among all members of the DMU, through PR?
9   If you were a food manufacturer that had just launched a new product and you wanted to gain the attention of distributors, how would you use social media to create a buzz around the campaign?
10 Examine the case studies. Consider alternative ways in which the campaign objectives could have been set and the how the outputs, outtakes and outcomes could have been measured.

NOTES

1   The interview with Tom Bowden-Green, Associate Director at Grayling was carried out by Loretta Smith.
2   The interview with Victoria Tomlinson, Managing Director of Northern Lights was carried out by Alison Theaker.

FURTHER READING

Kelly, D. (2009) 'Business to business public relations', in R. Tench and L. Yeomans (eds) *Exploring public relations*, Prentice Hall, pp. 426–440.
Fill, C. and K. (2004) *Business-to-business marketing: relationships, systems and communications* (4th edition), FT Press.
Phillips, D. and Young, P. (2009) *Online public relations* (2nd edition), Kogan Page.

CHAPTER 18

Not-for-profit public relations

Peter Brill and Cinzia Marrocco

CHAPTER AIMS

This chapter discusses public relations in the not-for-profit-sector with a focus on clarity and delivery of message, overcoming systemic tensions between information and propaganda, meeting the traditional and new media agenda and working with celebrities.

THE THIRD SECTOR

In the 1980s, increasing restrictions on government funding led to the 'opting out' of government control by some schools and NHS hospitals. This meant they were no longer part of the public sector and yet were not part of the commercial sector either; a third sector was created.

Today, there are more than 180,000 registered charities in England and Wales, 23,000 in Scotland and 5,000 in Northern Ireland.[1] However, there are other not-for-profit organisations that fall outside charitable status, such as Social Enterprises and Community Interest Companies (CICs). Combined, these groups of organisations are known as The Third Sector. If trade unions, political parties and educational institutions are added to the mix, the entire group is often referred to as Civil Society.

The Third Sector has evolved over time and ranges from small local community groups to large national, multi-branch organisations. They do, however, have certain key elements in common. They will have been established with a view to addressing a social need; be non-profit-making or reinvest the majority of their revenue to continue their work; use volunteers in some way and, while they must comply with certain statutory guidance or legislation, they will not be under direct political control.

In strict terms, a charity provides help in the form of money, food, goods or other aid to those in need, or for the benefit of a group – human or otherwise – but without exclusion. A not-for-profit is defined by the role it plays in society, but not all can register as charities as the term excludes any organisation that acts colely for the benefit of its membership as, for example, a housing association.

Social Enterprises, such as *The Big Issue* magazine, and CICs also fall into the not-for-profit category. While they operate to make financial profits, any profit, along with the organisation's assets, is locked so it can only be used to enhance the growth of the organisation itself and the community it is working for. Charities cannot be CICs, although they can apply to register a CIC as a subsidiary company, for example The Help For Heroes charity has also established a Help for Heroes Trading Company.

Charles Handy (1991) identified three broad types of voluntary activity: mutual support, service delivery and campaigning. 'The categorisation is crude, of course, and many voluntary organisations fit all three categories or slip unwittingly into a fourth . . . There lies the rub, for in this unconscious blending of the categories lies much organisational confusion.' Many of the issues discussed in this chapter are common to communications professionals across the Third Sector, regardless of organisational structure or purpose.

The regulators and lobbyists

The Charity Commission is the legal Regulator and Registrar of Charities in England and Wales. In Scotland and Northern Ireland the regulators are The Office of the Scottish Charity Regulator and the Charity Commission for Northern Ireland (established in 2009).

Since the Cabinet Office's review of the legal and regulatory framework of the Third Sector in 2002, the setting up and operation of charities has become more heavily regulated and monitored. In particular, scrutiny of each charity's objectives, or purpose for existing, has increased significantly.

Governance is a major concern for the charity regulators, ensuring that every organisation has a clearly defined structure for its management, financial and operational activities. The result has been a significant enhancement of the standards under which charities are allowed to operate and the support they receive to meet the standards.

As well as the regulators, lobby and support groups such as the National Council for Voluntary Organisations (NCVO), the Association of Chief Executives of Voluntary Organisations (ACEVO), Fundraising Standards Board and the Social Enterprise

Coalition also assist charities, not-for-profits and Civil Society groups in the increasingly complex tasks of governance, funding and operation.

RECENT HISTORY

A defining moment in the analysis and development of the charity sector came with the publication of the Wolfenden Committee Report in 1978. The report, entitled 'The Future of Voluntary Organisations', was co-funded by the Carnegie UK Trust and the Rowntree Foundation and explored the context, value and contribution of charities.

At the time of the Wolfenden Report, the position of charities according to David Wilson (1991) was: 'primarily one of securing strategic advantage through organisational flexibility. Voluntary organisations were characterised by their ability to respond rapidly to needs and to mobilise the entire organisation around events which were unpredictable and rapidly changing.'

More importantly, as Wilson notes, the biggest competitors to the voluntary sector were the state agencies; the very agencies that were employing or funding them to supply services they could not or would not supply themselves.

Described as 'welfare pluralism', this relationship changed in the 1980s fuelled both by the desire of the charities to become more autonomous in their funding and their relationship with the state agencies, and the desire of the government to move away from a culture of financial dependency by the charities. As Wilson states: 'The era of competitive strategies in the voluntary sector had arrived. The enterprise culture was predominant.'

Now the relationship has changed again. The charity sector remains highly competitive and has, on the whole, gained its independence from the state. However, the government has now turned facilitator and partner. The decentralisation of funding and service provision has allowed central government departments – such as the Home Office and its regional Government Offices – to assist with start-up funding, support initiatives and partnership matching. Kramer (1991) describes this relationship as: 'an entity called "the Contract State" has rapidly emerged as voluntary organisations have been used to deliver public services in the fields of health, education, personal social services, housing, the environment and community development.'

As the culture of charities and their communication has changed, so a number of common elements have emerged in charity strategy. One is the management of the organisations' reputation and image. Another is the need for charities to position themselves as effective service providers. This key message requires communication not just, in the case of healthcare related charities for example, to service purchasers, but also to existing and potential service users. With increasing emphasis being placed on 'user choice', the traditional interpretation of the two-step flow model with healthcare professionals as opinion-formers is now reversed, as service users gain influence on their choice of provider.

PUBLICS AND CLARITY OF MESSAGE

What are the messages?

As with any organisation, identifying and delivering key messages is essential for a Third Sector organisation. However, unlike most commercial organisations, the message itself can mean the difference between survival and failure. Clarity of message is vital.

Similar to a commercial organisation, a charity is likely to have a broad range of publics. In terms of communication, the primary publics are those individuals or groups represented by the charity and those needed for its survival, whether financial or resource-based, such as volunteers, donors or advocates for the organisation. An understanding of these publics and their relationship to the organisation is, again, vital.

According to Bruce (1996), the marketing of voluntary organisations

> first came in the late 1960s and early 1970s via the advertising agencies working with charities on publicity and fundraising campaigns. A marketing approach

FIGURE 18.1 Getting the message

Image: Marcin Wichary

Source: Licensed under a Creative Commons Attribution Licence

is now the dominant working method in the more professional fundraising and public relations arms of larger charities.

It is indeed true that most charities see their communications as marketing to existing or prospective stakeholders. The mix of traditional PR activity, such as the news release and media liaison, is coupled with viral or online marketing initiatives all driven by the PR function. As Bruce (1996) states: 'It is probably fair to say that voluntary organisations are as good as, if not better than, their commercial counterparts in achieving successful advertising and public relations.'

Often the most challenging task for a charity is identifying and maintaining focus on active or latent publics. As a charity grows it is easy to lose sight of the core publics in the chase for funding or resources to survive. Equally, as the charity's profile and visibility increases, additional publics are likely to become active; keen to be represented by a successful organisation, form an alliance to strengthen their own numbers, or campaign in opposition to the charity's purposes. These require close monitoring and careful development of messages to address them.

Bates and Pitkeathley (1996) state:

> to be an effective lobby a charity needs four things: a constituency; a clear and simple message; respect; and some success. You have to be clear about the group on whose behalf you are campaigning and you have to be seen to represent them.

Communicators need to express a need, and a solution to addressing it, in a way that is both economical and understandable by a non-expert audience. This is often hindered by the mainstream media's apparent indifference to the Third Sector and their need to often simplify complex issues. While all major newspapers have sections dedicated to business, finance fashion, the arts and sport, many editors are loathe to run more than one charity story a month. *The Guardian*'s Society section is a notable exception. This balance changes as the media becomes more regionally focused.

Features and stories about the corporate world, celebrity and sport appear consistently – the assumption being the public's appetite for such stories is matched by the coverage. However, research carried out by nfpSynergy (Brennan, 2009), a think tank and research consultancy for the not-for-profit sector, revealed that the public like to read stories about charities and their work over the activities of sport, fashion and celebrities, and only just behind business and the arts.

It is for this reason that not-for-profit PR practitioners are constantly repackaging their messages and trying to offer a hard news, political or commercial angle in the hope it will result in media coverage. Charities are largely viewed as either angels or devils, rather than being offered the opportunity to communicate successful service delivery or highlight the difference their work makes. It is not always easy to get this balance right.

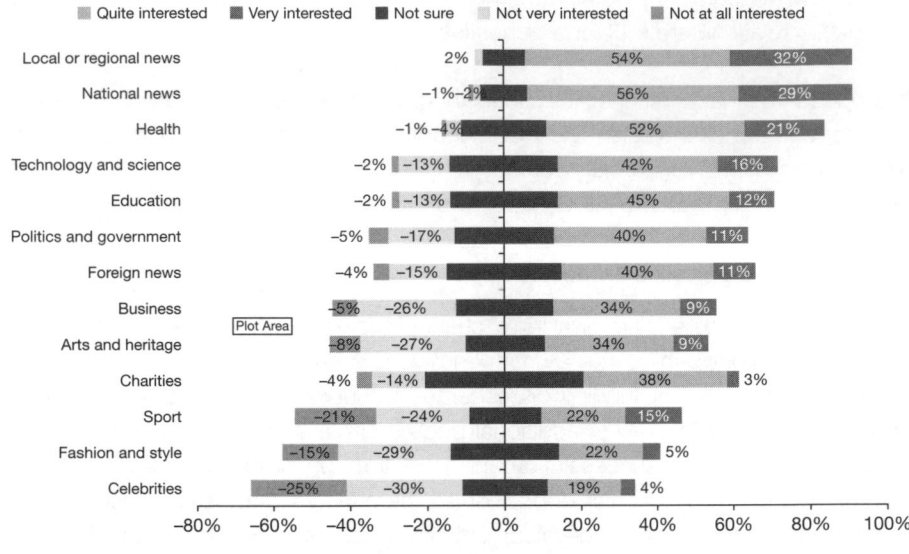

FIGURE 18.2 Chart based on 1000 adults 16+, Britain

Source: nfpSynergy, *Charity Awareness Monitor*, January 2009, by permission

ACTION FOR CHILDREN

In 2007, UK-based Action for Children launched a promotional campaign to re-brand the organisation from National Children's Homes and highlight its work with vulnerable children and young adults. With a policy of only using real life examples, while safeguarding the identities of any children involved in campaigns, the charity ran an internal and external communications strategy based around a series of interviews with beneficiaries telling their own stories.

The impact of the campaign was constantly measured and generally there was a positive response to the new brand and the messages being delivered. However, one small and, according to Action for Children's Director of Communication Gregg Vines, 'very vociferous and well organised' group took a different view of the examples used.

The group mobilised very quickly and, within 24 hours of the launch of the official campaign, had generated significant momentum for their own negative campaign through social media, e-mail and phone.

'We continued to monitor the activity but gave ourselves a couple of days' breathing space to assess the scale [of the negative campaign] and develop an appropriate response,' Vines explains. 'We were being advised to respond online but resisted, both to protect our message and the

C@SE STUDY

children. If this group didn't understand our campaign messages they were unlikely to understand our online response.'

Instead the organisation stayed offline, held face-to-face meetings and made numerous phone calls with the campaigning group, ensuring they recognised that the charity was listening to them and responding. Internal briefings were also held and senior staff attended the public meetings.

Although the campaigners remained troubled, they were placated by Action for Children's communication (which continued for some considerable time after the campaign had ended) and the social media activity died down. The charity itself became a strong advocate for social media, in particular Twitter, when used for particular target audiences.

For Gregg Vines, there were two key lessons learnt. The first was identifying and paying attention to key publics.

> Because we hadn't engaged with that particular group early enough, and it was a simple error of omission, we were vulnerable. What was surprising at the time was how fast an apparently disparate group were able to come together through social media and organise into a cohesive public.

The second lesson was in the strength and delivery of the messages. 'We had to hold our nerve,' says Vines.

> We believed in our messages, our values and stood our ground. While we withdrew one small element of the campaign because protection was the most important factor, our internal communication was strong and everyone had faith in the brand and the overall campaign. As with everything [in communications], online is simply another communications channel, but messages need to be tailored appropriately whatever the medium.'

C@SE STUDY

MESSAGE TENSIONS

Although most charities regularly review their objectives and the messages they deliver to, and on behalf of, their publics, increased scrutiny by the Charity Commission since 2006 has served to further focus charities' activities and governance around meeting their stated purposes.

The impact on communicators is to create even greater pressure to ensure that key messages clearly match the stated constituency in which the not-for-profit works. In addition, the task of maintaining the respect of the publics it claims to represent and keeping the organisation's core objectives can create tensions between the priorities of communicators, fundraisers and campaigners.

FIGURE 18.3 Tug-of-war
Image: Steve Snodgrass
Source: Licensed under a Creative Commons Attribution Licence

In some cases, regardless of the organisation's own communication and clarity of message, its role and constituency can be re-defined by external publics as something the organisation itself would not necessarily claim to be.

An example is the non-governmental organisation the Muslim Council of Britain (MCB). The MCB's charitable purposes include, according to their constitution (2002) the promotion of 'cooperation, consensus and unity on Muslim affairs in the UK'. Established in 1997 as an umbrella organisation for Muslim groups in the UK, the MCB quickly became the media and government's first point of contact as a commentator on Muslim affairs.

As a representative body and lobby group of around 300 Muslim organisations, it was only a short step to being perceived and identified as *the* representative body of British Muslims – a perception the government and media remain happy to foster as and when convenient. It is a constituency that some Muslim communities have argued is inaccurate, as has the MCB itself in its own constitution: 'The MCB's vision has never been to duplicate, supplant or belittle existing work or to seek to become the sole rallying point.'

However, the necessity of the MCB to remain proactive in representing its publics, has led to open criticism of the organisation by some Muslim communities who state that the MCB is not *their* representative body. This is a common challenge for many representative bodies that inevitably cannot reflect all views within their constituency. This is also true, for example, for the Church of England Synod and the Board of Deputies of British Jews. As an organisation grows in profile and visibility, so the opportunity for criticism and challenge to reputation and purpose also increases.

THE MESSENGERS

Often not-for-profits struggle to establish a clear role for communications within the organisation itself. The tension between a charity's communications or public relations team and other key departments is often determined by the level of influence the team has, for example, on fundraising and campaigns. It can be undermined by the perceived need to dilute key messages to tug at the heartstrings of potential donors or motivate a particularly inactive public.

Having said that, it is important that communicators, fundraisers and campaigners are the architects of organisational messages and that they work together on their delivery. These functions have similar objectives – promoting the work and purposes of the charity – but engage people in different ways. A common understanding of the agreed role of each department in the communications strategy in any Third Sector organisation is vital.

As Handy (1991) states, based on his three categories of charitable activity:

> Most organisations [have] grown like Topsy and end up as some sort of amalgam of all three categories. There is nothing wrong with that. It may indeed . . . be the only way to stay honest. It will, however, make life more complicated because the organisational assumptions will clash.

Organisational failure to agree a broad communication strategy will guarantee less effectiveness in the delivery of messages. The communication function needs to work closely with its internal publics – fundraisers, campaigns, operations and digital teams, and senior management – to agree their key external publics, how to communicate with them and desired responses from them.

Effective delivery of messages, particularly in the not-for-profit sector, is reliant on an integrated communication strategy based on mission and values and understood both internally and externally. Through this, positive impact can be achieved on the organisation's brand identity, fundraising, effectiveness of lobbying, coverage by the media and online presence.

As with organisations in many sectors, there is often a perception that communications/PR is only concerned with media activities. In smaller organisations, the boundary-spanning role of communicators is often extended through the amalgamation of fundraising and PR within the same department. This can lead to the organisation's messages becoming donation-biased as the fundraising element is given priority over the perceived functionary task of 'telling the press'. This boundary spanning tension can increase further when one individual or team is responsible for communication, fundraising *and* campaigning.

In larger not-for-profits, there is generally a separate communications department. While offering greater independence, the tensions with other key departments (in particular fundraising and campaigns) still remain and it is again important that communicators are not reduced to the role of functionaries and, at worst, communication technicians – simply delivering fundraising and campaign messages without strategic input.

It is essential for charity communicators, regardless of the size of organisation, to view and establish themselves and their function as managerial (even if their job titles do not actually reflect this) expert prescribers and facilitators. To that end, communicators need to establish a clearly defined role, ensuring that the board of trustees and senior management understand this role and actively seek the support of the communications function at a strategic level.

OPPORTUNITY AND OPPORTUNISM

Using the users

One of the most defining roles of not-for-profit communications is the portrayal of beneficiaries. How a charity – and the media – portrays this group has been the subject of fervent discussion for more than 30 years. Disabled writer and activist

FIGURE 18.4 The best of all worlds?
Image: Surian Soosay
Source: Licensed under a Creative Commons Attribution Licence

Paul Hunt wrote in the 1960s (quoted in Barnes, 1991): 'We are tired of being statistic cases, wonderfully courageous examples to the world, pitiful objects to stimulate funding.'

In some cases, the desire, or need, for not-for-profits to deliver impactful messages has created tensions among their own users. In the early 2000s, the Multiple Sclerosis Society in Britain ran advertising showing images of young, attractive males and females with their eyes and limbs torn away. The adverts told how the condition can result in paralysis, blindness and impaired speech. One advert referred to those diagnosed with the neurological condition as having 'a hope in hell'. Following research of its membership after the campaign, the MS Society found that rather than increasing, its membership was falling away. After a re-brand and change to more positive communication focus and visual identity, the organisation saw its membership increase by 30 per cent.

This issue of the portrayal of beneficiaries by not-for-profits, and indeed the media itself, is not confined to disabled people. It extends to all charities and organisations are sometimes criticised as behaving opportunistically when presenting beneficiaries as 'case studies' who need the help of the public. This is perceived to portray a vulnerability that calls on the goodwill of others, rather than highlighting the rights, choices and service needs of the beneficiaries within a 'normal' society.

The truth is, as long as there is the need to raise funds, not-for-profit communicators will tend towards images of their beneficiaries that maximise social, political and media opportunities. While this may create tensions between the organisation and its beneficiaries, not-for-profits by their very nature are dependent on the goodwill and understanding of publics beyond the beneficiaries themselves, who often do not understand the issues faced unless clearly and simply explained. In a highly competitive fundraising environment, communicators can be faced with a difficult moral and ethical dilemma.

Since the early 1990s, there has been a shift towards focusing communication on the achievements of the individual overcoming particular challenges. This is especially true in the portrayal of disabled people. The emphasis is more frequently on ability and survival rather than disability. In the case of organisations such as Help For Heroes and Livestrong, this has been effective.

However, Barnes (1991) argues that this is not always the most appropriate message:

> [this approach] achieves relatively little in terms of empowering disabled people. It is a clear denial of the status of the disabled person and disabled culture, obscures the need for change and perpetuates the impression that disabled people need to be supported by charitable organisations. The focus remains squarely on the disabled people rather than on the disabling society in which we live; the very opposite of what is needed.

Critics such as Barnes condemn the absence of involvement of beneficiaries in the development of communications. Addressing this imbalance is now commonly recognised by communicators. A proactive, consultative process helps to produce more informed communications. As demonstrated in the Action For Children case study (see above), this may not always put an end to the criticism, but will certainly go a long way towards strengthening understanding, relationships and alliances between the organisation and its beneficiaries.

The challenge for Third Sector communicators is to address the use of its beneficiaries in promotions or appeals in a positive but informative way. The internet generally, and social media in particular, has helped considerably in the development of beneficiary communities, fans and followers who can tell their own stories for and on behalf of the organisation without the communication necessarily being filtered by the organisation itself.

The opportunity box

The fine line between opportunism and opportunity is never more obvious than during a time of 'moral panic'. The idea of moral panics was first mooted in the early 1970s by social commentator Stan Cohen. In his book, *Folk Devils and Moral Panics* (1972), Cohen studied the culture of Mods and Rockers in the 1960s, including their regular battles on Brighton's beaches that he stated became self-fulfilling events fuelled by the reaction of the public, media and eventually the government.

Cohen defines a moral panic as: 'a condition, episode, person or groups of persons [that] emerges to become defined as a threat to societal values and interests.'

An example of this may be groups such as paedophiles, Yardies or football hooligans, or conditions such as AIDS, where issues of morality can be linked (rightly or wrongly) to the condition itself. Concern about the behaviours of these groups or spread of conditions, whether real or perceived, causes responses from the public, media and ultimately governments that may lead to moral panic. This in turn fuels further disproportionate fears and responses.

For charities, whether child protection agencies, football supporters associations or drugs advisory groups, the task of calmly communicating clear, understandable and objective messages can become caught up in, and influenced by, a state of moral panic. It should be stated that the outcomes of panics are not all necessarily negative. Tighter legislation, increased research and funding, greater public awareness of facts and enhanced processes and procedures can all result from panics.

The theory of moral panics can be extended to a broader socio-economic theory we will call 'social panic'. While not necessarily impinging on debates concerning morality (although often this becomes the case), social panics can be defined as a significantly increased awareness of, and concern for, a social or environmental

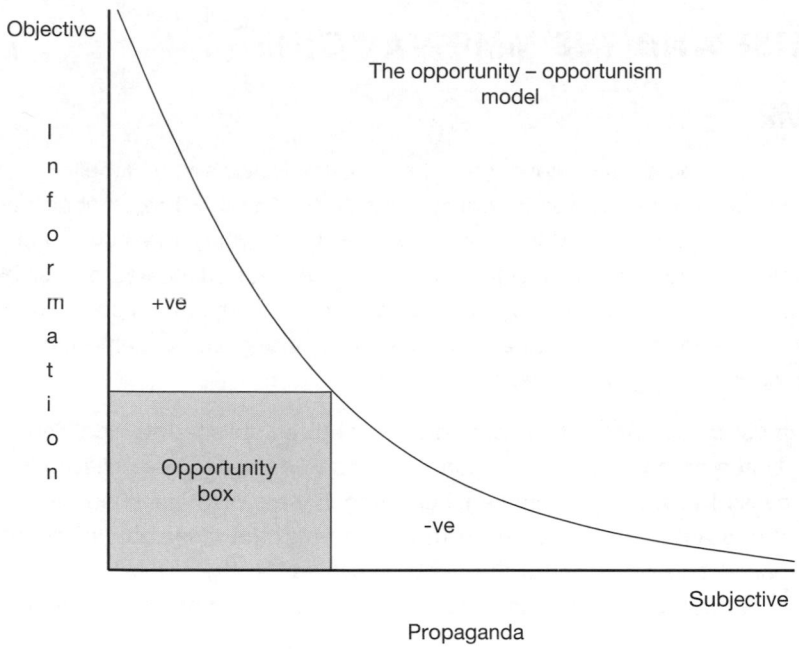

FIGURE 18.5 The opportunity–opportunism model
Source: Brill & Marrocco 2007

issue and the impact this may have on local, regional, national and global society. Examples of social panics might range from natural or human-made disasters to mad cows or technological failures.

There are two main dilemmas for Third Sector communicators when dealing with moral and social panics. The first is identifying the point at which objective information becomes subjective propaganda; the second is ensuring that opportunity does not become opportunism. The model below shows an Opportunity Box – the area where communicators need to apply the greatest use of skills as expert prescribers and where objectivity and information is balanced against a need to further the cause, purposes and awareness of the organisation itself.

While the more objective the information and the more positive the publics' perceptions of the information itself, the greater the loss of opportunity for the charity to transmit its own messages. However, travel too far down the scale towards subjectivity and propaganda, and communicators face the danger of an increasingly negative and even cynical response towards both the information and the charity and a perception that the organisation is simply being opportunistic.

SENSE AND THE MMR VACCINE

MMR

One recent social panic concerned the Measles Mumps and Rubella (MMR) vaccine, which was introduced into the UK in 1988 to combat the three most common childhood illnesses. Ten years later, a research paper was published in the medical journal *The Lancet* that suggested a possible link between the vaccine and autism and bowel disease in children. The research paper, and its lead author Dr Andrew Wakefield, became the subject of growing public debate.

A number of parent-led campaign groups were established to highlight their concerns about the MMR vaccine and the damage they believed it had caused to their children. Legal challenges were also launched on behalf of a number of children. At the same time, the research validity was questioned and a number of the doctors involved in the original paper distanced themselves from the link made between the vaccine and autism.

However, by the end of the 1990s, social panic had already set in and the debate became UK-wide, with many parents questioning the safety of the combined MMR vaccine. The Government, NHS, Chief Medical Officer and local GPs were put under significant pressure to provide separate vaccines. Public Health Laboratory Service (now the Health Protection Agency) figures, showed that by 2003 the uptake of vaccine had dropped to under 79 per cent, well below the stated 95 per cent required to protect the whole UK community. At the same time, the number of diagnosed cases of measles had increased significantly. The government and NHS refused to provide separate vaccines. Uptake has increased over subsequent years, and a significant number of research papers have failed to find evidence supporting the link between the vaccine and autism or bowel disease, while others suggest no links. After almost three years of formal investigation the General Medical Council found Dr Wakefield guilty of serious professional misconduct and in May 2010 he was struck off the medical register.

Throughout the time of social panic, Sense, the Deafblind and Rubella Association, faced the Opportunity Box dilemma. Naturally it was in the organisation's interests to promote the use, in particular, of a rubella-containing vaccine; as a major provider of services to the healthcare sector the organisation also needed to protect its relationship with local and national health authorities. Equally, a number of parents linked to the organisation were concerned about the research findings, or at least what they had read or heard about it, and the effects of the vaccine on their children.

C@SE STUDY

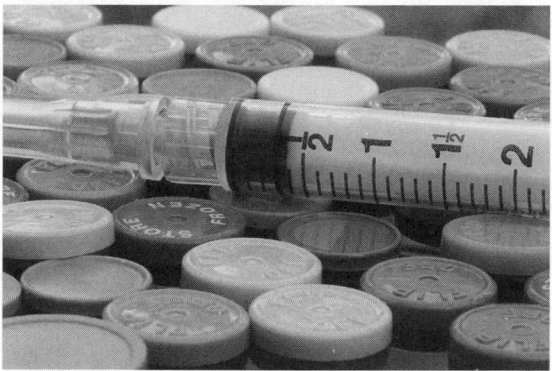

FIGURE 18.6 Vaccinations
Image: Dawn Huczek
Source: Licensed under a Creative Commons Attribution Licence

C@SE STUDY

The communications team at Sense acted as expert prescribers in the communications sense of the term, working with the senior managers and trustees. They took the decision to provide objective information via leaflets, the media and the organisation's website, while highlighting the dangers of not protecting children against rubella. Beneficiaries of the charity were able to provide case studies of the damaging effects of rubella and provide a human interest angle to why vaccinations are needed and the success they can have.

A decision was also taken to continue to support the combined vaccination when asked – a position that had been held by Sense since MMR's introduction. The organisation clearly communicated the fact that parents should make their own decision, based on the facts available.

While this could be perceived as 'sitting on the fence', the reality was that Sense quickly became recognised by its publics as a source of factual information. This gained the organisation significant credibility as an unbiased commentator on the debate and protected both its operational and fundraising income.

COMPASSION FATIGUE

A phrase much used in the media and among charities, 'compassion fatigue' in fact has two definitions. The clinical definition often applies to charity, medical or emergency service workers who regularly or suddenly treat large numbers of traumatised people. It is also known as Secondary Traumatic Stress Disorder.

However, the PR definition of compassion fatigue is best summed up by Simon Watney (1989) as a difficulty for: 'the media and their audience to sustain concern about individual crises over a period of months and maybe even years. Other more decisive – and short-term – events intervene, usurping attention, and meanwhile, little seems to change in the original scenario.'

Whether as a result of panics or crises, communicators in the charity sector fight a constant battle with compassion fatigue. Sometimes, according to Watney, 'fatigue is due to simple overexposure. The same thing that happens to movie stars and rock stars can happen to crises. They can get overexposed.'

In other cases, compassion fatigue has a more cynical or pragmatic edge: the crisis is geographically too remote to affect the charity's publics; there is not enough resource for the media to cover every event; or, worst of all, the scale is just too immense for people to comprehend.

The latter example Watney defines as number numbing:

> A single child at risk commands our attention and prompts our action. But one child, and then another, and another, and another and on and on and on is too much. A crowd of people in danger is faceless. Numbers alone can numb.

As with the challenge faced by the Opportunity Box, charity communications teams, along with their fundraising colleagues, are constantly required to balance reality with messages wrapped in a package that has impact for the media and donor publics. Generally, focusing human interest is deemed the best approach.

However, there are times when personal stories can invoke a different response, as highlighted by one listener to America's National Public Radio (NPR) post Hurricane Katrina: 'Instead of getting detailed news reports and analysis of the innumerable important national and international issues, I have been hearing long and uninformative human interest stories.'

This is further supported by NPR programme producer Chris Turpin who claimed:

> I wish it wasn't so, but I can understand why the audience is a tad jaded. Just look at the news cycle the last few years: Katrina, Iraq, tsunami, Kashmir quake, 9/11, the list goes on and on. There are days I wake up and, frankly, don't feel like turning the radio on.

At a briefing on charitable giving held by the Beacon Fellowship, Lord Bell, Chair of Chime Communications, commented:

> I do think that charities should spend more time explaining what they do with the money. It has always struck me that probably the weakest part of most charities' communication with their donors is what they actually do with the money. It tends to be rather calm, rather boring, and not at all very exciting.

The need for transparency is a common theme for critics of the Third Sector and has been levelled at organisations of all sizes, profiles and motivations. This leaves communicators with the dilemma of having to balance their time between explaining the primary need and demonstrating outputs and outcomes. The additional task of overcoming the 'compassion fatigue' of media and publics adds to the challenge. Finding new and dynamic ways of presenting key messages, needs to be combined with a keen sense of timing and an added desire to demonstrate the results of the charity's work.

MAKING THE MEDIA AGENDA

There is little doubt that the media is instrumental in setting the news agenda. Not only does it report the news, it also shapes public perceptions and raises and lowers the priority and volume of debate about particular issues. The press will generally feature one or two stories on the front page and broadcast bulletins will set a 'running order' that determines the importance and prominence of particular news items.

This notion of the power of the media to influence public opinion was explored by Lippmann in 1922. Lippmann discusses a world delivered by the media to the public that is beyond what most people see and do – another world that is 'out of reach' but is made accessible by the delivery of information by news agents. The public learns what journalists think are the important issues of the day. 'Attitudes and behaviour are usually governed by cognitions – what a person knows, thinks, believes. Hence, the agenda-setting function of the mass media implies a potentially massive influence.'

The influence of the media, even in this digital age, on a wide range of publics assists charity communicators to achieve their goals – fundraising, awareness, understanding, campaigning. The forming of opinions about causes by generating volume of exposure and creating the right tone, is the Holy Grail for any charity as this influences the personal behaviours of key target audiences.

The proliferation of information generated by the Third Sector is recognised as a powerful tool for media relations and stakeholder communication in general. Organisations are continually conducting research, developing new ways of working with or supporting their beneficiaries and launching new appeals. Within each organisation a plethora of stories can be found. Why is it, then, that charities struggle to influence the news agenda? Are they often seen as worthy but dull by journalists and editors? What is the key to finding the Holy Grail?

With the right elements in place, in particular strong messages, a shrewd sense of timing, and maximum use of available information and expertise, the news agenda can be influenced by charity communicators. This may require extensive research before, during and after the launch of a campaign, or in relation to the subject matter itself.

In March 2007, Mencap issued a report that claimed people with learning disabilities faced institutional discrimination in health care provision. The disability charity had spent three years researching and following up cases that resulted in a significant amount of detailed personal stories which set them apart from other news items at the time. The Mencap story, coupled with other related stories in the mental health field in the build-up to the Mencap campaign, persuaded Health Secretary Patricia Hewitt to set up an independent inquiry to examine the issues.

British charity Help for Heroes (H4H) has garnered significant media support since its launch in October 2007, including direct backing from *The Sun* and *The Sunday Times*. Established by husband and wife Bryn and Emma Parry, now both OBEs, the charity was established to help improve rehabilitation facilities for British servicemen and women wounded in recent conflicts around the world.

By taking deliberate and constant steps to avoid commenting on the conflicts themselves and focusing only on the individuals, their treatment and the facilities required, H4H has maintained a positive media presence that, in turn, has been further strengthened by support from a wide range of celebrities and high profile public figures and organisations.

A combination of good timing alongside careful message construction and positioning to a media for whom heroic deeds will always receive a positive response, has allowed H4H to largely overcome public objections on political grounds while meeting its charitable objectives of raising millions of pounds for facility improvements.

THE SOCIAL REVOLUTION

Digital space can be particularly useful for communications professionals as a vehicle for creating change and communicating with their organisation's publics. This is understandable when the phenomenal growth of online usage is considered. The ONS states that in 2010 30.1 million adults in the UK (approximately 60 per cent) accessed the internet every day and 43 per cent posted messages to social networking sites, chat sites or blogs.

Social networking or social media is web-based interaction that is highly accessible and potentially powerful. Kaplan and Haenlein (2010) describe it as: 'a group of Internet-based applications that build on the ideological and technological foundations of Web 2.0, which allows the creation and exchange of user-generated content.' It is the opportunity to exchange information and ideas that provides charities with an avenue to influence and, more importantly, listen to their publics wherever they are online.

While the private sector tries to identify methods of commercialising the use of tools such as Facebook, Twitter and YouTube, not-for-profits are also using social media to engage successfully key audiences for non-commercial purposes and there is a real opportunity for charities to be more innovative than the private sector in this arena. There are two key reasons for this: the financial pressures are different and there is a more frequent need to engage people in an issue, topic or theme rather than enter into a transactional relationship with them. However, many Third Sector organisations struggle to quantify the value of social media in their long-term communications strategies and use it to its full potential.

FIGURE 18.7 Social media icons

Image: webtreats.mysitemyway.com

Source: Licensed under a Creative Commons Attribution Licence

In late 2010, an individual set up a Facebook page asking people to change their profile picture on the social networking website to a cartoon character as a way of showing support for an end to worldwide violence against children. While not having any direct affiliation with a given charity, the individual simply added a link to the NSPCC website. The charity announced it had nothing to do with the campaign and acted only by making a few posts on the page. However, it did later recognise that some £100,000 had been donated to the NSPCC as a result of the campaign and the organisation's own Facebook supporters had jumped from 65,000 to more than 120,000 by the end of 2010. A spokesman from the NSPCC said 'we have been able to attract many new supporters which will help us with our work.'

The worldwide attention for NSPCC came with great speed and the impact of a seemingly simple campaign cannot be argued. However, such a response is rare for charities and highlights that many are not yet optimising the use of social media. One key question is whether the NSPCC can continue to keep its new 'friends' engaged and active as the result of a campaign it did not initiate itself. Are they now best served to broadcast messages proactively or continue to listen and react? In the case of social media, collaboration between fundraisers, campaigners and communications professionals is key in shaping a strategy to maintaining the organisation's relevance as an influencer of new and existing supporters.

The digital space has many unwritten rules and, rather than utilising refined PR or marketing messages, communicators need to be artful in honest discussion, the sharing of ideas, highlighting successes and being transparent about failures – a 'warts and all' approach. In truth this interaction is labour intensive and many organisations do not have the infrastructure, staff and expertise necessary to undertake it.

Therefore, as the Action for Children case study demonstrates, understanding the climate and responding appropriately to publics is more important than an organisation taking part in social media conversations for the sake of it.

There are signs that more not-for-profits are undertaking innovative digital campaigns but there is still limited data relating online interaction with offline commitment. It is dangerous for organisations to mistake this interaction as a successful shift in attitudes and opinion and detailed analysis is required to determine what approach really works and why.

Just as events, meetings with ministers and generating media coverage are tools in the communications kit, using the internet in general, and social media in particular, as a community mobiliser should be viewed as is an important additional tool. As always, strategies and objectives should be the basis for determining which tactics are best deployed. Cancer Research UK uses Facebook and Twitter successfully as key communications tools for its Race for Life programme by providing appropriate, relevant and timely information. Each year approximately 6,000 people register for the series through the charity's Facebook page, which offers training, information, prompts for registration and links to further engagement opportunities on the organisation's website. With more than 75,000 'likes', it is a shining example of how an online tool can be used to bring people together, organise and act.

In the same way, autism charities across the world united to highlight how communication is denied to millions of autistic people by appealing to social media users to opt out of using social networking sites for a day. The Beatbullying campaign held a digital 'march' across more than 60 websites to ask the British Government to help protect children against bullying and violence. The campaign used Facebook, Twitter and YouTube as part of an integrated campaign to drive more than 750,000 people to pledge their support.

An informed view, combined with activity built on strategic principles in the digital space is just as important for charities as ensuring they are using their supporters' donations wisely. Communicating with supporters, reaching out to people who need their services and finding new 'friends' can all be achieved through integrated online communications that remain centred on organisational and departmental objectives. The internet and social media also provides a positive monitoring tool to gauge where people might already be talking about and evaluating an organisation's brand and values. Once processes are established, communicators are well placed to advise senior teams on digital strategy and respond efficiently and effectively to opportunities that arise through social networks.

THE CELEBRITY FACTOR

The use of celebrities is a common practice for not-for-profits. Some Third Sector organisations even employ celebrity managers to nurture relationships with celebrities and their agents. Such relationships, when well developed and managed, can deliver positive benefits and long-lasting results.

Active courting of specific celebrities, use of their contacts, or carefully targeted communication likely to be read by them, can lead to celebrity awareness of an organisation so that they are at least open to an approach directly, or through their agent. Alternatively, celebrities can become involved having developed an interest because of some kind of personal experience of the issue itself.

In the latter case, celebrity relationships are often longer-lasting as they are more likely to have developed from a proactive approach by the celebrity themselves – seeking information from or about the organisation because they have a personal interest. For example, some medical charities have gained celebrity support through a family connection, such as footballer Gary Lineker's support of Leukaemia Research as a result of his son's illness. Equally, celebrities may have particular concerns or life values that move them towards specific campaigns such as animal welfare, poverty, or disaster relief.

Naturally, there are benefits that accrue to the celebrity as well, mostly in terms of their personal esteem and kudos. Many celebrities view charity work as a way of giving something back to the publics that have brought them success. Others view it as essential for their own promotion, so not all those willing to work with charities will be perceived as truly genuine in their motivation. This is an accusation that is often levelled at stars participating in emergency relief events or high profile 'telethons' such as the BBC's Children In Need, where, despite the significant sums of money raised, some celebrities are viewed as merely jumping on the bandwagon to boost their own popularity or showcase their latest production.

While this may or may not be true, public perception of individual celebrities can often present charity communicators with a fine balance of being inside or outside the Opportunity Box. More importantly, a tension is created between the opportunity perceived by the organisation and that of the celebrity who may feel that the more propagandist, subjective end of the scale is acceptable to further their careers.

The benefits

Whatever the motivation, the benefits of having strong links with a high-profile celebrity are manifold. As well as raising awareness of an organisation's specific campaign or general profile through media coverage, a celebrity can attract new audiences including other celebrities who may be keen to align themselves with both the organisation and their fellow celebrity.

When at its most positive, the relationship with a celebrity can contribute to the repositioning of an organisation and a step-change in public perceptions. As celebrities are often perceived as opinion-formers, their ability to mobilise public opinion, directly and indirectly reach a mass audience and sometimes speak from personal experience, are strong incentives for not-for-profits.

The growth of celebrity culture means that celebrities – whether 'A' or 'Z' list – are still held in awe by many people who come into contact with them. This often creates a power for the celebrity to ask 'the big question', a direct request for sponsorship or donations, which is greater than can be achieved by non-celebrity fundraisers.

The pitfalls

As with their own high-profile lives, when the relationship between celebrity and charity is happy, both sides benefit. However, when the relationship breaks down, the fallout can be spectacular and highly damaging, in particular to the charity.

The most important factor for charity communicators is to be extremely cautious of over-dependence on celebrity support. It is as easy for those working within the organisation to become as overawed by celebrity as it is for their target audiences. The danger is allowing the celebrity's story to overpower the charity's key messages.

It is easy to assume that because celebrities, or the characters they play, are familiar, their personal views match their public personas. In reality this is often not the case and it is important to ensure that research has been undertaken and checks made. Any potential celebrity relationship should be objectively assessed for risk – could the relationship discourage donors, damage the organisation's reputation through contradictory messages or 'bad behaviour', or simply fail to achieve impact? Fame does not automatically guarantee message resonance.

If using celebrities beyond more common promotional roles, as ambassadors or spokespeople, even greater care is required when considering an approach. Some are more skilful at handling complex issues and will promote a cause better than others. An ability to stay 'on message' is essential, even at times when they are not specifically working on behalf of the charity.

C@SE STUDY

LIVE**STRONG**

Livestrong is a charity and Foundation established in 1997 by cyclist, seven-times Tour de France winner and cancer survivor, Lance Armstrong. The charity supports, and has raised hundreds of millions of dollars for, survivors of cancer and those undergoing treatment.

It maximises personal, individual stories to create a global community for the survivors, their families and donors to the charity. It was also one of the first charities to produce the now-ubiquitous wristband and has distributed 70 million of the bright yellow Livestrong variety.

Livestrong's approach to communication has positively exploited the growth of social media to build a platform for campaigning, event organisation and story telling, including celebratory Tweets to and from survivors on the anniversary of their cancer diagnosis. Armstrong's celebrity, including creating his own Livestrong professional cycling team,

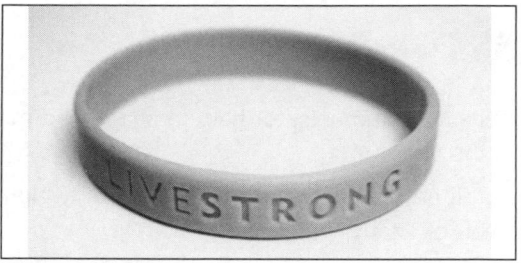

FIGURE 18.8 LiveStrong wristband
Image: dawnzy58
Source: Licensed under a Creative Commons Attribution Licence

has also created momentum by tapping into global brands for funding and world leaders for support.

However, Armstrong's own fame has also presented challenges for the charity and has required careful communications positioning. Drug taking – or doping – has become ingrained in the history of cycling sport. Despite being the most tested rider in the history of the sport with no single positive drugs tests to his name, rumours and allegations of doping have dogged Armstrong's career.

Armstrong and the organisation have always been conscious of the potential damage that any personal attack on Armstrong himself may have on the charity. This was forced into stark relief in 2010, when a former team-mate made doping allegations that sparked a US Federal investigation into Armstrong among others. Salter (2010) comments:

> Even if Armstrong isn't ultimately charged, a prolonged investigation that sullies the foundation's public face could take a toll on its fund-raising and, most important, its credibility. Will corporate sponsors and donors differentiate between the founder and his foundation? While [Livestrong CEO Doug] Ulman awaits the outcome, he's being forced to wrestle with a critical question about his boss: Is Livestrong's greatest asset also its greatest risk?

The reality, however, is that the charity itself has established such a strong community and positive core messages, that Armstrong has become almost secondary to the organisation and its major donors. This has allowed Livestrong to use Armstrong's celebrity to positive effect, but, where necessary, actively distance itself from personal issues. In talking to Salter, Ulman was clear: 'We wouldn't be where we are, a movement of millions, if we didn't have a visible founder and if he hadn't put the money and effort into this. The upside [of Armstrong] outweighs any potential downside.' But, he adds, 'as a cause and as an organization, we want to live beyond any one individual. Cancer is going to be around a long time.'

C@SE STUDY

QUESTIONS FOR DISCUSSION

1   How can a charity communicator help to shape and maintain the purposes of the charity?

2   At what point, if any, do commercial interests outweigh the communication of charity purpose?

3   How can a charity's PR function help to overcome 'compassion fatigue'?

4   At what point is the line crossed between opportunity and opportunism where charity communication is concerned?

5   What expert prescriber skills are required to keep communication within the Opportunity Box?

6   What moral or social panics are currently providing communication challenges to the charity sector? Which charities might be involved?

7   Are there examples where Third Sector organisations have significantly influenced the media agenda?

8   How do communicators ensure their charities remain relevant?

9   What is the role of a charity communicator in shaping an organisation's digital strategy?

10   How do you maximise the positives and minimise the risks of a relationship between a Third Sector organisation and a celebrity?

NOTE

1   Sources: The Charity Commission; The Office of the Scottish Charity Regulator; The Charity Commission for Northern Ireland.

FURTHER READING

Batsleer, J.S., Cornforth, C.J. & Payton, R. (eds) (1991), *Issues in voluntary & non-profit management: a reader*, Addison-Wesley/OU.

Cohen, S. (2002) *Folk devils and moral panics* (3rd edition), Routledge.

Li, C. and Bernoff, J. (2008), *Groundswell: winning in a world transformed by social technologies*, Harvard Business Press.

Moeller, S.D. (1999) *Compassion Fatigue*, Routledge.

O'Sullivan, T. and Jewkes, Y. (eds) (1997), *The media studies reader*, Hodder Arnold.

CHAPTER 19

Digital public relations – revolution or evolution?

Heather Yaxley

CHAPTER AIMS

Given the fast moving nature of developments in the digital world, this chapter takes a reflective look backwards, a wide look around, a deep look inside current practice and a long look ahead (to paraphrase Cutlip, Center and Broom 2000). It asks whether the influence of digital technology on public relations represents a revolution or evolution of theory and practice. Implications for communications theories, media relations, influencer engagement, and the role of professional bodies are assessed. Territorial arguments are considered along with suggestions that a new hybrid occupation will emerge from the dynamic online environment in which organisations seek to communicate, build relationships and manage reputations. The aim is to put this emerging area into context and present a pragmatic view of the opportunities and threats that practitioners face when engaging with digital public relations.

A GLOBAL AUDIENCE

In June 2010, according to Internet World Statistics, there were almost two thousand million users of the internet – compared to 360 million at the start of the decade. Over three-quarters of the population of North America, and six out of ten people in Oceania/Australia and Europe, are online. Although Africa (10.9 per cent), Asia (21.5 per cent) and the Middle East (29.8 per cent) lag behind, these are the areas of fastest growth. Indeed, 42 per cent of internet users are located in Asia – meaning in number terms three times as many people are online there as in North America.

News sources in China report it has 450 million internet users, representing a 20 per cent growth in 2010.

These numbers reflect a huge change in communications bringing global reach and immediate access, with content aggregated by a complex dynamic network of public and private relationships. This offers the potential for individuals and organisations to connect in order to disseminate and share information or express opinions, largely without gatekeepers (censorship and privacy are issues discussed later in this chapter). Alongside opportunities to build relationships, this mainly uncontrolled environment challenges reputations and the traditional role for public relations as a boundary spanning function between organisations and their publics.

At the same time, role competencies of public relations practitioners (Gregory 2008) indicate the occupation is well placed to take advantage of the online public sphere, where 'private people come together as a public' (Habermas 1989 cited in L'Etang 2008: 107). Whether this opportunity will be seized or if public relations will cede the territory to other disciplines, only time will tell.

LOOKING AROUND THE DIGITAL TERRAIN

The global reach of digital technology is undisputable but the figures presented above reveal two-thirds of the world's population are behind a digital divide, where they do not have access, or perhaps the ability, to take advantage of online communications. Even in countries where the majority have access, large sections of the population are excluded from the vast array of information and discussion taking place in the virtual world. The E-Learning Foundation (2010) claims 2 million school children in the UK are not able to access online resources at home; with the poorest least likely to have access to a computer.

Another consideration is the nature of online communities. Prensky (2001) distinguishes digital natives from digital immigrants; the former being the generation that has grown up immersed in a digital age. He argues the younger demographic not only prefers newer technology but engages differently with communications as a result. Pankraz (2010) identifies Gen C, a sub-set of digital natives who are interested in connecting with others in their 'tribes' (belonging to many simultaneously), derive social status by co-creating and sharing online (live streaming their experiences), 'swarm' around topics on the basis of peer approval, and are constantly connected via social media platforms.

As well as an age imbalance, Norris (2001) highlights that a digital divide adversely affects rural communities, and those with lower educational attainment and/or lower incomes. Other possible factors affecting digital engagement include gender, disability and ethnicity (Himma and Tavani 2008), leading to calls for positive action by government and businesses to increase access (OECD 2003).

From a public relations perspective, there continues to be a need to reach those who are not digitally equipped – and existing means of communication remain important (Kent 2010), even to publics who utilise newer technologies.

Arguments that the internet is a place with a primarily public goal of 'fostering conversation and connection between people' (Levine 2009: 25) are countered by observations of 'commercialization of cyberspace' (Curran and Seaton 2003: 235) as a consequence of which, the internet is 'pulled by opposed forces in different directions'. This debate is of relevance to public relations, which likewise is caught between the 'aggressive, competitive, hyperbolic, selling mind-set' of marketing and a 'more conciliatory, peacemaking approach' (Hutton 2010: 510).

In many ways the digital world reflects a frontier environment where 'the only certain thing is that everything is subject to change' (Fertik and Thompson 2010: 30); and there are inevitable tensions between 'early pioneers and late arrivals'. This can be seen in the way in which some internet users advocate social norms of behaviour; such as how the CIPR has established guidelines to reflect acceptable practice online. Governments and organizations likewise look to harness, or even control, the free-for-all nature of the online territory. For example, in the UK, the Digital Economy Act 2010 makes provision for online copyright protection and regulation of digital communications.

Technology also enables online movement to be tracked and monitored. For PR practitioners this facilitates examination of online debate, scrutiny of how issues develop, provides evidence of return on investment and enables evaluation of communications efforts. Such surveillance raises issues about privacy and security; impacting on the freedom to express opinions and potentially limiting the power of digital communications to enable greater public interaction in society.

Clearly digital terrain is uneven – with a lack of equal access to all sections of society, tensions between personal and commercial activity, and questions over ways in which online behaviour may be monitored, or potentially restricted. At the same time it has enabled unprecedented interconnection of the world's population, presented an opportunity for everyone (potentially) to express a public opinion and created an explosion in the availability of information and human knowledge.

A LOOK BACKWARDS: GETTING HERE FROM THERE

A reflective look backwards shows how developments in landline telephone technology; market competition and free access to the internet were responsible for widespread online access in the UK (Theaker 2007). Until faster connections became available the multimedia, 'writable web' (Phillips and Young 2009: 6) was inconceivable; while similar, recent changes in mobile access (smartphone technology and low cost data contracts) have brought online communications to pocket-sized devices that once only enabled telephone calls. The personal computer and mobile phone are not the only available platforms ('devices we use to access the internet and its knowledge', Phillips and Young 2009: 95) as laptop/tablet/notebook computers, e-readers, interactive television sets, gaming systems, in-car electronics, and hybrid or cross-platforms increasingly compete in providing online access.

Likewise, Phillips and Young (2009) observe a wide choice of channels by which information can now be obtained – from texting, instant messaging and email to social networks, blogging, micro-blogging (e.g. Twitter) and virtual environments. In 2010, with 81 million smartphones sold world-wide between October and the end of the year alone, the *Wall Street Journal* reported the rise of apps (micro-computer programmes); tens of thousands of which have been launched, making it even easier to access content through mobile devices. This includes news (via magazine, newspaper and broadcasting apps) and various social media enabling applications.

Many organizations are making their own information and services available in this way. The supermarket Waitrose launched an app in August 2010 featuring interactive recipes, video guides and technical kitchen tools. Motoring organization, the Automobile Association (AA), has a series of apps available including lifestyle, learn to drive and travel guides.

In the early days, organizations were interested in the internet as a means of publishing information for audiences – primarily using web pages as static online brochures where PR practitioners employed their traditional craft as wordsmiths. Today, they are increasingly forced to react, 24:7, to customers documenting their experiences with poor services instantly and globally via smartphone to a wide range of online channels – presenting a more strategic, reputation management and problem-solving role. Chaos at airports caused by extreme weather conditions at the end of 2010 saw stranded passengers turn to Twitter and YouTube to express their frustrations (which were re-reported by online and mainstream news channels); while some airlines (notably KLM) engaged with customers via social networking.

The primary use of the web in 1999 (according to data cited by Theaker 2007) was searching for information. This is still reflected in figures from Experian Hitwise (2010) showing the search engine Google as the most visited website in the UK. The dominance of search engines as a gateway to information has led to a new digital PR skill: search engine optimization (primarily using organic – i.e. content driven – rather than paid-for methods). Ensuring an organization's information is the most visible to searchers should be at the forefront of an online communications strategy (Phillips and Young 2009). This involves understanding how search engines work; researching the keywords used by stakeholders, including these within the organization's web pages (and other online presence), and ensuring information is regularly updated.

One change in the last decade has been the rise in social networks and entertainment media as online destinations. Facebook is now the second most visited site in the UK (overtaking Google as the most popular in the US at end of 2010), with YouTube in third place. These sites require a different strategic response from organizations as they allow for greater interactivity, but may also be seen as personal space where professional communicators are not welcome.

Public relations' role in building relationships, enacting dialogue, and working with 'earned media' (editorial coverage; Watson and Noble 2007: 231) suggests the function is best suited for such engagement rather than those with marketing or purely persuasive intent (Kent 2010).

In under a decade digital public relations has developed from crafting content to engaging 24:7 with online communities. This has been driven by changes in technology that enable publics to act as equals and amplify crisis situations. As well as continuing to provide accessible information for those undertaking online searches, PR practitioners need to be active in social networks to build relationships and managing organizational reputations. Looking backwards we can see how potentially the role of digital PR has changed from a tactical to a strategic one.

LOOKING AROUND: DIGITAL PR IN PRACTICE

Public relations pioneers broke digital ground by learning the lay of this new land, sometimes through trial and error. Unfortunately, technology enabled some poor practices to move online. Press release distribution became much easier, cheaper – and annoying to its recipients – with the advent of email and data management systems (which should enable personal contact and tailoring of information). As a result of complaints from journalists and online influencers (such as bloggers) about PR 'polluting' the online environment (Inconvenient PR Truth 2010), the CIPR, PRCA and Investor Relations Society, backed by the National Union of Journalists launched a 'media spamming charter' in September 2010.

The potential for deception online through the use of avatars (virtual identities) and campaign-specific micro-sites enables tactics in the less ethical style of Bernays' use of front groups (Palenchar and Fitzpatrick 2009). Theaker (2007) relates the case of a fake travel blog created by Edelman employees, which was portrayed as genuine advocacy supposedly involving two members of the public visiting Wal-Mart stores around the US. Kent (2010: 652) claims such 'ethical lapses' have received attention from journalists but primarily been ignored by public relations professionals.

Organizations have also experienced criticism of their behaviour from online communities using social media. Gilpin and Murphy (2010: 75) cite a mommy blogger (mothers who blog) campaign against the Johnson & Johnson Motrin painkiller brand to illustrate the consequences of failing to monitor online media over weekends and demonstrate a lack of recognition 'of the speed and reach of online social networks and their relationship to mainstream media'.

The ethics of practices such as ghost writing blogs, Tweeting on behalf of clients/ executives and paying bloggers to post favourable comments are other practices much debated online. Transparency is suggested as the best way of avoiding any confusion or deception, with regulation possible as a future control on such practices.

Despite these examples, Phillips and Young (2009: 222) argue 'there is no need for public relations to develop a new code of conduct for social media'. Nevertheless, they advocate public relations practitioners need to 'show the unseen hand' (ibid.: 223) in their work. The role of public relations historically has been as an invisible persuader (Mitchie 1998) but this is shifting towards a 'revealed identity' (Phillips and Young 2009: 232).

In terms of online and social media presence, the public relations practitioner may gain a higher profile, perhaps in having a Twitter account that carries their name or by openly contributing to a blog or other digital content. The alternative approach of anonymous organizational participation runs the risk of lacking personality, and probably reflects a one-way broadcasting approach to online communications.

Alongside cautionary examples, cases are used to make great claims for the success of social media campaigns. Public relations consultancy, Borkowski played a role in raising the profile of a Facebook campaign that influenced Cadbury's in reintroducing the Wispa chocolate bar in 2007. A student campaign on Facebook was successful in challenging an HSBC bank policy to rescind interest-free overdrafts (Shirky 2008). Such examples have been cited as evidence of the ability of social networks to change the behaviour of organizations. However, two anecdotal cases do not prove social media campaigns will necessarily be successful. Indeed, there are thousands of groups set up on Facebook (by organizations and activists) that do not generate much interest.

Looking at Facebook presence, at the end of 2010 Coca-Cola was the most popular commercial brand with almost 22 million fans/likes. Interestingly, the group was initially established by two members of the public and then supported by the company as an official site. Despite this popularity, the drink company has had problems using social media with a controversial Dr Pepper viral campaign being withdrawn following criticism including on the Mumsnet parents' forum.

Several awards schemes have been established to acknowledge best practice in social media campaigns by PR practitioners. Although helpful in highlighting practical examples, it is debatable whether there is sufficient evidence to assess the validity of award entries (or winners) in any meaningful manner. Also, this focus on praising campaigns presents a short-term, tactical focus for social media use rather than a 'coherent organization-wide online strategy' (Phillips and Young 2009: 180).

Numerous books, online resources, and training courses provide guidance for PR practitioners wishing to develop online strategies or campaigns; while the CIPR has established a social media panel to lead 'thinking and practice'. Such initiatives serve to underline a belief that 'professionals need to understand the strengths and limitations of the media so that, when appropriate they can use it' (Kent 2010: 654). There has been little examination of the risks and investment required in using social media, nor whether claims for its effectiveness are over-optimistic.

Another consideration for digital public relations practice is whether expertise should be developed in-house and/or if specialist consultancies should be engaged. There are practitioners (within consultancies and working in-house) with many years' experience in digital PR; while others have executed high profile campaigns or managed organizational online strategies. Their practical experience is used to advocate adoption of digital PR, with academic examination of the area generally lagging behind.

Theaker (2007) expressed a view that competency with new technology is a requirement for everyone working in PR. What this means in practice is unclear given the developing nature of technology. In 2001, Springston noted half of PR practitioners had no training in using email. By 2008, Eyrich *et al.* found this was a ubiquitous skill; although practitioners were 'slower to integrate more technologically complicated tools that cater to a niche audience (e.g., text messaging, social networks, virtual worlds)' (p. 413). This suggests that adoption of technologies will take time and may depend on ease of their integration into practice.

Kitchen and Panopoulos (2010) argue adoption of new technology should be seen as a continuous, long-term process; although they suggest organizations may prefer to employ 'young well-informed, technologically sophisticated professionals' (p. 226) rather than develop skills of more experienced PR practitioners. However, no difference in use of social media between those performing public relations manager and technician roles was found by Diga and Kelleher (2009). Grunig and Grunig (2010) dismiss employing a young person simply because they are technically adept to undertake social media; they also argue against a specialist social media function. As Holmes (2007) observed, the PR industry needs to find candidates who 'possess rare and perhaps even contradictory qualities' such as the good judgement that comes with age and experience alongside knowledge of new media opportunities.

It is vital that those responsible for online PR activities ensure they are 'part of a strategic, multi-participant, multi-media approach' (Phillips and Young 2009: 180). As such, digital public relations objectives need to be considered within a framework of the wider organizational and functional goals and strategies. This implies public relations practitioners need to have a strategic rather than only a tactical role; not least to ensure the function is able to work closely with other areas of the organization in developing an online strategy (such as IT, marketing, human resources and senior management). A holistic organizational approach enables a wide range of perspectives and skills to be involved in the process and ensures greater support for the resulting strategy.

Given the dynamic nature of online communications, those responsible for digital PR need to reflect a flexible attitude to ensure any issues identified by ongoing monitoring can be addressed promptly without creating a crisis situation. Risk assessment is particularly important when considering 'edgy' campaigns that may be felt appropriate to stimulate viral communications and engage younger audiences.

LEICESTER NHS TRUST

Leicester NHS Trust undertook a viral video campaign aiming to address the high levels of underage pregnancy in the area. The Teenage Kicks video shows the unexpected birth of a baby in a playground appearing to be filmed on a mobile phone. The campaign was made with the involvement of young people and received a positive reaction in conveying its message. Nevertheless, complaints received by YouTube resulted in the video being removed, albeit temporarily. Public relations practitioners need to consider the benefits and potential issues involved in engaging with social media and be prepared to handle any possible negative outcomes as appropriate for the organization and its aims. In this case, the opportunity to address a significant social issue appears to have outweighed any criticisms of the nature of the video.

DIGITAL MEDIA RELATIONS

One key area where the development of digital PR practice needs to be examined is media relations. In 2003, Callison observed that the majority of Fortune 500 company websites did not offer a dedicated online site for media content; those that did primarily included news releases and executive biographies/photographs.

Online press offices (or virtual media centres) can offer a wide range of electronic information in media-friendly form. However, the ability to transmit news and other company information direct to citizen journalists, bloggers and the general public raises the question of the value of a dedicated area with restricted access for traditional media contacts. Requiring registration and use of log-ins seems unadvisable; although protecting copyright or time-release sensitive material may necessitate limited access in some cases.

Technological developments also mean that organizations increasingly offer multimedia resources, links to additional information, and social media feeds within a media (or open access) website. Further, many organizations publish material that may once have been restricted to mainstream media on public sites such as YouTube, Flikr, Facebook and Twitter. The idea of an exclusive, media-only website is less important than ensuring timely, and accurate, information can be found by anyone interested in an issue or organization.

This all increases the challenge in ensuring information available is up to date and appropriately archived. Managing legacy issues is a considerable responsibility and extends to areas such as Wikipedia where inaccurate information may have a high profile. When engaging with third-party sites to correct information, PR practitioners must ensure they focus on fact not opinion or they could be accused of seeking censorship.

A more open approach means contact details for the PR team able to provide additional information should be readily available – and these are likely to include details of Twitter accounts. This does raise issues of providing personal contact details to the general public, which could be abused.

One option is that adopted by Ford Motor Company, which manages 24:7 global communications through its Content Factory; which supports media and in-house practitioners with a global news operation staffed by experts in PR, traditional journalism, multimedia and social media.

Open access also contributes towards search engine optimisation (SEO) as continuously updated news will be picked up; depending on how information is presented. Downloadable documents such as PDFs may not be readily searchable by search engines, whereas blog-style sites encourage frequent posting which does help boost SEO.

An interactive media-focused website could include the opportunity for instant messaging or online phone conversations, RSS (Really Simple Syndication) web feeds and other means for journalists (and other interested parties) to receive relevant communications from the press office.

This discussion highlights ongoing changes in the nature of journalism in the face of the online digital environment. News and other information that has traditionally been available only through print or broadcast media is now offered online, through search engines (e.g. Google News) and smartphone applications, as well as on the websites of familiar media organizations (such as the BBC). The ease of uploading and updating information means the online news world is a 24:7, global one. Technology also enables notification of news or specific information to be received immediately through RSS feeds, social media updates and emails from search engines and subscriptions on websites. At the same time, the public is increasingly invited to contribute to the development of news by sending in personal reports, photographs, experiences and comments.

Various models are evident in terms of how online media operate as businesses. The BBC is supported by the licence fee. Other media offer open access to information on the basis of attracting large audiences that are of interest to advertisers. Some media integrate their online and offline offerings with the income from one offsetting the other. Subscription only access and other financial models are being introduced, including paid-for smartphone applications. The success of relevant strategies is a matter of debate, and PR practitioners need to consider the implications of each model for their own media relations activities and communi-cations strategy. It could be that having a smaller audience that has paid to receive certain material is of greater value than more hits from those who are less interested in, or engaged with, the particular site.

The reach of online media is another important factor as blogs and social media may generate greater awareness of a story and add valuable engagement through comments and endorsement. This could apply equally to criticism and negative opinion, which may be transmitted by digital WOM. The symbiotic relationships between mainstream and online media interface is also of interest as online comment often relates to mainstream coverage and vice versa.

Monitoring online coverage can be problematic as content is frequently added, amended and removed. The use of RSS and email feeds from search engines and other sites for key search words can help PR practitioners keep up to date with what is being said online, both in websites and via social media. Expert companies also offer monitoring service, although the cost of employing them – and issues such as paying license fees – may need to be considered (although this second factor is being challenged legally in 2011 by the PRCA).

INFLUENCER ENGAGEMENT

One of the purposes of online monitoring is to identify those who are influential on an organization's key publics. This has traditionally been one reason why journalists were important as they were believed to provide valuable third party endorsement (Heath 2005), which was trusted and seen as credible by audiences.

The 2010 Edelman Trust Barometer reveals that trust in organizations (including media, government and NGOs) is fragile and affected by short-term concerns. This suggests that the ability of online communications to amplify awareness of, and discussion about issues, can readily impact on trust, and thereby, reputations.

The influence of social networks can be found in the high level of trust placed in those similar to ourselves in the Edelman survey (although experts are rated as more influential). The study concluded that multiple information sources enhance credibility, which argues against PR practitioners taking a narrow focus on journalists and media relations.

Bettinghaus and Cody (1994) identify that when considering a matter beyond their own experience, people are more likely to turn to experts. In contrast, the advice of friends or others like us is likely to be more influential for personal matters. The combination of expertise and similarity can be found online, where a conversational, narrative style evident particular in blogs, enhances trust (Brogan and Smith 2010).

PR practitioners have sought to engage the new online influencers, with the emergence of tactics such as 'blogger relations' (Solis and Breakenridge 2009: 102). This involves treating bloggers in the same way as journalists by providing information, building relationships, inviting on launches, and pitching stories. Not all bloggers have responded positively to such approaches, while the commercialization of bloggers has also been criticized. Solis and Breakenridge cite an example of mommy bloggers feeling they were being treated as a one-way communication channel by organizations' PR practitioners who had never read, let alone engaged with, their blogs.

The nature of engagement has changed with the maturation of blogs and other online communications. There has been discussion of regulation requiring openness about any commercial involvement, for example, payment or supply of goods in exchange for a positive review. In addition, organizations such as Mumsnet have emerged as an influential forum, growing from a website to share information into a significant commercial concern publishing books, making television programmes and attracting advertising on the basis of over 1.2 million unique visitors each month.

Public relations practitioners need to recognize that online influencers may react differently to mainstream journalist contacts. The latter establish relationships with PR practitioners as 'gate keepers' who provide access to information and resources within organizations, particularly when checking facts or other aspects of generating a story. In contrast, online communicators (such as bloggers or participants in social media) do not necessarily see themselves as writing for an audience or believe they need to check information beyond reference to existing online sources. Although some may welcome approaches from PR practitioners, others may resent such intrusion into their online space.

It is also worth reflecting that contact and engagement with PR practitioners may adversely affect the credibility of online influencers. As discussed above, there are tensions between those who see the internet as a place for open engagement in discussion and its increased commercialization. PR practitioners seeking to engage online influencers needs to consider whether their intent is persuasive, rather than informative or dialogic. If the former, they should tread lightly if they are not to potentially alienate those with whom they seek to engage.

LOOKING AHEAD

It is difficult to predict how digital PR will develop – but there are some indications that are worth exploring.

1   *Information overload*. At the end of 2010, there were 500 million members of Facebook and 200 million profiles on Twitter. Half of all active users of Facebook log on daily, spending an average of 32 minutes on the site. They upload over 2.5 billion photos each month, while Twitter users post 100 million comments every day. If the growth trends of these and other online sites continue, it is inevitable that information overload will make it harder and harder to monitor, engage and make an impact. There are also concerns about the ability of online technologies to cope with such volumes of information and discussion that a separate internet may need to be launched offering more selective, but faster, access – at a price. It should also be remembered that the increased volume of information contains much outdated and arguably decayed data. An analysis of accounts on Twitter in 2010 showed:

- 41 per cent of users have not tweeted since setting up an account
- 24 per cent of users have zero followers
- 79 per cent of users have fewer than 100 followers
- 81 per cent of users follow fewer than 100 people
- 80 per cent of users have made fewer than 500 tweets
- 22.5 per cent of users account for 90 per cent of all activity
- 2.2 per cent of users account for 58.3 per cent of all tweets (many of which are automatic feed generators).

2 *Privacy concerns*. With such a phenomenal increase in information online, existing worries about privacy and security of financial and other data will escalate. Organizations will not only need to protect their own data, but ensure anything provided by stakeholders is held securely. There will also be increasing concerns about ensuring veracity online to avoid fraudulent representation of an organization – or malicious attacks on its reputation.

3 *Censorship*. It may seem impossible with the volume of online information to shut the door, but governments and others may seek to use technology to censor information. The example of how the website Wikileaks has published confidential information may be used as justification for greater security and protection rather than serving to further open up public access.

4 *Micro-networks*. One solution to the scope and scale of the existing internet may be the development of more specialist, secure and personal networks. There is likely to be a cost, such as a subscription fee, for such services, but individuals may feel this is worth paying to avoid the increased noise and commercialization of the overloaded internet. This may be beneficial to organizations that may set up and own networks, or be welcome into other networks as valued partners.

5 *New influencers*. Faced with a vast array of opinion and information of questionable quality, people will need to turn to trusted sources of information. A new type of influencer may emerge – combining the best qualities of experts, journalists and people like ourselves. Whether or not the PR practitioner could fulfil this role is debatable (especially as they are partisan by nature of employment), but they could act as a facilitator of informed debate.

6 *Return on investment*. Everything online can be measured, and provided that systems can cope with the increasing volume and scope of the online world, it will be easier to consider return on investment. This presents a quantitative approach, unless qualitative measures that are able to analyse sentiment and other more subtle aspects of relationships and reputation can be developed.

7 *Ethics*. Underpinning all the above points is the issue of ethical behaviour. While the online landscape initially attracted pioneers and seems to be

undergoing a period of commercial development, it is possible this will result in a chaotic world where anything goes, particularly if government and organizations find they are unable to control or censor criminal and other behaviours that are socially or politically unacceptable. There is already plenty of opportunity for misrepresentation and other less ethical practices, and public relations has not been immune to transferring some of its own questionable tactics online.

IMPLICATIONS FOR COMMUNICATION THEORIES

Public relations is a communicative function – defined by Grunig and Hunt (1984: 6) as 'the management of communication between an organization and its publics'. Considering the impact of digital PR on communication theories enables us to assess the way in which practice is influenced by its development.

Fawkes and Gregory (2000: 109) stated that

> much public relations practice is still posited on dated theories of the system of communication along the linear lines of sender, channel, receiver (with feedback). The public relations professional is there to transmit a message with the purpose of persuading publics to the point of view being promulgated.

Clearly the multi-directional nature of online communications challenges the traditional idea of public relations involving a straightforward distribution of a message to a passive audience (through a compliant mediator).

The method of communications traditionally associated with public relations is one of an organization engaging in one-way communications of the press agentry or public information format identified by Grunig and Hunt (1984). This reflects a view of communications being transmitted by those with power over the source of communications (selectively) to the masses.

In contrast, the Cluetrain Manifesto (Levin, 1999) proposed digital communications sees a major directional change in messages where amateurs increasingly are the source with the elite (and presumably the PR practitioner) at the end of the process, responding to what is being generated online.

Using three levels of communication identified by Fawkes and Gregory (2000) we can reflect further on the nature of digital PR:

1   *inter-personal* – where individuals engage in conversation. Arguably, tools such as social media, forums and direct messaging, encourage this type of communication, even between organizations and publics.

2   *Group communications* – taking place within a group that shares a common aim and engaged in communication with others in the group and outside

it. Social networks by definition involve groups engaging in discussion around matters of interest – although discussion may not be limited to any group member as that can be fluid in the case of Twitter or open in the case of Facebook (although closed groups are also possible).

3   *society-wide* – traditionally seen as the level of mass media broadcast, it is evident in the global reach of websites, plus combining connections in social networks, or through the scale of some influencers (for example, at the end of 2010, Justin Bieber had almost 19 million members of his official Facebook group, while Lady Gaga has nearly 8 million followers on Twitter). The permanence of online communications also offers a 'long tail' where over time reach may grow cumulatively (for example, with YouTube views).

Three phenomena of online communications are noted by Gregory (1999b):

1   *transparency* – how organizations' activities are made more visible. This reflects increased openness in communications.

2   *porosity* – how organizations are increasingly 'leaky' with digital information easily distributed internally and externally.

3   *agency* – how information can be changed by others; who may act as positive or negative influencers in endorsing or challenging a message.

Fawkes and Gregory (2000) similarly note human interaction online whereby users can readily amend, adapt or add to original information, in the manner that Westley–Maclean (1957, cited in Baran and Davis 2008) describe, where feedback loops exist between all parties and there is opportunity for mutual influence.

This participation in the communication process is important as it extends and challenges simple transmission models of sender–message–receiver. Fawkes and Gregory (2000) emphasize consideration of how someone uses a communication channel, which further highlights that receivers are active not passive elements in the communications process.

What is missing from these simplified models – regardless of whether or not they allow for participation – is the wider social context within which the communications is taking place. This is important when monitoring online communications where discussion is taking place in a framework that may be personal or particular to the parties involved. Cultural and other dynamics need to be considered, particularly in respect of use of language, which may be affected by the informality of much of online communications.

Grunig and Grunig (2010) believe the impact of digital media emphasizes the importance of relationships, predicated on trust and mutual influence, as central to excellence in public relations. Social media, they argue (ibid.: 3), makes it possible to engage in 'two way balanced dialogue with publics' and so improve relationships. Such dialogue is not based on any "control", which they believe has never been

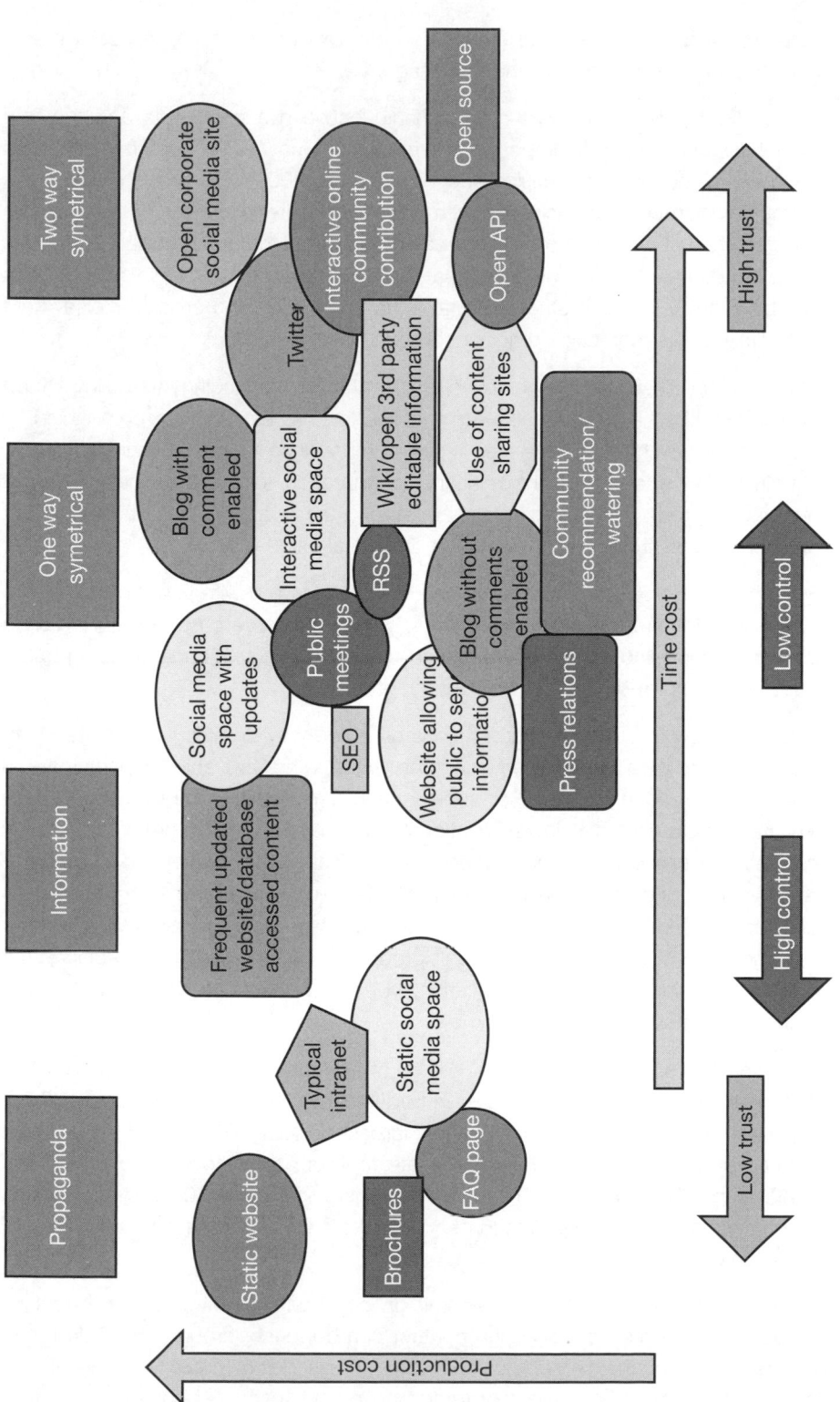

FIGURE 19.1 A new media adaptation of the models of public relations

Source: Dave Phillips, 2009. Used by permission

possible, despite the views of many in public relations who argue social media reflects a loss of control over their message.

Phillips (2009) demonstrates the relationship between social media and the four model paradigm originally proposed by Grunig and Hunt (1984). As shown in Figure 19.1, Phillips connects the illusion of control (Grunig 2009: 3) to propaganda (press agentry), which could be achieved with a static website where the PR practitioner (as discussed above) is employed in crafting messages that the organization wishes to communicate. It should be noted that there is no guarantee that this information can be controlled in that others can take the information and criticize it elsewhere (with links to the 'controlled' original source).

Phillips (2009) illustrates the increased time and cost of engaging in a dialogic form of public relations using open, engaging online techniques. This is accompanied by greater trust, which as we have seen is of vital importance for credibility and influence. Grunig (2009) also argues the relationship approach to social media requires a bridging approach to public relations rather than it acting as a buffer to act defensively and protect the organization from stakeholder views.

From a communications perspective this means engaging with social media needs to be undertaken as a two-way process; where the research and insight gained from monitoring and conversation is used to increase mutual understanding rather than simply inform defensive or persuasive strategies.

This advocacy for online communications as a two-way dialogic process needs to be considered in a dynamic environment where users are able to participate in interpersonal, group (network) or society-wide (broadcast) communications. One limitation of Grunig's considered relationship approach is that it omits the chaotic nature of the online environment where communication may be networked, ephemeral, taken out of context or lacking in veracity. Should – indeed, can – an organization develop a relationship with someone (who may be using an avatar alias) posting a superficial Tweet or joining a Facebook group just for fun? Arguably, Grunig is not talking about this type of communication, but it may reflect the dominant nature of online discussion.

Website Monitor Blogs reveals the nature of messaging on Twitter (Figure 19.2). The largest category of statement is an update of the user's current status (30 per cent) with personal conversation the next largest category (27 per cent). Messages where PR practitioners could engage relate to links posted to web content (3 per cent), images/video (3 per cent) and news stories/blog articles (10 per cent). Product recommendations or complaints (6 per cent) also offer organizations an opportunity to engage with a user.

Of course, given the 140 character limit on posts within Twitter, it is not really a medium for conversation, although contact can be made through retweeting, responding to or commenting on posts, or direct messages (if mutually following). The point is being made in respect of reminding practitioners that social media does

Twitter message types

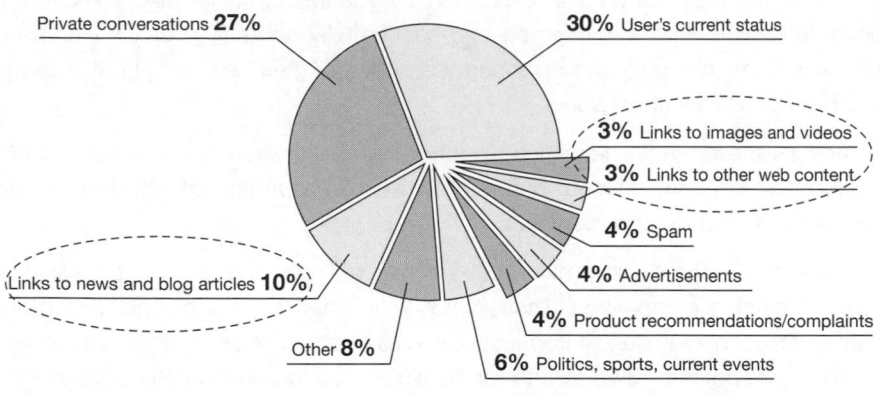

FIGURE 19.2 Twitter chart

Source: www.website-monitoring.com/blog/2010/05/04/twitter-facts-and-figures-history-statistics, used by permission

not necessarily offer the opportunity to build relationships in the same depth that traditional face-to-face methods allow. Nevertheless, combining online and offline communication means that relationships established in one medium can be enhanced in the other.

PROFESSIONAL BODIES IN AN ONLINE WORLD

The discussion of real and virtual relationships is relevant when looking at the impact of digital technology on professional public relations bodies. In the UK, membership of the CIPR, PRCA and similar bodies is not compulsory and a minority of practitioners make the commitment to join. Online communications offer both a challenge and an opportunity to such institutions.

Within social networks, such as Facebook and LinkedIn, there are many groups comprising public relations practitioners and other communication professionals. There is no cost to join these and a 'community of practice' (Wenger and Snyder 2000) can be formed offering personal and specific support as well as other opportunities. Other digital networks exclusively for communicators have been established such as MyRagan (www.myragan.com), which comprise discussion forums, personal blogs, bulletin boards, chatrooms and so forth.

In addition, PR practitioners can build their own personal network online, access a wide range of resources (many underpinned by solid research, such as the Institute for Public Relations) and participate in debate on specialist blogs (such as PR Conversations, www.prconversations.com).

Although these developments offer a threat to the long-established traditional PR bodies, in the main they have responded by integrating social media and other digital technology into their membership offering. Undoubtedly this has increased the value of membership and extended the ability for members to gain knowledge and build professional networks.

As well as these virtual networking opportunities, practitioners continue to build relationships in the 'real world' both as members of a professional body and with their colleagues and other contacts.

Undoubtedly, online developments have enhanced membership of a professional body by offering competition. Those who decide not to join an organization (for whatever reason) may benefit from accessing alternative online offerings and consequently, both options serve to offer professional development for the occupation.

TERRITORIAL ARGUMENTS

Grunig (2009) presents data claiming public relations departments in the US have responsibility for digital communications. Given the quoted figures of 49 per cent responsible for blogging, 48 per cent for social networking, and 52 per cent for micro blogging, the online territory is clearly not universally claimed by the PR function.

Several functions may legitimately lay claim to a piece of the digital terrain. IT functions naturally need to be involved in ensuring an organization has the technical capability to deliver an online communications strategy, as well as offering support for the development of relevant services. If an organization does not have relevant IT expertise in-house, or for specialist PR services, it may employ external consultancies. A media website may be more cost-effective to contract from an organization with expertise in this area.

Depending on the nature of the organization, the website may be under the responsibility of the sales or marketing function. This would be the case where the site is primarily involved in online retail. A marketing led approach will also be evident in paid-for search engine optimization and other online advertising. Marketing approaches are often used to establish micro-sites to support the introduction of a new product or service.

Customer relations may be involved in managing a corporate blog, particularly if its purpose is to focus on service issues and demonstrate a pro-active approach to managing any issues that arise.

Within the organization, an intranet and other communications technologies may be under the responsibility of the human resources function. This may involve providing employees with access to policies and procedures or other aspects of internal communications, if they fall under HR's control within the organization.

Even if public relations has primary control of digital communications, the function will need to work with others inside the organization (and externally where relevant).

It is unlikely that the PR function will have the expertise, or budget, to manage all areas of the organization's online presence. A collaborative approach is therefore recommended rather than fighting over territory.

Hutton (2010: 509) notes traditional rivalry between public relations and marketing 'in competing for organizational attention and resources'. He argues that in recent years, the marketing function has 'subsumed much or all of public relations', and while not considering the online environment specifically, his proposition that marketing has sought to 'manage relationships with a host of non-customer publics' (p. 519) would seem relevant.

Undoubtedly, the online world is one in which it is essential to manage communications cohesively with all stakeholders and publics. Unless restricted access is feasible (as discussed with media websites), information online is open to all. This means, for example, a Tweet intended for an individual journalist or to promote a particular product, or respond to a specific issue can be read by anyone. Even if access can be controlled, such as with membership of a LinkedIn group, once information is available digitally it can be readily re-communicated.

Rather than arguing over ownership of an organization's online presence, it is useful for public relations practitioners to focus on areas where their expertise is most relevant.

Hutton (2010) considers the relationship between marketing, advertising, marketing communications and public relations in terms of areas of responsibility and overlap. This shows PR specifically encompassing 'investor relations, community relations, employee communication, public affairs/government relations, media relations, crisis communications, corporate identity, executive communications, charitable donations, and the like' (ibid.: 514). Falling between marketing and public relations are corporate advertising, sponsorship and aspects of media relations, crisis communications, and corporate identity (notably relating to products or service delivery).

It may be helpful for the two functions to work together in developing online strategies for these areas of overlap, as well as ensuring a coherent approach for those areas that fall outside of joint responsibility.

Media relations should perhaps be extended to digital influencer relations to take account of citizen journalists, bloggers, and others who act as reliable sources online. When issues that relate to marketing, customer relations, or other functions arise, a joint approach would be taken as is common in managing similar matters when raised by offline media.

Public relations would also take a lead in online communications in managing emerging issues and crisis scenarios. This cannot be done in isolation where all the organization's digital collateral should be involved in communicating with relevant stakeholders and publics.

TOYOTA GB

During its global vehicle recall in 2010, Toyota GB set up a dedicated area of its website where customers could determine if their own model was involved. At the same time, the PR function undertook digital media relations, including using Twitter. Given the volume of online communications across the world, the company established a specific site, Toyota Communications (http://toyotaconversations.com) to aggregate links on Twitter mentioning the brand alongside video and other social media content, plus a copy of the Akio Plan to restore the company's reputation (named after Akio Toyoda, president and CEO of Toyota Motor Corporation).

A HYBRID FUTURE

Given discussion of the need for various functions to work together in the digital environment, it is worth considering whether the future will include a hybrid occupation rather than separate specialist functions.

Although Hutton (2010) argues IMC is a defensive strategy by the advertising industry, he observes fewer differences between marketing and PR in recent years. In looking at the relationship between the two, he notes that a model of a single combined function is 'appropriate to most situations where a high percentage of marketing issues are communication related and vice versa' (ibid.: 512), concluding this is 'typical of a small business'.

The historical difference between marketing and PR communications could be presented as a split between *paid* and *earned*. That is, marketing traditionally took responsibility for paid media, such as advertising, direct mail, brochures, etc. Public relations work with media and other non-consumer stakeholders was largely earned, by virtue of developing relationships or communicating useful information or narratives.

In the online world, this distinction is still evident, but blurring. Corcoran (2009) presents buzz, viral and WOM campaigns as earned media: 'when customers become the channel.' Further overlap can be seen in the area of *owned* or *created* media, which could include a YouTube channel, magazine, podcasts, Twitter accounts, corporate blog and so forth. Arguably PR's expertise in developing corporate narrative, understanding news and developing credible communications that are not exclusively sales/marketing oriented means that the discipline is best placed to manage owned/created media. The budgets involved in its generation may mean it falls under marketing's control. Such debate may reflect a need for a hybrid function, although as Grunig and Grunig (2010) have argued, it is important that online communications is not isolated from strategic management.

REVOLUTION OR EVOLUTION?

In many respects, the development of digital communications presents an opportunity for public relations to evolve in order to apply its existing strengths in earning coverage, building online relationships and managing corporate reputation. Simply transferring traditional PR tactics online would be naïve and arguably has already created problems of credibility.

On the other hand, an argument that 'the internet changes everything' (Phillips and Young 2009: 3) is simplistic, as the online terrain is not entirely an alien country. It may involve a 24:7 immediate global communications environment where everyone can be a publisher, but at its heart, digital PR is still about engaging people with interesting narratives, seeking to establish valuable relationships with key publics and ensuring positive reputations are understood and maintained.

For those who see the online arena as one that can be ignored or treated as the same as offline communications, perhaps it is useful to recognize the ways in which we are facing a revolution – not least because of the ease by which online communities can be networked and communicate independently.

For those who see the online arena as an entirely new terrain for public relations practice, it is important to recognise the discipline has a solid track record that can evolve in this new world. These strengths enable the function to integrate the skills and knowledge applied to mainstream media relations, community relations, public affairs and other areas of expertise to digital influencer relations, online issues/crisis management and stimulating WOM communications.

There are many opportunities and threats to public relations, not least in respect of its relationship with marketing where overlap is increasingly evident. Nevertheless, there is potential for PR practitioners to lead a hybrid strategic function that manages paid, earned and owned/created media communications both online and offline.

In conclusion, the fast-moving nature of the digital world can be seen as both an evolution and a revolution for PR theory and practice. It is something that cannot be ignored, but at the same time, it does not signal an end to everything we have ever known about working in this fascinating field.

QUESTIONS FOR DICUSSION

1 How does the digital divide impact on the work undertaken by PR practitioners?

2 Would you describe yourself as a digital native, a digital immigrant, a pioneer or a late arrival into the digital world? What does this mean for your own approach to digital PR?

3 In what ways might a PR function be affected by an increase in mobile access for online communications?

4 Research a brand (or your own employer) via Google, Facebook, YouTube and Twitter – what do the results tell you about its online reputation?

5 How could unethical digital PR practice be controlled?

6 What are the main arguments for and against young PR practitioners being given responsibility for managing an organization's social media communications?

7 What are the benefits and drawbacks of having open access to an online media centre?

8 Who do you trust online and why?

9 What challenges do you believe PR practitioners will experience if current online trends continue?

10 Look at the Ford Fiesta Movement campaign – www.ford.com/fiestamovement – is this a PR or marketing initiative?

FURTHER READING

Brogan, C. and Smith, J. (2010) *Trust agents: using the web to build influence, improve reputation, and earn trust*, John Wiley and Sons.

Phillips, D. and Young, P. (2009) *Online public relations* (2nd edition), Kogan Page.

Prensky, M. (2001) *Digital natives, digital immigrants*, from *On the Horizon* (MCB University Press, 9(5), October 2001).

Shirky, C. (2008) *Here comes everybody: the power of organizing without organizations*, Penguin Press.

Solis, B. and Breakenridge, D. (2009) *Putting the public back in public relations: how social media is reinventing the aging business of PR*, FT Press.

Part IV

Shaping the future

CHAPTER 20

Future challenges for PR

Alison Theaker

CHAPTER AIMS

This chapter concerns the development of the public relations industry itself. While the future cannot be divorced from the debates in previous chapters about the development of the media and globalisation, the reputation of public relations, improving education and the quality of entrants, the measurement of results and the impact of new technology continue to concern practitioners.

LOOKING BACK AT LOOKING FORWARD

In 1990, Peter Gummer, Chairman of Shandwick plc, stated: 'I believe that PR will increasingly be seen for what it really is – an indispensable tool of management' (Gummer 1990). In 1994, IBDO's survey suggested that 'PR is increasingly regarded as a serious discipline' (IBDO 1994). Like IBDO, White and Mazur (1995: 251) concentrated on the consultancy sector in their own look at the future of public relations: 'In future, public relations, involving skilful management of important relationships and communication with groups of people on whose support any organisation depends, will come to be regarded as a key task for senior management.' In order to take advantage of this, 'public relations practitioners will need to develop their qualifications and skills, or will find that their role will be usurped by others, possibly management consultants, or advisers from other areas such as marketing or law.'

In July 2000, the seventh International Research Symposium at Lake Bled, Slovenia, took the theme of the future of PR. Susanne Holmstrom from the University of Roskilde, Denmark, presented a view of the evolution of PR from an economic necessity to a normal part of the management process.

Gable (2003) set out 'five major PR issues for the next decade'. First, the need to improve strategic planning and the link to communications was stressed. The next issue was the encroachment on public relations services by other consultants such as management consultants, lawyers and accountants. This was connected to the third issue, credibility. Public relations was still seen as a profession of spin rather than strategic communications and reputation management. The fourth issue reverted back to the question of defining public relations and a feeling that it was still a misunderstood profession. One of the most important ways to improve understanding and relevance was felt to be an emphasis on evaluation and measuring long-term effectiveness. The last issue was finding enough properly qualified staff by promoting public relations as an attractive industry to college students. Gable added five other headings to this list: improving public relations curricula and education; overcoming the loss of faith in business ethics; countering the slump in the economy and resisting clients' tendency to want to do things cheaply rather than strategically; improving professional standards in agencies; and emphasising the public interest side of public relations to stress its contribution to society.

Woodall and Smith (2003) reported on a Future Trends study carried out for the IABC Research Foundation. The survey of more than 1,000 IABC members worldwide found that professional communicators were ideally placed to use their boundary-spanning role to provide critical information to organisational management to flag trends and changes in order to improve business performance. However, economic conditions were causing strategic planning to take a back seat to short-term issues. The use of new technology was the third theme, with mixed responses on whether practitioners were taking advantage of new communication methods. Evaluation and improving ways of measuring results was a common goal. Lastly, concern with demonstrating productivity in communications was cited as both an opportunity and a risk. On the one hand, it would demonstrate value for money and establish credibility, but on the other, would expose the fact that most practitioners had no formal mechanisms in place.

In February 2007, the Council of PR Firms' President, Kathy Cripps, was quoted as saying 'clients are increasingly using public relations firms more for their strategic communications, particularly in the marketing arena' (Shaw 2007).

THE REPUTATION OF PR

Despite concerns about the poor image of PR being related to the fact that anyone can claim to be a PR practitioner, the industry has consistently preferred self-regulation to statutory controls.

> It seems to me that when public relations can clearly demonstrate that it is a profession characterised by integrity, then the perceptions will change.
>
> (Professor Anne Gregory, LMU, 2004)

Danny Moss (MMU 2004), felt that the perception of PR was indeed changing:

> There is a greater recognition of the importance of communications and that reputation cannot be taken for granted. The mechanisms of communication are changing and this has forced a rethink of traditional media strategies. A new generation of better-educated practitioners are assuming positions of authority and bringing a greater understanding of the potential of PR into the boardroom.

Dr Dejan Verčič, (President, EUPRERA, 2004) was also optimistic:

> There can be no doubt that public relations entered the twenty-first century as one of the governing institutions of our post-modern society.

DOES PR OWN REPUTATION?

Ernst & Young (2003, cited in NHS 2009) found that 80–85 per cent of the market value of top US companies was in intangible assets such as reputation. They even suggested that a one point increase in the reputation of an airline could equate to customers willing to pay $18 more for a ticket. Reputation has concrete benefits. An Ipsos MORI study suggested that companies in the BITC CSR index outperformed others in the FTSE top 350 by 3.3–7.4 per cent annually (Murphy 2009a).

The CIPR definition of PR links the industry with the management of reputation. A good reputation is an intangible asset of immense financial worth suggests Kevin Murray, Chief Executive Officer of Bell Pottinger (2003). Loss of reputation was acknowledged as the single biggest risk facing organisations (Aon research 1999, cited in Murray 2003). Campbell *et al.* (2006) question whether an industry with a bad image and often not represented in the boardroom can be regarded as so influential. She suggests that reputation is uncontrollable, especially with the rise of non-traditional media sources.

Murray and White (2004) went on to examine what CEOs felt was the role of PR in reputation management and how they assessed its contribution. While they recognised that PR had a primary role in facilitating reputation management, CEOs saw that they could help generate employee effort, the real driver of good reputation. PR could enhance but not create reputation.

However, Murray (2006) later questioned the pursuit of reputation. He suggested that the key elements that should concern PR practitioners should be managing and interpreting relationships and building trust in organisations; which should create desired behaviours. He also recommended the need for practitioners to be more aware of where their audiences were getting information from and be more targeted in sending the right messages. Macleod (2009b) also made a call for the use of research, benchmarking and pre-testing to demonstrating how communication led to ultimate behavioural change and for research into understanding what audiences expect and find reasonable.

WHAT DO PRACTITIONERS DO?

Improving professional competence, based on greater investment in training, was one of the issues to emerge from the DTI/IPR research as mentioned in Chapter 5.

'Professionalisation of the industry is key to the future, and this is inextricably linked to education and CPD,' said Ralph Tench, then course leader at LMU (2004). 'This involves strong relationships between relevant professional bodies, educational institutions and practitioners. Old models and theories will need reflection and change which will best be transferred to the practitioner community through linking training and education with innovation in practice.'

With the emphasis on PR as a management function and the need to be taken seriously by the dominant coalition, De Santo and Moss (2004) recorded what PR managers actually did. They carried out interviews with practitioners in the UK and US and found that rather than fitting Broom's role typology, managers spent most of their time in meetings, both internal (UK, 16 per cent of time; US, 24 per cent) and external (UK, 31 per cent; US, 15 per cent). One fifth of managers' time was taken up by administration tasks, while troubleshooting took up 7 per cent of UK managers' time and 15 per cent in the US. While management theorists such as Fayol defined management as a set of activities designed to enable managers to forecast and plan, organise, command, coordinate and control, only 10 per cent of PR managers' time was spent in planning. While some of the respondents were members of the top management team and were taken seriously, most had little involvement in policy-making within organisations.

Several surveys have asked practitioners what they see as the most important issues affecting the profession. The Centre for Economics and Business Research published a definitive statement that the size of the UK PR profession was 48,000, with a turnover of £6.5 billion. Despite Genasi's (CEBR 2005) claim that public relations had 'developed well beyond traditional media work', 70 per cent of in-house work was then concerned with media relations and 48 per cent of consultancy work.

Bowden-Green (2006) carried out research into how CIPR members in the south west of England practised PR and how they perceived it. He found that two-thirds of them regarded PR as projecting favourable messages through managing relationships with the media. Fewer than half considered PR a profession.

While the 2006 *PR Week* Survey found that practitioners were working more hours (Johnson 2007), and the CEBR study in 2005 had found that a quarter of practitioners worked over 48 hours per week, it was questionable whether these long hours were productive. Research by Time Act Solutions with 50 agencies found that they were spending a staggering 45 per cent of their time on account management and reporting back, but less than 20 per cent on media relations – the main task recorded. Strategic counsel took up 0.6 per cent of their time. They seemed to be spending more time getting authorised than actually doing the job. While smaller agencies seemed to be more efficient, spending 42 per cent of time on media relations plus 15 per cent on writing press releases, still only 4 per cent was spent on counselling clients. This does not give a picture of an industry engaged in board level activity (Gray 2006b).

Research carried out for *PR Week* UK by Brands2Life also found a disparity between theory and practice. Senior communications people rated customers as their most important stakeholders, then employees and the media. However, media relations was ranked as the most time-consuming task, followed by corporate communications and then internal communications. Access to the CEO was felt to be more indicative of PR's influence than a seat on the board (Bashford 2006).

The EUPRERA research project, European Communication Monitor (Tench and Yeomans 2009), sampled 1,524 communications professionals, across 37 different European countries. Three quarters of them felt they were taken seriously by senior management, with 64 per cent involved in decision making. Most important disciplines in 2009 were marketing/brand management, corporate communications, crisis/issue management, investor relations and public affairs/lobbying. The top issue was felt to be how to link business strategy and communications. Coping with digital evolution and social media came third after sustainability and CSR. Double the number of practitioners thought that social networks were the most important channel of communication from the year before. However, practitioners were still mainly reliant on media monitoring to assess their effectiveness.

The CIPR's 2010 benchmarking study found that growth was expected in online reputation management, crisis management and internal communications. Sponsorship and events management were expected to decline. While members were broadly comfortable with their knowledge of social media, 23 per cent admitted that their knowledge was limited. The public sector budget cuts were beginning to bite, with half of in-house public sector practitioners concerned about redundancy. Media relations continued to be the most time-consuming task in both in-house (78 per cent) and consultancy (88 per cent). Strategy development and planning were the next main functions in consultancy, with internal communications and strategy development in-house.

Disappointingly, there continues to be a disparity between men and women, with more men in senior positions (18 per cent at director level as against 13 per cent of women), earning more (40 per cent of men earn more than £50,000, only 23 per cent of women). Women continue to make up the majority (65 per cent) of the profession, compared with the UK workforce as a whole (46 per cent). The industry continues to be overwhelmingly white (95 per cent) and only 0.4 per cent of Institute membership was disabled (CIPR 2010b). This recalls CIPR CEO Jane Wilson's comments in Chapter 5 about the industry not being reflective of the society it represents.

Zerfass *et al.* (2010) updated the European Communication Monitor and found that membership of professional organisations had fallen. Over 70 per cent thought communications were more important since the recession, but only 22 per cent had actually gained resources and 37 per cent had lost resources. Media relations with print journalists was expected to decrease by 9.5 per cent but actually increased by 5.2 per cent from 2007 to 2010. The growth of use of online channels was overestimated, as social media had been expected to rise by 41 per cent, but actually only increased by 15 per cent. Less than one third of organisations had implemented guidelines for social media communications. Challenges in the next three years were: coping with digital evolution; linking business strategy and communications (again); dealing with sustainable development and the need for transparency; building and maintaining trust. Evaluation still relied heavily on media response and internet/intranet usage. Only a quarter were tracking the impact of communications on financial strategic targets.

Arrow (2009) complained, 'Even the most professional of practitioners is still implementing regurgitated values, set elsewhere in the organisation.' Despite the high hopes expressed at the beginning of this chapter, the picture painted above still seems to be of an industry that continues to focus on tactical rather than strategic thinking, with media relations still regarded as the core activity rather than more 'excellent' pursuits.

REDRESSING THE BALANCE

Moloney (2006a) contests that the PR-isation of the media has created an imbalance in favour of corporate information. Material may be published without sourcing, and PR practitioners gain more power with the contraction of newsrooms. He feels that local government PR staff have assumed greater power in setting the local news agenda. The majority of practice is the one-sided presentation of data, using selective facts and emotions to construct corporate messages. He suggests that this weak propaganda is mainly used by the resource-rich to achieve self-advantage, rather than the 'mutual benefit' of PR definitions.

While Moloney sees this as an inevitable part of liberal democracy, he proposes communicative equality through public subsidy of PR for those organisations that cannot afford it. If all voices who want to speak are audible to all who want to listen, this would lead to more varied and informed public debates. In this way, the positive effects of PR techniques might outweigh the negative – just.

Tench and Yeomans (2009) suggested that with the rise of campaign and pressure groups and NGOs, publics are asserting more power. Social media gives these groups the ability to act swiftly and mobilise public support. However, they warn that PR techniques can be adopted by all organisations, including unpopular political regimes.

THE QUESTION OF TRUST

At the IPR International Symposium in May 1999, Larry Weber, CEO and Chairman of Weber Public Relations Worldwide, suggested that new technologies allowed PR practitioners to develop a dialogue with their constituencies, evolving towards Grunig's model of two-way symmetric communications.

As communications proliferate, audiences now require multiple exposures to a message before they will accept it. Organisations are being urged to engage their employees as advocates, as trust is shifting from authority figures to 'a person like myself'. CEOs, politicians, union representatives and PR practitioners were the least believed according to Edelman's Trust Survey 2005. Least credible sources of information were regarded as company websites and advertising. Corporate attributes driving trust were the quality of products, ethical management, attentiveness to customers, then labour relations and financial performance. Highly regarded behaviours were corporate philanthropy, visible senior management, listening to stakeholders, positive coverage in local media, using local employees as spokespersons, and changing the way they did business.

The effect of developing technology and social media has been to enable people to gather information from many sources and rely on their own judgements. Consumers are buying everything from books and music to hotels and air travel on the recommendations of people whom they have never met, but whose opinions they access through cyberspace. A study by Ipsos MORI found that one in three customers claimed not to buy because of negative WOM (cited in Millar 2009). The right thing to do often made complete business sense, such as Marks & Spencer's Plan A. Other writers agreed. Cathcart (2009) advised that regaining trust meant dispensing with the view that the only objective of management is to increase shareholder value, and Mcmillan (2009) stated that values and ethics were not irrelevant in a recession. Somerville (2011) reflected, 'Wikileaks has demonstrated that even the most secretive organisations in the world can suddenly have their inner workings exposed to the light instantaneously via the Internet.' However, many PR practitioners rated open dialogue as a threat (Zerfass *et al.* 2010). As Smith (2010) queried, 'If everyone can communicate with everyone, who needs PR professionals?'

CHANGING THE MODEL

Changes in technology and the development of social media have more recently been offered as both a driver and a reason for a fundamental shift in the way that public relations is being and should be practised.

Flint (2009) suggests that dialogue with stakeholders was the way forward and that the age of 'we talk you listen' was gone. Hutchinson (2011) feels there is 'a fundamental shift from monologue to dialogue'. Macleod (2009a) hoped that due to the connectivity of the internet, this was 'surely PR's time'. However, due to the unwillingness of practitioners to 'step in and step up', she felt that the 'jury is still sadly out'.

Watch (2009) suggested that in the first digital recession, digital channels were a godsend, providing a direct, effective and cheap means of targetting vital audiences. Brodie (2009) felt that the importance of online coverage matched traditional media. Smith (2010) likened the quality of communications via the internet as 'conversations, not shouting', but warned, 'We will actually have to know what we are talking about.' Murray (2010) felt that the use of social media gave a greater ability to track and monitor PR activity, encouraging organisations to shift resources from advertising into public relations.

Wright and Hinson (2010) found that 85 per cent of public relations practitioners believed that new communications media was changing the way that organisations communicate. They cited Gillan's (2009) opinion that social media had ended the age of one-way messaging. However, while 90 per cent of practitioners agreed that social media should be measured, only 38 per cent were actually doing it. While social media had grown dramatically, especially since the launch of Twitter in 2006, most internet users were still blending online and traditional sources to gather information. The latter were regarded as more likely to be accurate, truthful, credible and ethical. The use of social networks such as Facebook and LinkedIn continued to rise and provide an additional way of communicating with targetted audiences.

Waters *et al.* (2010) found that journalists are utilising digital media differently, contacting thousands of PR practitioners via blog postings and websites to gather content for stories they were working on. They suggested that the era of pitching stories to journalists was giving way to one of 'media catching' and recommended that practitioners should instead pitch their stories to influential bloggers. The HARO site (Shankman 2007 in ibid.) encourages journalists to ask for specific information and reach large numbers of practitioners who then 'catch' media placements for their organisation. Over 300 queries are issued each month through the site.

Kitchen and Schultz (2009) warned that as the amount of consumer to consumer marketing information was rising through social media, the marketer was no longer the only source of information about products. This required a more integrated approach to marketing communications throughout the organisation.

While it is certainly the case that social media offers an additional sheaf of communications methods to contact publics direct, the IPA TouchPoints survey (2010) found that adults still spend 75 per cent of their communication time talking face to face. While time on a mobile phone has stayed constant at 11 per cent, texting has grown to 4 per cent, although the latter showed the most growth in the 15–24 age group. Online time has grown by 38 per cent, but this represents a shift from 1.3 hours to 1.8 hours per week. Underlining Murray's point above, internet usage was still biased towards male users, ABC1s and London and the

South East. Emailing accounted for 20 per cent of internet activity, while social networking had risen to 11 per cent. Those who used social networks tended to be 15–24, studying or working full time and peak times were between 6.30–10pm. Only a low level of people claimed to be social networking while at work.

Internal communications will also be affected by developments in digital communications. Wright and Hinson (2010) found that the blogosphere was empowering employees, and that positive comments largely outweighed the negative. MacLeod and Clarke (2008) confirm that it will be hard for organisations to get through the recession without engaging the workforce. A survey for the IABC (2010) found that nearly half of employers communicate through Facebook, instant messaging and Twitter, but that when communicating with employees email and intranet are most common. Goals of communications still concentrated on increasing productivity, although retaining talent, improving employee morale and introducing a new culture were also important. While listening to employees was felt to be essential, 32 per cent of organisations rarely conducted employee listening activities. Byrne (2009) advised, 'Never stop listening to employees'. This would reduce the risk of active 'badvocates'. Smith (2010) felt

> The rise in the influence of employee brand ambassadors due to social media, and thus the importance of effectively engaging them through internal communication and protecting a company's internal reputation as much as the external reputation, shows that there is no such thing as 'internal only' and employees can be active defenders and promoters of the brand.

Kindersley (2009) pointed out that retention of talent in the communications industry was an issue for public relations itself. Zerfass *et al.* (2010) confirmed that only 40 per cent of practitioners were satisfied with their career opportunities, work–life balance and salary.

GLACIAL SHIFT

As we have seen, several issues continue to affect the profession. The calibre of entrants and the quality of the training they receive after they enter it must improve. This must involve both greater investment in staff and greater willingness to adopt new and more professional practices.

The opportunities offered by developments in new technology must be seized, both in the tactical area of media relations and direct communication with stakeholders through websites and in the strategic area of true company counsel. Awareness of the changing nature of business for clients and employers must lead to a global outlook. Senior PR managers need to strengthen their financial and general management skills to have any hope of being admitted to the top table. Once there, they need to support the trends in the increasing investment in corporate social responsibility programmes and ensure that they reflect a genuine response to stakeholder expectations rather than cosmetic surgery.

In the second edition, it was suggested that the phrase 'it's only a PR exercise' might even disappear from common usage as a recognition of the difference between PR and lying. This seems naïve in the face of the *PR Week* debate where the notion that lying was acceptable was supported. George Pilcher (2007), who proposed the motion that 'public relations has a duty to tell the truth' and lost, posed the question: 'How can we instruct the PR profession of the future to manage the truth if they don't know what it is?' The CIPR's achievement of Chartered status has not affected perceptions even of practitioners It seems, so how the Industry expects its reputation to improve is unclear.

Tench and Yeomans (2009) relate that academics are still continuing to try and define the field, while professional bodies continue to seek professional recognition to prevent encroachment from marketing, management consultancy, and in the US, the legal profession also. Gooderham's (2009) advice to clients, 'If you cannot communicate, how will anyone follow your lead?' could well be applied to the public relations industry itself.

QUESTIONS FOR DISCUSSION

1 Is it important to improve the reputation of PR? Who are the target audiences whose opinions need to be changed?

2 How can the value of public relations be demonstrated to board level management?

3 What skills are lacking in the curricula of public relations qualifications in higher education?

4 What forms of evaluation of public relations programmes are you familiar with? How could evaluation of public relations be improved?

5 Are social media a help or hindrance to public relations?

6 Is good PR essential to a good reputation? What else contributes to this?

7 PR can only give you the reputation you deserve. Do you agree?

8 How can the link be made between communications and strategic planning?

9 How might Moloney's subsidised PR resource work? Is this still necessary as social media becomes more prevalent?

10 What other issues affect the future of PR?

NOTE

1 All 2011 opinions expressed in this chapter are from interviews with or email responses to the author.

Bibliography

AA Foundation for Road Research (1999) *Unlicensed driving: a scoping study to identify potential areas for further research*, www.theaa.com/public_affairs/reports/AA-foundation-FDN26-unlicensed-driving.pdf, accessed 31 December 2010.

AccountAbility (2003) AA100 Assurance Standard.

Airbus (2010a) *The future by Airbus.*

Airbus (2010b) *Global Market Forecast: 2010–2029.*

Alfes, K., Truss, C., Soane, E., Rees, C. and Gatenby, M. (2010) *Creating an engaged workforce; findings from the Kingston employee engagement consortium project*, Chartered Institute of Personnel and Development, London.

Anderson, F.W., Hadley, L., Rockland, D. and Weiner, M. (2009) *Guidelines for setting measurable public relations objectives: an update,* September, www.instituteforpr.org/files/uploads/Setting_PR_Objectives.pdf, accessed 9 November 2010.

Anderson, R., Baxter, L.A. and Cissna, K.N. (2004) 'Texts and contexts of dialogue', in Anderson, R., Baxter, L.A. and Cissna, K.N. (eds) *Dialogue. Theorizing difference in communication studies*, 1–17, Thousand Oaks, California: Sage.

Andrews, L. (2006) 'Spin: from tactic to tabloid', *Journal of Public Affairs*, 6, pp. 31–45.

Ansell, J. and Wharton, F. (1992) *Risk: analysis assessment and management*, Chichester: John Wiley & Sons.

Apple (2011) www.apple.com/pr/library/2011/01/22appstore.html.

Appleyard, B. (2003) 'News review', *Sunday Times*, 18 May.

Arrow, C. (2009) 'The future practitoner', Submission for *Chartered Practitioner*, August, accessed via www.cipr.org.uk.

Arthur W. Page Society (2007) *The authentic enterprise*, www.awpagesociety.com.

Assinder (2002) at http//news.bbc.co.uk/1/hi/uk_politics/1965012.stm.

Austin, E.W. and Pinkleton, B.E. (2006) *Strategic public relations management* (2nd edition), Mahwah, NJ: Lawrence Erlbaum Associates.

Badhwar, N.K. (2009) 'The Milgram experiments, learned helplessness, and character traits', *Journal of Ethics*, 13(2/3), pp. 257–289.

Baker, M.J. and Balmer, J.M.T. (1997) 'Visual identity: trappings or substance?', *European Journal of Marketing*, 31 (5/5), pp. 366–382.

Balmer, J. and Greyser, S. (eds) (2003) *Revealing the corporation: perspectives on identity, image, reputation, corporate branding, and corporate level marketing*, London: Routledge.

Baran, S.J. and Davis, D.K. (2008) *Mass communication theory: foundations, ferment, and future,* Boston, MA: Cengage Learning.

Barnes, C. (1991) 'Discrimination: disabled people and the media', *Contact Magazine*, 70, pp. 45–48.

Barnett, M. (2010) 'Conversations on brands are vital', *Marketing Week*, 23 September.

Bashford, S. (2006) 'Juggling roles', *PR Week*, 7 July, pp. 25–27.

Baskin, O., Hahn, J., Seaman, S. and Reines, D. (2010) 'Perceived effectiveness and implementation of public relations measurement and evaluation tools among European providers and consumers of PR services', *Public Relations Review*, 36 (2), pp. 105–111.

Bates, F. and Pitkeathley, J. (1996) 'Standing up to be counted: campaigning and voluntary agencies', in C. Hanvey and T. Philpot (eds) *Sweet charity: the role and workings of voluntary organisations*, London: Routledge.

BBC (2007) *Guidelines for bloggers*, www.bbc.co.uk/guidelines/editorial guidelines/advice/weblogswebsites/guidelines, accessed 22 February 2007.

BBC (2011a) www.bbc.co.uk/newsbeat/12266806.

BBC (2011b) http://news.bbc.co.uk/local/gloucestershire/hi/people_and_places/newsid_9376000/9376322.stm.

BBC News (2007) 'Blair: In his own words', http://news.bbc.co.uk/1/hi/uk_politics/3750847.stm, accessed 29 December 2010.

Beatbullying (2010) www.beatbullying.org/bigmarch.

Beck, U. (1992) *Risk society: towards a new modernity* [translated from the German by Mark Ritter], London: Sage.

Beckman, S.C., Morsing, M. and Resch, L.A. (2006) 'Strategic CSR communication: an emerging field', in M. Morsing and S.C. Beckmann (eds) *Strategic CSR communication*, Copenhagen: DJOF Publishing.

Bell, Lord T. (2005) Speech at charitable giving post Tsunami briefing, www.beaconfellowship.org.uk/events_100305panel.asp.

Bengston, D.N. and Fang, D.P. (1999) 'An innovative method for evaluating strategic goals in a public agency', *Evaluation Review*, 23 (1), pp. 77–100.

Bennett, W.L. and Entman, R.M. (2001) 'Mediated politics: an introduction', in W.L. Bennett and R.L. Entman (eds) *Mediated politics: communication in the future of democracy*, Cambridge: Cambridge University Press.

Berger, A.A. (1995) *Essentials of mass communication theory*, London: Sage.

Berk, R.A. and Rossi, P.H. (1990) *Thinking about program evaluation*, Newbury Park, CA: Sage.

Berlo, D. (1960) *The process of communication*, New York: Holt, Rinehart and Winston.

Bernays, E.L. (1923) *Crystallizing public opinion*, New York: Boni and Liveright.

Bernays, E.L. (1928) *Propaganda*, (1995 edition, Chapter 1) IG Publishing: New York.

Bernays, E. (1992) www.prmuseum.com/bernays.

Bernstein, D. (1984) *Company image and reality*, London: Cassell.

Bettinghaus, E.P and Cody, M.J. (1994) *Persuasive communication* (5th edition), Wadsworth.

Billingsley, L.G. (2002) 'Healthy choices: reaching multicultural audiences', *Tactics*, August, p. 19.

Bines, H. and Watson, D. (1992) *Developing professional education*, Buckingham: Open University Press.

BIS (2009) *Digital Britain: the final report*, http://webarchive.nationalarchives.gov.uk/+/interactive.bis.gov.uk/digitalbritain/report, accessed 27 December 2010.

BITC (2007) *Corporate responsibility index* www.bitc.org.uk/crindex, May 2006.

Bland, M. (1980) *Employee Communication in the 1980's*, London: Kogan Page.

Bland, M., Theaker, A. and Wragg, D. (1996) *Effective media relations*, London: Kogan Page/IPR.

Boorstin, D. (1962) *The image*, Middlesex: Penguin Books.

Booth, R. (2010) 'PR firms make London world capital of reputation laundering', *Guardian*, 3 August.

Boulstridge, E. and Carrigan, M (2000) 'Do consumers really care about corporate responsibility? Highlighting the consumer attitude–behaviour gap', *Journal of Communication Management*, 4 (4), 355–368.

Bourdieu, P. (1983) 'Forms of capital', in J.C. Richards (ed.), *Handbook of theory and research for the sociology of education*, New York: Greenwood Press.

Bourland-Davis, P.G., Thompson, W. and Brooks, F.E. (2010) 'Activism in the 20th and 21st centuries', in R.L. Heath (ed.), *The Sage handbook of public relations* (2nd edition), London: Sage, pp. 409–420.

Bow, M. (2010) 'Former Cadbury chairman defends takeover price', *Professional Pensions*, www.professionalpensions.com/professional-pensions/news/1931114/cadbury-chairman-defends-takeover-price.

Bowden-Green, T. (2006) 'Public relations – a one way street?', *Profile*, November/December, p. 12.

Bowen S.A. (2007) *Ethics and public relations*, Institute for PR, http://instititeforpr.org/essentila_knowledge/detail/ethics_and_public_relations, accessed 25 August 2010.

Brennan, P. (2009) 'Charity awareness monitor', *nfpSynergy*, slide presentation, CAM@nfpSynergy.net.

Brodie, G. (2009) 'Previews', *CorpComms*, January, 4–7.

Brogan, C. and Smith, J. (2010) *Trust agents: using the web to build influence, improve reputation, and earn trust*, New Jersey: John Wiley and Sons.

Brooke, H. (2010a) http://heatherbrooke.org/2010/police-press-offices-are-a-public-insult.

Brooke, H. (2010b) *The Silent State*, London: William Heinemann.

Broom, G.M. (2009) *Cutlip and center's effective public relations* (10th edition), Upper Saddle River, NJ: Pearson.

Broom, G.M. and Dozier, D.M. (1990) *Using research in public relations*, Englewood Cliffs, NJ: Prentice Hall.

Bronn, P.S. (2010) 'Reputation, communication and the corporate brand' in R.L. Heath (ed.), *The SAGE handbook of public relations*, Los Angeles, CA.: Sage.

Bruce, I. (1996) 'Marketing force: meeting true need' in C. Hanvey and T. Philpot (eds) *Sweet charity: the role and workings of voluntary organisations*, London: Routledge.

Bruning, S.D. (2002) 'Relationship building as a retention strategy: linking relationship attitudes and satisfaction evaluations to behavioral outcomes,' *Public Relations Review*, 28 (1), pp. 39–48.

Bruning, S.D., DeMiglio, P.A. and Embry, K. (2006) 'Mutual benefit as outcome indicator: factors influencing perceptions of benefit in organization-public relationships', *Public Relations Review*, 32 (1), pp. 33–40.

Bruning, S.D., Dials, M. and Shirk, A. (2008) 'Using dialogue to build organization–public relationships, engage publics, and positively affect organizational outcomes', *Public Relations Review*, 34, pp. 25–31.

Budd, J.F. (1994) *A pragmatic examination of ethical dilemmas in public relations*, IPRA Gold Paper, No. 8.

Budge, I., Crewe, I., McKay, D. and Newton, K. (1998) *The new British politics*, London: Addison Wesley Longman.

Bundred, S. (2010) *Council periodicals and other communications with the public*, www.audit-commission.gov.uk/SiteCollectionDocuments/Downloads/20100122timms.pdf, accessed 27 December 2010.

Burgoon, M., Hunsaker, F. and Dawson, E.J. (1994) *Human communication*, Thousand Oaks, CA: Sage.

Burkitt B. and Ashton F. (1996) 'The birth of the stakeholder society', in *Critical Social Policy*, 16, pp. 3–16, London: Sage.

Bush, M. (2010) 'How social media is helping public relations sector not just survive but thrive', *Advertising Age*, 28 August.

Business in the Community (2007) www.bitc.org.uk/resources/publications/cr_index_2007.html.

Byrne, C. (2009) 'Beware of the badvocates. Corporate reputation thought leader series', *PR Week*, 18 September, p. 27.

Callison, C. (2003) 'Media relations and the Internet: how Fortune 500 company web sites assist journalists in news gathering', *Public Relations Review*, 29(1), pp. 29–41.

Campbell, C.B. (1993) 'Does public relations affect the bottom-line?' *Public Relations Journal*, October, 49 (10), pp. 14–17.

Campbell, F.E., Herman, R.A. and Noble, D. (2006) 'Contradictions in "reputation management"', *Journal of Communication Management*, 10(2), pp. 191–196.

Campbell, K.K. and Huxman, S.S. (2003) *The rhetorical act: thinking, speaking and writing critically*, (3rd edition), Belmont, CA: Thomson Wadworth.

Capriotti, P. and Moreno, A. (2007) 'Corporate citizenship and public relations: the importance and interactivity of social responsibility issues on corporate websites', *Public Relations Review*, 33, pp. 84–91.

Carrigan M. and Attalla, A. (2001) 'The myth of the ethical consumer. Do ethics matter in purchase behaviour?', *A Journal of Consumer Marketing*, 18 (7), pp. 560–578.

Carroll, A.B. and Buchholtz, A.K. (2009) *Business & society: ethics and stakeholder management*, Mason, Ohio: South-Western.

Cathcart, R. (2009) 'Business is a changed game. Corporate reputation thought leader series', *PR Week*. 18 September, p. 19.

Centre for Economics and Business Research (CEBR) (2005) *PR today: 48,000 professionals; £36.5 billion turnover. The economic significance of public relations*, www.cipr.co.uk/sites/default/files/CIPR%20full%20report%20-%20November%204%202005.pdf, accessed 16 December 2010.

Chapman, R. (1982) 'Measurement: it is alive and well in Chicago', *Public Relations Journal*, 38 (5), pp. 28–29.

Chen, N. and Cuthbertson, H. (2009) 'Public relations in mainland China : an adult with growing pains' in K. Sriramesh and D. Verčič (eds) (2009) *The global public relations handbook: theory, research, and practice*, London: Routledge.

Cheney, G. (1992) 'The corporate person (re)presents itself' in E.L. Toth and R.L. Heath (eds) *rhetorical and critical approaches to public relations*, Hillsdale, NJ: Lawrence Erlbaum.

Chomsky, N. (2002) *Media control*, New York: Seven Stories Press.

Christensen, L.T., Firat, A.F. and Torp, S. (2008) 'The organisation of integrated communications: toward flexible integration', *European Journal of Marketing*, 42, (3/4), pp. 423–452.

Christensen, L.T., Morsing, M. and Cheney, G. (2008) *Corporate communications: convention, challenge, complexity*, London: Sage.

Chryssides, G.D. and Kaler, J.H. (1993) *An introduction to business ethics*, London: Chapman and Hall.

CIPR (2005) 'Advancing the profession', *PR Week*, 22 July.

CIPR (2009a) *State of the profession report*: *CIPR*, www.cipr.co.uk/content/policy-resources/research-reports/state-pr-profession.

CIPR (2009b) *Social media guidelines*, www.cipr.co.uk/sites/default/files/Social%20Media%20Guidelines.pdf, accessed 31 December 2010.

CIPR (2010a) *Research, planning and measurement toolkit* (3rd edition), October 2010, www.cipr.co.uk/content/policy-resources/for-practitioners/research-planning-and-measurement/toolkit, accessed 18 November 2010.

CIPR (2010b) *State of the PR profession benchmarking survey*, www.cipr.co.uk, accessed 25 August 2010.

Clampitt, P. (2005) *Communicating for managerial effectiveness*, Thousand Oaks, CA: Sage.

Clarke, A. (2000) 'Globalisation – dancing to a new tune', presentation to students at Cardiff University, 12 October.

Clarke, T. (1997) 'Measuring and managing stakeholder relations', *Journal of Communication Management*, 2 (3), pp. 211–221.

Clifford, M. (2005) *PR Week*, 2 December, p. 44.

Cline, C. (1984) *Evaluation and measurement in public relations and organization communication: a literature review*, San Francisco, CA: International Association of Business Communicators Foundation.

Cockerell, M., Hennessy, P. and Walker, D. (1984) *Sources close to the Prime Minister*, London: Macmillan.

Cohen, D. (2009) 'Consumer PR thought leader series', *PR Week*, 24 July, p. 27.

Cohen, S. (1972) *Folk devils and moral panics*, London: MacGibbon and Kee.

COI (2010a) *COI announces redundancy programme*, http://coi.gov.uk/press.php?release=342, accessed 27 December 2010.

COI (2010b) *COI Annual Report 2009–10*, www.coi.gov.uk/documents/coi-annualreport2009–10.pdf, accessed 25 January 2011.

COI (2011) *History of COI*, http://coi.gov.uk/aboutcoi.php?page=87, accessed 18 January 2010.

Coleman, J.C. (1988) 'Social capital in the creation of human capital', *American Journal of Sociology* 94, S95-S120.

Coleman, J.C. (1990, 1994) *Foundations of social theory*, Cambridge, Mass.: Harvard University Press.

Coleman, R. and Wilkins, L. (2009) 'The moral development of PR practitioners: a comparison with other professions and influences on higher ethical reasoning', *Journal of PR Research* 21(3) pp. 318–340.

Commission of PR Education (1999) *A port of entry*, PRSA.

Conrad, C. and Poole M.S. (1985) *Strategic organisational communication into the twenty-first century*, Fort Worth: Hardcourt Brace & Co.

Coombs, W.T. (2010) 'Crisis communication: a developing field', in R.L. Heath (ed.), *The Sage handbook of public relations* (2nd edition), London: Sage, pp. 477–488.

Cooper, L. (2011) 'The year ahead . . .', *Marketing Week*, 6 January, pp. 12–16.

Corbett, J.E. (1988) 'Foreword', in R.R. Halford (ed.), *Oratorical encounters: selected studies and sources of twentieth century political accusations and apologies*, New York: Greenwood Publishing Group, pp. ix–xi.

Corcoran, S. (2009) *Defining earned, owned and paid media*, http://blogs.forrester.com/interactive_marketing/2009/12/defining-earned-owned-and-paid-media.html, accessed 31 December 2010.

Cornelissen, J.P. (2004) *Corporate communications*, London: Sage.

Cornelissen, J.P. (2008) *Corporate Communications* (3rd edition), London: Sage.

Cornelissen, J.P. (2009) *Corporate communications. A guide to theory and practice*, London: Sage.

Cornelissen, J.P. and Elving, W.J.L. (2003) 'Managing corporate identity: an integrative framework of dimensions and determinants', *Corporate Communications, An International Journal*, 8 (2), pp. 114–120.

Cornfield, M., Carson, J., Kalis, A. and Simon, E. (2005) *Buzz, blogs and beyond, pew Internet and American life project*, www.buzzmetrics.com.

Corporate Watch (2010). *All the rest is advertising: the public relations industry and the decline of trust*, www.corporatewatch.org.uk/?lid=412, accessed 22 November 2010.

Cortese, A. (2002) *The new accountability: tracking the social costs*, on www.nytimes.com, 24 March.

Costa, M. (2011) 'How to extend shelf life of your campaign', *Marketing Week*, 13 January, pp. 28–30.

Cottle, S. (2003) *News, public relations and power*, London: Sage.

Coulson-Thomas, C. (2004) 'Differing corporate communication practice in successful and unsuccessful companies', in S.M. Oliver (ed.) *Handbook of corporate communication and public relations*, London: Routledge, pp. 167–183.

Coupland, C. (2003) 'Corporate identities on the web: an exercise in the construction and development of "morality"', *Research Paper No. 2002–2003*, www.nottingham.ac.uk/business/iccsr/research/paperseries.html.

Court, D., Elzinga, D., Mulder, S., Jorgen, O. and Vik, V. (2009) 'The consumer decision journey', *McKinsey Quarterly*, www.mckinseyquarterly.com/The_consumer_decision_journey_2373, accessed 30 June 2011.

Cowlett, M. (2005) 'Is the training cupboard bare?', *PR Week*, 14 October, pp. 25–28.

Coxall, B. (2001) *Pressure groups and British politics*, London: Politicos.

Crush, P. (2005) 'Global PR: what does the world think?', *PR Week*, 11 November, pp. 23–29.

Curran, J. and Seaton, J. (2003) *Power without responsibility: the press, broadcasting, and new media in Britain*, London: Routledge.

Curtin, P.A., and Gaither, T.K. (2007) *International public relations: negotiating culture, identity, and power*, Thousand Oaks, CA: Sage.

Cutlip, S.M. (1994) *The unseen power: public relations, a history,* Hillsdalen NJ: Lawrence Erlbaum.

Cutlip, S.M., Center, A.H. and Broom, G.M. (1995) *Effective public relations* (7th edition), Englewood Cliffs, NJ: Prentice Hall.

Cutlip, S.M., Center, A.H. and Broom, G.M. (2000) *Effective public relations* (8th edition), Englewood Cliffs, NJ: Prentice Hall.

Cutlip, S., Center, A.H. and Broom, G. (2006) *Effective public relations* (9th edition), Upper Saddle River, NJ: Pearson Education International.

Dahlgren, P. (2001) 'The public sphere and the net: structure, space, and communication', in W.L. Bennett and R.L. Entman (eds) *Mediated politics: communication in the future of democracy*, Cambridge: Cambridge University Press.

Daily Mail (2011) *Labour restores official ties with Muslim Council of Britain*, www.dailymail. co.uk/news/article-1243588/Labour-restores-official-ties-Muslim-Council-Britain-despite-refusal-remove-deputy-accused-supporting-Hamas.html, accessed 10 January 2011.

Dainton, M. and Zelley, E.D. (2005) *Applying communication theory for professional life*, Thousand Oaks: Sage.

Daugherty, E.L. (2001) 'Public relations and social responsibility' in R.L. Heath (ed.) *Handbook of public relations*, London: Sage.

Davies, N. (2008) *Flat Earth news*, London: Chatto & Windus.

Davis, A. (2004) *Mastering public relations*, London: Palgrave.

Davis, A. (2006) 'Role of mass media in investor relations', *Journal of Communication Management*, 10 (1).

Davis, A. (2007) *The mediation of power, a critical introduction*, London: Routledge.

Dawkins, J. (2005) 'Corporate responsibility: the communication challenge', *Journal of Communication Management*, 9 (2), pp. 108–119.

Day, K.D., Dong, Q. and Robins, C. (2001) 'Public relations ethics: an overview and discussion of issues for the 21st century', in R.L. Heath (ed.) *Handbook of public relations*, London: Sage, pp. 403–409.

DCLG (2010) *Code of recommended practice on local authority publicity: consultation*, www.communities.gov.uk/publications/localgovernment/publicitycodeconsult2010, accessed 27 December 2010.

Deacon, D. and Golding, P. (1994) *Taxation and representation*, London: John Libbey.

De Bussy, N. (2008) 'Stakeholder theory' in W. Donsbach (ed.) *The international encyclopedia of communication,* Oxford: Wiley-Blackwell.

De Bussy, N. (2010) 'Dialogue as a basis for stakeholder engagement: defining and measuring core competencies', in R.L. Heath (ed.), *The SAGE handbook of public relations*, Los Angeles, CA.: Sage.

Deetz, S. and Simpson, J. (2004) 'Critical organizational dialogue', in R. Anderson, L. Baxter and K. Cissna, (eds), Dialogue. *Theorizing difference in communication studies*, Thousand Oaks, California: Sage, pp. 141–158.

Department of Health (2010) *Equity and excellence: liberating the NHS*, www.dh.gov.uk/en/Publicationsandstatistics/Publications/PublicationsPolicyAndGuidance/DH_117353, accessed 28 December 2010.

Department of Trade & Industry and the Chartered Institute of Public Relations (DTI/CIPR) (2003) *Unlocking the potential of public relations: developing good practice,* www.ecforbe.com/documents/papers/unlocking-potential-report.pdf, accessed 16 December 2010.

De Santo, B. and Moss D. (2004) 'Rediscovering what PR managers do: rethinking the measurement of managerial behaviour in the public relations context', *Journal of Communication Management*, 9(2), pp. 179–196.

Dewhurst, S. and FitzPatrick, L. (2007b) *How to develop outstanding internal communicators*, London: Melcrum.

Dezenhall, E. and Weber, J. (2007) *Damage control: why everything you know about crisis management is wrong*, New York: Portfolio.

Dienhart, J.W. (2000) *Business, institutions and ethics*, Oxford: Oxford University Press.

Diga, M. and Kelleher, T. (2009) 'Social media use, perceptions of decision-making power, and public relations roles', *Public Relations Review* 35(4), pp. 440–442.

Digital Economy Act (2010) www.legislation.gov.uk/ukpga/2010/24/contents, accessed 31 December 2010.

Dolphin, R. (2003) 'Approaches to investor relations: implementation in the British context', *Journal of Marketing Communications*.

Downs, C.W. and Allyson, D.A. (2004) *Assessing organizational communication: strategic communication audits*, New York, Guilford.

Dozier, D.M. (1984) 'Program evaluation and the roles of practitioners,' *Public Relations Review*, 10 (2), pp. 13–21.

Dozier, D.M. and Broom, G.M. (1995) 'Evolution of the manager role in public relations practice', *Journal of Public Relations Research*, 7 (1), pp. 3–26.

Dozier, D.M., Grunig, L.A. and Grunig, J.E. (1995) *Manager's guide to excellence in public relations and communication management*, Hillsdale, NJ: Lawrence Erlbaum.

Dozier, D.M., Grunig, L.A. and Gruning, J.E., (2001). 'Public relations as communication campaign', in R.E. Rica and C.K. Atkin (eds), *Public communication campaigns* (3rd edition), London: Sage.

Duncan, S. (2010) *Using web analytics to measure the impact of earned online media on business outcomes: a methodological approach*, February 2010, www.instituteforpr.org/files/uploads/Seth_Duncan_Web_Analytics.pdf, accessed: 17 February 2010.

Echo (2010) *EADS Farnborough airshow report*.

Economist (2010) *Rise of the image men,* December 16, www.economist.com/node/17722733, accessed 19 January 2011.

Edelman (2005) *Sixth Annual Edelman Trust Barometer.*

Edelman Trust Barometer, (2010) www.edelman.co.uk/trustbarometer/files/edelman-trust-barometer-2010.pdf, accessed 31 December 2010.

Edwards, L. (2010) *An exploratory study of the experiences of 'BAME' PR practitioners in the UK industry*: ESRC/Leeds Metropolitan University/CIPR.

Ehling, W.P. and Dozier, D.M. (1992) 'Public relations management and operations research', in J.E. Grunig (ed.) *Excellence in public relations and communication management*, Routledge, pp. 251–284.

E-Learning Foundation (2010) www.e-learningfoundation.com, accessed 31 December 2010.

Ellis, T. (2010) *A spoonful of sugar: health service communications*, www.behindthespin.com/careers/spoonfulofsugar, accessed 22 November 2010.

Elton, L. (1993) 'University teaching: a professional model for quality', in R. Ellis (ed.) *Quality assurance for university teaching*, Oxford: Open University Press.

Esman, M.J. (1972) 'The elements of institution building' in J.W. Eaton (ed.) *Institutional building and development*, London: Sage.

Evan, W.M. and Freeman, R.E. (1993) 'A stakeholder theory of the modern corporation: Kantian capitalism', in G.D. Chryssides and J.H. Kaler (eds) *An introduction to business ethics,* London: Chapman and Hall.

Ewen, S. (1996) *PR! A Social History of Spin*, New York: Basic Books.

Experian Hitwise (2010) www.hitwise.com/uk/datacentre/main/dashboard-7323.html, accessed 31 December 2010.

Eyrich, N., Padman, M.L. and Sweetser, K.D. (2008) 'PR practitioners use of social media tools and communication technology', *Public Relations Review*, 34(4), pp. 412–414.

Fairbanks, J., Plowman, K.D. and Rawlins, B.L. (2007) 'Transparency in government communication', *Journal of Public Affairs*, 7, pp. 23–37.

Fairchild, M. (1999) *The public relations research and evaluation toolkit*, Institute of Public Relations and Public Relations Consultants Association.

Fairclough, N. (2000) *New Labour, new language?,* London: Routledge.

Falconi, T.M. (2003) 'Europe – the PR challenge', *Profile*, May, pp. 12–13.

Farrington, C. (2003) 'Tomorrow the world', *Profile*, April, p. 11.

Farrington, C. (2005) 'Coming of age', *Profile*, March/April.

Fawkes, J. (2006a) 'Public relations, propaganda and the psychology of persuasion' in R. Tench, and L. Yeomans (eds) *Exploring public relations*, Harlow: Prentice Hall.

Fawkes, J. (2006b) 'Can ethics save public relations from the charge of propaganda?', *Ethical Space, Journal of the Institute of Communication Ethics*, 3 (1), pp. 32–42, Leicester: Troubadour Publishing.

Fawkes, J. (2010) 'The shadow of excellence: a Jungian approach to public relations ethics', *Review of Communication* (US), 10 (3) pp. 211–227.

Fawkes, J. and Gregory, A., (2000) 'Applying communication theories to the Internet', *Journal of Communication Management*, 5 (2), pp. 109–124.

Fawkes, J. and Tench, R. (2004) 'Does employer resistance to theory threaten the future of public relations? A consideration of research findings, comparing UK practitioner, academic and alumni attitudes to public relations education', *International Public Relations Research Symposium*, Bled, Slovenia, 11 July 2004.

FCIC (2011) *Financial crisis inquiry commission*, US, January 2011.

Fearn-Banks, K. (2007) *Crisis communications: a casebook approach*, London: Routledge.

Fedorcio, D., Heaton, P. and Madden, K. (1991) *Public relations for local Government*, Harlow: Longman.

Fekl, R. (2010) *Review: 2nd European summit on measurement*, Barcelona, www.communicationcontrolling.de/en/news/meldungen/measurement-summit-2010.html, accessed 9 November 2010.

Feldman, S. and Marks, V. (2005) *Panic nation*, London: Blake Publishing.

Ferrell, O.C., Fraedrich, J. and Ferrell, L. (2009) *Business ethics: ethical decision making and cases*, London: Cengage Learning.

Fertik, M. and Thompson, D. (2010) *Wild west 2.0: how to protect and restore your online reputation on the untamed social frontier*, AMACOM (Division of the American Management Association).

Fill, C. (2005) *Marketing communications: contexts, strategies and applications* (4th edition), Harlow: Pearson Education.

Fill, C. and Fill, K. (2004) *Business-to-business marketing: relationships, systems and communications* (4th edition), New Jersey : FT Press.

Financial Dynamics (2010) *Capital markets and investor relations*, www.fd.com/en/homepage/practice-areas/capital-markets-and-investor-relations.aspx, accessed 10 December 2010.

Finkelstein, D. (2003) *The Times*, 30 August, p. 6.

Finnegan, P. (2010) *A spoonful of sugar: health service communications*, www.behindthespin.com/careers/spoonfulofsugar, accessed 22 November 2010.

Fisher, F. (2003) *Reframing public policy: discursive politics and deliberative practices*, Oxford: Oxford University Press.

Fiske, J. (1990) *Introduction to communication studies*, London: Routledge.

FitzPatrick, K. (2006) 'Baselines for ethical advocacy in the "marketplace of ideas"' in K. FitzPatrick and C. Bornstein (eds) *Ethical public relations: responsible advocacy*, pp. 1–18.

FitzPatrick, K. and Bornstein, C. (eds) (2006) *Ethical public relations: responsible advocacy*, Thousand Oaks, CA: Sage.

Fleisher, G.S. (2002) 'Analysis and analytical tools for managing corporate public affairs', *Journal of Public Affairs*, 3 (4), pp. 371–382.

Fleisher, G.S. (2003) 'Managing the grassroots and assessing its performance', *Journal of Public Affairs*, 2 (3), pp. 167–172.

Fleisher, G.S. (2005) 'The measurement and evaluation of public affairs processes and performance' in P. Harris and C.S. Fleisher (eds) *The handbook of public affairs*, London: Sage, pp. 123–144.

Fleishman Hillard/National Consumers League (2007) 'Rethinking corporate social responsibility', http://fleishmanhillard.com/wp-content/uploads/2007/05/csr_white_paper.pdf.

Flint, J. (2009) 'The influencers are all around', Corporate Reputation Thought leader series, *PR Week*, 18 September, p. 9.

Fombrun, C.J. (1996) *Reputation: realizing value from corporate image*, Boston: Harvard Business School Press.

Foremski, T (2006) *Die press release, die! die! die!*, www.siliconvalleywatcher.com/mt/archives/2006/02/die_press_relea.php.

Frankental, P. (2001) 'Corporate social responsibility – a PR invention?', *Corporate Communications, An International Journal*, 6 (1).

Franklin, B. (1994) *Packaging politics*, London: Edward Arnold.

Franklin, B. (2004) *Packaging politics: political communications in Britain's media democracy* (2nd edition), London: Arnold.

Franklin, B., Hamer, M., Hanna, M., Kinsey, M. and Richardson, J.E. (2005) *Key concepts in journalism studies*, London: Sage.

Franklin, J. (2003) 'Review article social capital: policy and politics', *Social Policy & Society* 2 (4), pp. 349–352.

Freeman, R.E. (1984) *Strategic management: a stakeholder approach*, Boston, MA: Pitman.

Friedman, A.L. and Miles, S. (2002) 'Developing stakeholder theory', *Journal of Management Studies*, 39 (1), January.

Friedman, M. (1993) 'The social responsibility of business is to increase its profits', in G.D. Chryssides and J.H. Kaler (eds) *An introduction to business ethics*, London: Chapman and Hall.

Gaber, I. (1998) 'The new world of dogs and lamp-posts', *British Journalism Review*, 9 (2).

Gaber, I. (2000a) 'Lies, damn lies . . . and political spin', *British Journalism Review*, 11 (1), pp. 60–70.

Gaber, I. (2000b) 'Government by spin: an analysis of the process', *Media, Culture & Society*, 22 (4), pp. 507–518.

Gable, T. (2003) 'Five major PR issues for the next decade', *Strategist*, Spring, pp. 18–21.

Gallagher, D. (2007) 'Why UK agencies must think global', *PR Week*, 2 February, p. 15.

Galtung, J. and Ruge, M. (1973) 'Structuring and selecting news', in S. Cohen and J. Young (eds), *The manufacture of news*. London: Constable.

Gandy, O. (1992) 'Public relations and public policy: the structuration of dominance in the information age', in E. Toth and R. Heath (eds) *Rhetorical and critical approaches to public relations*, New Jersey: Lawrence Erlbaum.

Garrick, J. and Christie, R.F. (2008) *Quantifying and controlling catastrophic risks*, Amsterdam: Academic Press.

Gaunt, P. and Ollenburger, J. (1995) 'Issues management revisited: a tool that deserves another look', *Public Relations Review*, 21 (3), pp. 199–210.

Genasi, C. (2005) 'Professionalism and pride', *Profile*, January/February.

Getz, K.A. (2001) 'Public affairs and political strategy: theoretical foundations', *Journal of Public Affairs*, 1 (4) & 2 (1), pp. 305–329.

Giddens, A. (2007) *Over to you, Mr Brown*, Cambridge: Polity.

Gilpin, D.R. and Murphy, P.J. (2008) *Crisis management in a complex world*, Oxford: Oxford University Press.

Gilpin, D.R. and Murphy, P.J. (2010) 'Implications of complexity theory for public relations: Beyond crisis' in R.L. Heath (ed.), *The Sage handbook of public relations* (2nd edition), Sage, pp. 71–84.

Gladwell, M. (2000) *The tipping point: how little things can make a big difference*, London: Little Brown.

Global Alliance (2010) *Draft of the Stockholm accords*, www.globalalliancepr.org/content/1/486/draft-the-stockholm-accords, accessed 28 January 2011.

Global Reporting Initiative (2006) www.globalreporting.org/reportingframework/g3guidelines.

Gooderham, M. (2009) 'Brands people can believe in', Corporate Reputation Thought leader series, *PR Week*, 18 September, p. 23.

Goudge, P. (2006) *Employee research*, London: Kogan Page.

Grant, W. (2000) *Pressure groups, politics and democracy*, London: Macmillan.

Gray, R. (2006a) 'Agencies drawn by China's riches', *PR Week*, 21 July, pp. 24–26.

Gray, R. (2006b) 'Time well spent?', *PR Week*, 27 October, pp. 22–23.

Green, A. (2007) *Creativity in public relations*, London: Kogan Page.

Gregory, A. (1999), *Internet commission: the e-role for PR*, www.netreputation.co.uk/managementclarity/the_e_role_for_pr_part_1.pdf, accessed 31 December 2010.

Gregory, A. (2000a) 'Systems theories and public relations practice', *Journal of Communication Management*, 4 (3), pp. 266–277.

Gregory, A. (2000b) *Planning and managing public relations campaigns* (2nd edition), London: Kogan Page.

Gregory, A. (2001) 'Public relations and evaluation: does the reality match the rhetoric?', *Journal of Marketing Communications*, 7, pp. 171–189.

Gregory, A. (2004) 'PR in practice: the 21st century landscape', in A. Gregory (ed.) *Public Relations in Practice*, London: Kogan Page.

Gregory, A. (2007) 'Involving stakeholders in developing corporate brands', *Journal of Marketing Management*, 23 (1), pp. 59–73.

Gregory, A. (2008) 'The competencies of senior practitioners in the UK: an initial study', *Public Relations Review*, 34 (3), pp. 215–223.

Gregory, A. (2009) 'Ethics and professionalism in public relations' in R. Tench and L. Yeomans (eds) *Exploring public relations* (2nd edition), FT Prentice Hall.

Gregory, A. and Edwards, L. (2004) *Patterns of PR in Britain's 'most admired' companies*, Report commissioned by Eloqui PR from Leeds Business School.

Gregory, A. and White, J. (2008) 'Introducing the Chartered Institute of Public Relations initiative. Moving on from talking about evaluation to incorporating it into better management of the Practice', in B. van Ruler, A.T. Verčič and D. Verčič (eds) *Public relations metrics. Research and evaluation*, New York and London: Routledge, pp. 307–317.

Gregory, H. (2006) 'The grads are back', *PR Week*, 3 November, pp. 24–26.

Grundy, T. (1993) *Implementing strategic change*, London: Kogan Page.

Grunig, J.E. (1989) 'Symmetrical presuppositions as a framework for public relations theory', in C. Botan and V. Hazleton (eds) *Public relations theory*, Hillsdale, NJ: Lawrence Erlbaum.

Grunig, J.E. (2001) 'Two-way symmetrical public relations: past, present and future', in R.L. Heath (ed.) (2001) *The handbook of public relations*, Thousand Oaks, CA: Sage, pp. 11–30.

Grunig, J.E. (2009) Paradigms of global public relations in an age of digitalisation, *PRism* 6(2), http://praxis.massev.ac.nz/prism on-line iourn.html, accessed 31 December 2010.

Grunig, J.E. and Grunig, L.A. (2010) The Third Annual Grunig Lecture Series. Public Relations Excellence 2010, delivered at the PRSA International Conference, Sunday, October 17, 2010, Washington DC, www.instituteforpr.org/files/uploads/Third_Grunig_Lecture_Transcript.pdf, accessed 31 December 2010.

Grunig, J. E. and Huang, Y. H. (2000) 'From organizational effectiveness to relationship indicators: antecedents of relationships, public relations strategies, and relationship out-comes', in J.A. Ledingham and S.D. Bruning (eds) *Public relations as relationship management: a relational approach to the study and practice of public relations*. Mahwah, NJ: Lawrence Erlbaum, pp. 23–53.

Grunig, J.E. and Hung, C.J.F. (2002, March) The effect of relationships on reputation and reputation on relationships: a cognitive, behavioral study. Paper presented to the International, Interdisciplinary Public Relations Research Conference, Miami, Florida.

Grunig, J.E. and Hunt, T. (1984) *Managing Public Relations*, New York: Holt, Rinehart & Winston.

Grunig, J.E. and Repper, F. (1992) 'Strategic management, publics and issues', in J.E. Grunig (ed.) *Excellence in public relations and communications management*, Hillsdale, NJ: Lawrence Erlbaum.

Grunig, J.E., Dozier, D.M., Ehling, W.P., Grunig, L.A., Repper, F.C. and White, J. (eds) (1992) *Excellence in public relations and communication management*, Hillsdale, NJ: Lawrence Erlbaum.

Grunig, J.E., Grunig, L.A. and Toth, E.L. (2007) *The future of excellence in public relations and communication management: challenges for the next generation*, London: Lawrence Erlbaum.

Guardian (2005) *Blogger sacked for sounding off* (12 January 2005), www.guardian.co.uk/technology/2005/jan/12/books.newmedia, accessed 12 January 2011.

Guardian (2007) 'Brown promises new priorities as he accepts leadership', www.guardian.co.uk/politics/2007/may/17/labourleadership.labour2, accessed 20 December 2010.

Guither, H.D. (1998) *Animal rights: history and scope of a radical social movement*, Carbondale: SIU Press.

Gummer, P. (1990) 'PR in the year 2000', *CAM/TASC lecture*, 21 November.

Gurău, C. (2008) 'Integrated online marketing communication: implementation and man-agement', *Journal of communication management*, 12 (2), pp. 169–184.

Guthrie, J. and Kuchler, H. (2010) 'Cadbury deal puts lid on Quaker ties', *Financial Times*, 22 January.

Habermas, J. (1984) *The theory of communicative action: Vol. 1. Reason and the rationalization of society* [Die theorie des kommunikativen handelns. Handlungsrationalität und gesellschaftliche rationalisierung], Boston: Beacon Press.

Habermas, J. (1987) *The theory of communicative action: Vol. 2. Lifeworld and system: a critique of functionalist reason*, Boston: Beacon Press.

Habermas, J. (1989) *The structural transformation of the public sphere: an inquiry into a category of bourgeois society*, Cambridge: Polity Press.

Haimes, Y.Y. (2009), On the complex definition of risk: a systems-based approach, *Risk Analysis: An International Journal*, 29 (12), pp. 1647–1654.

Hall, P. (2010) *Careers in IR case studies. Investor relations society*. www.ir-soc.org.uk/index.asp?pageid=58.

Hall, S. (1980) 'Encoding, decoding in the television discourse' in S. Hall, D. Hobson and P. Lowe (eds) *Culture, Media, Language*, London: Macmillan.

Hall, S. and du Gay, P. (1996) *Questions of cultural identity*, London: Sage.

Hallahan, K. (2001) 'Improving public relations web sites through usability research', *Public Relations Review*, 27, pp. 223–239.

Hampden-Turner, C.M. and Trompenaars, F. (2000) *Building cross-cultural competence*, Yale University Press.

Handy, C. (1991) 'Types of voluntary organisations', in J. Batsleer, C. Cornforth and R. Payton (eds) (1991) *Issues in voluntary and non-profit management: a reader*, Addison-Wesley/Open University.

Hansen, G.E. (2003) 'Defrosting Europe', *Profile*, June, p. 13.

Harcup, T. and O'Neill, D. (2001) 'What is news? Galtung and Ruge revisited', *Journalism Studies*, 2 (2), pp. 261.

Hargie, O. and Tourish, D. (2000) *Handbook of communication audits for organisations*, London: Routledge.

Hargie O. and Tourish D. (eds), (2004) *Handbook of communication audits for organisations*, London: Routledge.

Harris, P. and Harris, I. (2005) 'Lobbying in the United Kingdom', in P. Harris and C.S. Fleisher (eds) *The handbook of public affairs*, London: Sage, pp. 224–246.

Harris, P. and Moss, D. (2001) 'Editorial. In search of public affairs: a function in search of an identity', *Journal of Public Affairs*, 1 (2), pp. 102–110.

Harrison, S. (1995) *Public relations – an introduction*, London: International Thomson Business Press.

Hartner J.K., Schmidt F.L. and Hayes T.L., (2002) 'Business-unit-level relationship between employee satisfaction, employee engagement, and business outcomes: a meta-analysis', *Journal of Applied Psychology 2002*, 87 (2), pp. 268–279.

Harvey, B. (1995) 'Public relations in local government', in S. Black (ed.) *The practice of public relations* (4th edition), London: Butterworth-Heinemann, pp. 73–86.

Hatch, M.J. and Schultz, M.S. (1997) 'Relations between organisational culture, identity and image', *European Journal of Marketing*, 31 (5/6), pp. 356–365.

Hatch, M.J. and Schultz, M.S. (2000) 'Scaling the Tower of Babel: relational differences between identity, image and culture in organizations', in M.S. Schultz, M.J. Hatch and M.H. Larsen (eds) *The expressive organization: linking identity, reputation, and the corporate brand*, Oxford: Oxford University Press, pp. 13–35.

Hauss, D. (1993) 'Measuring the impact of public relations', *Public Relations Journal*, 49 (2), pp. 14–20.

Hazelton, V. and Kennan W. (2000) 'Social capital: reconceptualising the bottom line', *Corporate Communications: An International Journal*, 5 (2), pp. 81–86.

Hearit, K.M. (1994) 'Apologies and public relations crises at Chrysler, Toshiba, and Volvo', *Public Relations Review*, 20 (2), pp. 113–125.

Hearit, K.M. (2001) 'Corporate apologia: when an organization speaks in defense of itself', in R.L. Heath and G. Vasquez (eds), *The handbook of public relations*, Sage, pp. 501–512.

Heath, R., Pearce, B., Shotter, J., Taykor, J., Kersten, A., Zorn, T., Roper, J., and Motion, J. (2006) 'The process of dialogue: participation and legitimation', *Management Communication Quarterly*, 19 (3), pp. 341–373.

Heath, R.G. (2007) 'Rethinking community collaboration through a dialogic lens: creativity, democracy, and diversity in community organizing', *Management Communication Quarterly*, 21, p. 145.

Heath, R.L. (1992) 'The wrangle in the marketplace: a rhetorical perspective of public relations', in E. Toth and R. Heath (eds) *Rhetorical and critical approaches to public relations*, Hillsdale, NJ: Lawrence Erlbaum.

Heath, R.L. (2001) 'Shifting foundations: public relations as relationship building', in R.L. Heath (ed.) (2001) *Handbook of public relations*.

Heath, R.L. (2005), *Encyclopedia of public relations* (Volume 2), Sage.

Heath, R.L. (ed.) (2010) *The SAGE Handbook of public relations*, London: Sage.

Heath, R.L. and Palenchar, M.J. (2009) *Strategic issues management: organizations and public policy challenges* (2nd edition), London: Sage.

HELiX (2008) www2.le.ac.uk/offices/press/advice-information/helix/helix-publications/Helix %20brochure%202008.pdf/view, accessed 14 January 2011.

Helm, C. and Jones, R. (2010) 'Brand governance', *Journal of Brand Managment*, 17, pp. 545–547.

Helsby, N. and Croton, M. (2009) *Internal communications – more to deliver?,* London: Watson Helsby Consulting.

Hendrix, J. (2006) *Public Relations Cases*, (7th edition), Belmont, CA: Wadsworth .

Heugens, P.P.M.A.R. (2002) 'Managing public affairs through storytelling', *Journal of Public Affairs*, 2, pp. 57–70.

Hiebert, R.E. (2005) 'Commentary: new technologies, PR, and democracy', *Public Relations Review*, 31, pp. 1–9.

Hill, M. (2005) *The Public policy process* (4th edition), Harlow: Pearson.

Himma, K.E. and Tavani, H.T. (2008) *The handbook of information and computer ethics*, London: John Wiley and Sons.

HL Paper 7 (2009) *House of Lords Select Committee on communication: first report of session, 2008–2009*, London: HMSO.

Hobsbawm, J. (2010) *Where the truth lies: trust and morality in the business of PR, journalism and communications* (2nd edition), London: Atlantic Books.

Holmes, P. (2007) *A manifesto for the 21st century public relations firm*, http://pr20.word press.com/2007/05/13/a-manifesto-for-the-21st-century-public-relations-firm/13 May, accessed 31 December 2010.

Holmstrom, S. (2010) 'Reflective management: seeing the organization as if from outside' in R.L. Heath (ed.), *The SAGE handbook of public relations*. Los Angeles, CA.: Sage.

Holtzhausen, D. (2000) 'Postmodern values in public relations', *Journal of Public Relations Research*, 12 (1), pp. 93–114.

Holtzhausen, D. (2007) 'Activism', in J.E., Grunig, L. A., Grunig and E.L., Toth, *The future of excellence in public relations and communication management: challenges for the next generation*, London: Routledge, pp. 357–379.

Holtzhausen, D.R. and Voto, R. (2002) 'Resistance from the margins: the postmodern public relations practitioner as organizational activist', *Journal of Public Relations Research*, 14 (1), pp. 57–84.

Hon, L.C. (1997) 'What have you done for me lately? Exploring effectiveness in public relations', *Journal of Public Relations Research*, 9 (1), pp. 1–30.

Hon, L.C. (1998) 'Demonstrating effectiveness in public relations: goals, objectives and evaluation', *Journal of Public Relations Research*, 10 (2), pp. 103–135.

Hon, L.C. and Grunig, J.E. (1999) 'Guidelines for measuring relationships in public relations', November, www.instituteforpr.org/files/uploads/guidelines_measuring_relationships.pdf, accessed 4 March 2010.

Horrox, M. (2010) 'Regulating the Profession', *Profile,* July/August.

Huang, Y. (2001) 'OPRA: a cross-cultural, multiple-item scale for measuring organization-public relationships,' *Journal of Public Relations Research*, 13 (1), pp. 61–90.

Hughes, G. (2009) 'Integrated marketing communications', in R. Tench and L. Yeomans (eds) *Exploring public relations*, pp. 498–516.

Hung, C.J.F. (2007) 'Towards the theory of relationship management: how to cultivate quality relationships?' in E.L. Toth (ed.) *The future of excellence in public relations and communication management: challenges to the next generation*, Mahwah, NJ: Lawrence Erlbaum, pp. 443–476.

Hunt, A (2010) *Mind the gap – assessing the impact of reduced government spending on the North East economy*, St Chads College, University of Durham.

Hutchinson, S. (2011) Personal email to author.

Hutton, J.G. (1999) 'The definition, dimensions and domain of public relations', *Public Relations Review*, 25 (2), pp. 199–214.

Hutton, J.G. (2001) 'Defining the relationship between public relations and marketing', in R.L. Heath, (ed.) *Handbook of public relations*, Thousand Oaks, CA: Sage.

Hutton, J.G. (2010) 'Defining the relationship between public relations and marketing: public relations' most important challenge', in R.L. Heath (ed.), *The Sage handbook of public relations* (2nd edition), Sage, pp. 509–522.

Hutton, W. (1996) *The state we're in*, London: Vintage.

Hutton, W. (2008) 'This terrifying moment is our one chance for a new world' (5 October) in *The Observer*, www.guardian.co.uk/business/2008/oct/05/banks.marketturmoil, accessed 1 January 2011.

IABC (2010) *Emails and intranet top communication methods used to engage employees*. 3 August. Http://news.iabc.com/index.php?s=43&item=239, accessed 25 August 2010.

IBDO (1994) *The public relations sector*. DTI, October.

IBM *Social media guidelines* www.ibm.com/blogs/zz/en/guidelines.html, accessed 12 January 2011.

Igan, D. Mishra, P., Tressel, T. (2009) *A fistful of dollars – lobbying and the financial crisis*. IMF Working Paper. www.imf.org/external/pubs/ft/wp/2009/wp09287.pdf, accessed 15 December 2010.

Ihlen, O. (2009) 'On Bourdieu: public relations in field struggles', in O. Ihlen, B. van Ruler and M. Fredriksson (eds) *Public relations and social theory*, New York: Routledge.

Ihlen, O. and Fredrikson, M. (eds) (2009) *Public relations and social theory: key figures and concepts*, Florence, KY, US: Routledge.

Ihlen, O. and van Ruler, B. (2009) 'Introduction: applying social theory to public relations', in O. Ihlen, (ed.), *Public relations and social theory: key figures and concepts*, Taylor & Francis.

Inconvenient PR Truth (2010) http://inconvenientprtruth.com, accessed 31 December 2010.

Ind, N. (1997) *The corporate brand*, Oxford: Macmillan.

Ingenhoff, D. and Koelling, A.M. (2009) 'The potential of web sites as a relationship building tool for charitable fundraising NPOs', *Public Relations Review*, 35, pp. 66–73.

Ingham, F. (2005) 'Pillar for future success', *Profile*, November/December, p. 20.

Internet World Statistics (2010) www.internetworldstats.com/stats.htm, accessed 31 December 2010.

IPA (2010) *Results of the third IPA touchpoints survey*, www.ipa.co.uk/Content/Results-of-third-IPA-TouchPoints-Survey, accessed 28 January 2011.

IPR (1999) *Developing Excellence*. IPR.

IPR (2003) *Factfile*, www.ipr.org.uk/news/index.htm, accessed 28 July 2003.

IPRA (1990) *Public relations education – recommendations and standards*, IPRA Gold Paper No. 7, September.

IPRA (1997) *The influence of globalisation: an analysis of the survey results*, IPRA Gold Paper No. 12, pp. 49–72.

Jandt, F.E. (2004) *An introduction to intercultural communication* (4th edition), Sage.

Jaques, T. (2002) 'Towards a new terminology: optimising the value of issue management', *Journal of Communication Management*, 7 (2), pp. 140–147.

Jaques, T. (2010), 'Embedding issue management: from process to policy', in R.L. Heath (ed.), *The Sage handbook of public relations* (2nd edition), Sage, pp. 435–446.

Jardine, A. (2006) 'MPR: the solution to the budget puzzle?', *PR Week*, 17 March, pp. 22–23.

Jeffrey, A., Jeffries-Fox, B. and Rawlins, B.L. (2010) *A new paradigm for media analysis: weighted media cost,* www.instituteforpr.org/files/uploads/A_New_Paradigm_Jeffries Fox.pdf, accessed: 25 November 2010.

Jeffries-Fox, B. (2003) *Advertising value equivalency (AVE)*, www.instituteforpr.org/files/uploads/2003_AVE.pdf, accessed 18 November 2010.

Joffe, M. (2003) 'Communicating globally', presentation to GMCA students, Emerson College, Boston, MA, 17 March.

Johnson, B. (2007) 'Blogs mark the first 10 years', *Guardian*, 7 April, p. 31.

Johnson, G., Scholes, K. and Whittington, R. (2005) *Exploring corporate strategy* (7th edition), Prentice Hall, Chapter 4.

Johnson, J., Scholes, K. and Whittington, R. (2008). *Exploring corporate strategy* (8th edition), Pearson Education.

Johnson, M. (2007) 'The pay gap widens', *PR Week*, 26 January.

Johnston, L. (2010) 'A good PR consultant is worth the money', *Financial Times*, 7 December, www.ft.com/cms/s/0/ca12e80c-024f-11e0-ac33-00144feabdc0.html#axzz1CtXqy3xc.

Jones, A. (2010) 'Cadbury steps up defence against Kraft' (12 January) in *The Financial Times*, [Online], www.ft.com/cms/s/0/c2ea9792-ff48-11de-823b-00144feab49a.html#axzz1Ct Xqy3xc.

Jones, N. (1999) *Sultans of spin: the media and the New Labour government*, Victor Gollancz.

Judd, L.R. (1990) 'Importance and Use of Formal Research and Evaluation', *Public Relations Review*, 16 (4), pp. 17–28.

Judge, Sir P. (2005) 'Globalisation', *7th Annual Cambridge Marketing College Lecture*, St John's College, Cambridge.

Kakabadse, A., Kakabadse, N., and Kouzmin, A. (2003) 'Reinventing the democratic governance project through information technology? A growing agenda for debate', *Public Administration Review*, 63 (1), pp. 44–60.

Kaletsky, A. (2010) *Capitalism 4.0*, Bloomsbury Publishing.

Kam, E. (2004) *Surprise attack: the victim's perspective*, Harvard University Press.

Kant, I. (1964) *Groundwork of the metaphysics of morals*, [trans. H.J. Paton], Harper and Row.

Kapein, M. and van Tulder, R. (2003). 'Toward effective stakeholder dialogue', *Business and Society Review* 108 (2), pp. 203–224.

Kaplan, A.M., Haenlein, M. (2010) 'Users of the world, unite! The challenges and opportunities of social media', *Business Horizons,* 53 (1), pp. 59–68.

Karian and Box (2007) *LG07 study 2007: a comprehensive view of local government communications today*, www.karianandbox.com/resources.php, accessed 3 January 2011.

Kasperson, R.E., Renn, O., Slovic, P., Brown, H.S., Emel, J., Goble, R., Kasperson, J.X. and Ratick, S. (1988), 'The social amplification of risk: a conceptual framework', *Risk Analysis*, 8 (2),pp. 177–187.

Katz, E. and Lazerfield, P.F. (1995) *Personal Influence*, Glencoe, IL: Free Press.

Kaul, J.M. (1976) *Public Relations in India*, Kolkata: Naya ProKash.

Kelleher, T. and Miller, B.M. (2006) 'Organizational blogs and the human voice: relational strategies and relational outcomes', *Journal of Computer-Mediated Communication*, 11, pp. 395–414.

Kelly, D. (2009) 'Business to business public relations', in R. Tench and L. Yeomans (eds) *Exploring public relations*, Prentice Hall, pp. 430–445.

Kelly, K., Laskin. A., Rosenstein, G. (2010) 'Investor relations: two way symmetrical practice', *Journal of Public Relations Research.*

Kelly, K.S. (2001) 'Stewardship: The Fifth Step in the Public Relations Process', in R.L. Heath (ed.) *Handbook of public relations*, Thousand Oaks, CA: Sage, pp. 279–289.

Kennan, W.R. and Hazleton, V. (2006) 'Internal public relations, social capital, and the role of effective organizational communication', in C.H. Botan and V. Hazleton (eds), *Public Relations Theory II* 311–338, Mahwah: Lawrence Erlbaum Associates.

Kent, M.L. (2010) 'Directions in social media for professionals and scholars', in R.L. Heath (ed.), *The Sage handbook of public relations* (2nd edition), Sage, pp. 643–656.

Kent, M.L. and Taylor, M. (2002) 'Toward a dialogic theory of public relations', *Public Relations Review* 28, pp. 21–37.

Kerr, G. (1999) 'How consistent are we in communication evaluation?' Paper presented at the Australia and New Zealand Communication Association Annual Conference, University of Western Sydney, July.

Kim, J.-N. and Ni, L. (2010) 'Seeing the forest through the trees: the behavioural, strategic management paradigm in public relations and its future', in R.L. Heath (ed.), *The Sage handbook of public relations* (2nd edition), Sage, pp. 35–57.

Kindersley, R. (2009) 'Previews', *CorpComms*, January, 4–7.

Kirdira, Y. (2008) 'The role of public relations for image creating in health services: a sample patient satisfaction survey', *Health Marketing Quarterly*, 24, (3 & 4), September.

Kirkpatrick, D. (1998) *Evaluating training programs*, Berrett-Koehler Publishers.

Kitchen, P. (ed.) (1997) *Public relations, principles and practice*, London: International Thomson Business Press.

Kitchen, P. and de Pelsmacker, P. (2004), *Integrated marketing communications – a primer*, Routledge, pp. 18–19.

Kitchen, P.J. and Panopoulos, A. (2010) 'Online public relations: The adoption process and innovation challenge, a Greek example', *Public Relations Review*, 36 (3), pp. 222–229.

Kitchen, P.J. and Schultz, D.E. (2009) 'IMC: new horizon/false dawn for a marketplace in turmoil?' *Journal of Marketing Communication* 15 (2–3), April-July pp. 197–204.

Kotter, J. (1996) 'Why transformation efforts fail', in *Harvard Business Review on Change* 1998, Harvard Business School Press, Harvard.

Kraft (2009) *Investor relations offer document: Cadbury*.

Kraft (2011) *Fact Sheet*, www.kraftfoodscompany.com/assets/pdf/kraft_foods_fact_sheet.pdf.

Kramer, R. (1991) 'Voluntary organisations, contracting and the Welfare State', in J. Batsleer, C. Cornforth and R. Payton (eds) (1991) *Issues in voluntary and non-profit management: a reader*, Addison-Wesley/Open University.

Kruckenberg, D. and Stark, K. (2001) 'Public relations and community: a reconstructed theory revisited', in R.L. Heath (ed.) *Handbook of Public Relations*, Thousand Oaks: Sage, pp. 51–61.

Kuteev-Moreira, J.P. and Eglin, G.J. (2004) 'Strategic challenges for corporate communicators in public service', in S.M. Oliver (ed.) *Handbook of corporate communication and public relations*, Routledge.

Kynaston, D. (1994) *The City of London*, Pimlico.

Larkin, T. and Larkin, S. (1994) *Communicating change*, Thousand Oaks, CA: McGraw Hill.

Lazare, A. (2005) *On apology*, US: OUP.

Leary-Joyce, J. (2004) *Becoming an employer of choice*, London: Chartered Institute of Personnel and Development.

Ledingham, J.A. (2003) 'Explicating relationship management on a general theory of public relations', *Journal of Public Relations Research*, 15 (2), pp. 181–198.

Ledingham, J.A. (2006a) *'Public relations a general theory of public relations'*, in C.H. Botan and V. Hazleton (eds) *Public relations II*, Mahwah, NJ: Lawrence Erlbaum.

Ledingham, J.A. (2006b) 'Toward a theory of relationship management in public relations: how to cultivate quality relationships?' in E. Toth (ed.) *The future of excellence in public relations and communication management,* Mahwah, NJ: Lawrence Erlbaum, pp. 477–506.

Ledingham, J.A. and Bruning, S. D. (2000) *Public Relations as relationship management: a relational approach to the study and practice of public relations*, Mahwah, NJ: Lawrence Erlbaum Associates.

Leitch, S. and Motion, J. (1999) 'Multiplicity in corporate identity strategy', *Corporate Communications, An International Journal*, 4 (4), pp. 193–199.

Leitch S. and Neilson, D. (2001) 'Bringing publics into public relations: new theoretical frameworks for practice', in D. Heath (ed.) (2001) *Handbook of public relations*, pp. 127–138.

Lerbinger, O. (2001) 'Diversity and global communication require social interactive approach', *Purview*, 8 January.

Lerpold, L., Ravasi, D., Van Rekom, J. and Soenen, G. (eds) (2007) *Organizational identity in practice*, Routledge Publishing.

L'Etang, J. (1996) 'Public relations and corporate responsibility', in J. L'Etang, and M. Pieczka, (eds) *Critical perspectives in public relations*, London: International Thomson Business Press, pp. 82–105.

L'Etang, J. (1998) 'State propaganda and bureaucratic intelligence: the creation of public relations in 20th century Britain', *Public Relations Review*, 24 (4), pp. 413–441.

L'Etang, J. (2003) 'The myth of the "ethical guardian": an examination of its origins, potency and illusions', *Journal of Communication Management*, 8 (1), pp. 53–67.

L'Etang, J. (2004) *Public relations in Britain: a history of the professional practice in the 20th century*, New Jersey: Lawrence Erlbaum.

L'Etang, J. (2005) 'Critical public relations: some reflections', *Public Relations Review*, 31, pp. 521–526.

L'Etang, J. (2006a) *'Corporate responsibility and public relations ethics'*, in J. L'Etang and M. Pieczka (eds) *Critical perspectives in public relations*, London: International Thomson Business Press.

L'Etang, J. (2006b) 'Public relations as diplomacy', in J. L'Etang and M. Pieczka (eds) *Critical perspectives in public relations*, London: International Thomson Business Press.

L'Etang, J. (2006c) 'Public relations and rhetoric', in J. L'Etang and M. Pieczka (eds) *Critical perspectives in public relations*, London: International Thomson Business Press.

L'Etang, J. (2008) *Public relations: concepts practice and critique*, London: Sage.

L'Etang, J. (2009) 'Radical PR – catalyst for change or an aporia?', *Ethical Space*, 6 (2), pp. 13–18.

L'Etang, J. and Pieczka, M. (eds) (2006a) *Critical perspectives in public relations*, London: International Thomson Business Press.

L'Etang, J. and Pieczka, M. (eds) (2006b) *Public relations, critical debates and contemporary practice,* Mahwah, NJ: Lawrence Erlbaum.

Levine, R. (2009) 'But how does it taste?' in R. Levine, C. Locke, D. Searls and D. Weinberger (eds) *The Cluetrain manifesto: 10th anniversary edition*, Basic Books, pp. 22–36.

Lewin, K. (1935) *A dynamic theory of personality*, McGraw Book Co.

Lewis, R. (2006) 'Should industry rogues fear CIPR?', *PR Week*, 17 November, p. 16.

Lewis, R.D. (1999) *When cultures collide: managing successfully across cultures* (2nd edition), Nicholas Brealey Publishing.

LGA (2005) *The original reputation campaign*, www.reputation.lga.gov.uk/lga/core/page.do?pageId=922700, accessed 27 December 2010.

LGA (2009) *Council papers 'no threat to local press'*, www.lga.gov.uk/lga/core/page.do?pageId=1770660, accessed 27 December 2010.

LGA/MORI (2005) *The business case for the reputation project*, www.reputation.lga.gov.uk/lga/aio/354546, accessed 27 December 2010.

LGCommunications (2009) *Proving communications works – the impact of council publications,* www.lgcomms.org.uk/documents/PrvngCommsWrks-ImptOfcnclPubs.pdf, accessed 27 December 2010.

LGCommunications (2010) *New Reputation Guide*, www.reputation.lga.gov.uk/lga/aio/11478942, accessed 2 January 2011.

Lindenmann, W.K. (1990) 'Research, evaluation and measurement: a national perspective', *Public Relations Review*, 16 (2), pp. 3–17.

Lindenmann, W.K. (1993) 'An "effectiveness yardstick" to measure public relations success', *PR Quarterly*, 38 (1), pp. 7–9.

Lindenmann, W.K. (1998) 'Only PR outcomes count – that is the real bottom-line', *Journal of Communication Management*, 3 (1), pp. 66–73.

Lindenmann, W.K. (2003) *Guidelines for measuring the effectiveness of PR programs and activities*, www.instituteforpr.org/files/uploads/2002_MeasuringPrograms_1.pdf, accessed 25 November 2010.

Lindenmann, W.K. (2005) *Putting PR measurement and evaluation into historical perspective*, February 2005, www.instituteforpr.org/files/uploads/PR_History2005.pdf, accessed 18 November 2010.

Lippmann, W. (1922) *Public opinion*, New York: Macmillan.

Liu, D. and Reddy, S. (2006) 'Times are changing', in WS.AW, Weber Shandwick.

London Stock Exchange (2010) *RNS*, www.londonstockexchange.com/products-and-services/rns/rns.htm.

Lucas, L. (2011) 'Cadbury people still chewing on Kraft culture', *Financial Times*, 14 January.

Ludlam, S. (2001) 'The making of New Labour', in S. Ludlam and M. Smith (eds) *New Labour in government*, Basingstoke: Macmillan, pp. 1–31.

Lukaszewski, J. (2010) *Why PRSA can't punish*, PRSA, www.prsa.org/aboutprsa/ethics/documents/why_prsa_cant_punish.pdf?utm_campaign=PRSASearch&utm_source=PRSAWebsite&utm_medium=SSearch&utm_term=why%20PRSA%20can%27t%20punish, accessed 25 August 2010.

McComas, K.A. (2010) 'Community engagement and risk management', in R.L. Heath (ed.), *The Sage handbook of public relations* (2nd edition), Sage, pp. 461–476.

McCoy, M. and Hargie, O. (2001) 'Evaluating evaluation: implications for assessing quality', *International Journal of Health Care Quality Assurance*, 14 (7), pp. 317–327.

McCoy, M. and Hargie, O. (2003) 'Implications of mass communication theory for asymmetric public relations evaluation', *Journal of Communication Management*, 7 (4), pp. 304–316.

McCusker, G. (2006) *Public relations disasters: talespin – inside stories and lessons learnt*, London: Kogan Page.

McElreath, M.P. (1996) *Managing systematic and ethical public relations campaigns*, Brown & Benchmark.

McGovern, G. (2011) www.gerrymcgovern.com, accessed 12 January 2011.

McGrath, C. (2005) *Lobbying in Washington, London and Brussels: the persuasive communication of political issues*, Lampeter: The Edwin Mellen Press.

McGrath, C. (2006) 'The ideal lobbyist', *Journal of Communication Management*, 10 (1), pp. 67–79.

McGrath, C. (2007) 'Framing lobbying messages: defining and communicating political issues persuasively', *Journal of Public Affairs*, 7 (3), pp. 269–280.

Mack, C.S. (1997) *Business, politics, and the practice of Government relations*, Westport: Quorum Books.

MacLeod, D. and Clarke, N. (2008) *Engaging for success: enhancing performance through employee engagement* – a report to Government, London: The Department for Business Innovation and Skills.

Macleod, S. (2009a) 'Letters', *PR Week*, 16 October.

Macleod, S. (2009b) 'It's time to connect the dots', Corporate Reputation Thought leader series, *PR Week*, 18 September, p. 15.

MacManus, T. (2000) 'Public relations, the cultural dimension', in D. Moss and B. De Santo (eds) *Perspectives on public relations research*, London: Routledge.

McMillan, G. (2009) 'Build a reputation that will last', Corporate Reputation Thought leader series, *PR Week*, 18 September, p. 21.

McNair, B. (1994) *Political communication: an introduction*, London: Routledge.

McNair, B. (1998) *The sociology of journalism*, London: Arnold.

McNair, B. (2000) *Journalism and democracy: an evaluation of the political public sphere*, London: Routledge.

McNair, B. (2003) *Political communication: an introduction* (3rd edition), London: Routledge.

McNair, B. (2003) *News and journalism in the UK* (4th edition), London: Routledge.

McNair, B. (2004) 'PR must die: spin, anti-spin and political public relations in the UK, 1997–2004', *Journalism Studies*, 5 (3), pp. 325–338.

Macnamara, J. (1992) 'Evaluation of public relations. The achilles heel of the profession', *International Public Relations Review*, 15 (4), pp. 17–31.

Macnamara, J. (2001) *Professional bodies condemn AVEs*, www.pria.com.au.

Macnamara, J. (2002a) 'An international perspective on priority issues in public relations', *IPRA World Congress*, Cairo, 14 November.

Macnamara, J. (2002b) 'Research and evaluation', in C. Tymson and P. Lazar (eds) *The new Australian and New Zealand public relations manual*, Sydney: Tymson Communications, pp. 100–134.

Macnamara, J. (2005) *Jim Macnamara's public relations handbook*, Sydney: Archipelago Press.

Macnamara, J. (2006) *PR metrics: research for planning & evaluation of PR & corporate communication*, www.carmaapac.com/downloads/PR%20Metrics%202006.pdf, accessed 11 November 2010.

Macnamara, J. (2007) *The fork in the road of media and communication theory and practice*, June 2007, www.instituteforpr.org/files/uploads/MacnamaraPaper_b.pdf, accessed 18 November 2010.

McQuail, D. (2000) *McQuail's mass communication theory*, London: Sage.

McQuail, D. and Windahl, S. (1993) *Communication models for the study of mass communication*, London: Longman.

McQuail, D., Blumler, J.G. and Brown, J. (1972) 'The television audience: a revised perspective', in D. McQuail (ed.) *Sociology of mass communication*, London: Penguin.

Magee, K. (2010) 'Measurement: what next for measurement?' *PR Week*. 18 August, www.prweek.com/news/1022935/Measurement-next-measurement/?DCMP=ILC-SEARCH, accessed 16 November 2010.

Magee, K. and O'Reilly, G. (2010) 'Charter sets "global standard" for calculating value of PR at European measurement summit', *PR Week*, 24 June, www.prweek.com/news/1011842/Charter-sets-global-standard-calculating-value-PR-European-Measurement-Summit/?DCMP=ILC-SEARCH, accessed 16 November 2010.

Margulies, W.P. (1977) 'Make the most of your corporate identity', *Harvard Business Review*, pp. 66–74.

Marketing Week (2010), Gap launch, 14 October.

Marklein, T. (2010) 'How to get started in measuring social media and what are the definitions of relevant metrics?' in *PR Measurement metrics: from concept to implementation reality*, London, 17 November, http://londonmeasurementconference.org/Presentations/Presentation4.pdf, accessed 18 November 2010.

Markwick, N. and Fill, C. (1997) 'Towards a framework for managing corporate identity', *European Journal of Marketing*, 31 (5), pp. 396–409.

Marr, A. (2004) *My trade*, London: Macmillan.

Marston, J.E. (1963) *The nature of public relations*, New York: McGraw-Hill.

Marx, E. (2001) *Breaking through culture shock*, London: Nicholas Brealey Publishing.

Maude, F. (2010) *Government spending data*, www.number10.gov.uk/news/latest-news/2010/11/government-spending-data-published-2-57257, accessed 2 January 2011.

May, S., Cheney, G. and Roper, J. (eds) (2007) *The debate over corporate social responsibility*, Oxford: Oxford University Press.

Melcrum (2006a) *Mastering audience segmentation*, London: Melcrum Publishing.

Melcrum (2006b) *Melcrum pulse; essential data on internal communications budgets, trends and salaries 2006–7*, London: Melcrum Publishing.

Melewar T.C. (2003) 'Determinants of the corporate identity construct: a review of the literature', *Journal of Marketing Communications* 9, pp. 195–220.

Melewar, T.C. (ed.) (2008) *Facets of corporate identity, communication and reputation*, Abingdon: Taylor & Francis.

Melewar, T.C. and Karaosmanoglu, E. (2006) 'Seven dimensions of corporate identity: a categorisation from practitioners' perspective', *European Journal of Marketing*, 40 (7/8), pp. 846–869.

Melewar, T.C. and McCann, C.D. (2004) 'Facets of the global corporate brand', in S.M. Oliver (ed.) *Handbook of corporate communication and public relations*, London: Routledge, pp. 158–166.

Michaelson, D. and Griffin, T.L. (2005) *A new model for media content analysis*, www.institute forpr.org/files/uploads/MediaContentAnalysis.pdf, accessed: 18 November 2010.

Michaelson, D. and Stacks, D.W. (2007) *Exploring the comparative communications effectiveness of advertising and public relations: an experimental study of initial branding advantage*, www.instituteforpr.org/files/uploads/Michaelson_Stacks.pdf, accessed 25 November 2010.

Milbraith, L.W. (1963) *The Washington Lobbyists*, Chicago: Rand McNally.

Millar, R. (2009) 'Connect with the customer', Corporate Reputation Thought leader series, *PR Week*, 18 September, p. 17.

Miller, D. (1998) 'Public relations and journalism', in A. Briggs and P. Cobley (eds) *The media: an introduction*, Harlow: Longman.

Miller, D. and Dinan, D. (2008) *A century of spin*, London: Pluto Press.

Miller, D., Kitzinger, J., Williams, K. and Beharrel, P. (1998) *The circuit of mass communication*, London: Sage.

Mitchell, R.K., Agle, B.R. and Wood, D.J. (1997) 'Towards a theory of stakeholder idntification and salience: defining the principle of who and what really counts', *Academy of Management Review*, 22 (4), pp. 853–886.

Mitchie, D. (1998) *The invisible persuaders*, London: Bantam Press.

Moingeon, B. and Ramanantsoa, B.R. (1997) 'Understanding corporate identity: the French school of thought', *European Journal of Marketing*, 31 (5), pp. 383–395.

Moloney, K. (2000) *Rethinking public relations: the spin and the substance*, London: Routledge.

Moloney, K. (2006a) *rethinking public relations: PR, propaganda and democracy*, London: Routledge.

Moloney, K. (2006b) 'Public affairs' in R. Tench and L. Yeomans (eds), *Exploring public relations*, Harlow: FT Prentice Hall, pp. 433–462.

Monck, A. and Hanley, M. (2008) *Can you trust the media?,* London: Icon.

Montagu Smith, N. (2006b) 'The value of education', *CorpComms*, May, pp. 15–17.

Morley, M. (2002a) *How to manage your global reputation* (2nd edition), New York: New York University Press.

Morley, M. (2002b) 'The Internet: medium, message, PR tool, manager', in *How to manage your global reputation*, New York: New York University Press, pp. 160–175.

Morley, M. (2009) 'A new career path for public relations professionals', *Institute for Public Relations,* wwwinstituteforpr.org.

Morris, D. (1999) *Vote.com*, Los Angeles: Renaissance Books.

Morris, T. and Goldsworthy, S. (2008) *PR: a persuasive industry?* London: Palgrave Macmillan.

Moss, D. and De Santo, B. (eds) (2002) *Public relations cases: international perspectives*, London: Routledge.

Moss, D. and Warnaby, G. (1997) 'A strategic perspective for public relations', in P.J. Kitchen (ed.) *Public relations: principles and practice*, pp. 43–73.

Moss, D.A., Newman, A. and De Santo, B (2005) 'What do communications managers do? Refining the core elements of management in a public relations/communications context', *Journal of Mass Communication Quarterly*, 82, pp. 873–890.

Moss, D.A., Warnaby, G. and Newman, A. (2000) 'Public relations practitioner role enactment at the senior management level within UK companies', *Journal of Public Relations Research*, 12 (4), pp. 277–307.

Motion, J. (2005) 'Participative public relations: power to the people or legitimacy for government discourse?', *Public Relations Review*, 31, pp. 505–512.

Motion, J. and Weaver, K. (2005) 'A discourse perspective for critical public relations research: life sciences network and the battle for truth', *Journal of Public Relations Research*, 17 (1), pp. 49–67.

Murphy, C. (2005) 'Equality brings results', *PR Week*, 1 April, pp. 23–24.

Murphy, C. (2009a) 'A question of reputation', Corporate Reputation Thought leader series, *PR Week*, 18 September, pp. 4–5.

Murphy, M. (1991) 'Game theory models for organizational/public conflict', *Canadian Journal of Communication*, 16 (2), URL: www.cjc-online.ca/index.php/journal/article/viewArticle/606, accessed 31 December 2010.

Murray, K. (2003) 'Reputation – managing the single greatest risk facing business today', *Journal of Communication Management*, 8 (2), pp. 142–149.

Murray, K. (2006) 'Reputation 2.0', *Behind the spin conference*, College of St Mark & St John, Plymouth, Devon, 8 September.

Murray, K. and White, J. (2004) *CEO views on reputation management*, London: Chime Communications.

Murray, K. and White, J. (2005) 'CEO views on reputation management', *Journal of Communication Management*, 9 (4), pp. 348–358.

Murray, W.M. (2010) *Future of the profession – what lies ahead?*, PRSA 1 July, www.prsa.org, accessed 25 August 2010.

Muslim Council of Britain (2002) *Constitution*, www.mcb.org.uk/downloads/MCBCON 2002.pdf.

Neef, D. (2004) *The supply chain imperative*, AMACOM (Division of the American Management Association).

Negrine, R. (1996) *The communication of politics*, London: Sage.

Neuendorf, K. (2002) *The content analysis guidebook*, Thousand Oaks, CA: Sage.

Newman, W. (1995) 'Community relations', in N.A. Hart (ed.) *Strategic public relations*, London: Macmillan.

Newsom, D., Turk, J.V. and Kruckeberg, D. (2000) *This is PR* (7th edition), Belmont, CA: Wadsworth.

Newspaper Society (2008) *Public sector competition*, www.newspapersoc.org.uk/default. aspx?page=4296, accessed 2 January 2011.

NHS (2009) *The communicating organisation*.

NIRI, (2010) *Origins of NIRI*, www.niri.org/FunctionalMenu/About/Origins/originsch1cfm.aspx, accessed 5 December 2010.

Norris, P. (2001) *Digital divide: civic engagement, information poverty, and the Internet worldwide*, Cambridge: Cambridge University Press.

NPR (2006) *Is 'compassion fatigue' setting in?*, 7 March, www.npr.org/templates/story/story.php?storyId=5249873, accessed 10 January 2011.

Nunn, M. (2006) 'The future's bright', *PR Business*, 22 June, pp. 16–17.

O'Connor, J. (2010) *The battle for reputation*, CIPR, www.cipr.co.uk, 9 August, accessed 25 August 2010.

O'Connor, N. and Falconi, T.M. (2004) 'Profiling the regulatory environment of public relations practice in the UK, Italy and South Africa', *Journal of Communications Management*, 9 (1), pp. 28–55.

O'Donovan, G.M., Armstrong, A., Mitchell, V. and Sweeney, M. (2001) *'Corporate social responsibility: do Australian banks toe the triple bottom line?'*, *Banking and Financial Services Journal*, June, pp. 6–10.

Olins, W. (1999) *Corporate identity*, Thames and Hudson.

Office for National Statistics ONS (2010) *Public sector – employment decreases in Q3 2010*, www.statistics.gov.uk/cci/nugget.asp?id=407, accessed 27 December 2010.

Organisation for Economic Co-operation and Development (OECD) (2003) *Closer government to business partnership urged to overcome digital divide in OECD-APEC*, www.oecd.org/dataoecd/34/26/2488661.pdf, accessed 31 December 2010.

Owen, D. (2005) *Corporate social reporting and stakeholder accountability: the missing link*, www.nottingham.ac.uk/business/ICCSR/research/paperseries.html.

Page, G. and Fearn. H. (2005) 'Corporate reputation: what do consumers really care about?', *Journal of Advertising Research*, Cambridge: Cambridge University Press, 45, pp. 305–313.

Paine, K.D. (2002) *Measures of success for cyberspace*, April 2002. www.instituteforpr.org/files/uploads/2002_Cyberspace.pdf, accessed 17 February 2010.

Paine, K. D. (2007*) How to measure social media relations: the more things change, the more they remain the same*, April 2007, www.instituteforpr.org/files/uploads/How_to_Measure_Blogs.pdf, accessed 17 February 2010.

Palenchar, M.J. (2010) 'Risk communication', in R.L. Heath (ed.), *The Sage handbook of public relations* (2nd edition), London: Sage, pp. 447–461.

Palenchar, M.J. and Fitzpatrick, K.R. (2009) 'Secret persuaders: ethical and rhetorical perspectives on the use of public relations front groups', in E.L. Toth (ed.) *Rhetorical and critical approaches to public relations II*, London: Taylor & Francis, pp. 272–289.

Pankraz, D. (27 October 2010) Introducing Generation C: The Connected Collective Consumer, http://blog.nielsen.com/nielsenwire/consumer/introducing-gen-c-%E2%80%93-the-connected-collective-consumer, accessed 31 December 2010.

Pauly, J.J. and Hutchison, L.L. (2005) 'Moral fables of public relations practice: The Tylenol and Exxon Valdez cases', *Journal of Mass Media Ethics*, 20 (4), pp. 231–249.

Pavlik, J.P. (1996) 'Managing the information superhighway – a report on the issues facing communications professionals', *Institute for Public Relations Research and Education.*

Pearson, R. (1989) 'Business ethics as communication ethics: public relations practice and the idea of dialogue', in C.H. Botan and V. Hazleton (eds) *Public relations theory*, Hillsdale, NJ: Lawrence Erlbaum.

Pearson, R. (1992) 'Perspectives on public relations history', in E. Toth and R. Heath (eds) *Rhetorical and critical approaches to public relations*, Hillsdale, NJ: Lawrence Erlbaum.

Peston, R. (2009). *Faith in banks*. www.bbc.co.uk/blogs/thereporters/robertpeston/2009/01/faith_in_banks.html#comments, accessed 5 December 2010.

Petty, R.E. and Cacioppo, J.T. (1986) 'The elaboration likelihood model of persuasion', in L. Berkowitz (ed.) *Advances in experimental social psychology* (Volume 19), Elsevier, pp. 123–192.

Phillips, D. (2001b) 'The public relations evaluationists', *Corporate Communications: An International Journal*, 6 (4), pp. 225–237.

Phillips, D. (2009) *A Grunigian view of modern PR*, http://leverwealth.blogspot.com/2009/01/grunigian-view-of-modern-pr.html, accessed 31 December 2010.

Phillips, D. and Young, P. (2009) *Online public relations: a practical guide to developing an online strategy in the world of social media*, London: Kogan Page.

Pieczka, M. (2000) 'Objectives and evaluation in public relations work: what do they tell us about expertise and professionalism?', *Journal of Public Relations Research*, 12 (3), pp. 211–233.

Pieczka, M. (2006) 'Paradigms, systems theory and public relations', in J. L'Etang, and M. Pieczka (eds) (2006) *Public relations, critical debates and contemporary practice*, Mahwah, NJ: Lawrence Erlbaum.

Pieczka, M. (forthcoming) *Public relations as dialogic expertise?*

Piekos, J.M. and Einsiedel, E.F. (1990) 'Roles and program evaluation techniques among canadian public relations practitioners', *Public Relations Research Annual*, 2, pp. 95–113.

Pilcher, G. (2007) 'Liar, liar, practitioners under fire', *Profile*, May/June, p. 12.

Pinkleton, B.E., Austin, E.W. and Dixon, A. (1999) 'Orientations in public relations research and campaign evaluation', *Journal of Marketing Communications*, 5 (2), pp. 85–95.

PRCA (2009) *84% of PR leaders say evaluation makes PR credible*, 3 March 2009, www.prca.org.uk/?pid=403&sid=8, accessed 9 December 2010.

PRCA (2010) *PRCA announces new action on evaluation*, 18 November 2010. www.prca.org.uk/PRCA-announces-new-action-on-evaluation-AMEC-PRSA, accessed 9 December 2010.

Prensky, M. (2001), *Digital natives, digital immigrants*, from on the horizon (MCB University Press, 9(5), October 2001), www.marcprensky.com/writing/Prensky%20-%20Digital%20Natives,%20Digital%20Immigrants%20-%20Part1.pdf, accessed 31 December 2010.

PriceWaterhouseCoopers (2010) *The 13th annual global CEO survey*, www.pwc.com/en_GX/gx/ceo-survey/pdf/13th-annual-global-ceo-survey_em.pdf, accessed 13 January 2010.

PR Week (2010) *Top PR 150 consultancies league table*, http://toppragencies.prweek.co.uk/Top150-leaguetable.aspx.

Putnam, R. (1996) 'The strange disappearance of civic America', *The American Prospect*, 7 (24).

Putnam, R. (2000) *Bowling alone: the collapse and revival of American community*, New York: Touchstone.

QMU (2011) www.qmu.ac.uk/the_university/mission_statement.htm.

Quigley, C. (2009) 'Empower, or lose power', *PR Week*, 4 November.

Quirke, B. (2003) *Making the connections*, Aldershot: Gower.

Ramsey, P. (2010) 'Journalism, deliberative democracy and government communication: normative arguments from public sphere theory', *Javnost-The Public*, European Institute for Communication and Culture, 17 (4), pp. 81–96.

Rawlins, B. (2010) *Report of the Advertising Value Equivalency (AVE) task force*, October 2010, www.instituteforpr.org/files/uploads/Position_on_AVE_10–08–2010.pdf, accessed 18 November 2010.

Regester, M. and Larkin, J. (1997) 'Issue and crisis management: fail-safe procedures', in P. Kitchen (ed.) *Public relations, principles and practice*, London: International Thomson Business Press.

Regester, M., and Larkin, J. (2008) *Risk issues and crisis management in public relations: a casebook of best practice*, London: Kogan Page.

Reidenbach, R.E. and Robin, D.P. (1991) 'A conceptual model of corporate moral development', *Journal of Business Ethics* 10, pp. 273–284.

Rethemeyer, R.K. (2007) 'The empires strike back: is the internet corporatizing rather than democratizing policy processes?', *Public Administration Review*, 67 (2), pp. 199–215.

Richards, B. (2004) 'Terrorism and PR', *Public Relations Review*, 2, pp. 169–179.

Robert, B. and Lajtha, C. (2002), A new approach to crisis management, *Journal of Contingencies and Crisis Management*, 10, pp. 181–191.

Robinson D., Perryman S. and Hayday, S. (2004) *The Drivers of Employee Engagement*. Report 408, Institute for Employment Studies.

Rogers, D. (2007a) 'Honesty on display at ethics debate', *PR Week*, 23 February, p. 19.

Rogers, D. (2007b) 'Global PR trends bode well for PR', *PR Week*, 9 March.

Rosborough, A. and Wakefield, R. (2000) 'Globalizing and diversifying public relations management', *PRSA/IPR World Congress*, Chicago.

Rossi, P.H., Freeman, H.E. and Lipsey, M.W. (2004) *Evaluation: a systematic approach* (7th edition), Thousand Oaks, CA: Sage.

Rossi, P.H. and Freeman H.E. (1989) *Evaluation: a systematic approach* (4th edition), Newbury Park, CA: Sage.

RSA Inquiry (1995) *Tomorrow's Company.*

Rucci, A.J, Kirn, S.P. and Quinn, R.T. (1998) 'The Employee-customer profit chain at Sears', *Harvard Business Review*.

Ruck. K. (ed.) (2010) *Exploring internal communication*, London: Pearson.

Rucker, D.D. and Petty, R.E. (2006) 'Increasing the effectiveness of communications to consumers: recommendations based on elaboration likelihood and attitude certainty perspectives', *American Marketing Association*, 25 (1), pp. 39–52.

Russo, D.F. (2010) *17 rules successful companies use to attract and keep top talent*: why engaged employees are your greatest sustainable advantage, Oxford: Pearson Education, p. 147.

Salter, C. (2010) *Can Livestrong survive Lance Armstrong and a doping scandal?,* Issue 150, and www.fastcompany.com/magazine/150/can-livestrong-survive-lance.html.

Scheider, S.C. and Barsoux, J.-L. (2003) *Managing across cultures* (2nd edition), London: Prentice Hall.

Schlesinger, P. (1990) 'Rethinking the sociology of journalism: source strategies and the limits of media-centrism', in M. Ferguson (ed.) *Public communication: the new imperatives – future directions for media research*, London: Sage.

Schmidt, K. (1997) 'Corporate identity: an evolving discipline', *Corporate Communications, An International Journal*, 2 (1), pp. 40–45.

Schultz, D.E., Tannenbaum, S.I. and Lauterborn, R.F. (1992) 'Integrated marketing communications', in P. Kitchen (1997) Chicago: NTC Business Books, pp. 2–13.

Schultz, M., Hatch, M.J. and Larsen, M. (2000) *The expressive organisation: linking indentity, reputation and the corporate brand*, Oxford: Oxford University Press.

Schwartz, P. and Gibb, B. (1999) *When good companies do bad things: responsibility and risk in an age of globalization*, London: John Wiley.

Scott, J. (2007) 'Relationship measures applied to Practice' in E.L. Toth (ed.) *The future of excellence in public relations and communication management*, Mahwah, NJ: Lawrence Erlbaum, pp. 263–275.

Scriven, M. (1996) 'The theory behind practical evaluation', *Evaluation*, 2 (4), pp. 393–404.

Sebenius, J.K. (2002) 'The hidden challenges of cross-border negotiations', *Harvard Business Review*, March, pp. 76–85.

Seitel, F. (1998) *The practice of public relations* (7th edition), London: Prentice Hall.

Sen, S. and Bhattacharya, C.B. (2001) 'Does doing good always lead to doing better? Consumer reactions to corporate social responsibility', *Journal of Marketing Research*, 38, pp. 225–244.

Shaw, M. (2007) *Council of PR firms survey shows growth in industry for 2006*, www.prfirms.org.

Shaw, P. (2005) 'The human resource dimensions of public affairs', in P. Harris and C.S. Fleisher (eds) *The Handbook of Public Affairs*, London: Sage, pp. 123–144.

Shirky, C. (2008) *Here comes everybody: the power of organizing without organizations*, London: Penguin Press.

Shirky, C. (2010) *Cognitive surplus: creativity and generosity in a connected age*, London: Allen Lane.

Showalter, A. and Fleisher, G.S. (2005) 'The tools and techniques of public affairs', in P. Harris and C.S. Fleisher (eds) *The handbook of public affairs*, London: Sage, pp. 145–159.

Singer, P. (1979) *Practical ethics*, Cambridge: Cambridge University Press.

Sinickas, A. (2006) *Evaluating communication structures*. Melcrum.

Sinickas, A (2009), *Measure your ROI—fast!*, www.sinicom.com/Sub%20Pages/pubs/articles/article127.pdf, accessed 13 January 2011.

Sireau, N. (2008) *Make poverty history: political communication in action*, London: Palgrave Macmillan.

Smith, A. (2010) *Plus ça change, plus c'est la meme chose for public relations*. Submission for Chartered PR practitioner, February. Accessed via www.cipr.co.uk.

Smith, B. (2008) 'Representing PR in the marketing mix – a study on public relations variables in marketing mix modeling', *Institute for Public Relations*, www.instituteforpr.org.

Smith, D. (2007) 'Enough! The Briton who is challenging the web's endless cacophony', *The Observer*, 29 April, http://media.guardian.co.uk/newmedia/story/0,,2068929,00.html, accessed 14 May 2007.

Smith, M.F. and Ferguson, D.P. (2001) 'Activism', in R.L. Heath and G. Vasquez (eds), *The handbook of public relations*, London: Sage, pp. 291–300.

Smith, M.F. and Ferguson, D.P. (2010) 'Activism 2.0', in R.L. Heath (ed.), *The Sage handbook of public relations* (2nd edition), London: Sage, pp. 395–408.

Smith, R.D. (2009) *Strategic planning for public relations* (3rd edition), New York and London: Routledge.

Smuddle, P.M. and Courtright, J.L. (2010) Public relations and power, in R.L. Heath (ed.), *The Sage handbook of public relations* (2nd edition), London: Sage, pp. 177–190.

Snell, K (1993) *Developing skills for ethical management*, Chapman Hall.

Solis, B. and Breakenridge, D. (2009) *Putting the public back in public relations: how social media is reinventing the aging business of PR*, London: FT Press.

Somerville, I. (2011) 'Managing public affairs and lobbying: persuasive communication in the policy sphere', in D. Moss and B. deSanto (eds) *Public relations: a managerial perspective*, London: Sage.

Somerville, I., Graham, M. and Wood, E. (2007) 'Public Relations and the free organizational publication: practitioner perspectives on the brave new (media) world', *Journal of Communication Management*, 11, pp. 198–211.

Sommerville, K.L. (2007) *Hospitality employee management and supervision: concepts and practical applications*, New Jersey: John Wiley and Sons.

Sowell, T. (2010) *Dismantling America: and other controversial essays*, New York: Basic Books.

Sparks, C. (2001) 'The Internet and the global public sphere', in W.L. Bennett and R.L. Entman (eds) *Mediated politics: communication in the future of democracy*, Cambridge: Cambridge University Press.

Sparrow, P.R. and Cooper C.L. (2003) *The employment relationship*, Oxford: Butterworth-Heinmann.

Spencer, C. and Jahansoozi, J. (2008) 'The role of research in shaping and measuring communication. London's bid to hold the 2012 james', in B. van Ruler, A.T. Verčič and D. Verčič (eds) *Public relations metrics. Research and evaluation*, New York and London: Routledge, pp. 182–206.

Springston, J.K. (2001) 'Public relations and new media technology', in R.L. Heath (ed.) *Handbook of public relations*, London: Sage, pp. 603–614.

Sriramesh, K. and Verčič, D. (eds) (2003) *The global public relations handbook: theory, research and practice*, New Jersey: Lawrence Erlbaum.

Sriramesh, K. and Verčič, D. (2009) *The global public relations handbook: theory, research, and practice* (Expanded and revised edition), London: Routledge.

Stanley, D.J., Meyer, J.P. and Topolntsky, L. (2005) 'Employee cynicism and resistance to organizational change', *Journal of Business and Psychology*, 19, pp. 429–459.

Stauber, J. and Rampton, S. (2004) *Toxic sludge is good for you* (3rd edition), London: Robinson.

Steyn, B. (2007) 'Contribution of public relations to organisational strategy formulation', in E.L. Toth (ed.), *The future of excellence in public relations and communication management*, New Jersey: Lawrence Erlbaum Associates.

Street, J. (2001) *Mass media, politics, and democracy*, Basingstoke: Palgrave.

Stufflebeam, D.L. and Shinkfield, A.J. (1985) *Systematic evaluation*, US: Kluwer-Nijhoff Publishing.

Sutherland, S. (1992), *Irrationality: The Enemy Within*, London: Constable.

Szondi, G. (2006) 'International context of public relations', in R. Tench and L. Yeomans (eds) *Exploring public relations*, London: FT Prentice Hall, pp. 113–140.

Taleb, N. (2007) *The black swan. The impact of the highly improbable*, London: Random House.

Tambini, D. (2008) *Financial journalism and the economic crisis*, www.imf.org/external/pubs/ft/wp/2009/wp09287.pdf, accessed 10 December 2010.

Taylor, M. (2001) 'International public relations: opportunities and challenges for the 21st century', in R.L. Heath (ed.) *Handbook of public relations*, London: Sage, pp. 629–637.

Taylor, M., Kent, M. L. and White, W.J. (2001) 'How activist organizations are using the internet to build relationships', *Public Relations Review*, 27 (3), pp. 263–284.

Tench, R. and Fawkes, J. (2005*)* 'Mind the gap, exploring different attitudes to public relations education from employers, academics and alumni', *Alan Rawel/CIPR Academic Conference*, Lincoln.

Tench, R. and Yeomans, L. (eds) (2006) *Exploring public relations*, Harlow: FT Prentice Hall.

Tench, R. and Yeoman, L. (2009) 'What next? Future issues for PR', in R. Tench and L. Yeomans (eds) *Exploring public relations* (2nd edition), Harlow: Prentice Hall, pp. 633–644.

Theaker, A. (2007) *Public relations handbook* (3rd edition), London: Routledge.

Thellusson, J. (2003) 'Measuring PR's value', *Admap*, February, Issue 436.

Thomas, C.S. (2004) *Research guide to US and international Interest groups*, Westport:, CT: Praeger.

Titley, S. (2003) 'How political and social change will transform the EU public affairs industry', *Journal of Public Affairs*, 3 (1), pp. 83–89.

Tobin, N. (2004) 'Can the professionalisation of the UK public relations industry make it more trustworthy?', *Journal of Communication Management*, 9 (1), pp. 56–64.

Toth, E.L. and Heath, R.L. (eds) (1992) *Rhetorical and critical approaches to public relations*, Hillsdale, NJ: Lawrence Erlbaum.

Toth, E.L., Serini, S.A., Wright, D.K. and Emig, A.G. (1998) 'Trends in public relations roles: 1990–1995', *Public Relations Review*, 24 (2), pp. 145–163.

Tremlett, G. and Topping, A. (2010) 'Ibiza police arrest 20 Britons in raid on major drug ring', *Guardian*, August 31, www.guardian.co.uk/world/2010/aug/31/ibiza-police-crack-drug-ring?INTCMP=SRCH.

Tuominen, P. (2007) 'Emerging metaphors in brand managment: towards a relational approach', *Journal of Communication Management*, 11 (2), pp. 182–191.

Turk, J.V. (2006) 'The professional bond, public relations education in the 21st century', *Report of the Commission on Public Relations Education*, www.commpred.org.

Turner, A. (2009) *How to tame global finance*, www.prospectmagazine.co.uk/2009/08/how-to-tame-global-finance, accessed 10 December 2010.

Tye, L. (1998) *The father of spin: Edward L. Bernays & the birth of public relations*, US: Owl Books.

Tyler, R.W. (1942) 'General Statement of Evaluation', *Journal of Educational Research*, 35 (7), pp. 492–501.

UK Treasury (2009) *A review of UK corporate governance in UK banks and other financial entities*, http://webarchive.nationalarchives.gov.uk/+/http://www.hm-treasury.gov.uk/d/walker_review_261109.pdf, accessed 10 December 2010.

United Nations Global Compact (2002) www.unglobalcompact.org/AboutTheGC/The TenPrinciples/index.html.

van der Laan, D. (2000) 'EU standards for PR', *CERP Newsletter*, January, pp. 11–16.

van Riel, C.B.M. (1995) *Principles of corporate communication*, London: Prentice Hall.

van Riel, C.B.M. and Fombrun, C.J. (2007) *Essentials of corporate communication*, London: Routledge.

van Ruler, B. and Verčič, D. (2002) 'The Bled manifesto on public relations', *9th International Public Relations Research Symposium*, Bled, Slovenia, July.

Varey, R. (1997) 'Public relations: the external publics context', in P.J. Kitchen (ed.) *Public relations, principles and practice*, London: International Thomson Business Press.

Veil, S.R., Littlefield, R.S. and Rowan, K.E. (2009) 'Dissemination as success: local emergency management communication practices', *Public Relations Review*, 35, pp. 449–461.

Vella, K.J. and Melewar, T.C. (2008) 'Explicating the relationship between identity and culture: a multi-perspective conceptual model', in TC. Melewar (ed.) *Facts of corporate identity, communication and reputation*, Abingdon: Routledge.

Vernelle, B. (1994) *Understanding and using groups*, London: Whiting and Birch.

Vines, G. (2010) Director of Communication, Action for Children. Personal interview with Peter Brill. 30 November.

Wachman, R. (2010) 'Rolls-Royce and BP need to get their message out – and say sorry', *Observer*, December 26, www.guardian.co.uk/business/2010/doc/26/bp rolls-royce-public-relations-record-comment?INTCMP=SRCH.

Wakefield, R.I. (2001) 'Effective public relations in the multinational organisation', in R.L. Heath (ed.) *Handbook of public relations*, London: Sage, pp. 639–647.

Wakefield, R.I. (2003) 'Preliminary Delphi research on international public relations programming', in D. Moss, D. Verčič and G. Warnaby (eds), *Perspectives on public relations research*, London: Routledge.

Walker, G. (1997) 'Public relations practitioners' use of research, measurement, and evaluation', *Australian Journal of Communication*, 24 (2), pp. 97–113.

Wallace, C. (2009) 'The AVE debate: measuring the value of PR', *PR Week*, 6 May. www.prweek.com/uk/news/903837/AVE-debate-Measuring-value-PR, accessed 16 November 2010.

Wall Street Journal (2010) The rise of apps, iPad and androids, 27 December, http://online.wsj.com/article/SB10001424052748704774604576035611315663944.html#printMode, accessed 31 December 2010.

Watch, S. (2009) Previews, *CorpComms*, January, pp. 4–7.

Waters, D., Tindall, N.T.J., Morton, T.S. (2010) 'Media catching and the journalist-PR practitioner relationship: how social media is changing the practice of media relations'. *Journal of Public Relations Research,* 22 (3), pp. 241–264.

Watney, S. (1989) 'Policing desire; pornography, AIDS and the media', in T. O'Sullivan and Y. Jewkes (eds) (1997) *The media studies reader*, London: Hodder Arnold.

Watson, T. (1995) *Evaluating public relations: the creation and validation of models of measurement for public relations practice*, Unpublished Doctoral Thesis, Southampton Institute.

Watson, T. (1997) 'Measuring the success rate: evaluating the PR process and PR programmes', in P. Kitchen (ed.) *Public relations, principles and practice*, London: International Thomson Business Press, pp. 283–306.

Watson, T. (2008) 'Public relations research priorities: a Delphi study', *Journal of Communication Management*, 12 (2), pp. 104–123.

Watson, T. and Noble, P. (2007) *Evaluating public relations* (2nd edition), London: Kogan Page.

Watts, R. (2004) 'The application of social semiotic theory to corporate positioning material', *Journal of Communication Management*, 8 (4).

Weaver, C.K., Motion, J. and Reaper J. (2006) 'From propaganda to discourse (and back again): truth, power, the public interest and public relations'. in J.L'Etang and M. Pieczka (eds) (2006) *Critical perspectives in public relations*, London: International Thomson Business Press.

Weber, M. (1968) *Economy and Society*, New York: Bedminster (original work published 1922).

Weiss, C.H. (1972) *Evaluation research*, New Jersey: Prentice-Hall.

Welch, M., Jackson, P.R. (2007) 'Rethinking internal communication: a stakeholder approach', *Corporate Communications*, 12 (2), pp. 117–198.

Wenger, E.C. and Snyder, W.M (2000) 'Communities of practice: the organizational frontier', *Harvard Business Review*, pp. 139–145, January–February.

Wheatcroft, C. (2010) *CIPR CEO commits to leading PR measurement best practice*, 18 November, www.cipr.co.uk/content/news-opinion/press-releases/6390/cipr-ceo-commits-to-leading-pr-measurement-best-practice, accessed 18 November 2010.

Whetten, D.A. & Godfrey, P.C. (1998) *Identity in organizations: building theory through conversations*, Thousand Oaks, California: Sage.

White, J. and Dozier, D.M. (1992) 'Public relations and management decision making' in J.F. Grunig (ed.) *Excellence in public relations and communication management*, New Jersey: Lawrence Erlbaum.

White, J. and Mazur, L. (1995) *Strategic communications management*, Harlow: Addison Wesley.

White, J. and Murray, K. (2004) 'Chief Executive Officers' expectations of a changing public relations practice', Paper presented at the BLED International Research Symposium.

Wiggins, J. (2009) 'Cadbury Vows to Fight Kraft Offer', *Financial Times*, 7 September.

Wiggins, J. and Guthrie, J. (2010) *Cadbury deal "the price of globalisation"*, 19 January, www.ft.com/cms/s/0/c022b2e0–053f-11df-a85e-00144feabdc0.html#axzz19y6KGfqz, accessed 10 December 2010.

Wilcox, D.L., Cameron, G.T., Ault, P.H. and Agee, W.K. (2003) *Public relations, strategies and tactics* (7th edition), New York: Allyn and Bacon.

Willis, P. (2009) 'Public relations and the consumer', in R. Tench and L. Yeomans (eds) *Exploring public relations*, pp. 409–424.

Wilson, D.C. (1991) 'Co-operation and competition in the voluntary sector: strategic challenges of the '90s and beyond', in Batsleer, Cornforth and Payton (eds) (1991) *Issues in voluntary & non-profit management: a reader*, Wokingham: Addison-Wesley/OU.

Wilson, D.C. (1992) *A strategy of change*, London: Routledge.

Wilson, J. and Eng, D. (2003) 'Wake up and smell the chai', *Profile*, June, p. 12.

Wim J.L. Elving (2005) 'The role of communication in organisational change', *Corporate Communications: An International Journal*, 10 (2), pp. 129–138.

Windahl, S., Signitzer, B. and Olsen, J.T. (1992) *Using communication theory*, London: Sage.

Wolf, K. (2005) 'PR career progression: the gap between traditional research and the UK industry's perception', *CIPR Academic* Conference, University of Lincoln, March.

Wood, E. (2006) 'Corporate communication' in R. Tench and L. Yeomans, *Public relations: concepts and applications*, London: Pearson.

Wood, E. (2007) 'Corporate communication', in R. Tench and L. Yeomans (eds) *Exploring public Relations*, Harlow: FT Prentice Hall.

Woodall, K. and Smith, S. (2003) 'What will the future hold?', *Communication World*, February–March, pp. 18–21.

World Bank (2006) http://go.worldbank.org/HZ9K9XO7L, accessed 8 February 2011.

World Business Council for Sustainable Development (2000) 'Corporate social responsibility: making good business sense', www.wbcsd.org/templates/TemplateWBCSD5/layout.asp?type=p&MenuId=MTE0OQ.

WPRF (2010) *Stockholm protocol, 2010*, www.wprf2010.se/draft-of-the-stockholm-accords, accessed 6 August 2010.

Wray, R. (2010) 'Deepwater horizon oil spill – BP gaffes', *Guardian*, July 27, www.guardian.co.uk/business/2010/jul/27/deepwater-horizon-oil-spill-bp-gaffes.

Wright, D.K. and Hinson, M.D. (2010) 'An analysis of new communications media use in PR: results of a 5 year trend study', *Public Relations Journal,* 4(2), Spring.

Wright, M., (ed.) (2009) *The Gower handbook of internal communication*, London: Gower.

Xavier, R., Johnston, K., Patel, A., Watson, T. and Simmons, P. (2005) 'Using evaluation techniques and performance claims to demonstrate public relationsimpact: an Australian perspective', *Public Relations Review*, 31, pp. 417–424.

Xavier, R., Mehta, A. and Gregory, A. (2006) 'Evaluation in use: the practitioner view of effective evaluation', *PRism* 4 (2), www.prismjournal.org/fileadmin/Praxio/Files/Journal_Files/Evaluation_Issue/XAVIER_ET_AL_ARTICLE.pdf, accessed 13 November 2009.

Yates, K. (2006) 'Internal communication effectiveness enhances bottom line results', *Journal of Organisational Excellence*, Summer, pp. 71–79.

Yeomans, L. (2006) 'Public sector communication', in R. Tench and L. Yeomans (eds) *Exploring public relations*, London: FT Prentice Hall.

Young, L.D. (2006) 'Urban myths and their disastrous effects on marketing', *Annual Cambridge Marketing Lecture*, CMC.

Zerfass, A. (2010) *Levels of impact and evaluation,* www.communicationcontrolling.de/en/knowledge/levels-of-impact-and-evaluation.html, accessed 9 November 2010.

Zerfass, A., Moreno, A., Tench, R., Verčič, D., and Verhoeven, P. (2009) *European communication Monitor 2009. Trends in communication management and public relations – results of a survey in 34 countries*, Brussels: EUPRERA, www.communicationmonitor.eu, accessed 23 February 2010.

Zerfass, A., Tench, R., Verhoeven, P., Verčič, D., and Moreno, A. (2010) *European Communication monitor 2010. Status quo and challenges for public relations in Europe. Results of an empirical survey in 46 countries* (Chart Version). Brussels: EACD, EUPRERA, www.communicationmonitor.eu, accessed 18 November 2010.

WEBSITES

www.bbc.co.uk

www.cipr.co.uk

www.coi.gov.uk

www.corporate-ir.net

www.corporatewatch.org.uk

www.csr.gov.uk

www.csreurope.com

www.fsa.gov.uk

www.holmesreport.com

www.cipr.co.uk

www.cyberatlas.com

www.fsa.gov.uk

www.idc.com

www.instat.com

www.irs.org.uk

www.jackmorton.com

www.lga.gov.uk

www.local.regions.odpm.gov.uk

www.london.gov.uk
www.londonstockexchange.co.uk
www.moreover.com
www.prca.org.uk
www.PRWatch.org
www.salford.gov.uk
www.sky.com
www.spannerworks.com
www.Spinwatch.com

Index